Supercharged Bitmapped Graphics

Supercharged Bitmapped Graphics

Steve Rimmer

Windcrest®/McGraw-Hill

FIRST EDITION
FIRST PRINTING

Library of Congress Cataloging-in-Publication Data

Rimmer, Steve.
    Supercharged bitmapped graphics / Steve Rimmer.
      p.   cm.
    Includes index.
    ISBN 0-8306-3788-5 (pbk.)
    1. Bitmapped graphics. I. Title.
T385.R554 1992
006.6—dc20   91-39711
                        CIP

TAB Books offers software for sale. For information and a catalog, please contact
TAB Software Department, Blue Ridge Summit, PA 17294-0850.

Acquisitions Editor: Brad J. Schepp
Managing Editor: Sandra L. Johnson
Book Editor: Alan Danis
Director of Production: Katherine G. Brown
Book Design: Jaclyn J. Boone
Cover: Sandra Blair Design and Brent Blair Photography, Harrisburg, PA.   WP1

To the memory of my father.

Contents

Preface

It was long, long ago—early in 1989, I think. A GIF file appeared called DRGNLDY.GIF, which turned out to contain a superb scan of a fantasy print, perhaps not surprisingly of a woman and a dragon. It was the sort of picture that people get framed and hang in the living room to see if it'll outrage the in-laws.

Back in 1989, the dragon lady was a pretty huge file—well over 300K—and too big to be displayed all at once on the available VGA cards of the period, which could go out to only 320×200 pixels in 256 colors. For a long time no one really knew what she looked like in her entirety. For reasons of decorum, she won't be shown in her entirety here, either.

As interesting as the dragon lady was to look at, she was more of a challenge. The challenge was to do something useful with her. Something useful eventually came down to figuring out a way to print her out, load her into PC Paintbrush to retouch a few misscanned pixels, and subsequently be able to pour her into Ventura chapters.

Having figured out a way to move the image in DRGNLDY.GIF into other applications, it seemed likely that the same set of tools would be useful in performing the translation for other—arguably less interesting—image files.

A lot of small, funky utilities sprang up around the dragon lady project. One program converted from GIF to PCX, another scaled up PCX files, yet another dithered PCX files down to monochrome, one translated

P-1 The respectable part of the dragon lady image file, more or less as it first appeared. It was downloaded from Rose Media, (416) 733-2285.

PCX files to MacPaint files—because the then-current version of Ventura wouldn't load the PCX files that the dithering program was creating—another program printed the MacPaint files to a LaserJet, and so on. The MacPaint files lopped off a bit of the picture, as it turned out, but this seemed a small concession.

Toward the end of 1989, the dragon lady finally wound up in a form which Ventura would accept. She languished comfortably in a dithered IMG file, and printed superbly.

P-2 Part of the dragon lady as she finally appeared in Ventura Publisher, dithered to mono-chrome.

After uncounted hours of meddling with the aforementioned funky utilities, I thought about writing my own, a sort of macro-funky utility which would convert everything to everything else. The resulting application, Graphic Workshop, transformed the dragon lady into a dithered file all ready to pour into Ventura in less than a minute.

This ignores the time it took to write, of course.

The accompanying source code disk contains the most recent descendent of Graphic Workshop. While very little of its original self remains, it is beginning to approach the ideal of being able to convert everything into everything else, so long as it's an image file.

At the same time as the quest to port the dragon lady into Ventura was going on, there were quite a few other projects about. For example, someone was working out a protocol for easily and reliably importing large databases into Ventura. It was very promising and had huge applications in publishing directories and guides. It was almost as exciting as watching paint dry, and almost nobody accosted the people involved in it to inquire as to how it was going.

Graphics—even if they're reprehensible, possibly sexist, mildly demonic graphics in poor taste and scanned with a slight visible moire pattern—speak to us in a language which we can understand a lot more readily than we understand words. As will be apparent in the explosive growth of graphics-based software, applications that attempt to communicate through pictures are more readily accepted by the people who have to use them.

Unfortunately, applications that communicate through pictures are also a pig to write, as compared to simple text mode programs. Images that can really express themselves seem to be somehow constrained by physical laws not to be manageable by conventional programming techniques. If there was a primary axiom of imaging, it would probably be "no image that fits in a single memory segment is worth looking at."

The converse is also true. No image that is worth looking at can be handled without some extremely tricky code.

In fact, however, the problems that cropped up in manipulating images like the dragon lady were not so much in learning to deal with huge amounts of memory as they were finding out how all the file formats involved were structured. Their specifications were frequently obscure and partially undocumented, and in most cases they turned out to have had several generations of patches, fixes, and modifications bolted onto them. Writing a program to read one image file is tricky. Writing a program to read all image files, no matter where they originate from, is a monumental challenge.

The great thing about graphics software is that it looks so slick when you finally do get it working. In the case of the code for Graphic Workshop, it entailed countless hours of long distance phone calls, faxes, and access to E-mail systems in which almost all the names started with at least three unprintable characters and a backslash. That's what this book is about, in a sense.

This book provides you with tight, comprehensible C code to do most of the things you're likely to want to do with bitmapped image files. It lets you read and write them, display them, print them, and manipulate them to an extent. Among other things, it lets you import the dragon ladies of your choice into WordPerfect documents, use them as Windows wallpaper, scan them into Targa files and print them to a LaserWriter—or a Color-Script if you're loaded. You can look at them in true color on a super VGA card or dither them down to eight colors and immortalize them on a Paint-Jet.

It should save you a lot of long distance calls, faxes, and time trying to figure out how to get unprintable characters into the command line of an E-mail system. If you just enjoy playing with graphics, it lets you rip past the frustrating bits and look at some pictures. If you're writing some serious software that deals with bitmapped images, it gives you the tools to handle the graphic code quickly and get down to the original parts of your application.

Using this book

In a sense, this book is a sequel. It expands on my previous book, *Bitmapped Graphics*, also published by Windcrest (book 3558). You might want to have a look at *Bitmapped Graphics* as well, as it offers code and explanations for a different group of image files as well as a more introductory explanation of graphic concepts in general.

Having said this, you won't have to be a wizard to use the code in this book. In a sense, it obviates the need to understand absolutely everything that's involved in using bitmapped graphics. Easily portable, it can be lifted and applied to your programming projects without your having to know how to manipulate a 12-bit string table, initialize a driver, or write in PostScript. You can treat much of it as a black box, using its functions without having to read the manual first.

Not reading the manual first is a long-standing tradition in microcomputer software, of course.

In order to use the code in this book, you should have at least a passing acquaintance with the C language. Actually, you should have a passing acquaintance with one of the Borland implementations of C in particular, because that's what the examples in this book are written in. If you do attempt to port some of them to a different dialect of C, such as Microsoft C, you should be pretty fluent in the lore of C compilers in general. While the code herein uses generic C for the most part, a few things are native to the Borland implementation of the language. The most notable of these is the way in which Borland's C compilers let you manipulate large model pointers, a central issue in dealing with large images.

You'll also want some dragon ladies of your own, some example image files to work with. A modem is a very powerful graphic programming tool in this regard.

Computer-based images are among the most fascinating applications of personal computers because they speak to precisely what a computer isn't. They're imprecise, luminous, sensuous, and serve to depict that which technology never can be—something human and alive. This might be why they're so appealing. After a long, hard day at the spreadsheets, it's comforting to realize that a computer can be something more than a glorified calculator.

Perhaps it's equally comforting to realize that computer users can still be moved by something more than "good numbers."

I hope that you have fun with *Supercharged Bitmapped Graphics*. Beyond their applications as expressive tools, communications accessories, visual media, and all the other frequently heard corporate terms, bitmapped graphics are fun. There never turned out to be any practical use for the dragon lady once she finally made it to Ventura; she was too scantily clad to actually make it to a printing press. The dragon didn't count as clothing. Nonetheless, several years after her arrival, she still turns up on the hard drives she once frequented.

None of the databases of the period have survived.

Steve Rimmer
CIS: 70451,2734
BBS: (416) 729-4609

1
Introduction

If a hammer doesn't work, get a bigger hammer.
—MURPHY'S LAWS OF COMPUTERS

Our visual perception of things has influenced the technology we've developed to enhance that vision. There is a fundamental difference between the way artists perceive things and the way everyone else does.

Artists are frequently limited in their craft by the tools they use. In time, they start to limit the way they see things to that which their tools allow them to render. At least, if they have any commercial sense they do. An artist who uses only pens will start to see the world in terms of lines.

People who look at things and don't have to reproduce them to make a living are more inclined to see those things as they actually appear to be: they don't impose a technical filter upon them. In considering new technologies that might prove interesting or useful, most of us evaluate them in terms of our own perceptions of their applicability. When confronted with ostensibly visual technologies, we don't tend to look at things the way artists do.

The human eye is a bitmapped device that likes to deal with the visual universe in this format. It appreciates television as a technology with which it has some kinship, because the lens of a camera is a technological analog of the human eye. On the other hand, the eye isn't quite sure what to do with line drawings. The intelligence of the eye's owner is required to make an artist's representation of reality look real, instead of just seeing marks on a page.

For this reason, pen plotters didn't catch on nearly as well as dot matrix graphic printers did, even if pen plotters are more fun to watch.

Television is easy to cope with because it looks somewhat like reality. Most of the graphic arts require a bit more mental effort. Artists will tell you—and rightly so—that this is good because by forcing people to appreciate the images of graphic arts the artists also force the people to perceive things at a much more conscious level.

Making people work to see a graphic wakes them up.

Computer-based bitmapped images are a digital extension of television, which is in turn an electronic extension of a real human eye. Bitmapped images represent one of two broad classes of graphics, the other being vector images, or line art. Bitmaps allow you to represent reality on a computer.

Vector art allows you to represent an artist's graphics on a computer. Both areas are equally interesting, but this book focuses on the former. In a sense, bitmapped graphics offer you the opportunity to misjudge reality for yourself rather than having an artist do it for you.

Figure 1-1 illustrates the difference between bitmapped and vector art.

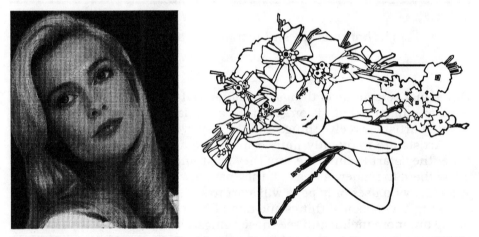

1-1 Bitmapped and vector art. The bitmapped example, on the left, came from a GIF file downloaded from Rose Media, (416) 733-2285. The vector example is one of the sample clip art files from CorelDRAW.

In its simplest sense, a bitmapped graphic is a matrix of dots. In a monochrome bitmapped image, such as the screen of your computer dispaying a monochrome or a page from a laser printer, each dot in the matrix is either on or off—black or white. When the matrix is sufficiently dense, images are formed.

Computer programmers who don't work for IBM call these dots *pixels*. Computer programmers who do work for IBM call them *pels*. There's no apparent reason for these two different names. Because most programmers don't work for IBM, this book refers to pixels.

For the purposes of this book, bitmapped graphic images come in four flavors: monochrome images, images with 4 to 16 colors, images with 32 to 256 colors, and images with an almost unlimited number of colors. The reasons for these distinctions will become clearer as you proceed through this chapter.

In discussing bitmapped color, the number of colors is often referred to by the number of bits required to store the color information. Monochrome images are referred to as 1-bit images because each pixel in the image requires 1 bit of information. The relationship between pixels and *bytes*, a more common unit of data storage, is explained further on in this chapter.

In order to represent 16 distinct colors, a pixel must consist of 4 bits; therefore, 16-color images are often referred to as having 4-bit color for this reason.

There are 2-bit and 3-bit colors as well, but they don't come up all very often because one of the broad classes of display adapters for PC systems are 16-color cards. There are no 4-color or 8-color cards of note. This situation is also dealt with in greater detail further on in this chapter.

The next common step up for PC color is 8 bits, or 256 colors. An image that consists of 256 unique colors can look like a color photograph. What is usually called 8-bit color, though, is actually 18-bit color. In order to understand why, you might have to suffer through a brief digression into the universe of PC display technology.

The most flexible form of color bitmapped image storage is called 24-bit color. The exact reason for this designation is given shortly. A 24-bit image can contain as many unique colors as there are pixels in the image, and a 24-bit image can represent a full-color photograph with the maximum possible fidelity. Unfortunately, as of this writing this display may be seen only if you have a $2000 display card.

Display technology

There are uses for bitmapped images that do not involve displaying them on a monitor. For example, you might print them or separate them onto film for use in commercial printing. For the most part, though, bitmapped pictures are meant to be seen. In this light, it's probably not surprising that the various bitmapped graphics formats that have appeared on the PC closely resemble the data structures of the various types of PC display cards.

The simplest form of graphics display is black and white. Note that this is not the same as a display that has gray levels. On a black-and-white display, every pixel on the screen is either fully on or fully off.

The old CGA card had a 640×200 pixel, black-and-white graphics mode—it was very ugly and won't be discussed. A bit less old-fashioned, the Hercules monochrome graphics adapter could manage a 720×348 monochrome display mode. An EGA card allows you to view 640×350 monochrome pixels. The VGA card standard allows for 640×480 pixels, and most super VGA cards can do even better than this. The high end at the moment, unless you want to look at a full-page display monitor for several thousand dollars, is 1024×768 pixels, which is available on some of the newer super VGA adapters.

A monochrome bitmap is very easy to understand. The picture itself is comprised of a two-dimensional matrix of pixels. It's convenient to think of the horizontal rows of pixels in the matrix as scan lines, just like the scan lines of a television set. In fact, they do correspond to the scan lines of a monitor.

Inasmuch as a byte has 8 bits, the first 8 bits of the image form the first byte, the second 8 bits form the second byte, and so on. By convention, if a monochrome image has a horizontal dimension that is not an even multiple of eight, the extra bits at the right edge are wasted because the horizontal lines always start on an even byte.

Figure 1-2 illustrates the bitmapped structure of a monochrome image.

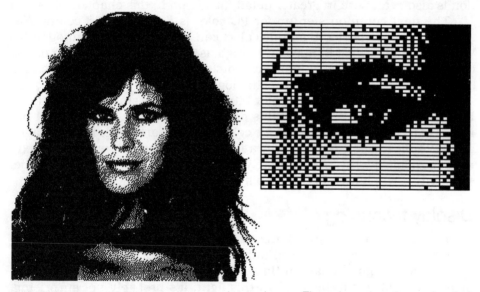

1-2 The bitmapped structure of a monochrome image. The enlarged section to the right illustrates how the pixels of the image are stored in bytes.

Colors are represented in one of two ways, depending upon what is doing the representing. The full-color cover of this book is the result of "subtractive" synthesis, this being the way that printing is done on paper. If you consider that a sheet of white paper reflects all colors of light perfectly, putting blue ink on a page subtracts some of the light the paper reflects. In fact, it subtracts everything but blue light: it serves as a filter that renders the paper a good reflector of blue and a poor reflector of everything else.

A computer monitor is black by default. Unless you bought a very cheap monitor with a screen that glares badly, a monitor that's off won't reflect anything. In order to make something appear, colored light must be added to its blackness. This sort of color is called "additive" synthesis.

Both of these color processes have three primary colors. Subtractive color uses cyan, magenta and yellow. Additive color uses red, green and blue. It's interesting to note that the additive set is the opposite of the subtractive set. For example, mixing equal amounts of cyan and yellow forms green.

While most of the examples of working with color given in this book deal with display applications, and hence additive color, subtractive color crops up in chapter 11 when we discuss color printing.

Additive color on a computer is represented by three values for every color—one for the red, one for the green, and one for the blue component. Additive color is also called RGB color for this reason. On a PC, it's common for color components to be defined by 3 bytes, one for each value. A single color defined this way consists of three 8-bit bytes, for a total of 24 bits.

The simplest way to represent a color image in data is to create a matrix of these 24-bit color pixels. Each pixel is represented by 3 bytes. While there is a growing number of 24-bit display cards, such as the Truevision Targa boards, the Hercules Graphics Station card and the Matrox card, 24-bit color has some technical and economic limitations.

The ATI-XL super VGA card, which is discussed in detail in chapter 10, offers a slightly less high-end true-color mode at a very much reduced price.

A picture that consists of 640×480 pixels of 24-bit color—these are fairly common dimensions for bitmapped graphics—would require 900K of storage. More to the point, a display card that could drive a monitor with such an image would require at least this much memory on board. It would also require that 900K of data be moved from your computer to the display card's memory every time your software wanted to update the screen.

As computers have become faster and memory has become cheaper, this prospect has become less daunting; however, most of the current color graphics standards were created on the slower computers.

Hardware designers have long cheated on the rather awkward memory requirements of full 24-bit color by using *palettes*. A display card based on palettes allows color images to be displayed without requiring all the memory of a full 24-bit card. This is done through some rather clever cheating, which you or I might not have thought of.

In a palette-driven image, the image data is accompanied by a *lookup table* of RGB color values, this being the palette. The largest commonly used color palette for bitmapped images contains 256 entries, or 256 distinct colors. Every pixel in the image in question is 1 of the 256 colors in the palette. As such, rather than representing each pixel as 3 bytes of RGB color, the display card stores the image as an array of single bytes. Each byte contains the number of the color in the palette in which it's to be displayed; that is, an index into the table of 3-byte color definitions.

This approach to color reduces the number of possible unique colors visible in an image at one time from 16 million or so down to 256—this being the number of entries in the color lookup table and the maximum number that can be stored in a single byte. However, from a hardware designer's point of view, it also cuts the memory requirement of the display card to one-third of what a true 24-bit card would require. This is the sort of tradeoff that hardware designers live and breathe and order pizzas for.

A standard VGA card, and all the super VGA cards that appeared in its wake, can display an image of 256 distinct colors at a resolution of 320×200 pixels. This is actually pretty coarse and was chosen because the entire image can fit into a single 64K memory segment, the relevance of which is seen a little later on. In fact, it's possible to make a stock VGA card display up to 320×480 pixels at 256 colors, but the results are very ugly.

Super VGA cards offer the same range of colors, but with the option of getting more pixels on your screen at once. The common next step up for super VGA card resolution is 640×480 pixels. Most super VGA cards also have a 640×400 pixel mode. You can calculate that 640×400 pixels will just fit in a quarter of a megabyte of memory (256K), whereas 640×480 won't. This slightly lower resolution mode is included in most super VGA cards so they can be offered in low-rent versions with only 256K of memory on board.

For reasons dealt with in chapter 10, when we discuss driving display cards in detail, the palette of a VGA card consists of three 6-bit numbers, rather than three 8-bit numbers. This is why a VGA card is said to have 18-bit color. It's common to refer to bitmapped images with 256 colors as 8-bit files because each pixel consists of 8 bits—the index into the color palette table—even though the actual colors are defined by 18 or 24 bits.

The other color display mode used in VGA cards, and the only one available on the older EGA cards, is the 16-color "business graphics" mode. This mode has a resolution of 640×480 pixels on a stock VGA card and 640×350 pixels on an EGA card. Most super VGA cards offer at least 800×600 pixel, 16-color modes.

The 16-color mode is the one normally used by Microsoft Windows, among other things.

The actual workings of 16-color display hardware is exceedingly weird, and is explained in chapter 10. However, for the moment it's sufficient to know that it can display 16 colors at once drawn from a palette of 64 possible colors. Its color resolution is thus a bit coarse: it's great for charts, text, a graphical user interface, and some other applications. It's not very good for displaying pictures, although there are ways to cheat on this a bit.

Bitmapped image files

Bitmapped images are just data, and as such can be stored in image files on your disk and displayed on your computer.

The simplest way to create and subsequently use an image file is to capture a binary dump of the screen buffer of your computer. When an image is displayed on your screen, the image data lives up in high memory, and can be dealt with just as you would any other data buffer. For example, if the picture in FIG. 1-3 is displayed on a VGA card, its data would live at address A000:0000H. Figure 1-3 is a monochrome image.

1-3   A bitmapped image displayed on a VGA screen.

You could make a file out of this image by copying the contents of the screen buffer to disk. Because there are 80 bytes in a 640-bit wide line and there are 480 lines, the file would be 38,400 bytes long. This is how it would be done:

```
FILE *fp;
char *p;
if((fp=fopen("PICTURE.BIN","wb")) != NULL) {
    p=MK_FP(0xa000,0);
    fwrite(p,1,38400,fp);
    fclose(fp);
} else puts("Error creating the file");
```

There are drawbacks to storing image files this way. First, if you attempt to display this picture on another VGA card by simply copying the contents of the file PICTURE.BIN back to location A000:0000H, all will be well only if the VGA card is in the appropriate graphics mode at that time.

If you attempt to use the same technique with a Hercules card, for example, the results look like a cat in a sandstorm because a Hercules card has different screen dimensions and several other characteristics that make it incompatible with the way a VGA card stores image data.

Second, all images stored in this format must have common dimensions. If it's confronted with a picture that is too big to fit in 640×480 pixels, it does not work.

The biggest problem with this format is that it wastes a lot of disk space. While this might not matter if you're dealing with 38K files on a 220Mb hard drive, it becomes considerably more relevant if you are working with 300K, full-color image files.

Consider the image in FIG. 1-3. The top line is all white. It occupies 80 bytes with totally redundant data. If the file format was a bit more intelligent, it might be replaced with some kind of code, or *token*, that would say "fill this line with 80 bytes of white data," but which would take up far fewer bytes.

The process of replacing redundant data in an image file with tokens is called *run-length compression*. It involves analyzing each line and finding places where there are consecutive bytes of identical data. Consecutive bytes can be replaced with tokens, called *run fields*. Nonconsecutive bytes are called *string fields*.

Figure 1-4 is an image that could be compressed this way, illustrating the byte structure and how the bytes would be compressed.

The structure of fields and tokens varies between the various commercial image file formats discussed in this book. Here's an illustration of how the principle works.

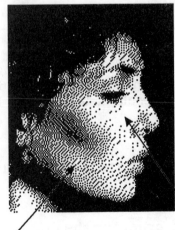

This area would be
compressed as a run
of bytes.

This area could be
run-length compressed.

1-4 An image fragment illustrating areas that could be compressed as a run of bytes and those that must be stored as string fields.

Let's allow that every field in a compressed file consists of one *key* byte followed by one or more data bytes. The key byte tells software that is decompressing the image how to treat each field. A key byte consists of the seven low-order bits, which define the field length, and the high-order bit, which is a flag. If the high-order bit is set, the field is a run of bytes. If it's not set, the field is a string.

Software that is to decode an image would begin by looking at the first byte of the image. If the high-order bit was set, it would AND off the flag and repeat the next byte in the file *n* times, where *n* is the value of the key byte with the flag bit removed. If the high-order bit was not set, the software would copy the next *n* bytes from the source file to the screen as is.

In practice, images are always compressed and subsequently decompressed one line at a time. Thus, for a 640×480 pixel image, the decompression function would expect the various runs to break at 80-byte intervals.

Run-length compression is relatively fast. Unfortunately, it's only modestly effective and easily fooled. There are potential pathological cases where a complex image might break up into lots of little fields in such a way that the addition of numerous key bytes combined with relatively little actual compression would result in a compressed file that was actually bigger than the original. This usually doesn't happen.

It's worth noting that there's a more effective way to compress image data, called *string table* compression, which is discussed in detail in chapter 2. It results in better overall compression and a much lower likelihood of the compression software being fooled into making compressed files that are bigger than uncompressed ones. However, it's much more complex to implement and much slower than run-length compression is.

This hypothetical image file format has two more problems to address. The first is that this format does not encompass any method for dealing with images of anything other than fixed dimensions. The second is that the format doesn't allow software that attempts to unpack it any way to know that what has been provided as an image file really isn't a text file or a spreadsheet or an old copy of WordStar 3.3. Both of these problems can be dealt with by adding a *header* to the beginning of the image data file.

A header is an arbitrary data structure that tells a program that knows what to do with the aforementioned image file something about what it's looking at. Here's a hypothetical header:

```
typedef struct {
        char signature[4];
        int width,depth;
        int number_of_colors;
        } HEADER;
```

In this format, assume that the signature field always contains the string "VGAP." As such, a function that wants to unpack one of these image files can know that it actually has an authentic one by checking to see if the first 4 bytes contain this string. Having established this, the next 2 bytes are the width in pixels and the following 2 bytes the depth in pixels. The last 2 bytes of the header are the number of colors, which is always 2 if this format only deals with monochrome images.

In real world image file formats, the header—if it exists—is usually quite a bit more complex than this.

Not all image file formats are structured like this last illustration. Some of the ones discussed in this book replace the single header and some image data with *tags*. Tags allow a complex image format to be much more flexible and expandable as you add more things to it. Tags crop up in chapters 2, 3, and 9. In a sense, tags are a whole array of custom headers, one for each of many different types of data that might relate to an image.

Commercial image file formats

This book deals with eight popular image file formats used in commercial software. You might want to regard it as a companion volume to my earlier book *Bitmapped Graphics*, which dealt with five other formats. There is some overlap, since three of them—GIF, PCX, and TIFF—appear in both books, although in slightly different ways. The eight formats are:

- CompuServe GIF. The GIF format was created by CompuServe to provide a way to exchange ostensibly public domain graphics by modem. The format has the most effective compression of any of the files discussed in this book: all other things being equal, GIF files are almost always smaller. It's also worth noting that the idea of sharing pictures by modem has become enormously popular, and more GIF files are floating around, usually free for the taking, than any other image file type.
- IFF/LBM. The IFF file format is native to the Commodore Amiga. When Electronic Arts, the creators of Amiga's Deluxe Paint application, ported their paint program over to the PC, the IFF format came with it. It was given the file extension LBM. Because Deluxe Paint is a very popular paint package, its files have proliferated as well.
- WordPerfect Graphics. The popular WordPerfect word processor accepts graphics inserted into its text chapters in the form of its proprietary WPG format. These files are a bit contentious, though, in that they can contain both bitmapped and vector elements. The discussion in this book treats them as purely bitmapped files.
- Windows BMP and Microsoft Paint. These are, to begin with, two wholly distinct formats. The Microsoft Paint MSP format is a monochrome-only file format that was native to Paint for Windows 2.0. It's still supported by the Paint program in Windows 3.0. The

approved native format of Windows 3.0, however, is BMP. This format can contain images from between 1 to 24 bits of color. It's interesting in that it's not compressed, making it quick to load but very wasteful of disk space.

- Pictor PIC. The PIC format, not to be confused with Lotus PIC, is a fairly old format that has recently found favor in PC animation circles. It's used by some Grasp applications, among other things. It can contain images with between 1 and 8 bits of color and provides moderate compression efficiency.
- Truevision Targa. The Targa, or TGA, format is used in high-end color applications, especially in professional digital color photograph retouching and color separation. It can support 24-bit images.
- PC Paintbrush PCX. The PCX file format is discussed at length in *Bitmapped Graphics*. It recently got a new aspect in that it can now support 24-bit images.
- TIFF. The TIFF format is also discussed at length in *Bitmapped Graphics*. Chapter 9 in this book deals with high-end color TIFF files.

As seen in this list, the image file formats discussed in this book were all created for specific purposes, in many cases as part of particular commercial applications.

A few years ago, most application software didn't talk to other programs. There was no perceived need for a word processor to share data with spreadsheet programs or with graphics programs, for example. This really isn't true anymore. There is a lot of software that all but insists on your having other applications, usually by other software manufacturers, to use them. For example, desktop publishing packages such as Ventura or PageMaker would be largely useless without word processors and graphics software to provide them with files.

If you want to make your application programs exchange files with commercial graphics packages, or generate graphic files that can be read by other programs, you'll have to understand how these files are structured. That's part of what this book is about.

If you know how to read and write graphic file formats, none of them are particularly hard to work with. A few, such as GIF and PIC, carry with them certain programming problems, but for the most part you may integrate them into your own software fairly transparently. When writing software to handle graphic files, it's worthwhile to provide your users with many choices of file formats to use.

If your program writes only PCX files and your users want to use the output of your software in WordPerfect, they can translate the files from PCX to WPG. However, this process gets tedious after a while. It's much more reasonable to provide everyone with a convenient file format.

Some color problems

There are a number of issues pertaining to color that arise throughout this book. As discussed previously in this chapter, the current generation of moderately priced PC display cards can display only a fixed number of colors. The high-end image files that make the best use of color scanning and paint technology cannot be displayed directly on a VGA card.

Toward the end of this book we look at the code to implement solutions to the problem of displaying an image with 16 million potential colors on a display adapter that can display only 256. It can be done, surprisingly well, by a process called *quantization*. While the details of this process are dealt with in chapter 12, it's worth knowing roughly what it's about because you'll encounter it in discussions of some of the file formats and printing techniques that appear in earlier chapters.

The problem of displaying a 24-bit image on a 256-color screen breaks down into three smaller problems. The first is that of finding a 256-color palette that best represents the mix of colors in the 24-bit image. Having done this, it should be possible to replace each pixel in the 24-bit image with a color from the palette and wind up with the least possible color shift for the overall image. In fact, this doesn't work well at all by itself, but it's where the solution to this problem begins.

A function that quantizes the colors in a 24-bit image creates a table of values for the image called a *histogram*. When it has been properly manipulated, the histogram specifies the 256 colors that are the most unique in the 24-bit image, weighted toward the most frequently used colors. This provides an optimum palette for a 256-color picture.

The second part of the solution to this problem involves *remapping* the colors in the 24-bit picture to the 256 possible colors of the quantized palette. This is actually pretty easy to do, as you can calculate the three-dimensional distance between two points in color-space and simply check all 256 combinations, choosing the one that results in the least distance. The details of process are discussed later in the book. Color-space is a concept that requires a few figures and diagrams to explain adequately.

The problem with simply quantizing and remapping a 24-bit image this way is that the results usually look really awful.

The reason that remapped pictures don't usually look particularly good and that properly reduced GIF files usually do has to do with a third and rather involved step in the process. This step, called *dithering*, creates the illusion of there being more colors in an image than actually exist, and in so doing sneaks around the 256-color limitation of a quantized 24-bit picture.

Here's a simple example of how dithering works. Consider that some code wants to display a green area on your screen, but that there is no green in the color palette that the program is using. However, cyan and yellow are in the palette. You can create a pretty convincing green area by first painting the area with yellow and then replacing the odd pixels with cyan. To anyone more than a few inches from your monitor, the area will appear green.

Dithered colors can be mixed in this way pretty accurately by varying the percentage of dots of the two colors used.

In dithering an image, a process called *error diffusion* is used to approximate colors that aren't really available by fudging the colors of adjacent pixels. The details of this process are dealt with later in this book, but you should be generally aware how it works as you go through the initial chapters. It turns up in a number of guises.

Some memory problems

One of the side issues of handling graphics that comes up repeatedly is that of memory management. While in many cases graphic files can be compressed to manageable sizes, they can't be worked with in this form. You have to decompress them into raw bitmaps to display, print, or otherwise manipulate them. Consider that a 640×480 pixel, 256-color image requires 300K of memory to store. A 24-bit image of the same dimensions occupies almost a megabyte.

Small bitmapped images can be dealt with using conventional DOS buffers. However, if your application itself is fairly large, or you anticipate working with big pictures, you'll unquestionably need a way to allocate buffers that are larger than the available DOS memory in your computer.

The memory situation on a PC is a trifle weird, and more than a bit awkward. For historical reasons that probably still provoke loud guffaws and ridicule in some circles, the architecture of a PC allows for up to only 640K of *conventional memory*. This is the memory where programs are run. It is also the memory that can be dealt with by a program using conventional pointers and allocation techniques.

There are two types of memory beyond conventional memory, both of which were grafted onto the system once it was obvious that a problem existed and that it was too late to change the cause. The two types are *expanded memory* and *extended memory*. To further confuse the issue, the authors of these two incompatible memory standards chose similar sounding names for them.

Expanded memory is also called EMS and LIM memory. The name LIM is derived from Lotus, Intel and Microsoft, the three parties who created it. Extended memory is also called XMS memory.

As discussed near the end of this section, the actual management of large image buffers for the code in this book is dealt with using a standard memory manager, the code for which can be found in the appendix. While you should understand the PC memory situation, you won't ultimately have to get too close to it as you develop your own graphics applications if you just swipe the memory manager.

Conventional memory

Conventional memory, or DOS memory, is the memory that exists in the first megabyte of the address space of your computer. Up to the first 640K of this memory is usable for programs and data. Some of it is taken up by DOS, resident programs, device drivers, and other low level things.

When a program loads, it sets up what's called a *heap* above itself. A heap is a pool of unused memory. Figure 1-5 illustrates the memory map of conventional memory when a program is loaded and running.

A program running under DOS is able to use as much of the heap as it needs for storing data. It does this by allocating blocks through a DOS call and subsequently accessing them with a pointer that DOS returns. When they're no longer needed, they can be deallocated, freeing them up for future use.

People who think about this sort of thing a lot will tell you that pointer-based memory allocation is somewhat crude, as it frequently results in a "fragmented" heap. If you allocate several small blocks and then deallocate some of them out of order, areas of free memory might become trapped between areas that are still allocated. These memory areas will then be unusable even though they aren't actually required any longer. This is not a problem for the code in this book, as it's concerned with allocating one enormous buffer, rather than numerous little ones.

There is, however, a problem with handling memory this way. It's not so much a function of DOS as it is a peculiarity of the memory addressing hardware that is part of the microprocessors used in PCs. In the days before the first IBM PC, the antecedents of its processors used linear memory addressing. Memory went from the 0 bytes up to the end of memory. The end of memory was 64K, or about as much memory is used by a conventional VGA card for a screen buffer in its full-color mode today.

It's possible to create a processor that can address several megabytes or more in the same way. The Motorola 68000 series chips, used in the Apple Macintosh, Commodore Amiga, and some other systems, work this way. However, there are a number of advantages to handling memory addressing for large amounts of memory in a slightly different manner. There are also a lot of mind-numbing complications inherent in doing so.

The slightly different way that the chips used in PC systems address memory is called *segmentation*. As with old-style 8-bit processors—the ones that could only address 64K—memory is addressed with 16-bit registers, which means that you can deal with only 64K at a time. However, there is a second register involved that determines which 64K you'll be dealing with. This second register is called the *segment* register.

A memory segment on a PC is a 64K block of memory that begins on an even 16-byte boundary. Incrementing the segment of an address moves the absolute address value up by 16 bytes.

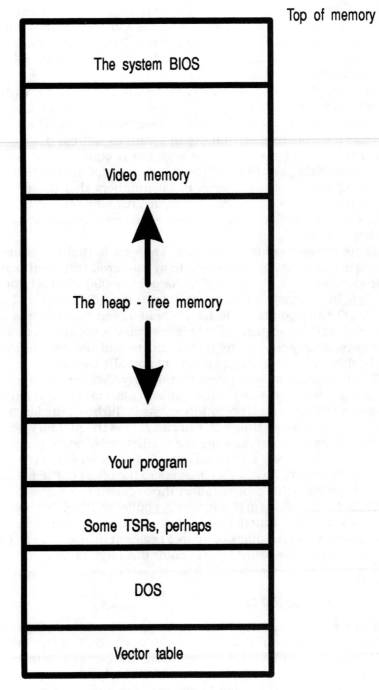

Top of memory

The system BIOS

Video memory

The heap - free memory

Your program

Some TSRs, perhaps

DOS

Vector table

1-5 How free memory is accessed as a heap by a program running under DOS.

On a processor with linear addressing, a pointer consists of a large number, usually 32 bits, that simply points somewhere between 0 and the top of memory. On a PC, it consists of two 16-bit numbers, the segment and the offset. The offset is the position within the current 64K segment that the pointer points to.

This notation is usually written as SEGMENT:OFFSET, with both values in hexadecimal.

There are a few peculiarities of segmented memory. The first is that if you write a small program that doesn't want to address more than 64K of memory, you can ignore it. If the segment is constant the program can handle everything as offsets. This means that for such small programs, everything can be handled with 16-bit numbers that the processor can work with more rapidly. A small program running on a PC can have the speed advantages of an older 8-bit processor even though it isn't actually running on one.

There are also some drawbacks. The first is that the same absolute address in memory may be pointed to by numerous different segment and offset combinations. For example, the pointer 0000:0010H points to the 16th byte in memory. It's the 16th byte in the 0th segment. The pointer 0001:0000H also points to the 16th byte in memory, but in this case to the 0th byte in the 1st segment. For this reason, it's not practical to compare pointers by simply comparing their segment and offset values. The values may be different even if the pointers are actually the same.

The real problem in segmented memory that turns up in this book, however, is inherent in most of the implementations of the C language that are used on PC systems. It certainly exists in Turbo C, the language of the examples in this book. Under C, you can access the memory pointed to by a pointer either by incrementing the pointer or by adding offsets to it. In both cases, what really happens is that C adds integers to the pointer.

To be more precise, C adds integers to the offset of the pointer. Under no condition does this process affect the segment value.

Consider the problem of allocating a buffer of 128K. You would have to use the `farmalloc` function to do this, as the conventional `malloc` function can only provide buffers of up to 1 segment in size, that is, 64K. If you do the following, the pointer p will point to a large buffer.

```
char *p;

p=farmalloc(131072L);
```

The argument to `farmalloc` is the actual number of bytes in 128K.

Using conventional C language, the upper 64K of the buffer at p is wholly unaddressable. Remember that C can add integers only to pointers, not to long integers. If you add 32K to p, that is $p+0 \times 8000$, the pointer will address the second quarter of the buffer. If you subsequently add this value to it a second time, the pointer will point to the base of its buffer again.

This may take a moment to figure out. Here's what's really happening. Initially, p points to SEGMENT:0000H. After adding 8000H to it, it points to SEGMENT:8000H. After adding 8000H to it again, it will be SEGMENT:0000H. Adding 8000H and 8000H will give you 10000H. However, because the offset value is a 16-bit number, it can hold only the equivalent of four hexadecimal digits, that high-order one will be lost. The C-language mechanism for adding to a pointer's offset does not include a way to deal with overflow and carry.

In order to address a buffer larger than 64K, then, the programs discussed in this book require a way to add long integers to pointers. In fact, there's a function to do it.

```
char *farPtr(p,l)   /* return a far pointer p + 1 */
    char *p;
    long l;
{
    unsigned int seg,off;

    seg = FP_SEG(p);
    off = FP_OFF(p);
    seg += (off / 16);
    off &= 0x000f;
    off += (unsigned int)(l & 0x000fL);
    seg += (l / 16L);
    p = MK_FP(seg,off);
    return(p);
}
```

The farPtr function adds a long integer to a pointer by splitting the pointer into its segment and offset components, and the long integer into two 16-bit values. It begins by *normalizing* the pointer; that is, by adjusting its segment and offset values so that the offset is as small as it can be. It then adds the new offset and segment values to the pointer components and recombines the pointer.

Note that farPtr returns a pointer, not an integer. It must be declared as such before it's used.

While it's important to understand something about segmented memory—enough to avoid some of the problems it causes the unwary—you'll probably find that you don't have to deal with it very much in this book. The memory management package in the appendix can do most of the work for you.

Expanded memory

Expanded memory is the older of the two approaches to extra memory. It was designed back in the dark prehistory of personal computers, when the 8088 processor was state-of-the-art. The 8088, the first generation of processors to drive PC systems, can address only 1Mb of memory space. In a

PC, the upper 384K is largely spoken for, as it contains the display buffer, the system BIOS and a few other things. Getting several megabytes of extra memory into this architecture called for some cheating, which is what expanded memory does.

In order to allow software running on an 8088 machine to access more memory than the processor could address, the authors of the EMS standard adopted a system of *paging*. Paging allows software that knows what's going on to get at a large pool of hidden memory by handling it in small sections. These sections are called *pages*, as you might expect. They're accessed through a memory window called a *page frame*.

The page frame may exist anywhere in the 1Mb memory range of the processor. For the sake of this discussion we'll assume that it exists at segment C000H, above the video card. In the initial EMS standard it was 16K long, although this changed in later versions.

Let's further assume that our machine has 8Mb of expanded memory, even if it isn't entirely obvious how it relates to the real memory address space that applications can address.

At any time, one 16K chunk of the 8Mb of memory is addressable because it is visible in the page frame. By tickling the registers of the EMS hardware, it's possible to make the current chunk vanish and another chunk appear in the page frame. In this way, all 8Mb can be written to and read from in 16K chunks, although a bit laboriously.

Consider that you have a picture that wants to unpack into 2Mb of memory. In order to store it in expanded memory, you would unpack the first 16K chunk and copy it to the page frame. You would then instruct the expanded memory hardware to take that page away and give you the next page. You would unpack the next 16K into that page frame and repeat the process. In this way, you could eventually store the whole image in expanded memory.

In reality this doesn't work out quite as easily as it might when you're dealing with bitmapped graphics. Few pictures have line lengths that end conveniently on 16K boundaries. For this reason, the expanded memory manager in the appendix does some cheating, using a table of expanded memory page and offset pointers to ensure that all the lines added to a buffer are stored properly.

Conventional DOS memory can be accessed by only one active program at a time—at least, this is true in the "real" processor mode, which suffices for this book. Expanded memory can be accessed by a number of programs simultaneously. Depending upon what your computer is doing, you might have resident programs and device drivers stored in expanded memory, as well as their buffers. If your program simply hogs all the expanded memory for itself, it might overwrite things that are already using the expanded memory, which can get a bit nasty if some of the other programs are using the expanded memory to store executable code that gets called for later.

In order to manage expanded memory properly, your system should be equipped with an EMS driver. An EMS driver is typically loaded through your CONFIG.SYS file. The driver provides a standard interface to your expanded memory and manages multiple users of the expanded memory.

The details of calling an EMS driver are discussed in the appendix.

There is an important difference between conventional memory and expanded memory. Conventional memory that has been allocated by an application program is automatically freed when you exit the program. This is not true of expanded memory. In fact, expanded memory that is allocated by an application program and not explicitly freed before you exit the application is orphaned and will be, inaccessible until your computer is rebooted.

For this reason, it's important to deallocate any expanded memory you use and to make sure that programs that use expanded memory can't be aborted unexpectedly by hitting Ctrl – Break, for example.

Extended memory

Extended memory appeared with the advent of 80286 processors, which support a secondary address bus. This extra bus allows 80286 and newer chips to address memory above 1Mb. Because of the immovable structure of a PC, with its video card, BIOS, EMS page frame, and other objects poised between conventional DOS memory and the space above 1Mb, this extra memory doesn't simply append itself to the 640K of conventional memory. It can be used only for storing data.

Once again, this is true for real mode programs. You can do clever things with extended memory and an 80386 series processor or better, but this subject is beyond the scope of this book.

Extended memory is also accessed through a suitable driver. Moving data in and out of extended memory is even easier than with expanded memory. You simply tell the driver where your data is stored in conventional memory and where you want the data to go in a previously allocated extended memory buffer. The driver moves all the data around.

When you allocate an extended memory buffer, the driver provides you with a memory *handle*. A handle is a number by which the driver refers to your memory block. If you then write data to your allocated memory, you'll really tell the driver to write it to the block referred to by that handle.

You never deal with the data in extended memory directly. It must always be done by the driver.

There is a very useful aspect to the handle-based memory management arrangement used by an extended memory driver. Because your program cannot access its data in extended memory directly, the driver is free to move its location in the extended memory heap around if it sees fit to do so. As long as it keeps track of your data, it will be able to get at it when you call for access to your buffer. As such, the driver can compact areas of deallocated memory, thereby avoiding the problem of a fragmented heap, which was discussed previously.

There are two things you must keep in mind about extended memory. First, like expanded memory, extended memory buffers are not freed until your program explicitly frees them. If your program fails to free them before it terminates, any allocated extended memory is orphaned. Second, most drivers allow for relatively few extended memory handles. The code in this book never wants to allocate more than a single extended memory buffer at a time. However, keep this in mind if you write a program that wants to deal with several extended memory buffers at once. You should also keep in mind that if your system software uses extended memory, as DOS 5 does, it loads some of itself into extended memory.

Virtual memory

Virtual memory is extra memory for people who don't have anything better. While a rather lofty sounding term, all it really involves is storing data in a temporary disk file if it won't fit in the available DOS memory. Virtual memory is very much slower than either expanded or extended memory. However, it's a way to let your programs work if they run out of DOS memory for image storage and can't find anywhere else to turn.

The memory interface

Since this book is about graphics, rather than the nuances and vagaries of memory drivers, it attempts to ignore the memory problems of PC systems as best it can. It can do this by calling the memory manager in the appendix to deal with image data.

Four functions are provided by the memory manager. The first is getbuffer. You can call this to allocate a large buffer in which to store the data for a picture. It's called as:

```
getbuffer(memory,linebytes,depth);
```

The memory argument to getbuffer is an unsigned long integer that contains the actual number of bytes the image will occupy. The linebytes argument is an unsigned integer that contains the number of bytes in 1 line of the image. The depth argument is an unsigned integer that contains the number of lines in the image.

If getbuffer is asked to allocate a buffer that does not fit in the available DOS memory, it allocates it in some sort of extra memory. The extra memory type is set by the external integer memorytype in the memory manager. It must contain one of the three constants:

```
#define    VIRTUAL     1
#define    EXTENDED    2
#define    EXPANDED    3
```

The `getbuffer` function returns a true value if it is able to allocate a buffer of some sort or 0 if it fails.

As an aside, it would be convenient to have the memory manager itself work out the sort of extra memory to use. It's possible to test for the presence of both extended and expanded memory drivers. Failing to find either, the memory manager could default to using virtual memory. In practice, this isn't a terribly good idea. Systems running with 80386 series and better processors frequently use extra memory drivers, such as Quarterdeck's QEMM, which can provide both extended and expanded memory. As such, testing for these two types of drivers usually results in both seeming to be present in this case.

Arguably, it's better to let the users of your software determine which type of extra memory to select when the applications are installed or configured.

Having used `getbuffer` to allocate a buffer, you can write image lines into it with the function `putline`. It's called as:

```
putline(line,number);
```

The `line` argument to `putline` is a pointer to the line data you want to write to the buffer. The `number` argument is an unsigned integer that specifies the line of the image to which you want to write. To get a line from the buffer, you call `getline`. It's used like this:

```
char *p;

p=getline(line);
```

The `line` argument to `getline` is an unsigned integer that specifies the line you want to get. The `getline` function returns a pointer to the data you're after.

Finally, the `freebuffer` function should be called to deallocate your buffer when you no longer need it.

Notice that no mention has been made of where all these lines are put and retrieved from. The memory manager transparently uses conventional memory or extra memory as it sees fit. You need not worry about where your image data is actually being stored, only that it's being stored somewhere.

Using the memory manager

The memory manager code in the appendix should be compiled to produce MEMMANGR.OBJ before you start working with the code in this book. You will require a project file for each of the complete programs in this book to link in MEMMANGR.OBJ and XMEM.OBJ, along with any other object modules as might be required. Alternately, as discussed in the appendix, you can combine the two modules of the memory manager into a LIB file and link to that.

You will require the following line in programs that use the memory manager.

```
#include "memmangr.h"
```

This include file, also shown in the appendix, has such things as the definition of the memory type constants above, prototypes for the memory manager functions, and so on.

It's worth noting that the memory manager allocates only one buffer at a time. Having called `getbuffer` once, you should not do so again until you've called `freebuffer`.

C-language considerations

The code in this book was developed under Borland's Turbo C language. It will compile without difficulty under Turbo C 2.0, Turbo C++ and Borland C++. If you wish to use it with other implementations of C, be prepared to do a bit of experimentation. The legendary portability of C is just that—mostly a legend. Each version of C is different, and the code in this book makes use of a few features of Turbo C that may not exist, or may work a bit differently, in other C compilers.

In using Turbo C with the code in this book, you should take care to set up Turbo C in accordance with the following guidelines. The programs herein generate compiler warnings, errors and frequently do not work properly if you do not.

Specifically, you must do the following:

- Turn off all the ANSI extensions
- Make `chars` unsigned by default
- Turn off case-sensitive linking
- Turn off register variables
- Use the large memory model

If you set up Turbo C correctly, all the programs in this book will compile, link and execute without warnings, errors or difficulties in execution.

While the graphics programs to be discussed in the ensuing chapters don't use any really exotic programming techniques—you won't have to dip into protected mode, for example, and none of the code in this book uses the object-oriented extensions of C++—they do involve some extensive C code in many cases. The C language has a lot of advantages for this sort of programming, but readability isn't one of them. It's frequently hard to read code you've written yourself after a few years. Reading code that someone else has written can be intimidating. This is especially true if you're trying to find a typing error or other problem.

The style in which you write C code can do a lot toward making it more readable and, therefore, easier for you to work with. Unless the application that you'll be applying the code to is part of a team effort, you can program in whatever style best suits you. In very few cases does your programming style have any bearing on the executable code that results from your work.

A few stylistic items are worth mentioning. Most of them are aspects of programming that I find work for me. They might not be as clear to you, and you should feel free to modify them as you wish.

Let's begin with the traditional way to declare a C function. I'm very fond of traditional things, even when they're technical and use microprocessors.

```
doSomething(p,n)
    char *p;
    int n;
{
    /* code goes here */
}
```

The approved ANSI way to do this is different.

```
doSomething(char *p,int n)
{
    /* code goes here */
}
```

Neither style makes any difference to your program. Use the one that makes the most sense to you. Note that if you use the traditional approach, you must turn off the "obsolete declaration" warning in Turbo C++.

In a somewhat related issue, you should decide what you want to do about prototyping functions. Some of the commonly used functions in this book, such as those of the memory manager, are supplied with prototypes. If you abstract the various other functions described herein for your own use, you're free to either use or not use prototypes with them as you see fit. In some respects prototypes can save you an awful lot of debugging by making the type checking in C a bit stronger.

Alternately, they can be a decided nuisance.

Under C, everything is an integer unless you explicitly tell C otherwise. For example, this is a legal—if somewhat sloppy—function declaration.

```
doSomething(n)
{
    /* code goes here */
}
```

In this example, the function doSomething is assumed to take one integer argument n, and to return an integer if the calling function cares to use it.

Here's another function.

```
doSomething(l,n)
    unsigned long l;
    int n;
```

```
{
    /* code goes here */
}
```

In this function, the function itself expects to be passed a `long` and an `int` in that order. Unfortunately, the function is the only thing that knows this. If you call it like this, bad things will probably happen.

```
int a,b;

doSomething(a,b);
```

In this case, the function will inhale both its erroneous `int` arguments into one largely meaningless `long` and then take the next 2 bytes of stack garbage as its `int`.

Here's a more catastrophic example.

```
doSomething(l,proc)
    long l;
    int (*proc)( );
{
    /* code goes here */
}
```

In this example, the second argument is a pointer to a function that `doSomething` will presumably execute sooner or later. If you call this function with an `int` instead of a `long` for its first argument, it will get the wrong data for the pointer and it will execute some undefined area in memory. This procedure will usually crash your computer really elegantly.

The way to get around this problem is to include prototypes for all the functions you use in a program, or at least for all the potentially nasty ones. This is a prototype for the last example of `doSomething`:

```
void doSomething(long l,int (*proc)( ));
```

This tells C that it's empowered to complain should you attempt to pass anything other than a `long` and a pointer to a function that returns integers as arguments to `doSomething`. It's also allowed to complain if the function that calls `doSomething` attempts to use its return value. By declaring it `void`, the prototype has told your C compiler that its return value is always meaningless.

You might not wish to use prototypes. If you're methodical and understand what you're doing, they're not necessary. On a large programming task, they represent a considerable undertaking to keep track of. I rarely use them myself.

In using the code in this book, you will not be working with functions you have written. One of the arguable advantages to buying a book that hands you prewritten functions to perform complex tasks is that you need not know what they're up to in detail. As such, you might want to engage in at least a limited use of prototypes, even if you don't ordinarily do so.

Finally, it's worth noting that any functions that don't return an int value must have prototypes for them to tell C that they'll be returning something else.

Assembly language considerations

With the exception of one linkable assembly language module in the memory manager, all of the assembly language in this book appears in a rather exotic form. It turns up in dealing with drivers, that is, with the code that interfaces an application to specific hardware. In this case, the drivers deal with specific super VGA cards. It's important that screen drivers be fast, as they govern the speed at which the screen can be updated. It's also important that the drivers be interchangeable, so that someone with a VGA card other than the one you have will be able to use your software.

For various reasons—some of them merely limitations to what you can do conveniently with Turbo C—the drivers in this book are all written in assembly language. Rather than being linked into your program, drivers are stored as binary disk files, loaded into buffers and executed from there. This makes the assembly language code a bit more obtuse than usual.

It's worth noting, as discussed in greater detail in the next section, that you don't actually have to write any drivers if you don't want to. The accompanying disk set for this book contains a complete set of preassembled drivers, all ready to use.

You may skip this section if you like.

Assembly language used with a C calling program, whether it's a linked module or a loaded driver, must work like a C function. The C language handles calls to functions in a way that may seem a trifle weird if you've never encountered it before. Specifically, C is a stack-oriented language. It passes arguments to functions on the stack and accepts return values from called functions in the processor registers.

Here's a typical C-language function call:

```
putch('a');
```

Here's how this would look in assembly language to do the same thing:

```
MOV   AX,0061H
PUSH  AX
CALL  _putch
POP   AX
```

The value 0061H puts the ASCII code for a lowercase a in the low-order byte of the AX register.

The function that does whatever putch must do, presumably printing a to the screen, will retrieve its argument by peeking back up the stack.

When a function is called in the large memory model, the processor pushes the current code segment and instruction pointer registers onto the stack, such that it is able to return to its former location when the function it's calling returns. As such, the argument will be 2 words, or 4 bytes, up the stack.

In fact, it will be 6 bytes, for reasons we get to in just a moment.

The stack always grows downward in its segment. If the stack pointer register, SP, initially points to FFFEH, executing a PUSH instruction will leave it pointing to FFFCH. As such, finding things that have been pushed onto the stack involves looking above the current contents of the SP register. In the foregoing example, the argument to putch might be retrieved by saying:

```
MOV    AX,[SP + 4]
```

In fact, it might be but it isn't. You can't index off the stack pointer: the above example is illegal and won't compile. There is a register called the base pointer, or BP register, that is specifically designed to take care of this situation, however. The BP register always implicitly addresses the stack segment.

Every C-language function uses the base pointer to address its own arguments. Because C stores its local variables on the stack too—something you won't have to get into in this book—the base pointer is involved in dealing with most of the data a function handles.

The first thing any assembly language function must do is to push the BP register onto the stack. Assuming that the function will modify it to allow its own arguments to be addressable, it must be restored such that the calling C-language function is able to continue to get at its own arguments and local variables when the assembly language function returns. As such, if the beginning of an assembly language function is:

```
PUSH    BP
MOV     BP,SP
```

the first argument to the function will be 6 bytes above BP. You could get at it like this:

```
MOV    AX,[BP + 6]
```

In fact, in this book we use a defined constant for the offset to the first argument, _AOFF, which is always 6. Therefore, this would get the first two arguments from the stack:

```
MOV    AX,[BP + _AOFF + 0]
MOV    BX,[BP + _AOFF + 2]
```

Under the large memory model, pointers are always far—that is, they're always 2 words long. This is how you'd retrieve a pointer from the stack, assuming it was the first argument to an assembly language function.

```
MOV    SI,[BP + _AOFF + 0]
MOV    DS,[BP + _AOFF + 2]
```

The offset is always first. In this example the pointer will be in DS:SI.

Even with its register variables switched off, Turbo C still expects you to preserve some registers through an assembly language call. Aside from the BP register, you should preserve the DS and ES registers by saving them on the stack also. Here, then, is a skeletal assembly language routine.

```
DOSOMETHING PROC   FAR
            PUSH   BP
            MOV    BP,SP
            PUSH   DS
            PUSH   ES

            MOV    SI,[BP + _AOFF + 0]
            MOV    DS,[BP + _AOFF + 2]

            LODSW

            POP    ES
            POP    DS
            POP    BP
            RET
DOSOMETHING ENDP
```

This function returns an integer from whatever is pointed to by its argument—a trivial function, to be sure.

Returned values from assembly language functions should be stored in the AX register for things that are 16 bits wide or smaller. In C, this bit of code:

```
a=getch( );
```

actually tells C to call getch and load the variable a with whatever getch leaves in the AX register.

If you wanted to return something larger than one register, such as a pointer or a long, you would use the AX register for the low-order word and the DX register for the high-order word. In the case of a pointer, the segment value would go in DX and the offset in AX.

It's worth noting that C does not know that an assembly language function that you've written is any different from its own library functions, and as such it takes no special precautions to protect itself from errant assembly language code. If you aren't careful to preserve the machine state through an assembly language function, your programs may crash a lot.

Debugging assembly language functions

Debugging assembly language code in a C-language program is particularly nettlesome, especially if you're chasing bugs in a loadable driver. It's very hard to find the part of a large program that contains the code in question, and higher level C-language debuggers aren't much use in this respect. There is a way to get around this.

The DOS DEBUG program allows you to single step or execute a specific area of a program by modifying your code behind your back. Specifically, if you issue an instruction like this to DEBUG:

```
-G=35F,366
```

the DEBUG program will replace whatever it finds at location 366 with the instruction INT 3. It will then start executing the program at location 35F. When DEBUG is active, the vector for INT 3 points back into DEBUG, allowing it to regain control of the computer when the code being executed reaches an INT 3. Having done so, it transparently replaces the original contents of the byte that has been displaced by the INT 3 instruction and returns you to a prompt.

You can use this feature to cause a program running under DEBUG to break anywhere you like. Simply put the instruction INT 3 where you'd like your code to stop. Figure 1-6 illustrates an example of this.

In FIG. 1-6, the program in question has actually stopped while it was in graphics mode. This won't be a problem most of the time, as the PC BIOS will display text in graphics mode, albeit more slowly than in text mode. The exception to this is the Hercules card, which does not have BIOS support.

Having been stopped by an INT 3 instruction, you can trace through a program under DEBUG by starting with the instruction beyond the INT 3. The DEBUG program will not remove the INT 3 from your code as it would one it had installed, as it didn't put it there to begin with.

Pictures of Lily

If you plan to work with the routines in this book, you might want to order the companion disk set for it. This disk provides you with the source code all typed in. It can also provide you with tested, ready to use super VGA drivers that support the following cards:

- Paradise Plus
- Paradise Professional
- ATI VGA Wonder
- ATI XL
- Trident
- Headland Video 7
- Tseng Labs

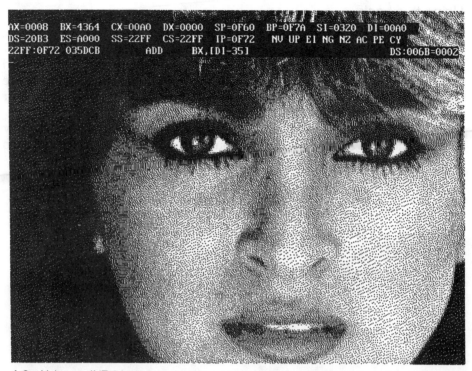

1-6 Using an INT 3 instruction to interrupt a program while it's running under DEBUG.

Equipped with these drivers, you can write graphics applications that will support cards you don't actually own. If your software handles the driver for your VGA card correctly, it will do so for other drivers as well.

The companion disk for this book also contains two large shareware applications—Graphic Workshop and Desktop Paint 256. Graphic Workshop embodies most of the things discussed in this book. Among other things, it allows you to print graphic files, to convert between image files of differing formats, to perform monochrome and color dithering, to rotate and scale files, to reverse them, and to inflict various sorts of special effects on them. Desktop Paint 256 is a super VGA paint program that drives Paradise, ATI, Video 7, Trident and Tseng VGA cards. It requires a Microsoft-compatible mouse.

Note that these programs are supplied in executable form only—they do not include source code. They're provided to help you generate example files to work with using the code in this book and to help you see what things like color dithering and PostScript printing should look like as you develop your own applications.

Finally, the disk set includes a variety of example pictures to work with. Using Graphic Workshop you can translate these into all the formats discussed in this book.

Using this book

The functions in this book have been written to be as portable as possible. As such, should you want to have your application display GIF files, for example, you need not really take the code in the next chapter apart and understand everything it's up to. Copy the functions, make sure you're passing them suitable arguments and get on with the real work of your own application.

There's enough information in this book to help you understand every line of code. However, there's also enough to allow you to forgo doing so unless you really want to.

2
GIF files

*Once you open a can of worms, the only
way to recan them is to use a bigger can.*
—MURPHY'S LAWS OF COMPUTERS

In the first chapter, the notion of a graphic file was largely that of a file to contain graphics. You might liken this to the notion of a word processor as being something to merely process words. Word processors no longer only process words: they also correct your spelling and grammar, add design elements to your pages, import pictures, and so on. Likewise, many graphic file formats do much more than just store pictures.

The most popular PC image file format currently in use is GIF. The GIF format was created by CompuServe, the on-line database company, in the hope that people would start uploading and downloading pictures, thereby increasing their use of CompuServe. This seems to have worked— GIF files exist in countless thousands.

The acronym GIF stands for *graphics interchange format*. It's pronounced "jif" if you believe the GIF standard documentation from CompuServe, or "gif" if you don't.

The intent in designing the GIF standard was to create a file format to hold images that were more or less in keeping with state-of-the-art PC display technology that could compress complex scanned images as tightly as possible and still be at least moderately extensible. Each of these issues probably deserves some discussion.

State-of-the-art PC display technology essentially involves VGA cards. A GIF file may contain between 1 and 8 bits of color information, or up to 256 colors. Color images are represented using a color palette, as discussed in chapter 1. The palette consists of a table of RGB byte values.

For reasons that become a little clearer in the discussion of the GIF encoding process, a GIF file can get away with storing images of any number of bits as whole bytes. This means that an image that requires only 4 bits of color is still stored in a GIF file with 1 byte per pixel. This actually presents a few logistical problems in displaying 16-color GIF images in the 16-color modes of an EGA or VGA card. Whereas the data that emerges from a GIF decoder matches the data structure of the screen buffer for 256-color modes, this is not the case for 16-color modes. Some bit swapping is necessary.

The example GIF decoder in this chapter cheats on this situation a bit by using the 256-color VGA mode to display all GIF files, no matter how many bits of color they contain.

Scanners frequently produce very complex images of photographs. A picture containing gradations of color—sunlight on a leaf, or flesh tones, for example—actually generates numerous different color values. When this sort of image is dithered down to 256 colors, the result frequently is image lines that don't compress at all using the run-length compression techniques discussed in chapter 1. In fact, the images frequently get bigger.

Figure 2-1 illustrates one of the example files from this book's companion disk set. This is a superb pathological case GIF file. If it's run-length compressed, such as when it's stored in the PCX format, it becomes substantially larger than if it is uncompressed. This 256-color image is reproduced here as a gray-scale picture.

When compressed as a GIF file, this image becomes smaller than its uncompressed size. The uncompressed file is 64K, the PCX file is 67K, and the GIF file is 62K.

2-1 A small GIF file. This picture exhibits negative compression if it's stored in a run-length compressed format.

This sort of image doesn't compress well because, while it might contain redundant data, it's more complex than simple strings of repeating bytes. Specifically, there are numerous patches of a few bytes that occur in the same order throughout the image, but they are of variable length and happen at irregular intervals.

The compression technique used in GIF files—to be elaborated upon shortly—is called *string table compression*. It's more popularly called LZW compression after Lempil-Ziv and Welch, who first postulated it. This is the same compression system used in the ARC and ZIP file-compression systems and in modified form in various limitations and derivatives.

String-table compression works by keeping a table of bit runs and replacing the runs with tokens (*codes*), just as in run-length compression. However, the strings may be of variable length, which improves upon the performance of the encoder considerably. In addition, because of the way that the table is built up, it can be recreated when a compressed file is decompressed without having the original table present. In effect, a GIF decoder can recreate the original list of tokens from the compressed data.

The extensibility criteria for the GIF standard might or might not matter to you. If you're only interested in the GIF format as a medium for moving single images around, arguably its most useful function, then the ability to store text with an image, for example, will not appeal to you. However, the flexibility of the GIF format allows you to use its "extensions" to considerably enhance the basic images that it embodies for some applications.

The current list of GIF extension standards allow for the following facilities:

- Graphic control extension: this block lets you define how an image will be displayed, the duration of the display, whether someone watching it can interrupt its display, and so on.
- Comment extension: this block lets you add text comments to an image.
- Plain text extension: this block contains text that is to be positioned and displayed on a graphic screen.
- Application extension: this block may contain anything you like to customize the GIF format for your applications.

Note that GIF extensions may all be ignored, if you like. If your use of GIF files doesn't include any of the foregoing facilities, you may simply write a GIF decoder that bypasses extension blocks.

GIF files can contain multiple images. Therefore, you can create animated videos in a single GIF file by using a combination of images and graphic control extension blocks. You can create GIF files that automatically add text to themselves, and it's quite possible to devise GIF readers that display the same text in different languages, or that allow you to step through a series of text and graphic menus by using the facilities of extension blocks.

Extension blocks are dealt with in greater detail later in this chapter.

GIF compression

You don't have to understand how a GIF file is compressed to work with one. Later in this chapter you'll find a complete GIF decoder in easy-to-use C source. The decoder may be added to your graphics applications without your knowing how it works. You can, therefore, skip the rest of this section if you'd like to avoid filling your head with string tables and 12-bit codes.

The basic approach to run-length compression discussed in chapter 1 suffers from numerous drawbacks when it's confronted with scanned image data instead of drawn data, as from a paint program. A drawn image tends to have a lot of fairly predictable filled space, while an image scanned from a photograph usually has a lot of pseudo-random pixels scattered about. Figure 2-2 illustrates examples of each file type.

2-2 Two clowns. The left image was drawn and will compress fairly well. The right image was scanned and probably won't compress well.

If you understood the discussion of run-length compression in chapter 1, you'll appreciate how the drawn image in FIG. 2-2 will compress effectively and the scanned one probably will not.

True 24-bit scanned images typically can't be compressed very much, no matter how exotic the code is that attempts to do so. Unless the original had a lot of area that was genuinely of a single color—and assuming that scanner errors didn't creep into the image—the process of scanning a photograph usually leaves little room for compression.

The 24-bit file formats in this book are very easy to work with for this reason. None of them support image file compression very much, mostly because it does little good. Full-color files are used almost exclusively to hold scanned images.

Dithering a 24-bit file down to 256 colors reduces the number of colors and the possibility of variations between pixels by an order of magnitude. In addition, dithering imposes a pattern on the image data to some extent. The resulting image probably won't be any more responsive to run-length compression than its 24-bit source file was, but one can typically expect somewhat reasonable compression ratios under slightly trickier compression techniques.

Note that when they work at all, different types of run-length compression systems work slightly better on different sorts of scanned and dithered images. For example, some of the run-length compression techniques in use for simpler image structures allow a "run of bytes" field to actually be a "run of strings" field; that is, to repeat a variable length string of bytes rather than just 1. This situation can nominally improve on the effectiveness of run-length compression in some circumstances.

String-table (LZW) compression works by letting the image data define the tokens to be used. As such, it optimizes the compression for each specific image. In a sense, it's run-length compression with as many as 4096 possible different types of "run of string" fields, which is very much more effective dealing with complex image data.

Any type of information can be LZW compressed. The PKZIP and LHARC file compression programs apply the same general approach to compressing any sort of disk files. As an aside, this might help to explain why GIF files don't compress when you ZIP them. Applying LZW compression to data that has already been LZW compressed doesn't make it any smaller.

In GIF files, image data is always stored, based on 1 byte per pixel. This might seem a bit wasteful, inasmuch as a picture with 16 colors would use only 4 bits out of the 8 bits in each byte. In fact, LZW compression doesn't actually compress the unused bits in a byte, so it ignores this extra real estate.

It's a lot easier to understand LZW compression if you begin with the decompression process. This example looks at the process of unpacking a GIF file. In fact, it assumes that the rather complex header of a GIF file has been dealt with previously, and that the data being looked at is in fact the beginning of a block of compressed image information. The header of a GIF file is discussed in detail shortly.

A function to decode LZW-compressed data works with three objects: to wit, a *code stream*, a *code table* and a *character stream*. The code stream is the data being read from the compressed file. The character stream is the uncompressed data. The code table consists of a stack of entries in which codes from the file are identified with strings of data. In a GIF file, the code table has 4096 entries. GIF image data file can be compressed with up to 12 bits per code. Two raised to the 12th power (2^{12}) is 4096.

Note that these 12 bits refer to the maximum number of bits that the LZW compression function that originally created the GIF file in question was allowed to squeeze into a code. This is not the same as the number of bits of color the file may contain. Compression always begins by assuming that there are no fewer than the number of color bits in the picture being compressed, but the bit count may be increased to a 12-bit maximum.

The effectiveness of string-table compression improves with the maximum number of bits allowed in a code; that is, in some cases you could achieve better compression with a 14-bit maximum code size rather than a 12-bit one. However, a 14-bit LZW compression function would require a string table with 16,384 entries. For practical purposes, each entry consists of two integers and a byte, for a total of 5 bytes per entry making the table 81,920 bytes long. Not only is this a substantial amount of memory to tie up in itself, but it's too large for C to address as a simple array.

Having 12 bits as the maximum code size is a reasonable compromise between file compression and the complexity of the code required to handle GIF files. A GIF decoder is a pretty nasty function as it stands. It's also fairly slow as file decompression functions go, and increasing the maximum code size would make it still slower.

There are a number of other bits of information that are important to keep in mind before you start trying to fathom GIF decoding. Specifically, there are several special codes that are defined before the decoding process starts working. These are as follows:

```
#define CODESIZE        (1 << bits_per_pixel)
#define CLEAR_CODE      CODESIZE
#define END_OF_IMAGE    (CLEAR_CODE + 1)
#define FREE_CODE       (CLEAR_CODE + 2)
```

Before the decoding process begins, the string table must be partially initialized. Specifically, the first CODESIZE entries must be initialized with their positions in the table: entry zero will contain 0, entry one will contain 1, and so on.

For an 8-bit picture, that is, one with 256 colors, entries 0 through 255 are initialized. Code 256 is the clear code and code 257 is the end-of-image code. Code 258 is the first free code in the table. If a GIF decoder encounters CLEAR_CODE in the code stream, it immediately re-initializes its string table. If it encounters END_OF_IMAGE in the code stream, it shuts down and goes home.

The use of CLEAR_CODE might not be entirely clear. As an image is compressed, the string table of the compression function gradually gets full of strings. For as long as there are fewer than 4,096 strings in it, it's free to use the existing strings if it finds duplicates of them in the data it's compressing, and to add new ones if it discovers strings it has not encountered previously. If the string table becomes filled, it deals with this condition by throwing away all its strings and starting over. However, it must signal this event so that when the file is decoded, the decoding function will know to throw away its string table at the same time. The signal for this is CLEAR_CODE.

Figure 2-3 illustrates what happens as a GIF file is uncompressed.

Unlike most formats, a GIF encoder doesn't really care about the ends of individual scan lines. It regards the entire image as a block of data and simply compresses it. A GIF decoder reconstructs the image one line at a time because this is how image data is generally used. However, this is a bit of fiction that the GIF decoder enacts for the benefit of whatever software will use the image data. As with a GIF encoder, it sees only a long stream of characters.

GIF file structure

A GIF file decoder confronted with a GIF file has several things to be concerned with. Specifically, it must make sure that it's looking at a real GIF file. Then it must determine the dimensions of the picture the file contains and the number of color bits it represents. It must locate the palette data if the picture has more than two colors, and then proceed to unpack the image data.

The first 6 bytes of a GIF file represents an identification string. The first 3 bytes are "GIF." The last 3 bytes might be either "87a" or "89a." The GIF 87a specification allows for extension blocks but doesn't define any types. The GIF 89a specification defines the extension block types and makes a few minor changes to the header structure.

A GIF reader can handle both variations on the GIF file format by looking at the identification field contents.

If you're writing a GIF decoder, you should also keep in mind that there is another potential variation on the beginnings of GIF files. It's discussed later in this chapter under Macintosh GIF images.

The first part of a GIF file, including the signature string, is described by the following C language structure:

```
typedef struct {
        char sig[6];
        unsigned int screenwidth,screendepth;
        char flags;
        char background;
        char aspect;
        } GIFHEADER;
```

A GIF header is properly referred to as a "screen descriptor" in GIF terminology.

The sig field of the GIFHEADER is, of course, the signature. The screenwidth and screendepth elements define the screen dimensions in pixels of the computer used to create the image or images in the file. The screen dimensions are not the same as the image dimensions. For practical purposes this information is rarely of any use in simply looking

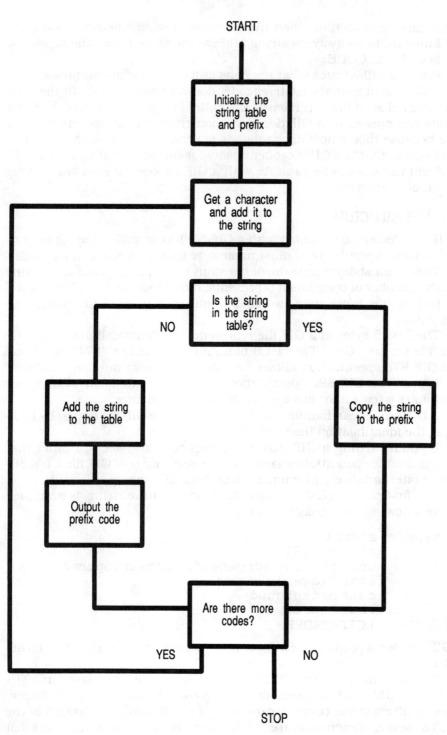

START

Initialize the string table and prefix

Get a character and add it to the string

Is the string in the string table?

NO

YES

Add the string to the table

Copy the string to the prefix

Output the prefix code

Are there more codes?

YES

NO

STOP

2-3 How a GIF file decoder works—simplified a bit.

at a GIF file's contents unless you find some comfort in knowing that your VGA card has a higher resolution graphics mode than anyone else's.

The `flags` field of the GIF header contains a number of bits of information. Specifically, if `gifheader->flags & 0x0080` is true, this data structure is followed by a color map. This is the same data that a display card defines as a "palette"; that is, a lookup table of 3-byte color values. The number of color bits it represents is `(gifheader->flags & 0x0007) + 1`. The number of colors in the table is `(1 << ((gifheader ->flags & 0x0007) + 1))`. There are 3 bytes for each color.

If `(gifheader->flags > 0x0008)` is true, the color palette is sorted with the most important colors first. As such, if you're confronted with looking at a 256-color GIF file with a sorted palette on a 16-color display, for example, you can remap all the colors in the image to the first 16 colors in the palette and the results should be only mildly ugly.

Finally `(1 << ((gifheader->flags >> 4) + 1)` is the number of color bits in the original image from which the GIF file was derived. This might not be the same as the number of color bits in the actual picture. Once again, this information is rarely of any practical use.

The latter two items are unique to the GIF 89a specification. These bits are set low in GIF 87a files. As discussed later in this chapter, GIF 87a files are quite adequate for simple image storage and most applications that generate GIF files still generate them with 87a specification. A huge body of these files exists. As such, it probably is not a good idea to write a GIF decoder that anticipates using the sort flag or the source color-palette-size fields if you anticipate it being presented with a variety of GIF files from the usual public domain sources.

The `background` field contains the color number of the background of the images in the file. If you want to display images from the file on a screen that might be larger than the images themselves, you should fill the screen with this value first. If you want to display them on a VGA card, you should also set the *overscan* to this value. The overscan is the color used to fill the border around the display area. It's black by default, and unless you've used software that specifically changes this, you might not have been aware of it.

Setting the overscan is discussed in chapter 10.

The `aspect` field is unique to GIF 89a files. It's always 0 in GIF 87a files. This specifies the aspect ratio of the pixels in the image. If this field isn't 0, the aspect ratio of the pixels in the image is `(gifheader ->aspect + 15) / 64`. Inasmuch as VGA cards allow for their default pixel aspect ratios only, this is another field that might or might not be of any real use.

If the `flags` field of the GIF header indicates that a color map is available, it comes next. This is called a *global* color map. It should be regarded as being a default set of colors that might be overridden by specific images in the file being read. In practice, most simple GIF files—GIF files with one image and no extensions—have a global color map as their only set of color definitions.

As the maximum number of colors in a GIF file is 256 and the number bytes of an RGB color is 3, the maximum amount of memory needed to hold the palette information of a GIF file is 768 bytes. If a global color map is available, you can work out the number of bytes it encompasses based on the number of color bits indicated by the `flags` field of the header, and read these bytes into a buffer.

Having read the GIF header and any global color map information that's present, the next byte in a GIF file should be a *block separator*. Block separators introduce the nature of a block of GIF information. There are three possible separators.

If the separator is a comma, the next block will be an image. If it's an exclamation point, it will be an extension. If it's a semicolon, you've reached the end of the GIF file and the decoder should retire.

This discussion deals with image blocks for the moment.

If you encounter a comma, the following data will be structured like this:

```
typedef struct {
        unsigned int left,top,width,depth;
        unsigned char flags;
        } IMAGEBLOCK;
```

An IMAGEBLOCK data structure defines the nature of a specific image, and anything that it includes that's in conflict with values in the GIF file header is considered to override the global values. Specifically, if an image block contains a color map, called a *local* color map, it supersedes the global map.

The `left` and `top` fields of the IMAGEBLOCK define the coordinates of the upper left corner of the displayed image relative to the upper left corner of your screen. In most cases these will be 0, and in most other cases you'll want to ignore them and pretend they're 0. However, if you're using GIF files to create a complex graphic display—perhaps using text added by an extension block—these values can be used to position a small image somewhere on the screen.

The `width` and `depth` fields define the actual dimensions of the image in this block in pixels. The `width` value also specifies the number of bytes in a line of unpacked image data, as a GIF decoder always packs and unpacks image lines with 1 byte per pixel, no matter how many bits of color are actually being used.

The `flags` field is similar to the `flags` field of the global header discussed earlier. The first 3 bits hold the number of bits of color information, so `(imageblock->flags & 0x0007) + 1` is the actual number of colors in the image for this block. Note that it's possible to create a multiple-image GIF file having images of differing numbers of colors.

If (imageblock->flags & 0x0040) is true, the image in this block is interlaced. The possibility of interlaced images greatly confuses the process of decoding GIF files in some applications. In an image where this bit is not set, the image lines are stored in the order they're displayed, so that the first line to be decoded is the first line displayed on your screen, and so on, just like normal human beings raised a safe distance from a nuclear power plant would have done it.

If this flag is set, the lines emerge from your GIF decoding function in a somewhat erratic order. Specifically, each image is split into four passes. On the first and second passes, every eighth line is written. The first pass starts with line zero and the second pass starts with line four. On the third pass, every fourth line is written, starting with line two. On the final pass, every second line is written, starting with line two.

There is actually a reason for ordering the lines of an image this way. You have to appreciate that CompuServe is a telecommunications system, and in creating the GIF format they foresaw the potential for people downloading GIF files with software that would display them as they were downloaded. If you download an interlaced image you can see a rough overview of the image contents in the first pass, and you can abort the transfer if you decide you don't like it.

You'll probably find that coping with GIF images having interlaced lines makes some programs a bit unwieldy. If you wanted to write a function to print GIF files, for example, you could read them into memory one line at a time, print that line and move on to the next line. However, this won't work if the image is interlaced. You'd have to read the whole image into a buffer and then read the lines from the buffer in a sensible order. If you're working with a really large GIF file, finding a big enough buffer might prove challenging.

If (imageblock->flags & 0x0080) is true, there is a local color map that is handled in the same way as the global color map. If (imageblock->flags & 0x0020) is true, the local color map is sorted, again similar to the global color map. This flag is defined only in the GIF 89a specification.

Following the IMAGEBLOCK structure and the local color map, if one is present, the next byte is the beginning of the LZW compressed-image information. It defines the initial image code size. The actual image data follows this byte and should be read until an end-of-image code appears.

Having correctly read an image block, the next byte to be read should be the next block separator. In a GIF file, the codes of LZW compressed-image data are stored in fields. Each field consists of a byte that defines the length of that field, followed by the data. As such, no field may be longer than 255 bytes. The last field in an image is always a zero-length block, indicating the end of the image data for a GIF reader.

You can work your way through a GIF file's image data as follows. This example assumes that fp is a file pointer for the GIF file being read, and that it initially points to the first byte of the first field of compressed data.

```
int i,n;
do {
  n=fgetc(fp);
  if(n != EOF) {
    for(i=0;i<n;++i) fgetc(fp);
  }
} while(n != 0 && n != EOF);
```

This is actually a quick way to check the integrity of a GIF file's image data. If the file is intact, running this bit of code should leave the file pointer ready to read the next block.

Extension blocks

If a block separator is an exclamation point, the block following is an extension. As their names might suggest, GIF extension blocks allow additional features to be tacked onto a basic GIF file. Extension blocks are most commonly used to attach some credits, a copyright notice, or a disclaimer to images. In the case of most GIF files—that is, ones that contain nudes—extension blocks are frequently used for the latter purpose. The following is an actual comment extension block from a GIF file.

priZm Image Center
P.O. Box 84
Bridgewater, MA 02324

508-697-3508 Hayes V9600
508-697-7771 USR HST/V.32
508-279-1552 USR HST

508-697-3575 Voice

Resemblance to people, places, or
things in our scans is purely coincidental.
priZm scans are electronic recreations
of pure fantasy.

Considering the nature of this disclaimer, you can probably imagine the nature of the GIF file in which it turned up. The "priZm Image Center" is one of many large bulletin boards that offer several gigabytes of GIF files for downloading. Because files tend to migrate between bulletin boards, you'll also find their work, complete with extension blocks like this one, on most local bulletin board systems.

As noted earlier in this chapter, a GIF file's extension blocks can serve many functions. The foregoing text came from a comment block, perhaps the simplest type of extension block. A comment block simply adds text to a GIF file in a predictable way. The text is not intended to be included as part of a graphic image, and does not include any formatting or control codes beyond simple text controls, such as carriage returns and line feeds.

There is a second text block type called "plain text," which allows text stored in a block to be added to an existing image. This type of block includes a header that defines where the text is to be placed on the screen and in what color it's to be drawn, among other things.

Image-control extension blocks define how an image should be handled after it is displayed. Specifically, an image-control extension block will allow a GIF file with multiple images to be set up so that a "smart" GIF viewer can display the whole works as the creator of the file intended. The file can display multiple images with pauses in between, for example, or with appearing and disappearing text.

In practice, this is a fairly exotic application for GIF files, and not one that is actually seen very often. Most of the activity surrounding GIF files has been to use the format to display pictures with increasingly high resolution. Having six 640×480 pixel scanned images in a single file, with each compressed image occupying approximately 200K, creates a rather unwieldy GIF file.

The GIF file that the previous disclaimer came out of did actually include an image-extension control block and a smaller second image. In this case, it would have caused a suitable GIF viewer to display the primary image in the file and then overlay it with the secondary one—predictably the logo of the priZm Image Center—until a key was hit, at which point the logo would go away.

Extension block structures

An extension block is structured as an exclamation point, which indicates the existence of an extension followed by a code that tells the reading software what type of extension it has encountered. By default, extension blocks are structured such that you may work your way around a block of unknown characteristics.

The simplest sort of GIF extension block is a comment. If the byte after the exclamation point is 0xfe, the extension is a comment block. A comment block consists of nothing but raw ASCII text. The text is stored in multiple data subblocks. A data subblock is defined as a byte to hold the length of the block, followed by as many bytes as defined by the length byte. A comment block may contain as many data subblocks required to hold its text. As a byte can hold numbers up to 255 only, larger amounts of text must be split up into multiple data subblocks. A comment extension is defined as ending when the first data subblock containing 0 bytes is encountered.

You can read the text out of a comment extension block as shown below. This example assumes that the 0xfe byte has just been read and that the file being read from has been opened with the file pointer in `fp`.

```
int i,n;
do {
```

```
       if(n=fgetc(fp)) != EOF) {
          for(i=0;i<n;++i)
          putch(fgetc(fp));
       }
    } while(n != 0 && n != EOF);
```

Note that this is the same approach used to skip over the fields of compressed data in an image block.

This bit of code will be embellished a bit when it turns up in a working GIF decoder.

A plain-text block—an extension to hold text that will be overlaid across a graphic—is identified by the byte 0x01 after the exclamation point that identifies the start of the extension. Following this byte is this data structure:

```
    typedef struct {
             char blocksize;
             unsigned int left,top;
             unsigned int gridwidth,gridheight;
             char cellwidth, cellheight;
             char forecolor,backcolor;
             } PLAINTEXT;
```

The left and top elements of this structure represent the starting position for the displayed text. The gridwidth and gridheight fields specify the distance in pixels from one character to the next for the text to be drawn. The cellwidth and cellheight fields specify the actual dimensions in pixels of the characters to be used. Note that GIF files do not provide a font in which to draw the text: they assume that a suitable font will be available to the viewer that interprets them.

You could store fonts as an application extension, which we'll discuss momentarily.

The forecolor and backcolor fields are the foreground and background color map indices respectively in which to draw the text.

Following this data structure is the text itself, stored as data sub-blocks, as previously described.

Any GIF file that contains more than one image block also contains control-block extensions so that a viewer encountering the pictures will know how they're to be displayed. The byte that identifies a graphic control block extension is 0xf9. Immediately after this byte you'll find the following data structure:

```
    typedef struct {
             char blocksize;
             char flags;
             unsigned int delay;
             char transparent_color;
             char terminator;
             } CONTROLBLOCK;
```

The blocksize field always contains the value 0x04.

If (controlblock->flags and 0x01) is true, controlblock ->transparent_color will contain a valid transparent color index. This color, when used in displaying the contents of the following image block, should be regarded as not being there, and should not be written to the screen. Anything below it should appear to show through the new graphic.

If (controlblock->flags and 0x02) is true, the viewing program that displays the following image block should wait for user input (that is, for a keypress) to allow the viewer to continue on to the next image in the file. If (controlblock->delay) is greater than zero and user input is expected, the viewer should wait for the number of seconds specified in the delay field or for a keypress, whichever comes first. If the delay value is greater than zero but user input is not specified, the viewer should wait for the number of seconds specified but ignore anything that happens at the keyboard.

The value provided by ((controlblock->flags >> 2) & 0x0007) represents the method by which the GIF viewer should remove the graphic in the next image block from the screen when it's time to dispose of it. The choices are as follows:

0 - do nothing
1 - leave it where it is
2 - restore the area beneath it to the background color
3 - restore the area beneath it to the previous graphic

It's quite acceptable for a GIF decoder to ignore those elements in a control block extension that it doesn't care about, or to ignore the whole extension.

Application blocks constitute the final type of GIF file extension. By definition, these are specific to the application that creates them. Unless your GIF file viewer is confronted with an application extension that has been put there by your software, you should probably ignore the contents of the block.

The byte that identifies an application extension is 0xff. The following data structure comes after the byte:

```
typedef struct {
        char blocksize;
        char applstring[8];
        char authentication[3];
        } APPLICATION;
```

The applstring field is an 8-byte string that identifies the software that should know what to do with the application block in question. The authentication field should contain 3 bytes based on the contents of the applstring field run through an algorithm of your choice. For example, you could perform a checksum of the applstring field, possibly XORing a few bits in the process, and store the results in the `authen-tication` field. This allows a GIF viewer that uses application extension blocks to store proprietary information, the opportunity to make sure that it's looking at one of its own application extensions, and not merely one that has the same `applstring` field.

Following this structure is the actual data in the extension, stored in data subblocks, as in the previous extension blocks.

Macintosh GIF files

Because of the ubiquitous nature of GIF files, they have also become popular in Macintosh circles. In fact, Macintosh color display hardware, and the Mac's 68000-series processors themselves, are very much out of keeping with the nature of GIF files. However, GIF readers and software to create GIF files do exist for Macintosh systems. As such, you might encounter Macintosh GIF files from time to time.

A Macintosh GIF file is identical to a PC GIF file internally. However, the rather peculiar file structure of the Mac might impose a slight complication on Macintosh GIF files that are ported to a PC environment. Whereas files on a PC are just files, the Macintosh makes a distinction between raw data, such as a GIF file, and data and executable code that have been structured to be loadable in blocks. The latter sort of data is referred to as "resources" on a Macintosh.

The Mac's file format divides all files into two "forks," the data fork and the resource fork. Image files typically consist of files with everything in the data forks and nothing in the resource forks. An application, such as a GIF viewer on the Macintosh, would have all its executable code stored as resources and usually little or nothing in its data fork.

You can think of these forked files as really being two different files that the Macintosh allows you to access through a single name. It works well for the Mac, but is relatively meaningless elsewhere.

Because the rest of the civilized universe gets by quite well with a single file fork, Macintosh files that are ported from a Mac to a PC system are at something of a loss as to the disposition of these two forks. This problem initially cropped up when Macintosh users started to connect their Macs to modems. The problem was dealt with by the author of an early Macintosh telecommunication package by adding what has come to be called the "MacBinary" header structure to the Mac's forked files.

In porting a file from a Macintosh to a PC using a MacBinary header, the resulting single-fork file consists of the contents of the original data fork followed by the contents of the original resource fork. The whole effort is preceded by a 128-byte header that specifies where the data fork ends and the resource fork begins, such that the single file may be split into two forks again should it ever find itself back on a Macintosh. The header also specifies some Macintosh-specific information, such as the original Macintosh file name and the Macintosh creation and modification dates.

It's worth noting that, unlike as with MS-DOS, the Macintosh's operating system allows for file names having up to 32 characters. Rather than naming a file "GIRL-RED.GIF," or something equally as cryptic, a Mac would let you call it "Girl in a red bathing suit.GIF."

There's a quick and nasty way to handle a GIF file that has a MacBinary header. If a program that reads GIF files attempts to read the GIF file header and fails to find the string "GIF" in the first 3 bytes of the signature, it should check the first byte to see if it's a 0. If it is, indicating the presence of a MacBinary header, it should seek to 128 bytes into the file and try to find the GIF file header again.

Alternately, you might want to peek about in the MacBinary header a bit. This is what it looks like:

```
typedef struct {
        char zerobyte;
        char name[64];
        char type[4];
        char creator[4];
        char filler[10];
        long datafork_size;
        long rsrcfork_size;
        long creation_date;
        long modif_date;
        char filler2[29];
        } MACBINARY;
```

If you encounter a GIF file with a MacBinary header, you can get at the header fields by seeking back to the beginning of the file and reading the first 128 bytes into a MacBinary structure. Some of the fields might need a bit of explanation.

The `name` field is the original Macintosh file name stored as a Pascal string—Apple is very fond of Pascal. Unlike as with a C-language string, a Pascal string has its length stored in the first byte of the string followed by the string's contents. There is no null-terminating byte.

The `type` and `creator` fields tell the Mac's operating system what sort of file this header belongs to. The `type` field contains the string "GIFf" for GIF files. The `creator` can contain any four printable characters: The most commonly used creator string for Macintosh GIF files is "BOZO." Make of this what you will.

By convention, the data for the data fork always comes first in a file with a MacBinary header. As such, the resource fork starts at `mac-binary->datafork_size+sizeof(MacBinary)` bytes into the file. In fact, there are two things to note about this. The resource fork should always be empty on a GIF file, and this expression is totally wrong on a PC.

Based on a microprocessor made by a different company, the Macintosh stores multiple-byte numbers differently from the way a PC does. Specifically, the bytes are backwards. In order to read a long integer created on a Mac, you must pass it through the following function:

```
long motr2intel(l)
    long l;
{
    return(((l & 0xff000000L) >> 24) +
           ((l & 0x00ff0000L) >> 8) +
           ((l & 0x0000ff00L) << 8) +
           ((l & 0x000000ffL) << 24));
}
```

Each of the long integers in a MacBinary header must be read using this function so that their contents can make sense in a PC environment. It's important to note, however, that the multiple-byte numbers in a GIF file are always stored in the Intel format that is used by PC systems, whether the file originated on a PC or a Mac. A Macintosh GIF file reader would have to use a function similar to the one above to read the multiple byte numbers in a GIF file, translating the Intel numbers into Motorola ones.

Finally, the `creation_date` and `modif_date` fields of a Mac-Binary header specify when the file was created and modified on the Macintosh that it came from. Both fields contain long integers. Apple and Microsoft differ in their beliefs as to when time began. Apple believes that this event took place on January 1, 1904. As any PC user who's found the CMOS batteries in his or her system dead one morning knows, Microsoft thinks that time began on January 1, 1980.

There is, of course, historical evidence to suggest that both of these dates are somewhat in error. This is probably irrelevant to the discussion of MacBinary headers.

You can work out the creation date of a GIF file with a MacBinary header by subtracting the number of seconds between January 1, 1904 and January 1, 1980 from the value in the `creation_date` field. This number is, in fact:

```
#define  mac2pc_date  2082830400L
```

The complete expression, then, would be as follows:

```
unsigned long t;

t=motr2intel(macbinary->creation_date)-
mac2pc_date;
```

The value in t will be a normal PC time value. You can see it in conventional time and date notation by passing it to the Turbo C `ctime` function, just as you would a value set by the Turbo C `time` function.

You can use the same approach for reading the modification date.

An example GIF reader

Writing a GIF file decoder that deals with image data in discrete lines is a bit awkward, which is not the case with most of the other file formats discussed in this book. In most formats, an image file can be decoded by working out whatever the header involves and then calling a function repeatedly to decode each line. Because of the way LZW compression works, this is not a practical method to use with GIF files. Instead, you must decode the entire file and deal with each line as it is completed, which is the opposite approach.

The most elegant and flexible way to approach a GIF file decoder is to set up function pointers for those functions that the decoder might need to perform once it has some data. For example, rather than hardwiring a function into the decoder to simply store lines in memory, the decoder could be passed a pointer to a function that it would call to store the lines. By replacing the function with a different one, something else could be done with the lines.

Figure 2-4 is the complete source code for a GIF decoder called READGIF. This one is written entirely in C. While not as fast as a GIF decoder written in assembly language, it's enormously easier to understand.

```
/*
        GIF reader - copyright (c) 1991
        Alchemy Mindworks Inc.
*/

#include "stdio.h"
#include "dos.h"
#include "alloc.h"

/*                              uncomment this line if you
#include "memmangr.h"           will be linking in the memory manager
*/

#define GOOD_READ       0       /* return codes */
#define BAD_FILE        1
#define BAD_READ        2
#define UNEXPECTED_EOF  3
#define BAD_CODE        4
#define BAD_FIRSTCODE   5
#define BAD_ALLOC       6
#define BAD_SYMBOLSIZE  7

#define NO_CODE         -1

#define SCREENWIDE      320     /* mode 13 screen dimensions */
#define SCREENDEEP      200
#define STEP            32      /* size of a step when panning */

#define HOME            0x4700  /* cursor control codes */
#define CURSOR_UP       0x4800
```

2-4 The complete source code for READGIF.

```
#define CURSOR_LEFT       0x4b00
#define CURSOR_RIGHT      0x4d00
#define END               0x4f00
#define CURSOR_DOWN        0x5000

typedef struct {
        char sig[6];
        unsigned int screenwidth,screendepth;
        unsigned char flags,background,aspect;
        } GIFHEADER;

typedef struct {
        unsigned int left,top,width,depth;
        unsigned char flags;
        } IMAGEBLOCK;

typedef struct {
        int width,depth,bits;
        int flags;
        int background;
        char palette[768];
        int (*setup)();
        int (*closedown)();
        int (*saveline)();
        int (*savext)();
        } FILEINFO;

typedef struct {
        char blocksize;
        char flags;
        unsigned int delay;
        char transparent_colour;
        char terminator;
        } CONTROLBLOCK;

typedef struct {
        char blocksize;
        unsigned int left,top;
        unsigned int gridwidth,gridheight;
        char cellwidth,cellheight;
        char forecolour,backcolour;
        } PLAINTEXT;

typedef struct {
        char blocksize;
        char applstring[8];
        char authentication[3];
        } APPLICATION;


char *farPtr(char *p,long l);
char *getline(unsigned int n);
```

2-4 Continued.

```
int putextension(FILE *fp);
int putline(char *p,unsigned int n);
int dosetup(FILEINFO *fi);
int doclosedown(FILEINFO *fi);

FILEINFO fi;
char *buffer=NULL;

main(argc,argv)
        int argc;
        char *argv[];
{
        FILE *fp;
        static char results[8][16] = {  "Ok",
                                        "Bad file",
                                        "Bad read",
                                        "Unexpected end",
                                        "Bad LZW code",
                                        "Bad first code",
                                        "Memory error",
                                        "Bad symbol size"
                                        };
        char path[81];
        int r;

        if(argc > 1) {
                strmfe(path,argv[1],"GIF");
                if((fp = fopen(path,"rb")) != NULL) {
                        fi.setup=dosetup;
                        fi.closedown=doclosedown;
                        fi.saveline=putline;
                        fi.savext=putextension;
                        r=unpackgif(fp,&fi);
                        printf("\%s",results[r]);
                        fclose(fp);
                } else printf("Error opening %s",path);
        } else puts("Argument:       path to a GIF file");
}

/* this function is called when the GIF decoder encounters an extension */
putextension(fp)
        FILE *fp;
{
        PLAINTEXT pt;
        CONTROLBLOCK cb;
        APPLICATION ap;
        int c,n,i;

        clrscr();
        switch((c=fgetc(fp))) {
                case 0x0001:                    /* plain text descriptor */
                        if(fread((char *)&pt,1,sizeof(PLAINTEXT),fp)
```

2-4 Continued.

```
                == sizeof(PLAINTEXT)) {
                    puts("PLAIN TEXT BLOCK\n_____");
                    printf("This block requires %u bytes\n",pt.blocksize);
                    printf("Text location at (%u,%u)\n",pt.left,pt.top);
                    printf("Grid dimensions are %u by %u\n",pt.gridwidth,pt.gridheight);
                    printf("Cell dimensions are %u by %u\n",pt.cellwidth,pt.cellheight);
                    printf("Foregound colour is %u\n",pt.forecolour);
                    printf("Background colour is %u\n",pt.backcolour);

                    do {
                        if((n=fgetc(fp)) != EOF) {
                            for(i=0;i<n;++i)
                                printchar(fgetc(fp));
                        }
                    } while(n > 0 && n != EOF);
            } else puts("Error reading plain text block");
            break;
case 0x00f9:              /* graphic control block */
        if(fread((char *)&cb,1,sizeof(CONTROLBLOCK),fp)
            == sizeof(CONTROLBLOCK)) {
                puts("CONTROL BLOCK\n_____");
                printf("This block requires %u bytes\n",cb.blocksize);
                switch((cb.flags >> 2) & 0x0007) {
                    case 0:
                            puts("No disposal specified");
                            break;
                    case 1:
                            puts("Do not dispose");
                            break;
                    case 2:
                            puts("Dispose to background colour");
                            break;
                    case 3:
                            puts("Dispose to previous graphic");
                            break;
                    default:
                            puts("Unknown disposal procedure");
                            break;
                }
                if(cb.flags & 0x0002)
                    printf("User input required - delay for %u seconds",
                        cb.delay);
                else puts("No user input required");

                if(cb.flags & 0x0001)
                    printf("Transparent colour: %u\n",
                        cb.transparent_colour);
                else puts("No transparent_colour");

        } else puts("Error reading control block");
        break;
case 0x00fe:              /* comment extension */
        puts("COMMENT BLOCK\n_____");
```

2-4 Continued.

```
                        do {
                                if((n=fgetc(fp)) != EOF) {
                                        for(i=0;i<n;++i)
                                                printchar(fgetc(fp));
                                }
                        } while(n > 0 && n != EOF);
                        break;
                case 0x00ff:                /* application extension */
                        if(fread((char *)&ap,1,sizeof(APPLICATION),fp)
                            == sizeof(APPLICATION)) {
                                puts("APPLICATION BLOCK\n_____");
                                printf("Application identification string: %0.8s",ap.applstring);
                                do {
                                        if((n=fgetc(fp)) != EOF) {
                                                for(i=0;i<n;++i) fgetc(fp);
                                        }
                                } while(n > 0 && n != EOF);
                        } else puts("Error reading application block");
                        break;
                default:                    /* something else */
                        printf("Skipping unknown extension type %02.2X\n",
                            c & 0x00ff);
                        n=fgetc(fp);
                        for(i=0;i<n;++i) fgetc(fp);
                        break;
                }
        getch();
}


/* unpack a GIF file */
unpackgif(fp,fi)
        FILE *fp;
        FILEINFO *fi;
{

        GIFHEADER gh;
        IMAGEBLOCK iblk;
        long t;
        int b,c;

        /* make sure it's a GIF file */
        if(fread((char *)&gh,1,sizeof(GIFHEADER),fp) != sizeof(GIFHEADER) ||
            memcmp(gh.sig, "GIF", 3)) return(BAD_FILE);

        /* get screen dimensions */
        fi->width=gh.screenwidth;
        fi->depth=gh.screendepth;
        fi->bits=(gh.flags & 0x0007) + 1;
        fi->background=gh.background;
        /* get colour map if there is one */
        if(gh.flags & 0x80) {
                c = 3 * (1 << ((gh.flags & 7) + 1));
                if(fread(fi->palette,1,c,fp) != c) return(BAD_READ);
```

2-4 Continued.

```
        }
        /* step through the blocks */
        while((c=fgetc(fp))==',' || c=='!' || c==0) {

                /* if it's an image block... */
                if (c == ',') {
                        /* get the start of the image block */
                        if(fread(&iblk,1,sizeof(IMAGEBLOCK),fp) !=
                            sizeof(IMAGEBLOCK)) return(BAD_READ);

                        /* get the image dimensions */
                        fi->width=iblk.width;
                        fi->depth=iblk.depth;

                        /* get the local colour map if there is one */
                        if(iblk.flags & 0x80) {
                                b = 3*(1<<((iblk.flags & 0x0007) + 1));
                                if(fread(fi->palette,1,b,fp) != c) return(BAD_READ);
                                fi->bits=(iblk.flags & 0x0007) + 1;
                        }

                        /* get the initial code size */
                        if((c=fgetc(fp))==EOF) return(BAD_FILE);

                        fi->flags=iblk.flags;

                        /* do the setup procedure */
                        if(fi->setup != NULL) {
                                if((t=(fi->setup)(fi)) != GOOD_READ)
                                        return(t);
                        }

                        /* unpack the image */
                        t=unpackimage(fp,c,fi);

                        /* do the close down procedure */
                        if(fi->closedown != NULL) (fi->closedown)(fi);

                        /* quit if there was an error */
                        if(t != GOOD_READ) return(t);
                }
                /* otherwise, it's an extension */
                else if(c == '!') (fi->savext)(fp);
        }
        return(GOOD_READ);
}

/* unpack an LZW compressed image */
unpackimage(fp,bits,fi)
        FILE *fp;
        int bits;
        FILEINFO *fi;
```

2-4 Continued.

```
{
        int bits2;              /* Bits plus 1 */
        int codesize;           /* Current code size in bits */
        int codesize2;          /* Next codesize */
        int nextcode;           /* Next available table entry */
        int thiscode;           /* Code being expanded */
        int oldtoken;           /* Last symbol decoded */
        int currentcode;        /* Code just read */
        int oldcode;            /* Code read before this one */
        int bitsleft;           /* Number of bits left in *p */
        int blocksize;          /* Bytes in next block */
        int line=0;             /* next line to write */
        int byte=0;             /* next byte to write */
        int pass=0;             /* pass number for interlaced pictures */

        char *p;                /* Pointer to current byte in read buffer */
        char *q;                /* Pointer past last byte in read buffer */
        char b[255];            /* Read buffer */
        char *u;                /* Stack pointer into firstcodestack */
        char *linebuffer;       /* place to store the current line */

        static char firstcodestack[4096];  /* Stack for first codes */
        static char lastcodestack[4096];   /* Stack for previous code */
        static int codestack[4096];        /* Stack for links */

        static int wordmasktable[] = {  0x0000,0x0001,0x0003,0x0007,
                                        0x000f,0x001f,0x003f,0x007f,
                                        0x00ff,0x01ff,0x03ff,0x07ff,
                                        0x0fff,0x1fff,0x3fff,0x7fff
                                        };

        static int inctable[] = { 8,8,4,2,0 }; /* interlace increments */
        static int startable[] = { 0,4,2,1,0 };  /* interlace starts */

        p=q=b;
        bitsleft = 8;

        if (bits < 2 || bits > 8) return(BAD_SYMBOLSIZE);
        bits2 = 1 << bits;
        nextcode = bits2 + 2;
        codesize2 = 1 << (codesize = bits + 1);
        oldcode=oldtoken=NO_CODE;

        if((linebuffer=malloc(fi->width)) == NULL) return(BAD_ALLOC);

        /* loop until something breaks */
        for(;;) {
                if(bitsleft==8) {
                        if(++p >= q &&
                        (((blocksize = fgetc(fp)) < 1) ||
                        (q=(p=b)+fread(b,1,blocksize,fp))< (b+blocksize))) {
                                free(linebuffer);
```

2-4 Continued.

```
                return(UNEXPECTED_EOF);
        }
        bitsleft = 0;
        }
        thiscode = *p;
        if ((currentcode=(codesize+bitsleft)) <= 8) {
                *p >>= codesize;
                bitsleft = currentcode;
        }
        else {
        if(++p >= q &&
          (((blocksize = fgetc(fp)) < 1) ||
          (q=(p=b)+fread(b,1,blocksize,fp)) < (b+blocksize))) {
                free(linebuffer);
                return(UNEXPECTED_EOF);
        }
        thiscode |= *p << (8 - bitsleft);
        if(currentcode <= 16) *p >>= (bitsleft=currentcode-8);
        else {
                if(++p >= q &&
                  (((blocksize = fgetc(fp)) < 1) ||
                  (q=(p=b) + fread(b,1,blocksize,fp)) < (b+blocksize))) {
                        free(linebuffer);
                        return(UNEXPECTED_EOF);
                }
                thiscode |= *p << (16 - bitsleft);
                *p >>= (bitsleft = currentcode - 16);
        }
}
thiscode &= wordmasktable[codesize];
currentcode = thiscode;

if(thiscode == (bits2+1)) break;     /* found EOI */
if(thiscode > nextcode) {
        free(linebuffer);
        return(BAD_CODE);
}

if(thiscode == bits2) {
        nextcode = bits2 + 2;
        codesize2 = 1 << (codesize = (bits + 1));
        oldtoken = oldcode = NO_CODE;
        continue;
}

u = firstcodestack;

if(thiscode==nextcode) {
        if(oldcode==NO_CODE) {
                free(linebuffer);
                return(BAD_FIRSTCODE);
        }
```

2-4 Continued.

```
                        *u++ = oldtoken;
                        thiscode = oldcode;
                }

                while (thiscode >= bits2) {
                        *u++ = lastcodestack[thiscode];
                        thiscode = codestack[thiscode];
                }

                oldtoken = thiscode;
                do {
                        linebuffer[byte++]=thiscode;
                        if(byte >= fi->width) {
                                (fi->saveline)(linebuffer,line);
                                byte=0;

                                /* check for interlaced image */
                                 if(fi->flags & 0x40) {
                                        line+=inctable[pass];
                                        if(line >= fi->depth)
                                                line=startable[++pass];
                                 } else ++line;
                        }

                        if (u <= firstcodestack) break;
                        thiscode = *--u;
                } while(1);

                if(nextcode < 4096 && oldcode != NO_CODE) {
                        codestack[nextcode] = oldcode;
                        lastcodestack[nextcode] = oldtoken;
                        if (++nextcode >= codesize2 && codesize < 12)
                            codesize2 = 1 << ++codesize;
                }
                oldcode = currentcode;
        }
        free(linebuffer);
        return(GOOD_READ);
}

/* This function is called before an image is decompressed. It must
   allocate memory, put the display in graphic mode and so on. */
dosetup(fi)
        FILEINFO *fi;
{
        union REGS r;

        if(!getbuffer((long)fi->width*(long)fi->depth,fi->width,fi->depth))
            return(BAD_ALLOC);

        r.x.ax=0x0013;
        int86(0x10,&r,&r);
```

2-4 Continued.

```
        setvgapalette(fi->palette,1<<fi->bits,fi->background);

        return(GOOD_READ);
}

/* This function is called after an image has been unpacked. It must
   display the image and deallocate memory. */
doclosedown(fi)
        FILEINFO *fi;
{

        union REGS r;
        int c,i,n,x=0,y=0;

        if(fi->width > SCREENWIDE) n=SCREENWIDE;
        else n=fi->width;

        do {
                for(i=0;i<SCREENDEEP;++i) {
                        c=y+i;
                        if(c>=fi->depth) break;
                        memcpy(MK_FP(0xa000,SCREENWIDE*i),getline(c)+x,n);
                }
                c=GetKey();
                switch(c) {
                        case CURSOR_LEFT:
                                if((x-STEP) > 0) x-=STEP;
                                else x=0;
                                break;
                        case CURSOR_RIGHT:
                                if((x+STEP+SCREENWIDE) < fi->width) x+=STEP;
                                else if(fi->width > SCREENWIDE)
                                        x=fi->width-SCREENWIDE;
                                else x=0;
                                break;
                        case CURSOR_UP:
                                if((y-STEP) > 0) y-=STEP;
                                else y=0;
                                break;
                        case CURSOR_DOWN:
                                if((y+STEP+SCREENDEEP) < fi->depth) y+=STEP;
                                else if(fi->depth > SCREENDEEP)
                                        y=fi->depth-SCREENDEEP;
                                else y=0;
                                break;
                        case HOME:
                                x=y=0;
                                break;
                        case END:
                                if(fi->width > SCREENWIDE)
                                        x=fi->width-SCREENWIDE;
                                else x=0;
                                if(fi->depth > SCREENDEEP)
                                        y=fi->depth-SCREENDEEP;
```

2-4 Continued.

```
                                                else y=0;
                                                break;
                                }
                        } while(c != 27);
                        freebuffer();

                        r.x.ax=0x0003;
                        int86(0x10,&r,&r);
                        return(GOOD_READ);
}

/* get one extended key code */
GetKey()
{
        int c;

        c = getch();
        if(!(c & 0x00ff)) c = getch() << 8;
        return(c);

}

/* set the VGA palette and background */
setvgapalette(p,n,b)
        char *p;
        int n,b;
{
        union REGS r;
        int i;
        outp(0x3c6,0xff);
        for(i=0;i<n;++i) {
                outp(0x3c8,i);
                outp(0x3c9,(*p++) >> 2);
                outp(0x3c9,(*p++) >> 2);
                outp(0x3c9,(*p++) >> 2);
        }
        r.x.ax=0x1001;
        r.h.bh=b;
        int86(0x10,&r,&r);
}


/* make file name with specific extension */
strmfe(new,old,ext)
        char *new,*old,*ext;
{
        while(*old != 0 && *old != '.') *new++=*old++;
        *new++='.';
        while(*ext) *new++=*ext++;
        *new=0;

}

printchar(c)                    /* print characters from extension blocks */
```

2-4 Continued.

```
            int c;
{
        if(c==9 || c==13 || c==10) putchar(c);
        else if(c >= 32) putchar(c);
        else if(c==EOF) printf("<EOF>");
        else printf("<%u>",c);
}


/* if you don't use in the memory manager, these functions
   will stand in for it */

#if !MEMMANGR

/* return a far pointer plus a long integer */
char *farPtr(p,l)
        char *p;
        long l;
{
        unsigned int seg,off;

        seg = FP_SEG(p);
        off = FP_OFF(p);
        seg += (off / 16);
        off &= 0x000f;
        off += (unsigned int)(l & 0x000fL);
        seg += (l / 16L);
        p = MK_FP(seg,off);
        return(p);
}

/* save one line to memory */
putline(p,n)
        char *p;
        unsigned int n;
{
        if(n >= 0 && n < fi.depth)
            memcpy(farPtr(buffer,(long)n*(long)fi.width),p,fi.width);
}

/* get one line from memory */
char *getline(n)
        unsigned int n;
{
        return(farPtr(buffer,(long)n*(long)fi.width));
}

#pragma warn -par
getbuffer(n,bytes,lines)
        unsigned long n;
        int bytes,lines;
{
```

2-4 Continued.

```
        if((buffer=farmalloc(n)) == NULL) return(0);
        else return(1);
}


freebuffer()
{
        if(buffer != NULL) farfree(buffer);
        buffer=NULL;

}
#endif /* !MEMMANGR */
```

Having worked your way through the discussion on GIF files structures, the decoder discussion should be pretty easy to follow. It's worth noting a few things about this code, however. To begin with, it can be self-contained: you won't need to use the memory-manager object module with it unless you'd like to work with files that must unpack into more conventional memory than you have available. If you want to use the memory manager, simply uncomment the include directive for its header file.

Because a complete discussion of display adapters doesn't turn up for several chapters, this GIF decoder gets by with a rudimentary-mode 13H VGA viewing function. It works only on a VGA card.

Chapter 10 also provides a complete explanation of what the display code in this program is actually up to. At the moment, you might want to use it and forget about what it's actually doing.

As an aside, one of the things that occasionally goes wrong with GIF file viewers like this one at the compiler level is a peculiar palette shift—an image appears, but its colors are wrong. This is usually caused by using signed rather than unsigned chars for the palette buffer and a few other things in the code that handle the palette and the GIF data. Make sure you set up Turbo C to default to unsigned characters.

In order to avoid hardwiring functions into the GIF decoder, it's passed a structure that, among other things, includes function pointers to handle the various things it might do with images and other types of blocks it encounters. The FILEINFO structure holds the dimensions of the current image block, its color depth and palette, and pointers to four functions. The setup function is called by the GIF decoder just before an image is to be unpacked. Typically, as in this example, this function should allocate a buffer in which to put the file, and perhaps put the screen in the appropriate graphics mode. You can see an example of a suitable function in dosetup.

It's important to note that GIF files frequently require more than 64K of memory to contain them once they're unpacked. For this reason, you must allocate the buffer for a GIF file with farmalloc, which can accept a long integer as its argument. It's also important to note that you must cast the width and depth values to long before you multiply them so that if the result exceeds what can be respectably stored in 16 bits, it won't be truncated.

The second function pointer, `closedown`, should point to a function to be called after an image has been displayed. This function typically deallocates the memory allocated by the setup function, and possibly restores the screen to text mode. In the case of the example GIF decoder in FIG. 2-4, it actually handles panning around the GIF file as well.

The `saveline` function is called by the GIF decoder each time a completed line has been decoded. It typically stores the line in memory or displays it on the screen. The function should accept two arguments: a pointer to the line data, and an integer representing the line number.

Finally, the `savext` function is called by the GIF decoder any time an extension block is encountered. It should do whatever is necessary to deal with the block. The `putextension` function in FIG. 2-4 illustrates one example of a suitable extension-block handler. It simply displays the relevant contents of any block it finds. If you want to implement a really sophisticated GIF viewer, one that actually overlays multiple images, displays text, waits for user input and so on, you have to modify this function to do a great deal more with extension blocks.

Note that it's essential that the extension-block handler be able to properly interpret, and skip over, all types of extension blocks, even if you have no interest in using the information extension blocks might contain.

To use this program, type it and compile it. Pass it the path to a GIF file as its command-line argument. You can use the companion source code disk for this book; the file ZOE.GIF makes a good initial test subject. It should display the picture in FIG. 2-1.

If you've elected to use the memory manager, you will require a project file to link it to READGIF.

Writing GIF files

Writing a function to create an image file and pack data into it is invariably easier than writing a decoder. In packing a file, your code knows what it will be doing. It need not interpret the contents of the image and figure out what's intended to happen. It's not surprising, then, that the example GIF writer discussed next is quite a bit smaller than the reader was.

Before you can experiment with a file writer, you need something to write. Specifically, you need some example image data for the writer program to pack into a GIF file. You can obtain this example image data in several ways. The easiest way, and perhaps the most useful, is to create a custom binary file format that contains it.

The program in FIG. 2-5 is clearly derivative of the foregoing GIF reader. In fact, if you've typed in the GIF reader you can make this program from it by simply replacing the `putextension`, `dosetup`, `doclosedown` and `putline` functions. There are also a few changes in the `main` function and a new data structure, BINARYHEADER, to add.

This program is called MAKEBIN.

```
/*
        GIF to binary converter - copyright (c) 1991
        Alchemy Mindworks Inc.
*/

#include "stdio.h"
#include "dos.h"
#include "alloc.h"

/*                              uncomment this line if you
#include "memmangr.h"           will be linking in the memory manager
*/

#define GOOD_READ       0       /* return codes */
#define BAD_FILE        1
#define BAD_READ        2
#define UNEXPECTED_EOF  3
#define BAD_CODE        4
#define BAD_FIRSTCODE   5
#define BAD_ALLOC       6
#define BAD_SYMBOLSIZE  7

#define NO_CODE         -1

#define BINARYSIG       "ALCHBINR"

typedef struct {
        char sig[6];
        unsigned int screenwidth,screendepth;
        unsigned char flags,background,aspect;
        } GIFHEADER;

typedef struct {
        unsigned int left,top,width,depth;
        unsigned char flags;
        } IMAGEBLOCK;

typedef struct {
        int width,depth,bits;
        int flags;
        int background;
        char palette[768];
        int (*setup)();
        int (*closedown)();
        int (*saveline)();
        int (*savext)();
        } FILEINFO;

typedef struct {
        char blocksize;
        char flags;
        unsigned int delay;
```

2-5 The complete source code for MAKEBIN.

```
             char transparent_colour;
             char terminator;
             } CONTROLBLOCK;

typedef struct {
             char blocksize;
             unsigned int left,top;
             unsigned int gridwidth,gridheight;
             char cellwidth,cellheight;
             char forecolour,backcolour;
             } PLAINTEXT;

typedef struct {
             char blocksize;
             char applstring[8];
             char authentication[3];
             } APPLICATION;

typedef struct {
             char sign[8];
             int width,depth,bits;
             char palette[768];
             } BINARYHEADER;

char *farPtr(char *p,long l);
char *getline(unsigned int n);

int putextension(FILE *fp);
int putline(char *p,unsigned int n);
int dosetup(FILEINFO *fi);
int doclosedown(FILEINFO *fi);

FILEINFO fi;
char *buffer=NULL;
FILE *out;

main(argc,argv)
        int argc;
        char *argv[];
{
        FILE *fp;
        static char results[8][16] = {  "Ok",
                                        "Bad file",
                                        "Bad read",
                                        "Unexpected end",
                                        "Bad LZW code",
                                        "Bad first code",
                                        "Memory error",
                                        "Bad symbol size"
                                        };

        char path[81];
        int r;
```

2-5 Continued.

```
                    if(argc > 1) {
                            strmfe(path,argv[1],"GIF");
                            if((fp=fopen(path,"rb")) != NULL) {
                                    strmfe(path,argv[1],"BIN");
                                    if((out=fopen(path,"wb")) != NULL) {
                                            fi.setup=dosetup;
                                            fi.closedown=doclosedown;
                                            fi.saveline=putline;
                                            fi.savext=putextension;
                                            r=unpackgif(fp,&fi);
                                            printf("\%s",results[r]);
                                            fclose(out);
                                    } else printf("Error creating %s",path);
                                    fclose(fp);
                            } else printf("Error opening %s",path);
                    } else puts("Argument:      path to a GIF file");
        }


        /* this function is called when the GIF decoder encounters an extension */
        putextension(fp)
                FILE *fp;
        {

                PLAINTEXT pt;
                CONTROLBLOCK cb;
                APPLICATION ap;
                int n,i;

                switch(fgetc(fp)) {
                        case 0x0001:              /* plain text descriptor */
                                if(fread((char *)&pt,1,sizeof(PLAINTEXT),fp)
                                    == sizeof(PLAINTEXT)) {

                                        do {
                                                if((n=fgetc(fp)) != EOF) {
                                                        for(i=0;i<n;++i)
                                                                fgetc(fp);
                                                }
                                        } while(n > 0 && n != EOF);
                                } else puts("Error reading plain text block");
                                break;
                        case 0x00f9:              /* graphic control block */
                                if(fread((char *)&cb,1,sizeof(CONTROLBLOCK),fp)
                                    != sizeof(CONTROLBLOCK))
                                    puts("Error reading control block");
                                break;
                        case 0x00fe:              /* comment extension */
                                do {
                                        if((n=fgetc(fp)) != EOF) {
                                                for(i=0;i<n;++i)
                                                        fgetc(fp);
                                        }
                                } while(n > 0 && n != EOF);
```

2-5 Continued.

```
                        break;
            case 0x00ff:                    /* application extension */
                    if(fread((char *)&ap,1,sizeof(APPLICATION),fp)
                        == sizeof(APPLICATION)) {
                            do {
                                    if((n=fgetc(fp)) != EOF) {
                                            for(i=0;i<n;++i) fgetc(fp);
                                    }
                            } while(n > 0 && n != EOF);
                    } else puts("Error reading application block");
                    break;
            default:                        /* something else */
                    n=fgetc(fp);
                    for(i=0;i<n;++i) fgetc(fp);
                    break;
        }
}


/* unpack a GIF file */
unpackgif(fp,fi)
        FILE *fp;
        FILEINFO *fi;
{
        GIFHEADER gh;
        IMAGEBLOCK iblk;
        long t;
        int b,c;

        /* make sure it's a GIF file */
        if(fread((char *)&gh,1,sizeof(GIFHEADER),fp) != sizeof(GIFHEADER) ||
            memcmp(gh.sig, "GIF", 3)) return(BAD_FILE);

        /* get screen dimensions */
        fi->width=gh.screenwidth;
        fi->depth=gh.screendepth;
        fi->bits=(gh.flags & 0x0007) + 1;
        fi->background=gh.background;
        /* get colour map if there is one */
        if (gh.flags & 0x80) {
                c = 3 * (1 << ((gh.flags & 7) + 1));
                if(fread(fi->palette,1,c,fp) != c) return(BAD_READ);
        }

        /* step through the blocks */
        while((c=fgetc(fp))==',' || c=='!' || c==0) {

                /* if it's an image block... */
                if (c == ',') {
                        /* get the start of the image block */
                        if(fread(&iblk,1,sizeof(IMAGEBLOCK),fp) !=
                            sizeof(IMAGEBLOCK)) return(BAD_READ);
```

2-5 Continued.

```c
                        /* get the image dimensions */
                        fi->width=iblk.width;
                        fi->depth=iblk.depth;

                        /* get the local colour map if there is one */
                        if(iblk.flags & 0x80) {
                                b = 3*(1<<((iblk.flags & 0x0007) + 1));
                                if(fread(fi->palette,1,b,fp) != c) return(BAD_READ);
                                fi->bits=(iblk.flags & 0x0007) + 1;
                        }

                        /* get the initial code size */
                        if((c=fgetc(fp))==EOF) return(BAD_FILE);

                        fi->flags=iblk.flags;

                        /* do the setup procedure */
                        if(fi->setup != NULL) {
                                if((t=(fi->setup)(fi)) != GOOD_READ)
                                        return(t);
                        }

                        /* unpack the image */
                        t=unpackimage(fp,c,fi);

                        /* do the close down procedure */
                        if(fi->closedown != NULL) (fi->closedown)(fi);

                                /* quit if there was an error */
                                if(t != GOOD_READ) return(t);
                }
                /* otherwise, it's an extension */
                else if(c == '!') (fi->savext)(fp);
        }
        return(GOOD_READ);
}


/* unpack an LZW compressed image */
unpackimage(fp,bits,fi)
        FILE *fp;
        int bits;
        FILEINFO *fi;
{
        int bits2;              /* Bits plus 1 */
        int codesize;          /* Current code size in bits */
        int codesize2;         /* Next codesize */
        int nextcode;          /* Next available table entry */
        int thiscode;          /* Code being expanded */
        int oldtoken;          /* Last symbol decoded */
        int currentcode;       /* Code just read */
        int oldcode;           /* Code read before this one */
        int bitsleft;          /* Number of bits left in *p */
        int blocksize;         /* Bytes in next block */
```

2-5 Continued.

```
int line=0;             /* next line to write */
int byte=0;             /* next byte to write */
int pass=0;             /* pass number for interlaced pictures */

char *p;                /* Pointer to current byte in read buffer */
char *q;                /* Pointer past last byte in read buffer */
char b[255];            /* Read buffer */
char *u;                /* Stack pointer into firstcodestack */
char *linebuffer;       /* place to store the current line */

static char firstcodestack[4096];   /* Stack for first codes */
static char lastcodestack[4096];     /* Stack for previous code */
static int codestack[4096];          /* Stack for links */

static int wordmasktable[] = {  0x0000,0x0001,0x0003,0x0007,
                                0x000f,0x001f,0x003f,0x007f,
                                0x00ff,0x01ff,0x03ff,0x07ff,
                                0x0fff,0x1fff,0x3fff,0x7fff
                                };

static int inctable[] = { 8,8,4,2,0 }; /* interlace increments */
static int startable[] = { 0,4,2,1,0 };  /* interlace starts */

p=q=b;
bitsleft = 8;

if (bits < 2 || bits > 8) return(BAD_SYMBOLSIZE);
bits2 = 1 << bits;
nextcode = bits2 + 2;
codesize2 = 1 << (codesize = bits + 1);
oldcode=oldtoken=NO_CODE;

if((linebuffer=malloc(fi->width)) == NULL) return(BAD_ALLOC);
/* loop until something breaks */
for(;;) {
        if(bitsleft==8) {
                if(++p >= q &&
                (((blocksize = fgetc(fp)) < 1) ||
                (q=(p=b)+fread(b,1,blocksize,fp))< (b+blocksize))) {
                        free(linebuffer);
                        return(UNEXPECTED_EOF);
                }
                bitsleft = 0;
        }
        thiscode = *p;
        if ((currentcode=(codesize+bitsleft)) <= 8) {
                *p >>= codesize;
                bitsleft = currentcode;
        }
        else {
                if(++p >= q &&
                  (((blocksize = fgetc(fp)) < 1) ||
```

2-5 Continued.

```
                (q=(p=b)+fread(b,1,blocksize,fp)) < (b+blocksize))) {
                        free(linebuffer);
                        return(UNEXPECTED_EOF);
                }
        thiscode |= *p << (8 - bitsleft);
        if(currentcode <= 16) *p >>= (bitsleft=currentcode-8);
        else {
                if(++p >= q &&
                  (((blocksize = fgetc(fp)) < 1) ||
                  (q=(p=b) + fread(b,1,blocksize,fp)) < (b+blocksize))) {
                        free(linebuffer);
                        return(UNEXPECTED_EOF);
                }
                thiscode |= *p << (16 - bitsleft);
                *p >>= (bitsleft = currentcode - 16);
        }
}
thiscode &= wordmasktable[codesize];
currentcode = thiscode;

if(thiscode == (bits2+1)) break;      /* found EOI */
if(thiscode > nextcode) {
        free(linebuffer);
        return(BAD_CODE);
}

if(thiscode == bits2) {
        nextcode = bits2 + 2;
        codesize2 = 1 << (codesize = (bits + 1));
        oldtoken = oldcode = NO_CODE;
        continue;
}

u = firstcodestack;

if(thiscode==nextcode) {
        if(oldcode==NO_CODE) {
                free(linebuffer);
                return(BAD_FIRSTCODE);

        }
        *u++ = oldtoken;
        thiscode = oldcode;
}

while (thiscode >= bits2) {
        *u++ = lastcodestack[thiscode];
        thiscode = codestack[thiscode];
}

oldtoken = thiscode;
do {
```

2-5 Continued.

```
                    linebuffer[byte++]=thiscode;
                    if(byte >= fi->width) {
                            (fi->saveline)(linebuffer,line);
                            byte=0;

                            /* check for interlaced image */
                            if(fi->flags & 0x40) {
                                    line+=inctable[pass];
                                    if(line >= fi->depth)
                                            line=startable[++pass];
                            } else ++line;
                    }

                    if (u <= firstcodestack) break;
                    thiscode = *--u;
            } while(1);

            if(nextcode < 4096 && oldcode != NO_CODE) {
                    codestack[nextcode] = oldcode;
                    lastcodestack[nextcode] = oldtoken;
                    if (++nextcode >= codesize2 && codesize < 12)
                        codesize2 = 1 << ++codesize;
            }
            oldcode = currentcode;
        }
    free(linebuffer);
    return(GOOD_READ);
}


/* This function is called before an image is decompressed. It must
   allocate memory, put the display in graphic mode and so on. */
dosetup(fi)
    FILEINFO *fi;
{
    if(!getbuffer((long)fi->width*(long)fi->depth,fi->width,fi->depth))
        return(BAD_ALLOC);

    return(GOOD_READ);
}


/* This function is called after an image has been unpacked. It must
   display the image and deallocate memory. */
doclosedown(fi)
    FILEINFO *fi;
{
    BINARYHEADER bh;
    int i;
    memcpy(bh.sign,BINARYSIG,8);
    bh.width=fi->width;
    bh.depth=fi->depth;
    bh.bits =fi->bits;
    memcpy(bh.palette,fi->palette,768);
```

2-5 Continued.

```
                    if(fwrite((char *)&bh,1,sizeof(BINARYHEADER),out) !=
                        sizeof(BINARYHEADER))
                            puts("Error writing binary header");
                    else {
                        for(i=0;i<fi->depth;++i) {
                            if(fwrite(getline(i),1,fi->width,out) !=
                                fi->width) {
                                    puts("Error writing line");
                                    break;
                            }
                        }
                    }

            freebuffer();

            return(GOOD_READ);
}


/* return a far pointer plus a long integer */
char *farPtr(p,l)
        char *p;
        long l;
{
        unsigned int seg,off;

        seg = FP_SEG(p);
        off = FP_OFF(p);
        seg += (off / 16);
        off &= 0x000f;
        off += (unsigned int)(l & 0x000fL);
        seg += (l / 16L);
        p = MK_FP(seg,off);
        return(p);
}

/* make file name with specific extension */
strmfe(new,old,ext)
        char *new,*old,*ext;
{
        while(*old != 0 && *old != '.') *new++=*old++;
        *new++='.';
        while(*ext) *new++=*ext++;
        *new=0;
}

/* if you don't use in the memory manager, these functions
   will stand in for it */

#if !MEMMANGR

/* save one line to memory */
```

2-5 Continued.

```
putline(p,n)
        char *p;
        unsigned int n;
{
        if(n >= 0 && n < fi.depth)
            memcpy(farPtr(buffer,(long)n*(long)fi.width),p,fi.width);
}

/* get one line from memory */
char *getline(n)
        unsigned int n;
{
        return(farPtr(buffer,(long)n*(long)fi.width));
}

#pragma warn -par
getbuffer(n,bytes,lines)
        unsigned long n;
        int bytes,lines;
{
        if((buffer=farmalloc(n)) == NULL) return(0);
        else return(1);
}

freebuffer()
{
        if(buffer != NULL) farfree(buffer);
        buffer=NULL;
}
#endif /* !MEMMANGR */
```

2-5 Continued.

The MAKEBIN program accepts the path to a GIF file as its argument and creates a file with the same name and the extension BIN. A BIN file begins with a BINARYHEADER data structure, followed by uncompressed image information. A BINARYHEADER looks like this:

```
typedef struct {
        char sign[8];
        int width,depth,bits;
        char palette[768];
        } BINARYHEADER;
```

Allowing that you can do without copyright information, secondary images, and user input, this is actually all the information you need to define an image. The palette buffer is large enough to hold up to 256 colors. Some of it will be ignored if your example image has fewer entries in its color map.

The sign field holds an 8-byte string to allow the software that reads these BIN files to know that it has an authentic, readable image.

Because this format does not attempt to compress its image data, GIF files with large dimensions will produce BIN files that occupy a lot of disk real estate. It's worth noting that images with fewer than 256 colors don't result in smaller BIN files. A monochrome file with the dimensions 576×720 bytes might occupy 20K or 30K as a GIF file. It requires something over 400K as a BIN file.

The BIN format serves only as test data for WRITEGIF, the example GIF writer to follow, and the other file writers in this book. You unquestionably will not want to store images this way.

The file ZOE.GIF on the disk accompanying this book makes a good test subject. It results in a 256-color image that occupies about 64K as a BIN file.

Packed file structure

By now, the structure of a GIF file should be pretty familiar. Assembling one really involves doing most of what took place in the discussion of READGIF earlier in this chapter, but in reverse. Specifically, to create a GIF file, you would do the following:

1. Write the header, or "screen descriptor."
2. Write an image block header.
3. Compress the image data.
4. Write a terminator block.

The terminator block is a single byte, a semicolon.

This list describes the most basic possible GIF file. Such a file contains one image and no extension blocks. The great majority of GIF files existing at the moment are structured like this. Despite the existence of the GIF 89a specification, most GIF writers still create GIF files with GIF 87a headers. There's a very good reason for this: the newer GIF 89a specification offers no advantages for single-image files. However, there are a lot of older applications about that were intended to read GIF 87a files, and might complain when confronted with files that use the GIF 89a specification.

There are a number of things about a GIF 89a file that might confuse an earlier GIF reader. For example, aside from the signature string, the GIF 87a specification defined the current aspect ratio field of the header as always being 0, something it need not be under the GIF 89a specification. Some GIF readers designed to read GIF 87a files checked this byte and assumed that the file being read was corrupted if it did not contain 0.

If your applications will be writing single-image GIF files, and you have no need for extension blocks or the other features of the GIF 89a standard, you should probably write GIF 87a files. The example GIF writer to be discussed here actually writes either type of file.

Writing a screen descriptor and an image block header both involve loading the appropriate data structures with their requisite values and writing them to the destination GIF files. The data structures are the same ones used in READGIF, and the values that inhabit their fields were explained earlier in this chapter.

Writing the actual compressed image data is, as you might expect, the most complicated part of creating a GIF file. You can view LZW compression as being the exact opposite of the decompression process described earlier. The code stream and the character stream are simply exchanged, and the whole process works as it did for the decompression algorithm.

If you do elect to write GIF 89a files, you can add as many additional extension and image blocks between the end of the first image and the final terminator block as you like. The example GIF writer adds a comment block. There are a few practical considerations to bear in mind, however. To begin with, unless all the images in a multiple-image file have a common palette, or unless they're all monochrome, you'll have to provide local color maps for the latter ones. If you set up a multiple-image GIF file such that the disposal of one image involves reverting to a previous one, keep in mind that both images must be stored somewhere. If both images are 640×480 pixel, 256-color GIF files, some GIF readers won't be able to find enough memory to deal with them.

Also keep in mind that many GIF readers don't read past the first image in a file.

Figure 2-6 is the complete source code for WRITEGIF. This program reads BIN files created by MAKEBIN. It begins by reading the header and then by passing the rest of the file to the compression code 1 byte at a time.

```
/*
        GIF writer - copyright (c) 1991
        Alchemy Mindworks Inc.
*/

#include "stdio.h"

#define GIF89          1                 /* set true for extensions */

#define BINARYSIG      "ALCHBINR"        /* binary identification */

#define largest_code   4095              /* largest possible code */
#define table_size     5003              /* table dimensions */

#if GIF89
#define GIFSIG         "GIF89a"
#define COMMENT        "This picture contains no artificial\r\n"\
                       "preservatives of any kind. It was\r\n"\
                       "made entirely without the use of\r\n"\
                       "polysorbate-80, monosodium glutimate\r\n"\
                       "or potassium cyanide, and it was not\r\n"\
                       "overpackaged, heat sealed or tested\r\n"\
                       "on animals. It's printed on recycled\r\n"\
                       "pixels and it was not bleached to make\r\n"\
                       "it white. None of the naughty bits\r\n"\
                       "(if present) have been digitally\r\n"\
```

2-6 The complete source code for WRITEGIF.

```
                                "enhanced to make them appear larger\r\n"\
                                "than they really are. Use no hooks.\r\n"
        #else
        #define GIFSIG          "GIF87a"
        #endif

        typedef struct {
                char sig[6];
                unsigned int screenwidth,screendepth;
                unsigned char flags,background,aspect,
                } GIFHEADER;

        typedef struct {
                unsigned int left,top,width,depth;
                unsigned char flags;
                } IMAGEBLOCK;

        typedef struct {
                char sign[8];
                int width,depth,bits;
                char palette[768];
                } BINARYHEADER;

        int getpixel();

        FILE *in,*out;
        BINARYHEADER bh;
        char code_buffer[259];          /* where the codes go */

        int oldcode[table_size];        /* the table */
        int currentcode[table_size];
        char newcode[table_size];
        int code_size;
        int clear_code;
        int eof_code;
        int bit_offset;
        int byte_offset;
        int bits_left;
        int max_code;
        int free_code;

        main(argc,argv)
                int argc;
                char *argv[];
        {
                char path[81];
                int n;

                if(argc > 1) {
                        strmfe(path,argv[1],"BIN");
                        strupr(path);
                        if((in=fopen(path,"rb")) != NULL) {
```

2-6 Continued.

```
                    if(fread((char *)&bh,1,sizeof(BINARYHEADER),in) ==
                        sizeof(BINARYHEADER)) {
                            if(!memcmp(bh.sign,BINARYSIG,8)) {
                                    strmfe(path,argv[1],"GIF");
                                    strupr(path);
                                    if((out=fopen(path,"wb")) != NULL) {
                                            puts("Writing");
                                            n=writeGif(out,getpixel,
                                                    bh.width,bh.depth,
                                                    bh.bits,bh.palette);
                                            printf("Return code: %d",n);
                                            fclose(out);
                                    } else printf("Error creating %s",path);
                            } else printf("%s is corrupted",path);
                    } else printf("Error reading %s",path);
                    fclose(in);
            } else printf("Error opening %s",path);
        } else puts("Argument:        path to a BIN file");
}


/* write a GIF file */
writeGif(fp,readpixel,width,depth,bits,palette)
        FILE *fp;
        int (readpixel)();
        unsigned int width,depth,bits;
        char *palette;
{

        /* write the header */
        if(writeScreenDesc(fp,width,depth,bits,0,palette)) return(1);

        /* write the image descriptor */
        if(writeImageDesc(fp,0,0,width,depth,bits,NULL)) return(2);

        /* write the image */
        if(compressImage(fp,readpixel,bits)) return(3);

        #if GIF89
        /* write the comment */
        if(writeComment(fp,COMMENT)) return(4);
        #endif

        /* write the terminator */
        fputc(';',fp);
        return(ferror(fp));
}


/* write the header */
writeScreenDesc(fp,width,depth,bits,background,palette)
        FILE *fp;
        unsigned int width,depth,bits,background;
        char *palette;
{
```

2-6 Continued.

```
                    GIFHEADER gh;

                    /* fill the header struct */
                    memset((char *)&gh,0,sizeof(GIFHEADER));
                    memcpy(gh.sig,GIFSIG,6);
                    gh.screenwidth=width;
                    gh.screendepth=depth;
                    gh.background=background;
                    gh.aspect=0;

                    /* set up the global flags */
                    if(palette == NULL) gh.flags=(((bits-1) & 0x07)<<4);
                    else gh.flags = (0x80 | ((bits-1)<<4) | ((bits-1) & 0x07));

                    /* write the header */
                    fwrite((char *)&gh,1,sizeof(GIFHEADER),fp);

                    /* write the colour map */
                    if(palette != NULL) fwrite(palette,1,3*(1<<bits),fp);

                    return(ferror(fp));
          }

/* write an image descriptor block */
writeImageDesc(fp,left,top,width,depth,bits,palette)
          FILE *fp;
          unsigned int left,top,width,depth;
          char *palette;
{

          IMAGEBLOCK ib;

          memset((char *)&ib,0,sizeof(IMAGEBLOCK));

          /* fill the image block struct */
          fputc(',',fp);
          ib.left=left;
          ib.top=top;
          ib.width=width;
          ib.depth=depth;

          /* set the local flags */
          if(palette==NULL) ib.flags=bits-1;
          else ib.flags=((bits-1) & 0x07) | 0x80;

          /* write the block */
          fwrite((char *)&ib,1,sizeof(IMAGEBLOCK),fp);
          /* write the colour map */
          if(palette != NULL) fwrite(palette,1,3*(1<<bits),fp);

          return(ferror(fp));
}
```

2-6 Continued.

```
/* initialize the code table */
init_table(min_code_size)
        int min_code_size;
{
        int i;

        code_size=min_code_size+1;
        clear_code=(1<<min_code_size);
        eof_code=clear_code+1;
        free_code=clear_code+2;
        max_code=(1<<code_size);

        for(i=0;i<table_size;i++) currentcode[i]=0;
}

/* flush the code buffer */
flush(fp,n)
        FILE *fp;
        int n;
{
        fputc(n,fp);
        fwrite(code_buffer,1,n,fp);
}

/* write a code to the code buffer */
write_code(fp,code)
        FILE *fp;
        int code;
{
        long temp;

        byte_offset = bit_offset >> 3;
        bits_left = bit_offset & 7;

        if(byte_offset >= 254) {
                flush(fp,byte_offset);
                code_buffer[0] = code_buffer[byte_offset];
                bit_offset = bits_left;
                byte_offset = 0;
        }

        if(bits_left > 0) {
                temp = ((long) code << bits_left) | code_buffer[byte_offset];
                code_buffer[byte_offset]=temp;
                code_buffer[byte_offset+1]=(temp >> 8);
                code_buffer[byte_offset+2]=(temp >> 16);
        }
        else {
                code_buffer[byte_offset] = code;
                code_buffer[byte_offset+1]=(code >> 8);
        }
        bit_offset += code_size;
```

2-6 Continued.

```
        }

/* compress an image */
compressImage(fp,readpixel,min_code_size)
        FILE *fp;
        int (*readpixel)();
        unsigned int min_code_size;
{
        int prefix_code;
        int suffix_char;
        int hx,d;

        /* make sure the initial code size is legal */
        if(min_code_size < 2 || min_code_size > 9) {
                /* monochrome images have two bits in LZW compression */
                if(min_code_size == 1) min_code_size = 2;
                else return(EOF);
        }

        /* write initial code size */
        fputc(min_code_size,fp);

        /* initialize the encoder */
        bit_offset=0;
        init_table(min_code_size);
        write_code(fp,clear_code);
        if((suffix_char=(readpixel)())==EOF) return(suffix_char);

        /* initialize the prefix */
        prefix_code = suffix_char;

        /* get a character to compress */
        while((suffix_char=(readpixel)()) != EOF) {

                /* derive an index into the code table */
                hx=(prefix_code ^ (suffix_char << 5)) % table_size;
                d=1;

                for(;;) {

                        /* see if the code is in the table */
                        if(currentcode[hx] == 0) {

                                /* if not, put it there */
                                write_code(fp,prefix_code);
                                d = free_code;

                                /* find the next free code */
                                if(free_code <= largest_code) {
                                        oldcode[hx] = prefix_code;
                                        newcode[hx] = suffix_char;
                                        currentcode[hx] = free_code;
```

2-6 Continued.

```
                                            free_code++;
                            }

                            /* expand the code size or scrap the table */
                            if(d == max_code) {
                                    if(code_size < 12) {
                                            code_size++;
                                            max_code <<= 1;
                                    }
                                    else {
                                            write_code(fp,clear_code);
                                            init_table(min_code_size);
                                    }
                            }
                            prefix_code = suffix_char;
                            break;
                    }
                    if(oldcode[hx] == prefix_code &&
                       newcode[hx] == suffix_char) {
                            prefix_code = currentcode[hx];
                            break;
                    }
                    hx += d;
                    d += 2;
                    if(hx >= table_size) hx -= table_size;
                }
        }

        /* write the prefix code */
        write_code(fp,prefix_code);

        /* and the end of file code */
        write_code(fp,eof_code);

        /* flush the buffer */
        if(bit_offset > 0) flush(fp, (bit_offset+7)/8);

        /* write a zero length block */
        flush(fp,0);

        return(ferror(fp));
}

#if GIF89
writeComment(fp,comment)
        FILE *fp;
        char *comment;
{
        int n;

        n=strlen(comment);
```

2-6 Continued.

```
        fputc('!',fp);              /* say it's an exntension block */
        fputc(0xfe,fp);             /* say it's a comment */

        do {
                if(n > 255) {
                        fputc(255,fp);
                        fwrite(comment,1,255,fp);
                        comment +=255;
                        n-=255;
                }
                else {
                        fputc(n,fp);
                        fwrite(comment,1,n,fp);
                        fputc(0,fp);
                        n=0;
                }
        } while(n);
        return(ferror(fp));
}
#endif

/* make file name with specific extension */
strmfe(new,old,ext)
        char *new,*old,*ext;
{
        while(*old != 0 && *old != '.') *new++=*old++;
        *new++='.';
        while(*ext) *new++=*ext++;
        *new=0;
}

/* get one pixel from the source image */
getpixel()
{
        return(fgetc(in));
}
```

2-6 Continued.

You can set WRITEGIF up to create either a basic GIF 87a file or a GIF
89a file with a comment block in addition to the basic image data. You're
free to change the contents of the comment or to modify the code to add
still more blocks if you like. The basic file structure is established in the
writeGif function—if you'd like to include additional blocks, this is
where to put the calls to create them.

Note that in this example, the call to writeImageDesc passes
NULL for the palette argument. This causes the image block being
created to not have a local color map. You should pass a pointer to a valid
palette buffer to this function if you want to create a multiple-image GIF
file with separate color maps for each image. If all the images have their
own color maps, you can pass NULL for the palette argument of
writeScreenDesc to inhibit the creation of a global color map. Note

that WRITEGIF creates noninterlaced files. You'd have to modify it quite substantially to change this. Specifically, you'd have to read the entire image into a buffer and then read the lines out in the appropriate order. At the moment, you'll find no calls to the memory manager functions in WRITEGIF. The image is read directly from the BIN file.

As with the READGIF program, a GIF compressor doesn't lend itself to being passed individual lines of image data to compress. It's a lot easier to write one such that it can get each byte of the source image as it's required. As such, the compressImage function is passed a pointer to a function that will return 1 byte of the source image at a time. It will return EOF when all the bytes have been compressed.

This turns out to be exceedingly easy to manage. Once the BINARY-HEADER structure of a BIN file has been read, the file pointer for the file points to the first byte of the image data. If fgetc is called once for each byte in the file and then once again, it will hit the end of the file and return EOF, telling compressImage that the jig's up.

If you'll be getting the bytes to be compressed from another source, you might have to be a bit more sophisticated in how you deal with signalling the end of the data to be compressed. For example, if you'll be reading bytes from a buffer, you should begin by multiplying the width of the image by its depth to obtain the total number of bytes to be compressed, casting both dimensions to long first, and then decrementing this value each time a byte is read. When the count hits 0, the function that gets bytes for compressImage should return EOF.

Note that when it reaches the end of the file, the compressor must write out the current block—it must "flush" its buffer—and it must write a zero-length block to tell the function that ultimately reads the file it's creating that all the image data has been read.

Writing a comment block is pretty tame. You can see it being done in writeComment. This function writes an exclamation point to indicate that the next block will be an extension and then 0xfe to indicate that it's a comment. The comment text itself is broken up into 255-byte chunks and written out to the file, with each chunk preceded by its length value. The final byte in the block must be 0. A GIF reader encountering this comment block interprets the 0 as the length byte of the final block, the signal to stop looking for more text.

Using GIF files

As you'll appreciate once you've had a chance to look at the other image-file formats discussed in this book, GIF files represent the most involved of the lot. They can also be the most difficult to implement even if you do have source code to work with them. Because they don't really work with separate, discrete lines of image data in the way that other files do, integrating them into an application designed to work with more conventional file formats can entail a bit of head scratching.

The ubiquitous nature of GIF files—and their impressive compression characteristics—arguably make them worth the effort.

In order to keep this discussion of GIF files down to a manageable level of hugeness, this chapter dealt with only the most rudimentary GIF viewer. The discussions of screen drivers and printing in later chapters involve GIF files again, but with more sophisticated ways to look at them.

Finally, it might well be argued that in the transitory culture of micro-computers, GIF files have acquired a rather sultry reputation. Just as the first high-speed European printing presses were used primarily to print erotica rather than Bibles, so too has this most sophisticated of popular image-file formats largely been used to contain pictures of nude women.

There is, unquestionably, a substantial body of people who'll regard this situation as being reprehensible. Many of them are still seething at the great injustices done to their ancestors during the nineteenth century; men who spent a lifetime laboring at the jackscrews of printing presses and ultimately found themselves out of work.

Desktop Paint 256, one of the applications on the companion disks for this book, is a full-color super VGA paint program that works with several image file formats, one of which is GIF. In fact, this appears to be the only format anyone cares to use it with. Inasmuch as Desktop Paint 256 is distributed as shareware, it turns up in catalogs with various descriptions of its functions. Several of them have appeared attesting that it's "the perfect tool to edit nude GIF files."

You might want to keep *this* in mind as well, should you undertake to create software that works with the GIF format.

Credits: The source code in this chapter is based on two C language functions to do LZW encoding and decoding that turned up on a bulletin board some years back. Their author was not mentioned in the file.

3

IFF/LBM files

If no one uses it, there's a reason.
—MURPHY'S LAWS OF COMPUTERS

I think I recall computers more for the games they can play than the work they can do. This is certainly true of computers that I've not found much to do with besides playing games. This seems to be true of computers that not only come with mice, but insist that they be used, often at gunpoint.

The only things I can recall about the Commodore Amiga are a single application, Electronic Arts' Deluxe Paint package, and a single game, Marble Madness. Of the two, Marble Madness was arguably more useful. The problem with Deluxe Paint, way back in the prehistory of the Amiga, was that it could create glorious pictures that could only be displayed on the screen of an Amiga. There was no way to print them and they were stored in a format that wasn't supported by any other computer. In fact, it was hardly even documented.

Marble Madness eventually succumbed to enough nights of bashing that reluctant marble into walls and dropping it screaming into precipices. Deluxe Paint was ported to the PC in time. At length we sold the Amiga for $25 at a garage sale to someone who initially wanted to swap us even for a box of kittens. He probably laughed all the way home, but it turns out that the Jones' dog had picked the Marble Madness disk off the top of the computer and buried it. We found it a year later in the begonias.

As with so many computers before it, the Amiga was clearly someone's vision of a system that would benefit from all the valuable work that went before it, scrap the rest, and start again with a powerful architecture and a set of fresh, expandable standards. In a sense it is, too, except that one of the valuable things that went before it *were* all those old standards. File formats, data structures and the other things that make information exchangeable are at least as important as the hardware and operating systems that people so frequently devise and then bury in favor of something supposedly better.

This is arguably more applicable to graphic file formats than to anything else, inasmuch as the actual graphic information doesn't vary much from one format to the next. The only differences one really encounters is the way in which the pixels are packed.

The Amiga trashed all the graphic file formats that preceded it and create its own, called IFF for *interchange format files*. The intent behind the IFF format was that it would be cleanly applicable not only to the 68000 processor architecture that the Amiga was designed around, but also to the Amiga's unique operating system. Something of a fusion of MS-DOS and the Macintosh's Finder, the Amiga's Workbench could be the topic of a book in itself. It's certainly beyond the scope of this one.

The principal feature of IFF files is that they're extensible in a way few other file formats can hope to match. They carry the notion of extension blocks that appeared in chapter 2 quite a bit further, with the result that IFF files can contain not only pictures but animation details, sampled sounds, word processing text and application-specific 68000 machine code.

If the idea of having a graphic talk to you seems disturbing, it's worth noting that this chapter deals with "pure" IFF files; that is, simple images. Much of the more exotic data that turns up in files ported directly from the Amiga—audio samples and such—is specific to hardware that exists on an Amiga and can't be simulated on a PC. The IFF file structure allows you to ignore data "chunks" that aren't of interest to you, much as GIF files let you ignore their extension blocks.

As previously noted, the Amiga Deluxe Paint program was eventually ported into a PC implementation. It looks like the Amiga version, at least superficially, and more to the point, it also uses a version of IFF files in its PC incarnation. Being a pretty respectable paint package, it has become reasonably popular, and IFF files have proliferated in PC circles. At the same time, Amiga users began to exchange files over bulletin boards. In a real sense, bulletin boards are genuinely machine-independent, and it wasn't long before there was a cultural exchange of sorts going on, an unnegotiated swap of IFF images for GIF files.

A whole lot of PC users got to see superb scanned impressionist art in IFF files and a plethora of Amiga owners found themselves staring at nudes from GIF files. It's hard to imagine the creators of the Amiga finding a way to work that situation into their advertising.

The IFF file format is actually pretty useful. It turns up not only as the native file format of Deluxe Paint, but it's also used by Splash from Spinnaker Software and by the ComputerEyes frame-grabber boards from Digital

Vision. Because it's designed around independent blocks of data, it lends itself to being adapted for specific uses. While you can extend GIF files to a certain extent through application-specific extensions, IFF files offer much more sophisticated ways to customize their format.

Alternately, you might just like scanned impressionist art.

Figure 3-1 illustrates some of the IFF graphics that come with Deluxe Paint.

The basic IFF file format allows for images of 2 to 256 colors, as with GIF files. There is no fixed limit to the dimensions that IFF files can attain. Some applications using IFF files like to see them padded upward to the next applicable set of Amiga screen dimensions. Early implementations of Deluxe Paint for the PC behaved erratically when confronted with IFF files that were of other dimensions, a problem that has since been fixed.

It's worth noting that there are a number of somewhat official variations on basic IFF files. One that you'll probably encounter is called HAM, for *hold and modify*. This file type is not discussed in this chapter, as it's relatively rare in PC circles and doesn't port very conveniently to PC display hardware. It's intended to take advantage of hardware unique to the Amiga. Another is called LBM. The LBM format is actually a variation on the "pure" IFF file used by Deluxe Paint. The difference between these two formats is discussed in detail later in this chapter. In dealing with 256-color files, Deluxe Paint reads both pure IFF files and LBM files. It always writes LBM files.

When you encounter IFF files that have been ported from an Amiga, they'll typically have the extension IFF. If you're using Deluxe Paint, the file extension is LBM.

The IFF file structure

Before you can begin to understand how an IFF file is put together, there are a number of concepts with which you'll probably want to become comfortable. The first, the problem of microprocessor number structures, was touched on in the brief discussion of Macintosh GIF files in chapter 2. It turns up with considerably more vehemence in dealing with IFF files—while the Amiga and the Mac are built by different manufacturers, they're based on the same series of processors, the Motorola 68000 series, which are different from the Intel processors that drive PC systems.

Motorola processors write multiple-byte numbers—integers and long integers—with their bytes in the inverse order of Intel's chips. This isn't a problem as long as you know that it's happening. As in chapter 2, you can read Motorola numbers on a PC by passing them through a conversion function, like this:

```
long motr2intl(l)
    long l;
{
```

3-1 Several LBM files from Deluxe Paint. (A) This image is entitled CELTIC.LBM, and is a 320 × 200, 256-color picture. (B) This image is called PHOENIX.LBM, and is a 640 × 480 pixel, 16-color picture.

```
return((( 1 & 0xff000000L) >> 24) +
      (( 1 & 0x00ff0000L) >> 8) +
      (( 1 & 0x0000ff00L) << 8) +
      (( 1 & 0x000000ffL) << 24));
}
```

It's worth noting, however, since working with IFF files is a lot more complicated than merely sneaking past the MacBinary header of a Macintosh GIF file, that forgetting to convert Motorola numbers is a prime source of bugs in IFF file decoders on a PC. If in writing your own code you find some weird values turning up, check to see if you've forgotten a call to motr2intl.

An IFF file consists of a very small header to identify it as such, followed by data chunks. Fortunately, the Amiga does not support the same two-forked file structure as the Macintosh does. An IFF file is a linear binary file, just as files are on a PC. Each chunk defines something about the file. A chunk might tell you what the file's dimensions are, how its palette is defined and, finally, what its actual image data is.

As with the Macintosh, the Amiga is fond of using 4-byte strings as identifiers for things. File types and the chunks within files are identified by these 4-byte strings. The beginning of an Amiga file can be defined by the following C-language structure.

```
typedef struct {
        char type[4];
        unsigned long size;
        char subtype[4];
} IFFHEADER;
```

If you read the first 12 bytes of an IFF file into an IFFHEADER variable, the type field should contain one of three strings: "FORM", "LIST", or "CAT ", with heavy emphasis on FORM. Note that "CAT " has a blank space at the end to pad it out to 4 bytes.

If you run the size value on an IFFHEADER through motr2intl, it turns out to be the size of the file in bytes. In fact, it might be off by a few bytes because some file-transfer protocols, file-copying programs, and such, pad out files by a few bytes when they're moved about.

The subtype field of an IFF file's IFFHEADER should contain one of two strings. If it's a pure IFF file, it holds the string "ILBM," for *interleaved bitmap*. If it's a Deluxe Paint LBM file with 256 colors in it, it holds the string "PBM ", again with a space to pad the length out to 4 bytes. This probably stands for *proprietary bitmap*.

In decoding an IFF file, you should begin by making sure that you've actually got one by checking that the type field of its header contains one of the three appropriate strings. You should then make note of the subtype contents, as this affects the way the image data will ultimately be dealt with.

The first byte after an IFFHEADER is the first byte of the first chunk. The chunks in an IFF file always consist of a 4-byte type field followed by a long integer. The long integer holds the size of the chunk's data. As such, if your IFF file reader encounters a chunk that it doesn't understand how to deal with, it can simply skip ahead to the following chunk.

The size value in a chunk may be off by 1 byte. Chunks are constrained to always have an even number of bytes in them. The size values are not constrained to reflect this. As such, if l is the size of a chunk, you should do the following to ensure that it reflects the real size of the chunk.

```
if(l & 1L) ++l;
```

There are actually only three chunk types that an IFF image file absolutely must contain. They are:

BMHD—The dimensions of the file
CMAP—The color map, or palette values
BODY—The image data itself

Files created by Deluxe Paint include numerous other chunks that are used by its slide show and animation facilities, aspects of the IFF format that don't really apply here. They also contain a chunk of the type TINY, which contains a reduced version of the file image. If you open the Load File box from within Deluxe Paint, a small preview version of the image in each selected LBM file appears on the screen. This preview image is stored in the TINY chunk and is discussed in detail later in this chapter.

The BMHD chunk

The order in which the IFF file chunks appear is important. For example, you would not know how to decode a BODY chunk unless you'd previously read a BMHD chunk that defined the dimensions, color depth, and other details of the BODY chunk image. A BMHD chunk is always the first essential IFF file chunk.

Having read the type and length fields of a BMHD chunk, the rest of the chunk is defined by the following structure:

```
typedef struct {
        unsigned int w,h;
        int x,y;
        char nPlanes;
        char masking;
        char compression;
        char pad1;
        unsigned int transparentColor;
        char xAspect,yAspect;
        int pageW,pageH;
        } BMHD;
```

Note that there are some Motorola integers in this data structure. This requires another function to convert them.

```
motr2inti(n)
    int n;
{
    return(((n & 0xff00) >> 8) |
           ((n & 0x00ff) << 8));
}
```

The w and x fields in a BMHD structure are the dimensions, in pixels, of the image it defines. The x and y values are the coordinates of the upper left corner of the image when it's displayed. These are usually both 0—the code in this chapter ignores them and displays all the images starting in the upper left corner of the screen.

The nPlanes value defines the number of color planes required to display the image. This value is the same as the number of color bits being used. On an Amiga, color images are always displayed as layered planes, similar to images in the 16-color modes of PC display adapters. There are certain advantages to doing this; for example, a 6-bit image can actually be smaller than an 8-bit image. A file format that defines each pixel as a byte requires as much raw storage for 6 bits as for 8 bits.

In fact, IFF files can be stored both ways. Files with the subtype "ILBM" are always stored as image planes. Files with the subtype "PBM " are stored byte-oriented, in the same way that GIF data was (see chapter 2). If you encounter an IFF or LBM file with the "PBM " subtype, the nPlanes field should contain a value of 8.

The masking field defines whether the image data in the file is interleaved with a mask. It can contain one of four values:

0—there is no mask
1—there is a mask
2—there is a mask with a transparent color
3—there is a lasso mask

The simplest instance is no mask, and most standard IFF files are set up this way. If one of the other three values is found in this field, an extra plane in each line serves as the mask.

Using the mask information in an IFF file is another area that is largely beyond the scope of this book. The Amiga has hardware called a *bit blitter* that makes masking fairly painless. Because such hardware is missing on a PC, handling masks and transparent colors is a bit of a pig to do in software.

The compression field may contain one of two values:

0—uncompressed image data
1—compressed image data

If the compression field contains 0, the image in the following BODY chunk will be raw data. If it's a 1, the image will be run-length encoded. The run-length encoding process used is called PackBits, and is, in fact, the one used to store MacPaint images on the Macintosh.

PackBits compression works well on drawn images but is appalling on scanned ones—compressing a sufficiently complex scanned image using PackBits may well create an IFF file that is notably bigger than the raw data being compressed. As such, it's often the case that scanned images are stored uncompressed.

Uncompressed images can also be loaded a lot faster.

The pad1 field is filler—it doesn't mean anything.

The transparentColor field of the header defines the color index in the image that should be considered transparent if the masking field indicates that a transparent color is being used. This is similar to the transparent colors used by GIF files. Transparent colors are not discussed here.

Finally, the xAspect and yAspect fields and the pageW and pageH fields define the aspect ratio and size of the source screen of the image being defined. These don't mean much to a PC, and can be safely ignored when you're reading an IFF file.

The CMAP chunk

The next essential chunk of an IFF file is a CMAP. The CMAP defines an array of RGB values to form a color palette. The data is in the same format as it appeared in the discussion of GIF files. Each color is defined as 3 bytes, one each for the red, green and blue light percentages. A 256-color image has 768 bytes of color-map information.

Note that monochrome IFF files (those with only 2 bits of color) usually also have a CMAP chunk. It defines a palette with two entries in it. The IFF format does not assume that all 2-color files use black and white as their two colors.

You can read a CMAP chunk by reading the type field, checking the length field to make sure that it contains a sensible value and then reading the data of the chunk into a buffer for later use in setting your display card's palette. A sensible value should be no more than 768 bytes, which is the maximum number of colors an IFF file can contain times the number of bytes in a color entry.

The BODY chunk

The image data stored in a BODY chunk is unstructured. If you've read the fields of its associated BMHD chunk properly, you should know how to deal with it.

In order to read the image data in a BODY chunk you should know the number of bytes in one line. If the IFF file in question has ILBM for its subtype, this value is:

```
bytes = pixels2bytes(motr2inti(bmhd.w))
* bmhd->nPlanes;
```

This assumes that bmhd is an object of the type BMHD and that it has been loaded with the contents of the image's BMHD chunk.

If the file has PBM as its subtype, the number of bytes in a line is:

```
bytes = motr2inti(bmhd.w);
```

If the file is uncompressed, you can read the lines into a buffer using the following bit of code. This assumes that bmhd is a BMHD object and that fp is a file pointer to the opened IFF file. The file pointer should begin by pointing to the first byte of the image data, having read the type and size fields of the BODY chunk.

```
char *p;
int i,n;

if((p=malloc(bytes)) != NULL) {
    n=motr2inti(bmhd.depth);
    for(i=0;i<n;++i) {
        fread(p,1,bytes,fp);
        putline(p,i);
    }
    free(p);
} else puts("Error allocating memory");
```

If the file is compressed, the foregoing bit of code should call a function to uncompress the file data.

```
char *p;
int i,n;

if((p=malloc(bytes)) != NULL) {
    n=motr2inti(bmhd.depth);
    for(i=0;i<n;++i) {
        readline(p,fp,bytes);
        putline(p,i);
    }
    free(p);
} else puts("Error allocating memory");
```

The readline function is a PackBits run-length decoder. This is what it looks like:

```
readline(p,fp,bytes)
    char *p;
    FILE *fp;
    int bytes;
{
    int c,i,n=0;

    do {
        c=fgetc(fp) & 0xff;
        if(c & 0x80) {
```

```
        if(c != 0x80) {
            i = ((c) & 0xff)+2;
            c=fgetc(fp);
            while(i--) p[n++] = c;
        }
    }
    else {
        i=(c & 0xff)+1;
        while(i--) p[n++] = fgetc(fp);
    }
} while(n < bytes);
return(n);
}
```

3-1 Continued.

The run-length encoding used by PackBits is particularly elegant, and only a bit obtuse. It works more or less like the hypothetical run-length encoding discussed in chapter 1. However, it uses the smallest possible number of bytes to do so, and usually results in pretty respectable compression of images that contain predictable runs of image data. It's also relatively fast to uncompress.

Here's how to decompress a line of PackBits data—this is essentially what the readline function, above, is doing.

The first byte read is treated as a key byte. If its high-order bit is set—if the byte AND 80H is true—the field following the byte is a run of bytes. The length of the run is defined as one more than the two's complement of the value in the byte. In a run-of-bytes field, the next byte is read and repeated for the length of the field.

If the high-order bit is not set, the field is a string. The length is one more than the value of the byte. In this case, the next n bytes should be read from the source file directly, where n is the length.

Once a field is read, the process should be repeated until the length of the decompressed line equals the calculated number of bytes in a line for the image being decoded, as discussed above. If the size of the line comes out too long, the image data has been corrupted or is not being unpacked properly.

Some implementations of PackBits like to pad out compressed lines to contain even numbers of bytes. Early implementations of the PC version of Deluxe Paint were very fussy about this. Compressed lines can be padded out with the value 80H. This is regarded as being neither a string key nor a run-of-bytes key, and is ignored upon reading it.

Note that the PackBits process doesn't really know what sort of data it's compressing. It's equally applicable to planes or byte-oriented lines. It's also worth noting that on its best day PackBits can't approach the compression efficiency of the string table compression used in GIF files.

Optional chunks

With the companion disk for this book, you can quickly see what chunks are in an IFF file by using the F4 details function of Graphic Workshop. If you don't have the disks, you might want to type in the program in FIG. 3-2, which is a small IFF file "walker." It lists all the chunks, identifying the ones it recognizes and ignoring the rest.

```
/*
        IFF lister - copyright (c) 1991
        Alchemy Mindworks Inc.
*/

#include "stdio.h"

long motr2intl(long l);

main(argc,argv)
        int argc;
        char *argv[];
{
        FILE *fp;
        char b[4];
        unsigned long l;

        if(argc > 1) {
                strupr(argv[1]);
                if((fp=fopen(argv[1],"rb")) != NULL) {

                        /* get the type */
                        fread(b,1,4,fp);
                        if(!memcmp(b,"FORM",4) ||
                            !memcmp(b,"LIST",4) ||
                            !memcmp(b,"CAT ",4)) {

                                /* get the size */
                                fread((char *)&l,1,4,fp);
                                printf("%s has %lu bytes of data\n",
                                    argv[1],motr2intl(l));

                                /* get the subtype */
                                fread(b,1,4,fp);

                                printf("File subtype: %4.4s\n",b);

                                /* read all the chunks */
                                do {
                                        fread(b,1,4,fp);
                                        fread((char *)&l,1,4,fp);
                                        l=motr2intl(l);
                                        if(l & 1L) ++l;
```

3-2 The source code for LISTIFF.

```
        fseek(fp,1,SEEK_CUR);

        printf("%6lu bytes: ",l);
        if(!memcmp(b,"BMHD",4))
            puts("BMHD - image deffinition");
        else if(!memcmp(b,"CMAP",4))
            puts("CMAP - palette deffinition");
        else if(!memcmp(b,"BODY",4))
            puts("BODY - image data");
        else if(!memcmp(b,"TINY",4))
            puts("TINY - Deluxe Paint preview");
        else if(!memcmp(b,"CRNG",4))
            puts("CRNG - Deluxe Paint colour range");
        else printf("%4.4s - unknown\n",b);

  } while(!ferror(fp) && memcmp(b,"BODY",4));

                    } else puts("This is not an IFF file");
                    fclose(fp);
            } else printf("Error opening %s\n",argv[1]);
        } else puts("Argument:       path to an IFF/LBM file");
}


long motr2intl(l)
        long l;
{
        return(((l & 0xff000000L) >> 24) +
               ((l & 0x00ff0000L) >> 8) +
               ((l & 0x0000ff00L) << 8) +
               ((l & 0x000000ffL) << 24));
}
```

3-2 Continued.

If you acquire IFF or LBM files from various sources, you'll probably find that they have widely varying numbers and types of tags. Here's a look at the tags generated by Deluxe Paint. This is a listing of CELTIC .LBM, one of the example images in FIG. 3-1:

```
CELTIC.LBM has 58660 bytes of data
File subtype:PBM
    20 bytes: BMHD - image definition
   768 bytes: CMAP - palette definition
   110 bytes: DPPS - unknown
     8 bytes: CRNG - Deluxe Paint color range
     8 bytes: CRNG - Deluxe Paint color range
     8 bytes: CRNG - Deluxe Paint color range
     8 bytes: CRNG - Deluxe Paint color range
     8 bytes: CRNG - Deluxe Paint color range
     8 bytes: CRNG - Deluxe Paint color range
     8 bytes: CRNG - Deluxe Paint color range
     8 bytes: CRNG - Deluxe Paint color range
```

```
        8 bytes: CRNG - Deluxe Paint color range
        8 bytes: CRNG - Deluxe Paint color range
        8 bytes: CRNG - Deluxe Paint color range
        8 bytes: CRNG - Deluxe Paint color range
        8 bytes: CRNG - Deluxe Paint color range
        8 bytes: CRNG - Deluxe Paint color range
        8 bytes: CRNG - Deluxe Paint color range
        8 bytes: CRNG - Deluxe Paint color range
     3828 bytes: TINY - Deluxe Paint preview
    53633 bytes: BODY - image data
```

Note that the LISTIFF program doesn't know what DPPS chunks are, nor does it care. The chunk structure of an IFF file allows unknown chunks to be ignored.

This is a READIFF listing of an IFF file that was found on a bulletin board, and comes from an Amiga application.

```
CINDY.LBM has 86964 bytes of data
File subtype: ILBM
        2 bytes: BHSM - unknown
       20 bytes: BMHD - image definition
       48 bytes: CMAP - palette definition
        4 bytes: CAMG - unknown
       98 bytes: BHCP - unknown
    86740 bytes: BODY - image data
```

This file has far fewer tags, but all the essential ones are there.

The most interesting optional chunk is the TINY preview. In fact, its discussion has to wait until after the complete process of dealing with IFF images has been beaten into submission.

An IFF/LBM viewer

Figure 3-3 is the source code for READIFF, a simple IFF file viewer. As with the GIF viewer in chapter 2, this one cheats a bit by using the VGA mode 13 to display all the images it finds, no matter how many colors they actually have. You might want to apply some of the screen-driver techniques discussed later in chapter 10 to the problem of creating a really universal IFF/LBM viewer.

```
/*
        IFF reader - copyright (c) 1991
        Alchemy Mindworks Inc.
*/

#include "stdio.h"
#include "dos.h"
#include "alloc.h"
```

3-3 The source code for READIFF.

```
/*                              uncomment this line if you
#include "memmangr.h"           will be linking in the memory manager
*/

#define GOOD_READ       0       /* return codes */
#define BAD_FILE        1
#define BAD_READ        2
#define MEMORY_ERROR    3


#define SCREENWIDE      320     /* mode 13 screen dimensions */
#define SCREENDEEP      200
#define STEP            32      /* size of a step when panning */


#define HOME            0x4700 /* cursor control codes */
#define CURSOR_UP       0x4800
#define CURSOR_LEFT     0x4b00
#define CURSOR_RIGHT    0x4d00
#define END             0x4f00
#define CURSOR_DOWN     0x5000


#define pixels2bytes(n)    ((n+7)/8)

typedef struct {
        int width,depth,bytes,bits;
        int flags;
        int background;
        char subtype[4];
        char palette[768];
        int (*setup)();
        int (*closedown)();
        } FILEINFO;

typedef struct {
        unsigned int w,h;
        int x,y;
        char nPlanes;
        char masking;
        char compression;
        char pad1;
        unsigned int transparentColor;
        char xAspect,yAspect;
        int pageW,pageH;
        } BMHD;

long motr2intl(long l);
char *farPtr(char *p,long l);
char *getline(unsigned int n);
char *planes2bytes(char *p,FILEINFO *fi);
int dosetup(FILEINFO *fi);
int doclosedown(FILEINFO *fi);
int putline(char *p,unsigned int n);
```

3-3 Continued.

```c
char masktable[8]={0x80,0x40,0x20,0x10,0x08,0x04,0x02,0x01};
char bittable[8] ={0x01,0x02,0x04,0x08,0x10,0x20,0x40,0x80};

FILEINFO fi;
char *buffer=NULL;

main(argc,argv)
        int argc;
        char *argv[];
{
        FILE *fp;
        static char results[8][16] = {  "Ok",
                                        "Bad file",
                                        "Bad read",
                                        "Memory error",
                                        };

        int r;

        if(argc > 1) {
                if((fp = fopen(argv[1],"rb")) != NULL) {
                        fi.setup=dosetup;
                        fi.closedown=doclosedown;
                        r=unpackiff(fp,&fi);
                        printf("\%s",results[r]);
                        fclose(fp);
                } else printf("Error opening %s",argv[1]);
        } else puts("Argument:        path to a IFF/LBM file");
}

/* unpack an IFF/LBM file */
unpackiff(fp,fi)
        FILE *fp;
        FILEINFO *fi;
{
        BMHD bmhd;
        unsigned long l;
        char *p,*pr,b[4];
        int i,n;

        /* get the type */
        fread(b,1,4,fp);
        if(!memcmp(b,"FORM",4) ||
           !memcmp(b,"LIST",4) ||
           !memcmp(b,"CAT ",4)) {

                /* ignore the size */
                fread((char *)&l,1,4,fp);

                /* get the subtype */
                fread(fi->subtype,1,4,fp);

                /* read all the chunks */
```

3-3 Continued.

```
do {
        fread(b,1,4,fp);
        fread((char *)&l,1,4,fp);
        l=motr2intl(l);
if(l & 1L) ++l;

/* check for a bitmap header */
if(!memcmp(b,"BMHD",4)) {
        if(fread((char *)&bmhd,1,sizeof(BMHD),fp)
            != sizeof(BMHD)) return(BAD_FILE);
        fi->width=motr2inti(bmhd.w);
        fi->depth=motr2inti(bmhd.h);
        fi->bits=bmhd.nPlanes;
        if(!memcmp(fi->subtype,"ILBM",4))
            fi->bytes=pixels2bytes(fi->width)*fi->bits;
        else
            fi->bytes=fi->width;
}

/* check for a palette */
else if(!memcmp(b,"CMAP",4)) {
        if((int)l <= 768) {
                if(fread(fi->palette,1,(int)l,fp) !=
                    (int)l) return(BAD_READ);
        }
        else {
                if(fread(fi->palette,1,768,fp) != 768)
                    return(BAD_READ);
                fseek(fp,l-768L,SEEK_SET);
        }
}

/* check for an image */
else if(!memcmp(b,"BODY",4)) {
        if((fi->setup)(fi) != GOOD_READ)
            return(MEMORY_ERROR);

        (fi->setup)(fi);
        if((p=malloc(fi->width)) != NULL) {
                for(i=0;i<fi->depth;++i) {
                        if(bmhd.compression)
                            n=readline(p,fp,fi->bytes);
                        else
                            n=fread(p,1,fi->bytes,fp);

                        if(n != fi->bytes) {
                                freebuffer();
                                free(p);
                                return(BAD_READ);
                        }

                        if(!memcmp(fi->subtype,"ILBM",4) ||
```

3-3 Continued.

```
                                               (!memcmp(fi->subtype,"PBM ",4) &&
                                                 fi->bits < 8)) {
                                                    if((pr=planes2bytes(p,fi)) == NULL) {
                                                        freebuffer();
                                                        free(p);
                                                        return(MEMORY_ERROR);
                                                    }
                                                    putline(pr,i);
                                                    free(pr);
                                             } else putline(p,i);
                                   }

                                   free(p);
                                   (fi->closedown)(fi);
                          } else return(MEMORY_ERROR);
                 }

                 /* skip an unknown chunk */
                 else fseek(fp,1,SEEK_CUR);

            } while(!ferror(fp) && memcmp(b,"BODY",4));
            return(GOOD_READ);

      } else return(BAD_FILE);
}

/* convert a planar line to a VGA line */
char *planes2bytes(line,fi)
      char *line;
      FILEINFO *fi;
{
      char *p,*pr;
      int i,j,n;

      /* allocate a place to put the line */
      if((p=malloc(fi->width)) != NULL) {

            /* get the width of one plane */
            n=pixels2bytes(fi->width);

            /* sscan through the pixels */
            for(i=0;i<fi->width;++i) {
                  pr=line;
                  p[i]=0;

                  /* fetch each planar pixel */
                  for(j=0;j<fi->bits;++j) {
                        if(pr[i>>3] & masktable[i & 0x0007])
                              p[i] |= bittable[j];
                        pr+=n;
                  }
            }
            return(p);
```

3-3 Continued.

```
                }
        return(NULL);
}


/* read a compressed PackBits line */
readline(p,fp,bytes)
        char *p;
        FILE *fp;
        int bytes;
{
        int c,i,n=0;

        do {
                c=fgetc(fp) & 0xff;
                if(c & 0x80) {
                        if(c != 0x80) {
                                i = ((~c) & 0xff)+2;
                                c=fgetc(fp);
                                while(i--) p[n++] = c;
                        }
                }
                else {
                        i=(c & 0xff)+1;
                        while(i--) p[n++] = fgetc(fp);
                }
        } while(n < bytes);
        return(n);
}


long motr2intl(l)
        long l;
{
        return(((l & 0xff000000L) >> 24) +
               ((l & 0x00ff0000L) >> 8) +
               ((l & 0x0000ff00L) << 8) +
               ((l & 0x000000ffL) << 24));
}

motr2inti(n)
        int n;
{
        return(((n & 0xff00) >> 8) | ((n & 0x00ff) << 8));
}


/* this function is called after the BMHD and CMAP chunks have
   been read but before the BODY is unpacked */
dosetup(fi)
        FILEINFO *fi;
{
        union REGS r;

        if(!getbuffer((long)fi->width*(long)fi->depth,fi->width,fi->depth))
```

3-3 Continued.

```
                return(MEMORY_ERROR);

        r.x.ax=0x0013;
        int86(0x10,&r,&r);

        setvgapalette(fi->palette,1<<fi->bits,fi->background);

        return(GOOD_READ);
}

/* This function is called after an image has been unpacked. It must
   display the image and deallocate memory. */
doclosedown(fi)
        FILEINFO *fi;
{
        union REGS r;
        int c,i,n,x=0,y=0;

        if(fi->width > SCREENWIDE) n=SCREENWIDE;
        else n=fi->width;

        do {
                for(i=0;i<SCREENDEEP;++i) {
                        c=y+i;
                        if(c>=fi->depth) break;
                        memcpy(MK_FP(0xa000,SCREENWIDE*i),getline(c)+x,n);
                }
                c=GetKey();
                switch(c) {
                        case CURSOR_LEFT:
                                if((x-STEP) > 0) x-=STEP;
                                else x=0;
                                break;
                        case CURSOR_RIGHT:
                                if((x+STEP+SCREENWIDE) < fi->width) x+=STEP;
                                else if(fi->width > SCREENWIDE)
                                    x=fi->width-SCREENWIDE;
                                else x=0;
                                break;
                        case CURSOR_UP:
                                if((y-STEP) > 0) y-=STEP;
                                else y=0;
                                break;
                        case CURSOR_DOWN:
                                if((y+STEP+SCREENDEEP) < fi->depth) y+=STEP;
                                else if(fi->depth > SCREENDEEP)
                                    y=fi->depth-SCREENDEEP;
                                else y=0;
                                break;
                        case HOME:
                                x=y=0;
                                break;
```

3-3 Continued.

```
                        case END:
                                if(fi->width > SCREENWIDE)
                                    x=fi->width-SCREENWIDE;
                                else x=0;
                                if(fi->depth > SCREENDEEP)
                                    y=fi->depth-SCREENDEEP;
                                else y=0;
                                break;
                }
        } while(c != 27);

        freebuffer();

        r.x.ax=0x0003;
        int86(0x10,&r,&r);
        return(GOOD_READ);
}

/* get one extended key code */
GetKey()
{
        int c;

        c = getch();
        if(!(c & 0x00ff)) c = getch() << 8;
        return(c);
}

/* set the VGA palette and background */
setvgapalette(p,n,b)
        char *p;
        int n,b;
{
        union REGS r;
        int i;

        outp(0x3c6,0xff);
        for(i=0;i<n;++i) {
                outp(0x3c8,i);
                outp(0x3c9,(*p++) >> 2);
                outp(0x3c9,(*p++) >> 2);
                outp(0x3c9,(*p++) >> 2);
        }
        r.x.ax=0x1001;
        r.h.bh=b;
        int86(0x10,&r,&r);
}

/* if you don't use in the memory manager, these functions
   will stand in for it */

#if !MEMMANGR
```

3-3 Continued.

```c
/* return a far pointer plus a long integer */
char *farPtr(p,l)
        char *p;
        long l;
{

        unsigned int seg,off;


        seg = FP_SEG(p);
        off = FP_OFF(p);
        seg += (off / 16);
        off &= 0x000f;
        off += (unsigned int)(l & 0x000fL);
        seg += (l / 16L);
        p = MK_FP(seg,off);
        return(p);


}


/* save one line to memory */
putline(p,n)
        char *p;
        unsigned int n;

{

        if(n >= 0 && n < fi.depth)
            memcpy(farPtr(buffer,(long)n*(long)fi.width),p,fi.width);

}

/* get one line from memory */
char *getline(n)
        unsigned int n;
{
        return(farPtr(buffer,(long)n*(long)fi.width));
}

#pragma warn -par
getbuffer(n,bytes,lines)
        unsigned long n;
        int bytes,lines;
{

    if((buffer=farmalloc(n)) == NULL) return(0);
    else return(1);
}

freebuffer()
{
        if(buffer != NULL) farfree(buffer);
        buffer=NULL;
}
#endif /* !MEMMANGR */
```

3-3 Continued.

The IFF viewer is a lot like the GIF viewer in the last chapter, although some of the data structures and constants are different. The IFF file decoding process is less cryptic than the GIF, although the variations on IFF files require that some format translation be done for some decoded lines. Specifically, mode 13 of a VGA card expects to see an array of bytes. This is how lines come out of an IFF file if its subtype is PBM (that is, if it's a proprietary Deluxe Paint file) but it's not how they emerge from a pure IFF file. In the latter case, the image is structured as a series of image planes, one for each color bit.

The translation between bit planes and bytes is discussed shortly.

The IFF file viewer does most of its work in the unpackiff function. You'll notice that it does much of what the LISTIFF program, discussed previously, did, but it's a bit more interested in the contents of some of the chunks. Specifically, if it encounters a BMHD chunk it reads its contents into a BMHD struct. It likewise deals with palette information in a CMAP chunk. Finally, it actually reads the image line data from a BODY chunk.

The image lines in an IFF BODY chunk are stored in a way common to most image-file formats, although not actually to the GIF file format discussed in chapter 2. Each line is packed as a distinct object, such that if you start decoding at the beginning of the image data, you can stop at the end of each integral line. As such, if depth is the number of lines in the file and readline is a function to unpack the lines, this unpacks them all:

```
int i;

for(i=0;i<depth;++i) {
    readline(buffer);
    putline(buffer,i);
}
```

In this example, buffer is assumed to be large enough to contain all the data for 1 line of the image.

In the case of an IFF file, the readline function can do one of two things. It can either decompress a line that has been encoded as PackBits run-length data or it can just read in raw bytes. In the portion of readiff that actually reads the BODY chunk, the code either calls readline to decode a PackBits line or fread to handle an uncompressed line. This decision is made based on the contents of bmhd.compression.

By convention, an IFF file that contains a single image that has its BODY chunk as the last chunk in the file. As such, the do loop in readiff that walks through the IFF chunks continues looping until a BODY chunk has been decoded. Note that inasmuch as all sorts of other data can be stored in IFF files, you would want to handle IFF decoding differently if you were writing a more universal IFF file handler. The test that determines whether the loop continues should actually compare the current file pointer to the number of bytes that the file is said to contain, based on the length value at the beginning. The file should not be considered read until the code reaches the end of it.

This is not an issue in decoding IFF files with bitmapped images in them, as these files *are* constrained to have their BODY chunks last.

The only issue that hasn't really been dealt with in this discussion of IFF images is the propensity of IFF image data to want to look like an Amiga's screen buffer in some cases. Unless you're working with 256-color IFF files that have come from the PC implementation of Deluxe Paint, your files will be planar. If you want to display them on a PC VGA card, you'll probably want them to be byte-oriented. Making the transition entails a bit of a digression.

A digression on bit fields

All IFF files that have ILBM as their subtype are stored so that each line is a series of image planes rather than as an array of bytes. The display code in `doclosedown` wants to work with image data in the latter form, as this corresponds to the structure of a VGA card's image buffer in mode 13. The function `planes2bytes` handles the translation in these cases. It allocates a new line buffer and creates an array of bytes that corresponds to the color information in an array of planes.

As an aside, if you're confronted with an IFF file having 16 colors or less, the planar structure of the line data as it emerges from the file corresponds exactly to the planar structure of an EGA or VGA card in a 16-color display mode. In this case, you would not want to translate the line data because it would be stuffed into the display buffer just as it emerged from the file. This is discussed in greater detail in chapter 10.

The `planes2bytes` function uses bit extraction, an area of bitmapped manipulation that we haven't discussed yet. This is something that need not come up when you're only working with byte-oriented formats such as GIF, but its almost inevitable if you're handling monochrome or planar images.

A planar image is one in which the pixels are held as individual bits within the bytes that make up the picture data. A monochrome image is the simplest sort of planar picture, but as discussed in chapter 1, 16-color images are often stored in this format as well. In this case, an image consists of four layered planes.

On an Amiga the display hardware can have still more layered planes, as all the Amiga's graphic display modes are planar. Just as with the PC, the Amiga's image file format corresponds somewhat to the structure of its display, such that a minimum of translation is required to display a stored image.

It's not that hard to understand how planar displays and planar files work, although it will probably occur to you to wonder why anyone would want to structure an image in so complex a way. In fact, there are good reasons for designing hardware to use image planes rather than bytes to store pixels. While a byte-oriented display such as mode 13H of a VGA card assumes that all images have 8 color bits, you can have as many planes as you like.

Figure 3-4 illustrates a monochrome image. This is, in fact, a planar image with one plane. Figure 3-4 also illustrates the palette for this image, which has two entries—black and white.

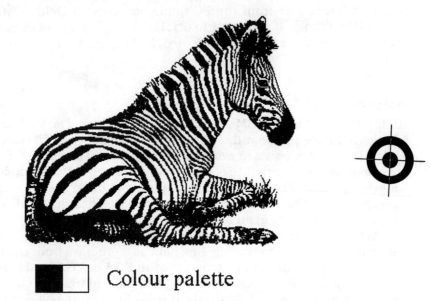

Colour palette

3-4 A monochrome image and its palette.

Figure 3-5 illustrates a 16-color image and its palette. Because this book is printed in black and white, this example has a gray-scale palette. A gray-scale palette is just like a color palette, except that all its entries happen to be varying densities of gray.

The picture in FIG. 3-5 has 4 bits of color, for a total of 16 gray levels. Every pixel in the picture has a value between 0 and 15.

To work out the value of the pixel at (x,y), you would locate that pixel in the first of the four planes. Start with a pixel value of 0. The first plane has a weight of 1. If the pixel is on in this plane, add 1 to the pixel value. The next plane has a weight of 2. If the pixel is on in this plane, add 2 to the pixel value. Repeat the process with the remaining two planes, which have weights of 4 and 8 respectively. Figure 3-6 illustrates this process.

A larger issue might be that of working out how to determine the value of a pixel in a bit plane. Unlike as with simply reading a byte out of an array, C does not provide any immediately obvious way to figure out whether a particular bit in an array of bytes is set.

As an aside, there's a useful macro that you'll probably encounter pretty often in working with bit fields. It's called `pixels2bytes`. It works out the number of bytes needed to contain a bit field of n pixels. This is

3-5 A 16-color image and its palette.

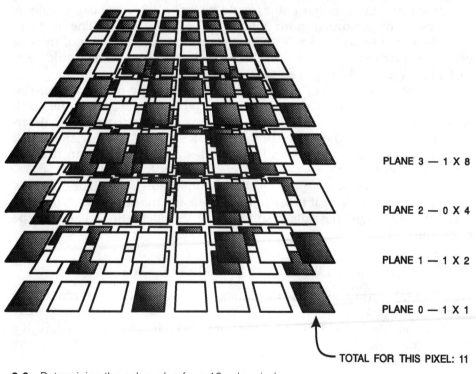

PLANE 3 — 1 X 8

PLANE 2 — 0 X 4

PLANE 1 — 1 X 2

PLANE 0 — 1 X 1

TOTAL FOR THIS PIXEL: 11

3-6 Determining the color value for a 16-color pixel.

n / 8 if the field length is evenly divisible by eight or 1 + n / 8 if it's not. The `pixels2bytes` macro is defined like this:

```
#define  pixels2bytes(n)  ((n+7)/8)
```

To begin the discussion of bit fields, let's assume that p points to a buffer that contains the image in FIG. 3-5. This image has the dimensions 640×480 pixels. You can work out the number of bytes in one line of one plane of the image as `pixels2bytes(640)`, or 80. As there are 4 bits of color in this picture, and hence four planes, there are four times this number of bytes in each complete line, for a total of 320.

By convention, a planar image is stored with its planes interleaved. As such, in decoding a planar image with 4 bits of color, you'll get the four plane lines for the first image line followed by the four plane lines for the second image line, and so on. This is *almost* always the case—the PIC file discussion in chapter 6 is an exception to it.

The buffer with the image in it has all its lines stored in the order in which they've come out of the source file. To work out the value of a pixel at (x,y), you would begin by locating line y. This is located at p+y*320. In practice, large planar images typically require more than 64K of storage, and you would want to use the `farPtr` function to access their lines, to wit, `farPtr(p,(long)y*320L)`.

If `pr` is a pointer into p, such that `pr` points to line y, the byte that contains pixel x in the first plane would be `pr[x / 8]`. You can divide by even powers of two much more quickly by using bit shifts. The byte can also be located as `pr[x >> 3]`. The byte in the second plane of the line would be at `pr[80 + (x >> 3)]`. The byte in the third plane would be at `pr[160 + (x >> 3)]`, and so on.

To determine whether a particular pixel is on or off in a byte, you would AND the byte with a mask that represents the position of the pixel. A mask is a byte with only 1 bit set. You can calculate the mask to determine the position of the pixel at (x,y) as `0x80 >> (x & 7)`. As such, if `pr` points to the line y, you would test to see if pixel x is set in the first plane by seeing if `(pr[x >> 3] & (0x80 >> (x & 7)))` is not 0.

Calculating `0x80 >> (x & 7)` is time-consuming if you'll be doing it a lot. You can cut the time it takes to work out each mask by observing that there are only eight possible results from this calculation. They can be stored in a table.

```
char masktable[8]=
{ 0x80,0x40,0x20,0x10,0x08,0x04,0x02,0x01 };
```

With this table available, the calculation of a bit mask can be reduced to `masktable[x & 7]`.

In translating planar lines to byte lines, as is the case in READIFF, it's also useful to have a table of weights for the various planes. This is the inverse of the mask table.

```
char bittable[8]=
{ 0x01,0x02,0x04,0x08,0x10,0x20,0x40,0x80 };
```

If pr points to line y of n planes, you can work out the actual palette
color number represented by the pixel (x,y) as shown here. In this case,
the lines are assumed to be 640 pixels wide, so each plane is 80 bytes long.
You will want to change this value for a real application.

```
int a=0,i;

for(i=0;i<n;++i) {
    if(pr[x>>3] & masktable[x & 7])
      a | = bittable[n];
    pr+=80;
}
```

The color palette number would be in a at the end of this calculation.

Bitwise manipulation can be used to test and manipulate bits in a bit
field. We've seen what's involved in testing bits. Much the same approach
is used when you want to modify the individual bits in a string of bytes. In
these examples, the string of bytes in question is pointed to by pr and the
position of the bit to be dealt with is x.

The easiest bitwise manipulation is setting a bit on. It's done by ORing
a mask with 1 byte of a bit field. This is how you do it:

```
pr[x >> 3] | ≅ masktable[x & 7];
```

To turn a bit off, you must AND the appropriate byte with the inverse
of the mask that you would have used to set the bit on by ORing it. This
has the effect of leaving all the existing bits unaffected except for the one
you wanted to turn off, which is masked. It's done like this:

```
pr[x >> 3] &= masktable[x & 7];
```

Finally, to flip a bit—that is, to invert its state—you can XOR a mask
with the bit field, like this:

```
pr[x >> 3] ^= masktable[x & 7];
```

In practice, writing functions such as planes2bytes takes some
head scratching. Bitwise manipulation is a bit finicky, especially if you're
used to thinking of bytes as being the smallest objects you're likely to confront. It's easy to miscalculate the length of a bit field in a multiple plane
line, which usually leaves you with pretty strange looking images.

The Deluxe Paint preview

One of the rather enviable features of the Deluxe Paint package is its file
previews. When you select an LBM file in the Deluxe Paint Load File dialog
box, it shows you a small preview image of the picture before you actually

load the complete image. The preview images, while hardly great art, are sufficiently detailed to let you decide whether you want to deal with that image. They certainly tell you a lot more than an eight-character file name can.

Figure 3-7 illustrates an LBM file and its preview image.

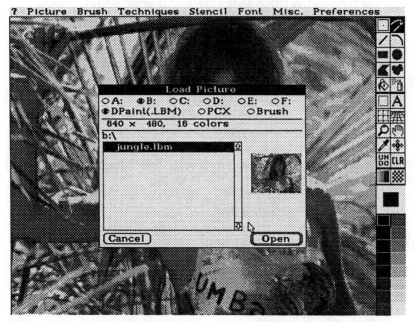

3-7 The preview of an LBM file as seen in the Deluxe Paint Load File dialog.

While it would be convenient to be able to simply scale the image in an LBM file on-the-fly to create a preview, this would be pretty time consuming and turns out not to be what Deluxe Paint is up to. It sneaks its way around the problem by storing a second, very much smaller version of the principal image in each file. The smaller image is stored in a chunk called TINY, which usually immediately precedes the BODY chunk.

A preview image stored as a TINY chunk is constrained to have the same palette, line structure and image compression type as the full-size picture it represents. These are quantities that have been established by the time a TINY chunk is encountered.

The contents of a TINY chunk consist of two integers to specify the dimensions of the image it contains, followed by the image data itself. Figure 3-8 illustrates a program called READTINY, which displays the preview in an LBM file. You'll note that this code really represents little more than a modification of the READIFF program previously discussed. The code to handle a BODY chunk has been replaced by code to deal with a TINY chunk. Everything else is pretty much the same.

```
/*
        IFF preview reader - copyright (c) 1991
        Alchemy Mindworks Inc.
*/

#include "stdio.h"
#include "dos.h"
#include "alloc.h"

/*                                  uncomment this line if you
#include "memmangr.h"               will be linking in the memory manager
*/

#define GOOD_READ         0         /* return codes */
#define BAD_FILE          1
#define BAD_READ          2
#define MEMORY_ERROR      3
#define NOT_FOUND         4

#define SCREENWIDE        320       /* mode 13 screen dimensions */
#define SCREENDEEP        200
#define STEP              32        /* size of a step when panning */

#define HOME              0x4700    /* cursor control codes */
#define CURSOR_UP         0x4800
#define CURSOR_LEFT       0x4b00
#define CURSOR_RIGHT      0x4d00
#define END               0x4f00
#define CURSOR_DOWN       0x5000

#define pixels2bytes(n)    ((n+7)/8)

typedef struct {
        int width,depth,bytes,bits;
        int flags;
        int background;
        char subtype[4];
        char palette[768];
        int (*setup)();
        int (*closedown)();
        } FILEINFO;

typedef struct {
        unsigned int w,h;
        int x,y;
        char nPlanes;
        char masking;
        char compression;
        char pad1;
        unsigned int transparentColor;
        char xAspect,yAspect;
```

3-8 The source code for READTINY.

```
        int pageW,pageH;
        } BMHD;

long motr2intl(long l);
char *farPtr(char *p,long l);
char *getline(unsigned int n);
char *planes2bytes(char *p,FILEINFO *fi);
int dosetup(FILEINFO *fi);
int doclosedown(FILEINFO *fi);

int putline(char *p,unsigned int n);

char masktable[8]={0x80,0x40,0x20,0x10,0x08,0x04,0x02,0x01};
char bittable[8] ={0x01,0x02,0x04,0x08,0x10,0x20,0x40,0x80};

FILEINFO fi;
char *buffer=NULL;

main(argc,argv)
        int argc;
        char *argv[];
{
        FILE *fp;
        static char results[8][16] = {  "Ok",
                                        "Bad file",
                                        "Bad read",
                                        "Memory error",
                                        "No preview"
                                        };

        int r;

        if(argc > 1) {
                if((fp = fopen(argv[1],"rb")) != NULL) {
                        fi.setup=dosetup;
                        fi.closedown=doclosedown;
                        r=unpackiff(fp,&fi);
                        printf("\%s",results[r]);
                        fclose(fp);
                } else printf("Error opening %s",argv[1]);
        } else puts("Argument:        path to a IFF/LBM file");
}

/* unpack an IFF/LBM file */
unpackiff(fp,fi)
        FILE *fp;
        FILEINFO *fi;
{
        BMHD bmhd;
        unsigned long l;
        char *p,*pr,b[4];
        int i,n;
```

3-8 Continued.

```
/* get the type */
fread(b,1,4,fp);
if(!memcmp(b,"FORM",4) ||
   !memcmp(b,"LIST",4) ||
   !memcmp(b,"CAT ",4)) {

        /* ignore the size */
        fread((char *)&l,1,4,fp);

        /* get the subtype */
        fread(fi->subtype,1,4,fp);

        /* read all the chunks */
        do {
                fread(b,1,4,fp);

                fread((char *)&l,1,4,fp);
                l=motr2intl(l);
                if(l & 1L) ++l;

                /* check for a bitmap header */
                if(!memcmp(b,"BMHD",4)) {
                        if(fread((char *)&bmhd,1,sizeof(BMHD),fp)
                            != sizeof(BMHD)) return(BAD_FILE);
                        fi->width=motr2inti(bmhd.w);
                        fi->depth=motr2inti(bmhd.h);
                        fi->bits=bmhd.nPlanes;
                        if(!memcmp(fi->subtype,"ILBM",4))
                                fi->bytes=pixels2bytes(fi->width)*fi->bits;
                        else
                                fi->bytes=fi->width;
                }

                /* check for a palette */
                else if(!memcmp(b,"CMAP",4)) {
                        if((int)l <= 768) {
                                if(fread(fi->palette,1,(int)l,fp) !=
                                    (int)l) return(BAD_READ);
                        }
                        else {
                                if(fread(fi->palette,1,768,fp) != 768)
                                    return(BAD_READ);
                                fseek(fp,l-768L,SEEK_SET);
                        }
                }

                /* check for a preview image */
                else if(!memcmp(b,"TINY",4)) {

                        /* read the preview width */
                        if(fread((char *)&n,1,sizeof(int),fp) != sizeof(int))
                            return(BAD_READ);
```

3-8 Continued.

```
                        fi->width=motr2inti(n);

                        /* read the preview depth */
                        if(fread((char *)&n,1,sizeof(int),fp) != sizeof(int))
                            return(BAD_READ);
                        fi->depth=motr2inti(n);

                        /* figure the bytes */
                        if(!memcmp(fi->subtype,"ILBM",4))
                            fi->bytes=pixels2bytes(fi->width)*fi->bits;
                        else
                            fi->bytes=fi->width;

                        (fi->setup)(fi);
                        if((p=malloc(fi->width)) != NULL) {
                                for(i=0;i<fi->depth;++i) {
                                        if(bmhd.compression)
                                            n=readline(p,fp,fi->bytes);
                                        else
                                            n=fread(p,1,fi->bytes,fp);

                                        if(n != fi->bytes) {
                                                free(p);
                                                freebuffer();
                                                return(BAD_READ);
                                        }

                                        if(!memcmp(fi->subtype,"ILBM",4) ||
                                          (!memcmp(fi->subtype,"PBM ",4) &&
                                          fi->bits < 8)) {
                                                if((pr=planes2bytes(p,fi)) == NULL) {
                                                        free(p);
                                                        freebuffer();
                                                        return(MEMORY_ERROR);
                                                }
                                                putline(pr,i);
                                                free(pr);
                                        } else putline(p,i);
                                }
                                free(p);
                                (fi->closedown)(fi);
                        } else return(MEMORY_ERROR);
                }

                /* skip an unknown chunk */
                else fseek(fp,1,SEEK_CUR);

        } while(!ferror(fp) && memcmp(b,"BODY",4) && memcmp(b,"TINY",4));
        if(!memcmp(b,"TINY",4)) return(GOOD_READ);
        else return(NOT_FOUND);
    } else return(BAD_FILE);
}
```

3-8 Continued.

```
                    /* convert a planar line to a VGA line */
                    char *planes2bytes(line,fi)
                            char *line;
                            FILEINFO *fi;
                    {
                            char *p,*pr;
                            int i,j,n;

                            /* allocate a place to put the line */
                            if((p=malloc(fi->width)) != NULL) {

                                    /* get the width of one plane */
                                    n=pixels2bytes(fi->width);

                                    /* sscan through the pixels */
                                    for(i=0;i<fi->width;++i) {
                                            pr=line;
                                            p[i]=0;

                                            /* fetch each planar pixel */
                                            for(j=0;j<fi->bits;++j) {
                                                    if(pr[i>>3] & masktable[i & 0x0007])
                                                        p[i] |= bittable[j];
                                                    pr+=n;
                                            }
                                    }
                                    return(p);
                            }
                            return(NULL);
                    }


                    /* read a compressed PackBits line */
                    readline(p,fp,bytes)
                            char *p;
                            FILE *fp;
                            int bytes;
                    {
                            int c,i,n=0;

                            do {
                                    c=fgetc(fp) & 0xff;
                                    if(c & 0x80) {
                                            if(c != 0x80) {
                                                    i = ((~c) & 0xff)+2;
                                                    c=fgetc(fp);
                                                    while(i--) p[n++] = c;
                                            }
                                    }
                                    else {
                                            i=(c & 0xff)+1;
                                            while(i--) p[n++] = fgetc(fp);
                                    }
```

3-8 Continued.

```
        } while(n < bytes);
        return(n);
}


long motr2intl(l)
        long l;
{
        return(((l & 0xff000000L) >> 24) +
                ((l & 0x00ff0000L) >> 8) +
                ((l & 0x0000ff00L) << 8) +
                ((l & 0x000000ffL) << 24));
}


motr2inti(n)
        int n;
{
        return(((n & 0xff00) >> 8) | ((n & 0x00ff) << 8));
}


/* this function is called after the BMHD and CMAP chunks have
   been read but before the BODY is unpacked */
dosetup(fi)
        FILEINFO *fi;
{
        union REGS r;

        if(!getbuffer((long)fi->width*(long)fi->depth,fi->width,fi->depth))
            return(MEMORY_ERROR);

        r.x.ax=0x0013;
        int86(0x10,&r,&r);

        setvgapalette(fi->palette,1<<fi->bits,fi->background);

        return(GOOD_READ);
}
/* This function is called after an image has been unpacked. It must
   display the image and deallocate memory. */
doclosedown(fi)
        FILEINFO *fi;
{
        union REGS r;
        int c,i,n,x=0,y=0;

        if(fi->width > SCREENWIDE) n=SCREENWIDE;
        else n=fi->width;

        do {
                for(i=0;i<SCREENDEEP;++i) {
                        c=y+i;
                        if(c>=fi->depth) break;
                        memcpy(MK_FP(0xa000,SCREENWIDE*i),getline(c)+x,n);
```

3-8 Continued.

```
			}
		c=GetKey();
		switch(c) {
			case CURSOR_LEFT:
				if((x-STEP) > 0) x-=STEP;
				else x=0;
				break;
			case CURSOR_RIGHT:
				if((x+STEP+SCREENWIDE) < fi->width) x+=STEP;
				else if(fi->width > SCREENWIDE)
					x=fi->width-SCREENWIDE;
				else x=0;
				break;
			case CURSOR_UP:
				if((y-STEP) > 0) y-=STEP;
				else y=0;
				break;
			case CURSOR_DOWN:
				if((y+STEP+SCREENDEEP) < fi->depth) y+=STEP;
				else if(fi->depth > SCREENDEEP)
					y=fi->depth-SCREENDEEP;
				else y=0;
				break;
			case HOME:
				x=y=0;
				break;
			case END:
				if(fi->width > SCREENWIDE)
					x=fi->width-SCREENWIDE;
				else x=0;
				if(fi->depth > SCREENDEEP)
					y=fi->depth-SCREENDEEP;
				else y=0;
				break;
		}
	} while(c != 27);

	freebuffer();

	r.x.ax=0x0003;
	int86(0x10,&r,&r);
	return(GOOD_READ);

}

/* get one extended key code */
GetKey()
{
	int c;

	c = getch();
	if(!(c & 0x00ff)) c = getch() << 8;
```

3-8 Continued.

```
                return(c);
}

/* set the VGA palette and background */
setvgapalette(p,n,b)
        char *p;
        int n,b;
{
        union REGS r;
        int i;

        outp(0x3c6,0xff);
        for(i=0;i<n;++i) {
                outp(0x3c8,i);
                outp(0x3c9,(*p++) >> 2);
                outp(0x3c9,(*p++) >> 2);
                outp(0x3c9,(*p++) >> 2);
        }
        r.x.ax=0x1001;
        r.h.bh=b;
        int86(0x10,&r,&r);
}

/* if you don't use in the memory manager, these functions
   will stand in for it */

#if !MEMMANGR

/* return a far pointer plus a long integer */
char *farPtr(p,l)
        char *p;
        long l;
{
        unsigned int seg,off;

        seg = FP_SEG(p);
        off = FP_OFF(p);
        seg += (off / 16);
        off &= 0x000f;
        off += (unsigned int)(l & 0x000fL);
        seg += (l / 16L);
        p = MK_FP(seg,off);
        return(p);
}

/* save one line to memory */
putline(p,n)
        char *p;
        unsigned int n;
{
        if(n >= 0 && n < fi.depth)
                memcpy(farPtr(buffer,(long)n*(long)fi.width),p,fi.width);
```
3-8 Continued.

```
        }

/* get one line from memory */
char *getline(n)
        unsigned int n;
{
        return(farPtr(buffer,(long)n*(long)fi.width));
}

#pragma warn -par
getbuffer(n,bytes,lines)
        unsigned long n;
        int bytes,lines;
{
        if((buffer=farmalloc(n)) == NULL) return(0);
        else return(1);
}

freebuffer()
{
        if(buffer != NULL) farfree(buffer);
        buffer=NULL;
}
#endif /* !MEMMANGR */
```

3-8 Continued.

In many applications, of course, you'll want to skip the contents of any TINY previews that you come across. As with all IFF chunks, you can do this by simply seeking forward in the file to the next chunk. Likewise, if you'll be writing software which creates IFF files, including a TINY chunk is optional. Deluxe Paint doesn't complain when it's confronted with an image file that lacks a preview; it simply leaves the preview area of its Load File dialog blank.

Writing IFF files

As with most image file formats, creating an IFF file is much less intimidating a task than unpacking all the permutations of IFF files can be. Having worked your way though the structure of IFF files in unpacking them, you can probably foresee how the process of writing one will take place.

The WRITEIFF program in FIG. 3-9 illustrates how to create an IFF file. This program uses the same binary files discussed in chapter 2. You'll want the MAKEBIN program to create a few as test subjects for this program. The MAKEBIN program, of course, converts images from GIF files, even though you are writing to IFF files.

```
/*
        IFF writer - copyright (c) 1991
```

3-9 The source code for WRITEIFF.

```
        Alchemy Mindworks Inc.
*/

#include "stdio.h"
#include "alloc.h"

#define ILBM            1                   /* set true for planar IFF */

#define BINARYSIG       "ALCHBINR"      /* binary identification */

#define GOOD_WRITE      0           /* return codes */
#define BAD_WRITE       1
#define BAD_READ        2
#define MEMORY_ERROR    3

#define TINYWIDE        80                  /* dimensions for DP TINY preview */
#define TINYDEEP        50
#define TINYBYTES       10

#define pixels2bytes(n)     ((n+7)/8)

typedef struct {
        char sign[8];
        int width,depth,bits;
        char palette[768];
        } BINARYHEADER;

typedef struct {
        unsigned int w,h;
        int x,y;
        char nPlanes;
        char masking;
        char compression;
        char pad1;
        unsigned int transparentColor;
        char xAspect,yAspect;
        int pageW,pageH;
        } BMHD;

int getline(char *p,int n,int line);
void fputlong(FILE *fp,long n);
char *bytes2planes(char *p,int width,int bytes,int bits);

FILE *in,*out;
BINARYHEADER bh;

char masktable[8]={0x80,0x40,0x20,0x10,0x08,0x04,0x02,0x01};
char bittable[8] ={0x01,0x02,0x04,0x08,0x10,0x20,0x40,0x80};

main(argc,argv)
        int argc;
        char *argv[];
```

3-9 Continued.

```
{
        static char results[4][16] = {   "Ok",
                                         "Bad write",
                                         "Bad read",
                                         "Memory error",
                                          };

        char path[81];
        int n;

        if(argc > 1) {
                strmfe(path,argv[1],"BIN");
                strupr(path);
                if((in=fopen(path,"rb")) != NULL) {
                        if(fread((char *)&bh,1,sizeof(BINARYHEADER),in) ==
                            sizeof(BINARYHEADER)) {
                                if(!memcmp(bh.sign,BINARYSIG,8)) {
                                        strmfe(path,argv[1],"LBM");
                                        strupr(path);
                                        if((out=fopen(path,"wb")) != NULL) {
                                                puts("Writing");
                                                n=writeIff(out,getline,
                                                        bh.width,bh.depth,
                                                        bh.bits,bh.palette);
                                                printf("\n%s",results[n]);
                                                fclose(out);
                                        } else printf("Error creating %s",path);
                                } else printf("%s is corrupted",path);
                        } else printf("Error reading %s",path);
                        fclose(in);
                } else printf("Error opening %s",path);
        } else puts("Argument:       path to a BIN file");
}

/* write an IFF/LBM file */
writeIff(fp,readline,width,depth,bits,palette)
        FILE *fp;
        int (*readline)();
        unsigned int width,depth,bits;
        char *palette;
{

        BMHD bmhd;
        double sx,sy,fx,fy;
        long l,pos;
        char *p,*pr,*pp,sb[TINYWIDE];
        int i,j,bytes;

        /* write the header */
        fwrite("FORM",1,4,fp);

        /* write a dummy long to hold the final length */
        fputlong(fp,0L);
```

3-9 Continued.

```c
/* write the subtype */
#if ILBM
fwrite("ILBM",1,4,fp);
#else
if(bits==8) fwrite("PBM ",1,4,fp);
else fwrite("ILBM",1,4,fp);
#endif

/* figure the plane width for ILBM files */
bytes=pixels2bytes(width);

/* allocate a line buffer */
if((p=malloc(width)) == NULL) return(MEMORY_ERROR);

/* write the bitmap header chunk */
fwrite("BMHD",1,4,fp);
fputlong(fp,(long)sizeof(BMHD));

/* load up the BMHD struct with this image's data */
memset((char *)&bmhd,0,sizeof(BMHD));
bmhd.w=motr2inti(width);
bmhd.h=motr2inti(depth);
bmhd.nPlanes=bits;
bmhd.compression=1;
bmhd.pageW=motr2inti(width);
bmhd.pageH=motr2inti(depth);
fwrite((char *)&bmhd,1,sizeof(BMHD),fp);

/* write the colour map*/
fwrite("CMAP",1,4,fp);
fputlong(fp,3*(1<<bits));
fwrite(palette,1,3*(1<<bits),fp);

/* write the preview */
fwrite("TINY",1,4,fp);
pos=ftell(fp);

/* write a dummy long for the chunk size */
fputlong(fp,0L);

/* write the preview dimensions */
fputword(fp,TINYWIDE);
fputword(fp,TINYDEEP);

/* work out the scale factors */
fy=(double)depth/(double)TINYDEEP;
fx=(double)width/(double)TINYWIDE;

sy=0.0;

/* scan through the lines and compress them */
for(i=0;i<TINYDEEP;++i) {
```

3-9 Continued.

```
                              /* get a line from the input file */
                              if(readline(p,width,(int)sy)) {
                                      free(p);
                                      return(BAD_READ);
                              }
                              sy+=fy;

                              /* scale it down */
                              sx=0.0;
                              for(j=0;j<TINYWIDE;++j) {
                                      sb[j]=p[(int)sx];
                                      sx+=fx;
                              }

                              /* write the line */
                              #if ILBM
                              if((pr=bytes2planes(sb,TINYWIDE,TINYBYTES,bits)) != NULL) {
                                      pp=pr;
                                      for(j=0;j<bits;++j) {
                                              writeline(fp,pp,TINYBYTES);
                                              pp+=TINYBYTES;
                                      }
                                      free(pr);
                              }  .
                              else {
                                      free(p);
                                      return(MEMORY_ERROR);
                              }
                              #else
                              if(bits==8) {
                                      writeline(fp,sb,TINYWIDE);
                              }
                              else {
                                      if((pr=bytes2planes(sb,TINYWIDE,TINYBYTES,bits)) != NULL) {
                                              pp=pr;
                                              for(j=0;j<bits;++j) {
                                                      writeline(fp,pp,TINYBYTES);
                                                      pp+=bytes;
                                              }
                                              free(pr);
                                      }
                                      else {
                                              free(p);
                                              return(MEMORY_ERROR);
                                      }
                              }
                              #endif
                      }

              /* file out where the file pointer is */
              l=ftell(fp)-8L;
```

3-9 Continued.

```
/* round it up to an even word */
if(l & 1L) {
        fputc(0,fp);
        ++l;
}


/* go back to the dummy */
fseek(fp,pos,SEEK_SET);

/* write in the size */
fputlong(fp,(l-pos)+4L);

/* and return to the end of the chunk */
fseek(fp,l+8L,SEEK_SET);

/* write the image */
fwrite("BODY",1,4,fp);
pos=ftell(fp);

/* put in a dummy long for the chunk size */
fputlong(fp,0L);

/* compress all the lines */
for(i=0;i<depth;++i) {

/* get a line */
if(readline(p,width,i)) {
        free(p);
        return(BAD_READ);
}

/* write the line */
#if ILBM
if((pr=bytes2planes(p,width,bytes,bits)) != NULL) {
        pp=pr;
        for(j=0;j<bits;++j) {
                writeline(fp,pp,bytes);
                pp+=bytes;
        }
        free(pr);
}
else {
        free(p);
        return(MEMORY_ERROR);
}
#else
if(bits==8) {
        writeline(fp,p,width);
}
else {
        if((pr=bytes2planes(p,width,bytes,bits)) != NULL) {
                pp=pr;
                for(j=0;j<bits;++j) {
```

3-9 Continued.

```
                                        writeline(fp,pp,bytes);
                                        pp+=bytes;
                                }
                                free(pr);
                        }
                        else {
                                free(p);
                                return(MEMORY_ERROR);
                        }
                }
                #endif
        }

        /* as with the TINY preview, the chunk size must be filled in */
        l=ftell(fp)-8L;
        if(l & 1L) {
                fputc(0,fp);
                ++l;
        }
        fseek(fp,pos,SEEK_SET);
        fputlong(fp,(l-pos)+4L);

        /* since this is the last chunk, the file size must also be filled in */
        fseek(fp,4L,SEEK_SET);
        fputlong(fp,l);

        free(p);

        if(ferror(fp)) return(BAD_WRITE);
        else return(GOOD_WRITE);
}

/* translates bytes into planes */
char *bytes2planes(p,width,bytes,bits)
        char *p;
        int width,bytes,bits;
{
        char *pr;
        int i,j,n;

        if((pr=malloc(bytes*bits)) != NULL) {
                for(i=0;i<width;++i) {
                        n=0;
                        for(j=0;j<bits;++j) {
                                if(p[i] & bittable[j])
                                    pr[n+(i>>3)] |= masktable[i & 0x0007];
                                else
                                    pr[n+(i>>3)] &= ~masktable[i & 0x0007];
                                n+=bytes;
                        }
                }
                return(pr);
```

3-9 Continued.

```
                } else return(NULL);
        }


        /* do packbits compression for one line of image data */
        writeline(fp,p,n)
                FILE *fp;
                char *p;
                int n;
        {
                char b[128];
                unsigned int bdex=0,i=0,j=0,t=0;

                do {
                        i=0;
                        while((p[t+i]==p[t+i+1]) &&
                                i < 127 &&
                                i < (n-1) &&
                                ((t+i+1) < n)) ++i;

                        if(i > 0 || bdex >= 127) {
                                if(bdex) {
                                        fputc(((bdex-1) & 0x7f),fp);
                                        ++j;
                                        fwrite(b,1,bdex,fp);
                                        j+=bdex;
                                        bdex=0;
                                }
                                if(i) {
                                        fputc((~i+1),fp);
                                        fputc(p[t+i],fp);
                                        j+=2;
                                        t+=(i+1);
                                }
                        } else b[bdex++]=p[t++];
                } while(t<n);

                if(bdex) {
                        fputc(((bdex-1) & 0x7f),fp);
                        ++j;
                        fwrite(b,1,bdex,fp);
                        j+=bdex;
                }
                if((j & 0x0001)) fputc(0x80,fp);
        }

        /* make file name with specific extension */
        strmfe(new,old,ext)
                char *new,*old,*ext;
        {
                while(*old != 0 && *old != '.') *new++=*old++;
                *new++='.';
                while(*ext) *new++=*ext++;
```

3-9 Continued.

```
                *new=0;
        }


/* fetch a line from the input file */
getline(p,n,line)
        char *p;
        int n,line;
{

        int i;

        /* seek past the binary file header to the line */
        fseek(in, (long)sizeof(BINARYHEADER) | (long)line * (long)n, SEEK_SET);
        i=fread(p,1,n,in);
        if(i==n) return(0);
        else return(1);
}


/* write one long to the file in motorola format */
void fputlong(fp,n)
        FILE *fp;
        long n;
{

        fputc((n >> 24),fp);
        fputc((n >> 16),fp);
        fputc((n >> 8),fp);
        fputc(n,fp);
}


/* write one integer to the file in motorola format */
fputword(fp,n)
        FILE *fp;
        int n;
{

        fputc((n >> 8),fp);
        fputc(n,fp);
}


motr2inti(n)
        int n;
{
        return(((n & 0xff00) >> 8) | ((n & 0x00ff) << 8));
}
```

3-9 Continued.

Note that, as with the GIF file example in the previous chapter, the data that comes out of a binary file created by MAKEBIN is byte oriented in that each pixel is represented by 1 byte. Depending upon the nature of your application for IFF files, the source image data in the programs you write based on the code in this chapter may be in another form. For example, once you have the code in this chapter working properly, you might wish to remove the function that translates byte-oriented lines to plane-oriented lines if your source images will be planar to start with.

You should also give some thought as to the file extension to use. The IFF extension is probably the most technically accurate one to use, but files so named will not appear in the Deluxe Paint Load File box. If you'll be creating IFF files with the intent of subsequently reading them with Deluxe Paint, you should probably name them with the extension LBM.

Before you start figuring out what all the code in WRITEIFF is about, you might want to consider one of the inherent problems in writing this type of file structure. Having each chunk with its size in an easily located place requires that you know the size before you write the chunk data. In some cases, this is pretty easy—a BMHD chunk is always 14 bytes long, and the size of a CMAP chunk can be worked out as being three times the number of colors in the image being compressed.

The size of a BODY chunk is pretty well impossible to predict if the file being written uses compression to store its lines. This is also true of a TINY preview chunk. Short of compressing it all twice, once to see how much space the compressed data takes and then a second time to write it to the file, there's no obvious way to know what to put in the size field when you write it.

The way around this problem is to write a dummy long integer for the chunk-size fields in chunks that are of an unpredictable length. When all the data for the chunk has been written, you can work out the length of the chunk by reading the file position and subtracting the position of the start of the chunk's data. You can then seek back in the file to where you put the dummy-size value, write in the real size value, and seek to the end of the chunk to proceed with writing the next chunk.

This should serve to explain what all the calls to `fseek` and `ftell` in the `writeiff` are about.

The `writeiff` function should be pretty easy to work through. It assembles an IFF file in a linear fashion. It begins by writing the type string ''FORM'' to the destination file, followed by a dummy long integer. It then writes the appropriate subtype field, either ''ILBM'' or ''PBM ''. If you set the ILBM define at the top of the source listing for WRITEIFF true, all the files it creates will be planar and have the subtype ''ILBM.'' If you set it false, 8-bit IFF files will be written as byte-oriented lines and have the subtype ''PBM .'' Images with fewer than 8 color bits are treated as normal ILBM files.

If you are creating IFF files that might have to be read by programs other than Deluxe Paint, or ones that might find themselves ultimately being ported back to an Amiga, you should write ILBM files. Choosing to write IFF files using the IFF subtype does not invalidate your files for use with Deluxe Paint—they simply load a bit slower.

Note also that the `fputlong` and `fputword` functions that write longs and integers to the destination file in this example have been designed to write them in the Motorola number format. If you abstract code from WRITEIFF to use somewhere else, make sure you keep this in mind.

The first chunk written to an IFF file is always a BMHD. It's pretty tame. The code that handles it writes the string BMHD and the chunk size to the file and then fills in and writes a BMHD data structure. Note that all the integers in a BMHD data structure must be run through `motr2inti` to make them respectable. While the `motr2inti` and `motr2intl` functions have been used to handle conversion from Motorola numbers until now, they are in fact suitable for translating in both directions, as the byte order of Motorola numbers is the reverse of that of Intel ones.

A BMHD chunk's length is always 14 bytes, which is conveniently an even number.

The next chunk is a CMAP. As mentioned earlier, this chunk should always be included, even if the file only has two colors. Deluxe Paint does not assume that an image with two colors necessarily uses black and white as its palette. If no CMAP chunk is included in a monochrome IFF file, Deluxe Paint usually uses the palette of whatever file was previously loaded.

A CMAP chunk's size can be calculated as three times the number of colors in the image, there being 3 bytes for each RGB value in a palette. Inasmuch as the number of colors in a palette must be an even power of two, the size of a CMAP chunk is always even.

The next chunk to be written is a TINY preview. If you are writing IFF files that will be read by something other than Deluxe Paint, you can excise the code to write previews if you like. Because the size of a preview can't be known until the data is written, this bit of code must write a dummy size value and seek around after the fact, as was discussed previously.

The TINY preview image is actually a scaled-down version of the full-size image in the file. It's not clear how Deluxe Paint derives the dimensions for its TINY previews. In this code, they're set to fixed values of 80 and 50 pixels for the width and depth respectively. The first 4 bytes in the preview are two integers that define its dimensions.

The final chunk to be written is a BODY. It works pretty much like the TINY chunk did, except that the image data isn't scaled down. Each line is read from the source file and written out by `writeline`, which handles the PackBits compression. When the whole image has been written, the code will pad out the chunk by 1 byte if it turns out to have an odd size and then fill in the chunk size field after the "BODY" string. Finally, it will seek back to the start of the file and fill in the file size field.

Working with IFF files

If you can live with its propensity for oddly structured numbers, the IFF format is a workable way to handle modest size images. It's much faster to work with than the GIF format and requires much less code. However, its PackBits compression isn't nearly as effective as the string-table compression used by GIF files when it's confronted by complex image data, and it's much more likely to exhibit negative compression if your source images get sufficiently detailed. This is a common situation if you work with scanned images.

You might want to see if you can come up with a workable IFF writer that stores images that behave themselves in compressed form and switches to the uncompressed version of the format when it's confronted with an awkward source file that refuses to squeeze.

One of the powerful features of the IFF format is that you may add your own custom chunks to it for your applications without anyone else having to know what they're supposed to do. Just as the code in this chapter can skip over chunks it doesn't know how to deal with, so too will Deluxe Paint and other software that reads IFF files be able to ignore your custom chunks if you form them correctly.

The Graphic Workshop package included on the companion disk set for this book writes a custom chunk called TEXT to the IFF files it creates. This chunk contains a string to identify the version of the software that created each IFF file it writes. While perhaps an obvious extension to the IFF format, this is not a defined chunk type. Nonetheless, it doesn't upset any other applications which read IFF image files.

Figure 3-10 illustrates the details window of Graphic Workshop displaying the chunk structure of one of its own IFF files.

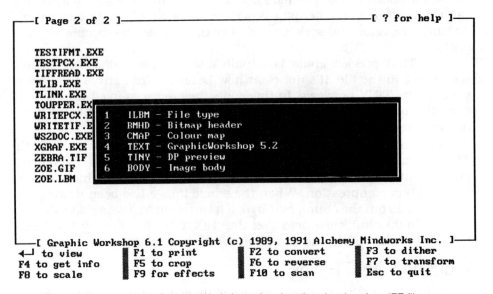

3-10 The details window of Graphic Workshop showing the chunks of an IFF file.

It's unlikely that anything you'll want to do with IFF files on a PC will require much beyond what has been discussed in this chapter. All the really exotic applications for these files assume that you are working on an Amiga. However, if you'd like to learn a bit more about the IFF format, you can buy a book called *EA IFF 85 Standard for Interchange Format Files* from Commodore Computers (1200 Wilson Dr., West Chester, PA 19380). This 1988 book is a bit thin in some respects in that it leaves out all sorts of things about the more recent chunk types and such. It's also written with an Amiga environment in mind, so you might have to read between the lines in places to make all its information applicable to working with a PC.

If you have access to a bulletin board with an Amiga section on it, you'll probably find several useful files dealing with the IFF format there, too. However, be aware that Amiga C compilers offer a lot of library functions that don't have counterparts on a PC. Also be aware that a discussion of IFF files might have nothing to do with images. They're also used to store music, text, and all sorts of application-specific data on the Amiga, so you might have to dig through a lot of inapplicable chunks.

The most frequently thought-of user of IFF files, Electronic Arts, probably will not prove to be of much assistance if you need information about anything specific to Deluxe Paint's application of this format. As of this writing, they appear to have a policy of not releasing any information about how their software works. For the most part, they let you listen to music on hold until you give up and look elsewhere.

4
WordPerfect graphics

A camel is a horse that's been designed by a committee.
—MURPHY'S LAWS OF COMPUTERS

WordPerfect has been described as a word processor for people who really want a database manager, an application sponsored by a consortium of keyboard manufacturers to help wear out your Alt key quicker, a 2K program with 500K of bolt-on accessories, and, perhaps most accurately, as the software equivalent of a camel. It's a word processor designed by a committee.

This book was written on a very old copy of WordStar.

In fairness, WordPerfect is a very powerful package: it can do almost anything if you know the right key combinations and you have long enough fingers to press all the keys involved simultaneously. The aspect of WordPerfect that is perhaps most relevant to this book actually has nothing at all to do with words. Aside from turning simple text into a typographer's worst nightmare, WordPerfect allows you to include graphics in your documents.

Figure 4-1 illustrates a WordPerfect document with an included graphic.

Just as the Amiga, discussed in chapter 3, abandoned all that had gone before it in favor of newer and more amusing file standards, so too have the authors of WordPerfect elected to create a proprietary graphic file format rather than adopting one of the existing ones. The resultant file structure, the WPG format, is an interesting example of image storage. For reasons that become clearer in a moment, it's not really a bitmapped file

Cocker spaniels are among the
least interesting of creatures.
Small, innocuous and incapable
of attacking anything much
larger than a golf ball, one
cannot help wondering why anyone
would go to the trouble of
breeding dogs which could only
have applications as chimney
brushes.

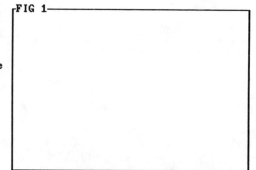

FIG 1

Bengal tigers are
considerably more interesting.
A typical Bengal tiger can eat
its own weight in cocker
spaniels in just under a week.
It will also eat house cats, annoying salesmen and, perhaps best of
all, poodles. None of these creatures is any match for an active
tiger, although some caution should be exercised in feeding your
tiger smaller poodles, as they might become stuck in its throat.
There are those who will suggest that large carnivorous
animals such as the Bengal tiger do not make suitable pets,
especially if you live in an apartment. You may hear the opinion
that these animals require large amounts of land to roam free in,

J:\WP\PETS.WP
Doc 1 Pg 1 Ln 1" Pos 1"

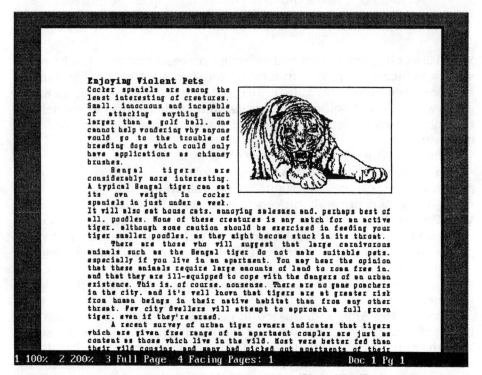

4-1 The text representation (A), and the graphic preview (B) of a WordPerfect document with
a WPG file included.

format at all. It regards bitmapped images as discrete graphic objects, one of many that WPG files can contain.

The WPG format is a very crude example of what's called a *metafile*. It's somewhat chunk oriented, in the way that IFF files are, but a WPG file can contain multiple sorts of graphic information. The format is primarily intended for storing vector drawings. A vector drawing is a collection of instructions to a drawing engine that tell it where to draw circles, lines, arcs and other graphic primitives. If you've watched AutoCAD or Corel-DRAW regenerate their screens one object at a time, you're probably familiar with the concept of vector art.

As with several other vector-based metafiles, one of the object types that a WPG file can contain is a bitmap fragment. In fact, it's quite allowable to have a WPG file containing nothing but a single bitmap fragment. As such, it's fair to regard WPG files as being capable of supporting bitmapped images, even if this facility seems to have been something of an afterthought in their design.

If you look at the complete WPG file format specification, it becomes obvious that the WPG format is really intended to provide a medium for importing charts, graphs and other corporate regalia into financial reports and memos to the stockholders. Having a few scanned photographs pop up in a WordPerfect document can certainly be eye-catching.

In fact, WordPerfect's treatment of bitmaps is rather unkind. It doesn't print them particularly well, especially if you import color images this way. While you can usually improve on its default treatment of bitmaps somewhat, as discussed at the end of this chapter, it's nowhere near as flexible as a true desktop publishing package in this regard. You can get much better results out of Ventura or even Microsoft Word.

The code in this chapter allows you to read and write bitmapped WordPerfect files. It's worth pointing out that it does *not* read vector WPG files. The example WPG files that come with WordPerfect contain vector graphics. Many of the public-domain WordPerfect graphics collections do as well.

It's also worth noting that DrawPerfect, WordPerfect's companion drawing package, is intended to work with vector images, not bitmaps.

Finally, the code in this chapter deals with WordPerfect graphics having 1, 4, and 8 color bits. The WPG file-format specification does allow for 8-bit WPG files. As of this writing, however, WordPerfect itself does not. Confronted with a 256-color WPG file, it often seems to read the image but does not display or print anything.

It might be that the WordPerfect Corporation allowed for 8-bit files in its specification because it intends to support them in a later product release. For this reason the discussion of WPG files in this chapter deals with them. However, if you write an application that generates WordPerfect files, you might want to limit its output to files with no more than 4 bits of color for the time being. Confronted with the ability to create WPG files that are not currently supported by WordPerfect, most people will probably assume that there's a bug in your software.

The WordPerfect graphic file structure

A WPG file consists of a header and a list of "records." There can be any number of records in a WPG file. They're analogous to the IFF chunks discussed in chapter 3. In a vector drawing, each record would be one graphic primitive. For example, in order to draw a five-pointed star with a WPG file using vector graphics, the file would require a minimum of five records.

In fact, it would actually require a few more than this. There are several record types required for housekeeping as well.

Because the majority of WPG record types contain vector drawing elements, and since this chapter won't be getting involved with vector art, it's possible to ignore most of the WPG file specification. The record types that concern you in dealing with the code in this chapter are as follows:

Type 15 - a start of records record
Type 14 - a color map record
Type 11 - a bitmap record
Type 16 - an end of records record

Specifically, a WordPerfect file that contains only a single bitmapped image, such as those dealt with here, has one each of the foregoing records in the order listed.

The record structure of a WPG file makes it about as tricky to work with as IFF files are. However, it's worth pointing out that WPG bitmapped images don't exhibit anything like the variations in their compression methods and other particulars that might confront an IFF viewer. Dealing with them is pretty tame.

To unpack a WPG file, you would start by reading its header. The header looks like this:

```
typedef struct {
        char id[4];
        long start;
        char product;
        char filetype;
        char majorversion;
        char minorversion;
        unsigned int encrypt;
        unsigned int reserved;
        } WPGHEAD;
```

The id field of a WPGHEAD structure always holds the string "\377WPC". Note that this is a 4-byte string—the first element in the string is an octal constant. Checking the contents of the id field is how a WPG file reader tells whether it has a real WPG file or something masquerading as one.

The start element specifies the offset from the beginning of the file to the start of the first record. This is usually 16L. The product field should be 1, and the filetype field should hold 16H. At present, the majorversion field is 1 and the minorversion field is 0. The encrypt field should hold a 0, indicating that the file is not encrypted. The reserved field is set to 0.

WordPerfect graphic records not only behave like IFF file chunks, they're also similarly structured. The first byte in a record is the record type, analogous to the 4-byte type field of an IFF chunk. The next several bytes define the size of the record. If the second byte in a record holds values from 0 through 254, it is the record length. If it holds 255, the next 2 bytes serve as an integer that defines the length of the record.

To further confuse this issue, WordPerfect graphic records can actually have long integers to define their lengths if they're big enough. If, in reading a record that has an integer to hold its length value, the high-order bit of the integer is set (that is, if the integer AND 8000H is true) the integer AND 7FFFH should be considered the high-order 2 bytes of a long integer, and the next 2 bytes in the WPG file being read should be considered the low-order 2 bytes.

Having determined the length and type of a record, a WPG reader can set about either decoding the beast if it happens to be of a relevant type or skipping it if it's of no interest. Skipping a record involves seeking forward in the WPG file being read to find the next record.

A "Start WPG Data" record will have 15 for its type value. It is always 6 bytes long. Its data looks like this:

```
typedef struct {
        char version;
        char flags;
        int screenwidth;
        int screendepth;
        } STARTRECORD;
```

The pversion field should be 1. If the flags field AND 01H is true, there's PostScript code tacked onto the WPG file being read. The screenwidth and screendepth fields specify the dimensions of the virtual space in which the current file's vector graphics are constrained, if any are present in the file.

None of this information is of much use to the code in this chapter.

A "Color Map" record has 14 as its type value. The data in the record is structured like this:

```
typedef struct {
        int startindex;
        int palettesize;
        } COLORMAP;
```

This data structure is followed by a number of 3-byte palette entries.

The `startindex` field defines the palette entry number in which the first color defined by this color map should be loaded. Typically, this is 0. The `palettesize` field defines the number of colors in this color map. Assuming that `startindex` is actually 0, the value of `palettesize` would be 16 for a 4-bit file and 256 for an 8-bit file.

A "Bitmap" record has 11 as its type. It contains this structure:

```
typedef struct {
        int width;
        int depth;
        int bits;
        int xresolution;
        int yresolution;
        } BITMAP;
```

The `width` and `depth` fields define the dimensions of the bitmapped image. The `bits` field holds the number of bits of color, which is 1, 2, 4, or 8. This chapter does not discuss 2-bit files. The `xresolution` and `yresolution` values specify the number of dots per inch in which the graphic in question is intended to be printed. This is fairly meaningless for the purposes of the code in this book.

Following this data structure is the actual encoded graphic data. A bitmap record is one that might require a long integer to specify its length. This record typically contains most of the data in a bitmap WPG file.

The image data in a WPG file is stored using a proprietary run-length encoding process. It's hard to say whether or not it's any more effective than simple PackBits encoding. It's certainly more complex.

As with other run-length encoded lines, a WPG line consists of a series of fields, of which there are four types. Each field consists of a key byte, to indicate its type, followed by the field data, as discussed in chapter 1. If the high-order bit of the key byte is set and any other bits are also set, the field is a run of bytes. In this case, the length is the key byte AND 7FH. The next byte in the file should be repeated this many times.

If the high-order bit of the key byte is set but no other bits are, this field is a solid run. The next byte in the file is the length. The byte FFH should be repeated this many times.

If the high-order bit of the key byte is not set but some of the other bits are, this field is a string. The length is the value of the key byte. This many bytes should be read as-is from the file.

Finally, if the key byte is 0, the next byte in the file is the repeat count. This means that the previously decoded line should be repeated as-is the number of times specified in the next byte.

Figure 4-2 illustrates a function to unpack WPG lines.

Monochrome WPG files have their lines stored as single monochrome planes, pretty well as you might expect. Eight-bit WPG files, if you decide that such things should exist, have their lines stored as arrays of bytes, just as GIF files and PBM-type IFF files do. Four-bit WPG files store their

```
readwpgline(p,fp,bytes)
        char *p;
        FILE *fp;
        int bytes;
{
        static int repeat;
        int c,d,i,n=0;

        if(repeat) {
                --repeat;
                n=bytes;
        }
        else {
            do {
                    c=fgetc(fp);
                    if((c & 0x0080) && (c & 0x007f)) {
                            d=fgetc(fp) & 0xff;
                            for(i=0;i<(c & 0x7f);++i) p[n++]=d;
                    }
                    else if((c & 0x0080) && !(c & 0x007f)) {
                            d=fgetc(fp) & 0xff;
                            for(i=0;i<d;++i) p[n++]=0xff;
                    }
                    else if(!(c & 0x0080) && (c & 0x007f)) {
                            for(i=0;i<(c & 0x7f);++i) p[n++]=fgetc(fp);
                    }
                    else {
                            repeat=fgetc(fp);
                            n=bytes;
                    }
            } while(n < bytes);
        }
        return(n);
}
```

4-2 A function to unpack one line of a compressed WordPerfect bitmapped image.

data in a way that is a little strange. As a rule, 4-bit image files usually cause most of the trouble when working with bitmaps, as there are several ways to store them and reasonable arguments to account for each approach.

The lines of a 4-bit WPG file come out of the readline function in FIG. 4-2 with each byte containing two pixels. The high-order 4 bits contain the first pixel and the low-order 4 bits contain the second. This is distinct from the way an IFF file stores a 4-bit image, as four planes. It's probably worth noting that this storage method doesn't correspond to any commonly used type of display hardware. It also doesn't lend itself to particularly effective run-length encoding. It becomes inefficient much more readily than planar lines do when it's confronted with complex scanned images.

As with the example file viewers discussed in the previous chapters, the viewer for WPG files discussed here uses mode 13H to display all the images it gets to look at. In this case, a 4-bit WPG line is in a more-or-less convenient form, as each byte that comes out of `readline` can be translated into two distinct bytes with nothing more than some bit shifting. In most cases you won't want to store image data in quite so inefficient a form, however.

A WPG file viewer

Figure 4-3 illustrates a simple viewer for bitmapped WPG files. It looks a lot like the previous file viewers discussed in this book—much of the code hasn't changed. The WordPerfect-specific routines should be easy to identify. The principal one is `unpackwpg`, which does all the work.

```
/*
        WPG reader - copyright (c) 1991
        Alchemy Mindworks Inc.
*/

#include "stdio.h"
#include "dos.h"
#include "alloc.h"

/*                              uncomment this line if you
#include "memmangr.h"           will be linking in the memory manager
*/

#define GOOD_READ       0       /* return codes */
#define BAD_FILE        1
#define BAD_READ        2
#define MEMORY_ERROR    3

#define SCREENWIDE      320     /* mode 13 screen dimensions */
#define SCREENDEEP      200
#define STEP            32      /* size of a step when panning */

#define HOME            0x4700  /* cursor control codes */
#define CURSOR_UP       0x4800
#define CURSOR_LEFT     0x4b00
#define CURSOR_RIGHT    0x4d00
#define END             0x4f00
#define CURSOR_DOWN     0x5000

#define RGB_RED         0
#define RGB_GREEN       1
#define RGB_BLUE        2
#define RGB_SIZE        3

#define pixels2bytes(n)    ((n+7)/8)

typedef struct {
```

4-3 The source code for READWPG.

```c
                   int width,depth,bytes,bits;
                   int background;
                   char palette[768];
                   int (*setup)();
                   int (*closedown)();
                   } FILEINFO;

         typedef struct {
                   char id[4];
                   long start;
                   char product;
                   char filetype;
                   char majorversion;
                   char minorversion;
                   unsigned int encrypt;
                   unsigned int reserved;
                   } WPGHEAD;

         char *farPtr(char *p,long l);
         char *getline(unsigned int n);
         char *mono2vga(char *p,int width);
         char *ega2vga(char *p,int width);

         int dosetup(FILEINFO *fi);
         int doclosedown(FILEINFO *fi);

         int putline(char *p,unsigned int n);

         char masktable[8]={0x80,0x40,0x20,0x10,0x08,0x04,0x02,0x01};

         FILEINFO fi;
         char *buffer=NULL;

         main(argc,argv)
                   int argc;
                   char *argv[];
         {
                   FILE *fp;
                   static char results[8][16] = {  "Ok",
                                                   "Bad file",
                                                   "Bad read",
                                                   "Memory error",
                                                   };
                   char path[81];
                   int r;

                   if(argc > 1) {
                           strmfe(path,argv[1],"WPG");
                           strupr(path);
                           if((fp = fopen(path,"rb")) != NULL) {
                                   fi.setup=dosetup;
                                   fi.closedown=doclosedown;
```

4-3 Continued.

```
                                r=unpackwpg(fp,&fi);
                                printf("\%s",results[r]);
                                fclose(fp);
                        } else printf("Error opening %s",path);
                } else puts("Argument:        path to a WPG file");
        }

/* unpack a WPG file */
unpackwpg(fp,fi)
        FILE *fp;
        FILEINFO *fi;
{
        WPGHEAD wpg;
        char *p,*pr;
        unsigned long offset=0L;
        int i;

        /* set the dimensions to illegal values */
        fi->width=fi->depth=fi->bytes=fi->bits=0;

        /* set a default monochrome palette */
        memcpy(fi->palette,"\000\000\000\377\377\377",6);

        /* get the header */
        if(fread((char *)&wpg,1,sizeof(WPGHEAD),fp)==sizeof(WPGHEAD)) {

                /* check the header */
                if(!memcmp(wpg.id,"\377WPC",4)) {

                        /* find the start of the records */
                        fseek(fp,wpg.start,SEEK_SET);

                        /* read all the records */
                        do {
                                i=readrecord(fi,fp,&offset);
                        } while(i != 16 && i != EOF);

                        /* see if there was a valid bitmap */
                        if(i==16 &&
                           fi->width != 0 &&
                           fi->depth != 0 &&
                           offset != 0L) {

                                /* allocate a line buffer */
                                if((p=malloc(fi->bytes)) != NULL) {

                                        if((fi->setup)(fi) != GOOD_READ) {
                                                free(p);
                                                return(MEMORY_ERROR);
                                        }

                                        /* find the start of the image data */
```

4-3 Continued.

```
                                        fseek(fp,offset,SEEK_SET);

                                        /* read all the lines */
                                        for(i=0;i<fi->depth;++i) {
                                                if(readwpgline(p,fp,fi->bytes)
                                                    != fi->bytes) {
                                                        freebuffer();
                                                        free(p);
                                                        return(BAD_READ);
                                                }

                                        /* translate the line types into VGA */
                                        switch(fi->bits) {
                                                case 1:
                                                        pr=mono2vga(p,fi->width);
                                                        if(pr != NULL) {
                                                                putline(pr,i);
                                                                free(pr);
                                                        }
                                                        else {
                                                                freebuffer();
                                                                free(p);
                                                                return(MEMORY_ERROR);
                                                        }
                                                        break;
                                                case 4:
                                                        pr=ega2vga(p,fi->width);
                                                        if(pr != NULL) {
                                                                putline(pr,i);
                                                                free(pr);
                                                        }
                                                        else {
                                                                freebuffer();
                                                                free(p);
                                                                return(MEMORY_ERROR);
                                                        }
                                                        break;
                                                case 8:
                                                        putline(p,i);
                                                        break;
                                        }
                                }
                                (fi->closedown)(fi);
                                free(p);
                                return(GOOD_READ);
                        } else return(MEMORY_ERROR);
                } else return(BAD_FILE);
            } else return(BAD_FILE);
        } else return(BAD_READ);
}

/* convert a monochrome line into an eight bit line */
```

4-3 Continued.

```
char *mono2vga(p,width)
        char *p;
        int width;
{

        char *pr;
        int i;

        if((pr=malloc(width)) != NULL) {
                for(i=0;i<width;++i) {
                        if(p[i >> 3] & masktable[i & 0x0007])
                            pr[i]=1;
                        else
                            pr[i]=0;
                }
                return(pr);
        } else return(NULL);
}


/* convert a four bit line into an eight bit line */
char *ega2vga(p,width)
        char *p;
        int width;
{

        char *pr;
        int i,j=0;

        if((pr=malloc(width)) != NULL) {
                for(i=0;i<width;) {
                        pr[i++]=(p[j] >> 4) & 0x0f;
                        pr[i++]=p[j] & 0x0f;
                        ++j;
                }
                return(pr);
        } else return(NULL);
}


/* read one record of a wpg file */
readrecord(fi,fp,offset)
        FILEINFO *fi;
        FILE *fp;
        unsigned long *offset;
{

        unsigned long l,t;
        unsigned int i,j,type,fc;
        type=fgetc(fp);
        t=ftell(fp);
        i=fgetc(fp) & 0x00ff;
        if(i == 0xff) {
                i=fgetword(fp);
                if(i & 0x8000) {
                        l = (unsigned long)(i & 0x7fff) << 16;
                        i = fgetword(fp);
```

4-3 Continued.

```
                              l += (((unsigned long)i)+4L);
                  } else l=(((unsigned int)i)+2L);
            } else l=(unsigned long)i;

            switch(type) {
                  case 11:                        /* bitmap */
                        fi->width=fgetword(fp);
                        fi->depth=fgetword(fp);
                        fi->bits=fgetword(fp);
                        fgetword(fp);
                        fgetword(fp);
                        *offset=ftell(fp);
                        if(fi->bits == 8) fi->bytes=fi->width;
                        else fi->bytes=pixels2bytes(fi->width)*fi->bits;
                        break;
                  case 14:                        /* palette */
                        fc=fgetword(fp);
                        j=fgetword(fp);

                        for(i=0;i<j;++i) {
                              if(((fc+i)*RGB_SIZE) >= 768) break;
                              fi->palette[((fc+i)*RGB_SIZE)+RGB_RED]=fgetc(fp);
                              fi->palette[((fc+i)*RGB_SIZE)+RGB_GREEN]=fgetc(fp);
                              fi->palette[((fc+i)*RGB_SIZE)+RGB_BLUE]=fgetc(fp);
                        }
                        break;
            }
            fseek(fp,t+1+1L,SEEK_SET);
            return(type);
}

/* uncompress one line of a wpg image */
readwpgline(p,fp,bytes)
      char *p;
      FILE *fp;
      int bytes;
{

      static int repeat;
      int c,d,i,n=0;

      if(repeat) {
            --repeat;
            n=bytes;
      }
      else {
            do {
                  c=fgetc(fp);
                  if((c & 0x0080) && (c & 0x007f)) {
                        d=fgetc(fp) & 0xff;
                        for(i=0;i<(c & 0x7f);++i) p[n++]=d;
                  }
                  else if((c & 0x0080) && !(c & 0x007f)) {
```

4-3 Continued.

```
                                  d=fgetc(fp) & 0xff;
                                  for(i=0;i<d;++i) p[n++]=0xff;
                          }
                          else if(!(c & 0x0080) && (c & 0x007f)) {
                                  for(i=0;i<(c & 0x7f);++i) p[n++]=fgetc(fp);
                          }
                          else {
                                  repeat=fgetc(fp);
                                  n=bytes;
                          }
                  } while(n < bytes);
          }
          return(n);
}


fgetword(fp)
          FILE *fp;
{
          return((fgetc(fp) & 0xff) + ((fgetc(fp) & 0xff) << 8));
}


/* This function is called before an image is unpacked */
dosetup(fi)
          FILEINFO *fi;
{
          union REGS r;

          if(!getbuffer((long)fi->width*(long)fi->depth,fi->width,fi->depth))
             return(MEMORY_ERROR);

          r.x.ax=0x0013;
          int86(0x10,&r,&r);

          setvgapalette(fi->palette,1<<fi->bits,fi->background);

          return(GOOD_READ);
}


/* This function is called after an image has been unpacked. It must
   display the image and deallocate memory. */
doclosedown(fi)
          FILEINFO *fi;
{
          union REGS r;
          int c,i,n,x=0,y=0;

          if(fi->width > SCREENWIDE) n=SCREENWIDE;
          else n=fi->width;

          do {
                  for(i=0;i<SCREENDEEP;++i) {
                          c=y+i;
```

4-3 Continued.

```
                        if(c>=fi->depth) break;
                        memcpy(MK_FP(0xa000,SCREENWIDE*i),getline(c)+x,n);
                }
                c=GetKey();
                switch(c) {
                        case CURSOR_LEFT:
                                if((x-STEP) > 0) x-=STEP;
                                else x=0;
                                break;
                        case CURSOR_RIGHT:
                                if((x+STEP+SCREENWIDE) < fi->width) x+=STEP;
                                else if(fi->width > SCREENWIDE)
                                    x=fi->width-SCREENWIDE;
                                else x=0;
                                break;
                        case CURSOR_UP:
                                if((y-STEP) > 0) y-=STEP;
                                else y=0;
                                break;
                        case CURSOR_DOWN:
                                if((y+STEP+SCREENDEEP) < fi->depth) y+=STEP;
                                else if(fi->depth > SCREENDEEP)
                                    y=fi->depth-SCREENDEEP;
                                else y=0;
                                break;
                        case HOME:
                                x=y=0;
                                break;
                        case END:
                                if(fi->width > SCREENWIDE)
                                    x=fi->width-SCREENWIDE;
                                else x=0;
                                if(fi->depth > SCREENDEEP)
                                    y=fi->depth-SCREENDEEP;
                                else y=0;
                                break;
                }
        } while(c != 27);

        freebuffer();

        r.x.ax=0x0003;
        int86(0x10,&r,&r);
        return(GOOD_READ);
}

/* get one extended key code */
GetKey()
{
        int c;

        c = getch();
```

4-3 Continued.

```c
        if(!(c & 0x00ff)) c = getch() << 8;
        return(c);
}


/* set the VGA palette and background */
setvgapalette(p,n,b)
        char *p;
        int n,b;
{
        union REGS r;
        int i;

        outp(0x3c6,0xff);
        for(i=0;i<n;++i) {
                outp(0x3c8,i);
                outp(0x3c9,(*p++) >> 2);
                outp(0x3c9,(*p++) >> 2);
                outp(0x3c9,(*p++) >> 2);
        }
        r.x.ax=0x1001;
        r.h.bh=b;
        int86(0x10,&r,&r);
}


/* make file name with specific extension */
strmfe(new,old,ext)
        char *new,*old,*ext;
{
        while(*old != 0 && *old != '.') *new++=*old++;
        *new++='.';
        while(*ext) *new++=*ext++;
        *new=0;
}


/* if you don't use in the memory manager, these functions
   will stand in for it */


#if !MEMMANGR

/* return a far pointer plus a long integer */
char *farPtr(p,l)
        char *p;
        long l;
{
        unsigned int seg,off;

        seg = FP_SEG(p);
        off = FP_OFF(p);
        seg += (off / 16);
        off &= 0x000f;
        off += (unsigned int)(l & 0x000fL);
        seg += (l / 16L);
```

4-3 Continued.

```
                p = MK_FP(seg,off);
                return(p);
}


/* save one line to memory */
putline(p,n)
        char *p;
        unsigned int n;
{
        if(n >= 0 && n < fi.depth)
            memcpy(farPtr(buffer,(long)n*(long)fi.width),p,fi.width);
}


/* get one line from memory */
char *getline(n)
        unsigned int n;
{
        return(farPtr(buffer,(long)n*(long)fi.width));
}
#pragma warn -par
getbuffer(n,bytes,lines)
        unsigned long n;
        int bytes,lines;
{
        if((buffer=farmalloc(n)) == NULL) return(0);
        else return(1);
}


freebuffer()
{
        if(buffer != NULL) farfree(buffer);
        buffer=NULL;
}
#endif /* !MEMMANGR */
```

4-3 Continued.

In writing a WPG file reader, keep in mind that despite warnings to the contrary, someone will unquestionably feed it some vector WPG files sooner or later. It would be convenient if the WPG file header included a flag to indicate whether a bitmap record was present in each file, but, sadly, this is not the case. However, since as a bitmap record is required to set the bitmap image dimensions, you can determine if a bitmap has been found by reading through all the records of a WPG file and checking the image dimensions when the dust settles.

The unpackwpg function starts by setting the dimensions and color bits values to 0, which are illegal values. If they're still 0 when all the records have been unpacked, the file being read lacks a bitmap record and can be assumed to contain only vector drawing elements.

The readrecord function handles each record in the file. In fact, as you'll note if you examine it, it cares only about two types—type 11 bitmap records and type 14 color-map records. It seeks past all the others. Note that upon encountering a bitmap record, it reads the fixed part of the bit-map data structure but it doesn't decode the bitmap data. Rather, it sets the value of offset to point to the bitmap data. Once all the records have been written, unpackwpg seeks back to where offset points and deals with the image data.

The readwpgline function is called once for each line in the file, just as in the case of the IFF files of the previous chapter. Because this viewer requires its line data to be stored in memory as 1 byte per pixel, mono-chrome lines must be passed through the mono2vga function and 4-bit lines are handled by ega2vga. You might want to look at the latter function carefully, as this illustrates how to unpack the 2-pixel-per-byte format of WPG file lines.

The ega2vga function is one of the few places where you can actually mangle a WPG file's image data if you're not careful. The function illus-trated here works properly. If you write one of your own, take care to see that the two pixels in each decoded byte are extracted in the correct order. Figure 4-4 illustrates the result of interchanging decoded bytes. In effect, each odd- and even-numbered pixel in the image have been swapped.

4-4 (A) A normal 16-color WPG bitmapped image, and (B) what happens if you unpack the pixels in the wrong order.

In most applications, you'll probably want to convert 4-bit WPG line data into planar lines. The bytes2planes function, discussed in chap-ter 2, illustrates how this is done. Planar lines would be required, for exam-ple, to display a 4-bit WPG file in the 16-color mode of an EGA or VGA card. This factor becomes somewhat more relevant in the discussion of display drivers in chapter 10.

Writing WPG files

There's not much to writing a WPG file—not unless you believe code to do so should include some sort of image-analysis function to permit only suitable subjects to be imported into WordPerfect documents. Ideally, such a function would refuse to write anything that didn't look like a bar chart or a Lotus graph.

This is, admittedly, a cynical bit of WordPerfect bashing.

In fact, depending upon the printer you use with WordPerfect, you might find that the above is almost true. WordPerfect can print fair-to-middling halftones to a PostScript printer, as a PostScript printer contains the intelligence to actually handle all the mechanics of screening a multiple-bit image. It's very much less adept at printing multiple-bit images to other types of output devices. Since you can have things other than bar charts and Lotus graphs in a WordPerfect document, restricting the WPG files you import to monochrome images might make your final documents a lot more attractive if you don't generate PostScript output.

The WRITEWPG program in FIG. 4-5 is a WPG file writer similar to the file writers discussed in previous chapters. It uses the binary files created by MAKEBIN (see chapter 2). Given a path to a binary file, it generates a WordPerfect graphics file of the same name and extension WPG.

The `writewpg` function of FIG. 4-5 does most of the work. It constructs a WPG file by writing a WPGHEAD header and each of the four records that makes up a basic bitmap image file.

Inasmuch as WPG files can deal only with images having 1, 4, or 8 bits, the actual number of bits in a source image presented to `writewpg` is rounded up.

```
/*
        WPG writer - copyright (c) 1991
        Alchemy Mindworks Inc.
*/

#include "stdio.h"
#include "alloc.h"

#define BINARYSIG       "ALCHBINR"       /* binary identification */

#define GOOD_WRITE      0       /* return codes */
#define BAD_WRITE       1
#define BAD_READ        2
#define MEMORY_ERROR    3

#define pixels2bytes(n)    ((n+7)/8)

typedef struct {
```

4-5 The source code for WRITEWPG.

```
                char sign[8];
                int width,depth,bits;
                char palette[768];
                } BINARYHEADER;

typedef struct {
                char id[4];
                long start;
                char product;
                char filetype;
                char majorversion;
                char minorversion;
                unsigned int encrypt;
                unsigned int reserved;
                } WPGHEAD;

int getline(char *p,int n,int line);

FILE *in,*out;
BINARYHEADER bh;

char masktable[8]={0x80,0x40,0x20,0x10,0x08,0x04,0x02,0x01};

main(argc,argv)
        int argc;
        char *argv[];
{
        static char results[4][16] = {  "Ok",
                                        "Bad write",
                                        "Bad read",
                                        "Memory error",
                                        };
        char path[81];
        int n;

        if(argc > 1) {
                strmfe(path,argv[1],"BIN");
                strupr(path);
                if((in=fopen(path,"rb")) != NULL) {
                        if(fread((char *)&bh,1,sizeof(BINARYHEADER),in) ==
                          sizeof(BINARYHEADER)) {
                        if(!memcmp(bh.sign,BINARYSIG,8)) {
                                strmfe(path,argv[1],"WPG");
                                strupr(path);
                                if((out=fopen(path,"wb")) != NULL) {
                                        puts("Writing");
                                        n=writeWpg(out,getline,
                                                bh.width,bh.depth,
                                                bh.bits,bh.palette);
                                        printf("\n%s",results[n]);
                                        fclose(out);
```

4-5 Continued.

```c
                                } else printf("Error creating %s",path);
                        } else printf("%s is corrupted",path);
                } else printf("Error reading %s",path);
                fclose(in);
        } else printf("Error opening %s",path);
    } else puts("Argument:       path to a BIN file");
}


/* write a WPG file */
writeWpg(fp,readline,width,depth,bits,palette)
        FILE *fp;
        int (*readline)();
        unsigned int width,depth,bits;
        char *palette;
{
        WPGHEAD wpg;
        unsigned long l,offset;
        char *p,*pr;
        int i,bytes;

        /* figure out the line size */
        if(bits==1) bytes=pixels2bytes(width);
        else if(bits > 1 && bits <=4) bytes=pixels2bytes(width) << 2;
        else bytes=width;

        /* allocate a line buffer */
        if((p=malloc(width)) == NULL) return(MEMORY_ERROR);

        /* allocate a scratch buffer */
        if((pr=malloc(bytes)) == NULL) {
                free(p);
                return(MEMORY_ERROR);
        }

        /* write the header */
        memcpy(wpg.id,"\377WPC",4);
        wpg.start=16L;
        wpg.product=1;
        wpg.filetype=0x16;
        wpg.majorversion=1;
        wpg.minorversion=0;
        wpg.encrypt=0;
        wpg.reserved=0;

        fwrite((char *)&wpg,1,sizeof(WPGHEAD),fp);

        /* write the starting record */
/*      fwrite("\017\006\001\000\000\044\000\030",1,8,fp);        */
        fwrite("\017\006\001\000",1,4,fp);
        fputword(fp,width);
        fputword(fp,depth);
```

4-5 Continued.

```c
/* write the palette record */
fputc(14,fp);

if(bits==1) {
        fputc(52,fp);
        fputword(fp,0);
        fputword(fp,16);
        for(i=0;i<48;++i) fputc(0,fp);
}
else if(bits > 1 && bits <=4) {
        fputc(52,fp);
        fputword(fp,0);
        fputword(fp,16);
        fwrite(palette,1,48,fp);
        bits=4;
}
else {
        fputc(0xff,fp);
        fputword(fp,772);
        fputword(fp,0);
        fputword(fp,256);
        fwrite(palette,1,768,fp);
        bits=8;
}

/* write the bitmap record */
fputc(11,fp);
fputc(0xff,fp);
offset=ftell(fp);
fputlong(fp,0L);
fputword(fp,width);
fputword(fp,depth);
fputword(fp,bits);
fputword(fp,0x004b);
fputword(fp,0x004b);

/* write the bitmap data */
for(i=0;i<depth;++i) {
        readline(p,width,i);
        if(bits==1) {
                packmonoline(pr,p,width);
                writewpgline(pr,fp,bytes);
        }
        else if(bits > 1 && bits <= 4) {
                packegaline(pr,p,width);
                writewpgline(pr,fp,bytes);
        }
        else writewpgline(p,fp,bytes);
}

/* write the end record */
l=(ftell(fp)-offset)-4L;
```

4-5 Continued.

```
                fputc(16,fp);
                fputc(0,fp);
                fseek(fp,offset,SEEK_SET);

                i=((unsigned int)(l >> 16)) | 0x8000;
                fputword(fp,i);
                fputword(fp,(unsigned int)l);

                free(pr);
                free(p);

                if(ferror(fp)) return(BAD_WRITD);
                else return(GOOD_WRITE);
        }

/* translate a vga line to a stacked pixel line */
packegaline(dest,source,width)
        char *dest,*source;
        int width;
        {

        int i,j=0;

        for(i=0;i<width;i+=2) {
                dest[j] = ((source[i] << 4) & 0xf0);
                dest[j] |= source[i+1] & 0x0f;
                ++j;
        }
}

/* translate a vga line to a monochrome line */
packmonoline(dest,source,width)
        char *dest,*source;
        int width;
        {

        int i;

        for(i=0;i<width;++i) {
                if(source[i]) dest[i >> 3] |= masktable[i & 0x0007];
                else dest[i >> 3] &= ~masktable[i & 0x0007];
        }
}

/* compress one WPG line */
writewpgline(p,fp,n)
        char *p;
        FILE *fp;
        int n;
        {

        char b[128];
        unsigned int bdex=0,i=0,j=0,t=0;

        do {
```

4-5 Continued.

```
                        i=0;
                        while((p[t+i]==p[t+i+1]) && ((t+i) < (n-1)) && i < 0x7d) ++i;
                        if(i>0 || bdex >= 0x7d) {
                                if(bdex) {
                                        fputc(bdex & 0x7f,fp);
                                        ++j;
                                        fwrite(b,1,bdex,fp);
                                        j+=bdex;
                                        bdex=0;
                                }
                                if(i) {
                                        fputc(((i+1) & 0x7f) | 0x80,fp);
                                        fputc(p[t+i],fp);
                                        j+=2;
                                        t+=(i+1);
                                }
                        } else b[bdex++]=p[t++];
                } while(t<n);
                if(bdex) {
                        fputc(bdex,fp);
                        ++j;
                        fwrite(b,1,bdex,fp);
                        j+=bdex;
                        bdex=0;
                }
}


/* make file name with specific extension */
strmfe(new,old,ext)
        char *new,*old,*ext;
{
        while(*old != 0 && *old != '.') *new++=*old++;
        *new++='.';
        while(*ext) *new++=*ext++;
        *new=0;
}


/* fetch a line from the input file */
getline(p,n,line)
        char *p;
        int n,line;
{
        int i;

        /* seek past the binary file header to the line */
        fseek(in,(long)sizeof(BINARYHEADER)+(long)line*(long)n,SEEK_SET);
        i=fread(p,1,n,in);
        if(i==n) return(0);
        else return(1);
}


/* write one long to the file in motorola format */
```

4-5 Continued.

```
fputlong(fp,n)
        FILE *fp;
        long n;
{
        fputc((n >> 24),fp);
        fputc((n >> 16),fp);
        fputc((n >> 8),fp);
        fputc(n,fp);
}

fputword(fp,n)                  /* write one word to the file */
        FILE *fp;
        int n;
{
        fputc(n,fp);
        fputc((n >> 8),fp);
}
```

4-5 Continued.

Creating a bitmap record entails most of the work in writing a WPG file, as this is where the image data must be compressed. As with IFF files, the source image is read one line at a time, converted to a suitable format, and compressed; in this case by calling `writewpgline`. The `writewpgline` function may look a lot like the compression function from the WRITEIFF program in chapter 3. In practice, both functions compress image data in the same way. They differ only in the way they express the fields they write.

Using WPG files

This chapter is relatively short because bitmapped WPG files are pretty simple to deal with. There are few variations on their structure, and not much to contend with in either reading or creating them. In addition, with only one principal application around that uses them, it's not difficult to check out whatever code you do write to work with them. If your copy of WordPerfect will deal with your files, no further beta testing should be necessary.

As an aside, the optimum print quality for any output device confronted with a bitmapped image is achieved by having each pixel of the bitmap printed as one pixel of the printer. The next best arrangement is to have each pixel of the source image printed as an integral number of destination pixels; for example, to have each source pixel printed as a 2×2 pixel block on your printer. This is discussed in greater detail in chapter 11.

WordPerfect has pretty crude bitmapped-image controls. It defaults to creating a graphic block that has no meaningful relationship to the size of the image that it will contain. As such, unless you get astronomically lucky, it will print your graphics with an arbitrary scaling factor, usually making them look pretty crunchy in the process.

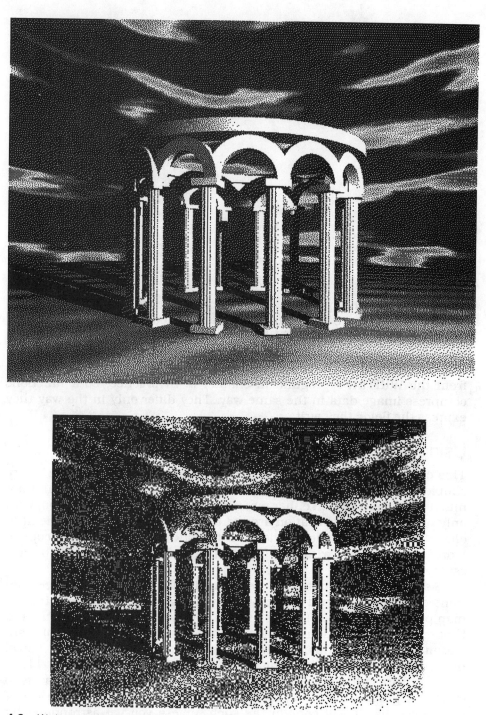

4-6 (A) A dithered monochrome WPG file, and (B) the result of using it in WordPerfect without being exceedingly careful about how it's sized.

You can get around this by taking note of the dimensions of each WPG file you plan to import into a WordPerfect document and adjusting the block dimensions accordingly. For example, if you wanted to import a 640×480 pixel image, you would divide each dimension by the resolution of your printer to get to optimum block size in inches. To print this graphic to a 300-dot-per-inch laser printer you would put it in a block that is 2.13×1.60 inches. If this is too small, the next step up would be 4.26×3.20 inches, and so on.

You may have to fiddle the scaling factors of each image as well to get your graphics to fit in their respective blocks.

Even if you won't be outputting your WPG files to a PostScript printer, you can still import multiple bit images into WordPerfect documents by first dithering them to monochrome WPG files. Monochrome dithering is discussed in detail in *Bitmapped Graphics*. Monochrome dithering simulates the effect of multiple-bit halftoning by using alternating black-and-white pixels to represent gray areas.

Dithered WPG files printed so that each source-image pixel in the source image is represented by an integral number of destination pixels can achieve quality approaching that of a true halftone. However, if Word-Perfect scales one arbitrarily, the results will probably look like bad spray-can art, as the distinct black pixels tend to run together. Figure 4-6 illustrates this.

This effect also turns up if you import a drawn monochrome image with gray areas that are represented by a screen of black-and-white pixels. You can make sure it doesn't affect your documents by calculating the size of WordPerfect's graphic blocks to make them suit your image dimensions.

If you'd like to learn more about WPG files—specifically about the vector-art records that haven't been discussed in this chapter—you can order the *WordPerfect Developer's Toolkit* from WordPerfect Corporation, 1555 North Technology Way, Orem, Utah 84057. Their phone number is (800) 222-9409.

5
Microsoft Windows BMP and MSP files

If something is not worth doing at all, it's not worth doing well.
—MURPHY'S LAWS OF COMPUTERS

Microsoft's Windows 3 is a bit like having a Macintosh without actually owning one. A high-end PC running Windows is every bit as user-friendly as a Mac—or every bit as user-obsequious, depending on how friendly you think a computer should be. It implements all sorts of things that DOS alone can't get together, the most notable of these being a tight integrated working environment and multitasking. To its credit, after having hired a team of consultants to successfully install Windows, anything with opposable thumbs can operate a computer running Windows.

Unlike earlier implementations of Windows, Windows 3 is genuinely fun. You can customize it to suit your taste, add applications to it somewhat easily, and make it reflect your needs, rather than allowing it to eventually cajole and browbeat you into accepting its own needs. This is distinct from the situation that most graphical user-interface environments seem determined to present you with. After a few days of work, you'll have a Macintosh exactly where it wants you.

In creating Windows, the software's authors developed two complete books of brand new data structures and file formats, unquestionably a record of some sort. Almost nothing about Windows existed before its inception. Perhaps not surprisingly, one of these many new standards was a new image-file format. Windows introduced BMP files. BMP is probably a condensation of "bitmap."

There are a number of uses for BMP files under Windows. The most commonly used one is as a source of "wallpaper." One of the features that Windows includes to allow you to personalize your virtual desktop is the ability to replace the solid color background of the screen with an image of your choice. The image can be inhaled from a BMP file.

Figure 5-1 illustrates Windows running with an image as wallpaper.

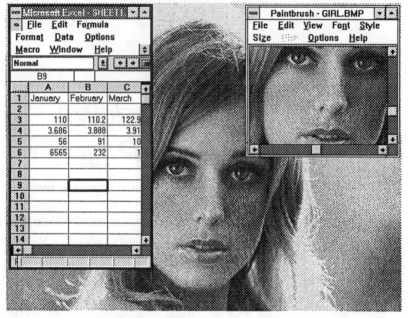

5-1 Using an image file as wallpaper in Windows 3.

The image in FIG. 5-1 started as a 256-color GIF file. It was translated to the BMP format so Windows could get along with it. While the translation was, in fact, done with Graphic Workshop (included with the companion disk set for this book), you can arrive at the same result using code discussed in this chapter and several later ones.

Should you have yet to encounter the buttons and boxes involved in setting up Windows to use BMP files as wallpaper, the control panel function involved is illustrated in FIG. 5-2.

In addition to serving as wallpaper, BMP files are becoming something of a standard file format among Windows applications. For reasons that are discussed in a moment, they're not likely to wholly supplant other file formats, but they are a convenient, common way for dealing with images in which speed of access and portability are more important than the amount of disk space taken up by your pictures.

Windows was clearly not written for people with small hard drives.

There are two features of BMP files that make them distinct from the file formats discussed in earlier chapters. The first is that they can contain images with up to 24 bits of color. The second is that their images are

5-2 Using the Windows control panel to choose some wallpaper.

stored uncompressed. By virtue of its header, a BMP file always occupies just a bit more room than its raw image data would have occupied all by itself.

This may seem pointedly wasteful, and in a sense it is. However, there are two drawbacks to image-file compression that the BMP format addresses. The first is that it takes significantly longer to read a compressed image from its file than it does to simply inhale raw image data. When they're used as wallpaper, BMP files can be read from the disk in almost no time. Having wallpaper installed in your system need not significantly affect the time it takes Windows to boot up. This would arguably not be the case if the wallpaper was stored in a compressed format.

The second drawback, and one that turns up in other formats that support 24-bit color, is that scanned 24-bit images rarely compress well and very often exhibit negative compression. It's usually the case that storing them uncompressed is as good as it gets.

Unlike the other formats discussed in this book, the BMP format really isn't intended for use as an archival image-file format. You would not want to store a lot of pictures this way. Rather, it's intended to store those few files which genuinely need to be retrieved as quickly as possible.

As it comes out of the box, there are relatively few ways to create BMP files under Windows. The package comes with several example files, and the Windows Paint application can be used to translate 16-color PCX files into the BMP format. As of this writing, no tools are provided with windows to translate 256-color images into the BMP format.

Third-party software is appearing that writes to the BMP format. Graphic Workshop translates other formats to it, and the Windows implementation of ZSoft's PC Paintbrush allows you to edit files directly in the BMP format. A growing number of Windows-based applications that accept graphic files are appearing with BMP import filters. Figure 5-3 illustrates the wallpaper BMP from FIG. 5-1 having migrated into CorelDRAW.

It's probably worth mentioning that the programs you write that deal with image files need not be running under Windows to work with BMP files. They can be created without any recourse to the Windows runtime,

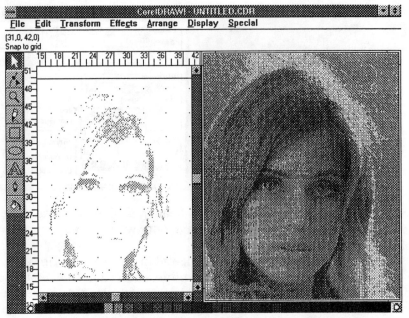

5-3 Loading a BMP file into CorelDRAW.

and there's no reason why a DOS-based application might not want to use them, perhaps for the same reasons that Windows does.

Windows and color

There is one peculiarity in using BMP files under Windows that can sneak up on you if you aren't aware of it. Windows is very dogmatic about the way it uses color and color palettes.

As discussed in chapter 1, a 16-color display card can display colors drawn from a larger palette, but only in chunks of 16 at a time. If you run multiple applications in multiple windows under Windows 3, they must all share a common 16-color palette. In fact, there is only one palette under Windows. While you can assign different colors from it to different screen areas, the colors themselves are fixed.

When you import a 16-color BMP file into Windows running with a 16-color display driver, the pixels in the BMP file's image are remapped to the nearest Windows palette colors. Color remapping is fairly simple. Given that you have a source image with a 16-color palette and a display with a different 16-color palette, each of the colors in the source palette is compared to the colors in the destination palette to find a replacement color that is as close as possible to the source color.

Color remapping can work very effectively in images where the source colors are all notably different and reasonably close to the destination colors. The Windows palette contains a good mix of colors, and as such most

16-color BMP files can be remapped to it without too noticeable a color shift.

There are specific instances in which color remapping starts to fall apart. For example, if you have an image of a green tree frog on a green leaf and you convert it to a BMP file for use in Windows, it will probably lose a great deal of detail when Windows gets hold of it. Windows has relatively few shades of green in its palette, and as such it's likely to remap many distinct shades of green in the source image to the same green when it displays the image.

Note that this does not permanently affect the contents of the BMP file in question; it changes only the way the file is displayed under Windows.

Another thing to watch out for is gray-scale pictures. It's possible to create pretty realistic gray-scale images with 16 distinct gray levels, something you can do in the 16-color modes of a VGA card. This is discussed in detail in chapter 10. Windows does not have 16 grays—it has two. If you attempt to use a gray-scale BMP file under Windows, all the grays are remapped to black, white or one of the available two gray levels. The result of this can be seen in FIG. 5-4.

5-4 Loading a gray-scale picture into a Windows application with only two grays available.

Having said this, it's probably worth noting that there are a few applications that really need 16 gray levels, and arrive at them by breaking Windows' palette rules and actually changing the palette to a series of grays. The ImageIn gray level image editor is an example of this application.

If you use Windows with a 256-color driver, only 16 of the 256 available colors are shanghaied by Windows. The remaining 240 colors are usually more than adequate to display a pretty respectable photographic image. As such, if you convert a scanned 256-color GIF file to a BMP file and use the resulting image as wallpaper with a 256-color Windows driver, you should encounter little discernible color shift in the image.

Quite a few of the GIF files that appear on bulletin boards are actually set up with the 16-color Windows palette as their first 16 colors and their scanned palette as the remaining 240 colors. This appears so that the bulletin board proprietors that do the scanning can add their own logos and phone numbers to the graphics in question.

Finally, 24-bit BMP files are a somewhat nebulous issue at the moment because there are no low-cost 24-bit display cards available, and hence, no 24-bit Windows drivers for them. If you attempt to import a 24-bit BMP file into a Windows application, such as Windows Paint, it will be remapped to use the available palette. The remapping algorithm that Paint uses is fast but dreadfully inaccurate. The resulting image will almost certainly exhibit a pronounced color shift. The remapping seems to shift towards blue much of the time.

This chapter discusses how you can create and use 24-bit BMP files. While they'll work properly without any color shift if you apply the code in this book to them, you'll probably find that importing them into Paint is largely pointless.

Getting photographic images into Windows when it's using a 16-color driver may seem a bit impractical. In fact, it's not—it just requires a bit of stealth. Whereas 16 inflexible colors are not really sufficient to display a convincing photograph per se, they're more than adequate to support color dithering. In chapter 12 we illustrate how to dither a full-color image down to one with a smaller, fixed palette. Such images make good Windows wallpaper. As long as you choose a dithering palette that corresponds to colors in Windows' own palette, there will be no color shift.

BMP file structure

Despite the rather convoluted names of their component parts, BMP files are very easy to work with. Having no compression to deal with, no tags, chunks, records or blocks to keep track of, and nothing secret or proprietary in their workings, they represent the least complicated file format discussed in this book.

A BMP file begins with a large header. It defines everything you could possibly want to know about the file except the names of the people pictured therein and the relative distance above sea level of the computer that created it. As with all the data structures associated with Windows, its elements have been named by Martians and many are, therefore, unpronounceable. This version renames the data structures that are actually used. Most of the remaining ones are no relevant to this discussion.

```
typedef struct {
        char id[2];
        long filesize;
        int reserved[2];
        long headersize;
        long infoSize;
        long width;
        long depth;
        int biPlanes;
        int bits;
        long biCompression;
        long biSizeImage;
        long biXPelsPerMeter;
        long biYPelsPerMeter;
        long biClrUsed;
        long biClrImportant;
        } BMPHEAD;
```

To begin with, the Windows 3 software developer's kit defines this header as several smaller headers. There's no good reason for splitting it up as such if you'll be working with BMP files exclusively, as all BMP files have all the smaller data structures glued together just as shown here.

The id field always contains the 2-byte string "BM," presumably once again for "bitmap". The filesize field contains, perhaps predictably, the size of the file. Note that it's a long integer, in that a file format that stores big images without compression is almost assured of exceeding the limits of common integers pretty early on.

The headersize represents the number of bytes in the file header. In fact, what it really defines is the offset in the file to the beginning of the bitmap. Everything before the bitmap is considered to be the file header.

These fields are considered to be the first header in a BMP file by the Windows software development kit. They're represented by a data structure called BITMAPFILEHEADER. The rest of the header discussed here is called a BITMAPINFOHEADER under Windows.

The infoSize is the number of bytes in a BITMAPINFOHEADER. It's a long integer, and is always 28H.

The width and depth elements define the dimensions of the image in the file in pixels. Note that these are both long integers; unless you have a few terabytes of hard drive space that aren't doing anything useful at the moment, you might not get to deal with any BMP files having dimensions that exceed 65,535 pixels, which is the limit to what you can get into an integer.

The biPlanes element is always 1. It represents the number of bits in the destination display device that ultimately gets to look at the bitmap in question. This doesn't actually make any sense, but it's the way Microsoft wants it.

The bits element is the number of bits of color in the source image. It can be 1, 4, 8, or 24.

The biCompression field is always 0L, which indicates that the file is uncompressed. The documentation for the BMP file format discusses a type of run-length compression for BMP image data. As of this writing it does not appear to be used under Windows.

The biSizeImage field contains the number of bytes in the image. One would think that this could be derived from all sorts of other fields in the header.

The biXPelsPerMeter and biYPelsPerMeter fields specify the resolution of the image, which really isn't relevant to this discussion. The biClrUsed and biClrImportant fields specify the number of colors that are actually used in the image and the number of colors that are important. You might, for example, create an 8-bit BMP file having 256 possible colors but only need 200 of them. It's unclear at the moment if Windows actually uses this information. If you set these fields to 0L, all the available colors are considered used and important.

Following the fixed portion of a BMP file header, you should find the color palette if the file has one or the start of the image data. The color palette of a BMP file is stored differently from palettes of other file formats. While it still specifies color as RGB indices, each entry is 4 bytes long. This is presumably because it's a lot quicker to get at a specific palette entry by multiplying by four—that is, shifting left by 2 bits—rather than by performing a true integer multiplication. To further confuse the issue, the order of the three color bytes in each entry is reversed.

This is how a BMP file stores one color entry:

```
typedef struct {
        char blue;
        char green;
        char red;
        char filler;
        } RGBQUAD;
```

The filler entry is always 0.

The bitmapped image data in a BMP file is stored in contiguous lines. It's probably not surprising that they're stored in the inverse order in which they're to be displayed; that is, the first line to be read from the file is the bottom line of the image, and so on. Anyone who's actually written any Windows code will probably marvel that the lines aren't packed sideways or with every alternate pixel inverted.

It's probably easiest to see how to unpack a monochrome BMP file. Assuming that the header has been read, you would seek to the start of image data, as specified by the headersize element, and then read out each line. This example assumes that the header is in a BMPHEAD object called bmp and that the file pointer fp is initially pointing to the start of the image data. There's a buffer at b that is big enough to hold one line of the image.

```
int i;

for(i=0;i<(int)bmp.depth;++i) {
  fread(b,1,pixels2bytes((int)bmp.width)fp);
  putline(b,(bmp.depth-1)-i);
}
```

In fact, this is a bit simplified. The actual number of bytes to read is always rounded up to the next-highest even long integer, or 4 bytes.

Monochrome image lines are stored as single plane bitmaps. Eight-bit lines are stored as arrays of bytes, such that each line is bmp.width->bytes long. The lines of a 24-bit image are bmp.width*3-bytes long. Each pixel is an RGB value. Note that these are not stored in the 4-byte RGBQUAD structure used by a BMP file's palette.

Four-bit lines are stored as they were in WPG files, that is, with each stored byte having one pixel in its lower 4 bits and a second in its upper 4 bits. The BMP file format is the only other format to be discussed in this book that handles 16-color images this way.

Handling 24-bit images—the short form

The simple nature of a BMP file's internal structure makes the workings of a BMP reader easy to follow. There's only one catch, although as catches go it's a pretty good one.

A BMP file with 24 color bits can support more colors than mode 13H of a VGA card can ever hope to display. Later, an involved discussion of techniques makes it possible to reduce 24-bit RGB images down to more manageable 8-bit files. However, the required code is complicated and relatively slow. In order to get past the simple process of unpacking and viewing 24-bit BMP files, a bit of cheating is in order.

This viewer cheats by displaying 24-bit files as gray-scale images. An RGB color value can be "summed" to its equivalent gray level by applying a weight to each of the three color components. The result will be a gray level that approximates what the color would have looked like had it been photographed with panchromatic black-and-white film. The formula is as follows:

```
gray = .30 * red + *.59 * green + .11 * blue
```

While this could be handled in C using floating point numbers, it's possible to use a bit of integer cheating that's just as effective. The grayvalue macro derives a gray level from an RGB color value.

```
#define   grayvalue(r,g,b) (((r*30)/100) + \
                            ((g*59)/100) + \
                            ((b*11)/100))
```

There are only 256 possible gray levels that grayvalue can produce if it's given legal RGB values. Therefore, if the palette of a VGA card is set up with 256 incremental levels of gray, the result of running each 3-byte pixel of a 24-bit image through `grayvalue` will be an array of index values into the gray palette. In effect, this process transforms 24-bit RGB lines into 8-bit palette driven lines.

This is how you'd create the palette:

```
int i;

for(i=0;i<256;++i) memset(palette+(i*3),i,3);
```

This assumes that `palette` is a buffer that is at least 768 bytes long. Note that the source code in this book that deals with RGB palette or pixel values uses constants to define the size of a palette entry and the offsets into each entry for the three color values, as follows:

```
#define    RGB_RED      0
#define    RGB_GREEN    1
#define    RGB_BLUE     2
#define    RGB_SIZE     3
```

Using these constants doesn't actually change the way your code works. It should help make your programs a bit more readable, though. Functions that work with RGB color data seem to be unusually mysterious.

As an aside, you can convert a color image with a palette into a gray-scale image really quickly by sending the palette through `grayvalue`. If `palette` is a 768-byte buffer containing the color palette lookup table of an image, the following remaps the whole image to gray:

```
int i,n;

for(i=0;i<256;++i)
    memset(palette+(i*RGB_SIZE),
            grayvalue(palette[i*RGB_SIZE+RGB_RED],
                    palette[i*RGB_SIZE+RGB_GREEN],
                    palette[i*RGB_SIZE+RGB_BLUE]),
            RGB_SIZE);
```

None of the actual pixel values in the image have to be changed. They'll still point to the same palette table entries, but the colors that the entries themselves define will have been changed to gray values.

It's worth noting that VGA cards, as mentioned in chapter 1, don't really display 24-bit colors. Their palette entries consist of 6-bit numbers, rather than the 8-bit ones that were discussed in conjunction with RGB color. If you look carefully at the `setvgapalette` function used in all the simple file viewers in this book, you'll note that the RGB color values are all shifted right by two places to accommodate this.

Inasmuch as the color registers of a VGA card can deal only with 6-bit numbers, they are actually capable of supporting a maximum of 64 discrete color intensity levels, rather than the 256 levels that can be specified in a true RGB color. Confronted with a completely gray palette with 256 distinct gray levels, a VGA card displays the first 4 levels in the palette as the same gray level on your screen, and the next 4 as 1 level, and so on. In a sense, a VGA card granulates color intensity by a factor of 4.

As there are only 64 distinct gray levels in a VGA card's palette, you need to provide only 64 grays. The remaining 192 color values can be used for something else.

You can compress gray levels by simply shifting the number provided by `grayvalue` right. By default, it produces gray levels that assume a 256-level gray palette. Shifting its results right by 1 will reduce the palette to 128 levels. Shifting it right by 2 will reduce the palette to 64 levels, and so on.

Note that 300-dot-per-inch PostScript laser printers, which ostensibly reproduce gray levels through halftoning, can only handle about 32 distinct shades of gray. Figure 5-5 illustrates the result of reducing the number of gray levels in a screened image. It's interesting to note that at the high end of the scale, doing so has little effect on laser printer output.

If you use the GEM version of Ventura Publisher with a VGA card screen driver and you set the Define Colors box to produce levels of gray, imported gray-scale TIFF files display on the screen as pretty convincing gray-scale photographs. These images have only 16 gray levels.

A BMP file viewer

The code in FIG. 5-6 illustrates READBMP, a simple BMP file viewer, which is clearly another derivative of the basic file-viewing program that appeared for each of the foregoing file formats. By now it should be pretty easy to see what it's up to. The unpackbmp function reads the first part of the file it's handed into a BMPHEAD object and extracts the relevant numbers from it. It reads the palette if there is one. Note that it translates from the RGBQUAD structure of a BMP file's palette entries into normal 3-byte palette entries. It then seeks to the start of the image data and inhales it.

As with WPG files, 4-bit BMP lines require some manipulation, inasmuch as they're packed with two pixels per byte. The same ega2vga function is used to convert them to VGA lines.

The READBMP program should allow you to display any Windows BMP files you come across. It's worth noting that it does not implement the run-length compression features of the BMP format and does not display run-length encoded BMP files if any turn up. It also does not deal with BMP files for the OS/2 presentation manager. While named with the BMP extension, these files are structured differently.

Writing BMP files

If reading BMP files is agreeably simple, writing them is almost trivial. The task involves no compression, options, gray-scale manipulation, and only a nominal amount of even rudimentary file handling. Once again, the example program in this chapter uses binary BIN files created by the MAKEBIN program in chapter 2. As such, your BMP files will probably look a lot like any GIF files you have on hand.

A

B

5-5 Reducing the number of gray levels in an image printed on a 300 dot per inch laser printer. (A) This image has 256 shades of gray, (B) this image has 64 shades of gray, (C) this image has 16 shades of gray, and (D) this image has 8 levels of gray.

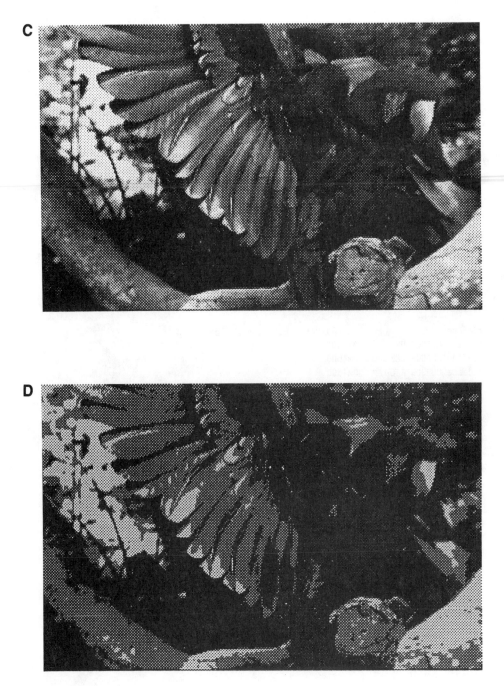

5-5 Continued.

```
/*
        BMP reader - copyright (c) 1991
        Alchemy Mindworks Inc.
*/

#include "stdio.h"
#include "dos.h"
#include "alloc.h"

/*                              uncomment this line if you
#include "memmangr.h"           will be linking in the memory manager
*/

#define GOOD_READ       0       /* return codes */
#define BAD_FILE        1
#define BAD_READ        2
#define MEMORY_ERROR    3

#define SCREENWIDE      320     /* mode 13 screen dimensions */
#define SCREENDEEP      200
#define STEP            32      /* size of a step when panning */

#define HOME            0x4700  /* cursor control codes */
#define CURSOR_UP       0x4800
#define CURSOR_LEFT     0x4b00
#define CURSOR_RIGHT    0x4d00
#define END             0x4f00
#define CURSOR_DOWN     0x5000

#define RGB_RED         0
#define RGB_GREEN       1
#define RGB_BLUE        2
#define RGB_SIZE        3

#define pixels2bytes(n)    ((n+7)/8)

#define greyvalue(r,g,b)          (((r*30)/100) + ((g*59)/100) + ((b*11)/100))

typedef struct {
        int width,depth,bytes,bits;
        int background;
        char palette[768];
        int (*setup)();
        int (*closedown)();
        } FILEINFO;

typedef struct {
        char id[2];
        long filesize;
        int reserved[2];
        long headersize;
        long infoSize;
```

5-6 The source code for READBMP.

```
                            long width;
                            long depth;
                            int biPlanes;
                            int bits;
                            long biCompression;
                            long biSizeImage;
                            long biXPelsPerMeter;
                            long biYPelsPerMeter;
                            long biClrUsed;
                            long biClrImportant;
                            } BMPHEAD;


        char *farPtr(char *p,long l);
        char *getline(unsigned int n);
        char *mono2vga(char *p,int width);
        char *ega2vga(char *p,int width);
        char *rgb2vga(char *p,int width);
        int dosetup(FILEINFO *fi);
        int doclosedown(FILEINFO *fi);

        int putline(char *p,unsigned int n);

        char masktable[8]={0x80,0x40,0x20,0x10,0x08,0x04,0x02,0x01};

        FILEINFO fi;
        char *buffer=NULL;

        main(argc,argv)
                int argc;
                char *argv[];
        {
                FILE *fp;
                static char results[8][16] = {  "Ok",
                                                "Bad file",
                                                "Bad read",
                                                "Memory error",
                                                };
                char path[81];
                int r;

                if(argc > 1) {
                        strmfe(path,argv[1],"BMP");
                        strupr(path);
                        if((fp = fopen(path,"rb")) != NULL) {
                                fi.setup=dosetup;
                                fi.closedown=doclosedown;
                                r=unpackbmp(fp,&fi);
                                printf("\%s",results[r]);
                                fclose(fp);
                        } else printf("Error opening %s",path);
                } else puts("Argument:       path to a BMP file");
        }
```

5-6 Continued.

```
/* unpack a BMP file */
unpackbmp(fp,fi)
        FILE *fp;
        FILEINFO *fi;
{

        BMPHEAD bmp;
        char *p,*pr;
        int i,n;

        /* set a default monochrome palette */
        memcpy(fi->palette,"\000\000\000\377\377\377",6);

        /* get the header */
        if(fread((char *)&bmp,1,sizeof(BMPHEAD),fp)==sizeof(BMPHEAD)) {

                /* check the header */
                if(!memcmp(bmp.id,"BM",2)) {

                        /* set the details */
                        fi->width=(int)bmp.width;
                        fi->depth=(int)bmp.depth;
                        fi->bits=bmp.bits;

                        /* work out the line width */
                        if(fi->bits==1) fi->bytes=pixels2bytes(fi->width);
                        else if(fi->bits==4) fi->bytes=pixels2bytes(fi->width)<<2;
                        else if(fi->bits==8) fi->bytes=fi->width;
                        else if(fi->bits==24) fi->bytes=fi->width*3;

                        /* round up to an even dword boundary */
                        if(fi->bytes & 0x0003) {
                                fi->bytes |= 0x0003;
                                ++fi->bytes;
                        }

                        /* get the palette */
                        if(fi->bits > 1 && fi->bits <=8) {
                                n=1<<fi->bits;
                                for(i=0;i<n;++i) {
                                        fi->palette[(i*RGB_SIZE)+RGB_BLUE]=fgetc(fp);
                                        fi->palette[(i*RGB_SIZE)+RGB_GREEN]=fgetc(fp);
                                        fi->palette[(i*RGB_SIZE)+RGB_RED]=fgetc(fp);
                                        fgetc(fp);
                                }
                        }
                        else if(fi->bits==24) {
                                for(i=0;i<256;++i)
                                    memset(fi->palette+(i*RGB_SIZE),i,RGB_SIZE);
                        }

                        /* allocate a line buffer */
                        if((p=malloc(fi->bytes)) != NULL) {
```

5-6 Continued.

```
                        if((fi->setup)(fi) != GOOD_READ) {
                                free(p);
                                return(MEMORY_ERROR);
                        }

                        /* find the start of the image data */
                        fseek(fp,bmp.headersize,SEEK_SET);

                        /* read all the lines */
                        for(i=0;i<fi->depth;++i) {
                                if(fread(p,1,fi->bytes,fp) != fi->bytes) {
                                        freebuffer();
                                        free(p);
                                        return(BAD_READ);
                                }

                                /* translate the line types into VGA */
                                switch(fi->bits) {
                                        case 1:
                                                pr=mono2vga(p,fi->width);
                                                if(pr != NULL) {
                                                        putline(pr,fi->depth-1-i);
                                                        free(pr);
                                                }
                                                else {
                                                        freebuffer();
                                                        free(p);
                                                        return(MEMORY_ERROR);
                                                }
                                                break;
                                        case 4:
                                                pr=ega2vga(p,fi->width);
                                                if(pr != NULL) {
                                                        putline(pr,fi->depth-1-i);
                                                        free(pr);
                                                }
                                                else {
                                                        freebuffer();
                                                        free(p);
                                                        return(MEMORY_ERROR);
                                                }
                                                break;
                                        case 8:
                                                putline(p,fi->depth-1-i);
                                                break;
                                        case 24:
                                                pr=rgb2vga(p,fi->width);
                                                if(pr != NULL) {
                                                        putline(pr,fi->depth-1-i);
                                                        free(pr);
                                                }
                                                else {
```

5-6   Continued.

```
                                                                freebuffer();
                                                                free(p);
                                                                return(MEMORY_ERROR);
                                                            }
                                                            break;

                                            }
                                        }
                                        (fi->closedown)(fi);
                                        free(p);
                                        return(GOOD_READ);
                                    } else return(MEMORY_ERROR);
                                } else return(BAD_FILE);
                        } else return(BAD_READ);
        }

/* convert a monochrome line into an eight bit line */
char *mono2vga(p,width)
        char *p;
        int width;
{
        char *pr;
        int i;

        if((pr=malloc(width)) != NULL) {
                for(i=0;i<width;++i) {
                        if(p[i >> 3] & masktable[i & 0x0007])
                            pr[i]=1;
                        else
                            pr[i]=0;
                }
                return(pr);
        } else return(NULL);
}

/* convert a four bit line into an eight bit line */
char *ega2vga(p,width)
        char *p;
        int width;
{
        char *pr;
        int i,j=0;

        if((pr=malloc(width)) != NULL) {
                for(i=0;i<width;) {
                        pr[i++]=(p[j] >> 4) & 0x0f;
                        pr[i++]=p[j] & 0x0f;
                        ++j;
                }
                return(pr);
        } else return(NULL);
}
```

5-6 Continued.

```
/* convert an RGB line into an eight bit line */
char *rgb2vga(p,width)
        char *p;
        int width;
{
        char *pr;
        int i;

        if((pr=malloc(width)) != NULL) {
                for(i=0;i<width;++i) {
                        pr[i]=greyvalue(p[RGB_RED],p[RGB_GREEN],p[RGB_BLUE]);
                        p+=RGB_SIZE;
                }
                return(pr);
        } else return(NULL);
}


/* This function is called before an image is unpacked */
dosetup(fi)
        FILEINFO *fi;
{
        union REGS r;

        if(!getbuffer((long)fi->width*(long)fi->depth,fi->width,fi->depth))
            return(MEMORY_ERROR);

        r.x.ax=0x0013;
        int86(0x10,&r,&r);

        setvgapalette(fi->palette,256,fi->background);

        return(GOOD_READ);
}
/* This function is called after an image has been unpacked. It must
   display the image and deallocate memory. */
doclosedown(fi)
        FILEINFO *fi;
{
        union REGS r;
        int c,i,n,x=0,y=0;

        if(fi->width > SCREENWIDE) n=SCREENWIDE;
        else n=fi->width;

        do {
                for(i=0;i<SCREENDEEP;++i) {
                        c=y+i;
                        if(c>=fi->depth) break;
                        memcpy(MK_FP(0xa000,SCREENWIDE*i),getline(c)+x,n);
                }
                c=GetKey();
                switch(c) {
```

5-6 Continued.

```
                case CURSOR_LEFT:
                        if((x-STEP) > 0) x-=STEP;
                        else x=0;
                        break;
                case CURSOR_RIGHT:
                        if((x+STEP+SCREENWIDE) < fi->width) x+=STEP;
                        else if(fi->width > SCREENWIDE)
                            x=fi->width-SCREENWIDE;
                        else x=0;
                        break;
                case CURSOR_UP:
                        if((y-STEP) > 0) y-=STEP;
                        else y=0;
                        break;
                case CURSOR_DOWN:
                        if((y+STEP+SCREENDEEP) < fi->depth) y+=STEP;
                        else if(fi->depth > SCREENDEEP)
                            y=fi->depth-SCREENDEEP;
                        else y=0;
                        break;
                case HOME:
                        x=y=0;
                        break;
                case END:
                        if(fi->width > SCREENWIDE)
                            x=fi->width-SCREENWIDE;
                        else x=0;
                        if(fi->depth > SCREENDEEP)
                            y=fi->depth-SCREENDEEP;
                        else y=0;
                        break;
        }
} while(c != 27);

freebuffer();

r.x.ax=0x0003;
int86(0x10,&r,&r);
return(GOOD_READ);
}

/* get one extended key code */
GetKey()
{
        int c;

        c = getch();
        if(!(c & 0x00ff)) c = getch() << 8;
        return(c);
}

/* set the VGA palette and background */
```

5-6 Continued.

```
setvgapalette(p,n,b)
        char *p;
        int n,b;
{

        union REGS r;
        int i;

        outp(0x3c6,0xff);
        for(i=0;i<n;++i) {
                outp(0x3c8,i);
                outp(0x3c9,(*p++) >> 2);
                outp(0x3c9,(*p++) >> 2);
                outp(0x3c9,(*p++) >> 2);
        }
        r.x.ax=0x1001;
        r.h.bh=b;
        int86(0x10,&r,&r);
}


/* make file name with specific extension */
strmfe(new,old,ext)
        char *new,*old,*ext;
{

        while(*old != 0 && *old != '.') *new++=*old++;
        *new++='.';
        while(*ext) *new++=*ext++;
        *new=0;
}


/* if you don't use in the memory manager, these functions
   will stand in for it */

#if !MEMMANGR

/* return a far pointer plus a long integer */
char *farPtr(p,l)
        char *p;
        long l;
{

        unsigned int seg,off;

        seg = FP_SEG(p);
        off = FP_OFF(p);
        seg += (off / 16);
        off &= 0x000f;
        off += (unsigned int)(l & 0x000fL);
        seg += (l / 16L);
        p = MK_FP(seg,off);
        return(p);
}


/* save one line to memory */
```

5-6 Continued.

```
putline(p,n)
        char *p;
        unsigned int n;
{
        if(n >= 0 && n < fi.depth)
            memcpy(farPtr(buffer,(long)n*(long)fi.width),p,fi.width);
}

/* get one line from memory */
char *getline(n)
        unsigned int n;
{
        return(farPtr(buffer,(long)n*(long)fi.width));
}

#pragma warn -par
getbuffer(n,bytes,lines)
        unsigned long n;
        int bytes,lines;
{
        if((buffer=farmalloc(n)) == NULL) return(0);
        else return(1);
}

freebuffer()
{
        if(buffer != NULL) farfree(buffer);
        buffer=NULL;
}
#endif /* !MEMMANGR */
```

5-6 Continued.

The only potential problem in creating a BMP file writer is that there is no immediate source of 24-bit binary source files to test it with. The MAKEBIN program from chapter 2 only reads GIF files, and GIF files, in turn, only supports images with up to 8 bits of color.

It's fairly easy to create 24-bit test BMP files. If you have Windows, you can load a file with less color depth into Windows Paint and export it as a 24-bit BMP file. It won't really make much use of all that color capacity, but it will be a genuine 24-bit BMP file, suitable for reading. If you have the companion source disks for this book, you'll find a 24-bit PCX file that can be converted into a 24-bit BMP file with Graphic Workshop.

The program in FIG. 5-7 is MAKEBIN2. Like the MAKEBIN program from chapter 2, it's just a distillation of the BMP file reader. Instead of displaying the BMP files it's given on the screen, it writes them to the same binary format that MAKEBIN did. In this case, it handles 24-bit binary files as well.

```c
/*
        BMP to BINARY - copyright (c) 1991
        Alchemy Mindworks Inc.
*/

#include "stdio.h"
#include "dos.h"
#include "alloc.h"

#define GOOD_READ        0       /* return codes */
#define BAD_FILE         1
#define BAD_READ         2
#define MEMORY_ERROR     3
#define BAD_WRITE        4

#define RGB_RED          0
#define RGB_GREEN        1
#define RGB_BLUE         2
#define RGB_SIZE         3

#define BINARYSIG        "ALCHBINR"

#define pixels2bytes(n)    ((n+7)/8)

#define greyvalue(r,g,b)        (((r*30)/100) + ((g*59)/100) + ((b*11)/100))

typedef struct {
        int width,depth,bytes,bits;
        char palette[768];
        } FILEINFO;

typedef struct {
        char id[2];
        long filesize;
        int reserved[2];
        long headersize;
        long infoSize;
        long width;
        long depth;
        int biPlanes;
        int bits;
        long biCompression;
        long biSizeImage;
        long biXPelsPerMeter;
        long biYPelsPerMeter;
        long biClrUsed;
        long biClrImportant;
        } BMPHEAD;

typedef struct {
        char sign[8];
        int width,depth,bits;
```

5-7 The source code for MAKEBIN2.

```
                char palette[768];
                } BINARYHEADER;

char *farPtr(char *p,long l);
char *getline(unsigned int n);
char *mono2vga(char *p,int width);
char *ega2vga(char *p,int width);

int putline(char *p,unsigned int n);

char masktable[8]={0x80,0x40,0x20,0x10,0x08,0x04,0x02,0x01};

FILEINFO fi;
char *buffer=NULL;
FILE *out;

main(argc,argv)
        int argc;
        char *argv[];
{
        FILE *fp;
        static char results[5][16] = {  "Ok",
                                         "Bad file",
                                         "Bad read",
                                         "Memory error",
                                         "Bad write"
                                         };
        char path[81];
        int r;

        if(argc > 1) {
                strmfe(path,argv[1],"BMP");
                strupr(path);
                if((fp = fopen(path,"rb")) != NULL) {
                        strmfe(path,argv[1],"BIN");
                        if((out=fopen(path,"wb")) != NULL) {
                                r=unpackbmp(fp,&fi);
                                printf("\%s",results[r]);
                                fclose(out);
                        } else printf("Error creating %s",path);
                        fclose(fp);
                } else printf("Error opening %s",path);
        } else puts("Argument:      path to a BMP file");
}

/* unpack a BMP file */
unpackbmp(fp,fi)
        FILE *fp;
        FILEINFO *fi;
{
        BINARYHEADER bh;
        BMPHEAD bmp;
```

5-7 Continued.

```
char *p,*pr;
int i,n;

/* set a default monochrome palette */
memcpy(fi->palette,"\000\000\000\377\377\377",6);

/* get the header */
if(fread((char *)&bmp,1,sizeof(BMPHEAD),fp)==sizeof(BMPHEAD)) {

        /* check the header */
        if(!memcmp(bmp.id,"BM",2)) {

                /* set the details */
                fi->width=(int)bmp.width;
                fi->depth=(int)bmp.depth;
                fi->bits=bmp.bits;

                /* work out the line width */
                if(fi->bits==1) fi->bytes=pixels2bytes(fi->width);
                else if(fi->bits==4) fi->bytes=pixels2bytes(fi->width)<<2;
                else if(fi->bits==8) fi->bytes=fi->width;
                else if(fi->bits==24) fi->bytes=fi->width*3;

                /* round up to an even dword boundary */
                if(fi->bytes & 0x0003) {
                        fi->bytes |= 0x0003;
                        ++fi->bytes;
                }

                /* get the palette */
                if(fi->bits > 1 && fi->bits <=8) {
                        n=1<<fi->bits;
                        for(i=0;i<n;++i) {
                                fi->palette[(i*RGB_SIZE)+RGB_BLUE]=fgetc(fp);
                                fi->palette[(i*RGB_SIZE)+RGB_GREEN]=fgetc(fp);
                                fi->palette[(i*RGB_SIZE)+RGB_RED]=fgetc(fp);
                                fgetc(fp);
                        }
                }

                /* set up the binary header */
                memcpy(bh.sign,BINARYSIG,8);
                bh.width=fi->width;
                bh.depth=fi->depth;
                bh.bits =fi->bits;
                memcpy(bh.palette,fi->palette,768);
                if(fwrite((char *)&bh,1,sizeof(BINARYHEADER),out) !=
                    sizeof(BINARYHEADER)) return(BAD_WRITE);

                if((p=malloc(fi->bytes)) == NULL) return(MEMORY_ERROR);

                /* read all the lines */
```

5-7 Continued.

```
                    for(i=0;i<fi->depth;++i) {

                         /* locate the line - upside down*/
                         fseek(fp,bmp.headersize+(long)(fi->depth-1-i)*fi->bytes,SEEK_SET);

                         if(fread(p,1,fi->bytes,fp) != fi->bytes) {
                              free(p);
                              return(BAD_READ);
                         }

                         switch(fi->bits) {
                              case 1:
                                   pr=mono2vga(p,fi->width);
                                   if(pr != NULL) {
                                        fwrite(pr,1,fi->width,out);
                                        free(pr);
                                   }
                                   else {
                                        free(p);
                                        return(MEMORY_ERROR);
                                   }
                                   break;
                              case 4:
                                   pr=ega2vga(p,fi->width);
                                   if(pr != NULL) {
                                        fwrite(pr,1,fi->width,out);
                                        free(pr);
                                   }
                                   else {
                                        free(p);
                                        return(MEMORY_ERROR);
                                   }
                                   break;
                              case 8:
                                   fwrite(p,1,fi->width,out);
                                   break;
                              case 24:
                                   fwrite(p,1,fi->width*RGB_SIZE,out);
                                   break;
                         }
                    }
                    free(p);
                    return(GOOD_READ);
               } else return(BAD_FILE);
          } else return(BAD_READ);
}

/* convert a monochrome line into an eight bit line */
char *mono2vga(p,width)
     char *p;
     int width;
{
```

5-7 Continued.

```
        char *pr;
        int i;

        if((pr=malloc(width)) != NULL) {
                for(i=0;i<width;++i) {
                        if(p[i >> 3] & masktable[i & 0x0007])
                                pr[i]=1;
                        else
                                pr[i]=0;
                }
                return(pr);
        } else return(NULL);
}


/* convert a four bit line into an eight bit line */
char *ega2vga(p,width)
        char *p;
        int width;
{
        char *pr;
        int i,j=0;

        if((pr=malloc(width)) != NULL) {
                for(i=0;i<width;) {
                        pr[i++]=(p[j] >> 4) & 0x0f;
                        pr[i++]=p[j] & 0x0f;
                        ++j;
                }
                return(pr);
        } else return(NULL);
}


/* make file name with specific extension */
strmfe(new,old,ext)
        char *new,*old,*ext;
{
        while(*old != 0 && *old != '.') *new++=*old++;
        *new++='.';
        while(*ext) *new++=*ext++;
        *new=0;
}
```

5-7 Continued.

In order to properly test the BMP writer program, you should create several binary files with MAKEBIN and MAKEBIN2, including at least one 24-bit file.

Note that MAKEBIN2 takes a BMP source file and writes a binary file with the same name and the extension BIN. The WRITEBMP program to be discussed in a moment essentially reverses the process, creating a file with the same name as the binary file it reads, but having the BMP extension. If either one does something improper, such that its destination file is mangled, the mangled image will perpetuate itself. If you start having problems, make sure that the BMP files that MAKEBIN2 is reading haven't become corrupted.

If you don't have a source of 24-bit BMP files to use with MAKEBIN2, you might want to look at chapter 7, which has a discussion of Targa files. It includes a program called MAKERGB, which can generate a synthetic 24-bit binary file.

Figure 5-8 is the source code for WRITEBMP. The `writebmp` function that does all the work shouldn't take too long to figure out. It creates a BMPHEAD object, filling in suitable parameters, and writes it to the destination file. It then writes a palette if the image to be stored has between 1 and 8 bits. Note that BMP files require a palette for monochrome files.

The image data is stored by reading it from the source binary file, packing it in the case of 4-bit lines, and writing it to the destination file.

```
/*
        BMP writer - copyright (c) 1991
        Alchemy Mindworks Inc.
*/

#include "stdio.h"
#include "alloc.h"

#define BINARYSIG       "ALCHBINR"      /* binary identification */

#define GOOD_WRITE      0       /* return codes */
#define BAD_WRITE       1
#define BAD_READ        2
#define MEMORY_ERROR    3

#define RGB_RED         0
#define RGB_GREEN       1
#define RGB_BLUE        2
#define RGB_SIZE        3

#define pixels2bytes(n)    ((n+7)/8)

typedef struct {
        char sign[8];
        int width,depth,bits;
        char palette[768];
        } BINARYHEADER;

typedef struct {
        char id[2];
        long filesize;
        int reserved[2];
        long headersize;
        long infoSize;
        long width;
```

5-8   The source code for WRITEBMP.

```
                    long depth;
                    int biPlanes;
                    int bits;
                    long biCompression;
                    long biSizeImage;
                    long biXPelsPerMeter;
                    long biYPelsPerMeter;
                    long biClrUsed;
                    long biClrImportant;
                    } BMPHEAD;

int getline(char *p,int n,int line);

FILE *in,*out;
BINARYHEADER bh;

char masktable[8]={0x80,0x40,0x20,0x10,0x08,0x04,0x02,0x01};

main(argc,argv)
        int argc;
        char *argv[];
{
        static char results[8][16] = {  "Ok",
                                        "Bad write",
                                        "Bad read",
                                        "Memory error",
                                        };
        char path[81];
        int n;

        if(argc > 1) {
                strmfe(path,argv[1],"BIN");
                strupr(path);
                if((in=fopen(path,"rb")) != NULL) {
                        if(fread((char *)&bh,1,sizeof(BINARYHEADER),in) ==
                          sizeof(BINARYHEADER)) {
                            if(!memcmp(bh.sign,BINARYSIG,8)) {
                                    strmfe(path,argv[1],"BMP");
                                    strupr(path);
                                    if((out=fopen(path,"wb")) != NULL) {
                                            puts("Writing");
                                            n=writebmp(out,getline,
                                                    bh.width,bh.depth,
                                                    bh.bits,bh.palette);
                                            printf("\n%s",results[n]);
                                            fclose(out);
                                    } else printf("Error creating %s",path);
                            } else printf("%s is corrupted",path);
                        } else printf("Error reading %s",path);
                        fclose(in);
                } else printf("Error opening %s",path);
        } else puts("Argument:       path to a BIN file");
```

5-8 Continued.

```
        }

        /* write a BMP file */
        writebmp(fp,readline,width,depth,bits,palette)
                FILE *fp;
                int (*readline)();
                unsigned int width,depth,bits;
                char *palette;
        {
                BMPHEAD bmp;
                char *p,*pr;
                int i,bytes;

                /* figure out the line size */
                if(bits==1) bytes=pixels2bytes(width);
                else if(bits > 1 && bits <= 4) bytes=pixels2bytes(width) << 2;
                else if(bits > 4 && bits <= 8) bytes=width;
                else bytes=width*RGB_SIZE;

                /* round up to an even dword boundary */
                if(bytes & 0x0003) {
                        bytes |= 0x0003;
                        ++bytes;
                }

                /* allocate a line buffer */
                if((p=malloc(width*RGB_SIZE)) == NULL) return(MEMORY_ERROR);

                /* allocate a scratch buffer */
                if((pr=malloc(bytes)) == NULL) {
                        free(p);
                return(MEMORY_ERROR);
        }

        /* write the header */
        memset((char *)&bmp,0,sizeof(BMPHEAD));
        memcpy(bmp.id,"BM",2);
        if(bits==1) {
                bmp.headersize=62L;
                bmp.filesize=bmp.headersize+(long)bytes*(long)depth;
        }
        else if(bits==4) {
                bmp.headersize=118L;
                bmp.filesize=bmp.headersize+(long)bytes*(long)depth;
        }
        else if(bits==8) {
                bmp.headersize=1078L;
                bmp.filesize=bmp.headersize+(long)bytes*(long)depth;
        }
        else {  /* 24 bit file */
                bmp.headersize=54L;
                bmp.filesize=bmp.headersize+(long)bytes*(long)depth;
```

5-8 Continued.

```
            }

            bmp.width=(long)width;
            bmp.depth=(long)depth;
            bmp.infoSize=0x28L;
            if(bits==1) bmp.bits=1;
            else if(bits > 1 && bits <= 4) bmp.bits=4;
            else if(bits > 4 && bits <= 8) bmp.bits=8;
            else bmp.bits=24;
            bmp.biPlanes=1;
            bmp.biCompression=0L;
            fwrite((char *)&bmp,1,sizeof(BMPHEAD),fp);

            /* write the palette */
            if(bmp.bits == 1)
                fwrite("\000\000\000\000\377\377\377\000",1,8,fp);
            else if(bmp.bits == 4) {
                    for(i=0;i<16;++i) {
                            fputc(palette[i*RGB_SIZE+RGB_BLUE],fp);
                            fputc(palette[i*RGB_SIZE+RGB_GREEN],fp);
                            fputc(palette[i*RGB_SIZE+RGB_RED],fp);
                            fputc(0,fp);
                    }
            }
            else if(bmp.bits == 8) {
                    for(i=0;i<256;++i) {
                            fputc(palette[i*RGB_SIZE+RGB_BLUE],fp);
                            fputc(palette[i*RGB_SIZE+RGB_GREEN],fp);
                            fputc(palette[i*RGB_SIZE+RGB_RED],fp);
                            fputc(0,fp);
                    }
            }

            /* write the bitmap */
            for(i=0;i<depth;++i) {
                    if(bits==24) readline(p,width*RGB_SIZE,depth-1-i);
                    else readline(p,width,depth-1-i);
                    if(bmp.bits==1) {
                    packmonoline(pr,p,width);
                    fwrite(pr,1,bytes,fp);
            }
            else if(bmp.bits == 4) {
                    packegaline(pr,p,width);
                    fwrite(pr,1,bytes,fp);
            }
            else if(bmp.bits == 8) fwrite(p,1,bytes,fp);
            else if(bmp.bits == 24) fwrite(p,1,bytes,fp);
    }

    free(pr);
    free(p);
```

5-8 Continued.

```
                if(ferror(fp)) return(BAD_WRITE);
                else return(GOOD_WRITE);
        }


/* translate a vga line to a stacked pixel line */
packegaline(dest,source,width)
        char *dest,*source;
        int width;
{
        int i,j=0;

        for(i=0;i<width;i+=2) {
                dest[j] = ((source[i] << 4) & 0xf0);
                dest[j] |= source[i+1] & 0x0f;
                ++j;
        }
}


/* translate a vga line to a monochrome line */
packmonoline(dest,source,width)
        char *dest,*source;
        int width;
{
        int i;

        for(i=0;i<width;++i) {
                if(source[i]) dest[i >> 3] |= masktable[i & 0x0007];
                else dest[i >> 3] &= ~masktable[i & 0x0007];
        }
}


/* make file name with specific extension */
strmfe(new,old,ext)
        char *new,*old,*ext;
{
        while(*old != 0 && *old != '.') *new++=*old++;
        *new++='.';
        while(*ext) *new++=*ext++;
        *new=0;
}


/* fetch a line from the input file */
getline(p,n,line)
        char *p;
        int n,line;

{
        int i;

        /* seek past the binary file header to the line */
        fseek(in, (long)sizeof(BINARYHEADER)+(long)line*(long)n,SEEK_SET);
        i=fread(p,1,n,in);
```

5-8 Continued.

```
        if(i==n) return(0);
        else return(1);
}
```

5-8 Continued.

The image data is stored by reading it from the source binary file, packing it (in the case of 4-bit lines), and writing it to the destination file. Note that it must be read from the source file in the inverse order it's to be packed—last line first—because this is the way BMP files like to view the universe.

When you have WRITEBMP working, you might want to test it by creating some BMP files and loading them into Windows Paint. Windows Paint is pretty good at spotting incorrectly structured BMP files. Because a BMP file is really just a header followed by a lot of unformatted data, a badly formed one usually has the real file size that doesn't correspond to the file size specified in the header. Windows Paint has little difficulty spotting the offenders in this case.

Figure 5-9 illustrates a GIF file that has been run through MAKEBIN and WRITEBMP, and subsequently loaded into Windows Paint.

5-9 The dragon lady sees the nineties.

Microsoft Windows MSP files

The observation that the current version of Windows is referred to as Windows 3 implies that there once was a Windows 2. In fact, there were several because Windows 2.0 was also available as Windows 286 and Windows

386 to support higher-end processors. None of these were any fun to use. They looked like giant, sort of user-friendly accounting packages and didn't do much of what Windows 3 gets people excited about.

Some of the current high-end Windows applications, such as Corel-DRAW, got their starts under Windows 2. As with Windows 3, some elementary applications were included with Windows 2, including Write and Paint. The Write application looked a lot like Windows 3 Write. The Paint program was somewhat crude, and later versions of Windows 2 included a Windows implementation of the then-current PC Paintbrush package to supplant it.

The Windows 2 Paint application had its own proprietary file format called MSP, presumably for "Microsoft Paint." Because MSP files are still supported in the Windows 3 Paint application and a lot of people used Windows 2 Paint for a long time, creating quite a few MSP files in the process, you might want to understand how MSP files work, along with checking out the current Windows BMP files.

Figure 5-10 illustrates an MSP file in Windows Paint.

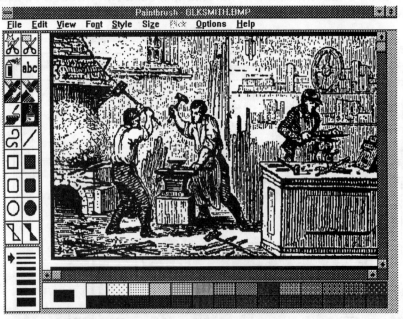

5-10 An MSP file in Windows Paint.

To begin with, MSP files have absolutely no meaningful variables beyond their dimensions. They support only monochrome images. They use still another form of run-length compression to squeeze things down. It's worth noting that way back in the dark prehistory of Windows, people tried to run it from floppy disks. Therefore, the amount of room that an MSP file occupied was clearly more important than the time it took to load. People without hard drives get used to waiting.

Unlike most of the earlier file formats discussed here, MSP files were never intended to be extensible. As such, their structures are pretty simple. An MSP file consists of a header, a line-size table and a heap of compressed image lines. Of these, the line-size table, explained in a moment can be ignored in reading an MSP image.

The first thing you'll encounter in an MSP file is its 32-byte header, which looks like this:

```
typedef struct {
        unsigned int key1,key2;
        unsigned int width,depth;
        unsigned int scraspx,scraspy;
        unsigned int prnaspx,prnaspy;
        unsigned int prndx,prndy;
        unsigned int aspcorx,aspcory;
        unsigned int wcheck;
        unsigned int res1,res2,res3;
        } MSPHEAD;
```

As seems to be common with image-file headers, very little of the information contained in the header is actually necessary.

The key1 and key2 fields of an MSPHEAD object are used to make sure that the file in question really is an MSP file. They also tell you what version of Windows was responsible for it. If the file came from Paint running under Windows 1, key1 will be 6144H and key2 will be 4D6EH. If it came from the Windows 2 version of Paint, key1 will be 694CH and key2 will be 536EH. The width and depth fields will be the dimensions of the image in pixels.

The scraspx and scraspy values specify the aspect ratio of the source screen. The prnaspx and prnaspy values specify the aspect ratio of the dots of the printer that the image in question would most enjoy being output to. The prndx and prndy values hold the resolution of this printer. None of these values is particularly meaningful in the context of this book.

The aspcorx and aspcory fields are not used.

The wcheck field is a checksum of the header, or, at least, it's reputed to be. Its value does not seem to be checked by Windows Paint, and is always 3AB2H.

The three reserved integers at the end of the header don't do anything.

Following the MSPHEAD object in an MSP file you'll find a line-size table. This consists of one integer for each of the scan lines in the file specifying the length of the compressed line. In reading a complete MSP file this information isn't needed, and the READMSP file viewer (to be discussed shortly) ignores it. However, unlike as with other compressed formats, an MSP file's line-size table allows software that is reading an MSP image to get at any lines it likes without having to read from the start of the image data.

Because the lengths of compressed lines can't be predicted, a compressed format such as IFF requires that all the lines up to the line in question be unpacked. Sneaking around this problem is an interesting ability of the MSP format: clearly, it was intended for use back when Windows could expect to have no more than 640K of memory to run in, and hence would be confronted with a perpetual shortage of closet space.

The actual image data of an MSP file is compressed one line at a time. The compression algorithm is pretty simple. Lines are compressed as a series of fields, with each field having a key byte as an identifier. The first byte of the image data is the first key byte. If it's 0, the field is a run of bytes. The first byte after the key is the length of the field. The second byte after the key should be repeated for the number times specified in the length byte.

If the key byte is not 0, the field is a string. The key byte is the length of the string. This number of bytes should be read as-is from the source file.

Having unpacked one field, the length of the unpacked data should be compared to the length of a complete scan line, that is, to `pixels2 bytes(msp.width)`. If the line is incomplete, the next field should be unpacked, and so on, until the whole line has been read.

An MSP file viewer

Figure 5-11 is a simple MSP file viewer, predictably called READMSP. While superficially like the other file viewers in this book so far, this one is designed to work with a file format that supports only monochrome images. As such, it uses the VGA mode 12H to display pictures instead of mode 13H. Mode 12H is a 16-color mode. However, for reasons discussed in detail in chapter 10. It defaults to behaving like a monochrome mode.

```
/*
        MSP reader - copyright (c) 1991
        Alchemy Mindworks Inc.
*/

#include "stdio.h"
#include "dos.h"
#include "alloc.h"

/*                              uncomment this line if you
#include "memmangr.h"           will be linking in the memory manager
*/

#define GOOD_READ       0       /* return codes */
#define BAD_FILE        1
#define BAD_READ        2
#define MEMORY_ERROR    3

#define SCREENWIDE      640     /* mode 12 screen dimensions */
```

5-11 The source code for READMSP.

```
#define SCREENDEEP      480
#define SCREENBYTES     80
#define STEP            32      /* size of a step when panning */

#define HOME            0x4700  /* cursor control codes */
#define CURSOR_UP       0x4800
#define CURSOR_LEFT     0x4b00
#define CURSOR_RIGHT    0x4d00
#define END             0x4f00
#define CURSOR_DOWN     0x5000

#define pixels2bytes(n)    ((n+7)/8)

typedef struct {
        int width,depth,bytes,bits;
        int (*setup)();
        int (*closedown)();
        } FILEINFO;

typedef struct {
        unsigned int key1,key2;
        unsigned int width,depth;
        unsigned int scraspx,scraspy;
        unsigned int prnaspx,prnaspy;
        unsigned int prndx,prndy;
        unsigned int aspcorx,aspcory;
        unsigned int wcheck;
        unsigned int res1,res2,res3;
        } MSPHEAD;

char *farPtr(char *p,long l);
char *getline(unsigned int n);
int dosetup(FILEINFO *fi);
int doclosedown(FILEINFO *fi);

int putline(char *p,unsigned int n);

char masktable[8]={0x80,0x40,0x20,0x10,0x08,0x04,0x02,0x01};

FILEINFO fi;

char *buffer=NULL;

main(argc,argv)
        int argc;
        char *argv[];
{
        FILE *fp;
        static char results[8][16] = {  "Ok",
                                        "Bad file",
                                        "Bad read",
                                        "Memory error",
```

5-11 Continued.

```
                                        };
          char path[81];
          int r;

          if(argc > 1) {
                  strmfe(path,argv[1],"MSP");
                  strupr(path);
                  if((fp = fopen(path,"rb")) != NULL) {
                          fi.setup=dosetup;
                          fi.closedown=doclosedown;
                          r=unpackmsp(fp,&fi);
                          printf("\%s",results[r]);
                          fclose(fp);
                  } else printf("Error opening %s",path);
          } else puts("Argument:       path to an MSP file");
}

/* unpack an MSP file */
unpackmsp(fp,fi)
          FILE *fp;
          FILEINFO *fi;
{
          MSPHEAD msp;
          char *p;
          int i;

          /* get the header */
          if(fread((char *)&msp,1,sizeof(MSPHEAD),fp)==sizeof(MSPHEAD)) {

                  /* check the header */
                  if((msp.key1==0x6144 || msp.key1==0x694c) &&
                     (msp.key2==0x4d6e || msp.key2==0x536e)) {
                          fi->width = msp.width;
                          fi->depth = msp.depth;
                          fi->bytes=pixels2bytes(fi->width);
                          fi->bits=1;

                          /* allocate a line buffer */
                          if((p=malloc(fi->bytes)) != NULL) {

                                  /* skip the line start table */
                                  fseek(fp,(long)(fi->depth*2)+32L,SEEK_SET);

                                  if((fi->setup)(fi) != GOOD_READ) {
                                          free(p);
                                          return(MEMORY_ERROR);
                                  }
                                  /* read all the lines */
                                  for(i=0;i<fi->depth;++i) {
                                          if(readline(p,fp,fi->bytes) != fi->bytes) {
                                                  freebuffer();
                                                  free(p);
```

5-11 Continued.

```
                                                    return(BAD_READ);
                                            }
                                            putline(p,i);
                                    }

                                    (fi->closedown)(fi);
                                    free(p);
                                    return(GOOD_READ);
                            } else return(MEMORY_ERROR);
                    } else return(BAD_FILE);
            } else return(BAD_READ);
    }


/* unpack one MSP line */
readline(p,fp,bytes)
        char *p;
        FILE *fp;
        int bytes;
    {
        int c,i=0,j,k;

        do {
                c=fgetc(fp);
                if(!c) {
                        k=fgetc(fp) & 0x00ff;
                        c=fgetc(fp);
                        for(j=0;j<k;++j) p[i++]=c;
                }
                else {
                        for(j=0;j<c;++j) p[i++]=fgetc(fp);
                }
        } while(i < bytes);
    }


/* this function is called before an image is unpacked */
dosetup(fi)
        FILEINFO *fi;
    {
        union REGS r;

        /* this is for monochrome files only */
        if(!getbuffer((long)pixels2bytes(fi->width)*(long)fi->depth,
                    pixels2bytes(fi->width),fi->depth))
            return(MEMORY_ERROR);

        r.x.ax=0x0012;
        int86(0x10,&r,&r);

        return(GOOD_READ);
    }


/* This function is called after an image has been unpacked. It must
```

5-11 Continued.

```
    display the image and deallocate memory. */
doclosedown(fi)
        FILEINFO *fi;
{

        union REGS r;
        int c,i,n,x=0,y=0;

        if(fi->width > SCREENWIDE) n=SCREENBYTES;
        else n=pixels2bytes(fi->width);

        do {
                for(i=0;i<SCREENDEEP;++i) {
                        c=y+i;
                        if(c>=fi->depth) break;
                        memcpy(MK_FP(0xa000,SCREENBYTES*i),getline(c)+(x>>3),n);
                }
                c=GetKey();
                switch(c) {
                        case CURSOR_LEFT:
                                if((x-STEP) > 0) x-=STEP;
                                else x=0;
                                break;
                        case CURSOR_RIGHT:
                                if((x+STEP+SCREENWIDE) < fi->width) x+=STEP;
                                else if(fi->width > SCREENWIDE)
                                    x=fi->width-SCREENWIDE;
                                else x=0;
                                break;
                        case CURSOR_UP:
                                if((y-STEP) > 0) y-=STEP;
                                else y=0;
                                break;
                        case CURSOR_DOWN:
                                if((y+STEP+SCREENDEEP) < fi->depth) y+=STEP;
                                else if(fi->depth > SCREENDEEP)
                                    y=fi->depth-SCREENDEEP;
                                else y=0;
                                break;
                        case HOME:
                                x=y=0;
                                break;
                        case END:
                                if(fi->width > SCREENWIDE)
                                    x=fi->width-SCREENWIDE;
                                else x=0;
                                if(fi->depth > SCREENDEEP)
                                    y=fi->depth-SCREENDEEP;
                                else y=0;
                                break;
                }
        } while(c != 27);
```

5-11 Continued.

```
                freebuffer();

                r.x.ax=0x0003;
                int86(0x10,&r,&r);
                return(GOOD_READ);
}

/* get one extended key code */
GetKey()
{
        int c;

        c = getch();
        if(!(c & 0x00ff)) c = getch() << 8;
        return(c);
}

/* make file name with specific extension */
strmfe(new,old,ext)
        char *new,*old,*ext;
{
        while(*old != 0 && *old != '.') *new++=*old++;
        *new++='.';
        while(*ext) *new++=*ext++;
        *new=0;
}


/* if you don't use in the memory manager, these functions
   will stand in for it */

#if !MEMMANGR

/* return a far pointer plus a long integer */
char *farPtr(p,l)
        char *p;
        long l;
{
        unsigned int seg,off;

        seg = FP_SEG(p);
        off = FP_OFF(p);
        seg += (off / 16);
        off &= 0x000f;
        off += (unsigned int)(l & 0x000fL);
        seg += (l / 16L);
        p = MK_FP(seg,off);
        return(p);
}

/* save one line to memory */
putline(p,n)
        char *p;
```

5-11 Continued.

```
            unsigned int n;
{
            if(n >= 0 && n < fi.depth)
                  memcpy(farPtr(buffer,(long)n*(long)fi.bytes),p,fi.bytes);
}

/* get one line from memory */
char *getline(n)
            unsigned int n;
{
            return(farPtr(buffer,(long)n*(long)fi.bytes));
}

#pragma warn -par
getbuffer(n,bytes,lines)
            unsigned long n;
            int bytes,lines;
{
            if((buffer=farmalloc(n)) == NULL) return(0);
            else return(1);
}

freebuffer()
{
            if(buffer != NULL) farfree(buffer);
            buffer=NULL;
}
#endif /* !MEMMANGR */
```

5-11 Continued.

The screen buffer of a VGA card in mode 12H is structured just like
the data that is uncompressed from an MSP file. Therefore, displaying an
MSP image on a VGA card in this mode involves little more than copying
the source lines to the appropriate lines of the screen buffer. As with mode
13H, the screen buffer lives at segment A000H. Its dimensions are
640×480 pixels, so each line is 80 bytes long.

The display and memory-management code toward the bottom of
READMSP has been modified to indicate that all the lines being handled
are only an eighth as long as they would have been under any of the full-
color formats.

The readmsp function does pretty much what you'd expect it to do. It
reads the header from the source image and works out the image dimensions. Just about everything else in the header is meaningless. It then
seeks past the line-size table and unpacks each of the compressed lines.
When all the lines are unpacked, it calls the closedown function to display the image and deallocate the image buffer.

Writing MSP files

The only thing that's even a bit tricky about writing an MSP file is creating
its line-size table. Because the table comes before the actual compressed

data, it must be filled in with dummy values initially and then replaced with correct values as the image lines are compressed. This requires a certain amount of seeking back and forth in the file being written, which slows down the compression process somewhat.

Because no current applications support MSP files, with the arguable exception of Windows Paint, which does so only somewhat, you might never have a reason to actually create one.

Figure 5-12 is the source code for WRITEMSP. It works just like all the other example file writer programs discussed thus far, except that it refuses to work with a BIN file having more than one bit of color. It begins by filling in the values of an MSPHEAD object and writing it to the destination file. It then writes a dummy line-size table and finally compresses the actual line data. Note that the line-size table is filled in one line at a time. The file position before writing a line is stored in `startpos`. The line is written and the file position is read again and stored in `endpos`. If the line number is in `i`, the line-size table entry for the current line will be at `32+i*2`. The difference between `endpos` and `startpos` is the length of the compressed line data for line `i`. It should be written to this location in the file and the file position restored to `endpos`, that is, the beginning of the next line.

```
/*
        MSP writer - copyright (c) 1991
        Alchemy Mindworks Inc.
*/

#include "stdio.h"
#include "alloc.h"

#define ILBM            1               /* set true for planar IFF */

#define BINARYSIG       "ALCHBINR"      /* binary identification */

#define GOOD_WRITE      0          /* return codes */
#define BAD_WRITE       1
#define BAD_READ        2
#define MEMORY_ERROR    3
#define TOO_MANY_BITS   4

#define pixels2bytes(n)    ((n+7)/8)

typedef struct {
        char sign[8];
        int width,depth,bits;
        char palette[768];
        } BINARYHEADER;

typedef struct {
        unsigned int key1,key2;
```

5-12 The source code for WRITEMSP.

```
                unsigned int width,depth;
                unsigned int scraspx,scraspy;
                unsigned int prnaspx,prnaspy;
                unsigned int prndx,prndy;
                unsigned int aspcorx,aspcory;
                unsigned int wcheck;
                unsigned int res1,res2,res3;
                } MSPHEAD;

int getline(char *p,int n,int line);
char *bytes2mono(char *p,int width,int bytes);

FILE *in,*out;
BINARYHEADER bh;

char masktable[8]={0x80,0x40,0x20,0x10,0x08,0x04,0x02,0x01};

main(argc,argv)
        int argc;
        char *argv[];

        static char results[5][16] = {  "Ok",
                                        "Bad write",
                                        "Bad read",
                                        "Memory error",
                                        "Too many bits"
                                        };
        char path[81];
        int n;

        if(argc > 1) {

                strmfe(path,argv[1],"BIN");
                strupr(path);
                if((in=fopen(path,"rb")) != NULL) {
                        if(fread((char *)&bh,1,sizeof(BINARYHEADER),in) ==
                            sizeof(BINARYHEADER)) {
                                if(!memcmp(bh.sign,BINARYSIG,8)) {
                                        strmfe(path,argv[1],"MSP");
                                        strupr(path);
                                        if((out=fopen(path,"wb")) != NULL) {
                                                puts("Writing");
                                                n=writemsp(out,getline,
                                                        bh.width,bh.depth,
                                                        bh.bits,bh.palette);
                                                printf("\n%s",results[n]);
                                                fclose(out);
                                        } else printf("Error creating %s",path);
                                } else printf("%s is corrupted",path);
                        } else printf("Error reading %s",path);
                        fclose(in);
                } else printf("Error opening %s",path);
```

5-12 Continued.

```
                } else puts("Argument:      path to a BIN file");
}

/* write an MSP file */
#pragma warn -par
writemsp(fp,readline,width,depth,bits,palette)
        FILE *fp;
        int (*readline)();
        unsigned int width,depth,bits;
        char *palette;
{
        MSPHEAD msp;
        long startpos,endpos;
        char *p,*pr;
        int i,bytes;

        if(bits > 1) return(TOO_MANY_BITS);

        /* write the header */
        memset((char *)&msp,0,sizeof(MSPHEAD));
        msp.key1=0x694c;
        msp.key2=0x536e;
        msp.width=width;
        msp.depth=depth;
        msp.scraspx=msp.scraspy=1;
        msp.prnaspx=msp.prnaspy=1;
        msp.wcheck=0x3ab2;
        fwrite((char *)&msp,1,sizeof(MSPHEAD),fp);

        for(i=0;i<depth;++i) fputword(fp,0);

        /* figure the line size */
        bytes=pixels2bytes(width);

        /* allocate a line buffer */
        if((p=malloc(width)) == NULL) return(MEMORY_ERROR);

        /* compress all the lines */
        for(i=0;i<depth;++i) {

        /* get the current position */
        startpos=ftell(fp);

        /* get a line */
        if(readline(p,width,i)) {
                free(p);
                return(BAD_READ);
        }

        /* convert and compress it */
        if((pr=bytes2mono(p,width,bytes)) != NULL) {
                writeline(fp,pr,bytes);
```

5-12 Continued.

```
                                   free(pr);
                          }
                   else {
                                   free(p);
                                   return(MEMORY_ERROR);
                   }
                   endpos=ftell(fp);

                   /* fill in the table entry */
                   fseek(fp,32L+(long)i*2L,SEEK_SET);
                   fputword(fp,(int)(endpos-startpos));
                   fseek(fp,endpos,SEEK_SET);
         }

         free(p);

         if(ferror(fp)) return(BAD_WRITE);
         else return(GOOD_WRITE);
}


/* translate bytes into planes for monochrome lines */
char *bytes2mono(p,width,bytes)
         char *p;
         int width,bytes;
{

         char *pr;
         int i;

         if((pr=malloc(bytes)) != NULL) {
                   for(i=0;i<width;++i) {
                            if(p[i])
                                 pr[i>>3] |= masktable[i & 0x0007];
                            else
                                 pr[i>>3] &= ~masktable[i & 0x0007];
                   }
                   return(pr);
         } else return(NULL);
}


/* write one MSP line to the destination file */
writeline(fp,p,n)
         FILE *fp;
         char *p;
         int n;
{

         char b[128];
         unsigned int bdex=0,i=0,j=0,t=0;

         do {
                   i=0;
                   while((p[t+i]==p[t+i+1]) && ((t+i) < (n-1)) && i < 0x7e) ++i;
                   if(i>0 || bdex >= 0x7e) {
```

5-12 Continued.

```
                                            if(bdex) {
                                                    fputc(bdex,fp);
                                                    ++j;
                                                    fwrite(b,1,bdex,fp);
                                                    j+=bdex;
                                                    bdex=0;
                                            }
                                            if(i) {
                                                    fputc(0x00,fp);
                                                    fputc(i+1,fp);
                                                    fputc(p[t+i],fp);
                                                    j+=3;
                                                    t+=(i+1);
                                            }
                                    } else b[bdex++]=p[t++];
                    } while(t<n);
                    if(bdex) {
                            fputc(bdex,fp);
                            ++j;
                            fwrite(b,1,bdex,fp);
                            j+=bdex;
                            bdex=0;
                    }
}

/* make file name with specific extension */
strmfe(new,old,ext)
        char *new,*old,*ext;
{
        while(*old != 0 && *old != '.') *new++=*old++;
        *new++='.';
        while(*ext) *new++=*ext++;
        *new=0;
}


/* fetch a line from the input file */
getline(p,n,line)
        char *p;
        int n,line;
{
        int i;

        /* seek past the binary file header to the line */
        fseek(in,(long)sizeof(BINARYHEADER)+(long)line*(long)n,SEEK_SET);
        i=fread(p,1,n,in);
        if(i==n) return(0);
        else return(1);
}

fputword(fp,n)                  /* write one word to the file */
        FILE *fp;
        int n;
```

5-12 Continued.

```
    {
        fputc(n,fp);
        fputc((n >> 8),fp);
    }
```

5-12 Continued.

In developing code that creates image files, it's handy to have a program to check them quickly. I usually use Graphic Workshop, which is
included on the companion disks. In testing the writer programs in this
chapter, you might be inclined to use the corresponding readers.

It's a lot quicker to use Graphic Workshop or READMSP to test your
MSP files, for example, than it is to boot up Windows and then run Windows Paint.

This is actually a bit dangerous. Neither Graphic Workshop nor the
readers in this book are anywhere near as fussy about the files they'll read
as are some of the applications that they're intended for. Windows is particularly fussy and checks the files it reads very carefully. In most cases, it
complains if you attempt to feed it an illegal file. Its most common form of
complaint is to display its "unrecoverable application error" box and terminate the program that is trying to read the errant file.

You might experience this, for example, if you modify WRITEMSP so
that it fills in its line-size table with illegal values: – 1 is a good choice.
Both Graphic Workshop and READMSP display files are created this way,
as neither one cares about the line-size table. Windows Paint will crash.

There's a useful moral in this observation. While it's quite acceptable
to use third-party graphic readers to test your code as you work, the final
check should really be the application for which the files are intended.

Closing Windows

The official documentation for Windows BMP files is the Windows software development kit. This is an expensive way to find out about BMP files
if that's the only element of Windows that you care about. In fact, there
isn't much in the software development kit on the subject that isn't covered in this chapter. Fortunately, there's a limit to what you can say about
a format as simple as BMP.

It used to be possible to write to Microsoft for a brief description of how
MSP files are structured. This probably is no longer the case. However, the
Microsoft technical note that dealt with MSP files didn't say anything that
isn't handled in this book. It just said it without any illustrations.

While arguably useful if you have designs on writing applications that
deal with bitmapped graphics for Windows, neither of the file formats dis-

cussed in this chapter really represents a useful way to store images for most applications beyond Windows. The most interesting element of BMP files—their ability to handle 24-bit color—is available in several other formats discussed in this book, most of which are more universally supported by third-party software.

6
PC Paint/Pictor PIC files

It's probably worth noting that the PIC file extension is used by a number of applications to mean widely different things in various applications. For example, PIC files hold the graphs that are generated by Lotus 1-2-3. Aside from being vector drawings rather than bitmaps (hence, beyond the scope of this book), Lotus graphs are among the least exciting of all visual displays. It's hard to be inspired to great poetry by a jagged line and some numbers.

The PIC format discussed in this chapter is PC Paint/Pictor PIC, which *is* a bitmapped format. It was originally created as the proprietary format for PC Paint 2.0. This program is not the same as Z-Soft's PC Paintbrush. While PC Paint has not proven to be quite as popular as PC Paintbrush, the PIC format is still healthy and frequently found in animation circles. It is used in Grasp packages, among other things.

Note that before version 2.0, PC Paint used simple binary image files with no structure and no compression. At present, PC Paint has undergone a name change to Pictor.

Figure 6-1 illustrates a PIC file taken from a Grasp package.

The PIC format has many of the characteristics of several other bitmap image formats discussed in this book, plus a few that are peculiar to itself. It can support images having 1, 4, or 8 bits of color, and any dimensions you like the look of. Unlike all the other formats in this book, it does not compress image data as lines per se, but as larger blocks. This can make unpacking a PIC file a bit more involved, but it also can make them

6-1 A PIC file from Grasp.

quicker to unpack and it can result in slightly better compression for some
sorts of drawn images.

The PIC format uses a variation on run-length encoding.

The most distinguishing—and potentially troublesome—characteristic of the PIC format is that it handles its 16-color images as discrete
planes rather than as interleaved lines. This means that in unpacking a
16-color PIC file you'll get all of the first plane followed by all of the second
plane and so on. All other formats discussed in this book that support planar images would give you the first plane of the first line, the second plane
of the first line, the third plane of the first line, and so on.

If you want to display a 16-color PIC file as quickly as possible, this
structure can actually prove very handy. As discussed in chapter 10,
updating a display card in its 16-color mode may be handled in two ways.
The first, and the one normally used, is to update one line at a time. This
involves swapping the four display pages on and off the address bus once
for each plane line being written, or four times for each complete image
line being displayed. If you're writing code to update a full screen at
640×480 pixels, you'd have to swap the display planes almost 2,000
times. While this involves only a few instructions per swap, writing the
image data to the screen slows down measurably.

The other way is to write each plane in its entirety; that is, to write all
of the first plane, swap the next display page in and write all of the second
plane, swap the pages again and so on. This is a lot faster to perform, but it
results in a screen display that is a bit weird while it's updating because
the colors keep changing.

Planar images with interleaved lines lend themselves to being displayed by the former approach. The four distinct planes that emerge from
a 16-color PIC file are ideal if you want to handle things as discrete planes.
It's possible to convert between these two structures.

Having said this, be aware that translating between an image with four discrete planes and one with interleaved lines requires that there be two large buffers available—one each for the source and destination image. This is not always practical, especially if you're working with potentially large images. Graphic Workshop deals with this issue by writing PIC data to a temporary disk file when it's packing or unpacking 16-color images, an arguably inelegant solution.

Finally, note that a 640×480 pixel, 16-color interleaved bitmap requires a single buffer of about 150K. As discussed in chapter 1, single-memory objects that require more than 64K are a bit tricky to handle on a PC. While you can sneak around this by using the *farPtr* function, there's a slight speed penalty inherent in doing so.

Each of the four planes of a PIC file can fit in about 38K. While you need four such buffers—just as much memory as you'd need to store an interleaved image of the same size—no one plane will require more than one memory segment. As such, the lines of each plane can be accessed using simple C-language pointer arithmetic.

Once again, it's possible to store interleaved planar images in multiple buffers as well. The structure of a 16-color PIC file simply lends itself more readily to doing so.

The PIC file structure

The PC Paint application that spawned PIC files dates back to the neolithic period of PC history, when CGA cards were high technology and floppy disks only came in one size. Its header structure also reflects this. Rather than simply defining the image dimensions and color depth of a file, the PIC format also allows a PIC file creator to specify a source display type that the file originated from, and hence a target display that is most suited to handling it.

With the growing number of display cards and display modes kicking around, attempting to match the display mode of a card to an image file is questionable at best. It's unlikely that you'll want to use the display mode information to select the display used to view it.

A PIC file starts with the following header. If you've read the previous chapters, chances are most of the elements in this structure should make sense to you even before you get through the following explanation. Despite their widely varying characteristics, all bitmapped image files deal with essentially the same information types.

```
typedef struct {
        unsigned int mark;
        unsigned int xsize;
        unsigned int ysize;
        unsigned int xoff;
        unsigned int yoff;
        char bitsinf;
```

```
    char emark;
    char evideo;
    unsigned int edesc;
    unsigned int esize;
    } PICHEAD;
```

The *mark* element is always 1234H. This key allows PIC readers to know that they have real PIC files rather than, for example, a masquerading Lotus graph. The *xsize* and *ysize* elements are the dimensions of the image in pixels. The *xoff* and *yoff* values are the coordinates of the upper left corner of the displayed image relative to the upper left corner of your screen. These are both 0 in most cases and are ignored in the example PIC reader discussed shortly.

The *bitsinf* element holds the number of bits of color in the picture about to be decoded. Unfortunately, it holds this value in a way that is very weird and complex. The lower 4 bits hold the number of bits per pixel per image plane and the upper 4 bits hold the number of image planes. This is how you'd derive a simple color-depth value from this number:

```
bits=(((pic.bitsinf & 0xf0)>> 4)+1)
*(pic.bitsinf & 0x0f);
```

This assumes that *pic* is an object of the type PICHEAD that has been loaded up with the beginning of a PIC file.

The *emark* element is always 0. The *evideo* element is a letter designation that indicates the type of display the PIC file would most like to be shown on. It might contain one of the following letters:

A—CGA 4 color
B—PCjr/Tandy 1000
C—CGA 2 color
D—EGA low resolution
E—EGA 2 color
F—EGA 4 color
G—EGA 16 color
H—Hercules monochrome
I—Plantronics
J—EGA low resolution
K—AT&T or Toshiba 3100
L—VGA 256 color
M—VGA 16 color
N—Hercules InColor
O—VGA monochrome

It's important to note that while your software can use the information in the *evideo* field if it wants to, you're quite free to ignore it. Bitmaps are essentially device-independent after they're unpacked. The PIC file reader discussed in this chapter displays PIC files with all of the above types in VGA mode 13H. This would be mode L from the PIC type list.

The *edesc* element defines how the palette information that follows the PICHEAD header should be interpreted. The choices are as follows:

0 - no palette
1 - one byte of color for a CGA border
2 - a PCjr palette
3 - an EGA palette
4 - a VGA palette

The code in this chapter does not deal with CGA and PCjr files.

Finally, the `esize` value specifies the number of bytes of palette information that follow the header. This is 0 for a monochrome file, 16 or 48 for a 16-color file, and 768 for a 256-color file.

As discussed in greater detail in chapter 10, the color palette for a 16-color display can be represented in two ways. The most obvious way to handle it would be as 16 3-byte RGB colors. A VGA card allows its 16-color palette to be set this way, with the result that its 16 colors can be drawn from the same 262,144 colors available in the 256-color display modes.

The older EGA card supported a much cruder way of setting its palette. Each color was defined as a single byte, with 2 bits for each of the three primary colors. A color could be set wholly off by having both of its bits off, wholly on by having both its bits on and to two intermediate intensity values by having one of its bits on. Figure 6-2 illustrates how an EGA color number is structured.

The PIC format allows you to define a 16-color image having either sort of palette. The PIC writer we deal with in this chapter writes 16-color PIC files with color numbers for their palettes. You can change this to use the more accurate RGB palette type if you like.

It's important to read the palette information correctly in a PIC file. At least, it's important to read exactly the number of palette bytes indicated in the *esize* element. The 2 bytes after the palette are an integer that defines the number of image blocks in the image. This will typically be a dozen or so, depending upon the complexity of the picture.

The block structure of PIC files might be a bit confusing. Blocks largely ignore the boundaries of image lines. A block can result in up to 8192 bytes of uncompressed image data—it's up to the software that unpacks a PIC file to split this up into lines correctly.

To further confuse this issue, the image data in a PIC file is stored beginning with the last line of the picture.

Each image block begins with the following header.

```
typedef struct {
        int pbsize;
        int bsize;
        char mbyte;
        } PICBLOCK;
```

7	Unused
6	Unused
5	High intensity red
4	High intensity green
3	High intensity blue
2	Low intensity red
1	Low intensity green
0	Low intensity blue

6-2　The bit fields of an EGA color number.

The *pbsize* element defines the size of the packed data in the block. The *bsize* element defines the amount of space the block unpacks into. This is constrained to not exceed 8192 bytes. Typically, all the blocks but the last one in an image or image plane have something approaching 8192 for their *bsize* values.

The *mbyte* value is a unique marker. Technically, it should be a byte that occurs as infrequently as possible in the block being compressed. In fact, this is fairly tedious to work out in creating a PIC file, and the PIC writer in this chapter cheats on this a bit.

The image data in a PIC block is run-length compressed using a pretty strange compression algorithm. The first byte after a PICBLOCK is the first byte of the first compressed field. If this byte is the same as the *mbyte* value of the PICBLOCK header for this block, the field is a run of bytes. The next byte is probably the length. If the next byte is a 0, the following 2 bytes are an integer representing the length. This allows for lengths of greater than 255 bytes if needed. The byte after the length is the byte to be repeated.

If the first byte in a field is not *mbyte*, the field is a 1-byte string. It's written directly to the block being unpacked.

Having unpacked one field, the process should be repeated until the entire block has been uncompressed.

If the image being read is monochrome or a 256-color picture, a completely uncompressed block can be split up into its component lines and written to its intended destination. If it's a 16-color picture, each planar line from a decoded block must be added to the complete image line it's bound for, assuming that you'll ultimately be storing the lines as interleaved planes. In the PIC reader discussed in this chapter, all the lines are converted to color bytes. Each byte has to be adjusted four times as its respective planes are read.

Note that a 16-color PIC file's planes are always stored as discrete blocks. As such, the end of a plane always coincides with the end of a block, and 16-color images typically have four short end blocks instead of one.

A PIC file reader

The READPIC program in FIG. 6-3 illustrates some code that handles the foregoing theoretical discussion of PIC files. You might find the code easier to follow, as PIC files don't lend themselves to explanation. Once again, this reader displays all the PIC files it encounters in the VGA card's mode 13H.

```
/*
        PIC reader - copyright (c) 1991
        Alchemy Mindworks Inc.
*/

#include "stdio.h"
#include "dos.h"
#include "alloc.h"

/*                              uncomment this line if you
#include "memmangr.h"           will be linking in the memory manager
*/

#define GOOD_READ       0       /* return codes */
#define BAD_FILE        1
#define BAD_READ        2
#define MEMORY_ERROR    3
```

6-3 The source code for READPIC.

```
#define SCREENWIDE        320     /* mode 13 screen dimensions */
#define SCREENDEEP        200
#define STEP               32     /* size of a step when panning */

#define HOME            0x4700   /* cursor control codes */
#define CURSOR_UP       0x4800
#define CURSOR_LEFT     0x4b00
#define CURSOR_RIGHT    0x4d00
#define END             0x4f00
#define CURSOR_DOWN     0x5000

#define pixels2bytes(n)    ((n+7)/8)

typedef struct {
        int width,depth,bytes,bits;
        int background;
        char palette[768];
        int (*setup)();
        int (*closedown)();
        } FILEINFO;

typedef struct {
        unsigned int mark;
        unsigned int xsize;
        unsigned int ysize;
        unsigned int xoff;
        unsigned int yoff;
        char bitsinf;
        char emark;
        char evideo;
        unsigned int edesc;
        unsigned int esize;
        } PICHEAD;

typedef struct {
        int pbsize;
        int bsize;
        char mbyte;
        } PICBLOCK;

char *farPtr(char *p,long l);
char *getline(unsigned int n);
char *mono2vga(char *p,int width);
int dosetup(FILEINFO *fi);
int doclosedown(FILEINFO *fi);

int putline(char *p,unsigned int n);

char masktable[8]={0x80,0x40,0x20,0x10,0x08,0x04,0x02,0x01};
char bittable[8] ={0x01,0x02,0x04,0x08,0x10,0x20,0x40,0x80};

FILEINFO fi;
```

6-3 Continued.

```
char *buffer=NULL;

main(argc,argv)
        int argc;
        char *argv[];
{
        FILE *fp;
        static char results[4][16] = {  "Ok",
                                         "Bad file",
                                         "Bad read",
                                         "Memory error",
                                         };
        char path[80];
        int r;

        if(argc > 1) {
                strmfe(path,argv[1],"PIC");
                strupr(path);
                if((fp = fopen(path,"rb")) != NULL) {
                        fi.setup=dosetup;
                        fi.closedown=doclosedown;
                        r=unpackpic(fp,&fi);
                        printf("\%s",results[r]);
                        fclose(fp);
                } else printf("Error opening %s",path);
        } else puts("Argument:       path to a PIC file");
}

/* unpack a PIC file */
unpackpic(fp,fi)
        FILE *fp;
        FILEINFO *fi;
{
        PICHEAD pic;
        PICBLOCK pbk;
        char b[768],*block,*p;
        unsigned long l;
        int bcount,c,i,j,ldex=0,len;
        int line=0,pass,pos,r=GOOD_READ;

        /* allocate a block buffer */
        if((block=malloc(8192)) == NULL) return(MEMORY_ERROR);

        /* read in the header */
        if(fread((char *)&pic,1,sizeof(PICHEAD),fp) == sizeof(PICHEAD)) {

                /* is it a real header? */
                if(pic.mark == 0x1234) {
                        /* get the values */
                        fi->width = pic.xsize;
                        fi->depth = pic.ysize;
                        fi->bits=(((pic.bitsinf & 0xf0)>>4)+1)*(pic.bitsinf & 0x0f);
```

6-3 Continued.

```
/* if there are more than 256 colours... */
if(pic.esize > 768) return(BAD_FILE);

/* get the line byte size */
if(fi->bits==8) fi->bytes=fi->width;
else fi->bytes=pixels2bytes(fi->width);

/* read the palette if there is one */
fread(b,1,pic.esize,fp);

/* adjust the palette as needs be */
if(fi->bits==1)
    memcpy(fi->palette,"\000\000\000\377\377\377",6);
else if(fi->bits==4 && pic.evideo != 'M')
    ega2vgapalette(fi->palette,b,16);
else {
        memcpy(fi->palette,b,768);
        for(i=0;i<pic.esize;++i)
            fi->palette[i]=fi->palette[i] << 2;
}

/* do the setup */
if((fi->setup)(fi) != GOOD_READ) {
        free(block);
        return(MEMORY_ERROR);
}

/* clear out the lines */
if((p=malloc(fi->width)) != NULL) {
        memset(p,0,fi->width);
        for(i=0;i<fi->width;++i) putline(p,i);
        free(p);
}
else {
        free(block);
        return(MEMORY_ERROR);
}

/* get the number of blocks */
bcount=fgetword(fp);

/* read all the blocks */
if(bcount) {
        for(i=0;i<bcount;++i) {
                l=ftell(fp);
                pos=0;

                /* get one block */
                if(fread((char *)&pbk,1,sizeof(PICBLOCK),fp) != sizeof(PICBLOCK)) {
                        freebuffer();
                        free(block);
                        return(BAD_READ);
```

6-3 Continued.

```
                    }
                    /* unpack it */
                    do {
                            c=fgetc(fp);
                            len=1;
                            if(c==pbk.mbyte) {
                                    len=fgetc(fp);
                                    if(len==0) len=fgetword(fp);
                                    c=fgetc(fp);
                                    memset(block+ldex,c,len);
                                    ldex+=len;
                            } else block[ldex++]=c;
                            pos+=len;
                            while(ldex >= fi->bytes) {
                                    ldex-=fi->bytes;
                                    if(fi->bits==8) putline(block,fi->depth-line-1);
                                    else if(fi->bits==1) {
                                            if((p=mono2vga(block,fi->width)) != NULL) {
                                                    putline(p,fi->depth-line-1);
                                                    free(p);
                                            }
                                            else {
                                                    freebuffer();
                                                    free(block);
                                                    return(MEMORY_ERROR);
                                            }
                                    }
                                    else {
                                            if((p=getline(fi->depth-(line%fi->depth)-1)) !=
                                                    pass=line/fi->depth;
                                                    for(j=0;j<fi->width;++j) {
                                                            if(block[j>>3] & masktable[j & (
                                                                    p[j] |= bittable[pass];
                                                            else
                                                                    p[j] &= ~bittable[pass];
                                                    }
                                                    putline(p,fi->depth-(line%fi->depth)-1),
                                            }
                                    }
                                    ++line;
                                    movmem(block+fi->bytes,block,ldex);
                            }
                    } while(pos < pbk.bsize && c != EOF);
                    fseek(fp,1+(long)pbk.pbsize,SEEK_SET);
            }
            (fi->closedown)(fi);
        } else r=BAD_FILE;
    } else r=BAD_FILE;
} else r=BAD_READ;
free(block);

return(r);
```

6-3 Continued.

```
        }

/* convert a monochrome line into an eight bit line */
char *mono2vga(p,width)
        char *p;
        int width;
{
        char *pr;
        int i;

        if((pr=malloc(width)) != NULL) {
                for(i=0;i<width;++i) {
                        if(p[i >> 3] & masktable[i & 0x0007])
                                pr[i]=1;
                        else
                                pr[i]=0;
                }
                return(pr);
        } else return(NULL);
}


fgetword(fp)
        FILE *fp;
{
        return((fgetc(fp) & 0xff) + ((fgetc(fp) & 0xff) << 8));
}


/* This function is called after the BMHD and CMAP chunks have
   been read but before the BODY is unpacked */
dosetup(fi)
        FILEINFO *fi;
{
        union REGS r;

        if(!getbuffer((long)fi->width*(long)fi->depth,fi->width,fi->depth))
            return(MEMORY_ERROR);

        r.x.ax=0x0013;
        int86(0x10,&r,&r);

        setvgapalette(fi->palette,1<<fi->bits,fi->background);

        return(GOOD_READ);
}

/* This function is called after an image has been unpacked. It must
   display the image and deallocate memory. */
doclosedown(fi)
        FILEINFO *fi;
{
        union REGS r;
        int c,i,n,x=0,y=0;
```

6-3 Continued.

```
                if(fi->width > SCREENWIDE) n=SCREENWIDE;
                else n=fi->width;

                do {
                        for(i=0;i<SCREENDEEP;++i) {
                                c=y+i;
                                if(c>=fi->depth) break;
                                memcpy(MK_FP(0xa000,SCREENWIDE*i),getline(c)+x,n);
                        }
                        c=GetKey();
                        switch(c) {
                                case CURSOR_LEFT:
                                        if((x-STEP) > 0) x-=STEP;
                                        else x=0;
                                        break;
                                case CURSOR_RIGHT:
                                        if((x+STEP+SCREENWIDE) < fi->width) x+=STEP;
                                        else if(fi->width > SCREENWIDE)
                                            x=fi->width-SCREENWIDE;
                                        else x=0;
                                        break;
                                case CURSOR_UP:
                                        if((y-STEP) > 0) y-=STEP;
                                        else y=0;
                                        break;
                                case CURSOR_DOWN:
                                        if((y+STEP+SCREENDEEP) < fi->depth) y+=STEP;
                                        else if(fi->depth > SCREENDEEP)
                                            y=fi->depth-SCREENDEEP;
                                        else y=0;
                                        break;
                                case HOME:
                                        x=y=0;
                                        break;
                                case END:
                                        if(fi->width > SCREENWIDE)
                                            x=fi->width-SCREENWIDE;
                                        else x=0;
                                        if(fi->depth > SCREENDEEP)
                                            y=fi->depth-SCREENDEEP;
                                        else y=0;
                                        break;
                        }
                } while(c != 27);

                freebuffer();

                r.x.ax=0x0003;
                int86(0x10,&r,&r);
                return(GOOD_READ);
}
```

6-3 Continued.

```c
/* get one extended key code */
GetKey()
{
        int c;

        c = getch();
        if(!(c & 0x00ff)) c = getch() << 8;
        return(c);
}

/* set the VGA palette and background */
setvgapalette(p,n,b)
        char *p;
        int n,b;
{
        union REGS r;
        int i;

        outp(0x3c6,0xff);
        for(i=0;i<n;++i) {
                outp(0x3c8,i);
                outp(0x3c9,(*p++) >> 2);
                outp(0x3c9,(*p++) >> 2);
                outp(0x3c9,(*p++) >> 2);
        }
        r.x.ax=0x1001;
        r.h.bh=b;
        int86(0x10,&r,&r);
}

ega2vgapalette(dest,source,n)
        char *dest,*source;
        int n;
{
        int i,r,g,b;

        for(i=0;i<n;++i) {
                r=g=b=0;
                if(*source & 0x01) b+=0x80;
                if(*source & 0x08) b+=0x40;
                if(*source & 0x02) g+=0x80;
                if(*source & 0x10) g+=0x40;
                if(*source & 0x04) r+=0x80;
                if(*source & 0x20) r+=0x40;
                ++source;
                *dest++=r;
                *dest++=g;
                *dest++=b;
        }
}

/* make file name with specific extension */
```

6-3 Continued.

```
strmfe(new,old,ext)
        char *new,*old,*ext;
{
        while(*old != 0 && *old != '.') *new++=*old++;
        *new++='.';
        while(*ext) *new++=*ext++;
        *new=0;
}

/* if you don't use in the memory manager, these functions
   will stand in for it */

#if !MEMMANGR

/* return a far pointer plus a long integer */
char *farPtr(p,l)
        char *p;
        long l;
{
        unsigned int seg,off;

        seg = FP_SEG(p);
        off = FP_OFF(p);
        seg += (off / 16);
        off &= 0x000f;
        off += (unsigned int)(l & 0x000fL);
        seg += (l / 16L);
        p = MK_FP(seg,off);
        return(p);
}

/* save one line to memory */
putline(p,n)
        char *p;
        unsigned int n;
{
        if(n >= 0 && n < fi.depth)
            memcpy(farPtr(buffer,(long)n*(long)fi.width),p,fi.width);
}

/* get one line from memory */
char *getline(n)
        unsigned int n;
{
        return(farPtr(buffer,(long)n*(long)fi.width));
}

#pragma warn -par
getbuffer(n,bytes,lines)
        unsigned long n;
        int bytes,lines;
{
```

6-3 Continued.

```
        if((buffer=farmalloc(n)) == NULL) return(0);
        else return(1);
}

freebuffer()
{
        if(buffer != NULL) farfree(buffer);
        buffer=NULL;
}
#endif /* !MEMMANGR */
```

6-3 Continued.

The *unpackpic* function of READPIC does most of the work. It begins by reading the header and making some sense of it. Note that it must set a default monochrome palette for 1-bit files because the VGA card wants a palette, even if it's a very short one. If you display monochrome PIC files in a genuinely monochrome screen mode you won't need this.

The tricky part of this code is the block reader down toward the bottom of *unpackpic*. Aside from uncompressing the block information, it has to parcel out the line data. In fact, what it really does is to uncompress fields until at least one line's worth of image data is in the *block* buffer. It then writes the line to the main image buffer and moves whatever's left over to the start of the *block* buffer. The uncompressed data from subsequent fields is appended to this.

Note that 16-color lines must be read from the main image buffer, updated and written back to the buffer four times.

It's probably worth observing that READPIC is a bit more of a memory pig than were the previous file readers covered. Aside from allocating an image buffer, it must also have 8K of memory available to use as a block buffer. This probably will not pose a problem if you're running it on a system with most of the 640K of memory available. If you attempt to run it shelled out of something else, such as Turbo C, it could complain if it's presented with a moderately large file. Because READPIC stores everything as VGA lines, it requires pretty substantial amounts of memory even if you're only working with monochrome files. For example, a 576×720 pixel monochrome image requires a bit over 50K of storage as a planar 1-bit image. The READPIC program requires 405K.

If you're working in the Turbo C integrated-programming environment and find that memory is a problem, you might want to create some small example files to use while you're testing your code. The F5 crop function of Graphic Workshop allows you to excise chunks from larger images and write them to PIC files—or to any other format you want to work with.

Writing PIC files

Writing a PIC file is more like reading one in reverse than is the case for most formats. There are few holes in this concept, of course. Packing up image data as blocks rather than lines requires a slightly different approach than that which has appeared in dealing with the other run-length encoded formats in this book. In addition, the notion of a "least frequently used byte"—the *mbyte* field in the PICBLOCK structure discussed previously—presents something of a problem for a line-oriented packing arrangement. The WRITEPIC program cheats on this by using a constant byte value. You might want to add some analysis code to the function to create a histogram of all the byte values and choose the best one for each block being compressed.

As a rule, this adds considerably to the time it takes to write a PIC file and does almost nothing to improve its compression. The run-length compression used in PIC files does passably well in compressing drawn images of the sort you'd expect to find coming from a paint program. It typically handles scanned images with the poorest compression of any of the run-length compression algorithms discussed in this book, although it is quite fast. Figure 6-4 illustrates the code for WRITEPIC.

```
/*
        PIC writer - copyright (c) 1991
        Alchemy Mindworks Inc.
*/

#include "stdio.h"
#include "alloc.h"

#define BINARYSIG       "ALCHBINR"      /* binary identification */

#define GOOD_WRITE      0       /* return codes */
#define BAD_WRITE       1
#define BAD_READ        2
#define MEMORY_ERROR    3

#define RGB_RED         0
#define RGB_GREEN       1
#define RGB_BLUE        2
#define RGB_SIZE        3

#define pixels2bytes(n)    ((n+7)/8)

typedef struct {
        char sign[8];
        int width,depth,bits;
        char palette[768];
        } BINARYHEADER;

typedef struct {
        unsigned int mark;
        unsigned int xsize;
        unsigned int ysize;
        unsigned int xoff;
        unsigned int yoff;
```

6-4 The source code for WRITEPIC.

```
                char bitsinf;
                char emark;
                char evideo;
                unsigned int edesc;
                unsigned int esize;
                } PICHEAD;

typedef struct {
                int pbsize;
                int bsize;
                char mbyte;
                } PICBLOCK;

int getline(char *p,int n,int line);

FILE *in,*out;
BINARYHEADER bh;

char masktable[8]={0x80,0x40,0x20,0x10,0x08,0x04,0x02,0x01};
char bittable[8] ={0x01,0x02,0x04,0x08,0x10,0x20,0x40,0x80};

main(argc,argv)
        int argc;
        char *argv[];
{
        static char results[8][16] = {  "Ok",
                                        "Bad write",
                                        "Bad read",
                                        "Memory error",
                                        };
        char path[81];
        int n;


        if(argc > 1) {
                strmfe(path,argv[1],"BIN");
                strupr(path);
                if((in=fopen(path,"rb")) != NULL) {
                        if(fread((char *)&bh,1,sizeof(BINARYHEADER),in) ==
                            sizeof(BINARYHEADER)) {
                                if(!memcmp(bh.sign,BINARYSIG,8)) {
                                        strmfe(path,argv[1],"PIC");
                                        strupr(path);
                                        if((out=fopen(path,"wb")) != NULL) {
                                                puts("Writing");
                                                n=writepic(out,getline,
                                                        bh.width,bh.depth,
                                                        bh.bits,bh.palette);
                                                printf("\n%s",results[n]);
                                                fclose(out);
                                        } else printf("Error creating %s",path);
                                } else printf("%s is corrupted",path);
```

6-4 Continued.

```
                                        } else printf("Error reading %s",path);
                                        fclose(in);
                            } else printf("Error opening %s",path);
                } else puts("Argument:        path to a BIN file");
}

/* write a PIC file */
writepic(fp,readline,width,depth,bits,palette)
        FILE *fp;
        int (*readline)();
        unsigned int width,depth,bits;
        char *palette;
{

        PICHEAD pic;
        unsigned long offset;
        char *block,*p,*pr;
        int i,j,pblock=0,bytes,ttl=0;

        /* allocate some buffers */
        if((block=malloc(8192)) == NULL) return(MEMORY_ERROR);

        if((p=malloc(width)) == NULL) {
                free(block);
                return(MEMORY_ERROR);
        }

        if((pr=malloc(width)) == NULL) {
                free(p);
                free(block);
                return(MEMORY_ERROR);
        }

        /* clear out the PICHEAD */
        memset((char *)&pic,0,sizeof(PICHEAD));

        /* fill in the values */
        pic.mark=0x1234;
        pic.xsize=width;
        pic.ysize=depth;

        switch(bits) {
                case 1:
                        bytes=pixels2bytes(width);
                        pic.bitsinf=0x01;
                        pic.evideo='O';
                        pic.edesc=0;
                        pic.esize=0;
                        break;
                case 8:
                        bytes=width;
                        pic.bitsinf=0x08;
                        pic.evideo='L';
```

6-4 Continued.

```
                pic.edesc=4;
                pic.esize=768;
                break;
        default:
                bytes=pixels2bytes(width);
                pic.bitsinf=((bits-1) << 4) | 0x01;
                pic.evideo='G';
                pic.edesc=3;
                pic.esize=16;
                break;
    }

pic.emark=0xff;

/* write the header */
if(fwrite((char *)&pic,1,sizeof(PICHEAD),fp) != sizeof(PICHEAD))
    return(BAD_WRITE);

/* write the palette */
if(bits > 1 && bits <=4) {
        for(i=0;i<16;++i) {
                j=0;
                if(palette[0] > 0xbb) j |= 0x24;
                else if(palette[0] > 0x77) j |= 0x04;
                else if(palette[0] > 0x33) j |= 0x20;
                if(palette[1] > 0xbb) j |= 0x12;
                else if(palette[1] > 0x77) j |= 0x02;
                else if(palette[1] > 0x33) j |= 0x10;
                if(palette[2] > 0xbb) j |= 0x09;
                else if(palette[2] > 0x77) j |= 0x01;
                else if(palette[2] > 0x33) j |= 0x08;
                fputc(j,fp);
                palette+=3;
        }
}
else if(bits > 4 && bits <=8) {
        for(i=0;i<pic.esize;++i)
            fputc(palette[i]>>2,fp);
}
/* put in the dummy block count */
offset=ftell(fp);
fputword(fp,0);

/* pack the file */
if(bits==1 || bits==8) {
        for(i=0;i<depth;++i) {

                /* get a line */
                if((*readline)(p,width,depth-1-i)) {
                        free(pr);
                        free(p);
                        free(block);
```

6-4 Continued.

```
                                        return(BAD_READ);
                            }

                            /* translate it if needs be */
                            if(bits==1) packmonoline(pr,p,width,0);
                            else memcpy(pr,p,width);

                            /* add it to the block if there's room */
                            if((ttl+bytes) < 8192) {
                                    memcpy(block+ttl,pr,bytes);
                                    ttl+=bytes;
                            }
                            else {
                                    /* write the block when it's full */
                                    if(writepicblock(block,fp,ttl) != 0) {
                                            free(pr);
                                            free(p);
                                            free(block);
                                            return(BAD_WRITE);
                                    }

                                    /* fetch the leftovers */
                                    memcpy(block,pr,bytes);
                                    ttl=bytes;
                                    ++pblock;
                            }
                    }

                    /* write any leftovers */
                    if(ttl) {
                            if(writepicblock(block,fp,ttl) != 0) {
                                    free(pr);
                                    free(p);
                                    free(block);
                                    return(BAD_WRITE);
                            }
                            ++pblock;
                    }
            }
            else {
                    /* handle a four plane file */
                    for(j=0;j<bits;++j) {
                            /* read each line */
                            for(i=0;i<depth;++i) {
                                    if((*readline)(p,width,depth-1-i)) {
                                            free(pr);
                                            free(p);
                                            free(block);
                                            return(BAD_READ);
                                    }

                                    /* make a plane of it */
```

6-4　Continued.

```
                        packmonoline(pr,p,width,j);

                        /* add it to the block if there's room */
                        if((ttl+bytes) < 8192) {
                                memcpy(block+ttl,pr,bytes);
                                ttl+=bytes;
                        }
                        else {
                                /* or write the block when it's full */
                                if(writepicblock(block,fp,ttl) != 0) {
                                        free(pr);
                                        free(p);
                                        free(block);
                                        return(BAD_WRITE);
                                }
                                memcpy(block,pr,bytes);
                                ttl=bytes;
                                ++pblock;
                        }
                }

                /* write leftovers */
                if(ttl) {
                        if(writepicblock(block,fp,ttl) != 0) {
                                free(pr);
                                free(p);
                                free(block);
                                return(BAD_WRITE);
                        }
                        ++pblock;
                        ttl=0;
                }
        }
    }

    /* go set the block count */
    fseek(fp,offset,SEEK_SET);
    fputword(fp,pblock);

    free(pr);
    free(p);
    free(block);

    if(ferror(fp)) return(BAD_WRITE);
    else return(GOOD_WRITE);
}

/* translate a vga line to a monochrome line */
packmonoline(dest,source,width,plane)
        char *dest,*source;
        int width;
{
```

6-4 Continued.

```
        int i;
        for(i=0;i<width;++i) {
                if(source[i] & bittable[plane]) dest[i >> 3] |= masktable[i & 0x0007];
                else dest[i >> 3] &= ~masktable[i & 0x0007];
        }
}

/* write one PIC block */
writepicblock(p,fp,n)
        char *p;
        FILE *fp;
        int n;
{
        PICBLOCK pbk;
        long l,tl;
        unsigned int i=0,t=0;

        l=ftell(fp);
        pbk.pbsize=sizeof(PICBLOCK);
        pbk.bsize=n;
        pbk.mbyte=0x81;
        fwrite((char *)&pbk,1,sizeof(PICBLOCK),fp);
        do {
                i=0;
                while((p[t+i]==p[t+i+1]) && ((t+i) < n))++i;
                if(i>0) {
                        fputc(pbk.mbyte,fp);
                        if(i < 256) fputc(i,fp);
                        else {
                                fputc(0,fp);
                                fputWord(fp,i);
                                pbk.pbsize+=2;
                        }
                        fputc(p[t],fp);
                        pbk.pbsize+=3;
                        t+=i;
                }
                else {
                        if(p[t] != pbk.mbyte) {
                                fputc(p[t++],fp);
                                ++pbk.pbsize;
                        }
                        else {
                                fputc(pbk.mbyte,fp);
                                fputc(1,fp);
                                fputc(p[t],fp);
                                pbk.pbsize+=3;
                                ++t;
                        }
                }
        } while(t<n);
        tl=ftell(fp);
```

6-4 Continued.

```
            fseek(fp,1,SEEK_SET);
            fwrite((char *)&pbk,1,sizeof(PICBLOCK),fp);
            fseek(fp,tl,SEEK_SET);
            return(ferror(fp));
}


fputword(fp,n)                   /* write one word to the file */
        FILE *fp;
        int n;
{
        fputc(n,fp);
        fputc((n >> 8),fp);
}


/* make file name with specific extension */
strmfe(new,old,ext)
        char *new,*old,*ext;
{
        while(*old != 0 && *old != '.') *new++=*old++;
        *new++='.';
        while(*ext) *new++=*ext++;
        *new=0;
}


/* fetch a line from the input file */
getline(p,n,line)
        char *p;
        int n,line;
{
        int i;

        /* seek past the binary file header to the line */
        fseek(in,(long)sizeof(BINARYHEADER)+(long)line*(long)n,SEEK_SET);
        i=fread(p,1,n,in);
        if(i==n) return(0);
        else return(1);
}
```

6-4 Continued.

The WRITEPIC program reads binary files created by MAKEBIN or MAKEBIN2. If you use files from MAKEBIN2, make sure that they have no more than 8 bits of color. The `writepic` function creates one of three file types, depending upon the number of bits of color it encounters. As mentioned earlier in this chapter, it writes 16-color files using EGA color numbers to define the palette. This is inherently less accurate than using real RGB palette values, but some PIC readers do not display 16-color files with RGB palettes on old-style EGA display cards. If you want to change this, modify the `default` case of the `switch` at the top of `writepic` so that `pic.evideo` is 'M' and `pic.edisc` is 4. You must also change the code that writes the palette data below this to write an RGB palette for 16-color files, just as is presently done for 256-color files.

Note that `writepic` does not know the number of blocks a file contains until after all the blocks have been created. Therefore, it must write a dummy count to the file initially and then seek back and fill in the real count when all the image data has been compressed.

All of the file readers and writers in this book have been based on handling image data as discrete lines. This is how most applications will want to use it, and how the memory manager code described in this book expects it to be handled as well. Because PIC files are not inherently line oriented, the code in `writepic` is a bit more convoluted than it would have to be in a function that could deal with PIC files as blocks rather than as lines. While you're free to modify `writepic` to handle whole image blocks at a time, do so with the risk of confusion later on. While PIC files themselves might be comfortable with large blocks of image data, almost everything you're likely to want to display or print their images on will expect to see one line at a time.

The code to pack blocks works with one line at a time, keeping track of the aggregate block size in `ttl`. When adding another line to the current block would cause it to exceed 8192 bytes unpacked, the current block is ended and a new one is started. Note that, as has been discussed, no attempt is made in `writepic` to find an optimum *mbyte* value for each block. The value 0x81 is used, which is as good as any.

The function that is used to implement PIC format run-length encoding is `writepicblock`, and is a derivative of the other run-length compression functions seen earlier in this book, with the exception that it usually gets to write a great deal more data. Because there is no run of bytes field in a PIC block, `writepicblock` doesn't require any meaningful amount of string storage.

Using PIC files

Unless you're particularly enamored of PC Paint, Pictor or Grasp animation, you might have little use for PIC. As with Windows BMP and WordPerfect WPG files, it's a format dedicated to a specific task and has little application outside of that task. Because it's particularly unkind to scanned images, the most frequent inhabitant of bitmapped image files at the moment, there are few discrete PIC files floating about on bulletin boards.

7
Truevision TGA files

Never repeat a successful experiment.
—MURPHY'S LAWS OF COMPUTERS

The Truevision Targa board was among the first high-end display devices for PC systems that could display RGB color, as opposed to the palette color of a VGA card. Capable of representing up to 16-million discrete colors and bankrupting small countries all in one convenient, easy-to-open package, the Targa board is a model of expensive high technology. While still widely used in high-end color retouching and prepress applications, the Truevision hardware has been augmented by several other 24-bit display devices, many based on the Texas Instruments TIGA chip. Most of the TIGA boards cost less.

There are numerous flavors of Targa boards, and discussing them is beyond the scope of this book. You may get some idea of their complexities if you immerse yourself in the details of the files that accompany them.

In addition to developing the Targa hardware, Truevision also came up with a specification for a high-end file format that would support images of a caliber suitable for display on Targa hardware. The Targa format, or TGA, supports images of any dimensions with between 1 and 32 bits of color. The extra 8 bits at the high end take some explaining.

While the Targa format originated with Truevision's hardware, it has migrated to many other applications. It's probably the most universally supported 24-bit file format for PC applications. Unlike TIFF, for example, it's subject to relatively few variations. Software that reads Targa files should be able to read all Targa files. This is unquestionably not the case for 24-bit TIFF files.

My favorite application for Targa files is David Buck's DKB ray tracer. Ray tracing is a process in which a mathematical model of solid objects and light sources is created. The computer then rasterizes an image by figuring out how each ray of light generated by the light source is absorbed or reflected by the objects in the model. The DKB ray tracer generates its resultant images as 24-bit Targa files. An example of its work can be seen in FIG. 7-1.

7-1 A Targa file generated by the DKB ray tracer.

As an aside, it took several hours to generate FIG. 7-1 with the DKB ray tracer running on a 33-MHz, 80486-based system.

Targa files are relatively complicated to work with because they have numerous options and modes. Specifically, a Targa file can support images with 1, 8, 16, 24 or 32 bits of color. Its lines can be compressed using a simple run-length encoding procedure or they can be stored uncompressed. They can be stored starting at either the top or the bottom of the image, and they can be reversed right to left or packed normally.

Predictably, a Targa reader should be able to handle all these permutations. It's not a trivial undertaking.

Targa files and color

Before discussing the details of a Targa reader, it's worth looking at a few things that are peculiar to the Targa format. Most of these have to do with the way color is handled in a Targa file. The variations on the Targa format are intended to allow stored Targa image data to reflect the actual nature of the display hardware it was created on, and is intended to be displayed on in the future.

This discussion assumes that you have a Targa board. If you don't, you might feel that the variations on the Targa format are intended to confuse programmers, a likely alternate explanation.

To begin with, Targa files store the 3 bytes of an RGB color value in the inverse order to the way the rest of the civilized universe does. Whereas a normal pixel or palette entry would be stored in the order red, green, blue, they're packed as blue, green, red in a Targa file.

You might well think that forgetting this would be pretty easy to spot, but this is not always the case. Bear in mind that at this point in the discussion of image files the only way to look at 24-bit images has been to reduce them to gray. Color errors are not readily apparent in a gray-scale picture. If you use ray-traced Targa files as test images, since they're very easy to obtain, you might not notice that the colors are wrong even if you view the pictures in color. Ray tracing isn't known for treating its subjects with conventional notions of color and illumination.

Eight-bit Targa files are stored in the same way that 8-bit files in the other formats we've looked at are; that is, as indices into a palette, which are pretty easy to handle. Files with more than 8 bits are stored as arrays of RGB values. However, unlike 24-bit BMP files, for example, each pixel need not require 3 bytes.

Targa files with RGB color, or "true color," as the Targa documentation calls it, can be stored with 16, 24 or 32 bits of color information. A 16-bit Targa file stores each color index in 5 bits, for a total of 15 bits, which can be squeezed into 2 bytes, with 1 bit left over. The first 5 bits represent the blue intensity, the next 5 bits the green intensity and the last 5 bits the red intensity, as shown in FIG. 7-2.

The high-order bit of a 16-bit Targa pixel is used if the image in question is to serve as an overlay on an existing image. It defines image transparency. In this case, if the high-order bit is set, the pixel is to be written to the display. If it's not set, the pixel is not to be written and the existing pixel in its location "shows through" the overlay.

This chapter does not discuss the use of overlaid images and transparency.

Targa files with 24 bits of color behave in the same way that 24-bit BMP files do, except that their order of the 3 bytes in each pixel is backwards. As such, each pixel consists of 3 bytes representing the blue, green, and red intensity. Each line of a 24-bit Targa image has a byte length that is three times the image width.

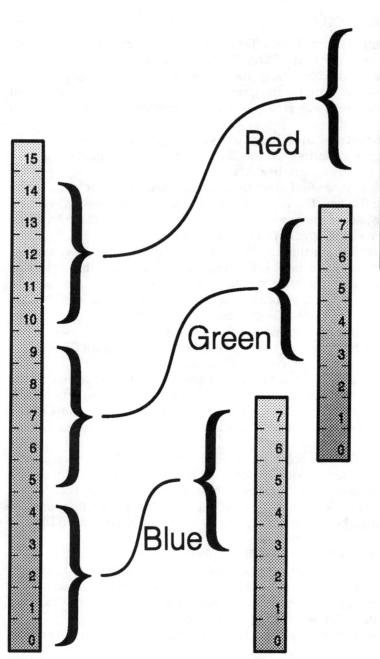

7-2 The structure of a 16-bit Targa pixel.

Targa files with 32 bits of color are structured just like 24-bit Targa files, except that there are 4 bytes of color information per pixel, instead of 3 bytes. The forth byte is called a blend value. If the high-order bit of a pixel is clear, the pixel consists of the three RGB values and the 4th byte is ignored. If it's set, the low-order 7 bits specify the degree to which the pixel color is to be blended with the color of the image being overlaid. This allows each pixel to range from completely transparent to completely opaque.

Blending colors to this extent is something that you can do with a Targa board. It's not really within the scope of the display hardware discussed in this book. As such, the fourth bit of a 32-bit Targa file's pixels is ignored in this discussion of the Targa format.

Targa storage issues

The most common applications for Targa images are in high-end photographic retouching, as a common output file for color scanning, and for complex computer-generated art (such as ray tracing). These applications all behave in much the same way whether or not they began with scanned photographs. The image data they involve is exceedingly complex and exhibits very little redundancy.

As touched on previously, 256-color pictures that started life as scanned originals can frequently be compressed to some degree using string-table compression. Bear in mind that not only do such images have an upper limit of 256 possible pixel values, but that the error-diffusion dithering process that got them into a 256-color format to begin with imposes a pattern of sorts on them. This makes it more likely that they'll be receptive to attempts to compress them.

True 24-bit images are very much less likely to compress. It's quite possible to create a Targa file in which no two pixels represent exactly the same color.

The Targa format does allow for a simple type of run-length compression, which compresses drawn Targa images to some extent. It invariably exhibits negative compression when it's confronted with a scanned picture. For this reason, compression is rarely used in Targa files. Scanned full-color images take up a lot of disk space—there isn't much you can do about this. To fully understand why scanned images are so troublesome, you should probably experience how a color scanner works. If this isn't practical, you might want to consider the image fragment in FIG. 7-3.

Figure 7-3 has been excised from another of those really useful test images. It's a scanned file of enormous dimensions and considerable resolution. The entire picture, 1024×768 pixels of it, is occupied by a woman's face. While looking at someone's face ''in real life'' might suggest that flesh tones are relatively homogeneous, a scanner sees them otherwise. Your eye tends to ignore minor variations in color and luminance unless you're deliberately looking for them. A scanner isn't quite this selective.

Consider that it takes only a variation of 1 bit in a row of pixels to break up a run-of-bytes field and reduce the compression efficiency of that line of image data.

There are fairly exotic compression algorithms, called *lossy* compres-

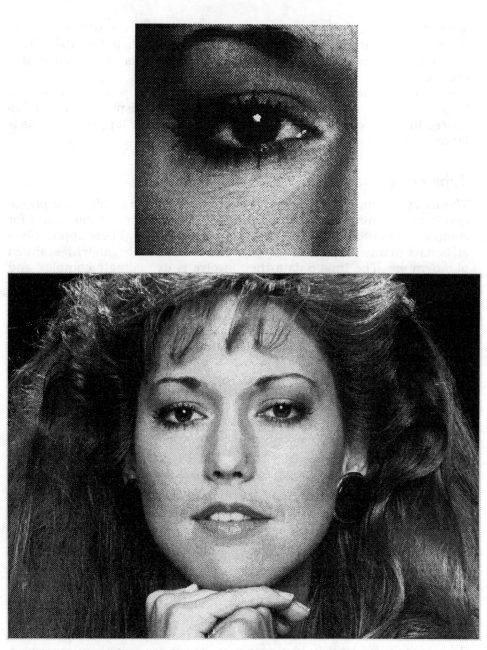

7-3 (A) A fragment of a scanned image, and (B) the image it was removed from. The original image bore the notice "AF Digits by Millard Brown."

sion, that seek to improve on the compression of images by throwing away small, arguably extraneous details and variations in color. One of the popular algorithms as of this writing is called JPEG compression. This sort of compression unquestionably does not allow you to unpack exactly the same image as you compressed; when it works well, it produces almost the same image, but with a substantial saving in storage space.

It's possible to choose source images that can be compressed this way with little or no apparent loss of detail. It's equally possible to choose images that deteriorate markedly. There's no obvious way to have your software tell them apart.

When your eye ignores minor color variations and presents you with relatively even flesh tones or color gradations, it's doing so with the benefit of a remarkably sophisticated intelligent processing system, something that computer software can't begin to duplicate. While your eye performs a type of lossy compression, it uses a very clever adaptive algorithm to do so.

The Targa format is intended to be used in high-end imaging applications—situations in which you would arguably value the quality of the images you'll be working with over the amount of storage space they require. Huge Targa files are something that users of high-end color-image processing software must live with.

As a final note in discussing image-file compression, you might consider that most of the images you'll find on bulletin boards exhibit artificially impressive compression ratios simply because they consist of a lot of blank space. Figure 7-4 is a typical GIF file.

This picture requires 126,463 bytes of disk storage and unpacks into 307,200 bytes of memory. The compressed file is about 41 percent of the size of the uncompressed image, which is a pretty substantial reduction.

7-4 This is a GIF file downloaded from Rose Media, (416) 733-2285, quite some time ago. It's illustrative of the art form in that it's a portrait mode image set into a landscape mode matte.

However, like most GIF files, this one really consists of a portrait-mode picture inset into a larger landscape mode matte so it can be displayed on a VGA monitor, which is a landscape mode display. If you were to crop out the actual image area and compress it as a separate file, it would occupy 126,463 bytes of disk space and unpack into 150,841 bytes of memory. The compressed image is 83 percent of the size of the source image, which isn't much compression to speak of. Note that this is an 8-bit image: as was noted previously, compression is even less effective when it's confronted with 24-bit pictures.

Targa file structure

A Targa file consists of a header, an optional palette area, and the stored image data for the picture it contains. Eight-bit color-mapped Targa files have a palette. The other formats don't require one.

The Targa specification from Truevision actually divides the Targa header into several smaller data structures. For the sake of this discussion, it's sufficient to view them as a single one. This is what it looks like:

```
typedef struct {
        char identsize;
        char colormaptype;
        char imagetype;
        unsigned int colormapstart;
        unsigned int colormaplength;
        char colormapbits;
        unsigned int xstart;
        unsigned int ystart;
        unsigned int width,depth;
        char bits;
        char descriptor;
        } TGAHEAD;
```

Note that a Targa file does not have an identification string or signature per se. If you rename some other sort of file with the extension ".TGA," a Targa reader could not immediately spot the switch. It should be able to figure out that its leg is being pulled as it analyzes the header data, however.

It might be that along with assuming that people who use high-end graphics hardware have large hard drives, the Targa designers also decided that these people were less absent-minded than people who were content to look at VGA cards.

The identsize field of a TGAHEAD structure represents the number of bytes that separate the header and whatever comes next. In most cases this will be a 0. However, some software that creates Targa files will put some identification after the header so you'll know where the files come from. For example, if you look at one of the example Targa files in

Truevision's Targa development kit, you'll find an instance of the `ident-size` field being used, as shown in FIG. 7-5.

Having read the first part of a Targa file into a TGAHEAD object, a Targa reader should seek forward by `identsize` bytes. If `identsize` is 0, this will have no effect. If it isn't a 0, it keeps the reader from attempting to interpret Truevision's notice in FIG. 7-5, for example, as the first few lines of image data.

```
17C8:0100  1A 00 0A 00 00 00 00 00-00 00 00 00 80 00 80 00   ................
17C8:0110  18 00 54 72 75 65 76 69-73 69 6F 6E 28 52 29 20   ..Truevision(R)
17C8:0120  53 61 6D 70 6C 65 20 49-6D 61 67 65 87 00 00 FF   Sample Image....
17C8:0130  87 00 FF 00 87 FF 00 00-87 00 00 00 87 00 00 FF   ................
17C8:0140  87 00 FF 00 87 FF 00 00-87 FF FF FF 87 00 00 FF   ................
17C8:0150  87 00 FF 00 87 FF 00 00-87 00 00 00 87 00 00 FF   ................
17C8:0160  87 00 FF 00 87 FF 00 00-87 FF FF FF 87 00 00 FF   ................
17C8:0170  87 00 FF 00 87 FF 00 00-87 00 00 00 87 00 00 FF   ................
```

7-5 Peeking at the beginning of a Truevision Targa test file.

The `colormaptype` field defines the type of color map being used in the file, assuming that one is being used at all. This will be a 0 for a file with monochrome or RGB color information, or 1 if there's a color map present. If there is a color map present, the `colormapstart` field specifies the color map index of the first color that the palette data defines and the `colormaplength` field specifies the number of colors that the color map contains. In most cases, these will be 0 and 256 respectively. It is, however, quite allowable for an image to define only some of the 256 colors in a palette, assuming that it won't be using the others.

The `imagetype` field of a Targa header defines the type and storage of the image in the file being read. It can contain one of several values, as follows:

1—Uncompressed palette-driven image
2—Uncompressed RGB image
3—Uncompressed monochrome image
9—Run-length encoded palette-driven image
10—Run-length encoded RGB image
11—Run-length encoded monochrome image

The Targa specification notes that values of 0 through 127 should be considered legal proprietary codes for image storage that Truevision might dream up in the future. Values from 128 and up can be used for custom storage types. In fact, these six values are all you're likely to encounter. As such, checking for the presence of one of these numbers in this field is a moderately safe way to make sure that your software actually has been given a Targa file to read.

The `xstart` and `ystart` fields represent the offset between the upper left corner of the image being read and the upper left corner of the screen it's to be displayed on. As with the other file formats discussed here, these fields are usually 0; they are ignored in the code in this chapter that reads Targa files.

The `width` and `depth` values represent the dimensions of the image in pixels. The `bits` value defines the number of bits of color it uses. This value will be 1, 8, 16, 24, or 32.

Note that it's possible to have an 8-bit Targa file without a color map. If you encounter one, you should assume that it has a gray-scale palette of the sort used in the 24-bit file readers discussed thus far.

Finally, the `descriptor` field is a collection of flags that indicate how the image data should be handled. Only 2 bits of the field are important for this discussion. Assuming that `tga` is an object of the type TGAHEAD, if `tga.descriptor AND 20H` is true, the file has been stored beginning with the last line of the source image. Otherwise, it has been stored normally. If `tga.descriptor AND 10H` is true, each line has been stored reversed left to right, such that it would look like a mirror image if it were displayed normally.

Figure 7-6 is a table that associates the effective origin, the location of the first displayed pixel of an image, with the setting of these 2 bits of the `descriptor` field.

The lower 4 bits of the `descriptor` field indicate the number of bits available for overlays, something that isn't relevant to this chapter. The upper 2 bits are currently unused.

Once the Targa header and the color-map information, if it exists, have been read, the next byte in the file is the first byte of the image.

Most of the Targa files you'll encounter will be stored uncompressed, for reasons previously discussed. In this case, the number of bytes to read for each line can be worked out from the width of the file and the number of bits of color it supports, as follows:

```
 1 bit – bytes = (width + 7) / 8
 8 bit – bytes = width
16 bit – bytes = width * 2
24 bit – bytes = width * 3
32 bit – bytes = width * 4
```

Reading a line from an uncompressed Targa file involves little more than inhaling the appropriate number of bytes into a buffer. However, note that the format of lines with more than 8 color bits is peculiar to the Targa format. In most cases you'll want to deal with them all as normal 24-bit RGB lines, as discussed when we looked at 24-bit BMP files. This is the way the later code in this book expects to see them.

If you encounter a 16-bit Targa file, its 2-byte pixels should be unpacked into 3-byte RGB pixels. The order of the 3-byte RGB pixels in a 24-bit Targa line should be adjusted. The 4-byte pixels in a 32-bit Targa line should be reduced to 3 bytes. As such, full-color Targa lines, while easy to read, do require some massaging before you can use them with code that expects to work with standard RGB color information.

Bit 5 = 1, bit 4 = 0   Bit 5=1, bit 4 = 1

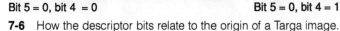

Bit 5 = 0, bit 4 = 0   Bit 5 = 0, bit 4 = 1

7-6 How the descriptor bits relate to the origin of a Targa image.

Run-length encoded Targa files must be unpacked in addition to the foregoing data manipulation. This is pretty simple; Targa run-length encoding is agreeably uncomplicated. It might be argued that a function that is almost never used can get away without doing very much.

Compressed Targa lines appear in Targa files with `imagetype` values of 9, 10, and 11. In this case, the first byte of a line is the first byte of a compressed field, and should be regarded as a key byte. The length of the field will be one more than the value held in the low-order 7 bits. If the high-order bit is set, the field is a run of pixels. If it's not set, the field is a string.

It's important to keep in mind, when you're looking at Targa run-length compression, that with the exception of monochrome TGA files, all the fields work in pixels rather than in bytes. The number of bytes in a pixel varies with the number of bits of color in the file. As such, a compressed field with a length of 10 in a file with 24 bits of color would actually involve 30 bytes of uncompressed data—that's ten pixels of 3-bytes each.

Once one field of a line has been uncompressed, the next byte read from the file should be regarded as being the key byte of the next field. The process should be repeated until a whole line is unpacked. As with most other image file formats, compressed Targa lines are constrained to end on even line boundaries.

The only thing that makes Targa files even mildly complicated to deal with is their relatively large number of modes and pixel formats. None of this is really unworkable, however, and despite their fairly exotic, high-end aspects, Targa files are among the least involved image files to write code for.

Just make sure that all the blue and red areas in your test images are as they should be, lest you turn out to have forgotten to reverse the RGB byte order.

A Targa reader

As with 24-bit BMP files, the following simple Targa reader will handle files having more than 8 bits of color as gray-scale images. This is a shame in looking at Targa files, as one encounters such interesting images in them. Code that allows you to do more with the RGB color file facilities can be found later. Figure 7-7 illustrates the code for READTGA.

```
/*
        TGA reader - copyright (c) 1991
        Alchemy Mindworks Inc.
*/

#include "stdio.h"
#include "dos.h"
#include "alloc.h"

/*                              uncomment this line if you
#include "memmangr.h"           will be linking in the memory manager
*/

#define GOOD_READ       0       /* return codes */
#define BAD_FILE        1
#define BAD_READ        2
#define MEMORY_ERROR    3

#define SCREENWIDE      320     /* mode 13 screen dimensions */
#define SCREENDEEP      200
#define STEP            32      /* size of a step when panning */

#define HOME            0x4700  /* cursor control codes */
#define CURSOR_UP       0x4800
#define CURSOR_LEFT     0x4b00
#define CURSOR_RIGHT    0x4d00
#define END             0x4f00
#define CURSOR_DOWN     0x5000
```

7-7 The source code for READTGA.

```
#define RGB_RED         0
#define RGB_GREEN       1
#define RGB_BLUE        2
#define RGB_SIZE        3

#define pixels2bytes(n)    ((n+7)/8)

#define greyvalue(r,g,b)         (((r*30)/100) + ((g*59)/100) + ((b*11)/100))

typedef struct {
        int width,depth,bytes,bits;
        int background;
        char palette[768];
        int (*setup)();
        int (*closedown)();
        } FILEINFO;

typedef struct {
        char identsize;
        char colourmaptype;
        char imagetype;
        unsigned int colourmapstart;
        unsigned int colourmaplength;
        char colourmapbits;
        unsigned int xstart;
        unsigned int ystart;
        unsigned int width,depth;
        char bits;
        char descriptor;
        } TGAHEAD;
        char *farPtr(char *p,long l);
        char *getline(unsigned int n);
        char *mono2vga(char *p,int width);
        char *rgb2vga(char *p,int width);
        int dosetup(FILEINFO *fi);
        int doclosedown(FILEINFO *fi);

        int putline(char *p,unsigned int n);

        char masktable[8]={0x80,0x40,0x20,0x10,0x08,0x04,0x02,0x01};

        FILEINFO fi;
        char *buffer=NULL;

        main(argc,argv)
                int argc;
                char *argv[];
        {
                FILE *fp;
                static char results[8][16] = {  "Ok",
                                                "Bad file",
                                                "Bad read",
```

7-7 Continued.

```
                                        "Memory error",
                                };

        char path[81];
        int r;

        if(argc > 1) {
                strmfe(path,argv[1],"TGA");
                strupr(path);
                if((fp = fopen(path,"rb")) != NULL) {
                        fi.setup=dosetup;
                        fi.closedown=doclosedown;
                        r=unpacktga(fp,&fi);
                        printf("\%s",results[r]);
                        fclose(fp);
                } else printf("Error opening %s",path);
        } else puts("Argument:       path to a TGA file");
}

/* unpack a TGA file */
unpacktga(fp,fi)
        FILE *fp;
        FILEINFO *fi;
{

        TGAHEAD tga;
        char *p,*pr;
        int i,n,startline,endline,incline;

        /* set a default monochrome palette */
        memcpy(fi->palette,"\000\000\000\377\377\377",6);

        /* get the header */
        if(fread((char *)&tga,1,sizeof(TGAHEAD),fp)==sizeof(TGAHEAD)) {

                if(tga.imagetype==0x01 ||
                   tga.imagetype==0x02 ||
                   tga.imagetype==0x03 ||
                   tga.imagetype==0x09 ||
                   tga.imagetype==0x0a ||
                   tga.imagetype==0x0b) {

                        /* set the details */
                        fi->width=tga.width;
                        fi->depth=tga.depth;
                        fi->bits=tga.bits;

                        /* work out the line width */
                        if(fi->bits==1) fi->bytes=pixels2bytes(fi->width);
                        else if(fi->bits==8) fi->bytes=fi->width;
                        else fi->bytes=fi->width*3;

                        fseek(fp,(long)tga.identsize,SEEK_CUR);
```

7-7 Continued.

```
                /* get the palette */
                if(tga.colourmaptype) {
                        switch(tga.colourmapbits) {
                                case 24:
                                        for(i=tga.colourmapstart;i<tga.colourmaplength;++i) {
                                                if(i >= 768) break;
                                                fi->palette[i*RGB_SIZE+RGB_BLUE]=fgetc(fp);
                                                fi->palette[i*RGB_SIZE+RGB_GREEN]=fgetc(fp);
                                                fi->palette[i*RGB_SIZE+RGB_RED]=fgetc(fp);
                                        }
                                        break;
                                case 16:
                                        for(i=tga.colourmapstart;i<tga.colourmaplength;++i) {
                                                if(i >= 768) break;
                                                n=fgetword(fp);
                                                fi->palette[i*RGB_SIZE+RGB_BLUE]=((n >> 10) & 0x1f) << ॏ
                                                fi->palette[i*RGB_SIZE+RGB_GREEN]=((n >> 5) & 0x1f) << ॏ
                                                fi->palette[i*RGB_SIZE+RGB_RED]=(n & 0x1f) << 3;
                                        }
                                        break;
                        }
                }

                if(fi->bits > 8) {
                        for(i=0;i<256;++i)
                            memset(fi->palette+(i*RGB_SIZE),i,RGB_SIZE);
                }
                else if(fi->bits==1) memcpy(fi->palette,"\000\000\000\377\377\377",6);

                /* allocate a line buffer */
                if((p=malloc(fi->bytes)) != NULL) {

                        if((fi->setup)(fi) != GOOD_READ) {
                                free(p);
                                return(MEMORY_ERROR);
                        }

                        if(!(tga.descriptor & 0x20)) {
                                startline=fi->depth-1;
                                endline=-1;
                                incline=-1;
                        }
                        else {
                                startline=0;
                                endline=fi->depth;
                                incline=1;
                        }

                        /* read all the lines */
                        for(i=startline;i != endline;i+=incline) {
                                if(readtgaline(p,fp,&tga)) {
                                        free(p);
```

7-7 Continued.

```
                                        freebuffer();
                                        return(BAD_READ);
                        }

                        /* translate the line types into VGA */
                        switch(fi->bits) {
                                case 1:
                                        pr=mono2vga(p,fi->width);
                                        if(pr != NULL) {
                                                reverse(pr,&tga);
                                                putline(pr,i);
                                                free(pr);
                                        }
                                        else {
                                                free(p);
                                                return(MEMORY_ERROR);
                                        }
                                        break;
                                case 8:
                                        reverse(p,&tga);
                                        putline(p,i);
                                        break;
                                case 16:
                                case 24:
                                case 32:
                                        pr=rgb2vga(p,fi->width);
                                        if(pr != NULL) {
                                                reverse(pr,&tga);
                                                putline(pr,i);
                                                free(pr);
                                        }
                                        else {
                                                free(p);
                                                return(MEMORY_ERROR);
                                        }
                                        break;
                        }
                }
                (fi->closedown)(fi);
                free(p);
                return(GOOD_READ);
        } else return(MEMORY_ERROR);
    } else return(BAD_FILE);
  } else return(BAD_READ);
}

/* reverse one line left for right needs be */
reverse(p,tga)
        char *p;
        TGAHEAD *tga;
{
        char *pr;
```

7-7 Continued.

```
                   int i;

                   if(!(tga->descriptor & 0x10)) return;
                   if((pr=malloc(tga->width)) != NULL) {
                           for(i=0;i<tga->width;++i) pr[i]=p[tga->width-1-i];
                           memcpy(p,pr,tga->width);
                           free(pr);
                   }
          }

          /* read one line in the appropriate mode */
          readtgaline(p,fp,tga)
                   char *p;
                   FILE *fp;
                   TGAHEAD *tga;
          {

                   int c,i,n=0,size;
                   int r,g,b,linesize;

                   if(tga->bits==1) linesize=pixels2bytes(tga->width);
                   else linesize=tga->width;

                   /* handle uncompressed lines */
                   if(tga->imagetype==0x01 ||
                      tga->imagetype==0x02 ||
                      tga->imagetype==0x03) {
                           switch(tga->bits) {
                                   case 1:
                                           fread(p,1,pixels2bytes(tga->width),fp);
                                           break;
                                   case 8:
                                           fread(p,1,tga->width,fp);
                                           break;
                                   case 16:
                                           for(i=0;i<tga->width;++i) {
                                                   c=fgetword(fp);
                                                   r=((c >> 10) & 0x1f) << 3;
                                                   g=((c >> 5) & 0x1f) << 3;
                                                   b=(c & 0x1f) << 3;
                                                   *p++=r;
                                                   *p++=g;
                                                   *p++=b;
                                           }
                                           break;
                                   case 24:
                                           for(i=0;i<tga->width;++i) {
                                                   b=fgetc(fp);
                                                   g=fgetc(fp);
                                                   r=fgetc(fp);
                                                   *p++=r;
                                                   *p++=g;
                                                   *p++=b;
```

7-7 Continued.

```
                        }
                        break;
        case 32:
                        for(i=0;i<tga->width;++i) {
                                b=fgetc(fp);
                                g=fgetc(fp);
                                r=fgetc(fp);
                                fgetc(fp);
                                *p++=r;
                                *p++=g;
                                *p++=b;
                        }
                        break;
        }
}

/* handle compressed lines */
else {
        do {
                c=fgetc(fp);
                size=(c & 0x7f)+1;
                n+=size;
                if(c & 0x80) {
                        switch(tga->bits) {
                                case 1:
                                case 8:
                                        c=fgetc(fp);
                                        for(i=0;i<size;++i) *p++=c;
                                        break;
                                case 16:
                                        c=fgetword(fp);
                                        r=((c >> 10) & 0x1f) << 3;
                                        g=((c >> 5) & 0x1f) << 3;
                                        b=(c & 0x1f) << 3;
                                        for(i=0;i<size;++i) {
                                                *p++=r;
                                                *p++=g;
                                                *p++=b;
                                        }
                                        break;
                                case 24:
                                        b=fgetc(fp);
                                        g=fgetc(fp);
                                        r=fgetc(fp);
                                        for(i=0;i<size;++i) {
                                                *p++=r;
                                                *p++=g;
                                                *p++=b;
                                        }
                                        break;
                                case 32:
                                        b=fgetc(fp);
```

7-7 Continued.

```
                              g=fgetc(fp);
                              r=fgetc(fp);
                              fgetc(fp);
                              for(i=0;i<size;++i) {
                                     *p++=r;
                                     *p++=g;
                                     *p++=b;
                              }
                              break;
                    }
            }
            else {
                 switch(tga->bits) {
                      case 1:
                      case 8:
                              for(i=0;i<size;++i) *p++=fgetc(fp);
                              break;
                      case 16:
                              for(i=0;i<size;++i) {
                                     c=fgetword(fp);
                                     r=((c >> 10) & 0x1f) << 3;
                                     g=((c >> 5) & 0x1f) << 3;
                                     b=(c & 0x1f) << 3;
                                     *p++=r;
                                     *p++=g;
                                     *p++=b;
                              }
                              break;
                      case 24:
                              for(i=0;i<size;++i) {
                                     b=fgetc(fp);
                                     g=fgetc(fp);
                                     r=fgetc(fp);
                                     *p++=r;
                                     *p++=g;
                                     *p++=b;
                              }
                              break;
                      case 32:
                              for(i=0;i<size;++i) {
                                     b=fgetc(fp);
                                     g=fgetc(fp);
                                     r=fgetc(fp);
                                     fgetc(fp);
                                     *p++=r;
                                     *p++=g;
                                     *p++=b;
                              }
                              break;
                  }
            }
} while(n < linesize);
```

7-7 Continued.

```
                }

                return(ferror(fp));
}

/* convert a monochrome line into an eight bit line */
char *mono2vga(p,width)
        char *p;
        int width;
{

        char *pr;
        int i;

        if((pr=malloc(width)) != NULL) {
                for(i=0;i<width;++i) {
                        if(p[i >> 3] & masktable[i & 0x0007])
                                pr[i]=1;
                        else
                                pr[i]=0;
                }
                return(pr);
        } else return(NULL);
}

/* convert an RGB line into an eight bit line */
char *rgb2vga(p,width)
        char *p;
        int width;
{

        char *pr;
        int i;

        if((pr=malloc(width)) != NULL) {
                for(i=0;i<width;++i) {
                        pr[i]=greyvalue(p[RGB_RED],p[RGB_GREEN],p[RGB_BLUE]);
                        p+=RGB_SIZE;
                }
                return(pr);
        } else return(NULL);
}

fgetword(fp)
        FILE *fp;
{
        return((fgetc(fp) & 0xff) + ((fgetc(fp) & 0xff) << 8));
}

/* This function is called before an image is unpacked */
dosetup(fi)
        FILEINFO *fi;
{
        union REGS r;
```

7-7 Continued.

```
                    if(!getbuffer((long)fi->width*(long)fi->depth,fi->width,fi->depth))
                        return(MEMORY_ERROR);

                    r.x.ax=0x0013;
                    int86(0x10,&r,&r);

                    setvgapalette(fi->palette,256,fi->background);

                    return(GOOD_READ);
            }

/* This function is called after an image has been unpacked. It must
    display the image and deallocate memory. */
doclosedown(fi)
            FILEINFO *fi;
{
            union REGS r;
            int c,i,n,x=0,y=0;

            if(fi->width > SCREENWIDE) n=SCREENWIDE;
            else n=fi->width;

            do {
                    for(i=0;i<SCREENDEEP;++i) {
                            c=y+i;
                            if(c>=fi->depth) break;
                            memcpy(MK_FP(0xa000,SCREENWIDE*i),getline(c)+x,n);
                    }
                    c=GetKey();
                    switch(c) {
                            case CURSOR_LEFT:
                                    if((x-STEP) > 0) x-=STEP;
                                    else x=0;
                                    break;
                            case CURSOR_RIGHT:
                                    if((x+STEP+SCREENWIDE) < fi->width) x+=STEP;
                                    else if(fi->width > SCREENWIDE)
                                        x=fi->width-SCREENWIDE;
                                    else x=0;
                                    break;
                            case CURSOR_UP:
                                    if((y-STEP) > 0) y-=STEP;
                                    else y=0;
                                    break;
                            case CURSOR_DOWN:
                                    if((y+STEP+SCREENDEEP) < fi->depth) y+=STEP;
                                    else if(fi->depth > SCREENDEEP)
                                        y=fi->depth-SCREENDEEP;
                                    else y=0;
                                    break;
                            case HOME:
                                    x=y=0;
```

7-7 Continued.

```
                                     break;
                          case END:
                                     if(fi->width > SCREENWIDE)
                                          x=fi->width-SCREENWIDE;
                                     else x=0;
                                     if(fi->depth > SCREENDEEP)
                                          y=fi->depth-SCREENDEEP;
                                     else y=0;
                                     break;
                    }
          } while(c != 27);

          freebuffer();

          r.x.ax=0x0003;
          int86(0x10,&r,&r);
          return(GOOD_READ);
}

/* get one extended key code */
GetKey()
{
          int c;

          c = getch();
          if(!(c & 0x00ff)) c = getch() << 8;
          return(c);
}

/* set the VGA palette and background */
setvgapalette(p,n,b)
          char *p;
          int n,b;
{
          union REGS r;
          int i;

          outp(0x3c6,0xff);
          for(i=0;i<n;++i) {
                    outp(0x3c8,i);
                    outp(0x3c9,(*p++) >> 2);
                    outp(0x3c9,(*p++) >> 2);
                    outp(0x3c9,(*p++) >> 2);
          }
          r.x.ax=0x1001;
          r.h.bh=b;
          int86(0x10,&r,&r);
}

/* make file name with specific extension */
strmfe(new,old,ext)
          char *new,*old,*ext;
```

7-7 Continued.

```
        {
                while(*old != 0 && *old != '.') *new++=*old++;
                *new++='.';
                while(*ext) *new++=*ext++;
                *new=0;
        }

/* if you don't use in the memory manager, these functions
   will stand in for it */

#if !MEMMANGR

/* return a far pointer plus a long integer */
char *farPtr(p,l)
        char *p;
        long l;
{
        unsigned int seg,off;

        seg = FP_SEG(p);
        off = FP_OFF(p);
        seg += (off / 16);
        off &= 0x000f;
        off += (unsigned int)(l & 0x000fL);
        seg += (l / 16L);
        p = MK_FP(seg,off);
        return(p);
}

/* save one line to memory */
putline(p,n)
        char *p;
        unsigned int n;
{
        if(n >= 0 && n < fi.depth)
            memcpy(farPtr(buffer,(long)n*(long)fi.width),p,fi.width);
}

/* get one line from memory */
char *getline(n)
        unsigned int n;
{
        return(farPtr(buffer,(long)n*(long)fi.width));
}

#pragma warn -par
getbuffer(n,bytes,lines)
        unsigned long n;
        int bytes,lines;
{
        if((buffer=farmalloc(n)) == NULL) return(0);
        else return(1);
```

7-7 Continued.

```
        }

freebuffer()
{
        if(buffer != NULL) farfree(buffer);
        buffer=NULL;
}
#endif /* !MEMMANGR */
```

7-7 Continued.

The unpacktga function in READTGA contains most of the Targa-specific code in the program. It begins by reading the Targa header into a TGAHEAD object and checking to see that the file purports to contain an image type that it recognizes. It then extracts the file dimensions and works out how big a line buffer it needs. Next, it seeks past anything tacked onto the end of the header.

The color map, if it exists, gets read next. In this reader, because images with more than 8 bits of color must be displayed in gray scale, a synthetic gray-level color map is created if no proper palette is read.

Each line is read from the source file by calling readtgaline, which handles reading raw bytes or uncompressing lines as is required. It also translates lines with 16, 24 and 32-bit pixels into a standard 24-bit RGB format.

Note that the line numbers may increase or decrease with each line, depending upon the contents of the TGAHEAD descriptor byte. Likewise, the unpacked lines may be reversed.

The actual display code is unchanged from that of the readers presented in previous chapters.

In creating READTGA, a number of the features of Targa files have clearly been ignored. Most notably, this code throws away all the Targa overlay and transparency information, inasmuch as it's not needed to merely view Targa images. You might want to augment the Targa reader code to work these facilities back in if you can come up with a use for them.

As a rule, you can utilize the specific extensions of particular formats such as Targa if you'll be writing programs that work only with one image-file format. For example, the Graphic Workshop package included on the companion disk is limited to using those things common to all formats. It would be impractical to have it work with transparency and overlays in 24-bit images when only one of the several 24-bit formats it supports knows anything about them.

A standard 24-bit test file

While the color data structure of 24-bit BMP files, discussed in chapter 5, was pretty standard, the odd pixel order of Targa files makes it possible to correctly read a TGA file without necessarily interpreting its colors correctly. As touched on earlier, this is not necessarily easy to spot in many types of test images because the subjects may not make it obvious in which colors they're intended to be rendered.

A standard 24-bit test file is very useful in this regard, as it's easy to interpret and not open to any ambiguities as to what colors it should contain. If you generate a binary file with fixed colors, they should appear as you'd expect them in a subsequent test Targa file that your TGA writer code generates, assuming that your Targa writer is working correctly.

Such a file can also be used as a source file for WRITEBMP, discussed in chapter 5.

It's pretty easy to create saturated solid RGB colors mathematically. Allowing that each of the three color indices can be either 0 or 255 (0 is fully off and 255 is fully on), the following eight colors can be generated:

Color	Red	Green	Blue
Black	0	0	0
Red	255	0	0
Green	0	255	0
Blue	0	0	255
Cyan	0	255	255
Magenta	255	0	255
Yellow	255	255	0
White	255	255	255

It's possible to create lines with specific color areas by simply filling them in with 3-byte pixels drawn from this list.

You can generate different intensities of these colors by using some value other than 255 for the nonzero intensity elements. For example, the pixel (128,0,0) would be half intensity red, (64,0,0) would be very dark red and so on.

The source code in FIG. 7-8 illustrates a simple program called MAKERGB.C that generates a standard binary file containing a synthetic test image. The image has eight horizontal bands. The top band consists of eight saturated blocks in the eight colors specified above. They're also stored in the above order. If your Targa writer doesn't produce them this way, you'll know that something's amiss.

```
/*
        RGB binary test file generator - copyright (c) 1991
        Alchemy Mindworks Inc.
*/

#include "stdio.h"
#include "dos.h"
#include "alloc.h"

#define GOOD_WRITE      0       /* return codes */
```

7-8 The source code for MAKERGB.

```
#define MEMORY_ERROR      1
#define BAD_WRITE         2

#define RGB_RED           0
#define RGB_GREEN         1
#define RGB_BLUE          2
#define RGB_SIZE          3

#define BINARYSIG         "ALCHBINR"

#define FILEWIDTH         320     /* the file diemsnions - make */
#define FILEDEPTH         400     /* these anything you like */

#define BANDCOUNT         8
#define BANDSIZE          (FILEDEPTH/BANDCOUNT)

#define pixels2bytes(n)   ((n+7)/8)

typedef struct {
        char sign[8];
        int width,depth,bits;
        char palette[768];
        } BINARYHEADER;

char *getline(unsigned int n);

char masktable[8]={0x80,0x40,0x20,0x10,0x08,0x04,0x02,0x01};

char *buffer=NULL;

main()
{
        FILE *fp;
        static char results[3][16] = {  "Ok",
                                        "Memory error",
                                        "Bad write"
                                        };

        int r;

        if((fp = fopen("RGBTEST.BIN","wb")) != NULL) {
                r=writergb(fp);
                printf("\%s",results[r]);
        } else puts("Error creating RGBTEST");
}
/* write a test file */
writergb(fp)
        FILE *fp;
{
        BINARYHEADER bh;
        char *p;
        double r,g,b;
        int i,j,bytes,depth=0;
```

7-8 Continued.

```
                        /* work out the line size */
                        bytes=FILEWIDTH * RGB_SIZE;

                        /* set up the binary header */
                        memset((char *)&bh,0,sizeof(BINARYHEADER));
                        memcpy(bh.sign,BINARYSIG,8);
                        bh.width=FILEWIDTH;
                        bh.depth=FILEDEPTH;
                        bh.bits=24;

                        /* write the header */
                        if(fwrite((char *)&bh,1,sizeof(BINARYHEADER),fp) !=
                            sizeof(BINARYHEADER)) return(BAD_WRITE);

                        /* allocate a buffer */
                        if((p=malloc(bytes)) == NULL) return(MEMORY_ERROR);

                        /* make a line with eight colour blocks in it */
                        i=0;
                        j=FILEWIDTH/8;

                        /* make black band */
                        for(;i<(j*1);++i) {
                                p[i*RGB_SIZE+RGB_RED]=0;
                                p[i*RGB_SIZE+RGB_GREEN]=0;
                                p[i*RGB_SIZE+RGB_BLUE]=0;
                        }

                        /* make red band */
                        for(;i<(j*2);++i) {
                                p[i*RGB_SIZE+RGB_RED]=0xff;
                                p[i*RGB_SIZE+RGB_GREEN]=0;
                                p[i*RGB_SIZE+RGB_BLUE]=0;
                        }

                        /* make green band */
                        for(;i<(j*3);++i) {
                                p[i*RGB_SIZE+RGB_RED]=0;
                                p[i*RGB_SIZE+RGB_GREEN]=0xff;
                                p[i*RGB_SIZE+RGB_BLUE]=0;
                        }

                        /* make blue band */
                        for(;i<(j*4);++i) {
                                p[i*RGB_SIZE+RGB_RED]=0;
                                p[i*RGB_SIZE+RGB_GREEN]=0;
                                p[i*RGB_SIZE+RGB_BLUE]=0xff;
                        }

                        /* make cyan band */
                        for(;i<(j*5);++i) {
                                p[i*RGB_SIZE+RGB_RED]=0;
```

7-8 Continued.

```
                p[i*RGB_SIZE+RGB_GREEN]=0xff;
                p[i*RGB_SIZE+RGB_BLUE]=0xff;
        }


        /* make magenta band */
        for(;i<(j*6);++i) {
                p[i*RGB_SIZE+RGB_RED]=0xff;
                p[i*RGB_SIZE+RGB_GREEN]=0;
                p[i*RGB_SIZE+RGB_BLUE]=0xff;
        }


        /* make yellow band */
        for(;i<(j*7);++i) {
                p[i*RGB_SIZE+RGB_RED]=0xff;
                p[i*RGB_SIZE+RGB_GREEN]=0xff;
                p[i*RGB_SIZE+RGB_BLUE]=0;
        }


        /* make white band */
        for(;i<(j*8);++i) {
                p[i*RGB_SIZE+RGB_RED]=0xff;
                p[i*RGB_SIZE+RGB_GREEN]=0xff;
                p[i*RGB_SIZE+RGB_BLUE]=0xff;
        }


        /* write the saturated colour stripe band */
        for(;depth<(BANDSIZE*1);++depth) fwrite(p,1,bytes,fp);


        /* write the gradated red band */
        r=g=b=0.0;
        for(i=0;i<FILEWIDTH;++i) {
                p[i*RGB_SIZE+RGB_RED]=(char)r;
                p[i*RGB_SIZE+RGB_GREEN]=(char)g;
                p[i*RGB_SIZE+RGB_BLUE]=(char)b;
                r+=(double)256/FILEWIDTH;
        }
        for(;depth<(BANDSIZE*2);++depth) {
                printf("\rWriting line %u",depth);
                fwrite(p,1,bytes,fp);
        }


        /* write the gradated green band */
        r=g=b=0.0;
        for(i=0;i<FILEWIDTH;++i) {
                p[i*RGB_SIZE+RGB_RED]=(char)r;
                p[i*RGB_SIZE+RGB_GREEN]=(char)g;
                p[i*RGB_SIZE+RGB_BLUE]=(char)b;
                g+=(double)256/FILEWIDTH;
        }
        for(;depth<(BANDSIZE*3);++depth) {
                printf("\rWriting line %u",depth);
                fwrite(p,1,bytes,fp);
```

7-8 Continued.

```
                }

                /* write the gradated blue band */
                r=g=b=0.0;
                for(i=0;i<FILEWIDTH;++i) {
                        p[i*RGB_SIZE+RGB_RED]=(char)r;
                        p[i*RGB_SIZE+RGB_GREEN]=(char)g;
                        p[i*RGB_SIZE+RGB_BLUE]=(char)b;
                        b+=(double)256/FILEWIDTH;

                }
                for(;depth<(BANDSIZE*4);++depth) {
                        printf("\rWriting line %u",depth);
                        fwrite(p,1,bytes,fp);
                }

                /* write the gradated cyan band */
                r=g=b=0.0;
                for(i=0;i<FILEWIDTH;++i) {
                        p[i*RGB_SIZE+RGB_RED]=(char)r;
                        p[i*RGB_SIZE+RGB_GREEN]=(char)g;
                        p[i*RGB_SIZE+RGB_BLUE]=(char)b;
                        g+=(double)256/FILEWIDTH;
                        b+=(double)256/FILEWIDTH;
                }
                for(;depth<(BANDSIZE*5);++depth) {
                        printf("\rWriting line %u",depth);
                        fwrite(p,1,bytes,fp);
                }

                /* write the gradated magenta band */
                r=g=b=0.0;
                for(i=0;i<FILEWIDTH;++i) {
                        p[i*RGB_SIZE+RGB_RED]=(char)r;
                        p[i*RGB_SIZE+RGB_GREEN]=(char)g;
                        p[i*RGB_SIZE+RGB_BLUE]=(char)b;
                        r+=(double)256/FILEWIDTH;
                        b+=(double)256/FILEWIDTH;
                }
                for(;depth<(BANDSIZE*6);++depth) {
                        printf("\rWriting line %u",depth);
                        fwrite(p,1,bytes,fp);
                }

                /* write the gradated yellow band */
                r=g=b=0.0;
                for(i=0;i<FILEWIDTH;++i) {
                        p[i*RGB_SIZE+RGB_RED]=(char)r;
                        p[i*RGB_SIZE+RGB_GREEN]=(char)g;
                        p[i*RGB_SIZE+RGB_BLUE]=(char)b;
                        r+=(double)256/FILEWIDTH;
                        g+=(double)256/FILEWIDTH;
```

7-8 Continued.

```
    }
for(;depth<(BANDSIZE*7);++depth) {
        printf("\rWriting line %u",depth);
        fwrite(p,1,bytes,fp);
    }


/* write the gradated white band */
r=g=b=0.0;
for(i=0;i<FILEWIDTH;++i) {
        p[i*RGB_SIZE+RGB_RED]=(char)r;
        p[i*RGB_SIZE+RGB_GREEN]=(char)g;
        p[i*RGB_SIZE+RGB_BLUE]=(char)b;
        r+=(double)256/FILEWIDTH;
        g+=(double)256/FILEWIDTH;
        b+=(double)256/FILEWIDTH;
    }
for(;depth<(BANDSIZE*8);++depth) {
                printf("\rWriting line %u",depth);
                fwrite(p,1,bytes,fp);
        }

        free(p);
        if(!ferror(fp)) return(GOOD_WRITE);
        else return(BAD_WRITE);
    }
```

7-8 Continued.

The remaining seven bands are gradations from black to full intensity of the latter seven colors.

If you run the TESTRGB.BIN file that MAKERGB creates through WRITEBMP or WRITETGB, discussed momentarily, it should leave you with the same image in whatever format you've selected. The best way to make sure that all the colors are correct is to use the 24-bit preview mode of Graphic Workshop. While it does a fairly crunchy 8-color dither, it shows you fairly accurate approximations of 24-bit colors. If you attempt to view RGBTEST.TGA with Graphic Workshop, the menu in FIG. 7-9 will appear.

There are three color dithers available in the 24-bit preview mode of Graphic Workshop. As discussed later in this book, these are presented in order of increasing image quality and decreasing processing speed. For the sake of a simple color check, the first one (the Floyd color dither), is accurate enough. If you select it you'll see an image like the one in FIG. 7-10, except that it will be in color.

Note that the rounded corners in the graduated blocks are an irregularity introduced by the 8-color dither of Graphic Workshop. The actual image in the file doesn't look like this.

```
┌─[ Adjust colours ]─────────────┐
│ Display normally               │
│ ████Display as grey████████████│
│ Remap fixed                    │
│ Remap quantized                │
│ Bayer dither mono              │
│ Floyd dither mono              │
│ Burkes dither mono             │
│ Stucki dither mono             │
│ Threshold                      │
│ Floyd dither colour            │
│ Burkes dither colour           │
│ Stucki dither colour           │
│ Display reversed               │
└────────────────────────────────┘
```

7-9 The view options menu of Graphic Workshop.

7-10 The 8-color preview mode of Graphic Workshop displaying the MAKERGB test file. Of course, there were eight colors in the display, rather than eight levels of gray.

Writing Targa files

While it's arguably important to be able to read run-length-encoded Targa files because your software might find itself confronted by one, there's little practical reason to create them. For previously discussed reasons, the sorts of applications Targa files are typically used for don't require them. This discussion of a Targa writer looks at creating type 1, 2, and 3 TGA files—that is, uncompressed images.

Likewise, inasmuch as most RGB color images are dealt with using 24-bit pixels, there isn't much reason for creating Targa files with 16 or 32 bits of color. The Targa writer discussed here writes 24-bit Targa files when it's confronted with a 24-bit source binary file.

You might have cause to add these omitted features back into the writer code if your application calls for them. A function to run-length encode Targa lines can be easily derived from the run-length encoding used for other formats discussed in this book, such as the one in chapter 3. Converting 24-bit color pixels to the other two RGB formats supported by Targa files involves little more than some bit shifting for 16-bit files and simply tacking an extra byte onto each 3-byte RGB value for 32-bit ones.

The WRITETGA program is illustrated in FIG. 7-11. It reads binary files created by MAKEBIN and MAKEBIN2, discussed in chapter 6, and by MAKERGB. The latter is probably the best source of test images if you'll be modifying this code, and subsequently find that you have to debug it.

The most interesting part of the WRITETGA program is the function `writetga`. It probably won't require much explanation if you've worked your way through the file writers previously discussed in this book. Inasmuch as the Targa format isn't all that complex to begin with, and as many of its potentially awkward features can be ignored in writing TGA files, very little data manipulation actually need take place in `writetga`.

```
/*

        TGA writer - copyright (c) 1991
        Alchemy Mindworks Inc.
*/

#include "stdio.h"
#include "alloc.h"

#define BINARYSIG       "ALCHBINR"       /* binary identification */

#define GOOD_WRITE      0       /* return codes */
#define BAD_WRITE       1
#define BAD_READ        2
#define MEMORY_ERROR    3

#define RGB_RED         0
#define RGB_GREEN       1
#define RGB_BLUE        2
```

7-11 The source code for WRITETGA.

```
#define RGB_SIZE        3

#define pixels2bytes(n)     ((n+7)/8)

typedef struct {
        char sign[8];
        int width,depth,bits;
        char palette[768];
        } BINARYHEADER;

typedef struct {
        char identsize;
        char colourmaptype;
        char imagetype;
        unsigned int colourmapstart;
        unsigned int colourmaplength;
        char colourmapbits;
        unsigned int xstart;
        unsigned int ystart;
        unsigned int width,depth;
        char bits;
        char descriptor;
        } TGAHEAD;

int getline(char *p,int n,int line);

FILE *in,*out;
BINARYHEADER bh;

char masktable[8]={0x80,0x40,0x20,0x10,0x08,0x04,0x02,0x01};

main(argc,argv)
        int argc;
        char *argv[];
{
        static char results[8][16] = {  "Ok",
                                        "Bad write",
                                        "Bad read",
                                        "Memory error",
                                        };
        char path[81];
        int n;

        if(argc > 1) {
                strmfe(path,argv[1],"BIN");
                strupr(path);
                if((in=fopen(path,"rb")) != NULL) {
                        if(fread((char *)&bh,1,sizeof(BINARYHEADER),in) ==
                            sizeof(BINARYHEADER)) {
                                if(!memcmp(bh.sign,BINARYSIG,8)) {
                                        strmfe(path,argv[1],"TGA");
                                        strupr(path);
```

7-11 Continued.

```
                                          if((out=fopen(path,"wb")) != NULL) {
                                                  puts("Writing");
                                                  n=writetga(out,getline,
                                                             bh.width,bh.depth,
                                                             bh.bits,bh.palette);
                                                  printf("\n%s",results[n]);
                                                  fclose(out);
                                          } else printf("Error creating %s",path);
                                  } else printf("%s is corrupted",path);
                          } else printf("Error reading %s",path);
                          fclose(in);
                  } else printf("Error opening %s",path);
          } else puts("Argument:        path to a BIN file");
}


/* write a TGA file */
writetga(fp,readline,width,depth,bits,palette)
        FILE *fp;
        int (*readline)();
        unsigned int width,depth,bits;
        char *palette;
{

        TGAHEAD tga;
        char *p,*pr;
        int i,j,r,b,bytes;

        /* figure out the line size */
        if(bits==1) bytes=pixels2bytes(width);
        else if(bits > 1 && bits <= 8) bytes=width;
        else bytes=width*RGB_SIZE;

        /* allocate a line buffer */
        if((p=malloc(width*RGB_SIZE)) == NULL) return(MEMORY_ERROR);

        /* allocate a scratch buffer */
        if((pr=malloc(bytes)) == NULL) {
                free(p);
                return(MEMORY_ERROR);
        }

        /* write the header */
        memset((char *)&tga,0,sizeof(TGAHEAD));
        if(bits==1) {
                tga.imagetype=0x03;
                tga.width=width;
                tga.depth=depth;
                tga.bits=1;
                tga.descriptor=0x20;
}
else if(bits > 1 && bits <=8) {
        tga.colourmaptype=0x01;
        tga.imagetype=0x01;
```

7-11 Continued.

```
                        tga.colourmaplength=256;
                        tga.colourmapbits=24;
                        tga.width=width;
                        tga.depth=depth;
                        tga.bits=8;
                        tga.descriptor=0x20;
        }
        else {   /* 24 bit file */
                        tga.imagetype=0x02;
                        tga.width=width;
                        tga.depth=depth;
                        tga.bits=24;
                        tga.descriptor=0x20;
        }

        fwrite((char *)&tga,1,sizeof(TGAHEAD),fp);

        /* write the palette */
        if(tga.bits == 8) {
                for(i=0;i<256;++i) {
                        fputc(palette[i*RGB_SIZE+RGB_BLUE],fp);
                        fputc(palette[i*RGB_SIZE+RGB_GREEN],fp);
                        fputc(palette[i*RGB_SIZE+RGB_RED],fp);
                }
        }

        /* write the bitmap */
        for(i=0;i<depth;++i) {
                if(bits==24) readline(p,bytes,i);
                else readline(p,width,i);

                if(tga.bits==1) {
                        packmonoline(pr,p,width);
                        fwrite(pr,1,bytes,fp);
                }
                else if(tga.bits == 8) fwrite(p,1,bytes,fp);
                else if(tga.bits == 24) {
                        for(j=0;j<width;++j) {
                                r=p[j*RGB_SIZE+RGB_RED];
                                b=p[j*RGB_SIZE+RGB_BLUE];
                                p[j*RGB_SIZE+RGB_RED]=b;
                                p[j*RGB_SIZE+RGB_BLUE]=r;
                        }
                        fwrite(p,1,bytes,fp);
                }
        }

        free(pr);
        free(p);

        if(ferror(fp)) return(BAD_WRITE);
        else return(GOOD_WRITE);
```

7-11 Continued.

```
}

/* translate a vga line to a monochrome line */

packmonoline(dest,source,width)
        char *dest,*source;
        int width;
{
        int i;

        for(i=0;i<width;++i) {
                if(source[i]) dest[i >> 3] |= masktable[i & 0x0007];
                else dest[i >> 3] &= ~masktable[i & 0x0007];
        }
}

/* make file name with specific extension */
strmfe(new,old,ext)
        char *new,*old,*ext;
{
        while(*old != 0 && *old != '.') *new++=*old++;
        *new++='.';
        while(*ext) *new++=*ext++;
        *new=0;
}

/* fetch a line from the input file */
getline(p,n,line)
        char *p;
        int n,line;
{
        int i;

        /* seek past the binary file header to the line */
        fseek(in,(long)sizeof(BINARYHEADER)+(long)line*(long)n,SEEK_SET);
        i=fread(p,1,n,in);
        if(i==n) return(0);
        else return(1);
}
```

7-11 Continued.

After it has set up its buffers and such, the `writetga` function begins by filling in a TGAHEAD object. The Targa format doesn't concern itself with images having between 2 and 7 bits of color. Such pictures should be "promoted" to 8-bit pictures. You could write a partial color map in such cases, although this version of the Targa writer does not. In a file format that requires a quarter of a megabyte to store a modest size picture, saving 500 bytes just doesn't seem to be worth it.

If the image being created has 8 bits of color, the `writetga` function creates a palette for it after the header. Note that the palette entries are written with their red and blue entries exchanged.

The loop at the bottom of the `writetga` function handles sending the actual image data out to the destination file. It isn't up to much. However, once again keep in mind that the byte order of 24-bit RGB values has to be kept track of.

As an aside, note that all the file readers and writers in this book use the C-language streamed file functions—`fopen`, `fread` and so on. These make it easy to write and understand the functions that employ them, but they're less than blindingly fast. Some formats really do need them, as they require that you handle their data 1 byte at a time or in unpredictable blocks.

Formats such as TGA—especially in writing uncompressed Targa files—lend themselves to handling large blocks of formatted data. If you implement the code in this chapter in your own programs, you might want to replace the streamed file functions with conventional low-level C-language file-handling calls, such as `open`, `read` and so on, if you're concerned about the speed at which everything operates.

Using Targa files

Aside from ray tracing, Targa files frequently turn up without the benefit of a Targa board as one of the output options for color scanners. While there are several formats that support 24-bit color, TGA files are less likely to be misinterpreted than, say, 24-bit TIFF files. It's very disappointing indeed to scan several pages of originals into TIFF files to subsequently find that your scanner software and the intended recipient of your TIFF files don't have the same notion of how a TIFF file should be structured.

Some of the ambiguity of TIFF is discussed later in this book.

As will also be apparent from the RGBTEST program in this chapter, you can use the Targa format as a convenient way to write synthetic images—pictures in which the image details result from data manipulations rather than from the light show of a scanner. You could, for example, store 24-bit fractals or other sorts of data plots this way.

8

24-bit PCX files

When the going gets tough, the tough go shopping.
—Murphy's Laws of Computers

Through its numerous incarnations, rewrites, ports, and bug fixes, Z-Soft's PC Paintbrush program remains as one of the most popular PC drawing tools short of yellow highlighters that draw on a monitor. In its present form, PC Paintbrush is a Microsoft Windows application of mammoth dimensions that edits files having up to 24 bits of color. The problem of editing a 24-bit picture on a 16-color display is beyond the scope of this book.

Although PC Paintbrush for Windows works with a number of image file formats, PCX is still its native format. Because PC Paintbrush has been so popular, PCX files have come as close to being a standard image file format for PC applications in general as anything is likely to get. They're imported by most desktop publishing software, used as templates by several drawing packages, and exported by a host of other applications.

This chapter deals with one of the many flavors of PCX files—the new 24-bit PCX standard. Reading and writing all PCX files is a fairly large topic, discussed in detail in *Bitmapped Graphics*.

Figure 8-1 illustrates a 24-bit PCX file, reproduced here in living black and white. This file was downloaded from Z-Soft's bulletin board.

The PCX standard, although still evolving, has been around for a long time, as is the case with the software that was originally designed to work with PCX files. Actually, "evolving" might not be the best word to describe it. It's been having things bolted onto it for quite some time, with 24-bit

8-1 A 24-bit hummingbird, downloaded from the Z-Soft bulletin board.

PCX files being one of the more elegant additions. By comparison, 8-bit PCX files are decidedly funky. They won't be dealt with here.

The PCX format is the only 24-bit standard discussed in this book that insists on compressing the images it works with whether or not you think they'll get any smaller. As briefly discussed earlier, run-length compression doesn't usually reduce the size of complex 24-bit images, and it's not uncommon to find 24-bit PCX files that unpack to raw images that are smaller than the files from which they came.

In fact, as you'll observe in the following discussion of PCX files, the run-length encoding procedure used to store PCX images is heavily weighted toward drawn rather than scanned images. It's good at dealing with large areas of unbroken color, rather than a lot of variegated pixels.

Figure 8-2 illustrates another 24-bit PCX file downloaded from Z-Soft's bulletin board. This is a picture drawn in PC Paintbrush, rather than scanned. The hummingbird in FIG. 8-1 took up 461,002 bytes as a disk file and 456,966 bytes in memory. It exhibited about 8 percent negative compression. The marquee in FIG. 8-2 took up 330,670 bytes as a 24-bit PCX file and 402,300 bytes of memory. In this case, compression reduced it by about 21 percent.

One might argue that PC Paintbrush purports to be a drawing package rather than a scanner driver. As such, having its file format favor drawn images makes sense to some degree.

One of the notable advantages to using PCX compression over other run-length compression designs, such as Targa run-length encoding, is

8-2 A 24-bit PC Paintbrush drawing downloaded from the Z-Soft bulletin board.

that PCX encoding is blindingly fast to unpack. The 24-bit version has a clever twist in this respect, which is dealt with momentarily.

The PCX file structure

A PCX file consists of a 128-byte header followed by a lot of compressed image data. The 8-bit PCX file structure was clearly created after the fact; it has a 768-byte palette tacked onto the end of the image data along with a marker to help locate the beast. Since this chapter only discusses 24-bit PCX files, you won't have to deal with PCX palettes at all in working with the code discussed here.

The chapter in *Bitmapped Graphics* that deals with PCX files explains all the mutations and variations of this ubiquitous file format.

No matter how many color bits a PCX file supports, it starts with the same header, which looks like the following:

```
typedef struct   {
        char manufacturer;
        char version;
        char encoding;
        char bits_per_pixel;
        int xmin,ymin;
        int xmax,ymax;
        int hres;
        int vres;
        char palette[48];
        char reserved;
```

```
      char color_planes;
      int bytes_per_line;
      int palette_type;
      char filler[58];
      } PCXHEAD;
```

While somewhat nasty looking, the PCXHEAD structure is actually pretty easy to understand if you know about its peculiarities.

The manufacturer element of a PCXHEAD object is always 10. This is how a PCX reader knows it's looking at a PCX file. The version varies, and indicates something about how the file being read is structured and the age of the software that wrote it. Assuming that the PCX file in question was generated by PC Paintbrush, the following values for the versions field apply:

0—version 2.5 of PC Paintbrush
2—version 2.8 of PC Paintbrush, palette included
3—version 2.8 of PC Paintbrush, use default palette
5—version 3.0 of PC Paintbrush or better

All the files discussed in this chapter have version values of 5.

The encoding field is always 1, indicating run-length encoding. At present this is the only type of encoding that PCX files support.

The bits_per_pixel element indicates the number of bits of color required by each pixel of the image in question. Oddly, this is 8 bits for 24-bit files.

The xmin and ymin elements specify the coordinates of the upper left corner of the image relative to the upper left corner of your screen, and are usually both 0. The xmax and ymax elements specify the distance from the upper left corner to the lower right corner. Therefore, if pcx is an object of the type PCXHEAD that has been loaded with a PCX file header, you can calculate the actual dimensions of a PCX image like this:

```
int width,depth;

width=pcx.xmax-pcx.xmin+1;
depth=pcx.ymax-pcx.ymin+1;
```

The hres and yres elements of the header indicate the horizontal and vertical resolution respectively. These values normally aren't used.

The palette field of the header holds the color palette for the picture being unpacked—assuming, of course, that it has one. This also assumes that the image supports no more than 16 colors. The next step up, 256 colors, requires a palette that is added to the end of the image data, as previously mentioned. Since 24-bit files don't have palettes at all, this field can be ignored for the code in this chapter.

The color_planes field specifies the number of color planes in the image. In a 16-bit image, this would be 4. In a 24-bit image, it's 3, which is what makes the way PCX files treat 24-bit image data rather clever.

Run-length encoding 3-byte RGB pixels is a somewhat questionable undertaking. There are several ways to go at it, each with its own set of trade-offs. You might consider the way that 24-bit pixels are compressed in Targa files; that is, as fields and runs of 3-byte objects. This is a fairly obvious approach, but its speed suffers a bit in unpacking compressed lines, as the code that does so is forced to work with three, a very inconvenient number for a computer. Multiplying something by three involves real multiplication, which is slow.

A PCX file compresses a single line of RGB pixels as three planes. The first plane consists of all the red pixels, the second of all the green pixels and the third of all the blue pixels. In this way, no one line actually requires working with objects bigger than 1 byte. As such, you can unpack 24-bit PCX files very quickly.

Having said this, it's worth noting that 24-bit PCX files unpack into a format that isn't anything like what most of the code that works with RGB color expects to see. The process of converting the planar lines of a 24-bit PCX file into RGB pixel lines of the sort discussed throughout this book might soak up most of the time savings.

The `bytes_per_line` value represents the number of bytes in one plane of the image being unpacked. Depending upon the application that created them, the number of bytes in a single RGB plane might not be the same as the number of pixels on a line. In some cases you'll find that the number of bytes is rounded up to an even number, with a dummy byte added to the end of the line, if needed. As such, when you're unpacking a PCX file, you should unpack each line to the value in this field, not one derived from the image width.

The `palette_type` field only applies to 256-color PCX files and doesn't pertain to the code in this chapter. It indicates whether the image in question is to be displayed in color or as a gray-scale picture. If it's to be displayed in color, this field value will be 2. Gray-scale images will have a value of 1.

Following the PCX file header, the next byte in the file is the first byte of the first compressed red plane. The run-length compression used in PCX files is very easy to understand. To uncompress a line, you would read a byte and see if its two high-order bits are set. If they are, AND off the two high bits and call the remaining value a length specifier. Read in the next byte and repeat it this many times.

If the two high-order bits are not set, the byte should be written as is to the decoded data.

Having read one field of the line being decoded, you then repeat the process until a full line has been read. A full line will be an uncompressed string of bytes equal to the value in `pcx.bytes_per_line`.

This is a function that reads one line of a PCX file.

```
readpcxline(p,fp,bytes)
    char *p;
    FILE *fp;
```

```
        int bytes;
    {

        int n=0,c,i;
        do {
        c=fgetc(fp) & 0xff;
            if((c & 0xc0) == 0xc0) {
                i=c & 0x3f;
                c=fgetc(fp);
                while(i--) p[n++]=c;
            }
            else p[n++]=c;
        } while(n < bytes);
        return(n);
    }
```

Clearly, one of the specific advantages to PCX compression is that it doesn't require a lot of complex code to work with.

Note that all PCX files use the same type of run-length compression, no matter how many color bits they have.

A PCX file reader

A PCX file reader for 24-bit files works pretty well, as all the previous readers have, except that its format-specific code has been replaced with functions to handle PCX files. As with the earlier readers discussed in this book, READPCX displays 24-bit color on a VGA card by reducing the 24-bit pixels to gray values.

The READPCX program shown in FIG. 8-3 is only intended to deal with 24-bit files and will refuse to work with PCX files having fewer color bits. In fact, handling some of the lesser species of PCX files is particularly tricky. Sixteen-color files are perhaps the nastiest; at least three distinct types of them are in common use along with numerous lesser-seen varieties. Once again, if you want to get deeply into the myth and folklore of PCX files, you should refer to *Bitmapped Graphics*.

```
/*
        24 bit PCX reader - copyright (c) 1991
        Alchemy Mindworks Inc.
*/

#include "stdio.h"
#include "dos.h"
#include "alloc.h"

/*                              uncomment this line if you
#include "memmangr.h"           will be linking in the memory manager
*/

#define GOOD_READ       0       /* return codes */
```

8-3 The source code for READPCX.

```
#define BAD_FILE        1
#define BAD_READ        2
#define MEMORY_ERROR    3
#define WRONG_BITS      4

#define SCREENWIDE      320     /* mode 13 screen dimensions */
#define SCREENDEEP      200
#define STEP            32      /* size of a step when panning */

#define HOME            0x4700  /* cursor control codes */
#define CURSOR_UP       0x4800
#define CURSOR_LEFT     0x4b00
#define CURSOR_RIGHT    0x4d00
#define END             0x4f00
#define CURSOR_DOWN     0x5000

#define RGB_RED         0
#define RGB_GREEN       1
#define RGB_BLUE        2
#define RGB_SIZE        3

#define greyvalue(r,g,b)        (((r*30)/100) + ((g*59)/100) + ((b*11)/100))

typedef struct {
        int width,depth,bytes,bits;
        char palette[768];
        int (*setup)();
        int (*closedown)();
        } FILEINFO;

typedef struct {
        char manufacturer;
        char version;
        char encoding;
        char bits_per_pixel;
        int xmin,ymin;
        int xmax,ymax;
        int hres;
        int vres;
        char palette[48];
        char reserved;
        char colour_planes;
        int bytes_per_line;
        int palette_type;
        char filler[58];
        } PCXHEAD;

char *farPtr(char *p,long l);
char *getline(unsigned int n);
int dosetup(FILEINFO *fi);
int doclosedown(FILEINFO *fi);
int putline(char *p,unsigned int n);
```

8-3 Continued.

```
        FILEINFO fi;
        char *buffer=NULL;


        main(argc,argv)
                int argc;
                char *argv[];
        {
                FILE *fp;
                static char results[5][16] = {  "Ok",
                                                "Bad file",
                                                "Bad read",
                                                "Memory error",
                                                "Too few colours"
                                                };
                char path[80];
                int r;

                if(argc > 1) {
                        strmfe(path,argv[1],"PCX");
                        strupr(path);
                        if((fp = fopen(path,"rb")) != NULL) {
                                fi.setup=dosetup;
                                fi.closedown=doclosedown;
                                r=unpackpcx(fp,&fi);
                                printf("\%s",results[r]);
                                fclose(fp);
                        } else printf("Error opening %s",path);
                } else puts("Argument:       path to a PCX file");
        }


        /* unpack an PCX file */
        unpackpcx(fp,fi)
                FILE *fp;
                FILEINFO *fi;
        {
                PCXHEAD pcx;
                char *p,*pr;
                int i,j,bytes;

                for(i=0;i<256;++i)
                    memset(fi->palette+(i*RGB_SIZE),i,RGB_SIZE);


                if(fread((char *)&pcx,1,sizeof(PCXHEAD),fp) == sizeof(PCXHEAD) &&
                    pcx.manufacturer==10) {
                        if(pcx.bits_per_pixel==8 && pcx.colour_planes==3) {
                                bytes=pcx.bytes_per_line;
                                fi->width=pcx.xmax-pcx.xmin+1;
                                fi->depth=pcx.ymax-pcx.ymin+1;
                                fi->bytes=bytes*RGB_SIZE;

                                if((p=malloc(fi->bytes)) == NULL) return(MEMORY_ERROR);
```

8-3 Continued.

```
                        if((pr=malloc(fi->width)) == NULL) {
                                free(p);
                                return(MEMORY_ERROR);
                        }

                        if((fi->setup)(fi) != GOOD_READ) {
                                free(pr);
                                free(p);
                                return(MEMORY_ERROR);
                        }

                        for(i=0;i<fi->depth;++i) {
                                for(j=0;j<RGB_SIZE;++j) {
                                        if(readpcxline(p+(j*bytes),fp,bytes) != bytes) {
                                                freebuffer();
                                                free(pr);
                                                free(p);
                                                return(BAD_READ);
                                        }
                                }

                                for(j=0;j<fi->width;++j)
                                        pr[j]=greyvalue(p[j],
                                                p[RGB_GREEN*bytes+j],
                                                p[RGB_BLUE*bytes+j]);

                                putline(pr,i);
                        }
                        (fi->closedown)(fi);
                        freebuffer();
                        free(pr);
                        free(p);
                } else return(WRONG_BITS);
        } else return(BAD_READ);
        return(GOOD_READ);
}

/* read and decode a PCX line into p */
readpcxline(p,fp,bytes)
        char *p;
        FILE *fp;
        int bytes;
{
        int n=0,c,i;

        do {
                c=fgetc(fp) & 0xff;
                if((c & 0xc0) == 0xc0) {
                        i=c & 0x3f;
                        c=fgetc(fp);
                        while(i--) p[n++]=c;
                }
                else p[n++]=c;
```

8-3 Continued.

```
            } while(n < bytes);
            return(n);
}


/* This function is called after the BMHD and CMAP chunks have
    been read but before the BODY is unpacked */
dosetup(fi)
            FILEINFO *fi;
{

            union REGS r;

            if(!getbuffer((long)fi->width*(long)fi->depth,fi->width,fi->depth))
                return(MEMORY_ERROR);

            r.x.ax=0x0013;
            int86(0x10,&r,&r);

            setvgapalette(fi->palette,256,0);

            return(GOOD_READ);
}


/* This function is called after an image has been unpacked. It must
    display the image and deallocate memory. */
doclosedown(fi)
            FILEINFO *fi;
{

            union REGS r;
            int c,i,n,x=0,y=0;

            if(fi->width > SCREENWIDE) n=SCREENWIDE;
            else n=fi->width;

            do {
                    for(i=0;i<SCREENDEEP;++i) {
                            c=y+i;
                            if(c>=fi->depth) break;
                            memcpy(MK_FP(0xa000,SCREENWIDE*i),getline(c)+x,n);
                    }
                    c=GetKey();
                    switch(c) {
                            case CURSOR_LEFT:
                                    if((x-STEP) > 0) x-=STEP;
                                    else x=0;
                                    break;
                            case CURSOR_RIGHT:
                                    if((x+STEP+SCREENWIDE) < fi->width) x+=STEP;
                                    else if(fi->width > SCREENWIDE)
                                        x=fi->width-SCREENWIDE;
                                    else x=0;
                                    break;
                            case CURSOR_UP:
```

8-3 Continued.

```
                                        if((y-STEP) > 0) y-=STEP;
                                        else y=0;
                                        break;
                        case CURSOR DOWN:
                                if((y+STEP+SCREENDEEP) < fi->depth) y+=STEP;
                                else if(fi->depth > SCREENDEEP)
                                    y=fi->depth-SCREENDEEP;
                                else y=0;
                                break;
                        case HOME:
                                x=y=0;
                                break;
                        case END:
                                if(fi->width > SCREENWIDE)
                                    x=fi->width-SCREENWIDE;
                                else x=0;
                                if(fi->depth > SCREENDEEP)
                                    y=fi->depth-SCREENDEEP;
                                else y=0;
                                break;
                    }
            } while(c != 27);

            freebuffer();

            r.x.ax=0x0003;
            int86(0x10,&r,&r);
            return(GOOD_READ);
    }

    /* get one extended key code */
    GetKey()
    {
            int c;

            c = getch();
            if(!(c & 0x00ff)) c = getch() << 8;
            return(c);
    }

    /* set the VGA palette and background */
    setvgapalette(p,n,b)
            char *p;
            int n,b;
    {
            union REGS r;
            int i;

            outp(0x3c6,0xff);
            for(i=0;i<n;++i) {
                    outp(0x3c8,i);
                    outp(0x3c9,(*p++) >> 2);
```

8-3 Continued.

```
                outp(0x3c9,(*p++) >> 2);
                outp(0x3c9,(*p++) >> 2);
        }
        r.x.ax=0x1001;
        r.h.bh=b;
        int86(0x10,&r,&r);
}


/* make file name with specific extension */
strmfe(new,old,ext)
        char *new,*old,*ext;
{
        while(*old != 0 && *old != '.') *new++=*old++;
        *new++='.';
        while(*ext) *new++=*ext++;
        *new=0;
}


/* if you don't use in the memory manager, these functions
   will stand in for it */

#if !MEMMANGR

/* return a far pointer plus a long integer */
char *farPtr(p,l)
        char *p;
        long l;
{
        unsigned int seg,off;

        seg = FP_SEG(p);
        off = FP_OFF(p);
        seg += (off / 16);
        off &= 0x000f;
        off += (unsigned int)(l & 0x000fL);
        seg += (l / 16L);
        p = MK_FP(seg,off);
        return(p);
}


/* save one line to memory */
putline(p,n)
        char *p;
        unsigned int n;
{
        if(n >= 0 && n < fi.depth)
            memcpy(farPtr(buffer,(long)n*(long)fi.width),p,fi.width);
}


/* get one line from memory */
char *getline(n)
        unsigned int n;
```

8-3 Continued.

```
{
        return(farPtr(buffer,(long)n*(long)fi.width));
}

#pragma warn -par
getbuffer(n,bytes,lines)
        unsigned long n;
        int bytes,lines;
{
        if((buffer=farmalloc(n)) == NULL) return(0);
        else return(1);
}

freebuffer()
{
        if(buffer != NULL) farfree(buffer);
        buffer=NULL;
}
#endif /* !MEMMANGR */
```
8-3 Continued.

All the PCX-specific code in READPCX lives in the unpackpcx function, which does pretty much what you'd expect it to do. It begins by reading the first 128 bytes of the file passed to it into a PCXHEAD object and then extracts the appropriate information from the header. The rest of the code reads the image planes. The process of converting the three planes of a PCX 24-bit line to one 8-bit gray-scale line requires quite a bit of byte-juggling. It's handled here in a way that is easy to understand but not as fast as it could be. If you want to manipulate PCX planes, you'll find it a lot faster to read each plane into a separate line buffer. Having done this, you can get at the individual bytes with simple indexing, which entails no multiplication.

This code is artificially simple in that it only has to deal with one type of PCX file. Perhaps more to the point, the 24-bit PCX standard has no variations on its structure as yet. You'll note the absence of the case statements and complex if else decision trees that seem to sprout like mushrooms around any file format that offers many choices.

If this version of READPCX actually supported all types of PCX files, the unpackpcx function would contain enough branches to be declared a national park.

Writing PCX files

Writing a 24-bit PCX file isn't any more difficult than reading one. The WRITEPCX program in FIG. 8-4 works like the other file writers discussed thus far, except that it writes only 24-bit files. It accepts 24-bit binary files, as created by MAKEBIN2 or MAKERGB, and creates a corresponding 24-bit PCX file. You can't use binary files from MAKEBIN because MAKEBIN reads GIF files, which only support a maximum color depth of 8 bits. If you use binary files from MAKEBIN2, be certain that the BMP files you used as source images did, in fact, have 24-bits of color.

If you attempt to have WRITEPCX read a binary file with less than 24 bits of color, it complains and returns you to DOS.

```
/*
        24-bit PCX writer - copyright (c) 1991
        Alchemy Mindworks Inc.
*/

#include "stdio.h"
#include "alloc.h"

#define BINARYSIG       "ALCHBINR"      /* binary identification */

#define GOOD_WRITE      0               /* return codes */
#define BAD_WRITE       1
#define BAD_READ        2
#define MEMORY_ERROR    3
#define WRONG_BITS      4

#define RGB_RED         0
#define RGB_GREEN       1
#define RGB_BLUE        2
#define RGB_SIZE        3

typedef struct {
        char sign[8];
        int width,depth,bits;
        char palette[768];
        } BINARYHEADER;

typedef struct {
        char manufacturer;
        char version;
        char encoding;
        char bits_per_pixel;
        int xmin,ymin;
        int xmax,ymax;
        int hres;
        int vres;
        char palette[48];
        char reserved;
        char colour_planes;
        int bytes_per_line;
        int palette_type;
        char filler[58];
        } PCXHEAD;

int getline(char *p,int n,int line);

FILE *in,*out;
```

8-4 The source code for WRITEPCX.

```
        BINARYHEADER bh;

main(argc,argv)
        int argc;
        char *argv[];
{
        static char results[5][16] = {  "Ok",
                                        "Bad write",
                                        "Bad read",
                                        "Memory error",
                                        "Too few colours"
                                        };

        char path[81];
        int n;

        if(argc > 1) {
                strmfe(path,argv[1],"BIN");
                strupr(path);
                if((in=fopen(path,"rb")) != NULL) {
                        if(fread((char *)&bh,1,sizeof(BINARYHEADER),in) ==
                          sizeof(BINARYHEADER)) {
                                if(!memcmp(bh.sign,BINARYSIG,8)) {
                                        strmfe(path,argv[1],"PCX");
                                        strupr(path);
                                        if((out=fopen(path,"wb")) != NULL) {
                                                puts("Writing");
                                                n=writepcx(out,getline,
                                                        bh.width,bh.depth,
                                                        bh.bits,bh.palette);
                                                printf("\n%s",results[n]);
                                                fclose(out);
                                        } else printf("Error creating %s",path);
                                } else printf("%s is corrupted",path);
                        } else printf("Error reading %s",path);
                        fclose(in);
                } else printf("Error opening %s",path);
        } else puts("Argument:       path to a BIN file");
}

/* write a PCX file */
#pragma warn -par
writepcx(fp,readline,width,depth,bits,palette)
        FILE *fp;
        int (*readline)();
        unsigned int width,depth,bits;
        char *palette;
{
        PCXHEAD pcx;
        char *p,*pr;
        int i,j,bytes;

        if(bits != 24) return(WRONG_BITS);
```

8-4 Continued.

```
        bytes=width*RGB_SIZE;

        /* allocate a line buffer */
        if((p=malloc(bytes)) == NULL) return(MEMORY_ERROR);

        /* allocate a scratch buffer */
        if((pr=malloc(width)) == NULL) {
                free(p);
                return(MEMORY_ERROR);
        }

        /* write the header */
        memset((char *)&pcx,0,sizeof(PCXHEAD));
        pcx.manufacturer=10;
        pcx.encoding=1;
        pcx.xmin=0;
        pcx.ymin=0;
        pcx.xmax=width-1;
        pcx.ymax=depth-1;
        pcx.colour_planes=3;
        pcx.bytes_per_line=width;
        pcx.bits_per_pixel=8;
        pcx.version=5;

        fwrite((char *)&pcx,1,sizeof(PCXHEAD),fp);

        /* write the bitmap */
        for(i=0;i<depth;++i) {
                readline(p,bytes,i);
                for(j=0;j<width;++j) pr[j]=p[j*RGB_SIZE+RGB_RED];
                writepcxline(pr,fp,width);
                for(j=0;j<width;++j) pr[j]=p[j*RGB_SIZE+RGB_GREEN];
                writepcxline(pr,fp,width);
                for(j=0;j<width;++j) pr[j]=p[j*RGB_SIZE+RGB_BLUE];
                writepcxline(pr,fp,width);
        }

        free(pr);
        free(p);

        if(ferror(fp)) return(BAD_WRITE);
        else return(GOOD_WRITE);
}

writepcxline(p,fp,n)
        char *p;
        FILE *fp;
        int n;
{

        unsigned int i=0,j=0,t=0;

        do {
                i=0;
```

8-4 Continued.

```
                while((p[t+i]==p[t+i+1]) && ((t+i) < n) && (i < 63))++i;
                if(i>0) {
                        fputc(i | 0xc0,fp);
                        fputc(p[t],fp);
                        t+=i;
                        j+=2;
                }
                else {
                        if(((p[t]) & 0xc0)==0xc0) {
                                fputc(0xc1,fp);
                                ++j;
                        }
                        fputc(p[t++],fp);
                        ++j;
                }
        } while(t<n);
        return(ferror(fp));
}

/* make file name with specific extension */
strmfe(new,old,ext)
        char *new,*old,*ext;
{
        while(*old != 0 && *old != '.') *new++=*old++;
        *new++='.';
        while(*ext) *new++=*ext++;
        *new=0;
}

/* fetch a line from the input file */
getline(p,n,line)
        char *p;
        int n,line;
{
        int i;

        /* seek past the binary file header to the line */
        fseek(in, (long) sizeof (BINARYHEADER) + (long) line* (long) n, SEEK_SET);
        i=fread(p,1,n,in);
        if(i==n) return(0);
        else return(1);
}
```

The process of writing a 24-bit PCX file is pretty simple. You should begin by filling in a PCXHEAD object and writing it to the destination file. There are several important things to keep in mind when doing this. Note that the xmax and ymax fields should be one less than their respective image dimensions. You must fill in the version and encoding fields properly. The unused portions of the file header should be set to 0. This is most easily accomplished by filling the whole PCXHEAD with zeros before you set the relevant fields.

Keep in mind that PCX files, perhaps more so than any other PC image file format, are read by an enormous number of applications that weren't written by the creator of the format. Third-party PCX readers might or might not check all the fields in the header, and they might not be smart enough to know when they're confronted with ridiculous data in some of the fields. You can help ensure that the PCX files you create will be universally welcomed by other software by making sure that you handle the PCX header correctly, even when you aren't sure why.

The Graphic Workshop package included with the companion disk for this book is written to read as many PCX files as possible, even ones with questionable header information. In a sense, it's the worst possible check to make sure that a PCX writer is behaving itself. It's designed to be as forgiving as possible, probably more so than other applications. Having a current copy of PC Paintbrush on hand is a particularly good check, although you might not want to boot up Windows and run it periodically as you develop your code.

As of this writing, the Windows Paint application reads PCX files and 24-bit files, but it does not read 24-bit PCX files. Most of the time it retaliates with an unrecoverable application error box if you attempt to feed it a 24-bit PCX file.

Having successfully dispensed with the PCX header, writing the lines is pretty elementary. The lines that come out of a binary image file of the type discussed in this book are stored as 3-byte RGB pixels. As such, each line must be split into three planes to be compressed. This is more-or-less the opposite to what happened in the READPCX program discussed earlier.

The `writepcxline` function works just like the other run-length encoding functions discussed in this book. It searches for runs of bytes and writes out the appropriate fields if it finds them. Data that cannot be treated as a run of bytes is written 1 byte at a time. Note, however, that if a byte with both its high-order bits turns up it must be written as a run of bytes field that is 1 byte long.

Using 24-bit PCX files

Most of the image-file formats that support 24-bit color are somewhat exotic or unapproachable. They lack popularly available applications to create and edit them. By comparison, PC Paintbrush for Windows is pretty easy to come by, and can be used with non-stratospheric display hardware. While you might need a moderately high-end machine to run Windows and PC Paintbrush for Windows, you won't have to mortgage your cat for a Targa board.

If you plan to support 24-bit color in a program you're writing, the PCX format isn't a bad choice for this reason. It's not as flexible as Targa or TIFF, but it's probably a lot more likely to find widespread acceptance because it's easily accessible.

9

Color TIFF files

Things equal to nothing else are equal to each other.
—MURPHY'S LAWS OF COMPUTERS

The dictionary defines *tiff* as "a slight fit of annoyance." This is probably inappropriate, as most sentient life forms confronted with TIFF files become insanely furious over them with time. The justification for this obvious understatement is that TIFF is an acronym that stands for *tagged image file format*. It might have been more appropriate to call the associated image-file standard something like "enrage," or "chaos," or "plague." Regrettably, none of these terms lends itself to having its letters stand for anything.

The TIFF standard is a good example of what happens when a large group of people try to create a system that does everything. The TIFF specification is that of a perfect image-file format. It's flexible, extensible, capable of supporting all sorts of special features and application-specific information, portable into other machine environments, but it's not easily workable.

The very flexibility that makes TIFF look really appealing when you first tear the shrink wrap off the TIFF developer's toolkit turns out to be its major limitation. There are hundreds of ways to construct a TIFF file. The TIFF standard supports a half-dozen or so different types of image compression. Images with 1 bit of color can be stored inverted or normally. Images with more than 1 bit of color can be stored in planes, in bytes, in nibbles, and in RGB triplets. Individual parameters like image dimensions and aspect ratios may be stored as long integers, short integers, rational numbers, and probably even as text strings, all without really violating the TIFF standard. The list of options could run for pages.

Common sense might lead you to ascertain that storing numbers written out as text strings is pushing the point; however, many of the less extreme TIFF options are not governed by common sense.

The drawback to TIFF files is that if someone hands you one on disk, there's a fair-to-middling chance that your software won't be able to read it. Likewise, if you write a program that generates TIFF files, the odds are easily as good that at least one major PC application that claims to import TIFF files will not import yours.

All this aside, TIFF is a useful format, even if it is a somewhat perilous one. It's particularly well suited to mid-range imaging applications, and most desktop publishing packages will import TIFF files to use as color or halftoned gray-scale art.

You might think of TIFF as being everyone's second favorite image-file format, there being no meaningful consensus on a candidate for first place. It has the advantage of not being tied to a specific manufacturer, application, or particular computer. TIFF files are designed to be equally readable (or unreadable) by Macintosh and PC systems.

As with the PCX format discussed in chapter 8, TIFF files are handled at length in *Bitmapped Graphics*. This chapter deals specifically with color TIFF files, something that the chapter on TIFF files in *Bitmapped Graphics* doesn't cover.

TIFF files are capable of supporting up to 24 bits of color. You can store an image of any dimensions in one. In fact, you can store multiple images in a TIFF file, along with just about any other information you can think of. If you liked the chunk structure of IFF files, you'll find TIFF very appealing.

Unlike the other image file formats discussed in this book, using TIFF files with real-world applications usually requires you to create files with some knowledge of the specific software that will be reading them. There is no practical way to write a universal TIFF reader, a program that will decode every weird TIFF file around. As such, when you work with TIFF files it's usually necessary to know what created them. This becomes more of a concern as you begin to work with color images because color TIFF files have more parameters to become confused.

The Graphic Workshop package on the companion disk for this book has been fine-tuned to read and write TIFF files for a number of specific applications. It creates TIFF files that can be imported by Ventura Publisher and CorelDRAW, for example. It reads TIFF files from a larger source of software, including PC Paintbrush and most Macintosh applications. It also reads and writes files for other software, although there's no saying which software.

As an aside, the format-specific code for Graphic Workshop is completely written in assembly language. It's stored as a type of code overlays called *resources*, so that the main program can load the appropriate chunk of code when it's needed and then dispose of it, reducing the amount of memory the program occupies while it's working. One of the limitations to this system as it's implemented in Graphic Workshop is that no single code resource can exceed 64K in length.

This has only proven to be a limitation once. The TIFF format resource became bigger than 64K during an attempt to have it handle two addition forms of image-file compression that the TIFF standard defines. Most other image file formats require Graphic Workshop code resources of about 10K in length.

It probably does not need to be said that the code in this chapter does not read all TIFF files, nor does it write ones that are universally accepted by other applications. It explains the basic structure of TIFF files. You might find that you have to fine-tune the code or the TIFF files it deals with for specific applications.

In fairness, you should probably regard this chapter as an introduction to TIFF files, rather than an exhaustive study of them. If you want to know more about using the TIFF standard, you should probably read the standard, which is discussed at the end of this chapter.

Figure 9-1 illustrates CorelDRAW with a TIFF file generated by the WRITETIF program discussed later in this chapter. CorelDRAW displays TIFF images pretty crudely: they look a lot better than this when they're printed.

In one sense, working with color TIFF files should make the prospect of overcoming the TIFF standard's plethora of variations a bit less intimi-

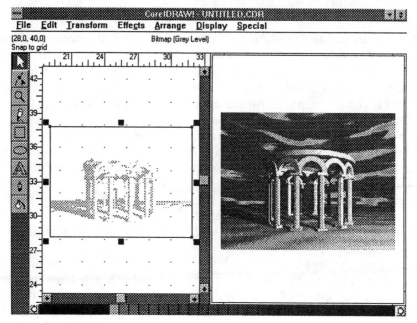

9-1 CorelDRAW having imported a TIFF file.

dating. Born in the days when most images had only 1 bit of color, a lot of its more puzzling options are intended for use with black-and-white pictures. Several of its troublesome compression procedures aren't applicable to color files.

The TIFF file structure

As previously discussed, the Intel microprocessors that drive PC-compatible systems handle multiple-byte numbers in the inverse order that they appear on Motorola microprocessor systems, most notably the Apple Macintosh. This procedure is something that rarely turns up outside of graphic files, since there are relatively few data types that can be ported between systems. Raw text is by its nature machine independent: words mean much the same thing whether or not your system came with a mouse and a mortgage.

The TIFF standard is designed to allow PCs to work with Intel numbers in TIFF files, Macintoshes to work with Motorola numbers, and to allow both systems to read the other's TIFF files in a pinch on days when the network isn't down. As such, every TIFF file carries with it information about the machine used to create it. In fact, it's the first thing in the file.

A TIFF file begins with a deceptively simple header, which looks like:

```
typedef struct {
        unsigned int numbertype;
        unsigned int version;
        unsigned long offset;
        } TIFFHEAD;
```

If you go ahead and read the first 8 bytes of a TIFF file into one of these things, `tiffhead.numbertype` will be 4949H if the file uses Intel numbers and 4D4DH if it uses Motorola numbers. To make this a bit easier to remember, 49H is the ASCII code for I and 4DH is the ASCII code for M.

A TIFF reader requires functions to fetch words and long integers from the file as it's being read. These functions should set the byte order based on what turns up in the `numbertype` field of the header.

The `version` element will always be 42. However, the value 42 can appear in either byte of the integer, depending upon the contents of the `numbertype` field. Likewise, the long integer `offset` may also be either an Intel or a Motorola number. For this reason, while it's convenient to regard the start of a TIFF file as a header, it's not usually the case that it is actually read into a data structure, as would be the case for most file headers.

Note that the `numbertype` element is hardware-independent. The byte order with which it's read doesn't matter, as both bytes are the same.

The `offset` element of a TIFF file header represents the distance from the start of the file to the first "image file directory." Image file directories are what give TIFF files their laudable flexibility and daunting level of confusion. Each directory can contain any number of "tags." Each tag specifies something about the image to be unpacked. Some of them specify some pretty exotic things. There is, for example, a special tag to specify the name of the artist that drew the picture, one for the model number of the scanner that digitized it and two to specify the dimensions of the optimum spot size to halftone it. The latter two are, in fairness, now considered to be obsolete.

An image file directory begins with an integer that defines the number of tags in the directory. Each tag is 12-bytes long. It's structured like this:

```
typedef struct {
        unsigned int tag;
        unsigned int type;
        unsigned long length;
        unsigned long offset;
        } TIFFTAG;
```

Once again, note that each of these elements can be stored as either an Intel or a Motorola number. As such, you would not normally read them into a struct.

The `tag` field specifies the identity of the tag from several dozen defined TIFF tags. For example, if the tag number is 256, the tag is called `ImageWidth`, and defines the width in pixels of the image being unpacked. A list of the most commonly used TIFF tags appears later in this chapter.

The `type` field specifies the type of numbers used to define the information in the current tag. Currently, there are five data types defined for TIFF tags:

1—The tag defines data as a byte.
2—The tag defines a string of ASCII characters.
3—The tag defines data as an unsigned integer.
4—The tag defines data as an unsigned long integer.
5—The tag defines data as a rational number consisting of two long integers, one each for the numerator and the denominator of a fraction.

The `length` field defines the length of the data in the current tag. Note, however, that it doesn't actually define the length in bytes, but defines it in the unit of storage specified by the tag. As such, the length value for a tag that specifies 1 integer would be 1, for 1 integer. The length value for a tag that specifies a 500-byte string would also be 1, for one string.

The `offset` value of a tag defines the actual information the tag represents. If the `length` element specifies data that will fit into 4 bytes, the actual size of the `offset` element, the data is stored in that `offset` element. Alternately, it will be stored somewhere in the TIFF file, with its location specified by the `offset` field relative to the start of the file.

This is more than a little tricky to implement in practice. It doesn't appear to take into account the phase of the moon or the average number of hairs per square centimeter on the inside thigh of a mature female polar bear in July, but one can never be certain. At the very least, there's probably a tag type defined to specify those things.

Of the numerous defined TIFF tags, almost all of them are optional. Here are the tags that must exist in a TIFF file in order to provide enough information to make sense of the file:

- `NewSubfileType` defines the nature of the image.
- `ImageWidth` defines the width of the picture in pixels.
- `ImageDepth` defines the depth of the picture in pixels.
- `BitsPerSample` defines the number of bits per pixel.
- `StripOffsets` specifies where the image data starts in the file.

Other tags that probably should appear are `Compression`, which defines numerous TIFF compression types that have been used and `PhotometricInterpretation`, which defines whether the image data has been stored normally or inverted or how its color pixels should be interpreted. You can build on the list to suit your fancy.

The `Compression` tag represents one of the more irritating options of the TIFF format. A hypothetical TIFF reader that could deal with absolutely every TIFF file in the western spiral arm of the milky way would have to be able to interpret all of the TIFF compression types. The value of the `Compression` tag may be one of the following as of this writing:

1—no compression
2—CCITT group 3 Huffman encoding
3—CCITT group 3 FAX compression
4—CCITT group 4 FAX compression
5—LZW string-table compression
32773—Macintosh PackBits run-length encoding

A few additional options are now, mercifully, obsolete.

Of the compression options, type 1 and type 32773 compression are dealt with in this chapter. The three CCITT compression types require some pretty monstrous makeup code tables to work, and don't apply to color TIFF files in any case. The LZW compression type, essentially the same compression used in GIF files, also requires some pretty enormous heaps of code. It's not being widely used currently.

Having read all the tags in an image file directory, you should encounter a long integer that most likely will be 0. This value indicates that all the tags in the file have been read. If it's not 0, there's another image file directory lurking around. The long integer in question represents its offset.

You will not ordinarily encounter TIFF files with more than one image file directory. It's been suggested that such files could exist to support preview images such as the ones that IFF files store in their TINY chunks, transparency masks, or animation cells. You might want to experiment with these types of applications if you're adventurous.

A TIFF Tag walker

The substantial variations among TIFF files makes software that is capable of exploring the little brutes almost essential. If a TIFF file does not read, or does not read correctly, being able to see what its tags are up to is exceedingly useful. Perhaps even more useful is being able to see the structure of the tags of a TIFF file that can be read by an application you wish to support. If you want to create TIFF files that will be read successfully by Aldus PageMaker, for example, peeking at the tags of one of the TIFF images that comes with the PageMaker package is a good place to start.

If you understand the structure of a TIFF file, you should be able to figure out how to read the tags from an image file directory and expand them to display their meanings. The details function of Graphic Workshop can do this. Figure 9-2 illustrates the details window with the tags of a TIFF file revealed.

```
1              SubfileType:  00000001 00000001
2               ImageWidth:  00000280 00000001
3              ImageLength:  000001E0 00000001
4            BitsPerSample:  00000008 00000001
5              Compression:  RUNLENGTH
6         PhotometricInterp:  REVERSED MONO
7              StripOffsets:  0000021C 00000001
8        PlanarConfiguration:  CONTIGUOUS
9           GrayResponseUnit:  00000003 00000001
10         GrayResponseCurve:  0000001C 00000100
11                 Software:  GraphicWorkshop 5.2
12            Number format:  INTEL
```

9-2 The Graphic Workshop details window with the tags of a TIFF file displayed.

In fact, a program to "walk" the tag structure of a TIFF file offers a good example of how to deal with TIFF files in general. All it omits is the process of actually unpacking pictures. Compared to making sense of the voluminous assortment of TIFF tags, a bit of line decoding is trivial.

Figure 9-3 illustrates the source code for LISTTIF. This is a simple tag walker. It can read all the tags in a TIFF file and present the information they contain in a more-or-less readable manner.

If you've been following the discussion of the basic structure of a TIFF file, you should be able to work your way through LISTTIF pretty effortlessly. It begins by reading in the first word of a TIFF file to determine the type of processor that created it. It throws away the version number and reads the offset value. It then seeks to the first image file directory and decodes it.

```
/*
        TIFF lister - copyright (c) 1991
        Alchemy Mindworks Inc.
*/

#include "stdio.h"

/* TIFF sizes */
#define TIFFbyte            1
#define TIFFascii           2
#define TIFFshort           3
#define TIFFlong            4
#define TIFFrational        5

#define TAGCOUNT        45

typedef struct {
        int number;
        char name[20];
        } TAGNAME;

unsigned long fgetlong(FILE *fp);
unsigned int fgetword(FILE *fp);
char *tagname(int n);

unsigned int numbertype='II';

TAGNAME tagnames[TAGCOUNT] = {
        { 254,"         NewSubFile"},
        { 255,"        SubfileType"},
        { 256,"         ImageWidth"},
        { 257,"        ImageLength"},
        { 278,"        RowsPerStrip"},
        { 273,"        StripOffsets"},
        { 279,"     StripByteCounts"},
        { 277,"     SamplesPerPixel"},
        { 258,"       BitsPerSample"},
        { 284,"PlanarConfiguration"},
        { 259,"         Compression"},
        { 292,"        Group3Options"},
        { 293,"        Group4Options"},
        { 266,"          FillOrder"},
        { 263,"       Threshholding"},
        { 264,"          CellWidth"},
        { 265,"         CellLength"},
        { 280,"      MinSampleValue"},
        { 281,"      MaxSampleValue"},
        { 262,"   PhotometricInterp"},
```

9-3 The source code for LISTTIF.

```
                { 290,"    GrayResponseUnit"},
                { 291,"   GrayResponseCurve"},
                { 300,"   ColorResponseUnit"},
                { 301,"ColorResponseCurves"},
                { 282,"         XResolution"},
                { 283,"         YResolution"},
                { 296,"      ResolutionUnit"},
                { 274,"         Orientation"},
                { 269,"       DocumentName"},
                { 285,"           PageName"},
                { 286,"          XPosition"},
                { 287,"          YPosition"},
                { 297,"         PageNumber"},
                { 270,"   ImageDescription"},
                { 271,"               Make"},
                { 272,"              Model"},
                { 288,"         FreeOffsets"},
                { 320,"          ColourMap"},
                { 289,"     FreeByteCounts"},
                { 315,"             Artist"},
                { 306,"           DateTime"},
                { 316,"       HostComputer"},
                { 270,"   ImageDescription"},
                { 305,"           Software"},
                { 000,"            Unknown"}
                };

main(argc,argv)
        int argc;
        char *argv[];
{

        FILE *fp;
        char path[80];
        unsigned long l;
        unsigned int i,n;

        if(argc > 1) {
                strmfe(path,argv[1],"TIF");
                strupr(path);
                if((fp=fopen(path,"rb")) != NULL) {
                        numbertype=fgetword(fp);
                        if(numbertype=='II' || numbertype=='MM') {

                                printf("TIFF tag listing for %s\n",path);

                                if(numbertype=='II') puts("Intel number format");
                                else puts("Motorola number format");

                                fgetword(fp);

                                while((l=fgetlong(fp)) != 0L) {
                                        fseek(fp,l,SEEK_SET);
```

9-3 Continued.

```
                                        n=fgetword(fp);

                                        for(i=0;i<n;++i) readtag(fp);
                                }

                        } else printf("%s isn't a TIFF file\n",path);
                        fclose(fp);
                } else printf("Error opening %s\n",path);
        } else puts("Argument:      path to a TIFF file");
}

/* expand one tag */
readtag(fp)
        FILE *fp;
{
        double nm,dm;
        char b[65];
unsigned long length,offset,pos;
int tag,type,i;

tag=fgetword(fp);
type=fgetword(fp);

if(type == TIFFlong) {
        length=fgetlong(fp);
        offset=fgetlong(fp);
}
else {
        length=(unsigned long)fgetword(fp);
        fgetword(fp);
        offset=(unsigned long)fgetword(fp);
        fgetword(fp);
}

pos=ftell(fp);
switch(type) {
        case TIFFascii:
                fseek(fp,offset,SEEK_SET);
                for(i=0;i<64;++i) {
                        if((b[i]=fgetc(fp)) == 0) break;
                }
                break;
        case TIFFshort:
                if(length <= 1L) sprintf(b,"%u",offset);
                else sprintf(b,"Offset = %-6u Length = %-6u",(int)offset,(int)length);
                break;
        case TIFFrational:
                fseek(fp,offset,SEEK_SET);
                nm=(double)fgetLong(fp);
                dm=(double)fgetLong(fp);
                sprintf(b,"%g",nm/dm);
                break;
```

9-3 Continued.

```c
                default:
                        if(length <= 1L) sprintf(b,"%lu",offset);
                        else sprintf(b,"Offset = %-6lu Length = %-6lu",offset,length);
                        break;
        }

        printf("%s - %s\n",tagname(tag),b);

        fseek(fp,pos,SEEK_SET);
}

char *tagname(n)
        int n;
{
        int i;

        for(i=0;i<TAGCOUNT;++i) {
                if(n==tagnames[i].number)
                        return(tagnames[i].name);
        }
        return(tagnames[TAGCOUNT-1].name);
}

/* get a word from a TIFF file */
unsigned int fgetword(fp)
        FILE *fp;
{
        if(numbertype == 'II') return((fgetc(fp) & 0xff) + ((fgetc(fp) & 0xff) << 8));
        else return(((fgetc(fp) & 0xff) << 8) + (fgetc(fp) & 0xff));
}


/* get a long integer from a TIFF file */
unsigned long fgetlong(fp)
        FILE *fp;
{
        if(numbertype == 'II')
            return((unsigned long)(fgetc(fp) & 0xff) +
                ((unsigned long)(fgetc(fp) & 0xff) << 8) +
                ((unsigned long)(fgetc(fp) & 0xff) << 16) +
                ((unsigned long)(fgetc(fp) & 0xff) << 24));
        else
            return(((unsigned long)(fgetc(fp) & 0xff) << 24) +
                ((unsigned long)(fgetc(fp) & 0xff) << 16) +
                ((unsigned long)(fgetc(fp) & 0xff) << 8) +
                (unsigned long)(fgetc(fp) & 0xff));
}

/* make file name with specific extension */
strmfe(new,old,ext)
        char *new,*old,*ext;
{
        while(*old != 0 && *old != '.') *new++=*old++;
```

9-3 Continued.

```
        *new++='.';
        while(*ext) *new++=*ext++;
        *new=0;
}
```

9-3 Continued.

Displaying the contents of a tag really involves reading the two integers and two long integers that comprise it and figuring out what the tag is up to. The tag value is used as the search key in a lookup table of tag names. The tag type determines how to interpret the data defined by the tag. Note that for tags with ASCII data it's necessary to seek to where the data is stored, deal with it, and then seek back to the end of the tag so that the next tag can be properly read.

It's quite allowable to have unknown tag types. Special applications for TIFF files can use proprietary tags to store data not defined in the basic TIFF specification. For this reason, a TIFF reader that encounters a tag type that it doesn't recognize should ignore it, rather than aborting.

You might want to run some TIFF files from various sources through LISTTIF. It's interesting to see what turns up. The following is the listing for a monochrome TIFF file created by a fairly old version of Graphic Workshop:

```
TIFF tag listing for SUNTAN.TIF
Intel number format
SubfileType          -   1
ImageWidth           -   576
ImageLength          -   720
BitsPerSample        -   1
Compression          -   32773
PhotometricInterp    -   1
StripOffsets         -   28
PlanarConfiguration  -   1
Software             -   GraphicWorkshop 5.2
```

Following is a TIFF file that I found on a bulletin board. It has no ASCII fields to suggest where it might have come from.

```
TIFF tag listing for FLWRGIRL.TIF
Intel number format
SubfileType          -   1
ImageWidth           -   816
ImageLength          -   1472
BitsPerSample        -   1
Compression          -   32773
PhotometricInterp    -   1
StripOffsets         -   Offset = 241    Length = 1472
SamplesPerPixel      -   1
RowsPerStrip         -   1
```

```
StripByteCounts        -   Offset=6129   Length=1472
MinSampleValue         -   0
MaxSampleValue         -   1
XResolution            -   300
YResolution            -   300
PlanarConfiguration    -   1
```

The next file is a Motorola TIFF file. It comes from the example test files of Adobe's Streamline tracing package, and was ported to a PC system over a TOPS network:

```
TIFF tag listing for ZEBRA.TIF
Motorola number format
ImageWidth       -    945
ImageLength      -    662
BitsPerSample    -    1
StripOffsets     -    102
XResolution      -    5.25
YResolution      -    5.25
```

The `BitsPerSample` tags of these listings indicate that they all are monochrome TIFF files. While the LISTTIF program will read the tags of monochrome files, the READTIF program, to be discussed next, will not display monochrome images. See *Bitmapped Graphics* for a thorough discussion of monochrome TIFF files.

A TIFF file reader

As discussed earlier, a program to read all the various types and permutations of TIFF files would be an enormous, and probably quixotic, undertaking. The READTIF program in FIG. 9-4 is hardly enormous. It's also hardly universal. You won't have to look very far for a TIFF file that it won't read.

```
/*
        TIFF reader - copyright (c) 1991
        Alchemy Mindworks Inc.
*/


#include "stdio.h"
#include "dos.h"
#include "alloc.h"


/*                          uncomment this line if you
#include "memmangr.h"        will be linking in the memory manager
*/


#define GOOD_READ      0      /* return codes */
```

9-4   The source code for READTIF.

```
#define BAD_FILE          1
#define BAD_READ          2
#define MEMORY_ERROR      3

#define SCREENWIDE        320    /* mode 13 screen dimensions */
#define SCREENDEEP        200
#define STEP              32     /* size of a step when panning */

#define HOME              0x4700 /* cursor control codes */
#define CURSOR_UP         0x4800
#define CURSOR_LEFT       0x4b00
#define CURSOR_RIGHT      0x4d00
#define END               0x4f00
#define CURSOR_DOWN        0x5000

#define RGB_RED           0
#define RGB_GREEN         1
#define RGB_BLUE          2
#define RGB_SIZE          3

/* TIFF object sizes */
#define TIFFbyte                  1
#define TIFFascii                 2
#define TIFFshort                 3
#define TIFFlong                  4
#define TIFFrational              5

/* TIFF tag names */
#define NewSubFile                254
#define SubfileType               255
#define ImageWidth                256
#define ImageLength               257
#define RowsPerStrip              278
#define StripOffsets              273
#define StripByteCounts           279
#define SamplesPerPixel           277
#define BitsPerSample             258
#define Compression               259
#define PlanarConfiguration       284
#define Group3Options             292
#define Group4Options             293
#define FillOrder                 266
#define Threshholding             263
#define CellWidth                 264
#define CellLength                265
#define MinSampleValue            280
#define MaxSampleValue            281
#define PhotometricInterp         262
#define GrayResponseUnit          290
#define GrayResponseCurve         291
#define ColorResponseUnit         300
#define ColorResponseCurves       301
```

9-4 Continued.

```
#define XResolution            282
#define YResolution            283
#define ResolutionUnit         296
#define Orientation            274
#define DocumentName           269
#define PageName               285
#define XPosition              286
#define YPosition              287
#define PageNumber             297
#define ImageDescription       270
#define Make                   271
#define Model                  272
#define FreeOffsets            288
#define FreeByteCounts         289
#define ColorMap               320
#define Artist                 315
#define DateTime               306
#define HostComputer           316
#define ImageDescription       270
#define Software               305

#define pixels2bytes(n)     ((n+7)/8)

#define greyvalue(r,g,b)           (((r*30)/100) + ((g*59)/100) + ((b*11)/100))

typedef struct {
        unsigned int width,depth,bytes,bits;
        unsigned int flags;
        unsigned int background;
        unsigned int rowsperstrip;
        unsigned int count;
        unsigned int samples;
        unsigned int planarconfig;
        unsigned int compression;
        unsigned int bitspersample;
        unsigned long bytecount;
        unsigned long offset;
        char palette[768];
        int (*setup)();
        int (*closedown)();
        } FILEINFO;

char *farPtr(char *p,long l);
char *getline(unsigned int n);
char *planes2bytes(char *p,FILEINFO *fi);
int dosetup(FILEINFO *fi);
int doclosedown(FILEINFO *fi);

int putline(char *p,unsigned int n);

unsigned long fgetlong(FILE *fp);
unsigned int fgetword(FILE *fp);
```

9-4 Continued.

```
        unsigned int numbertype='II';

        FILEINFO fi;
        char *buffer=NULL;

        main(argc,argv)
                int argc;
                char *argv[];
        {
                FILE *fp;
                static char results[8][16] = {   "Ok",
                                                 "Bad file",
                                                 "Bad read",
                                                 "Memory error",
                                                 };
                char path[80];
                int r;

                if(argc > 1) {
                        strmfe(path,argv[1],"TIF");
                        strupr(path);
                        if((fp = fopen(path,"rb")) != NULL) {
                                fi.setup=dosetup;
                                fi.closedown=doclosedown;
                                r=unpacktiff(fp,&fi);
                                printf("\%s",results[r]);
                                fclose(fp);
                        } else printf("Error opening %s",path);
                } else puts("Argument:        path to a TIFF file");
        }

        /* unpack a TIFF file */
        unpacktiff(fp,fi)
                FILE *fp;
                FILEINFO *fi;
        {
                char *p,*pr;
                unsigned long l;
                int i,j,n;

                /* get the number types */
                numbertype=fgetword(fp);

                /* see if it's real */
                if(numbertype=='II' || numbertype=='MM') {

                        /* trash the version */
                        fgetword(fp);

                        /* seek through the image directories */
                        while((l=fgetlong(fp)) != 0L) {
                                fseek(fp,l,SEEK_SET);
```

9-4 Continued.

```
/* set default values */
setdefaults(fi);

/* decode all the tags */
n=fgetword(fp);

for(i=0;i<n;++i) decodetag(fi,fp);

/* save the file position */
l=ftell(fp);

/* figure the bits - no monochrome pictures */
fi->bits=fi->samples*fi->bitspersample;
if(fi->bits==1) continue;

/* figure the bytes */
if(fi->bits <= 8)
    fi->bytes=pixels2bytes(fi->width)*fi->bits;
else fi->bytes=fi->width*RGB_SIZE;

if(fi->width != 0 &&
   fi->depth != 0 &&
   fi->offset != 0L) {

        if((p=malloc(fi->bytes)) == NULL)
            return(MEMORY_ERROR);

        if((pr=malloc(fi->width)) == NULL) {
                free(p);
                return(MEMORY_ERROR);
        }

        (fi->setup)(fi);

        if(fi->count==1L) {
                fseek(fp,fi->offset,SEEK_SET);
                for(i=0;i<fi->depth;++i) {
                        if(readline(p,fp,fi->bytes,fi) != fi->bytes) {
                                free(pr);
                                free(p);
                                freebuffer();
                                return(BAD_READ);
                        }
                        convertline(pr,p,fi);
                        putline(pr,i);
                }
        }
        else {
                for(l=0L;l<fi->count;++l) {
                        fseek(fp,fi->offset+(l*sizeof(long)),SEEK_SET);
                        fseek(fp,fgetlong(fp),SEEK_SET);
                        for(j=0;j<(int)fi->rowsperstrip;++j) {
                                if((int)((l*fi->rowsperstrip)+j) >= fi->depth) break;
```

9-4 Continued.

```
                                                if(readline(p,fp,fi->bytes,fi) != fi->bytes) {
                                                        free(pr);
                                                        free(p);
                                                        freebuffer();
                                                        return(BAD_READ);
                                                }
                                                convertline(pr,p,fi);
                                                putline(pr,(int)(l*fi->rowsperstrip)+j);
                                        }
                                }
                        }
                        free(pr);
                        free(p);
                        (fi->closedown)(fi);
                        fseek(fp,l,SEEK_SET);
                }
        }
        return(GOOD_READ);
    } else return(BAD_FILE);
}


convertline(dest,source,fi)
        char *dest,*source;
        FILEINFO *fi;
{
        int i;


        switch(fi->bits) {
                case 24:
                        for(i=0;i<fi->width;++i) {
                                dest[i]=greyvalue(source[RGB_RED],source[RGB_GREEN],source[RGB_BLUE]);
                                source+=RGB_SIZE;
                        }
                        break;
                case 8:
                        memcpy(dest,source,fi->width);
                        break;
                case 4:
                        for(i=0;i<fi->width;) {
                                dest[i++]=(*source>>4) & 0x0f;
                                dest[i++]=*source & 0x0f;
                                ++source;
                        }
                        break;
        }
}


setdefaults(fi)
        FILEINFO *fi;
{
        int i;
```

9-4 Continued.

```
                    fi->width=0;
                    fi->depth=0;
                    fi->bits=0;
                    fi->planarconfig=1;
                    fi->samples=1;
                    fi->compression=1;
                    fi->offset=0L;

                    for(i=0;i<256;++i)
                        memset(fi->palette+(i*RGB_SIZE),i,RGB_SIZE);
    }

decodetag(fi,fp)
        FILEINFO *fi;
        FILE *fp;
    {
        long length,offset,pos;
        int tag,type,i;

        tag=fgetword(fp);
        type=fgetword(fp);

        if(type == TIFFlong) {
                length=fgetlong(fp);
                offset=fgetlong(fp);
        }
        else {
                length=(unsigned long)fgetword(fp);
                fgetword(fp);
                offset=(unsigned long)fgetword(fp);
                fgetword(fp);
        }

        switch(tag) {
                case SubfileType:
                        break;
                case ImageWidth:
                        fi->width=(unsigned int)offset;
                        break;
                case ImageLength:
                        fi->depth=(unsigned int)offset;
                        break;
                case RowsPerStrip:
                        if(type==TIFFlong) fi->rowsperstrip=offset;
                        else fi->rowsperstrip=offset & 0xffffL;
                        break;
                case StripOffsets:
                        if(type==TIFFlong) fi->offset=offset;
                        else fi->offset=offset & 0xffffL;
                        fi->count=(int)length;
                        break;
                case StripByteCounts:
```

9-4 Continued.

```
                    if(type==TIFFlong) fi->bytecount=offset;
                    else fi->bytecount= offset & 0xffffL;
                    break;
        case SamplesPerPixel:
                    fi->samples=(int)offset;
                    break;
        case BitsPerSample:
                    if(length > 1L) {
                            pos=ftell(fp);
                            fseek(fp,offset,SEEK_SET);
                            fi->bitspersample=fgetword(fp);
                            fseek(fp,pos,SEEK_SET);
                    } else fi->bitspersample=(int)offset;
                    break;
        case PlanarConfiguration:
                    fi->planarconfig=(int)offset;
                    break;
        case Compression:
                    fi->compression=(int)offset;
                    break;
        case Group3Options:
                    break;
        case Group4Options:
                    break;
        case FillOrder:
                    break;
        case Threshholding:
                    break;
        case CellWidth:
                    break;
        case CellLength:
                    break;
        case MinSampleValue:
                    break;
        case MaxSampleValue:
                    break;
        case PhotometricInterp:
                    break;
        case GrayResponseUnit:
                    break;
        case GrayResponseCurve:
                    break;
        case ColorResponseUnit:
                    break;
        case ColorResponseCurves:
                    break;
        case XResolution:
                    break;
        case YResolution:
                    break;
        case ResolutionUnit:
                    break;
```

9-4 Continued.

```
                    case Orientation:
                            break;
                    case DocumentName:
                            break;
                    case PageName:
                            break;
                    case XPosition:
                            break;
                    case YPosition:
                            break;
                    case PageNumber:
                            break;
                    case ImageDescription:
                            break;
                    case Make:
                            break;
                    case Model:
                            break;
                    case FreeOffsets:
                            break;
                    case FreeByteCounts:
                            break;
                    case ColorMap:
                            pos=ftell(fp);
                            fseek(fp,offset,SEEK_SET);
                            for(i=0;i<(1<<fi->bitspersample);++i) {
                                    if(i >= 256) break;
                                    fi->palette[i*RGB_SIZE+RGB_RED]=
                                        fgetword(fp) >> 8;
                            }
                            for(i=0;i<(1<<fi->bitspersample);++i) {
                                    if(i >= 256) break;
                                    fi->palette[i*RGB_SIZE+RGB_GREEN]=
                                        fgetword(fp) >> 8;
                            }
                            for(i=0;i<(1<<fi->bitspersample);++i) {
                                    if(i >= 256) break;
                                    fi->palette[i*RGB_SIZE+RGB_BLUE]=
                                        fgetword(fp) >> 8;
                            }
                            fseek(fp,pos,SEEK_SET);
                            break;
            }
    }

/* read a compressed PackBits line */
readline(p,fp,bytes,fi)
        char *p;
        FILE *fp;
        int bytes;
        FILEINFO *fi;
{
```

9-4 Continued.

```
            int c,i,n=0;


        if(fi->compression==1) return(fread(p,1,bytes,fp));
        else if(fi->compression==0x8005) {
                do {
                        c=fgetc(fp) & 0xff;
                        if(c & 0x80) {
                                if(c != 0x80) {
                                        i = ((~c) & 0xff)+2;
                                        c=fgetc(fp);
                                        while(i--) p[n++] = c;
                                }
                        }
                        else {
                                i=(c & 0xff)+1;
                                while(i--) p[n++] = fgetc(fp);
                        }
                } while(n < bytes);
                return(n);
        }
        else return(0);
}


/* get a word from a TIFF file */
unsigned int fgetword(fp)
        FILE *fp;
{
        if(numbertype == 'II') return((fgetc(fp) & 0xff) + ((fgetc(fp) & 0xff) << 8));
        else return(((fgetc(fp) & 0xff) << 8) + (fgetc(fp) & 0xff));
}


/* get a long integer from a TIFF file */
unsigned long fgetlong(fp)
        FILE *fp;
{
        if(numbertype == 'II')
            return((unsigned long)(fgetc(fp) & 0xff) +
                ((unsigned long)(fgetc(fp) & 0xff) << 8) +
                ((unsigned long)(fgetc(fp) & 0xff) << 16) +
                ((unsigned long)(fgetc(fp) & 0xff) << 24));
        else
            return(((unsigned long)(fgetc(fp) & 0xff) << 24) +
                ((unsigned long)(fgetc(fp) & 0xff) << 16) +
                ((unsigned long)(fgetc(fp) & 0xff) << 8) +
                (unsigned long)(fgetc(fp) & 0xff));
}


/* make file name with specific extension */
strmfe(new,old,ext)
        char *new,*old,*ext;
{
```

9-4 Continued.

```
                while(*old != 0 && *old != '.') *new++=*old++;
                *new++='.';
                while(*ext) *new++=*ext++;
                *new=0;
        }

/* This function is called after the BMHD and CMAP chunks have
   been read but before the BODY is unpacked */
dosetup(fi)
        FILEINFO *fi;
{
        union REGS r;

        if(!getbuffer((long)fi->width*(long)fi->depth,fi->width,fi->depth))
            return(MEMORY_ERROR);

        r.x.ax=0x0013;
        int86(0x10,&r,&r);

        setvgapalette(fi->palette,256,fi->background);

        return(GOOD_READ);
}

/* This function is called after an image has been unpacked. It must
   display the image and deallocate memory. */
doclosedown(fi)
        FILEINFO *fi;
{
        union REGS r;
        int c,i,n,x=0,y=0;

        if(fi->width > SCREENWIDE) n=SCREENWIDE;
        else n=fi->width;

        do {
                for(i=0;i<SCREENDEEP;++i) {
                        c=y+i;
                        if(c>=fi->depth) break;
                        memcpy(MK_FP(0xa000,SCREENWIDE*i),getline(c)+x,n);
                }
                c=GetKey();
                switch(c) {
                        case CURSOR_LEFT:
                                if((x-STEP) > 0) x-=STEP;
                                else x=0;
                                break;
                        case CURSOR_RIGHT:
                                if((x+STEP+SCREENWIDE) < fi->width) x+=STEP;
                                else if(fi->width > SCREENWIDE)
                                    x=fi->width-SCREENWIDE;
                                else x=0;
```

9-4 Continued.

```
                               break;
                   case CURSOR_UP:
                           if((y-STEP) > 0) y-=STEP;
                           else y=0;
                           break;
                   case CURSOR_DOWN:
                           if((y+STEP+SCREENDEEP) < fi->depth) y+=STEP;
                           else if(fi->depth > SCREENDEEP)
                               y=fi->depth-SCREENDEEP;
                           else y=0;
                           break;
                   case HOME:
                           x=y=0;
                           break;
                   case END:
                           if(fi->width > SCREENWIDE)
                               x=fi->width-SCREENWIDE;
                           else x=0;
                           if(fi->depth > SCREENDEEP)
                               y=fi->depth-SCREENDEEP;
                           else y=0;
                           break;
               }
       } while(c != 27);

       freebuffer();

       r.x.ax=0x0003;
       int86(0x10,&r,&r);
       return(GOOD_READ);
}

/* get one extended key code */
GetKey()
{
       int c;

       c = getch();
       if(!(c & 0x00ff)) c = getch() << 8;
       return(c);
}

/* set the VGA palette and background */
setvgapalette(p,n,b)
       char *p;
       int n,b;
{
       union REGS r;
       int i;

       outp(0x3c6,0xff);
       for(i=0;i<n;++i) {
```

9-4 Continued.

```
                    outp(0x3c8,i);
                    outp(0x3c9,(*p++) >> 2);
                    outp(0x3c9,(*p++) >> 2);
                    outp(0x3c9,(*p++) >> 2);
             }
             r.x.ax=0x1001;
             r.h.bh=b;
             int86(0x10,&r,&r);
    }


/* if you don't use in the memory manager, these functions
   will stand in for it */

#if !MEMMANGR

/* return a far pointer plus a long integer */
char *farPtr(p,l)
             char *p;
             long l;
    {
             unsigned int seg,off;

             seg = FP_SEG(p);
             off = FP_OFF(p);
             seg += (off / 16);
             off &= 0x000f;
             off += (unsigned int)(l & 0x000fL);
             seg += (l / 16L);
             p = MK_FP(seg,off);
             return(p);
    }


/* save one line to memory */
putline(p,n)
             char *p;
             unsigned int n;
    {
             if(n >= 0 && n < fi.depth)
                  memcpy(farPtr(buffer,(long)n*(long)fi.width),p,fi.width);
    }


/* get one line from memory */
char *getline(n)
             unsigned int n;
    {
             return(farPtr(buffer,(long)n*(long)fi.width));
    }


#pragma warn -par
getbuffer(n,bytes,lines)
             unsigned long n;
             int bytes,lines;
```

9-4 Continued.

```
{
        if((buffer=farmalloc(n)) == NULL) return(0);
        else return(1);
}

freebuffer()
{
        if(buffer != NULL) farfree(buffer);
        buffer=NULL;
}
#endif /* !MEMMANGR */
```

9-4 Continued.

READTIF illustrates the basic approach to reading all TIFF files. It will handle a lot of the commonly encountered color TIFF files, as these don't seem to exhibit the peculiarities found in some of the more exotic monochrome TIFF images. Because color data doesn't compress very well, most of the color TIFF files around don't attempt to compress their image data, which is especially true of RGB color TIFF images.

This is the LISTTIF output for an 8-bit color TIFF file of the sort that READTIF can read:

```
TIFF tag listing for F:ZOE.TIF
Intel number format
SubfileType            -    1
ImageWidth             -    320
ImageLength            -    200
BitsPerSample          -    8
Compression            -    32773
PhotometricInterp      -    3
StripOffsets           -    1568
PlanarConfiguration -    1
Software               -    GraphicWorkshop 6.1
ColorMap               -    Offset = 32   Length = 1536
```

Before plunging into the workings of READTIF, look at exactly what some of these tags are intended to express, since a few of them have not been discussed previously.

The SubFileType tag should be the first tag in an image file directory. In fact, it has been superseded by one called NewSubFile. These tags specify what the image being defined by the directory in question is to be used for. The arguments to SubFileType can be one of the following values:

1—A single full size picture
2—A reduced resolution picture of an image defined in another directory in the current TIFF file
3—One page of a multiple-page document

The `NewSubFile` tag defines much the same information, but does so using bits set in its argument, as follows:

Bit 0—A reduced resolution picture of an image defined in another directory in the current TIFF file

Bit 1—One page of a multiple-page document

Bit 2—A transparency mask

If no bits are set, the image defaults to a full size picture, that is, the equivalent of a `SubFileType` tag with an argument of one.

The `PhotometricInterpretation` tag tells a TIFF reader how to deal with the image data it finds in a TIFF file. Its arguments are as follows:

0—The image is a reversed black-and-white picture.

1—The image is a normal black-and-white picture.

2—The image uses RGB color.

3—The image uses palette color.

4—The image is a black-and-white transparency mask.

Finally, the `ColorMap` tag specifies the offset of the color map, or palette table. Based on the general level of awkwardness of the TIFF specification, you might assume that the palette data would not be stored in the usual 3-byte RGB format that appears elsewhere in this book. This would be a pretty safe bet, although you might not have anticipated the lengths to which it goes to be unique.

The color map is stored with 48 bits of color per entry, of which 24 bits are virtually never used. Each RGB value is stored as three integers. However, they're not stored sequentially—all the red values are stored first, followed by all the green values, and finally by all the blue values. Converting the 16-bit color intensity values to 8-bit ones is pretty easy. All you have to do is shift them right by 8 bits, essentially discarding the lower 8 bits of color resolution.

It's worth noting that TIFF tags are always stored in numerical order, based on the values of their tag numbers. This method was set up so that if you read through an image file directory you'll encounter the tags with the most important information first.

The line format of TIFF files is arguably the single weirdest part of the TIFF specification. As noted, there are lots of ways to compress line information. There are also several ways to pack the pixels in a line, depending upon how the tags are set. Once again, the code in this chapter does not deal with all the permutations.

A TIFF file with 24-bits of color has its lines stored as 3-byte RGB values, just as they've appeared elsewhere in this book. Lines of an 8-bit color file are stored as an array of bytes that serve as indices into the color map, as was the case in the GIF format, for example. A TIFF file with 4 bits of color is also stored as an array of bytes, with each byte holding 2 pixels.

This is the same storage format used in the BMP and WPG formats for 4-bit images.

Images of 5 to 7 bits of color should be stored as 8-bit files. Images with 2 or 3 bits of color should be stored as 4-bit files.

The TIFF specification does allow for planar color lines as well, structured in the way that planar IFF lines are. I've yet to encounter a commercial application that could read planar TIFF files properly.

As a final note, determining the number of bits per pixel in a 24-bit TIFF file requires a level of cunning that arguably surpasses any other single bit of graphic decoding discussed in this book. No human being could have thought this up without help.

The number of bits of color in a TIFF file is defined as the number of bits per sample multiplied by the number of samples per pixel. In a 24-bit file, these values are 8 and 3 respectively—at least, they might be. It's more often the case that you'll find 24-bit files with `BitsPerSample` tags having lengths greater than 1, indicating that their offset values are really offsets. If you look where such an offset points, you'll find a table of three values, usually 8,8,8. Each one of these represents the number of bits per pixel in each of the 3 bytes of an RGB color. In theory, this would allow you to have different numbers of pixels in the red, green and blue values of a 24-bit image. It's exceedingly hard to imagine any situation where this would be of much use.

If a TIFF reader encounters a 24-bit image structured this way, it should work out the number of bits per pixel by adding up each of the three values in the table pointed to by the `BitsPerSample` tag. However, inasmuch as each of the values is usually the same, you can cheat and simply find the first entry in the table and multiply it by the argument to the `SamplesPerPixel` tag, arriving at the same results. Dogmatic TIFF acolytes will no doubt wring their hands in consternation at the thought of taking such liberties, but it always works and it certainly simplifies the code that reads TIFF tags, something that is complex enough as it stands.

Understanding TIFF files largely involves understanding their tags. Once you have these monsters by the throat, the task of unpacking a TIFF file's image data is almost trivial. You can see how it all works in READTIF.

The READTIF viewer begins by opening a prospective TIFF file, determining its number type, and finding the first image file directory. It then steps through each of the tags, working out those values that are important to unpacking the image. You'll notice that there are a lot of blank cases in the large `switch` statement in `decodetag`. These represent tags that have information that might be interesting or even useful in other contexts, but that isn't important to READTIF.

Having decoded all the tags in an image file directory, the dimensions and color depth of the image being read should be known, as well as the offset in the image data file. Assuming that none of these things are 0, the picture can be unpacked.

It's worth noting that some parameters of a TIFF file have default values, which are to be used in the event that a tag does not exist to explicitly define them. For example, the default value of the `Compression` tag is 1 (no compression) and if you wanted to be lazy, you could create a legal uncompressed TIFF file with the `Compression` tag omitted. The `setdefaults` function in READTIF establishes the relevant default values as well as setting the dimensions, color depth and offset values to 0.

The offset at which the image data in a TIFF file is located is defined by the `StripOffsets` tag. If you have become attuned to the eccentricities of TIFF, you might regard this observation with some suspicion. You might well ask why such a tag would not be called `ImageOffset`. This is, of course, yet another can of worms—carnivorous, evil-tempered worms who've been sitting in that can for months practicing to be leeches.

The TIFF specification notes that it's probably a lot easier to deal with big images if the image data is broken up into "strips," such that no individual strip requires more than 64K of memory to store it. A TIFF file so structured would consist of a number of packed strips and then by a table of offsets into the file to locate each one. The `StripOffsets` tag would supply the offset to the table of offsets.

Most TIFF files are not stored this way. They're stored as one large image (a single strip) and the `StripOffsets` tag provides the offset to the image directly. However, to be certain that your TIFF reader will read the greatest number of TIFF files, you should provide code to handle both types of images. This should explain the rather complex `for` loop in READTIF that actually unpacks the image lines. It seeks around a lot in files with multiple strips as it must move repeatedly from the table to the image data and back, with one peregrination for each strip in the file.

If you set about to design a more complete TIFF reader, you might consider reading the strip offset table into an array of long integers before you start unpacking strips. This inarguably makes the reader faster, although it requires allocating another memory buffer. This should not be a problem if you are really dealing with one strip at a time. In real-world applications, an image file reader that is designed to store all of a large image in memory probably should not expect to allocate lots of little scratch buffers as well, lest it find that its image buffer has hogged all of the available real estate.

A program that works slowly is arguably preferable to one that doesn't work at all.

As with all the file readers discussed thus far, the READTIF program uses mode 13H of a VGA card to display all the TIFF files it encounters, reducing 24-bit files to gray.

Writing TIFF files

With the exception of the small TIFF header, you may place the various elements of TIFF files anywhere you like. In most cases, the location is determined by the complexity of the code needed to handle the TIFF elements in a particular order. The WRITETIF program, discussed in this chapter, will create TIFF files in the following order:

1—The header.
2—The palette or bits per sample table.
3—The image data.
4—The tags.

There's nothing magical about this structure: if you have a good reason to place the tags before the image data, for example, you can do so without upsetting the TIFF standard. The only thing to keep in mind is that the long integer beginning with the 4th byte of the file must point to them.

The TIFF files created in this chapter are pretty rudimentary, containing image data, the minimum number of tags needed to define it, and nothing else. As mentioned earlier, you can add a great deal more to a TIFF file if you're so inclined.

Finally, the WRITETIF program creates Intel format TIFF files, as this is usually what PC applications can read with the least amount of fuss. You may modify it to create Motorola format TIFF files if you can think of a good reason for doing so. You'll have to change the number type written to the first word in the file and the code for `fputword` and `fputlong`.

The WRITETIF program can be found in FIG. 9-5.

```
/*
        TIFF writer - copyright (c) 1991
        Alchemy Mindworks Inc.
*/

#include "stdio.h"
#include "alloc.h"

#define BINARYSIG       "ALCHBINR"      /* binary identification */

#define GOOD_WRITE      0       /* return codes */
#define BAD_WRITE       1
#define BAD_READ        2
#define MEMORY_ERROR    3
#define WRONG_BITS      4

#define RGB_RED         0
#define RGB_GREEN       1
#define RGB_BLUE        2
#define RGB_SIZE        3

/* TIFF object sizes */
#define TIFFbyte                1
#define TIFFascii               2
#define TIFFshort               3
#define TIFFlong                4
```

9-5 The source code for WRITETIF.

```
                                    #define TIFFrational              5

                                    /* TIFF tag names */
                                    #define NewSubFile               254
                                    #define SubfileType              255
                                    #define ImageWidth               256
                                    #define ImageLength              257
                                    #define RowsPerStrip             278
                                    #define StripOffsets             273
                                    #define StripByteCounts          279
                                    #define SamplesPerPixel          277
                                    #define BitsPerSample            258
                                    #define Compression              259
                                    #define PlanarConfiguration      284
                                    #define Group3Options            292
                                    #define Group4Options            293
                                    #define FillOrder                266
                                    #define Threshholding            263
                                    #define CellWidth                264
                                    #define CellLength               265
                                    #define MinSampleValue           280
                                    #define MaxSampleValue           281
                                    #define PhotometricInterp        262
                                    #define GrayResponseUnit         290
                                    #define GrayResponseCurve        291
                                    #define ColorResponseUnit        300
                                    #define ColorResponseCurves      301
                                    #define XResolution              282
                                    #define YResolution              283
                                    #define ResolutionUnit           296
                                    #define Orientation              274
                                    #define DocumentName             269
                                    #define PageName                 285
                                    #define XPosition                286
                                    #define YPosition                287
                                    #define PageNumber               297
                                    #define ImageDescription         270
                                    #define Make                     271
                                    #define Model                    272
                                    #define FreeOffsets              288
                                    #define FreeByteCounts           289
                                    #define ColorMap                 320
                                    #define Artist                   315
                                    #define DateTime                 306
                                    #define HostComputer             316
                                    #define ImageDescription         270
                                    #define Software                 305

                                    #define pixels2bytes(n)    ((n+7)/8)

                                    typedef struct {
                                            char sign[8];
```

9-5 Continued.

```
            int width,depth,bits;
            char palette[768];
            } BINARYHEADER;

    int getline(char *p,int n,int line);
    int fputword(FILE *fp,int n);
    int fputlong(FILE *fp,long n);

    FILE *in,*out;
    BINARYHEADER bh;

    main(argc,argv)
            int argc;
            char *argv[];
    {
            static char results[5][16] = {  "Ok",
                                            "Bad write",
                                            "Bad read",
                                            "Memory error",
                                            "Too few colours"
                                            };

            char path[81];
            int n;

            if(argc > 1) {
                    strmfe(path,argv[1],"BIN");
                    strupr(path);
                    if((in=fopen(path,"rb")) != NULL) {
                            if(fread((char *)&bh,1,sizeof(BINARYHEADER),in) ==
                                sizeof(BINARYHEADER)) {
                                    if(!memcmp(bh.sign,BINARYSIG,8)) {
                                            strmfe(path,argv[1],"TIF");
                                            strupr(path);
                                            if((out=fopen(path,"wb")) != NULL) {
                                                    puts("Writing");
                                                    n=writetif(out,getline,
                                                            bh.width,bh.depth,
                                                            bh.bits,bh.palette);
                                                    printf("\n%s",results[n]);
                                                    fclose(out);
                                            } else printf("Error creating %s",path);
                                    } else printf("%s is corrupted",path);
                            } else printf("Error reading %s",path);
                            fclose(in);
                    } else printf("Error opening %s",path);
            } else puts("Argument:      path to a BIN file");
    }

    /* write a TIFF file */
    writetif(fp,readline,width,depth,bits,palette)
            FILE *fp;
            int (*readline)();
```

9-5 Continued.

```
                unsigned int width,depth,bits;
                char *palette;
{

                char *p,*pr;
                long pos;
                int i,bytes;

                if(bits==1) return(WRONG_BITS);

                /* figure out the line size */
                if(bits > 1 && bits <= 4) bytes=pixels2bytes(width) << 2;
                else if(bits > 4 && bits <= 8) bytes=width;
                else bytes=width*RGB_SIZE;

                /* allocate a line buffer */
                if((p=malloc(width*RGB_SIZE)) == NULL) return(MEMORY_ERROR);

                /* allocate a scratch buffer */
                if((pr=malloc(bytes)) == NULL) {
                        free(p);
                        return(MEMORY_ERROR);
                }

                /* write the header */
                fputword(fp,'II');
                fputword(fp,42);
                fputlong(fp,0L);

                /* write the palette */
                if(bits > 1 && bits <= 4) {
                        for(i=0;i<16;++i) fputword(fp,palette[i*RGB_SIZE+RGB_RED]<<8);
                        for(i=0;i<16;++i) fputword(fp,palette[i*RGB_SIZE+RGB_GREEN]<<8);
                        for(i=0;i<16;++i) fputword(fp,palette[i*RGB_SIZE+RGB_BLUE]<<8);
                }
                else if(bits > 4 && bits <=8) {
                        for(i=0;i<256;++i) fputword(fp,palette[i*RGB_SIZE+RGB_RED]<<8);
                        for(i=0;i<256;++i) fputword(fp,palette[i*RGB_SIZE+RGB_GREEN]<<8);
                        for(i=0;i<256;++i) fputword(fp,palette[i*RGB_SIZE+RGB_BLUE]<<8);
                }
                else {
                        for(i=0;i<RGB_SIZE;++i) fputword(fp,8);
                }

                /* write the bitmap */
                for(i=0;i<depth;++i) {
                        if(bits==24) readline(p,width*RGB_SIZE,i);
                        else readline(p,width,i);
                        if(bits == 4) {
                                packegaline(pr,p,width);
                                writeline(fp,pr,bytes);
                        }
                        else if(bits == 8) writeline(fp,p,bytes);
```

9-5 Continued.

```
                    else if(bits == 24) fwrite(p,1,bytes,fp);
        }

        pos=ftell(fp);
        /* write the tags */
        if(bits > 1 && bits <=4) {
                fputword(fp,9);
                writetiftag(fp,SubfileType,TIFFshort,1L,1L);
                writetiftag(fp,ImageWidth,TIFFshort,1L,(long)width);
                writetiftag(fp,ImageLength,TIFFshort,1L,(long)depth);
                writetiftag(fp,BitsPerSample,TIFFshort,1L,4L);
                writetiftag(fp,Compression,TIFFshort,1L,32773L);
                writetiftag(fp,PhotometricInterp,TIFFshort,1L,3L);
                writetiftag(fp,StripOffsets,TIFFlong,1L,104L);
                writetiftag(fp,PlanarConfiguration,TIFFshort,1L,1L);
                writetiftag(fp,ColorMap,TIFFshort,96L,8L);
        }
        else if(bits > 4 && bits <=8) {
                fputword(fp,9);
                writetiftag(fp,SubfileType,TIFFshort,1L,1L);
                writetiftag(fp,ImageWidth,TIFFshort,1L,(long)width);
                writetiftag(fp,ImageLength,TIFFshort,1L,(long)depth);
                writetiftag(fp,BitsPerSample,TIFFshort,1L,8L);
                writetiftag(fp,Compression,TIFFshort,1L,32773L);
                writetiftag(fp,PhotometricInterp,TIFFshort,1L,3L);
                writetiftag(fp,StripOffsets,TIFFlong,1L,1544L);
                writetiftag(fp,PlanarConfiguration,TIFFshort,1L,1L);
                writetiftag(fp,ColorMap,TIFFshort,1536L,8L);
        }
        else {
                fputword(fp,10);
                writetiftag(fp,NewSubFile,TIFFshort,1L,0L);
                writetiftag(fp,ImageWidth,TIFFshort,1L,(long)width);
                writetiftag(fp,ImageLength,TIFFshort,1L,(long)depth);
                writetiftag(fp,BitsPerSample,TIFFshort,3L,8L);
                writetiftag(fp,Compression,TIFFshort,1L,1L);
                writetiftag(fp,PhotometricInterp,TIFFshort,1L,2L);
                writetiftag(fp,StripOffsets,TIFFlong,1L,14L);
                writetiftag(fp,SamplesPerPixel,TIFFshort,1L,3L);
                writetiftag(fp,RowsPerStrip,TIFFlong,1L,(long)depth);
                writetiftag(fp,PlanarConfiguration,TIFFshort,1L,1L);
        }
        fputlong(fp,0L);
        fseek(fp,4L,SEEK_SET);
        fputlong(fp,pos);

        free(pr);
        free(p);

        if(ferror(fp)) return(BAD_WRITE);
        else return(GOOD_WRITE);
}
```

9-5 Continued.

```
                    /* write one TIFF tag to the IFD */
                    writetiftag(fp,tag,type,length,offset)
                            FILE *fp;
                            int tag,type;
                            long length,offset;
                    {
                            fputword(fp,tag);
                            fputword(fp,type);
                            fputlong(fp,length);
                            fputlong(fp,offset);

                            return(ferror(fp));
                    }

                    /* do packbits compression for one line of image data */
                    writeline(fp,p,n)
                            FILE *fp;
                            char *p;
                            int n;
                    {
                            char b[128];
                            unsigned int bdex=0,i=0,j=0,t=0;

                            do {
                                    i=0;
                                    while((p[t+i]==p[t+i+1]) &&
                                            i < 127 &&
                                            i < (n-1) &&
                                            ((t+i+1) < n)) ++i;

                                    if(i > 0 || bdex >= 127) {
                                            if(bdex) {
                                                    fputc(((bdex-1) & 0x7f),fp);
                                                    ++j;
                                                    fwrite(b,1,bdex,fp);
                                                    j+=bdex;
                                                    bdex=0;
                                            }
                                            if(i) {
                                                    fputc((~i+1),fp);
                                                    fputc(p[t+i],fp);
                                                    j+=2;
                                                    t+=(i+1);
                                            }
                                    } else b[bdex++]=p[t++];
                            } while(t<n);

                            if(bdex) {
                                    fputc(((bdex-1) & 0x7f),fp);
                                    ++j;
                                    fwrite(b,1,bdex,fp);
                                    j+=bdex;
```

9-5 Continued.

```
                }
        if((j & 0x0001)) fputc(0x80,fp);
}

/* translate a vga line to a stacked pixel line */
packegaline(dest,source,width)
        char *dest,*source;
        int width;
{
        int i,j=0;

        for(i=0;i<width;i+=2) {
                dest[j] = ((source[i] << 4) & 0xf0);
                dest[j] |= (source[i+1] & 0x0f);
                ++j;
        }
}

/* make file name with specific extension */
strmfe(new,old,ext)
        char *new,*old,*ext;
{
        while(*old != 0 && *old != '.') *new++=*old++;
        *new++='.';
        while(*ext) *new++=*ext++;
        *new=0;
}

/* fetch a line from the input file */
getline(p,n,line)
        char *p;
        int n,line;
{
        int i;

        /* seek past the binary file header to the line */
        fseek(in,(long)sizeof(BINARYHEADER)+(long)line*(long)n,SEEK_SET);
        i=fread(p,1,n,in);
        if(i==n) return(0);
        else return(1);
}

int fputword(fp,n)
        FILE *fp;
        int n;
{
        fputc(n,fp);
        fputc((n >> 8),fp);
        return(ferror(fp));
}

int fputlong(fp,n)
```

9-5 Continued.

```
        FILE *fp;
        long n;

    {
        fputc(n,fp);
        fputc((n >> 8),fp);
        fputc((n >> 16),fp);
        fputc((n >> 24),fp);
        return(ferror(fp));

    }
```
9-5 Continued.

The WRITETIF program can be found in FIG. 9-5.

The WRITETIF program accepts binary files from any of the programs discussed in this book that created them. The files can have between 4 and 24 bits of color. It creates 4, 8, or 24-bit TIFF files accordingly. The 4-bit and 8-bit TIFF files are stored using run-length compression. As run-length compressing the bytes of an RGB line is all but certain to create a file with thunderously apparent negative compression, 24-bit files are written uncompressed.

The `writeline` function that packs lines for WRITETIF has been lifted from the WRITEIFF program several chapters back. Both formats use the same run-length compression procedure, having both, in turn, lifted it from the MacPaint file format.

The `writetif` function handles creating a TIFF file from a binary source file. It writes the Intel number type specifier, the TIFF version (integer containing 42) and then a dummy long integer that will eventually hold the offset of the image file directory, once it's determined where this is to be stored.

Depending upon the number of bits of color the file being written will support, the next element in the file will either be the color palette information or three integers, each containing the value 8, this latter being the data for the `SamplesPerPixel` tag of a 24-bit file. If you wanted to add some additional descriptive tags, such as some ASCII information, this is probably where you'd put their data.

Having written the palette information or the samples-per-pixel table, the code then writes the image information. As you'll observe if you look at the principal `for` loop of the `writetif` function, image lines are handled in one of three ways, depending upon their color depth. Four-bit lines are translated from 1 pixel per byte lines—the way they come from a binary source file—into lines with two pixels stacked in each byte. The resulting packed lines are then compressed by `writeline`. Eight-bit lines are compressed by `writeline` directly. Lines of 24-bit images are written directly to the file.

The last thing to write is an image file directory. This consists of an integer indicating the number of tags in the directory followed by the tags themselves. The tags are handled individually by the `writetiftag` function. The use of the symbolic constants defined at the top of the file makes defining these things fairly straightforward.

It's very important to make sure that there's a long integer containing the value 0 after the last tag in the image file directory, so that a TIFF reader that reads files having multiple image file directories will know that it has reached the end of the line. If it doesn't find 4 bytes of 0, it will interpret whatever random bytes it does find as an offset and go searching for a second, nonexistent, set of tags.

Having written its tags, the `writetif` code must seek back to the dummy long integer at the beginning of the file and write in the offset of the start of the image file directory.

Commonly used TIFF tags

The following is a list of TIFF tags you're likely to encounter in TIFF files, and may want to use yourself. It's by no means exhaustive.

`Artist`   315 (13BH)   ASCII
This tag specifies who created the image.

`BitsPerSample`   258 (102H)   SHORT
This tag defines the number of bits per sample. The default is 1.

`ColorMap`   320 (140H)   SHORT
This tag defines the offset to a color map for palette color images.

`ColorResponseCurves`   301 (12DH)   SHORT
This tag defines three color response curves. These curves allow TIFF readers to redefine the color in an image, such as to compensate for specific output or display hardware.

`Compression`   259 (103H)   SHORT
This tag defines the type of compression used in a TIFF image. The default is 1. Its values can be as follows:

> 1—no compression.
> 2—CCITT group 3 one-dimensional modified Huffman run-length encoding.
> 3—CCITT group 3 FAX compression.
> 4—CCITT group 4 FAX compression.
> 5—LZW compression.
> 32773—PackBits run-length encoding.

`DateTime`   306 (132)   ASCII
This tag defines the date and time at which the image was created.

`GrayResponseCurve`   291 (123H)   SHORT
This tag defines the offset of a gray-response curve, which modifies the gray levels of a gray-scale image to compensate for specific output or display hardware.

GrayResponseUnit   290 (122H)   SHORT

This tag modifies the gray-response curve. The default value is 2. The recognized values are as follows:

     1—tenths of a unit.
     2—hundredths of a unit.
     3—thousandths of a unit.
     4—ten-thousandths of a unit.
     5—hundred-thousandths of a unit.

HostComputer   316 (13CH)   ASCII

This tag defines the type of computer used to create the image.

ImageDescription   270 (10EH)   ASCII

This tag defines a text description of the image.

ImageLength   257 (101H)   SHORT or LONG

This tag defines the image depth in pixels.

ImageWidth   256 (100H)   SHORT or LONG

This tag defines the image width in pixels.

Make   271 (10FH)   ASCII

This tag defines the name of the manufacturer of the hardware that digitized the image.

Model   272 (110H)   ASCII

This tag defines the model number of the hardware that digitized the image.

NewSubfileType   254 (FEH)   LONG

This tag defines the nature of an image in a TIFF file. Its data is made up of a set of 32 flag bits. The unused bits are set low. The default is 0, indicating a single, stand-alone image. The bits are defined as follows:

     Bit 0—set if the image is a reduced version of another image stored elsewhere in the file
     Bit 1—set if the image is one of several pages stored in this file
     Bit 2—set if this image is a transparency mask.

PhotometricInterpretation 262 (106H)

This tag indicates how an image has been stored. Its values can be as follows:

     0—If the image is black and white, it's stored reversed.
     1—If the image is black and white, it's stored normally.
     2—The image uses RGB color.
     3—The image uses palette color.
     4—The image is a black-and-white transparency mask.

`PlanarConfiguration`   284 (11CH)   SHORT
This tag defines whether images are stored contiguously or in discrete planes. The default value is 1. The recognized values are:

1—The pixels are stored contiguously in a single plane.
2—The pixels are stored as multiple planes.

`Predictor`   317 (13DH)   SHORT
This tag defines whether a prediction process is used if image data is compressed by LZW encoding. The default is 1, meaning that prediction is not used.

`ResolutionUnit`   296 (128H)   SHORT
This tag defines resolution units for `XResolution` and `YResolution` tags. The default value is 2. The recognized values are:

1—No absolute unit of measurement is used.
2—Resolution is defined in inches.
3—Resolution is defined in centimeters.

`RowsPerStrip`   278 (116H)   SHORT or LONG
This tag defines the number of rows per strip.

`SamplesPerPixel`   277 (115H)   SHORT
This tag defines the number of samples per pixel. The default is 1.

`StripByteCounts`   279 (117H)   SHORT or LONG
This tag defines the number of bytes in each strip of an image.

`StripOffsets`   273 (111H)   SHORT or LONG
This tag defines the offset to each strip of image information relative to the start of the file.

`XResolution`   282 (11AH)   RATIONAL
This tag defines the number of horizontal pixels per `ResolutionUnit`.

`YResolution`   283 (11BH)   RATIONAL
This tag defines the number of vertical pixels per `ResolutionUnit`.

`Software`   305 (131H)   ASCII
This tag defines the name of the software used to create the image.

Using TIFF files

It's probably possible to write a moderately large book on the vagaries and nuances of TIFF. Such a book, while an invaluable reference if you really wanted to make the TIFF specification get up and dance, would probably be extremely difficult to read and would require supreme nerve and willpower to open.

While this chapter does not even begin to really get into the TIFF standard, it probably contains enough information to allow you to use TIFF files in most imaging applications. It omits things such as a detailed description of group 3 CCITT FAX encoding and how to create an RGB image having different bit depths for its three color indices, but these are things that you probably won't need.

If you'd like to know everything there is to know about TIFF files, you should probably spring for a copy of the Aldus *TIFF Developer's Kit*. It's available from Aldus Corporation, 411 First Ave. South, Seattle, WA 98104. Aldus can be reached at (206) 628-6593.

10
High-speed screen drivers

Telepathy means never having to say you're sorry.

—GRAFFITI

Several years ago, computer store proprietors discovered a better way to attract attention to their hardware. Rather than having vulgar day-glow signs proclaim the number of megabytes, milliseconds, ports, and other paraphernalia offered by the systems they were trying to sell, they put VGA graphics on the screens of their demonstration computers.

While being able to multitask 12 applications under Windows is useful, being able to display a full color scan of a white mouse on your monitor is genuinely interesting. That scan of a mouse has probably sold more computers than all the polyester computer salesmen in the western hemisphere.

Figure 10-1 illustrates the mouse in question, should you be one of the few who's not encountered it yet.

As people grew more sophisticated, they began to look at the mouse graphic and remark "hmm . . . standard VGA mode . . . not very impressive," or words to this effect. Regrettably, the mouse really is a pretty low resolution scan, weighing in at 320×200 pixels in 256 colors. The computer store proprietors began to up the ante, which they were able to do because new super VGA cards were appearing at about that time. Initially capable of displaying 256 colors with 640×400 pixel resolution, the currently available cards support up to 1Mb of memory and 256-color display modes handling 1024×768 pixels.

10-1 A scanned mouse. This file was originally downloaded from Rose Media, (416) 733-2285.

Figure 10-2 illustrates the relative sizes of the commonly available super VGA modes. It's worth noting that the larger mouse is a synthetic derivative of the original. No higher resolution mice have appeared to date, and computer store displays have diversified into other subjects.

This chapter looks at driving standard VGA cards and some of the more popular super VGA cards to display the graphics discussed earlier in this book. Specifically, it deals with code to handle the following display hardware:

- The standard IBM VGA 320×200 pixel display
- The Paradise cards
- The ATI VGA Wonder cards
- The Tseng Labs 4000 series chips
- Thc Trident 8900 series chips
- VGA monochrome and 16-color modes
- The ATI XL 15-bit color hardware
- The Paradise 15-bit color hardware

This list might require a bit of elaboration. The original IBM VGA card supported the 256-color, 320×200 pixel mode, mode 13H, which was used informally in the early chapters of this book. All super VGA cards support it as well.

Super VGA cards are based on a superset of the original VGA card's facilities. In most cases, this superset provides for 16- and 256-color modes having higher resolutions than the original IBM hardware could

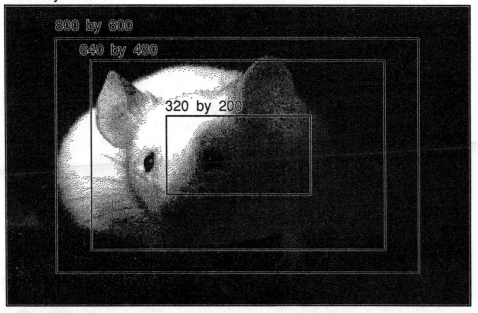

10-2 Attack of the incredible expanding rodent—the relative sizes of the popular 256-color super VGA modes.

manage. A few of the super VGA cards designed for use primarily in business applications confine themselves to having higher resolution 16-color modes only, as this is what's used to run Microsoft Windows in a business environment. These cards are not discussed here.

A number of fairly standard resolution modes are supported by super VGA cards at 256 colors. They are:

- 640×400 pixels
- 640×480 pixels
- 800×600 pixels
- 1024×768 pixels

The 640×400, 256-color mode is useful in that it allows you to display a large graphic on a super VGA card having only 256K on board. If your card has 512K on board, it should support 640×480 pixels at 256 colors, and probably 800×600 pixels as well. If you have 1Mb of memory on your display card, you should be able to manage 1024×768 pixels in 256 colors.

Note that not all monitors can synchronize at these higher resolutions. In fact, very low-end, non-multisync monitors will not even handle the 640×400 pixel, 256-color mode of a super VGA card. If you find that the code in this chapter doesn't display stable pictures, you might want to determine if your monitor is capable of handling these modes.

Most mid-range multisync monitors can handle up to 800×600 pixels. You need a pretty good monitor to get up to 1024×768 pixels. I use a Sony HG monitor, which can handle this resolution.

It's important to note that driving a VGA card and monitor at a resolution that the monitor cannot support can damage both the card and the monitor if you let the card remain in the unsupported mode long enough. It's a good idea to be ready to reboot your computer when you're initially trying out code to drive a super VGA card.

If you attempt to select a super VGA mode that your card does not support or doesn't have enough memory to manage, the text on your screen will change colors, but nothing nasty should happen.

In order to keep both the complexity of this chapter and the risk of smoking your monitor down to a minimum, the code discussed here deals with the 640×400 or 640×480 pixel modes of each of the super VGA cards dealt with.

While the code in this chapter deals with monochrome and 16-color modes as well as the 256-color VGA modes, it specifically looks at these modes as they pertain to VGA cards. If you're interested in driving a CGA, EGA or Hercules card, you can find a discussion of screen drivers for them in *Bitmapped Graphics*.

The latter two cards in the previous list of display adapters, the ATI XL and the newest Paradise D series cards, represent something of a departure from the other cards discussed in this chapter. While they each support super VGA modes out to 1024×768 pixels at 256 colors, they have additional modes that aren't currently available on most other super VGA display hardware. These "true color" modes handle color without the use of a palette. In reality, they force you to reduce the 24-bit images provided by most true color file formats down to only 15 bits of color, but as discussed shortly this doesn't turn out to be much worse than the color resolution of a VGA card's palette-driven modes.

The thing that makes these true color cards so useful in display applications, such as those discussed in this book, is that they allow you to view 24-bit files without resorting to gray scales or going for a Coke while your images are quantized and dithered. This chapter looks at drivers for these cards as well.

There are lots of available super VGA cards based on a fairly restricted number of chip sets. The chip sets are the very large scale integration devices (VLSI) that give super VGA cards their features. In many cases, the chip manufacturers sell them to third-party board makers in addition to using them in their own hardware.

As of this writing, only ATI in the above list was not doing this. As such, it's possible to buy low-cost super VGA cards with Paradise, Tseng Labs and Trident chips on them. These cards behave just like genuine Paradise, Tseng Labs and Trident hardware, although they usually cost less.

Should you be uncertain which type of display card you have, you can usually work it out by staring at the markings on the large square chips on your card for a while. The Paradise chip set is made by Western Digital and usually has the letters "WD" on it. The current generation of Tseng Labs chips is identified by the number 4000 as of this writing. The current generation of Trident chips is identified by the number 8900. They also bear the logo of their manufacturer, a stylized trident.

The Graphic Workshop drivers

Assuming that you're not content to display 256-color images in mode 13H, a feature common to all VGA cards but arguably too ugly to think about seriously, you'll be confronted with a problem of some magnitude. There are at least a half-dozen popular super VGA cards, and over a half-dozen more that might crop up. Each one comes in various revisions and flavors, with different maximum resolutions based on the amount of memory particular cards support.

You should realize that no two of these disparate cards are in any way compatible. Software designed to drive the super VGA modes of a Paradise card, for example, does not drive an ATI card. Mode 13H is common to both cards in that software that supports mode 13H, such as the code in earlier chapters, does work on both devices. However, while both cards support a 640×480, 256-color mode, different software is required to drive them at this resolution.Writing C-language code to support all the permutations of super VGA cards, while possible, is something well worth avoiding. Aside from being somewhat huge, this library of functions would be difficult to maintain. Every time a new display card appeared you'd have to recompile your software.

A better possible way to deal with this swamp is to use device-independent code to display the images in question and then to write loadable device drivers to handle the hardware-specific aspects of the whole juggling act. Because Turbo C doesn't really have a convenient provision for dealing with this from within C, the drivers must be written in assembly language. Doing this requires a little more work, but the drivers will be both smaller and faster.

The basis of this process is pretty easy to understand; the drivers will prove a bit more complicated. Consider that there is an unpacked image in a buffer pointed to by p. There's also some machine language code pointed to by gd that displays it. The pointers involved would be declared like this:

```
char *p;
void (*gd)( );
```

Because this is device-independent code, the calling function need not know which super VGA card you're using; that's the concern of the code at gd. For practical purposes, the code at gd is an assembly language routine that has been loaded from a disk file.

In order to display the image, then, the language calling program would do this:

```
(gd)(p);
```

This means that it will call the assembly language driver at gd and pass it the pointer to the image. It's the driver's responsibility to display the picture.

This arrangement allows you to support multiple VGA cards by simply having multiple drivers on hand. In order to display a picture on an ATI card, you would load up the ATI driver. In order to display a picture on a Paradise card, you'd load the Paradise driver, and so on. The C-language calling program remains independent of the driver.

You face a lot of nasty practical considerations in translating this concept to a real-world driver standard that supports the wide range of available display cards.

The Graphic Workshop package on the companion disks for this book deals with the problem of supporting a wide variety of display cards in exactly the way just discussed. It has a set of loadable machine-language drivers and device-independent code to call them. While the Graphic Workshop drivers do have some features that aren't really called for in the context of this chapter, they do offer a good example of a workable, real-world driver standard. You might find that you have to modify this standard for your applications.

There are some decided advantages to using this driver standard if you find that your programs work with it. Graphic Workshop and its drivers have been around for a long time, and have been tested on many cards, some of which were pretty peculiar. In addition, there are a number of Graphic Workshop drivers for cards not discussed here. If you wish to support the cards they are written for, you can extract them from Graphic Workshop's resource file. The procedure for doing this is discussed near the end of this chapter.

A Graphic Workshop screen driver provides the following functions to the calling code:

- RGB on
- RGB off
- RGB line
- VGA on
- VGA off
- VGA line
- VGA palette
- VGA overscan
- EGA on
- EGA off
- EGA palette
- monochrome on

- monochrome off
- monochrome line
- monochrome functions

The three RGB functions are used to display 24-bit files, assuming that the card being used can handle true color images. In all but the ATI XL and Paradise D drivers, discussed later in this chapter, these three functions aren't implemented.

The five VGA functions handle 256-color images, or more precisely, images having from 5 to 8 bits of color. The on and off functions turn the appropriate mode on and off. The line function displays one line. The palette function sets the VGA palette and the overscan sets the border.

The EGA functions handle 16-color images. This chapter does not cover EGA cards per se; it's common to regard 16-color pictures as being EGA images and 256-color pictures as being VGA images because these values are the upper limits of color depth of the two cards respectively. In fact, the EGA 16-color mode, while available on a VGA card, is pretty ugly. The drivers in this chapter use the VGA 16-color mode.

The monochrome functions handle monochrome images in the same way that EGA and VGA images were supported. The monochrome functions call is actually a catch-all for things that Graphic Workshop needs and which none of the code in this chapter uses.

In addition to these function calls, a driver tells the calling code the dimensions of the screen it's working with. It also has a name and a version number that are useful to Graphic Workshop but not all that important to other programs.

The C language provides for a very elegant way to interface to loadable machine-language modules—at least it does on a PC. A screen driver can be defined by the following struct:

```
typedef struct {
        int (*vga_on)( );
        int (*vga_line)( );
        int (*vga_off)( );
        int (*vga_palette)( );
        int (*vga_overscan)( );
        int (*ega_on)( );
        int (*ega_line)( );
        int (*ega_off)( );
        int (*ega_palette)( );
        int (*mono_on)( );
        int (*mono_functions)( );
        int (*mono_line)( );
        int (*mono_off)( );
        int (*rgb_on)( );
        int (*rgb_line)( );
        int (*rgb_off)( );
        int rgb_wide, rgb_deep,
        int vga_wide, vga_deep, vga_screenseg;
```

```
int ega_wide, ega_deep, ega_bytes;
int ega_screenseg;
int mono_wide, mono_deep, mono_bytes;
int mono_screenseg;
int driver_version, driver_subversion;
char name[25];
} GRAFDRIVER;
```

If gd is a pointer of the type GRAFDRIVER and is presently pointing to a loaded, initialized Graphic Workshop screen driver, you could change to the VGA graphics mode that the driver supports by doing this:

```
(gd->vga_on)( );
```

Each of the function pointers in a GRAFDRIVER object can be used the same way. While it might not be clear what calling one of these functions actually does until you've had a look at the source code for a driver, it's sufficient to know that as far as a C-language program is concerned, each of these pointers behaves as if it were pointing to a normal, large model C function.

Keep in mind that a GRAFDRIVER object is not the entire driver. It's just the header, the predictable part that interfaces with a C program. As such, if gd points to an object of the type GRAFDRIVER, the object is a lot bigger than sizeof(GRAFDRIVER). A simple mode 13H screen driver requires a bit less than 2K of code.

Note that the GRAFDRIVER standard has evolved a lot and that some of its rather haphazard appearance is due to its maintaining a degree of backwards compatibility. Specifically, RGB support is a new addition. Originally, 4 NULL pointers in a GRAFDRIVER structure allowed for future expansion. As a large-model pointer is 2 integers in reality, it was possible to convert these to 3 pointers for the RGB functions and 2 integers to define the current RGB mode screen size.

The (*mono_functions)( ) pointer used to be a pointer to a function that would update the entire monochrome screen in one pass, rather than line by line. The current revision of Graphic Workshop no longer needs that facility, and was changed to its current use.

The version and sub-version numbers tell Graphic Workshop how to use a driver, but a lot of old drivers for special purpose cards still exist. Drivers with major version numbers of 1 still support the old call for (*mono_functions)( ). This call is obsolete. You shouldn't use it in your code. The version 2.0 drivers support the (*mono_functions)( ) that appear in the driver source code in this chapter. Version 2.1 drivers support mode tables, which allow Graphic Workshop to know the modes available in a particular driver. Once again, these are not things you're likely to want to implement in your code. Because none of these things pertain to the basic function of the screen drivers, you can safely ignore them.

Calling the driver functions

Much of the discussion of screen-handling code dealt with here gets into some fairly evil looking assembly language. It's worth noting that you don't have to confront a single pseudo-op or indirect addressing mode if you don't want to. The screen drivers that the assembly language code in this chapter creates are included with the companion disk set for this book. Using nothing more than the C calling code dealt with here, you can load them and use them without getting involved in seeing how they work.

Of course, if you have the leisure to dig through the assembly language listings, you'll have a first-hand glimpse at some very weird hardware and the code that works with it.

Before you immerse yourself in the source code for a screen driver, it's helpful to know what the various callable parts of a driver are intended to do. This section deals with the arguments for the driver functions as seen from the safe, comfortable world of a C program. In all of these examples, it's assumed that gd is a pointer to a GRAFDRIVER object that is loaded and initialized. Loading and initializing one is dealt with after we've had a look at an actual driver. For the moment, the details of how a driver works can be ignored.

Because not all drivers may be assumed to support all four basic screen modes (monochrome, 16 colors, 256 colors, and 24 bits), you should treat the four on functions of a GRAFDRIVER as flags. For example, if gd->rgb_on is NULL, your code should assume that the current driver does not have 24-bit color support, and make other arrangements to handle 24-bit images.

The on functions should be passed two integer arguments that represent the dimensions of the image to be displayed. This would be a proper call to gd->vga_on. This example assumes that fi is a pointer to a FILEINFO structure of the type that has been turning up in each of the file readers in this book.

```
(gd->vga_on)(fi->width,fi->depth);
```

Having the image dimensions available to a driver's on functions allows it to automatically select one of several driver modes. For example, a super VGA card that supports both the standard mode 13H, 256-color mode and a proprietary 640×480 pixel, 256-color mode could select the former for small images and the latter for images having dimensions larger than 320×200 pixels.

Alternately, you can pass constant values to force a driver into a particular mode if you know the mode you want to use. For example, if you want to force a driver into its 640×480 pixel, 256-color mode, you would select the 256-color mode like this:

```
(gd->vga_on)(640,480);
```

The four off functions don't have any arguments. They simply return the screen to text mode. The gd->vga_line function accepts three arguments: a pointer to the graphic information to be written to the screen, the length of the data, and the line number. Here's how you'd copy an image from a buffer to the screen, assuming that the screen has previously been put into a VGA graphics mode using gd->vga_on. This example uses the memory manager getline call that appeared in the file reader programs earlier in this book.

```
int i;

for(i=0;i<gd->vga_deep;++i)
    (gd->vga_line)(getline(i),gd->vga_wide,i);
```

In fact, this is a bit simplistic. It assumes that the picture being displayed is at least as big as the screen. The GIF file reader discussed later in this chapter illustrates a somewhat more complete implementation of this bit of code. The gd->rgb_line call works the same way.

The gd->ega_line call assumes that the lines it displays are stored as four planes, as discussed in chapter 3 in conjunction with IFF/LBM files. Here's how it's called.

```
int i;

for(i=0;i<gd->ega_deep;++i)
    (gd->ega_line)(getline(i),pixels2bytes
    (gd->ega_wide),i);
```

The argument that specifies the width of the line to be moved should be the number of bytes in a plane, rather than in the complete line.

The gd->mono_line call works the same way, except that its latter two arguments are interchanged.

```
int i;
for(i=0;i<gd->mono_deep;++i)
    (gd->mono_line)(getline(i),i,pixels2bytes
    (gd->mono_wide));
```

Note that the third argument to gd->mono_line is the number of bytes to move, not the number of pixels.

The gd->vga_palette function sets the 256-color palette. It's called with two arguments, these being a pointer to the RGB palette table to be used, and an integer that defines the number of colors in the table, to a maximum of 256. It's acceptable to let this second argument remain at 256 no matter how many colors are actually in your picture. A picture with 7 bits of color would have only 128 valid colors in its palette. If you tell gd->vga_palette to set 256 colors, the upper 128 colors will be meaningless. If the image only has 7 bits of color, none of its pixels will attempt to use the upper 128 colors and they'll be safely ignored.

Note that the palette color table should be stored as three 8-bit bytes per color, in the order red, green, blue. While VGA cards only use the upper 6 bits of color, it's the driver's responsibility to convert this internally.

The gd->vga_overscan call sets the color of the border in the display card's 256-color mode. It takes one integer as an argument. The integer should hold the color index of the border color.

The gd->ega_palette call probably deserves some extra discussion. It's another aspect of the Graphic Workshop screen driver standard that has evolved somewhat.

The original EGA card supported a 16-color mode that allowed 16 colors to be selected from a 64-color palette. It used 2 bits to define each of the three color components of a color, for a total of 6 bits per color. A color could thus be defined as a single byte, called EGA color numbers.

The 16-color modes of a VGA card can be set up to use EGA color numbers if you so wish. However, the degree of control that color numbers provide you with is crude. You can, in fact, have 18 bits of color control in the 16-color mode of a VGA card, just as you can in its 256-color mode. This means that you can select 16 colors from a palette of 262,144 colors.

The Graphic Workshop screen driver standard allows for both forms of setting the 16-color palette. It's assumed that the driver knows which one to use. A driver written to support old EGA cards would use EGA color numbers. A driver to handle a VGA or super VGA card can use real RGB colors.

The call to gd->ega_palette takes three arguments. The first is a pointer to a table of EGA color numbers. The second is an integer containing the actual number of colors to be set, with a maximum of 16. The third is a pointer to a table of RGB color values.

Inasmuch as the drivers in this chapter are all working with various VGA cards, the EGA color numbers can safely be ignored. The example code later in this chapter passes NULL for the first argument of gd->ega_palette, although if you want to fully implement the driver standard in your programs you should probably provide a real table of EGA color numbers, just in case someone with a cranky old EGA card turns up.

Should you be curious about just how the 16-color palette is set on a VGA card, you might want to peek behind the window dressing of a VGA card to understand just what it's doing in its 16-color modes. The designers of the VGA card appreciated that it should be backwards-compatible with the older EGA card, although the actual color-management hardware of an EGA card is not present in a VGA card. In fact, the EGA color numbers turn out to be supported in software to some extent.

A VGA card has 256 color registers, all of which are used in the 256-color mode. Only 16 colors are used in the 16-color mode, but not necessarily the first 16.

An EGA color number uses the first 6 bits of a byte, so there are 64 permutations of bits. In order to support the older EGA color numbers, should someone wish to use them, the default palette of a VGA card in its 16-color mode is set up so that there are 64 colors in its first 64 color registers that correspond to all the colors available on an EGA card. Which of these colors are actually used is determined by how the EGA color numbers are set.

In order to set up a VGA card's 16-color palette using RGB values, then, you load the RGB values into the first 16 color registers, just as in the case for the color registers in the 256-color mode. You then load the numbers 0 though 15 into the EGA color number registers, as this causes the card to use the first 16 colors in its color map. Normally these would be the first 16 EGA colors; however, since you just reprogrammed them, they'll be your colors.

The gd->mono_functions call is somewhat complex, and because it's not used by any of the code in this chapter, its arguments can probably be ignored. If you're curious as to what it's up to, you can check out the source code for the screen drivers, each of which has the function to implement it.

This, then, is a summary of the GRAFDRIVER screen calls:

```
(gd->rgb_on)(int width, int depth);
(gd->rgb_off)( );
(gd->rgb_line)(char *line, int width,
int line_number);

(gd->vga_on)(int width, int depth);
(gd->vga_palette)(char *palette,
int number_of_colors);
(gd->vga_overscan)(int color);
(gd->vga_line)(char *line, int width, int
line_number);
(gd->vga_off)( );

(gd->ega_on)(int width, int depth);
(gd->ega_palette)(char *egapallete,
                    int number_of_colors,
char *rgb_palette);
(gd->ega_line)(char *line, int width, int
line_number);
(gd->ega_off)( );

(gd->mono_on)(int width, int depth);
(gd->mono_line)(char *line, int line_number, int
width);
(gd->mono_off)( );
```

If a few of these things don't make total sense just yet, you might want to peek ahead at the example GIF reader discussed later in this chapter, which makes calls to the screen driver code.

An assembly language mode 13 VGA driver

Assembly language is never a pretty sight at the best of times. The code that implements a loadable driver rivals mutant swamp turtles and several small foreign cars for absolute ugliness. It's weird, very tricky to figure out and seems to use at least three different memory models all at the same time. If you're thinking of skipping over part of this chapter, this is the part to skip.

Having said this, if you abstract the code in this chapter for your own applications, you won't actually have to write any assembly language.

If you've done assembly language programming before, you'll know that assembly language code is position-dependent. It's written so that it knows where it starts and where everything relative to its start should be. If you tell an assembly language function to address a static buffer, for example, it assumes that the buffer is located relative to the start of the known universe where it was when the program was assembled.

If you allocate a buffer, load some assembly language into it, and then call it, you might imagine that the assembly language would probably crash. The absolute location of an allocated buffer in memory is unpredictable, and as such, calling some code stored in one would only have a $1/655,360$ chance of functioning properly. This is a questionable level of reliability.

Needless to say, you can cheat on this. The way around it lies in the segmented memory structure of a PC's processor.

A small model program consists of code that addresses everything pertaining to itself using 16-bit numbers, that is, as offsets from its current segment. In fact, such a program doesn't really know what its current segment is—it only knows that it has one.

In a large-model program, things are addressed using 32-bit pointers, in which the high-order word represents the segment. A program that uses large model pointers addresses things relative to byte 0 of memory.

If you allocate memory in a large-model program by calling the DOS memory allocation function, the pointer will have an unpredictable segment, to be sure. Its offset, however, is predictable. It is always 0.

Under the large-memory model, then, it's possible to allocate a buffer, load a small model program into the buffer, and execute it without worrying about where the program thinks its bottom of memory is. Because the small model program knows only about its current segment, this being the segment of the allocated buffer, it need not know that it's living in some allocated memory fairly high up in the absolute address space of your computer. This is the basis for loadable screen drivers.

Under Turbo C 2.0, the language that Graphic Workshop was originally written in, calling the `malloc` library function always returned a buffer with an offset of 8. As such, loadable drivers could start safely at location 8. This was handled by having an 8-byte signature string before the first part of the assembly language, something that also served as a check to make sure that something claiming to be a screen driver really was one.

Later versions of Turbo C, and subsequently Borland C++, proved not to be very consistent in this respect. They returned allocated buffers with all sorts of offset values. As such, the code in this chapter allocates the buffer to hold its screen drivers by calling DOS directly. This has something of a side effect in that it seems to conflict with the `farmalloc` function in some Turbo C versions. Therefore, allocating an image buffer is also handled by calling DOS directly.

As discussed in chapter 1, an assembly language function that is to be called by a C-language program must behave itself as would a real C-language function, lest the whole works crash colorfully into oblivion. This might seem to be a bit difficult to arrive at in a driver of the type just discussed, in that the calling program uses the large memory model and the driver the small model.

In fact, all a C-language program really insists on is that assembly language functions treat the stack properly, preserve the BP, DS, and ES registers, and return as would real large model functions, even if they can't operate like them. This latter requirement merely involves replacing the RET instruction at the end of an assembly language function that is to be called from a C program with RETF—that is, a far return.

Normally, declaring an assembly language PROC as FAR would cause the assembler to use a RETF implicitly. Inasmuch as the PROCs in a driver must be declared NEAR to work, you must explicitly use a far return.

One convenient side effect of using a small model driver is that all the data associated with it is effectively in the same segment as the code, providing you with an extra addressable segment to put things in. As such, in a function such as `gd->vga_line`, which essentially copies data from one large pointer to another large pointer, tying up the DS and ES registers in the process, you can use the CS register to address any scratch variables you need while the code is running.

Figure 10-3 illustrates the source code for VGA.ASM, a screen driver to handle a stock VGA card, that is, to use mode 13H as its full color mode.

```
;
;                       Graphic Workshop VGA screen driver
;                       Copyright (C) 1989, 1991 Alchemy Mindworks Inc.
;


VERSION         EQU     2               ;VERSION NUMBER
SUBVERSION      EQU     1               ;SUBVERSION NUMBER


_AOFF           EQU     6               ;STACK OFFSET


VGA_WIDE        EQU     320             ;WIDTH OF VGA SCREEN IN PIXELS
VGA_DEEP        EQU     200             ;DEPTH OF VGA SCREEN IN PIXELS
VGA_SCREENSEG   EQU     0A000H          ;SEGMENT OF VGA SCREEN
EGA_WIDE        EQU     640             ;WIDTH OF EGA SCREEN IN PIXELS
EGA_DEEP        EQU     480             ;DEPTH OF EGA SCREEN IN PIXELS
EGA_BYTES       EQU     80              ;WIDTH OF EGA SCREEN IN BYTES
EGA_SCREENSEG   EQU     0A000H          ;SEGMENT OF EGA SCREEN
MONO_WIDE       EQU     640             ;WIDTH OF MONO SCREEN IN PIXELS
```

10-3 The source code for VGA.ASM.

```
MONO_DEEP        EQU      480              ;DEPTH OF MONO SCREEN IN PIXELS
MONO_BYTES       EQU      80               ;WIDTH OF MONO SCREEN IN BYTES
MONO_SCREENSEG   EQU      0A000H           ;SEGMENT OF MONO SCREEN

;THIS MACRO SELECTS AN EGA PLANE
EGAPLANE         MACRO    ARG1
                 MOV      AL,2
                 MOV      DX,03C4H
                 OUT      DX,AL
                 INC      DX
                 MOV      AL,ARG1
                 OUT      DX,AL
                 ENDM


CODE             SEGMENT PARA PUBLIC 'CODE'
                 ASSUME  CS:CODE


                 ORG      0000H            ;ORIGIN FOR LOADABLE DRIVER

                 DB       'ALCHDRV2'       ;SIGNATURE - DON'T CHANGE THIS

;THE FOLLOWING ARE THE POINTERS TO THE CALLABLE ROUTINES AND THE COMMON
;DATA. THE SEGMENTS ARE FILLED IN BY GRAPHIC WORKSHOP. DON'T CHANGE ANYTHING.
DISPATCH         PROC     FAR
                 DW       VGA_ON           ;FAR POINTER TO VGA MODE SELECT
                 DW       ?
                 DW       VGA_LINE         ;FAR POINTER TO VGA LINE DISPLAY
                 DW       ?
                 DW       VGA_OFF          ;FAR POINTER TO VGA MODE DESELECT
                 DW       ?
                 DW       VGA_PALETTE      ;FAR POINTER TO VGA PALETTE SET
                 DW       ?
                 DW       VGA_OVERSCAN     ;FAR POINTER TO VGA OVERSCAN SET
                 DW       ?
                 DW       EGA_ON           ;FAR POINTER TO EGA MODE SELECT
                 DW       ?
                 DW       EGA_LINE         ;FAR POINTER TO EGA LINE DISPLAY
                 DW       ?
                 DW       EGA_OFF          ;FAR POINTER TO EGA MODE DESELECT
                 DW       ?
                 DW       EGA_PALETTE      ;FAR POINTER TO EGA PALETTE SET
                 DW       ?
                 DW       MONO_ON          ;FAR POINTER TO MONO MODE SELECT
                 DW       ?
                 DW       MONO_FUNCTIONS   ;FAR POINTER TO MONO EXTRA FUNCTIONS
                 DW       ?
                 DW       MONO_LINE        ;FAR POINTER TO MONO LINE DISPLAY
                 DW       ?
                 DW       MONO_OFF         ;FAR POINTER TO MONO MODE DESELECT
                 DW       ?
                 DW       0,0              ;RGB ON
                 DW       0,0              ;RGB LINE
```

10-3 Continued.

```
                    DW      0,0             ;RGB OFF
                    DW      0               ;RGB WIDE
                    DW      0               ;RGB DEEP

V_VGAWIDE           DW      VGA_WIDE        ;VGA SCREEN WIDTH
V_VGADEEP           DW      VGA_DEEP        ;VGA SCREEN DEPTH
V_VGASCRNSEG        DW      VGA_SCREENSEG   ;VGA SCREEN SEGMENT
V_EGAWIDE           DW      EGA_WIDE        ;EGA SCREEN WIDTH
V_EGADEEP           DW      EGA_DEEP        ;EGA SCREEN DEPTH
V_EGABYTES          DW      EGA_BYTES       ;EGA SCREEN BYTES
V_EGASCRNSEG        DW      EGA_SCREENSEG   ;EGA SCREEN SEGMENT
V_MONOWIDE          DW      MONO_WIDE       ;MONO SCREEN WIDTH
V_MONODEEP          DW      MONO_DEEP       ;MONO SCREEN DEPTH
V_MONOBYTES         DW      MONO_BYTES      ;BYTE WIDTH ON MONOCHROME SCREEN
V_MONOSCRNSEG       DW      MONO_SCREENSEG  ;MONOCHROME SCREEN SEGMENT

                    DW      VERSION
                    DW      SUBVERSION

;THE DESCRIPTION APPEARS IN THE F10 "ABOUT" BOX IN GRAPHIC
;WORKSHOP WHEN AN EXTERNAL DRIVER IS BEING USED. IT CAN'T
;EXCEED 24 CHARACTERS AND MUST BE NULL TERMINATED
                    DB      'Standard VGA 320 x 200 ',0
DISPATCH            ENDP

VGAMODETABLE        DW      -1,-1

EGAMODETABLE        DW      -1,-1

MONOMODETABLE       DW      -1,-1

;THIS FUNCTION IS CALLED TO PUT THE SCREEN IN ITS 256-COLOUR MODE
VGA_ON              PROC    NEAR
                    PUSH    BP
                    PUSH    DS
                    PUSH    ES
                    MOV     CX,200          ;DEPTH OF SCREEN
                    SUB     DX,DX
                    SUB     BX,BX

VGA_ON1:            PUSH    DX
                    MOV     AX,320          ;WIDTH OF SCREEEN
                    MUL     DX
                    MOV     CS:[SCREENTABLE+BX],AX
                    ADD     BX,0002H
                    POP     DX
                    INC     DX
                    LOOP    VGA_ON1

                    MOV     AX,0013H
                    INT     10H
```

10-3 Continued.

```
                        POP      ES
                        POP      DS
                        POP      BP
                        RETF
        VGA_ON          ENDP

        ;THIS FUNCTION IS CALLED TO DISPLAY ONE LINE
        VGA_LINE        PROC     NEAR
                        PUSH     BP
                        MOV      BP,SP
                        PUSH     DS
                        PUSH     ES

                        MOV      SI,[BP + _AOFF + 0]      ;OFFSET OF SOURCE
                        MOV      DS,[BP + _AOFF + 2]      ;SEGMENT OF SOURCE

                        MOV      BX,[BP + _AOFF + 6]      ;GET LINE NUMBER
                        CMP      BX,VGA_DEEP              ;MAKE SURE IT'S A
                        JGE      SHOWVGAX                 ;GOOD NUMBER
                        CMP      BX,0000H
                        JL       SHOWVGAX

                        SHL      BX,1                     ;GET THE OFFSET INTO THE
                        MOV      DI,CS:[SCREENTABLE+BX]   ;SCREEN BUFFER

                        CLD
                        MOV      CX,[BP + _AOFF + 4]      ;LENGTH OF MOVE IN BYTES
                        CMP      CX,0
                        JE       SHOWVGAX                 ;CHECK FOR NASTIES
                        CMP      CX,320
                        JL       SHOWVGA1
                        MOV      CX,320

        SHOWVGA1:       MOV      AX,0A000H                ;MOVE THE LINE
                        MOV      ES,AX
                REPNE   MOVSB

        SHOWVGAX:       POP      ES
                        POP      DS
                        POP      BP
                        RETF
        VGA_LINE        ENDP

        ;THIS ROUTINE DESELECTS THE VGA 256 COLOUR MODE
        VGA_OFF         PROC     NEAR
                        PUSH     BP
                        PUSH     DS
                        PUSH     ES
                        MOV      AX,1200H
                        MOV      BX,0031H
                        INT      10H
```

10-3 Continued.

```
                MOV     AX,0003H
                INT     10H
                POP     ES
                POP     DS
                POP     BP
                RETF
VGA_OFF         ENDP

;THIS ROUTINE SETS THE VGA PALETTE
VGA_PALETTE     PROC    NEAR
                PUSH    BP
                MOV     BP,SP
                PUSH    DS
                PUSH    ES

                MOV     SI,[BP + _AOFF + 0]     ;OFFSET OF SOURCE
                MOV     DS,[BP + _AOFF + 2]     ;SEGMENT OF SOURCE

                MOV     CX,[BP + _AOFF + 4]     ;NUMBER OF COLOURS

                CMP     CX,0000H                ;CHECK FOR NASTIES
                JG      GVP0
                JMP     GVPX

GVP0:           MOV     DX,03C6H                ;GET THE PALETTE REGISTER
                MOV     AL,0FFH
                OUT     DX,AL

                MOV     BX,0                    ;FIRST ENTRY

GVP1:           PUSH    CX
                MOV     DX,03C8H
                MOV     AL,BL
                INC     BX
                OUT     DX,AL

                INC     DX

                LODSB                           ;GET THE RED VALUE
                SHR     AL,1                    ;TO SIX BITS
                SHR     AL,1
                OUT     DX,AL                   ;SET IT

                LODSB                           ;GET THE GREEN VALUE
                SHR     AL,1                    ;TO SIX BITS
                SHR     AL,1
                OUT     DX,AL                   ;SET IT

                LODSB                           ;GET THE BLUE VALUE
                SHR     AL,1                    ;TO SIX BITS
                SHR     AL,1
                OUT     DX,AL                   ;SET IT
```

10-3 Continued.

```
                          POP     CX
                          LOOP    GVP1

        GVPX:             POP     ES
                          POP     DS
                          POP     BP
                          RETF
        VGA_PALETTE       ENDP

        ;THIS ROUTINE SETS THE VGA OVERSCAN.
        VGA_OVERSCAN      PROC    NEAR
                          PUSH    BP
                          MOV     BP,SP
                          PUSH    DS
                          PUSH    ES
                          MOV     AX,1001H
                          MOV     BX,[BP + _AOFF + 0]
                          XCHG    BH,BL
                          INT     10H
                          POP     ES
                          POP     DS
                          POP     BP
                          RETF
        VGA_OVERSCAN      ENDP

        ;THIS ROUTINE SELECTS THE EGA 16 COLOUR MODE
        EGA_ON            PROC    NEAR
                          PUSH    BP
                          PUSH    DS
                          PUSH    ES
                          MOV     CX,480              ;DEPTH OF SCREEN
                          SUB     DX,DX
                          SUB     BX,BX

        EGA_ON1:          PUSH    DX
                          MOV     AX,80               ;WIDTH OF SCREEEN
                          MUL     DX
                          MOV     CS:[SCREENTABLE+BX],AX
                          ADD     BX,2
                          POP     DX
                          INC     DX
                          LOOP    EGA_ON1

                          MOV     AX,0012H
                          INT     10H
                          POP     ES
                          POP     DS
                          POP     BP
                          RETF
        EGA_ON            ENDP

        ;THIS ROUTINE DISPLAYS AN EGA LINE
```

10-3 Continued.

```
EGA_LINE        PROC    NEAR
                PUSH    BP
                MOV     BP,SP
                PUSH    DS
                PUSH    ES

                MOV     SI,[BP + _AOFF + 0]     ;OFFSET OF SOURCE
                MOV     DS,[BP + _AOFF + 2]     ;SEGMENT OF SOURCE
                MOV     BX,[BP + _AOFF + 6]     ;GET LINE NUMBER

                CMP     BX,480                  ;CHECK FOR NASTIES
                JGE     SHOWEGAX

                CMP     BX,0000H
                JL      SHOWEGAX

                SHL     BX,1                    ;GET THE OFFSET
                MOV     DI,CS:[SCREENTABLE+BX]

                MOV     AX,0A000H
                MOV     ES,AX
                MOV     BX,[BP + _AOFF + 4]     ;LENGTH OF MOVE IN BYTES

                MOV     CX,BX                   ;SHOW PLANE 0
                EGAPLANE        1
                CLD
                PUSH    DI
        REPNE   MOVSB
                POP     DI

                MOV     CX,BX                   ;SHOW PLANE 1
                EGAPLANE        2
                PUSH    DI
        REPNE   MOVSB
                POP     DI

                MOV     CX,BX                   ;SHOW PLANE 2
                EGAPLANE        4
                PUSH    DI
        REPNE   MOVSB
                POP     DI

                MOV     CX,BX                   ;SHOW PLANE 3
                EGAPLANE        8
                PUSH    DI
        REPNE   MOVSB
                POP     DI
                EGAPLANE        0FH

SHOWEGAX:       POP     ES
                POP     DS
                POP     BP
```

10-3 Continued.

```
                        RETF
EGA_LINE                ENDP

;THIS ROUTINE SETS THE EGA PALETTE
EGA_PALETTE             PROC    NEAR
                        PUSH    BP
                        MOV     BP,SP
                        PUSH    DS
                        PUSH    ES

                        MOV     SI,[BP + _AOFF + 6]     ;OFFSET OF SOURCE
                        MOV     DS,[BP + _AOFF + 8]     ;SEGMENT OF SOURCE

                        MOV     CX,[BP + _AOFF + 4]     ;NUMBER OF COLOURS

                        CMP     CX,16
                        JLE     EGA_PALETTE1            ;CHECK FOR NASTIES
                        MOV     CX,16

EGA_PALETTE1:           PUSH    CX
                        MOV     BX,0000H

EGA_PALETTE2:           PUSH    CX
                        LODSB
                        SHR     AL,1
                        SHR     AL,1
                        MOV     DH,AL

                        LODSB
                        SHR     AL,1
                        SHR     AL,1
                        MOV     CH,AL

                        LODSB
                        SHR     AL,1
                        SHR     AL,1
                        MOV     CL,AL
                        MOV     AX,1010H

                        INT     10H                     ;DO A BIOS PALETTE SET
                        INC     BX
                        POP     CX
                        LOOP    EGA_PALETTE2

                        POP     CX
                        MOV     BX,0000H

EGA_PALETTE3:           PUSH    CX                      ;SET THE DUMMY EGA NUMBERS
                        MOV     AX,1000H
                        INT     10H
                        ADD     BX,0101H
                        POP     CX
```

10-3 Continued.

```
                    LOOP     EGA_PALETTE3

                    POP      ES
                    POP      DS
                    POP      BP
                    RETF
EGA_PALETTE         ENDP

;THIS ROUTINE DESELECTS THE EGA 16 COLOUR MODE
EGA_OFF             PROC     NEAR
                    PUSH     BP
                    PUSH     DS
                    PUSH     ES
                    MOV      AX,0003H
                    INT      10H
                    POP      ES
                    POP      DS
                    POP      BP
                    RETF
EGA_OFF             ENDP

;THIS ROUTINE SELECTS THE 2 COLOUR MODE
MONO_ON             PROC     NEAR
                    PUSH     BP
                    PUSH     DS
                    PUSH     ES

                    MOV      AX,CS
                    MOV      DS,AX
                    MOV      ES,AX
                    MOV      AX,0012H
                    INT      10H

                    MOV      CX,480
                    SUB      DX,DX
                    SUB      BX,BX

MONO_ON1:           PUSH     DX
                    MOV      AX,80
                    MUL      DX
                    MOV      CS:[SCREENTABLE+BX],AX
                    ADD      BX,2
                    POP      DX
                    INC      DX
                    LOOP     MONO_ON1

                    SUB      AX,AX

                    POP      ES
                    POP      DS
                    POP      BP
                    RETF
```

10-3 Continued.

```
MONO_ON          ENDP

;THIS FUNCTION PERFORMS VARIOUS GRAPHIC OPERATIONS
;       ARGUMENTS         -       FUNCTION CODE
;                         -       VARIABLE
;
;       FUNCTIONS         -       0       RETURN SCREEN SEG
;                         -       1       RETURN OFFSET TO SCREEN TABLE
;                         -       2       RETURN MONOCHROME SCREEN WIDTH
;                         -       3       RETURN MONOCHROME SCREEN DEPTH
;                         -       4       INVERT FRAME RECT - ARGS ON STACK
;                         -       5       RETURN OFFSET OF VGAMODETABLE
;                         -       6       RETURN OFFSET OF EGAMODETABLE
;                         -       7       RETURN OFFSET OF MONOMODETABLE
;                         -       8       RETURN OFFSET OF RGBMODETABLE
;
MONO_FUNCTIONS   PROC     NEAR
                 PUSH     BP
                 MOV      BP,SP
                 PUSH     DS
                 PUSH     ES

                 CMP      WORD PTR [BP + _AOFF + 0],0000H
                 JNE      MF1

                 MOV      AX,MONO_SCREENSEG
                 JMP      MF_EXIT

MF1:             CMP      WORD PTR [BP + _AOFF + 0],0001H
                 JNE      MF2

                 MOV      AX,OFFSET SCREENTABLE-8
                 JMP      MF_EXIT

MF2:             CMP      WORD PTR [BP + _AOFF + 0],0002H
                 JNE      MF3

                 MOV      AX,MONO_WIDE
                 JMP      MF_EXIT

MF3:             CMP      WORD PTR [BP + _AOFF + 0],0003H
                 JNE      MF4

                 MOV      AX,MONO_DEEP
                 JMP      MF_EXIT

MF4:             CMP      WORD PTR [BP + _AOFF + 0],0004H
                 JE       MF5
                 JMP      MF6

MF5:             MOV      AX,MONO_SCREENSEG
                 MOV      ES,AX
```

10-3 Continued.

```
            MOV     BX,[BP + _AOFF + 4]     ;GET TOP
            SHL     BX,1
            MOV     DI,CS:[SCREENTABLE+BX]

            MOV     BX,[BP + _AOFF + 2]     ;GET LEFT
            MOV     CX,[BP + _AOFF + 6]     ;GET RIGHT
            SUB     CX,BX

MF5A:       PUSH    BX
            AND     BX,0007H
            MOV     AL,CS:[MASKTABLE+BX]
            POP     BX

            PUSH    BX
            SHR     BX,1
            SHR     BX,1
            SHR     BX,1
            XOR     ES:[DI+BX],AL
            POP     BX
            INC     BX
            LOOP    MF5A

            MOV     BX,[BP + _AOFF + 4]     ;GET TOP
            INC     BX
            MOV     CX,[BP + _AOFF + 8]     ;GET BOTTOM
            DEC     CX
            SUB     CX,BX

MF5B:       PUSH    BX
            SHL     BX,1
            MOV     DI,CS:[SCREENTABLE+BX]
            MOV     BX,[BP + _AOFF + 2]     ;GET LEFT
            PUSH    BX
            AND     BX,0007H
            MOV     AL,CS:[MASKTABLE+BX]
            POP     BX
            PUSH    BX
            SHR     BX,1
            SHR     BX,1
            SHR     BX,1
            XOR     ES:[DI+BX],AL
            POP     BX
            MOV     BX,[BP + _AOFF + 6]     ;GET RIGHT
            DEC     BX
            PUSH    BX
            AND     BX,0007H
            MOV     AL,CS:[MASKTABLE+BX]
            POP     BX
            PUSH    BX
            SHR     BX,1
            SHR     BX,1
            SHR     BX,1
```

10-3 Continued.

```
                        XOR        ES:[DI+BX],AL
                        POP        BX
                        POP        BX
                        INC        BX
                        LOOP       MF5B

                        MOV        BX,[BP + _AOFF + 8]      ;GET BOTTOM
                        DEC        BX
                        SHL        BX,1
                        MOV        DI,CS:[SCREENTABLE+BX]

                        MOV        BX,[BP + _AOFF + 2]      ;GET LEFT
                        MOV        CX,[BP + _AOFF + 6]      ;GET RIGHT
                        SUB        CX,BX

MF5D:                   PUSH       BX
                        AND        BX,0007H
                        MOV        AL,CS:[MASKTABLE+BX]
                        POP        BX

                        PUSH       BX
                        SHR        BX,1
                        SHR        BX,1
                        SHR        BX,1
                        XOR        ES:[DI+BX],AL
                        POP        BX
                        INC        BX
                        LOOP       MF5D

MF6:                    CMP        WORD PTR [BP + _AOFF + 0],0005H
                        JNE        MF7

                        MOV        AX,OFFSET VGAMODETABLE
                        JMP        MF_EXIT

MF7:                    CMP        WORD PTR [BP + _AOFF + 0],0006H
                        JNE        MF8

                        MOV        AX,OFFSET EGAMODETABLE
                        JMP        MF_EXIT

MF8:                    CMP        WORD PTR [BP + _AOFF + 0],0007H
                        JNE        MF_EXIT

                        MOV        AX,OFFSET MONOMODETABLE
                        JMP        MF_EXIT

MF_EXIT:                POP        ES
                        POP        DS
                        POP        BP
                        RETF
MONO_FUNCTIONS          ENDP
```

10-3 Continued.

```
MASKTABLE        DB      80H,40H,20H,10H,08H,04H,02H,01H

;THIS ROUTINE DISPLAYS A SINGLE MONOCHROME LINE
MONO_LINE       PROC    NEAR
                PUSH    BP
                MOV     BP,SP

                PUSH    DS
                PUSH    ES

                MOV     AX,0A000H                ;POINT TO THE SCREEN
                MOV     ES,AX

                MOV     CX,[BP + _AOFF + 6]      ;GET THE WIDTH OF MOVE

                CMP     CX,0                     ;CHECK FOR NASTIES
                JE      MONO_LINE2

                CMP     CX,80
                JL      MONO_LINE1
                MOV     CX,80

MONO_LINE1:     MOV     SI,[BP + _AOFF + 0]      ;OFFSET OF BITMAP
                MOV     DS,[BP + _AOFF + 2]      ;SEGMENT OF BITMAP
                MOV     BX,[BP + _AOFF + 4]      ;NUMBER OF LINE
                SHL     BX,1

                CLD                              ;CLEAR DIRECTION FLAG

                MOV     DI,CS:[SCREENTABLE+BX]   ;FETCH THE OFFSET
        REPNE   MOVSB                            ;DO THE MOVE

MONO_LINE2:     POP     ES
                POP     DS

                POP     BP
                RETF
MONO_LINE       ENDP

;THIS ROUTINE DESELECTS THE 2 COLOUR MODE
MONO_OFF        PROC    NEAR
                PUSH    BP
                PUSH    DS
                PUSH    ES

                MOV     AX,0003H
                INT     10H
                SUB     AX,AX

                POP     ES
```

10-3 Continued.

```
                 POP      DS
                 POP      BP
                 RETF
MONO_OFF         ENDP


;THIS IS A LINE START LOOKUP TABLE

SCREENTABLE      DW       480 DUP(0)        ;LINE START TABLE

CODE             ENDS
                 END
```

10-3 Continued.

The first part of VGA.ASM is its dispatch table, which corresponds to the structure in a GRAFDRIVER object. Each of the function pointers is actually the integer offset into the driver for the function in question and a segment value. As discussed shortly, the segment value cannot be known when the driver is assembled, and is left blank.

Note that the first 8 bytes of the driver are the string "ALCHDRV2." By ignoring this string when the driver is loaded, the driver effectively has an ORG of 8. This works out properly if the buffer to hold the driver has an offset of 8, which it does.

Following the dispatch table of the driver are three very short screen-mode tables. In a more complex driver, these would indicate all the available modes of the super VGA card being supported, such that Graphic Workshop could create a menu of them. As noted previously, they don't pertain to the discussion in this chapter and can be ignored.

The rest of the driver consists of the actual code that makes it go. The code may be up to 64K long, although no driver requires anything like this to handle even really complex display cards. The functions are structured as C-language functions written in assembly language.

As was pointed out informally in the file readers in this book, the offset of a particular line in a VGA card's buffer can be worked out by multiplying the line number by the byte width of one displayed line in the current screen mode. This is easy to do, but relatively time-consuming as it involves the use of the dreaded 8088 MUL instruction, a processor hog of considerable magnitude. Therefore, when one of the on functions is called, part of the work of the corresponding machine code is to create a table of all of the possible offsets into the screen buffer that could point to the starts of lines. In mode 13H there are 200 of them.

Having stored these values in a table, the subsequent line display functions can figure out the byte offset from the base of the display buffer for any line by finding its entry in the table. As the table is actually an array of words, if BX is the line number, this loads the offset of the line in the screen buffer into DI:

```
SHL   BX,1
MOV   DI,CS:[SCREENTABLE+BX]
```

This takes about 24 machine cycles to perform. A MUL takes 133.

Becoming more apparent later in this chapter, using a screen table also makes it possible to address the screen buffer of higher resolution 256-color modes, in which the buffer is structured as multiple pages.

The monochrome screen mode and the 16-color screen mode used in VGA.ASM are, in fact, the same modes. In order to properly understand how this works, you need a bit of insight into how the 16-color modes behave. This is somewhat peculiar and in many respects awkward to deal with, but it does have a few advantages as well.

In its 16-color display mode, a VGA card's screen buffer begins at A000:0000H and runs for 38,400 bytes. If you have a calculator handy you'll find that this is not enough memory to contain a 640×480 pixel, 4-bit picture. In fact, such a picture requires 153,600 bytes. Unfortunately, a VGA card is only allowed to have a video buffer that occupies a maximum of 64K.

To get around this memory restriction, the 16-color screen buffer is paged. As with expanded memory (see chapter 1), the 64K address space of a VGA card's screen buffer serves as a page frame. In this case each page is effectively 38,400 bytes long.

In writing a planar 16-color image to a VGA card in its 16-color mode, the first plane would go in the first page, the second plane in the second page and so on. This is, in fact, why many PC image formats store 16-color pictures as planes.

You can tickle some of a VGA card's registers to determine which page or pages are visible in the page frame. When a page is visible, moving data into the address space beginning at A000:0000H affects what's in that page, and hence what appears on the screen. Note that all the pages are always visible to the screen itself.

This is a function to set the page to be written to:

```
plane(n)
  int n;
{
  outportb(0x3c4,0x02);
  outportb(0x3c5,n);
}
```

In fact, what this function does is to set bits in the VGA card's "barrel register." Each of the four low-order bits in the barrel register corresponds to one of the four pages, causing the first page to appear in the page frame:

```
plane(1);
```

This causes the second page to appear:

```
plane(2);
```

This causes the fourth page to appear:

```
plane(8);
```

Finally, the following call causes all the pages to appear. This is the default state of the card.

```
plane(15);
```

Writing to the page frame affects the data in all the visible pages, even if there is more than one page visible at the moment.

If all the pages are visible, any area of the page frame that contains unset bits will display color 0 in the current 16-color palette. Any area that has set bits displays color 15, as all the bits in all 4 pages are set. When you first select the 16-color mode, the default palette has black as color 0 and white as color 15. As such, the display behaves as a monochrome screen until you either reset the palette or start moving pages in and out of the page frame.

You can see this at work in assembly language in the EGA_LINE function of VGA.ASM. It changes pages four times for each line it displays.

Once you have VGA.ASM in a text file, you can assemble it using MASM or TASM. You'll also need TLINK and EXE2BIN. This is a batch file that handles the whole works.

```
ECHO OFF
BREAK ON
MASM %1 %1 NUL NUL
IF ERRORLEVEL 1 GOTO PROBLEM
TLINK %1
EXE2BIN %1 %1.DRV
DEL %1.EXE
DEL %1.OBJ
:PROBLEM
BREAK OFF
```

If no errors have crept into the source file, you should be left with VGA.DRV.

Whether or not you plan to work with any of the more involved VGA drivers discussed in this chapter, you should probably get VGA.DRV going. It serves as a good benchmark to make sure that the C-language code that calls the screen drivers is functioning as it should. The code in VGA.DRV is pretty simple.

Loading a driver

Once you have a screen driver properly assembled, it must be loaded into a buffer and initialized. There are several things to keep in mind about this process. First, the executable code of the driver must be loaded into a buffer with an offset value of 8 or very nasty things will happen.

If you're using the old Turbo C 2.0, calling `malloc` should provide you with a suitable buffer. However, code that's written this way isn't particularly portable, as recompiling it under, say, one of the new Borland C++ compilers produces a program that only knows how to crash. It's a lot more sensible to use a custom memory allocation function that always returns a suitable buffer.

The `dosalloc` function allocates memory using a direct call to the DOS INT 21H memory manager. It has a fixed offset of 8 for all the buffers it returns. While it behaves just like `malloc`, it may have a few catches, depending upon the version of Turbo C or Borland C++ you're using. Specifically, it might not get along with `farmalloc` and it might refuse to work on programs that are run from within the integrated development environment.

Both of these difficulties, should they arise, are easily dealt with. Rather than using `farmalloc`, you can allocate large buffers using this same interrupt call. The INT 21H memory manager is hardly likely to conflict with itself. If you find that programs that use `dosalloc` won't run from the integrated environment of your compiler, you'll have to return to DOS to try them.

```
char *dosalloc(n)
    unsigned int n;
{
    union REGS r;

    n+=8;
    r.x.ax=0x4800;
    r.x.bx=1+(n>>4);
    int86(0x21,&r,&r);
    if(r.x.cflag) return(NULL);
    else return(MK_FP(r.x.ax,0x0008));
}
```

Note that since it returns a `char` pointer, you need a prototype for `dosalloc`:

```
char *dosalloc(unsigned int n);
```

Having allocated memory using a direct call to DOS, you must free it using the appropriate DOS call, rather than calling the Turbo C `free` function. Here's the code to do this.

```
dosfree(p)
    char *p;
{
    union REGS r;
    struct SREGS sr;
```

```
        r.x.ax=0x4900;
        sr.es=FP_SEG(p);
        int86x(0x21,&r,&r,&sr);
    }
```

As you'll have noticed if you've had a go at VGA.ASM, the pointers in a driver's dispatch table are only partially complete. They represent the offsets into the driver of each routine, but they don't include the segments. The segments of the individual functions of the driver are the same as that of the driver in general. This, in turn, is the segment of the buffer in which it resides, something that is different each time a driver is loaded.

After it has been loaded, a driver must be initialized. The segment values for each of the supplied functions must be filled in, which is pretty easy to do under Turbo C. The segment of a buffer can be determined with the FP_SEG macro.

The loadDriver function in FIG. 10-4 handles the complete loading and initialization process for a driver. It accepts the path to a driver as its argument and returns a pointer of the type GRAFDRIVER if it has successfully loaded and initialized the driver. Alternately, it returns NULL if it couldn't allocate memory for the driver or if the driver couldn't be found.

The loadDriver function is actually pretty easy to follow. It opens the driver as a binary file and works out how big it is. The quickest way to find the size of a file is to seek to the end of it and read the file pointer position with ftell. It then reads in the first 8 bytes to make sure that the file is actually a Graphic Workshop screen driver. Finally, it allocates a buffer with dosalloc and loads in the rest of the driver.

```
GRAFDRIVER *loadDriver(s)
        char *s;
{
        GRAFDRIVER *gd;
        char *grafDriver=NULL;
        FILE *fp;
        long l;
        char b[8];
        unsigned int seg;

        /* open the driver */
        if((fp=fopen(s,"rb")) != NULL) {

                /* seek to the end to see how big it is */
                fseek(fp,0L,SEEK_END);
                l=ftell(fp);

                /* return to the beginning */
                rewind(fp);

                /* check the signiture */
                fread(b,1,8,fp);
```

10-4 The loadDriver function.

```
if(!memcmp(b,"ALCHDRV2",8)) {
        l-=8L;

        /* load the driver */
        if(l < 0xffffL &&
           (grafDriver=dosalloc((unsigned int)l)) != NULL) {
                if(fread(grafDriver,1,(unsigned int)l,fp)==
                   (unsigned int)l) {
                        gd=(GRAFDRIVER *)grafDriver;
                        seg=FP_SEG(grafDriver);

                        /* fil i th  segment  */
                        if(gd->vga_on != NULL) {
                                grafDriver[2]=seg;
                                grafDriver[3]=(seg >> 8);
                                grafDriver[6]=seg;
                                grafDriver[7]=(seg >> 8);
                                grafDriver[10]=seg;
                                grafDriver[11]=(seg >> 8);
                                grafDriver[14]=seg;
                                grafDriver[15]=(seg >> 8);
                                grafDriver[18]=seg;
                                grafDriver[19]=(seg >> 8);
                        }

                        if(gd->ega_on != NULL) {
                                grafDriver[22]=seg;
                                grafDriver[23]=(seg >> 8);
                                grafDriver[26]=seg;
                                grafDriver[27]=(seg >> 8);
                                grafDriver[30]=seg;
                                grafDriver[31]=(seg >> 8);
                                grafDriver[34]=seg;
                                grafDriver[35]=(seg >> 8);
                        }

                        if(gd->mono_on != NULL) {
                                grafDriver[38]=seg;
                                grafDriver[39]=(seg >> 8);
                                grafDriver[42]=seg;
                                grafDriver[43]=(seg >> 8);
                                grafDriver[46]=seg;
                                grafDriver[47]=(seg >> 8);
                                grafDriver[50]=seg;
                                grafDriver[51]=(seg >> 8);
                        }

                        if(gd->rgb_on != NULL) {
                                grafDriver[54]=seg;
                                grafDriver[55]=(seg >> 8);
                                grafDriver[58]=seg;
                                grafDriver[59]=(seg >> 8);
```

10-4 Continued.

```
                                        grafDriver[62]=seg;
                                        grafDriver[63]=(seg >> 8);
                            }
                    }
                    else {
                            dosfree(grafDriver);
                            grafDriver=NULL;
                    }
            }
        }
        fclose(fp);
    }
    return((GRAFDRIVER *)grafDriver);
}
```

10-4 Continued.

The largest part of `loadDriver` is the initialization code for all the segments. It's important to initialize only those pointers that actually reflect workable functions. For example, you wouldn't want to initialize the RGB function pointers in VGA.ASM, as it doesn't have RGB color support. A complex viewing program, such as Graphic Workshop, can decide whether the driver it finds itself working with can display particular levels of color by checking to see if the appropriate on function is NULL or not.

You'll probably want to implement the same sort of checking yourself if you'll be supporting a lot of different drivers and multiple screen modes.

As with `dosalloc`, the `loadDriver` function needs a prototype, as it returns a pointer.

```
GRAFDRIVER *loadDriver(char *s);
```

The GIF file viewer in the next section of this chapter illustrates all the previous code at work.

A better GIF viewer

The GIF viewer discussed in chapter 2 had its principal limitation in the way it managed its screen, and hence its memory. The way that GIF files compress images makes it easy to display them in mode 13H even if they don't require the availability of 256 colors. While this made for a reasonably small and easily understood program at the start of this book, chances are you wouldn't want to work with images this way in a real-world application.

With the availability of a screen driver that works with each of the three VGA graphics modes, it's possible to write a more sensible GIF viewer. The READGIF2 program in FIG. 10-5 stores monochrome files as a single image plane and displays them using the mono functions of the screen driver. It stores images having between 2 and 4 bits of color as 16-color images, and displays them with the ega functions. Finally, images with more than 4 bits of color are stored as they were in chapter 2, and displayed using the vga functions.

The READGIF2 program works pretty much the same way as the original READGIF program did, except that it uses direct DOS calls to allocate and free memory and GRAFDRIVER calls to display things.

```
/*
        GIF reader - copyright (c) 1991
        Version using device independant screen drivers
        Alchemy Mindworks Inc.
*/

#include "stdio.h"
#include "dos.h"

/*                              uncomment this line if you
#include "memmangr.h"           will be linking in the memory manager
*/

#define GOOD_READ       0       /* return codes */
#define BAD_FILE        1
#define BAD_READ        2
#define UNEXPECTED_EOF  3
#define BAD_CODE        4
#define BAD_FIRSTCODE   5
#define BAD_ALLOC       6
#define BAD_SYMBOLSIZE  7
#define NO_DRIVER       8

#define NO_CODE         -1

#define SCREENWIDE      320     /* mode 13 screen dimensions */
#define SCREENDEEP      200
#define STEP            32      /* size of a step when panning */

#define HOME            0x4700  /* cursor control codes */
#define CURSOR_UP       0x4800
#define CURSOR_LEFT     0x4b00
#define CURSOR_RIGHT    0x4d00
#define END             0x4f00
#define CURSOR_DOWN     0x5000

#define pixels2bytes(n)    ((n+7)/8)

typedef struct {
        char sig[6];
        unsigned int screenwidth,screendepth;
        unsigned char flags,background,aspect;
        } GIFHEADER;

typedef struct {
```

10-5 The source code for READGIF2.

```
                unsigned int left,top,width,depth;
                unsigned char flags;
                } IMAGEBLOCK;

        typedef struct {
                int width,depth,bytes,bits;
                int flags;
                int background;
                char palette[768];
                int (*setup)();
                int (*closedown)();
                int (*saveline)();
                int (*savext)();
                } FILEINFO;

        typedef struct {
                char blocksize;
                char flags;
                unsigned int delay;
                char transparent_colour;
                char terminator;
                } CONTROLBLOCK;

        typedef struct {
                char blocksize;
                unsigned int left,top;
                unsigned int gridwidth,gridheight;
                char cellwidth,cellheight;
                char forecolour,backcolour;
                } PLAINTEXT;

        typedef struct {
                char blocksize;
                char applstring[8];
                char authentication[3];
                } APPLICATION;

        typedef struct {
                int (*vga_on)();
                int (*vga_line)();
                int (*vga_off)();
                int (*vga_palette)();
                int (*vga_overscan)();
                int (*ega_on)();
                int (*ega_line)();
                int (*ega_off)();
                int (*ega_palette)();
                int (*mono_on)();
                int (*mono_functions)();
                int (*mono_line)();
                int (*mono_off)();
                int (*rgb_on)();
```

10-5 Continued.

```
        int (*rgb_line)();
        int (*rgb_off)();
        int rgb_wide;
        int rgb_deep;
        int vga_wide;
        int vga_deep;
        int vga_screenseg;
        int ega_wide;
        int ega_deep;
        int ega_bytes;
        int ega_screenseg;
        int mono_wide;
        int mono_deep;
        int mono_bytes;
        int mono_screenseg;
        int driver_version;
        int driver_subversion;
        char name[25];
        } GRAFDRIVER;

GRAFDRIVER *loadDriver(char *s);

        char *farPtr(char *p,long l);
        char *getline(unsigned int n);
        char *dosalloc(unsigned int n);

        int putextension(FILE *fp);
        int putline(char *p,unsigned int n);
        int convertline(char *p,unsigned int n);
        int dosetup(FILEINFO *fi);
        int doclosedown(FILEINFO *fi);

        char masktable[8]={0x80,0x40,0x20,0x10,0x08,0x04,0x02,0x01};
        char bittable[8] ={0x01,0x02,0x04,0x08,0x10,0x20,0x40,0x80};

        GRAFDRIVER *gd;
        FILEINFO fi;
        char *buffer=NULL;

        main(argc,argv)
                int argc;
                char *argv[];
        {
                FILE *fp;
                static char results[9][16] = {  "Ok",
                                                "Bad file",
                                                "Bad read",
                                                "Unexpected end",
                                                "Bad LZW code",
                                                "Bad first code",
                                                "Memory error",
                                                "Bad symbol size",
```

10-5 Continued.

```
                                    "No driver mode"
                                    };

        char path[81];
        int r;

        if(argc > 2) {
                strmfe(path,argv[2],"DRV");
                if((gd=loadDriver(path))== NULL) {
                        printf("Error loading driver %s\n",path);
                        exit(1);
                }
                strmfe(path,argv[1],"GIF");
                if((fp = fopen(path,"rb")) != NULL) {
                        fi.setup=dosetup;
                        fi.closedown=doclosedown;
                        fi.saveline=convertline;
                        fi.savext=putextension;
                        r=unpackgif(fp,&fi);
                        dosfree((char *)gd);
                        printf("\%s",results[r]);
                        fclose(fp);
                } else printf("Error opening %s",path);
        } else puts("Arguments:      path to a GIF file\r\n"
                    "                path to a driver");
}

/* this function is called when the GIF decoder encounters an extension */
putextension(fp)
        FILE *fp;

{

        PLAINTEXT pt;
        CONTROLBLOCK cb;
        APPLICATION ap;
        int c,n,i;

        clrscr();
        switch((c=fgetc(fp))) {
                case 0x0001:                /* plain text descriptor */
                        if(fread((char *)&pt,1,sizeof(PLAINTEXT),fp)
                          == sizeof(PLAINTEXT)) {
                                puts("PLAIN TEXT BLOCK\n_____");
                                printf("This block requires %u bytes\n",pt.blocksize);
                                printf("Text location at (%u,%u)\n",pt.left,pt.top);
                                printf("Grid dimensions are %u by %u\n",pt.gridwidth,pt.gridheight);
                                printf("Cell dimensions are %u by %u\n",pt.cellwidth,pt.cellheight);
                                printf("Foregound colour is %u\n",pt.forecolour);
                                printf("Background colour is %u\n",pt.backcolour);

                                do {
                                        if((n=fgetc(fp)) != EOF) {
                                                for(i=0;i<n;++i)
                                                        printchar(fgetc(fp));
```

10-5 Continued.

```
                              }
                     } while(n > 0 && n != EOF);
              } else puts("Error reading plain text block");
              break;
case 0x00f9:                /* graphic control block */
         if(fread((char *)&cb,1,sizeof(CONTROLBLOCK),fp)
              == sizeof(CONTROLBLOCK)) {
                     puts("CONTROL BLOCK\n_____");
                     printf("This block requires %u bytes\n",cb.blocksize);
                     switch((cb.flags >> 2) & 0x0007) {
                            case 0:
                                   puts("No disposal specified");
                                   break;
                            case 1:
                                   puts("Do not dispose");
                                   break;
                            case 2:
                                   puts("Dispose to background colour");
                                   break;
                            case 3:
                                   puts("Dispose to previous graphic");
                                   break;
                            default:
                                   puts("Unknown disposal procedure");
                                   break;
                     }
                     if(cb.flags & 0x0002)
                        printf("User input required - delay for %u seconds",
                            cb.delay);
                     else puts("No user input required");

                     if(cb.flags & 0x0001)
                        printf("Transparent colour: %u\n",
                            cb.transparent_colour);
                     else puts("No transparent_colour");
              } else puts("Error reading control block");
              break;
case 0x00fe:               /* comment extension */
         puts("COMMENT BLOCK\n_____");
         do {
                     if((n=fgetc(fp)) != EOF) {
                            for(i=0;i<n;++i)
                                   printchar(fgetc(fp));
                     }
         } while(n > 0 && n != EOF);
         break;
case 0x00ff:               /* application extension */
         if(fread((char *)&ap,1,sizeof(APPLICATION),fp)
              == sizeof(APPLICATION)) {
                     puts("APPLICATION BLOCK\n_____");
                     printf("Application identification string: %0.8s",ap.applstring);
                     do {
```

10-5 Continued.

```
                                        if((n=fgetc(fp)) != EOF) {
                                                for(i=0;i<n;++i) fgetc(fp);
                                        }
                                } while(n > 0 && n != EOF);
                        } else puts("Error reading application block");
                        break;
                default:                        /* something else */
                        printf("Skipping unknown extension type %02.2X\n",
                            c & 0x00ff);
                        n=fgetc(fp);
                        for(i=0;i<n;++i) fgetc(fp);
                        break;
                }
        getch();
}


/* unpack a GIF file */
unpackgif(fp,fi)
        FILE *fp;
        FILEINFO *fi;
{

        GIFHEADER gh;
        IMAGEBLOCK iblk;
        long t;
        int b,c;

        /* make sure it's a GIF file */
        if(fread((char *)&gh,1,sizeof(GIFHEADER),fp) != sizeof(GIFHEADER) ||
            memcmp(gh.sig, "GIF", 3)) return(BAD_FILE);

        /* get screen dimensions */
        fi->width=gh.screenwidth;
        fi->depth=gh.screendepth;
        fi->bits=(gh.flags & 0x0007) + 1;
        fi->background=gh.background;
        /* get colour map if there is one */
        if (gh.flags & 0x80) {
                c = 3 * (1 << ((gh.flags & 7) + 1));
                if(fread(fi->palette,1,c,fp) != c) return(BAD_READ);
        }

        /* step through the blocks */
        while((c=fgetc(fp))==',' || c=='!' || c==0) {

                /* if it's an image block... */
                if (c == ',') {
                        /* get the start of the image block */
                        if(fread(&iblk,1,sizeof(IMAGEBLOCK),fp) !=
                            sizeof(IMAGEBLOCK)) return(BAD_READ);

                        /* get the image dimensions */
                        fi->width=iblk.width;
```

10-5 Continued.

```
                fi->depth=iblk.depth;

                if(fi->bits==1) fi->bytes=pixels2bytes(fi->width);
                else if(fi->bits > 1 && fi->bits <= 4)
                    fi->bytes=pixels2bytes(fi->width)<<2;
                else fi->bytes=fi->width;

                /* get the local colour map if there is one */
                if(iblk.flags & 0x80) {
                        b = 3*(1<<((iblk.flags & 0x0007) + 1));
                        if(fread(fi->palette,1,b,fp) != c) return(BAD_READ);
                        fi->bits=(iblk.flags & 0x0007) + 1;
                }

                /* get the initial code size */
                if((c=fgetc(fp))==EOF) return(BAD_FILE);

                fi->flags=iblk.flags;

                /* do the setup procedure */
                if(fi->setup != NULL) {
                        if((t=(fi->setup)(fi)) != GOOD_READ)
                            return(t);
                }

                /* unpack the image */
                t=unpackimage(fp,c,fi);

                /* do the close down procedure */
                if(fi->closedown != NULL) (fi->closedown)(fi);

                /* quit if there was an error */
                if(t != GOOD_READ) return(t);
            }
            /* otherwise, it's an extension */
            else if(c == '!') (fi->savext)(fp);
        }
        return(GOOD_READ);
}


/* unpack an LZW compressed image */
unpackimage(fp,bits,fi)
        FILE *fp;
        int bits;
        FILEINFO *fi;
{
        int bits2;          /* Bits plus 1 */
        int codesize;       /* Current code size in bits */
        int codesize2;      /* Next codesize */
        int nextcode;       /* Next available table entry */
        int thiscode;       /* Code being expanded */
        int oldtoken;       /* Last symbol decoded */
```

10-5 Continued.

```
int currentcode;      /* Code just read */
int oldcode;          /* Code read before this one */
int bitsleft;         /* Number of bits left in *p */
int blocksize;        /* Bytes in next block */
int line=0;           /* next line to write */
int byte=0;           /* next byte to write */
int pass=0;           /* pass number for interlaced pictures */

char *p;              /* Pointer to current byte in read buffer */
char *q;              /* Pointer past last byte in read buffer */
char b[255];          /* Read buffer */
char *u;              /* Stack pointer into firstcodestack */
char *linebuffer;     /* place to store the current line */

static char firstcodestack[4096];  /* Stack for first codes */
static char lastcodestack[4096];   /* Statck for previous code */
static int codestack[4096];        /* Stack for links */

static int wordmasktable[] = {  0x0000,0x0001,0x0003,0x0007,
                                0x000f,0x001f,0x003f,0x007f,
                                0x00ff,0x01ff,0x03ff,0x07ff,
                                0x0fff,0x1fff,0x3fff,0x7fff
                                };

static int inctable[] = { 8,8,4,2,0 }; /* interlace increments */
static int startable[] = { 0,4,2,1,0 };  /* interlace starts */

p=q=b;
bitsleft = 8;

if (bits < 2 || bits > 8) return(BAD_SYMBOLSIZE);
bits2 = 1 << bits;
nextcode = bits2 + 2;
codesize2 = 1 << (codesize = bits + 1);
oldcode=oldtoken=NO_CODE;

if((linebuffer=dosalloc(fi->width)) == NULL) return(BAD_ALLOC);

/* loop until something breaks */
for(;;) {
        if(bitsleft==8) {
                if(++p >= q &&
                (((blocksize = fgetc(fp)) < 1) ||
                (q=(p=b)+fread(b,1,blocksize,fp))< (b+blocksize))) {
                        dosfree(linebuffer);
                        return(UNEXPECTED_EOF);
                }
                bitsleft = 0;
        }
        thiscode = *p;
        if ((currentcode=(codesize+bitsleft)) <= 8) {
                *p >>= codesize;
```

10-5 Continued.

```
                bitsleft = currentcode;
        }
        else {
                if(++p >= q &&
                   (((blocksize = fgetc(fp)) < 1) ||
                    (q=(p=b)+fread(b,1,blocksize,fp)) < (b+blocksize))) {
                        dosfree(linebuffer);
                        return(UNEXPECTED_EOF);
                }
                thiscode |= *p << (8 - bitsleft);
                if(currentcode <= 16) *p >>= (bitsleft=currentcode-8);
                else {
                        if(++p >= q &&
                           (((blocksize = fgetc(fp)) < 1) ||
                            (q=(p=b) + fread(b,1,blocksize,fp)) < (b+blocksize))) {
                                dosfree(linebuffer);
                                return(UNEXPECTED_EOF);
                        }
                        thiscode |= *p << (16 - bitsleft);
                        *p >>= (bitsleft = currentcode - 16);
                }
        }
        thiscode &= wordmasktable[codesize];
        currentcode = thiscode;

        if(thiscode == (bits2+1)) break;      /* found EOI */
        if(thiscode > nextcode) {
                dosfree(linebuffer);
                return(BAD_CODE);
        }

        if(thiscode == bits2) {
                nextcode = bits2 + 2;
                codesize2 = 1 << (codesize = (bits + 1));
                oldtoken = oldcode = NO_CODE;
                continue;
        }

        u = firstcodestack;

        if(thiscode==nextcode) {
                if(oldcode==NO_CODE) {
                        dosfree(linebuffer);
                        return(BAD_FIRSTCODE);
                }
                *u++ = oldtoken;
                thiscode = oldcode;
        }

        while (thiscode >= bits2) {
                *u++ = lastcodestack[thiscode];
                thiscode = codestack[thiscode];
```

10-5 Continued.

```
                }

                oldtoken = thiscode;
                do {
                        linebuffer[byte++]=thiscode;
                        if(byte >= fi->width) {
                                (fi->saveline)(linebuffer,line);
                                byte=0;

                                /* check for interlaced image */
                                if(fi->flags & 0x40) {
                                        line+=inctable[pass];
                                        if(line >= fi->depth)
                                                line=startable[++pass];
                                } else ++line;
                        }

                        if (u <= firstcodestack) break;
                        thiscode = *--u;
                } while(1);

                if(nextcode < 4096 && oldcode != NO_CODE) {
                        codestack[nextcode] = oldcode;
                        lastcodestack[nextcode] = oldtoken;
                        if (++nextcode >= codesize2 && codesize < 12)
                            codesize2 = 1 << ++codesize;
                }
                oldcode = currentcode;
        }
        dosfree(linebuffer);
        return(GOOD_READ);
}

convertline(p,line)
        char *p;
        unsigned int line;
{

        char *pr;
        int i,j,n;

        if(fi.bits==1) {
                if((pr=dosalloc(fi.bytes)) != NULL) {
                        memset(pr,0,fi.bytes);
                        for(i=0;i<fi.width;++i)
                            if(p[i]) pr[i>>3] |= masktable[i & 0x0007];
                        putline(pr,line);
                        dosfree(pr);
                }
        }
        else if(fi.bits > 1 && fi.bits <=4) {
                if((pr=dosalloc(fi.bytes)) != NULL) {
                        memset(pr,0,fi.bytes);
```

10-5 Continued.

```
                                    n=0;
                                    for(j=0;j<fi.bits;++j) {
                                            for(i=0;i<fi.width;++i)
                                                    if(p[i] & bittable[j])
                                                            pr[n+(i>>3)] |= masktable[i & 0x0007];
                                            n+=pixels2bytes(fi.width);
                                    }
                                    putline(pr,line);
                                    dosfree(pr);
                            }
                    }
                else putline(p,line);
        }


/* This function is called before an image is decompressed. It must
   allocate memory, put the display in graphic mode and so on. */
dosetup(fi)
        FILEINFO *fi;
{
        if(!getbuffer((long)fi->bytes*(long)fi->depth,fi->bytes,fi->depth))
            return(BAD_ALLOC);

        if(fi->bits==1) {
                if(gd->mono_on==NULL) {
                        freebuffer();
                        return(NO_DRIVER);
                }
                (gd->mono_on)(fi->width,fi->depth);
        }
        else if(fi->bits > 1 && fi->bits <= 4) {
                if(gd->ega_on==NULL) {
                        freebuffer();
                        return(NO_DRIVER);
                }
                (gd->ega_on)(fi->width,fi->depth);
                (gd->ega_palette)(NULL,1<<fi->bits,fi->palette);
        }
        else {
                if(gd->vga_on==NULL) {
                        freebuffer();
                        return(NO_DRIVER);
                }
                (gd->vga_on)(fi->width,fi->depth);
                (gd->vga_palette)(fi->palette,1<<fi->bits);
                (gd->vga_overscan)(fi->background);
        }

        return(GOOD_READ);
}


/* This function is called after an image has been unpacked. It must
   display the image and allocate memory. */
```

10-5 Continued.

```
doclosedown(fi)
        FILEINFO *fi;
{
        int screenwide,screendeep;
        int c,i,n,x=0,y=0;

        if(fi->bits==1) {
                screenwide=gd->mono_wide;
                screendeep=gd->mono_deep;
                if(fi->width > screenwide) n=pixels2bytes(screenwide);
                else n=pixels2bytes(fi->width);
        }
        else if(fi->bits > 1 && fi->bits <= 4) {
                screenwide=gd->ega_wide;
                screendeep=gd->ega_deep;
                n=pixels2bytes(fi->width);
        }
        else {
                screenwide=gd->vga_wide;
                screendeep=gd->vga_deep;
                if(fi->width > screenwide) n=screenwide;
                else n=fi->width;
        }
  do {
        for(i=0;i<screendeep;++i) {
                c=y+i;
                if(c>=fi->depth) break;
                if(fi->bits==1)
                        (gd->mono_line)(getline(y+i)+(x>>3),i,n);
                else if(fi->bits > 1 && fi->bits <= 4)
                        (gd->ega_line)(getline(y+i)+(x>>3),n,i);
                else
                        (gd->vga_line)(getline(y+i)+x,n,i);
        }
        c=GetKey();
        switch(c) {
                case CURSOR_LEFT:
                        if((x-STEP) > 0) x-=STEP;
                        else x=0;
                        break;
                case CURSOR_RIGHT:
                        if((x+STEP+screenwide) < fi->width) x+=STEP;
                        else if(fi->width > screenwide)
                            x=fi->width-screenwide;
                        else x=0;
                        break;
                case CURSOR_UP:
                        if((y-STEP) > 0) y-=STEP;
                        else y=0;
                        break;
                case CURSOR_DOWN:
                        if((y+STEP+screendeep) < fi->depth) y+=STEP;
```

10-5 Continued.

```
                                else if(fi->depth > screendeep)
                                        y=fi->depth-screendeep;
                                else y=0;
                                break;
                        case HOME:
                                x=y=0;
                                break;
                        case END:
                                if(fi->width > screenwide)
                                        x=fi->width-screenwide;
                                else x=0;
                                if(fi->depth > screendeep)
                                        y=fi->depth-screendeep;
                                else y=0;
                                break;
                }
        } while(c != 27);

        freebuffer();

        if(fi->bits==1) (gd->mono_off)();
        else if(fi->bits > 1 && fi->bits <= 4) (gd->ega_off)();
        else (gd->vga_off)();

        return(GOOD_READ);
}


/* get one extended key code */
GetKey()
{
        int c;

        c = getch();
        if(!(c & 0x00ff)) c = getch() << 8;
        return(c);
}

/* make file name with specific extension */
strmfe(new,old,ext)
        char *new,*old,*ext;
{
        while(*old != 0 && *old != '.') *new++=*old++;
        *new++='.';
        while(*ext) *new++=*ext++;
        *new=0;
}

printchar(c)                    /* print characters from extension blocks */
        int c;
{
        if(c==9 || c==13 || c==10) putchar(c);
        else if(c >= 32) putchar(c);
```

10-5 Continued.

```
            else if(c==EOF) printf("<EOF>");
            else printf("<%u>",c);
}

GRAFDRIVER *loadDriver(s)               /* load an external graphics driver */
        char *s;
{
        GRAFDRIVER *gd;
        char *grafDriver=NULL;
        FILE *fp;
        long l;
        char b[8];
        unsigned int seg;

        if((fp=fopen(s,"rb")) != NULL) {
                fseek(fp,0L,SEEK_END);
                l=ftell(fp);
                rewind(fp);

                fread(b,1,8,fp);
                if(!memcmp(b,"ALCHDRV2",8)) {
                        l-=8L;
                        if(l < 0xffffL &&
                            (grafDriver=dosalloc((unsigned int)l)) != NULL) {
                                if(fread(grafDriver,1,(unsigned int)l,fp)==
                                    (unsigned int)l) {
                                        gd=(GRAFDRIVER *)grafDriver;
                                        seg=FP_SEG(grafDriver);

                                        if(gd->vga_on != NULL) {
                                                grafDriver[2]=seg;
                                                grafDriver[3]=(seg >> 8);
                                                grafDriver[6]=seg;
                                                grafDriver[7]=(seg >> 8);
                                                grafDriver[10]=seg;
                                                grafDriver[11]=(seg >> 8);
                                                grafDriver[14]=seg;
                                                grafDriver[15]=(seg >> 8);
                                                grafDriver[18]=seg;
                                                grafDriver[19]=(seg >> 8);
                                        }

                                        if(gd->ega_on != NULL) {
                                                grafDriver[22]=seg;
                                                grafDriver[23]=(seg >> 8);
                                                grafDriver[26]=seg;
                                                grafDriver[27]=(seg >> 8);
                                                grafDriver[30]=seg;
                                                grafDriver[31]=(seg >> 8);
                                                grafDriver[34]=seg;
                                                grafDriver[35]=(seg >> 8);
                                        }
```

10-5 Continued.

```
                                    if(gd->mono_on != NULL) {
                                            grafDriver[38]=seg;
                                            grafDriver[39]=(seg >> 8);
                                            grafDriver[42]=seg;
                                            grafDriver[43]=(seg >> 8);
                                            grafDriver[46]=seg;
                                            grafDriver[47]=(seg >> 8);
                                            grafDriver[50]=seg;
                                            grafDriver[51]=(seg >> 8);
                                    }

                                    if(gd->rgb_on != NULL) {
                                            grafDriver[54]=seg;
                                            grafDriver[55]=(seg >> 8);
                                            grafDriver[58]=seg;
                                            grafDriver[59]=(seg >> 8);
                                            grafDriver[62]=seg;
                                            grafDriver[63]=(seg >> 8);
                                    }
                            }
                            else {
                                    dosfree(grafDriver);
                                    grafDriver=NULL;
                            }
                    }
            }
            fclose(fp);
    }
    return((GRAFDRIVER *)grafDriver);
}

/* if you don't use in the memory manager, these functions
   will stand in for it */

#if !MEMMANGR

char *dosalloc(n)
        unsigned int n;
{
        union REGS r;

        n+=8;
        r.x.ax=0x4800;
        r.x.bx=1+(n>>4);
        int86(0x21,&r,&r);
        if(r.x.cflag) return(NULL);
        else return(MK_FP(r.x.ax,0x0008));
}

dosfree(p)
        char *p;
{
```

10-5 Continued.

```
        union REGS r;
        struct SREGS sr;

        r.x.ax=0x4900;
        sr.es=FP_SEG(p);
        int86x(0x21,&r,&r,&sr);
}

/* return a far pointer plus a long integer */
char *farPtr(p,l)
        char *p;
        long l;
{
        unsigned int seg,off;

        seg = FP_SEG(p);
        off = FP_OFF(p);
        seg += (off / 16);
        off &= 0x000f;
        off += (unsigned int)(l & 0x000fL);
        seg += (l / 16L);
        p = MK_FP(seg,off);
        return(p);
}

/* save one line to memory */
putline(p,n)
        char *p;
        unsigned int n;
{
        if(n >= 0 && n < fi.depth)
            memcpy(farPtr(buffer,(long)n*(long)fi.bytes),p,fi.bytes);
}

/* get one line from memory */
char *getline(n)
        unsigned int n;
{
        return(farPtr(buffer,(long)n*(long)fi.bytes));
}

#pragma warn -par
getbuffer(n,bytes,lines)
        unsigned long n;
        int bytes,lines;
{
        union REGS r;

        r.x.ax=0x4800;
        r.x.bx=1+(int)(n>>4);
        int86(0x21,&r,&r);
```

10-5 Continued.

```
              if(r.x.cflag) return(0);
              else {
                      buffer=MK_FP(r.x.ax,0x0000);
                      return(1);
              }
      }

freebuffer()
{
      union REGS r;
      struct SREGS sr;

      if(buffer != NULL) {
              r.x.ax=0x4900;
              sr.es=FP_SEG(buffer);
              int86x(0x21,&r,&r,&sr);
      }
      buffer=NULL;
}
#endif /* !MEMMANGR */
```

10-5 Continued.

Note that this program requires two command line arguments, these
being the name of the GIF file to be displayed and the name of the driver to
use. Both arguments can include complete DOS paths if you like. For
example, to display the ZOE.GIF file from the companion disks for this
book, you would type:

READGIF2 ZOE.GIF VGA.DRV

The ZOE.GIF file actually has the dimensions 320×200 pixels, that is, it's
no bigger than the screen of a VGA card in mode 13H. If you attempt to
display a larger 256-color GIF file with READGIF2 using the VGA driver,
you'll have to pan around it using the arrow keys on your keyboard.

Should you have one of the super VGA cards that the drivers in this
chapter support, you'll be able to see more of your larger GIF images on it.
The EXAMPLE3.GIF file that comes with Graphic Workshop has the
dimensions 640×400 pixels in 256 colors. If you display it using
READGIF2 and the VGA driver, you'll see something like the image in FIG.
10-6.

If you have a Paradise card, for example, and you peek ahead at the
section that describes the Paradise super VGA driver — or get it from the
companion disks for this book—you can run READGIF2 like this:

READGIF2 EXAMPLE2.GIF PARADISE.DRV

This should show you the entire image, as in FIG. 10-7.

You should also try READGIF2 with some monochrome and 16-color
GIF files to make sure that the other screen modes work properly.

10-6 Part of the EXAMPLE3.GIF file from Graphic Workshop.

The frog, originally a GIF file, was converted to an LBM file and imported into Deluxe Paint. The gradient in "Graphic Workshop" was added, and the result was exported to PC Paintbrush IV Plus. The Alchemy Mindworks logo was created in Corel Draw and exported as a PCX file.

10-7 All of the EXAMPLE3.GIF file from Graphic Workshop.

Once READGIF2 is working, you might want to have a shot at adapting the other file readers discussed in this book to use the screen drivers, rather than being hard-wired into using mode 13H.

A Paradise Super VGA driver

Super VGA cards typically offer anything from 640×400 pixels and up at 256 colors. You can calculate that this presents some memory problems. Whereas the screen page of a VGA card is constrained to occupy no more than 1 segment of memory (64K), the screen buffer for 640×400 pixels needs about 256K.

Unlike the 16-color modes, which naturally break up into planes requiring less than 64K each, a 256-color picture is a single matrix of bytes. There are two obvious ways of splitting up such a large buffer of data—you can break it either after enough even lines to fill 64K or right on a 64K boundary.

The first approach makes for a screen driver that's a lot easier to work with, and hence, operates a lot faster. The second has some advantages in the way a super VGA card uses its on-board memory.

The Paradise chip sets from Western Digital are actually the only ones that allow you to force the pages to break anywhere you like, and hence to make their breaks fall at the ends of lines. All the other super VGA cards discussed in this chapter have three or four lines in which page changes are located somewhere along the line.

Paradise cards are perhaps not the least expensive super VGA cards available at present (although they are found in disguise as numerous low-cost third-party cards), but they are the easiest ones to write code for. For reasons you'll probably appreciate once you've had a chance to look at the other drivers discussed in this chapter, software that drives a super VGA card can typically drive a Paradise card faster than it can more conventional super VGA hardware, as it's required to do less data manipulation to handle page breaks.

As an aside, the Paradise cards, as with the other super VGA cards discussed, offer a higher resolution 16-color mode as well. This works just like the standard VGA 640×480, 16-color mode discussed previously in conjunction with VGA.ASM, except that it has different dimensions. The driver dealt with here also illustrates how to use it.

Because Paradise cards allow you to have page breaks fall at the ends of lines, a driver can be written to assign every line on the screen both an offset and a page number. As with VGA.ASM, it's preferable to put each of these values in a table, so that they need to be calculated only once. Having done this, when the VGA_LINE function is called, the code can fetch both the page number and the offset into the page, call up the appropriate page, and copy the new line data into it.

In fact, it's preferable to keep track of the current page and only actually change pages when a different page needs to be addressed. In updating the entire screen, this reduces the page changes from 400 to 3, a considerable time savings.

The Paradise driver discussed here supports the Paradise Plus card specifically, although it's equally suitable for later Paradise hardware. The

Paradise Plus card is a fairly low-end card with only 256K of memory on board. It's also essentially the card that tends to show up as OEM cards in complete computer systems, such as the Dell machines. It has a super VGA 256-color mode that supports 640×400 pixels.

As discussed later you can easily expand this driver to support a higher-resolution Paradise card if you have one. A card with more memory, and hence one that is capable of handling more 256-color modes, will still support the 640×400 pixels mode that this driver works with.

Note that the early Paradise chip sets had a bit of a timing problem in their 640×400 pixel, 256-color mode, which will result in some screen noise as the driver updates its screen.

Figure 10-8 illustrates the source code for PARADISE.ASM. It should be assembled using the same batch file that dealt with VGA.ASM earlier in this chapter, to leave you with PARADISE.DRV.

```
;
;               Graphic Workshop Paradise screen driver
;               Copyright (C) 1989, 1991 Alchemy Mindworks Inc.
;


VERSION         EQU     2               ;VERSION NUMBER
SUBVERSION      EQU     1               ;SUBVERSION NUMBER

_AOFF           EQU     6               ;STACK OFFSET

VGA_WIDE        EQU     640             ;WIDTH OF VGA SCREEN IN PIXELS
VGA_DEEP        EQU     400             ;DEPTH OF VGA SCREEN IN PIXELS
VGA_SCREENSEG   EQU     0A000H          ;SEGMENT OF VGA SCREEN
EGA_WIDE        EQU     640             ;WIDTH OF EGA SCREEN IN PIXELS
EGA_DEEP        EQU     480             ;DEPTH OF EGA SCREEN IN PIXELS
EGA_BYTES       EQU     80              ;WIDTH OF EGA SCREEN IN BYTES
EGA_SCREENSEG   EQU     0A000H          ;SEGMENT OF EGA SCREEN
MONO_WIDE       EQU     800             ;WIDTH OF MONO SCREEN IN PIXELS
MONO_DEEP       EQU     600             ;DEPTH OF MONO SCREEN IN PIXELS
MONO_BYTES      EQU     80              ;WIDTH OF MONO SCREEN IN BYTES
MONO_SCREENSEG  EQU     0A000H          ;SEGMENT OF MONO SCREEN

PROA_REG        EQU     9               ;PROA REGISTER

;THIS MACRO SELECTS AN EGA PLANE
EGAPLANE        MACRO   ARG1
                MOV     AL,2
                MOV     DX,03C4H
                OUT     DX,AL
                INC     DX
                MOV     AL,ARG1
                OUT     DX,AL
```

10-8 The source code for PARADISE.ASM.

```
              ENDM

;SET THE PROA REGISTER TO THE VALUE IN AL
SET_PROA      MACRO
              PUSH    AX
              MOV     DX,03CEH
              MOV     AX,050FH
              OUT     DX,AX
              POP     AX
              MOV     AH,AL
              MOV     AL,PROA_REG
              OUT     DX,AX
              MOV     AX,000FH
              OUT     DX,AX
              ENDM


CODE          SEGMENT PARA PUBLIC 'CODE'
              ASSUME  CS:CODE

              ORG     0000H           ;ORIGIN FOR LOADABLE DRIVER

              DB      'ALCHDRV2'

;THE FOLLOWING ARE THE POINTERS TO THE CALLABLE ROUTINES AND THE COMMON
;DATA. THE SEGMENTS ARE FILLED IN BY GRAPHIC WORKSHOP. DON'T CHANGE ANYTHING.
DISPATCH      PROC    FAR
              DW      VGA_ON          ;FAR POINTER TO VGA MODE SELECT
              DW      ?
              DW      VGA_LINE        ;FAR POINTER TO VGA LINE DISPLAY
              DW      ?
              DW      VGA_OFF         ;FAR POINTER TO VGA MODE DESELECT
              DW      ?
              DW      VGA_PALETTE     ;FAR POINTER TO VGA PALETTE SET
              DW      ?
              DW      VGA_OVERSCAN    ;FAR POINTER TO VGA OVERSCAN SET
              DW      ?
              DW      EGA_ON          ;FAR POINTER TO EGA MODE SELECT
              DW      ?
              DW      EGA_LINE        ;FAR POINTER TO EGA LINE DISPLAY
              DW      ?
              DW      EGA_OFF         ;FAR POINTER TO EGA MODE DESELECT
              DW      ?
              DW      EGA_PALETTE     ;FAR POINTER TO EGA PALETTE SET
              DW      ?
              DW      MONO_ON         ;FAR POINTER TO MONO MODE SELECT
              DW      ?
              DW      MONO_FUNCTIONS  ;FAR POINTER TO MONO PAGE DISPLAY
              DW      ?
              DW      MONO_LINE
              DW      ?
              DW      MONO_OFF        ;FAR POINTER TO MONO MODE DESELECT
```

10-8 Continued.

```
                        DW      ?
                        DW      0,0                 ;RGB ON
                        DW      0,0                 ;RGB OFF
                        DW      0,0                 ;RGB LINE
                        DW      0                   ;RGB WIDTH
                        DW      0                   ;RGB DEPTH

V_VGAWIDE               DW      VGA_WIDE            ;VGA SCREEN WIDTH
V_VGADEEP               DW      VGA_DEEP            ;VGA SCREEN DEPTH
V_VGASCRNSEG            DW      VGA_SCREENSEG       ;VGA SCREEN SEGMENT
V_EGAWIDE               DW      EGA_WIDE            ;EGA SCREEN WIDTH
V_EGADEEP               DW      EGA_DEEP            ;EGA SCREEN DEPTH
V_EGABYTES              DW      EGA_BYTES           ;EGA SCREEN BYTES
V_EGASCRNSEG            DW      EGA_SCREENSEG       ;EGA SCREEN SEGMENT
V_MONOWIDE              DW      MONO_WIDE           ;MONO SCREEN WIDTH
V_MONODEEP              DW      MONO_DEEP           ;MONO SCREEN DEPTH
V_MONOBYTES             DW      MONO_BYTES          ;BYTE WIDTH ON MONOCHROME SCREEN
V_MONOSCRNSEG           DW      MONO_SCREENSEG      ;MONOCHROME SCREEN SEGMENT
                        DW      VERSION
                        DW      SUBVERSION
                        DB      'Paradise Plus Card 2.1 ',0
DISPATCH                ENDP


VGAMODETABLE            DW      320,200
                        DW      640,400
                        DW      -1,-1


EGAMODETABLE            DW      640,480
                        DW      800,600
                        DW      -1,-1


MONOMODETABLE           DW      640,480
                        DW      800,600
                        DW      -1,-1


;THIS ROUTINE SELECTS THE VGA 256 COLOUR MODE
VGA_ON                  PROC    NEAR
                        PUSH    BP
                        MOV     BP,SP
                        PUSH    DS

                        CMP     WORD PTR [BP + _AOFF + 0],320
                        JG      PARA_ON
                        CMP     WORD PTR [BP + _AOFF + 2],200
                        JG      PARA_ON

                        MOV     CS:[V_VGAWIDE],320
                        MOV     CS:[V_VGADEEP],200
                        MOV     CX,200                      ;DEPTH OF SCREEN
                        SUB     DX,DX
                        MOV     SI,OFFSET SCREENTABLE
```

10-8 Continued.

```
VGA_ON1:        PUSH    DX
                MOV     AX,320                  ;WIDTH OF SCREEEN
                MUL     DX
                MOV     CS:[SI],AX
                ADD     SI,2
                POP     DX
                INC     DX
                LOOP    VGA_ON1

                MOV     AX,0013H
                INT     10H

                JMP     PARA_EXIT

PARA_ON:        MOV     CS:[V_VGAWIDE],VGA_WIDE
                MOV     CS:[V_VGADEEP],VGA_DEEP
                MOV     CS:[CODEPAGE],0FFFFH

                MOV     CX,400                  ;DEPTH OF SCREEN
                SUB     BX,BX                   ;ZERO LINE COUNTER
                MOV     SI,OFFSET SCREENTABLE   ;POINT TO TABLE

PVGAG1:         PUSH    CX
                MOV     AX,640                  ;WIDTH OF SCREEEN
                MUL     BX                      ;TIMES LINE NUMBER

                MOV     CL,4                    ;SHIFT HIGH ORDER
                SHL     DX,CL                   ;WORD OVER BY A BYTE
                AND     DX,0070H

                CMP     AX,(0FFFEH-640)          ;SEE IF WE WILL
                JB      PVGAG2                  ;HIT A 64K BOUNDARY
                SUB     AX,1000H                ;AND ADJUST THE
                INC     DX                      ;HIGH ORDER WORD

PVGAG2:         MOV     CS:[SI],AX              ;SAVE THE VALUES
                MOV     CS:[SI+2],DX            ;IN OUR LOOKUP TABLE
                ADD     SI,4                    ;AND POINT TO THE
                INC     BX                      ;NEXT LINE AND
                POP     CX                      ;ENTRY
                LOOP    PVGAG1

                MOV     AX,005EH
                INT     10H

PARA_EXIT:      POP     DS
                POP     BP
                RETF
VGA_ON          ENDP

;THIS ROUTINE DISPLAYS A VGA LINE
VGA_LINE        PROC    NEAR
```

10-8 Continued.

```
                    PUSH    BP
                    MOV     BP,SP

                    PUSH    DS
                    PUSH    ES

                    CMP     V_VGAWIDE,320
                    JNE     PARASHOW

                    MOV     SI,[BP + _AOFF + 0]     ;OFFSET OF SOURCE
                    MOV     DS,[BP + _AOFF + 2]     ;SEGMENT OF SOURCE

                    MOV     BX,[BP + _AOFF + 6]     ;GET LINE NUMBER
                    CMP     BX,200
                    JGE     PSHOWVGAX

                    SHL     BX,1
                    MOV     DI,CS:[SCREENTABLE+BX]

                    CLD
                    MOV     CX,[BP + _AOFF + 4]     ;LENGTH OF MOVE IN BYTES
                    CMP     CX,0
                    JE      PSHOWVGAX               ;CHECK FOR NASTIES
                    CMP     CX,320
                    JL      SHOWVGA1
                    MOV     CX,320
SHOWVGA1:           MOV     AX,VGA_SCREENSEG
                    MOV     ES,AX
        REPNE       MOVSB

                    JMP     PSHOWVGAX

PARASHOW:           CMP     WORD PTR [BP + _AOFF + 6],400
                    JGE     PSHOWVGAX               ;IS THIS A LEGAL LINE?
                    MOV     SI,[BP + _AOFF + 0]     ;OFFSET OF SOURCE
                    MOV     DS,[BP + _AOFF + 2]     ;SEGMENT OF SOURCE
                    MOV     CX,[BP + _AOFF + 4]     ;LENGTH OF MOVE IN BYTES

                    CMP     CX,640                  ;IS IT TOO LONG?
                    JL      PSHOWVGA0

                    MOV     CX,640

PSHOWVGA0:          MOV     BX,[BP + _AOFF + 6]     ;GET INDEX INTO LINE TABLE
                    SHL     BX,1
                    SHL     BX,1

                    MOV     DI,CS:[SCREENTABLE + BX]
                    MOV     AX,CS:[SCREENTABLE + 2 + BX]
                    CMP     CS:[CODEPAGE],AX
                    JE      PSHOWVGA1
                    MOV     CS:[CODEPAGE],AX
```

10-8 Continued.

```
                SET_PROA                         ;SET HIGH ORDER WORD

PSHOWVGA1:      MOV     AX,0A000H                ;POINT TO VIDEO BUFFER
                MOV     ES,AX                    ;WITH ES

                CLD
        REPNE   MOVSB                            ;MOVE IN THE LINE DATA

PSHOWVGAX:      POP     ES
                POP     DS
                POP     BP
                RETF
VGA_LINE        ENDP

;THIS ROUTINE DESELECTS THE VGA 256 COLOUR MODE
VGA_OFF         PROC    NEAR
                MOV     AX,1200H
                MOV     BX,0031H
                INT     10H

                MOV     AX,0003H
                INT     10H
                RETF
VGA_OFF         ENDP

;THIS ROUTINE SETS THE VGA PALETTE
VGA_PALETTE     PROC    NEAR
                PUSH    BP
                MOV     BP,SP
                PUSH    DS
                PUSH    ES

                MOV     SI,[BP + _AOFF + 0]      ;OFFSET OF SOURCE
                MOV     DS,[BP + _AOFF + 2]      ;SEGMENT OF SOURCE

                MOV     CX,[BP + _AOFF + 4]      ;NUMBER OF COLOURS

                CMP     CX,0                     ;CHECK FOR NASTIES
                JG      GVP0
                JMP     GVPX

GVP0:           MOV     DX,03C6H
                MOV     AL,0FFH
                OUT     DX,AL

                MOV     BX,0

GVP1:           PUSH    CX
                MOV     DX,03C8H
                MOV     AL,BL
                INC     BX
                OUT     DX,AL
```

10-8 Continued.

```
                        LODSB
                        SHR     AL,1
                        SHR     AL,1
                        OUT     DX,AL

                        LODSB
                        SHR     AL,1
                        SHR     AL,1
                        OUT     DX,AL

                        LODSB
                        SHR     AL,1
                        SHR     AL,1
                        OUT     DX,AL

                        POP     CX
                        LOOP    GVP1

GVPX:                   POP     ES
                        POP     DS
                        POP     BP
                        RETF
VGA_PALETTE             ENDP

;THIS ROUTINE SETS THE VGA OVERSCAN.
VGA_OVERSCAN            PROC    NEAR
                        PUSH    BP
                        MOV     BP,SP

                        MOV     AX,1001H
                        MOV     BX,[BP + _AOFF + 0]
                        XCHG    BH,BL
                        INT     10H

                        POP     BP
                        RETF
VGA_OVERSCAN            ENDP

;THIS ROUTINE SELECTS THE EGA 16 COLOUR MODE
EGA_ON                  PROC    NEAR
                        PUSH    BP
                        MOV     BP,SP
                        PUSH    DS

EGA480:                 CMP     WORD PTR [BP + _AOFF + 2],640
                        JG      EGA600
                        CMP     WORD PTR [BP + _AOFF + 2],480
                        JG      EGA600

                        MOV     CS:[V_EGAWIDE],640
                        MOV     CS:[V_EGADEEP],480
                        MOV     CS:[V_EGABYTES],80
```

10-8 Continued.

```
                 MOV     CX,480              ;DEPTH OF SCREEN
                 SUB     DX,DX
                 MOV     SI,OFFSET SCREENTABLE

EGA_ON2:         PUSH    DX
                 MOV     AX,80               ;WIDTH OF SCREEEN
                 MUL     DX
                 MOV     CS:[SI],AX
                 ADD     SI,2
                 POP     DX
                 INC     DX
                 LOOP    EGA_ON2

                 MOV     AX,0012H
                 INT     10H

                 JMP     EGA_EXIT

EGA600:          MOV     CS:[V_EGAWIDE],800
                 MOV     CS:[V_EGADEEP],600
                 MOV     CS:[V_EGABYTES],100

                 MOV     CX,600              ;DEPTH OF SCREEN
                 SUB     DX,DX
                 MOV     SI,OFFSET SCREENTABLE

EGA_ON3:         PUSH    DX
                 MOV     AX,100              ;WIDTH OF SCREEEN
                 MUL     DX
                 MOV     CS:[SI],AX
                 ADD     SI,2
                 POP     DX
                 INC     DX
                 LOOP    EGA_ON3

                 MOV     AX,0058H
                 INT     10H

EGA_EXIT:        POP     DS
                 POP     BP
                 RETF
EGA_ON           ENDP

;THIS ROUTINE DISPLAYS AN EGA LINE
EGA_LINE         PROC    NEAR
                 PUSH    BP
                 MOV     BP,SP
                 PUSH    DS
                 PUSH    ES

                 MOV     SI,[BP + _AOFF + 0]     ;OFFSET OF SOURCE
                 MOV     DS,[BP + _AOFF + 2]     ;SEGMENT OF SOURCE
```

10-8 Continued.

```
                    MOV     BX,[BP + _AOFF + 6]      ;GET LINE NUMBER
                    CMP     BX,CS:[V_EGADEEP]
                    JGE     SHOWEGAX

                    SHL     BX,1
                    MOV     DI,CS:[SCREENTABLE+BX]

                    MOV     AX,0A000H
                    MOV     ES,AX
                    MOV     BX,[BP + _AOFF + 4]      ;LENGTH OF MOVE IN BYTES

                    MOV     CX,BX
                    EGAPLANE        1
                    CLD
                    PUSH    DI
          REPNE     MOVSB
                    POP     DI

                    MOV     CX,BX
                    EGAPLANE        2
                    PUSH    DI
          REPNE     MOVSB
                    POP     DI

                    MOV     CX,BX
                    EGAPLANE        4
                    PUSH    DI
          REPNE     MOVSB
                    POP     DI

                    MOV     CX,BX
                    EGAPLANE        8
                    PUSH    DI
          REPNE     MOVSB
                    POP     DI
                    EGAPLANE        0FH

SHOWEGAX:           POP     ES
                    POP     DS
                    POP     BP
                    RETF
EGA_LINE            ENDP

;THIS ROUTINE SETS THE EGA PALETTE
EGA_PALETTE         PROC    NEAR
                    PUSH    BP
                    MOV     BP,SP
                    PUSH    DS
                    PUSH    ES

                    MOV     SI,[BP + _AOFF + 6]      ;OFFSET OF SOURCE
                    MOV     DS,[BP + _AOFF + 8]      ;SEGMENT OF SOURCE
```

10-8 Continued.

```
              MOV      CX,[BP + _AOFF + 4]     ;NUMBER OF COLOURS
              CMP      CX,16
              JLE      EGA_PALETTE1
              MOV      CX,16

EGA_PALETTE1: PUSH     CX
              MOV      BX,0000H

EGA_PALETTE2: PUSH     CX
              LODSB
              SHR      AL,1
              SHR      AL,1
              MOV      DH,AL
              LODSB
              SHR      AL,1
              SHR      AL,1
              MOV      CH,AL
              LODSB
              SHR      AL,1
              SHR      AL,1
              MOV      CL,AL
              MOV      AX,1010H
              INT      10H
              INC      BX
              POP      CX
              LOOP     EGA_PALETTE2

              POP      CX
              MOV      BX,0000H

EGA_PALETTE3: PUSH     CX
              MOV      AX,1000H
              INT      10H
              ADD      BX,0101H
              POP      CX
              LOOP     EGA_PALETTE3

              POP      ES
              POP      DS
              POP      BP
              RETF
EGA_PALETTE   ENDP

;THIS ROUTINE DESELECTS THE EGA 16 COLOUR MODE
EGA_OFF       PROC     NEAR
              MOV      AX,0003H
              INT      10H
              RETF
EGA_OFF       ENDP

;THIS ROUTINE SELECTS THE 2 COLOUR MODE
MONO_ON       PROC     NEAR
              PUSH     BP
```

10-8 Continued.

```
                          MOV      BP,SP
                          PUSH     DS
                          PUSH     ES

                          CMP      WORD PTR [BP + _AOFF + 2],640
                          JG       MONO600
                          CMP      WORD PTR [BP + _AOFF + 2],480
                          JG       MONO600

                          MOV      CS:[V_MONOWIDE],640
                          MOV      CS:[V_MONODEEP],480
                          MOV      CS:[V_MONOBYTES],80

                          MOV      AX,0012H
                          INT      10H

                          MOV      CX,480
                          SUB      DX,DX
                          MOV      SI,OFFSET SCREENTABLE

MONO_ON1:                 PUSH     DX
                          MOV      AX,80
                          MUL      DX
                          MOV      CS:[SI],AX
                          ADD      SI,2
                          POP      DX
                          INC      DX
                          LOOP     MONO_ON1

                          JMP      MONOEXIT

MONO600:                  MOV      CS:[V_MONOWIDE],800
                          MOV      CS:[V_MONODEEP],600
                          MOV      CS:[V_MONOBYTES],100

                          MOV      AX,0059H
                          INT      10H

                          MOV      CX,600
                          SUB      DX,DX
                          MOV      SI,OFFSET SCREENTABLE

MONO_ON3:                 PUSH     DX
                          MOV      AX,100
                          MUL      DX
                          MOV      CS:[SI],AX
                          ADD      SI,2
                          POP      DX
                          INC      DX
                          LOOP     MONO_ON3

MONOEXIT:                 POP      ES
                          POP      DS
```

10-8 Continued.

```
                POP     BP
                SUB     AX,AX
                RETF
MONO_ON         ENDP

;THIS FUNCTION PERFORMS VARIOUS GRAPHIC OPERATIONS
;        ARGUMENTS        -       FUNCTION CODE
;                         -       VARIABLE
;
;        FUNCTIONS        -       0       RETURN SCREEN SEG
;                         -       1       RETURN OFFSET TO SCREEN TABLE
;                         -       2       RETURN MONOCHROME SCREEN WIDTH
;                         -       3       RETURN MONOCHROME SCREEN DEPTH
;                         -       4       INVERT FRAME RECT - ARGS ON STACK
;                         -       5       RETURN OFFSET OF VGAMODETABLE
;                         -       6       RETURN OFFSET OF EGAMODETABLE
;                         -       7       RETURN OFFSET OF MONOMODETABLE
;                         -       8       RETURN OFFSET OF RGBMODETABLE
;
MONO_FUNCTIONS  PROC    NEAR
                PUSH    BP
                MOV     BP,SP
                PUSH    DS
                PUSH    ES

                CMP     WORD PTR [BP + _AOFF + 0],0000H
                JNE     MF1

                MOV     AX,MONO_SCREENSEG
                JMP     MF_EXIT

MF1:            CMP     WORD PTR [BP + _AOFF + 0],0001H
                JNE     MF2

                MOV     AX,OFFSET SCREENTABLE-8
                JMP     MF_EXIT

MF2:            CMP     WORD PTR [BP + _AOFF + 0],0002H
                JNE     MF3

                MOV     AX,MONO_WIDE
                JMP     MF_EXIT

MF3:            CMP     WORD PTR [BP + _AOFF + 0],0003H
                JNE     MF4

                MOV     AX,MONO_DEEP
                JMP     MF_EXIT

MF4:            CMP     WORD PTR [BP + _AOFF + 0],0004H
                JE      MF5
                JMP     MF6
```

10-8 Continued.

```
MF5:            MOV     AX,MONO_SCREENSEG
                MOV     ES,AX

                MOV     BX,[BP + _AOFF + 4]     ;GET TOP
                SHL     BX,1
                MOV     DI,CS:[SCREENTABLE+BX]

                MOV     BX,[BP + _AOFF + 2]     ;GET LEFT
                MOV     CX,[BP + _AOFF + 6]     ;GET RIGHT
                SUB     CX,BX

MF5A:           PUSH    BX
                AND     BX,0007H
                MOV     AL,CS:[MASKTABLE+BX]
                POP     BX

                PUSH    BX
                SHR     BX,1
                SHR     BX,1
                SHR     BX,1
                XOR     ES:[DI+BX],AL
                POP     BX
                INC     BX
                LOOP    MF5A

                MOV     BX,[BP + _AOFF + 4]     ;GET TOP
                INC     BX
                MOV     CX,[BP + _AOFF + 8]     ;GET BOTTOM
                DEC     CX
                SUB     CX,BX

MF5B:           PUSH    BX
                SHL     BX,1
                MOV     DI,CS:[SCREENTABLE+BX]
                MOV     BX,[BP + _AOFF + 2]     ;GET LEFT
                PUSH    BX
                AND     BX,0007H

                MOV     AL,CS:[MASKTABLE+BX]
                POP     BX
                PUSH    BX
                SHR     BX,1
                SHR     BX,1
                SHR     BX,1
                XOR     ES:[DI+BX],AL
                POP     BX
                MOV     BX,[BP + _AOFF + 6]     ;GET RIGHT
                DEC     BX
                PUSH    BX
                AND     BX,0007H
                MOV     AL,CS:[MASKTABLE+BX]
                POP     BX
```

10-8 Continued.

```
                    PUSH    BX
                    SHR     BX,1
                    SHR     BX,1
                    SHR     BX,1
                    XOR     ES:[DI+BX],AL
                    POP     BX
                    POP     BX
                    INC     BX
                    LOOP    MF5B

                    MOV     BX,[BP + _AOFF + 8]      ;GET BOTTOM
                    DEC     BX
                    SHL     BX,1
                    MOV     DI,CS:[SCREENTABLE+BX]

                    MOV     BX,[BP + _AOFF + 2]      ;GET LEFT
                    MOV     CX,[BP + _AOFF + 6]      ;GET RIGHT
                    SUB     CX,BX

MF5D:               PUSH    BX
                    AND     BX,0007H
                    MOV     AL,CS:[MASKTABLE+BX]
                    POP     BX

                    PUSH    BX
                    SHR     BX,1
                    SHR     BX,1
                    SHR     BX,1
                    XOR     ES:[DI+BX],AL
                    POP     BX
                    INC     BX
                    LOOP    MF5D

MF6:                CMP     WORD PTR [BP + _AOFF + 0],0005H
                    JNE     MF7

                    MOV     AX,OFFSET VGAMODETABLE
                    JMP     MF_EXIT

MF7:                CMP     WORD PTR [BP + _AOFF + 0],0006H
                    JNE     MF8

                    MOV     AX,OFFSET EGAMODETABLE
                    JMP     MF_EXIT

MF8:                CMP     WORD PTR [BP + _AOFF + 0],0007H
                    JNE     MF_EXIT

                    MOV     AX,OFFSET MONOMODETABLE
                    JMP     MF_EXIT
```

10-8 Continued.

```
MF_EXIT:          POP      ES
                  POP      DS
                  POP      BP
                  RETF
MONO_FUNCTIONS    ENDP

MASKTABLE         DB       80H,40H,20H,10H,08H,04H,02H,01H

MONO_LINE         PROC     NEAR
                  PUSH     BP
                  MOV      BP,SP

                  PUSH     DS
                  PUSH     ES

                  MOV      AX,0A000H              ;POINT TO THE SCREEN
                  MOV      ES,AX

                  MOV      CX,[BP + _AOFF + 6]    ;GET THE WIDTH OF MOVE
                  CMP      CX,CS:[V_MONOBYTES]
                  JL       MONO_LINE1
                  MOV      CX,CS:[V_MONOBYTES]

MONO_LINE1:       MOV      SI,[BP + _AOFF + 0]    ;OFFSET OF BITMAP
                  MOV      DS,[BP + _AOFF + 2]    ;SEGMENT OF BITMAP
                  MOV      BX,[BP + _AOFF + 4]    ;NUMBER OF LINE
                  SHL      BX,1

                  CLD                             ;CLEAR DIRECTION FLAG
                  MOV      DI,CS:[SCREENTABLE + BX]
         REPNE    MOVSB                           ;DO THE MOVE

                  POP      ES
                  POP      DS

                  POP      BP
                  RETF
MONO_LINE         ENDP

;THIS ROUTINE DESELECTS THE 2 COLOUR MODE
MONO_OFF          PROC     NEAR
                  MOV      AX,0003H
                  INT      10H
                  SUB      AX,AX
                  RETF
MONO_OFF          ENDP

;THIS IS A LINE START LOOKUP TABLE

SCREENTABLE       DW       800 DUP(?)          ;LINE START TABLE
```

10-8 Continued.

```
CODEPAGE        DW      0

CODE            ENDS
                END
```

10-8 Continued.

As all super VGA cards, Paradise cards support both mode 13H and their proprietary higher-resolution 256-color modes. The PARADISE.ASM driver automatically selects one of the available display modes based on the actual dimensions of the image to be displayed, as passed to VGA_ON. If the picture fits in 320×200 pixels, the driver will use mode 13H. If it does not, the driver will call for the 640×400 pixel mode.

The VGA_ON routine sets up a screen table. In the case of the higher-resolution mode, it uses two words for each entry. The first one represents the offset into the current page for the line in question. The second one represents the page to use. A single 64K segment can hold 102 complete 640-byte lines, so this mode uses 4 pages of display memory.

Thus far, all the Paradise-specific code has involved a bit of sneaky integer math and little more. There are actually two things that are important to know about in driving a Paradise card. They involve two hardware registers called PRO_A and PRO_B, which handle changing pages.

A complete discussion of all the registers and options of a Paradise card could fill this chapter. The only time you'll need to use PRO_A is when you're changing pages. The code to do this is agreeably simple. It's handled in PARADISE.ASM by the macro SET_PROA. This macro sets the PRO_A register to whatever value is in AX. As the card is set up by VGA_ON, this causes the page whose number is in AX to be selected and appear in the VGA page frame.

```
SET_PROA MACRO
PUSH     AX
MOV      DX,03CEH
MOV      AX,050FH
OUT      DX,AX
POP      AX
MOV      AH,AL
MOV      AL,09H
OUT      DX,AX
MOV      AX,000FH
OUT      DX,AX
ENDM
```

The other bit of code you'll want to know about is the one that selects the 640×400 pixel, 256-color mode and tells the Paradise chip set to use its convenient page break mode. Here's what it looks like:

```
MOV  AX,005EH
INT  10H
```

By convention, if the AH register is 0 when your code throws an INT 10H call, the BIOS assumes that you're asking for a screen mode change of some sort. The screen mode to be used is in the AL register. Mode 5EH is a proprietary Paradise mode.

Expanding the Paradise driver

As with many of the available super VGA chip sets, the ones from Western Digital have gone through several revisions. At present, there are three distinct chip sets around, called the 1B, 1C, and 1D sets, and are marked as follows:

```
1B    90C00
1C    90C11
1D    90C30
```

The 1B chips support up to 640×480 pixels in 256 colors and up to 800×600 pixels in 16 colors. The 1C chips support up to 800×600 pixels in both 256 and 16 colors. The 1D chips support up to 1024×768 pixels in 256 and 16 colors, as well as the Paradise true color modes.

If you have a card with one of the newer Western Digital chips on it, you can modify PARADISE.ASM to support it. You will also need enough memory on your card to support the modes you're interested in. Multiply the screen dimensions together to find out how much memory is required for any of the 256-color modes.

The only things about PARADISE.ASM that need changing to allow it to handle a higher resolution 256-color mode are the mode value in the INT 10H call, as discussed above, the screen dimension equates, and the size of the screen table at the bottom of the file to allow for more line entries.

These are the mode numbers that correspond to the Paradise card's 256-color display modes:

```
005EH    640×400 pixels, 256 colors
005FH    640×480 pixels, 256 colors
005CH    800×600 pixels, 256 colors
0060H    1024×768 pixels, 256 colors
```

If you decide to provide higher-resolution modes for PARADISE.ASM, you might want to add them to the existing code, so that all of the intermediate modes will still be available. Having said this, the 640×400 line mode is a decided compromise, implemented so that a minimum super VGA full color mode would be available on cards having only 256K of display memory. If you have 512K or better, a strong argument can be made for dispensing with this mode, as it tends to display images that look a bit elongated vertically.

There's a section at the end of this chapter that discusses a driver for the Paradise true color modes.

Finally, note that some lower end multisync monitors that come bundled with computers seem to consider that anything larger than 640×480 pixels isn't worth looking at. The lower-end color VGA monitors offered by Dell computers are like this. If you use the PARADISE.ASM driver as it stands, 800×600 pixels, 16-color pictures will send such a monitor into paroxysms of horizontal barrel rolls and screen flotsam. If you have such a monitor, disable the higher resolution 16 color and monochrome mode options in the driver.

If you'd like more information about driving the Paradise chip set, you might want to write to Western Digital directly. They can send you a data sheet, although you should be warned that it's a very inscrutable document. They can be reached at Western Digital Imaging, 800 East Middlefield Rd., Mountain View, CA 94043.

A Tseng Labs Super VGA driver

The Tseng Labs 4000 series chip set is one of the more popular ones at the moment, and it turns up in a number of third-party VGA cards. In fact, while it implements a pretty fast VGA card and supports lots of modes, it's a fairly uncomplicated design. It's representative of the rest of the super VGA cards discussed in this chapter.

Depending upon how much memory is on your card, the Tseng Labs chips provide you with 256-color screen modes ranging from the coarse pixels of mode 13H up to 1024×768 pixels. This last one, as has been noted before, is a real monitor killer if your tube isn't expecting it.

The TSENG.ASM driver illustrated in FIG. 10-9 implements the 640×480 pixel, 256-color mode of the Tseng Labs 4000 chip set. This one is fairly safe. It assumes that you'll have at least 512K of display memory on your VGA card.

```
;
;               Graphic Workshop Tseng screen driver
;               Copyright (C) 1989, 1991 Alchemy Mindworks Inc.
;


VERSION         EQU     2               ;VERSION NUMBER
SUBVERSION      EQU     1               ;SUBVERSION NUMBER


_AOFF           EQU     6               ;STACK OFFSET


VGA_WIDE        EQU     640             ;WIDTH OF VGA SCREEN IN PIXELS
VGA_DEEP        EQU     480             ;DEPTH OF VGA SCREEN IN PIXELS
VGA_SCREENSEG   EQU     0A000H          ;SEGMENT OF VGA SCREEN
EGA_WIDE        EQU     640             ;WIDTH OF EGA SCREEN IN PIXELS
EGA_DEEP        EQU     480             ;DEPTH OF EGA SCREEN IN PIXELS
EGA_BYTES       EQU     80              ;WIDTH OF EGA SCREEN IN BYTES
```

10-9 The source code for TSENG.ASM.

```
EGA_SCREENSEG    EQU      0A000H           ;SEGMENT OF EGA SCREEN
MONO_WIDE        EQU      640              ;WIDTH OF MONO SCREEN IN PIXELS
MONO_DEEP        EQU      480              ;DEPTH OF MONO SCREEN IN PIXELS
MONO_BYTES       EQU      80               ;WIDTH OF MONO SCREEN IN BYTES
MONO_SCREENSEG   EQU      0A000H           ;SEGMENT OF MONO SCREEN

;THIS MACRO SELECTS AN EGA PLANE
EGAPLANE         MACRO    ARG1
                 MOV      AL,2
                 MOV      DX,03C4H
                 OUT      DX,AL
                 INC      DX
                 MOV      AL,ARG1
                 OUT      DX,AL
                 ENDM

CODE             SEGMENT PARA PUBLIC 'CODE'
                 ASSUME  CS:CODE

                 ORG      0000H            ;ORIGIN FOR LOADABLE DRIVER

                 DB       'ALCHDRV2'       ;SIGNATURE - DON'T CHANGE THIS

;THE FOLLOWING ARE THE POINTERS TO THE CALLABLE ROUTINES AND THE COMMON
;DATA. THE SEGMENTS ARE FILLED IN BY GRAPHIC WORKSHOP. DON'T CHANGE ANYTHING.
DISPATCH         PROC     FAR
                 DW       VGA_ON           ;FAR POINTER TO VGA MODE SELECT
                 DW       ?
                 DW       VGA_LINE         ;FAR POINTER TO VGA LINE DISPLAY
                 DW       ?
                 DW       VGA_OFF          ;FAR POINTER TO VGA MODE DESELECT
                 DW       ?
                 DW       VGA_PALETTE      ;FAR POINTER TO VGA PALETTE SET
                 DW       ?
                 DW       VGA_OVERSCAN     ;FAR POINTER TO VGA OVERSCAN SET
                 DW       ?
                 DW       EGA_ON           ;FAR POINTER TO EGA MODE SELECT
                 DW       ?
                 DW       EGA_LINE         ;FAR POINTER TO EGA LINE DISPLAY
                 DW       ?
                 DW       EGA_OFF          ;FAR POINTER TO EGA MODE DESELECT
                 DW       ?
                 DW       EGA_PALETTE      ;FAR POINTER TO EGA PALETTE SET
                 DW       ?
                 DW       MONO_ON          ;FAR POINTER TO MONO MODE SELECT
                 DW       ?
                 DW       MONO_FUNCTIONS   ;FAR POINTER TO MONO PAGE DISPLAY
                 DW       ?
                 DW       MONO_LINE
                 DW       ?
                 DW       MONO_OFF         ;FAR POINTER TO MONO MODE DESELECT
                 DW       ?
```

10-9 Continued.

```
                DW          0,0                 ;RGB ON
                DW          0,0                 ;RGB OFF
                DW          0,0                 ;RGB LINE
                DW          0                   ;RGB WIDTH
                DW          0                   ;RGB DEPTH

V_VGAWIDE       DW          VGA_WIDE            ;VGA SCREEN WIDTH
V_VGADEEP       DW          VGA_DEEP            ;VGA SCREEN DEPTH
V_VGASCRNSEG    DW          VGA_SCREENSEG       ;VGA SCREEN SEGMENT
V_EGAWIDE       DW          EGA_WIDE            ;EGA SCREEN WIDTH
V_EGADEEP       DW          EGA_DEEP            ;EGA SCREEN DEPTH
V_EGABYTES      DW          EGA_BYTES           ;EGA SCREEN BYTES
V_EGASCRNSEG    DW          EGA_SCREENSEG       ;EGA SCREEN SEGMENT
V_MONOWIDE      DW          MONO_WIDE           ;MONO SCREEN WIDTH
V_MONODEEP      DW          MONO_DEEP           ;MONO SCREEN DEPTH
V_MONOBYTES     DW          MONO_BYTES          ;BYTE WIDTH ON MONOCHROME SCREEN
V_MONOSCRNSEG   DW          MONO_SCREENSEG      ;MONOCHROME SCREEN SEGMENT
                DW          VERSION
                DW          SUBVERSION
                DB          'Tseng 4000 640x480 2.1',0
DISPATCH        ENDP


VGAMODETABLE    DW          320,200
                DW          640,480
                DW          -1,-1


EGAMODETABLE    DW          -1,-1


MONOMODETABLE   DW          -1,-1


;THIS ROUTINE SELECTS THE VGA 256 COLOUR MODE
;THE HEIGHT AND WIDTH OF THE IMAGE ARE ON THE STACK - THESE
;MAY BE USEFUL IF YOU WANT TO PICK ONE OF SEVERAL AVAILABLE
;MODES BASED ON THE AREA OF THE PICTURE TO BE DISPLAYED
VGA_ON          PROC        NEAR
                PUSH        BP
                MOV         BP,SP
                PUSH        DS

                CMP         WORD PTR [BP + _AOFF + 0],320
                JG          EXT_ON
                CMP         WORD PTR [BP + _AOFF + 2],200
                JG          EXT_ON

                MOV         CS:[V_VGAWIDE],320
                MOV         CS:[V_VGADEEP],200
                MOV         CX,200                          ;DEPTH OF SCREEN
                SUB         DX,DX
                MOV         SI,OFFSET SCREENTABLE

VGA_ON1:        PUSH        DX
                MOV         AX,320                          ;WIDTH OF SCREEEN
```

10-9 Continued.

```
                      MUL      DX
                      MOV      CS:[SI],AX
                      ADD      SI,2
                      POP      DX
                      INC      DX
                      LOOP     VGA_ON1

                      MOV      AX,0013H
                      INT      10H

                      JMP      EXT_EXIT

EXT_ON:               MOV      CS:[V_VGAWIDE],640
                      MOV      CS:[V_VGADEEP],480

                      MOV      CX,480                      ;DEPTH OF SCREEN
                      SUB      BX,BX                       ;ZERO LINE COUNTER
                      MOV      SI,OFFSET SCREENTABLE       ;POINT TO TABLE

EXT_1:                PUSH     CX
                      MOV      AX,640                      ;WIDTH OF SCREEEN
                      MUL      BX                          ;TIMES LINE NUMBER

                      AND      DX,00FFH

                      CMP      AX,(0FFFEH-640)              ;SEE IF WE WILL
                      JB       EXT_2

                      MOV      DH,0FFH

EXT_2:                MOV      CS:[SI],AX                  ;SAVE THE VALUES
                      MOV      CS:[SI+2],DX                ;IN OUR LOOKUP TABLE
                      ADD      SI,4                        ;AND POINT TO THE
                      INC      BX                          ;NEXT LINE AND
                      POP      CX                          ;ENTRY
                      LOOP     EXT_1

                      MOV      DX,03C4H                    ;SET TSENG REGISTERS
                      MOV      AL,0
                      OUT      DX,AL
                      MOV      DX,03C5H
                      IN       AL,DX
                      AND      AL,0FEH
                      OUT      DX,AL
                      MOV      DX,03CEH
                      MOV      AL,06H
                      OUT      DX,AL
                      MOV      DX,03CFH
                      IN       AL,DX
                      XOR      AL,06H
                      OR       AL,02H
                      OUT      DX,AL
```

10-9 Continued.

```
                MOV        AX,CS:[MODEBYTE]
                INT        10H
                MOV        CS:[BANK],0000H

EXT_EXIT:       POP        DS
                POP        BP
                RETF
VGA_ON          ENDP

;THIS ROUTINE DISPLAYS A VGA LINE
VGA_LINE        PROC       NEAR
                PUSH       BP
                MOV        BP,SP

                PUSH       DS
                PUSH       ES

                CMP        CS:[V_VGAWIDE],320
                JNE        EXTSHOW

                MOV        SI,[BP + _AOFF + 0]      ;OFFSET OF SOURCE
                MOV        DS,[BP + _AOFF + 2]      ;SEGMENT OF SOURCE

                MOV        BX,[BP + _AOFF + 6]      ;GET LINE NUMBER
                CMP        BX,200
                JG         VGASHOW2

                SHL        BX,1
                MOV        DI,CS:[SCREENTABLE + BX]

                CLD
                MOV        CX,[BP + _AOFF + 4]      ;LENGTH OF MOVE IN BYTES
                CMP        CX,0
                JE         VGASHOW2

                CMP        CX,320
                JL         VGASHOW1
                MOV        CX,320

VGASHOW1:       MOV        AX,0A000H
                MOV        ES,AX
         REPNE  MOVSB

VGASHOW2:       JMP        EXTSHOWX

EXTSHOW:        CMP        WORD PTR [BP + _AOFF + 6],480
                JL         EXTSHOW1
                JMP        EXTSHOWX

EXTSHOW1:       MOV        SI,[BP + _AOFF + 0]      ;OFFSET OF SOURCE
                MOV        DS,[BP + _AOFF + 2]      ;SEGMENT OF SOURCE
                MOV        CX,[BP + _AOFF + 4]      ;LENGTH OF MOVE IN BYTES
```

10-9 Continued.

```
                CMP       CX,640                    ;IS IT TOO LONG?
                JL        EXTSHOW2

                MOV       CX,640

EXTSHOW2:       MOV       BX,[BP + _AOFF + 6]       ;GET INDEX INTO LINE TABLE
                SHL       BX,1
                SHL       BX,1

                MOV       DI,CS:[SCREENTABLE + BX]
                MOV       AX,CS:[SCREENTABLE + 2 + BX]

                CALL      VGA_BANK

                CMP       AH,00H
                JNE       EXTSHOW3

                MOV       AX,0A000H                 ;POINT TO VIDEO BUFFER
                MOV       ES,AX                     ;WITH ES

                CLD
        REPNE   MOVSB                               ;MOVE IN THE LINE DATA
                JMP       EXTSHOWX

EXTSHOW3:       MOV       AX,0A000H                 ;POINT TO VIDEO BUFFER
                MOV       ES,AX                     ;WITH ES

                PUSH      CX
                MOV       AX,DI
                MOV       CX,0000H
                SUB       CX,AX
                MOV       BX,CX

                CMP       CX,[BP + _AOFF + 4]       ;ARE THERE ENOUGH BYTES LEFT?
                JL        EXTSHOW4                  ;IF SO, GO JUMP THE FRAME

                MOV       CX,[BP + _AOFF + 4]
                CLD
        REPNE   MOVSB                               ;MOVE IN THE LINE DATA

                POP       CX
                JMP       EXTSHOWX

EXTSHOW4:       CLD
        REPNE   MOVSB                               ;MOVE IN THE LINE DATA

                POP       CX
                SUB       CX,BX
                CMP       CX,0
                JLE       EXTSHOWX

                MOV       BX,[BP + _AOFF + 6]       ;GET INDEX INTO LINE TABLE
```

10-9 Continued.

```
                    SHL     BX,1
                    SHL     BX,1
                    MOV     AX,CS:[SCREENTABLE + 2 + BX]
                    INC     AX

                    CALL    VGA_BANK

                    MOV     AX,0A000H
                    MOV     ES,AX

                    MOV     DI,0

                    CLD
          REPNE     MOVSB                              ;MOVE IN THE LINE DATA

EXTSHOWX:           POP     ES
                    POP     DS
                    POP     BP
                    RETF
VGA_LINE            ENDP

;THIS ROUTINE DESELECTS THE VGA 256 COLOUR MODE
VGA_OFF             PROC    NEAR
                    MOV     AX,1200H
                    MOV     BX,0031H
                    INT     10H

                    MOV     AX,0003H
                    INT     10H
                    RETF
VGA_OFF             ENDP

;THIS SETS THE VGA PAGE
VGA_BANK            PROC    NEAR
                    CMP     AX,CS:[BANK]
                    JNE     VGABANK1
                    RET

VGABANK1:           MOV     CS:[BANK],AX

                    PUSH    AX
                    PUSH    DX
                    MOV     AH,AL
                    MOV     DX,3BFH
                    MOV     AL,3
                    OUT     DX,AL
                    MOV     DL,0D8H
                    MOV     AL,0A0H
                    OUT     DX,AL
                    AND     AH,15
                    MOV     AL,AH
                    SHL     AL,1
```

10-9 Continued.

```
                        SHL     AL,1
                        SHL     AL,1
                        SHL     AL,1
                        OR      AL,AH
                        MOV     DL,0CDH
                        OUT     DX,AL
                        POP     DX
                        POP     AX
                        RET
        VGA_BANK        ENDP


        ;THIS ROUTINE SETS THE VGA PALETTE
        VGA_PALETTE     PROC    NEAR
                        PUSH    BP
                        MOV     BP,SP
                        PUSH    DS
                        PUSH    ES

                        MOV     SI,[BP + _AOFF + 0]     ;OFFSET OF SOURCE
                        MOV     DS,[BP + _AOFF + 2]     ;SEGMENT OF SOURCE

                        MOV     CX,[BP + _AOFF + 4]     ;NUMBER OF COLOURS
                        CMP     CX,0                    ;CHECK FOR NASTIES
                        JG      GVP0
                        JMP     GVPX

        GVP0:           MOV     DX,03C6H
                        MOV     AL,0FFH
                        OUT     DX,AL

                        MOV     BX,0

        GVP1:           PUSH    CX
                        MOV     DX,03C8H
                        MOV     AL,BL
                        INC     BX
                        OUT     DX,AL

                        INC     DX

                        LODSB
                        SHR     AL,1
                        SHR     AL,1
                        OUT     DX,AL

                        LODSB
                        SHR     AL,1
                        SHR     AL,1
                        OUT     DX,AL

                        LODSB
                        SHR     AL,1
```

10-9 Continued.

```
             SHR      AL,1
             OUT      DX,AL

             POP      CX
             LOOP     GVP1

GVPX:        POP      ES
             POP      DS
             POP      BP
             RETF
VGA_PALETTE  ENDP

;THIS ROUTINE SETS THE VGA OVERSCAN.
VGA_OVERSCAN PROC     NEAR
             PUSH     BP
             MOV      BP,SP
             MOV      AX,1001H
             MOV      BX,[BP + _AOFF + 0]
             XCHG     BH,BL
             INT      10H
             POP      BP
             RETF
VGA_OVERSCAN ENDP


;THIS ROUTINE SELECTS THE EGA 16 COLOUR MODE
EGA_ON       PROC     NEAR
             PUSH     BP
             MOV      BP,SP
             PUSH     DS

EGA480:      MOV      CS:[V_EGAWIDE],640
             MOV      CS:[V_EGADEEP],480
             MOV      CS:[V_EGABYTES],80

             MOV      CX,640                 ;DEPTH OF SCREEN
             SUB      DX,DX
             MOV      SI,OFFSET SCREENTABLE

EGA_ON2:     PUSH     DX
             MOV      AX,80                  ;WIDTH OF SCREEEN
             MUL      DX
             MOV      CS:[SI],AX
             ADD      SI,2
             POP      DX
             INC      DX
             LOOP     EGA_ON2

             MOV      AX,0012H
             INT      10H

             POP      DS
             POP      BP
```

10-9 Continued.

```
                        RETF
EGA_ON                  ENDP

;THIS ROUTINE DISPLAYS AN EGA LINE
EGA_LINE                PROC    NEAR
                        PUSH    BP
                        MOV     BP,SP
                        PUSH    DS
                        PUSH    ES

                        MOV     SI,[BP + _AOFF + 0]     ;OFFSET OF SOURCE
                        MOV     DS,[BP + _AOFF + 2]     ;SEGMENT OF SOURCE
                        MOV     BX,[BP + _AOFF + 6]     ;GET LINE NUMBER
                        CMP     BX,CS:[V_EGADEEP]
                        JGE     SHOWEGAX

                        SHL     BX,1
                        MOV     DI,CS:[SCREENTABLE + BX]

                        MOV     AX,0A000H
                        MOV     ES,AX
                        MOV     BX,[BP + _AOFF + 4]      ;LENGTH OF MOVE IN BYTES

                        MOV     CX,BX
                        EGAPLANE        1
                        CLD
                        PUSH    DI
        REPNE           MOVSB
                        POP     DI

                        MOV     CX,BX
                        EGAPLANE        2
                        PUSH    DI
        REPNE           MOVSB
                        POP     DI

                        MOV     CX,BX
                        EGAPLANE        4
                        PUSH    DI
        REPNE           MOVSB
                        POP     DI

                        MOV     CX,BX
                        EGAPLANE        8
                        PUSH    DI
        REPNE           MOVSB
                        POP     DI
                        EGAPLANE        0FH

SHOWEGAX:               POP     ES
                        POP     DS
                        POP     BP
```

10-9 Continued.

```
                    RETF
EGA_LINE            ENDP

;THIS ROUTINE SETS THE EGA PALETTE
EGA_PALETTE         PROC    NEAR
                    PUSH    BP
                    MOV     BP,SP
                    PUSH    DS
                    PUSH    ES

                    MOV     SI,[BP + _AOFF + 6]    ;OFFSET OF SOURCE
                    MOV     DS,[BP + _AOFF + 8]    ;SEGMENT OF SOURCE

                    MOV     CX,[BP + _AOFF + 4]    ;NUMBER OF COLOURS
                    CMP     CX,16
                    JLE     EGA_PALETTE1
                    MOV     CX,16

EGA_PALETTE1:       PUSH    CX
                    MOV     BX,0000H

EGA_PALETTE2:       PUSH    CX
                    LODSB
                    SHR     AL,1
                    SHR     AL,1
                    MOV     DH,AL
                    LODSB
                    SHR     AL,1
                    SHR     AL,1
                    MOV     CH,AL
                    LODSB
                    SHR     AL,1
                    SHR     AL,1
                    MOV     CL,AL
                    MOV     AX,1010H
                    INT     10H
                    INC     BX
                    POP     CX
                    LOOP    EGA_PALETTE2

                    POP     CX
                    MOV     BX,0000H

EGA_PALETTE3:       PUSH    CX
                    MOV     AX,1000H
                    INT     10H
                    ADD     BX,0101H
                    POP     CX
                    LOOP    EGA_PALETTE3

                    POP     ES
                    POP     DS
```

10-9 Continued.

```
                                POP       BP
                                RETF
            EGA_PALETTE         ENDP


            ;THIS ROUTINE DESELECTS THE EGA 16 COLOUR MODE
            EGA_OFF             PROC      NEAR
                                MOV       AX,0003H
                                INT       10H
                                RETF
            EGA_OFF             ENDP


            ;THIS ROUTINE SELECTS THE 2 COLOUR MODE
            MONO_ON             PROC      NEAR
                                PUSH      BP
                                MOV       BP,SP
                                PUSH      DS
                                PUSH      ES

                                MOV       CS:[V_MONOWIDE],640
                                MOV       CS:[V_MONODEEP],480
                                MOV       CS:[V_MONOBYTES],80

                                MOV       AX,0012H
                                INT       10H

                                MOV       CX,480
                                SUB       DX,DX
                                MOV       SI,OFFSET SCREENTABLE

            MONO_ON1:           PUSH      DX
                                MOV       AX,80
                                MUL       DX
                                MOV       CS:[SI],AX
                                ADD       SI,2
                                POP       DX
                                INC       DX
                                LOOP      MONO_ON1

                                POP       ES
                                POP       DS
                                POP       BP
                                SUB       AX,AX
                                RETF
            MONO_ON             ENDP


            ;THIS FUNCTION PERFORMS VARIOUS GRAPHIC OPERATIONS
            ;       ARGUMENTS         -       FUNCTION CODE
            ;                         -       VARIABLE
            ;
            ;       FUNCTIONS         -       0       RETURN SCREEN SEG
            ;                         -       1       RETURN OFFSET TO SCREEN TABLE
            ;                         -       2       RETURN MONOCHROME SCREEN WIDTH
```

10-9 Continued.

```
;                      -     3        RETURN MONOCHROME SCREEN DEPTH
;                      -     4        INVERT FRAME RECT - ARGS ON STACK
;                      -     5        RETURN OFFSET OF VGAMODETABLE
;                      -     6        RETURN OFFSET OF EGAMODETABLE
;                      -     7        RETURN OFFSET OF MONOMODETABLE
;                      -     8        RETURN OFFSET OF RGBMODETABLE
;
MONO_FUNCTIONS  PROC    NEAR
                PUSH    BP
                MOV     BP,SP
                PUSH    DS
                PUSH    ES

                CMP     WORD PTR [BP + _AOFF + 0],0000H
                JNE     MF1

                MOV     AX,MONO_SCREENSEG
                JMP     MF_EXIT

MF1:            CMP     WORD PTR [BP + _AOFF + 0],0001H
                JNE     MF2

                MOV     AX,OFFSET SCREENTABLE-8
                JMP     MF_EXIT

MF2:            CMP     WORD PTR [BP + _AOFF + 0],0002H
                JNE     MF3

                MOV     AX,MONO_WIDE
                JMP     MF_EXIT

MF3:            CMP     WORD PTR [BP + _AOFF + 0],0003H
                JNE     MF4

                MOV     AX,MONO_DEEP
                JMP     MF_EXIT

MF4:            CMP     WORD PTR [BP + _AOFF + 0],0004H
                JE      MF5
                JMP     MF6

MF5:            MOV     AX,MONO_SCREENSEG
                MOV     ES,AX

                MOV     BX,[BP + _AOFF + 4]      ;GET TOP
                SHL     BX,1
                MOV     DI,CS:[SCREENTABLE+BX]

                MOV     BX,[BP + _AOFF + 2]      ;GET LEFT
                MOV     CX,[BP + _AOFF + 6]      ;GET RIGHT
                SUB     CX,BX
```

10-9 Continued.

```
MF5A:          PUSH    BX
               AND     BX,0007H
               MOV     AL,CS:[MASKTABLE+BX]
               POP     BX
               PUSH    BX
               SHR     BX,1
               SHR     BX,1
               SHR     BX,1
               XOR     ES:[DI+BX],AL
               POP     BX
               INC     BX
               LOOP    MF5A

               MOV     BX,[BP + _AOFF + 4]     ;GET TOP
               INC     BX
               MOV     CX,[BP + _AOFF + 8]     ;GET BOTTOM
               DEC     CX
               SUB     CX,BX

MF5B:          PUSH    BX
               SHL     BX,1
               MOV     DI,CS:[SCREENTABLE+BX]
               MOV     BX,[BP + _AOFF + 2]     ;GET LEFT
               PUSH    BX
               AND     BX,0007H
               MOV     AL,CS:[MASKTABLE+BX]
               POP     BX
               PUSH    BX
               SHR     BX,1
               SHR     BX,1
               SHR     BX,1
               XOR     ES:[DI+BX],AL
               POP     BX
               MOV     BX,[BP + _AOFF + 6]     ;GET RIGHT
               DEC     BX
               PUSH    BX
               AND     BX,0007H
               MOV     AL,CS:[MASKTABLE+BX]
               POP     BX
               PUSH    BX
               SHR     BX,1
               SHR     BX,1
               SHR     BX,1
               XOR     ES:[DI+BX],AL
               POP     BX
               POP     BX
               INC     BX
               LOOP    MF5B

               MOV     BX,[BP + _AOFF + 8]     ;GET BOTTOM
               DEC     BX
               SHL     BX,1
```

10-9 Continued.

```
                MOV     DI,CS:[SCREENTABLE+BX]

                MOV     BX,[BP + _AOFF + 2]     ;GET LEFT
                MOV     CX,[BP + _AOFF + 6]     ;GET RIGHT
                SUB     CX,BX

MF5D:           PUSH    BX
                AND     BX,0007H
                MOV     AL,CS:[MASKTABLE+BX]
                POP     BX
                PUSH    BX
                SHR     BX,1
                SHR     BX,1
                SHR     BX,1
                XOR     ES:[DI+BX],AL
                POP     BX
                INC     BX
                LOOP    MF5D

MF6:            CMP     WORD PTR [BP + _AOFF + 0],0005H
                JNE     MF7

                MOV     AX,OFFSET VGAMODETABLE
                JMP     MF_EXIT

MF7:            CMP     WORD PTR [BP + _AOFF + 0],0006H
                JNE     MF8

                MOV     AX,OFFSET EGAMODETABLE
                JMP     MF_EXIT

MF8:            CMP     WORD PTR [BP + _AOFF + 0],0007H
                JNE     MF_EXIT

                MOV     AX,OFFSET MONOMODETABLE
                JMP     MF_EXIT

MF_EXIT:        POP     ES
                POP     DS
                POP     BP
                RETF
MONO_FUNCTIONS  ENDP

MASKTABLE       DB      80H,40H,20H,10H,08H,04H,02H,01H

MONO_LINE       PROC    NEAR
                PUSH    BP
                MOV     BP,SP

                PUSH    DS
                PUSH    ES
```

10-9 Continued.

```
                      MOV      AX,0A000H            ;POINT TO THE SCREEN
                      MOV      ES,AX

                      MOV      CX,[BP + _AOFF + 6]  ;GET THE WIDTH OF MOVE
                      CMP      CX,CS:[V_MONOBYTES]
                      JL       MONO_LINE1
                      MOV      CX,CS:[V_MONOBYTES]

MONO_LINE1:           MOV      SI,[BP + _AOFF + 0]  ;OFFSET OF BITMAP
                      MOV      DS,[BP + _AOFF + 2]  ;SEGMENT OF BITMAP
                      MOV      BX,[BP + _AOFF + 4]  ;NUMBER OF LINE
                      SHL      BX,1

                      CLD                           ;CLEAR DIRECTION FLAG
                      MOV      DI,CS:[SCREENTABLE + BX]
         REPNE        MOVSB                         ;DO THE MOVE

                      POP      ES
                      POP      DS

                      POP      BP
                      RETF
MONO_LINE             ENDP

;THIS ROUTINE DESELECTS THE 2 COLOUR MODE
MONO_OFF              PROC     NEAR
                      MOV      AX,0003H
                      INT      10H
                      SUB      AX,AX
                      RETF
MONO_OFF              ENDP

;THIS IS A LINE START LOOKUP TABLE

SCREENTABLE           DW       1600 DUP(?)          ;LINE START TABLE

BANK                  DW       ?
MODEBYTE              DW       002EH

CODE                  ENDS
                      END
```

10-9 Continued.

In fact, as you'll notice when the next super VGA card driver is discussed, the only things about TSENG.ASM that dedicated it to the Tseng Labs chips are the code to switch to the proprietary 640×480 pixel, 256-color mode and a procedure called VGA_BANK, which handles the screen memory paging. In writing the Trident driver, dealt with in the next section, only these two elements are changed.

Unlike the Paradise chips, the Tseng Labs chips want to change screen pages on hard-wired 64K segment boundaries. This requires a slightly trickier code. The screen table for the high-resolution 256-color modes consists of 2 words per entry. The first word is again the offset into the current page. The second word has the page number in its low-order byte and a flag in its high-order byte. The flag is set only for those lines that have page changes in them.

The VGA_LINE function deals with the lines it's to write based on the screen table flags. If the flag is not set, it knows it can copy the whole line to the screen in one shot, as none of it will cross a page boundary. If the flag is set, it will copy the portion of the line that falls in the current page, change banks, and then copy the rest of the line.

Having assembled TSENG.ASM to TSENG.DRV, you would be able to look at the EXAMPLE3.GIF file from Graphic Workshop using READGIF2 like this:

```
READGIF2 EXAMPLE3.GIF TSENG.DRV
```

Expanding the Tseng Labs driver

Assuming that your card has enough memory, all you need do to get at the higher-resolution super VGA modes of a Tseng Labs card is to select the appropriate arguments for the mode change code and create the screen table for the dimensions of the mode you're interested in up in VGA_ON. Make sure you increase the size of the screen table at the bottom of the source listing appropriately if you do add more modes to TSENG.ASM. The code that changes screen modes can be found in VGA_LINE, and looks like this:

```
MOV    AX,CS:[MODEBYTE]
INT    10H
```

The number stored in MODEBYTE selects the screen mode—something of a misnomer, perhaps, as MODEBYTE is actually a word. Here's a list of the mode numbers to use for the available screen modes on a Tseng Labs 4000 series card:

```
002EH    640×480 pixels, 256 colors
0030H    800×600 pixels, 256 colors
0038H    1024×768 pixels, 256 colors
0029H    800×600 pixels, 16 colors
0037H    1024×768 pixels, 16 colors
```

Note that if you attempt to use the 1024×768 pixel, 16-color mode you'll have to provide for page switching part way through each image plane, something that is not dealt with in TSENG.ASM.

A Trident Super VGA driver

Trident-based super VGA cards are among the least expensive third-party cards at the moment. Third-party cards using Trident chips with 256K of memory on them cost well under $100 as of this writing. Despite their low cost, Trident cards are fast, capable display adapters with no peculiarities. If you get one with lots of memory on it, you'll find that it offers the same types of high-resolution graphics modes as the other cards discussed in this chapter.

Figure 10-10 illustrates the code for TRIDENT.ASM. This implements the 640×400 pixel, 256-color super VGA mode of this card. It behaves exactly as did TSENG.ASM in the previous section, except for the argument to the INT 10H screen mode change function and the VGA_BANK code that switches display pages.

```
;
;                       Graphic Workshop Trident screen driver
;                       Copyright (C) 1989, 1991 Alchemy Mindworks Inc.
;


VERSION          EQU    2                  ;VERSION NUMBER
SUBVERSION       EQU    0                  ;SUBVERSION NUMBER


_AOFF            EQU    6                  ;STACK OFFSET


VGA_WIDE         EQU    640                ;WIDTH OF VGA SCREEN IN PIXELS
VGA_DEEP         EQU    400                ;DEPTH OF VGA SCREEN IN PIXELS
VGA_SCREENSEG    EQU    0A000H             ;SEGMENT OF VGA SCREEN
EGA_WIDE         EQU    640                ;WIDTH OF EGA SCREEN IN PIXELS
EGA_DEEP         EQU    480                ;DEPTH OF EGA SCREEN IN PIXELS
EGA_BYTES        EQU    80                 ;WIDTH OF EGA SCREEN IN BYTES
EGA_SCREENSEG    EQU    0A000H             ;SEGMENT OF EGA SCREEN
MONO_WIDE        EQU    640                ;WIDTH OF MONO SCREEN IN PIXELS
MONO_DEEP        EQU    480                ;DEPTH OF MONO SCREEN IN PIXELS
MONO_BYTES       EQU    80                 ;WIDTH OF MONO SCREEN IN BYTES
MONO_SCREENSEG   EQU    0A000H             ;SEGMENT OF MONO SCREEN

;THIS MACRO SELECTS AN EGA PLANE
EGAPLANE         MACRO  ARG1
                 MOV    AL,2
                 MOV    DX,03C4H
                 OUT    DX,AL
                 INC    DX
                 MOV    AL,ARG1
                 OUT    DX,AL
                 ENDM

CODE             SEGMENT PARA PUBLIC 'CODE'
                 ASSUME  CS:CODE

                 ORG    0000H              ;ORIGIN FOR LOADABLE DRIVER

                 DB     'ALCHDRV2'         ;SIGNATURE - DON'T CHANGE THIS
```

10-10 The source code for TRIDENT.ASM.

```
;THE FOLLOWING ARE THE POINTERS TO THE CALLABLE ROUTINES AND THE COMMON
;DATA. THE SEGMENTS ARE FILLED IN BY GRAPHIC WORKSHOP. DON'T CHANGE ANYTHING.
DISPATCH         PROC    FAR
                 DW      VGA_ON          ;FAR POINTER TO VGA MODE SELECT
                 DW      ?
                 DW      VGA_LINE        ;FAR POINTER TO VGA LINE DISPLAY
                 DW      ?
                 DW      VGA_OFF         ;FAR POINTER TO VGA MODE DESELECT
                 DW      ?
                 DW      VGA_PALETTE     ;FAR POINTER TO VGA PALETTE SET
                 DW      ?
                 DW      VGA_OVERSCAN    ;FAR POINTER TO VGA OVERSCAN SET
                 DW      ?
                 DW      EGA_ON          ;FAR POINTER TO EGA MODE SELECT
                 DW      ?
                 DW      EGA_LINE        ;FAR POINTER TO EGA LINE DISPLAY
                 DW      ?
                 DW      EGA_OFF         ;FAR POINTER TO EGA MODE DESELECT
                 DW      ?
                 DW      EGA_PALETTE     ;FAR POINTER TO EGA PALETTE SET
                 DW      ?
                 DW      MONO_ON         ;FAR POINTER TO MONO MODE SELECT
                 DW      ?
                 DW      MONO_FUNCTIONS  ;FAR POINTER TO MONO PAGE DISPLAY
                 DW      ?
                 DW      MONO_LINE
                 DW      ?
                 DW      MONO_OFF        ;FAR POINTER TO MONO MODE DESELECT
                 DW      ?
                 DW      0,0             ;RGB ON
                 DW      0,0             ;RGB OFF
                 DW      0,0             ;RGB LINE
                 DW      0               ;RGB WIDTH
                 DW      0               ;RGB DEPTH

V_VGAWIDE        DW      VGA_WIDE        ;VGA SCREEN WIDTH
V_VGADEEP        DW      VGA_DEEP        ;VGA SCREEN DEPTH
V_VGASCRNSEG     DW      VGA_SCREENSEG   ;VGA SCREEN SEGMENT
V_EGAWIDE        DW      EGA_WIDE        ;EGA SCREEN WIDTH
V_EGADEEP        DW      EGA_DEEP        ;EGA SCREEN DEPTH
V_EGABYTES       DW      EGA_BYTES       ;EGA SCREEN BYTES
V_EGASCRNSEG     DW      EGA_SCREENSEG   ;EGA SCREEN SEGMENT
V_MONOWIDE       DW      MONO_WIDE       ;MONO SCREEN WIDTH
V_MONODEEP       DW      MONO_DEEP       ;MONO SCREEN DEPTH
V_MONOBYTES      DW      MONO_BYTES      ;BYTE WIDTH ON MONOCHROME SCREEN
V_MONOSCRNSEG    DW      MONO_SCREENSEG  ;MONOCHROME SCREEN SEGMENT
                 DW      VERSION
                 DW      SUBVERSION
                 DB      'Trident 256K VGA 2.0  ',0
DISPATCH         ENDP

;THIS ROUTINE SELECTS THE VGA 256 COLOUR MODE
```

10-10 Continued.

```
VGA_ON          PROC    NEAR
                PUSH    BP
                MOV     BP,SP
                PUSH    DS

                CMP     WORD PTR [BP + _AOFF + 0],320
                JG      EXT_ON
                CMP     WORD PTR [BP + _AOFF + 2],200
                JG      EXT_ON

                MOV     CS:[V_VGAWIDE],320
                MOV     CS:[V_VGADEEP],200
                MOV     CX,200                  ;DEPTH OF SCREEN
                SUB     DX,DX
                MOV     SI,OFFSET SCREENTABLE

VGA_ON1:        PUSH    DX
                MOV     AX,320                  ;WIDTH OF SCREEEN
                MUL     DX
                MOV     CS:[SI],AX
                ADD     SI,2
                POP     DX
                INC     DX
                LOOP    VGA_ON1

                MOV     AX,0013H

                INT     10H

                JMP     EXT_EXIT

EXT_ON:         MOV     CS:[V_VGAWIDE],640
                MOV     CS:[V_VGADEEP],400

                MOV     CX,400                  ;DEPTH OF SCREEN
                SUB     BX,BX                   ;ZERO LINE COUNTER
                MOV     SI,OFFSET SCREENTABLE   ;POINT TO TABLE

EXT_1:          PUSH    CX
                MOV     AX,640                  ;WIDTH OF SCREEEN
                MUL     BX                      ;TIMES LINE NUMBER

                AND     DX,00FFH

                CMP     AX,(0FFFEH-640)
                JB      EXT_2

                MOV     DH,0FFH

EXT_2:          MOV     CS:[SI],AX              ;SAVE THE VALUES
                MOV     CS:[SI+2],DX            ;IN OUR LOOKUP TABLE
                ADD     SI,4                    ;AND POINT TO THE
```

10-10 Continued.

```
            INC     BX                              ;NEXT LINE AND
            POP     CX                              ;ENTRY
            LOOP    EXT_1

            MOV     AX,005CH
            INT     10H

            MOV     CS:[BANK],0000H

EXT_EXIT:   POP     DS
            POP     BP
            RETF
VGA_ON      ENDP

;THIS ROUTINE DISPLAYS A VGA LINE
VGA_LINE    PROC    NEAR
            PUSH    BP
            MOV     BP,SP

            PUSH    DS
            PUSH    ES

            CMP     CS:[V_VGAWIDE],320
            JNE     EXTSHOW

            MOV     SI,[BP + _AOFF + 0]     ;OFFSET OF SOURCE
            MOV     DS,[BP + _AOFF + 2]     ;SEGMENT OF SOURCE

            MOV     BX,[BP + _AOFF + 6]     ;GET LINE NUMBER
            CMP     BX,200
            JG      VGASHOW2

            SHL     BX,1
            MOV     DI,CS:[SCREENTABLE+BX]

            CLD
            MOV     CX,[BP + _AOFF + 4]     ;LENGTH OF MOVE IN BYTES
            CMP     CX,0
            JE      VGASHOW2

            CMP     CX,320
            JL      VGASHOW1
            MOV     CX,320
VGASHOW1:   MOV     AX,0A000H
            MOV     ES,AX
     REPNE  MOVSB

VGASHOW2:   JMP     EXTSHOWX

EXTSHOW:    CMP     WORD PTR [BP + _AOFF + 6],400
            JL      EXTSHOW1
            JMP     EXTSHOWX
```

10-10 Continued.

```
EXTSHOW1:        MOV    SI,[BP + _AOFF + 0]      ;OFFSET OF SOURCE
                 MOV    DS,[BP + _AOFF + 2]      ;SEGMENT OF SOURCE
                 MOV    CX,[BP + _AOFF + 4]      ;LENGTH OF MOVE IN BYTES

                 CMP    CX,640                   ;IS IT TOO LONG?
                 JL     EXTSHOW2

                 MOV    CX,640

EXTSHOW2:        MOV    BX,[BP + _AOFF + 6]      ;GET INDEX INTO LINE TABLE
                 SHL    BX,1
                 SHL    BX,1

                 MOV    DI,CS:[SCREENTABLE + BX]
                 MOV    AX,CS:[SCREENTABLE + 2 + BX]

                 CALL   VGA_BANK

                 CMP    AH,00H
                 JNE    EXTSHOW3

                 MOV    AX,0A000H
                 MOV    ES,AX

                 CLD
        REPNE    MOVSB                           ;MOVE IN THE LINE DATA
                 JMP    EXTSHOWX

EXTSHOW3:        MOV    AX,0A000H                ;POINT TO VIDEO BUFFER
                 MOV    ES,AX                    ;WITH ES

                 PUSH   CX
                 MOV    AX,DI
                 MOV    CX,0000H
                 SUB    CX,AX
                 MOV    BX,CX

                 CMP    CX,[BP + _AOFF + 4]      ;ARE THERE ENOUGH BYTES LEFT?
                 JL     EXTSHOW4                 ;IF SO, GO JUMP THE FRAME

                 MOV    CX,[BP + _AOFF + 4]
                 CLD
        REPNE    MOVSB                           ;MOVE IN THE LINE DATA

                 POP    CX
                 JMP    EXTSHOWX

EXTSHOW4:        CLD
        REPNE    MOVSB                           ;MOVE IN THE LINE DATA

                 POP    CX
                 SUB    CX,BX
```

10-10 Continued.

```
            CMP     CX,0
            JLE     EXTSHOWX

            MOV     BX,[BP + _AOFF + 6]     ;GET INDEX INTO LINE TABLE
            SHL     BX,1
            SHL     BX,1
            MOV     AX,CS:[SCREENTABLE + 2 + BX]
            INC     AX

            CALL    VGA_BANK

            MOV     AX,0A000H
            MOV     ES,AX

            MOV     DI,0

            CLD
    REPNE   MOVSB                           ;MOVE IN THE LINE DATA

EXTSHOWX:   POP     ES
            POP     DS
            POP     BP
            RETF
VGA_LINE    ENDP

;THIS ROUTINE DESELECTS THE VGA 256 COLOUR MODE
VGA_OFF     PROC    NEAR
            MOV     AX,1200H
            MOV     BX,0031H
            INT     10H

            MOV     AX,0003H
            INT     10H
            RETF
VGA_OFF     ENDP

VGA_BANK    PROC    NEAR
            CMP     AX,CS:[BANK]
            JNE     VGABANK1
            RET

VGABANK1:   MOV     CS:[BANK],AX

            PUSH    AX
            PUSH    BX
            PUSH    DX
            CLI

            MOV     DX,3CEH         ;SET PAGE SIZE TO 64K
            MOV     AL,6
            OUT     DX,AL
            INC     DL
```

10-10 Continued.

```
                       IN       AL,DX
                       DEC      DL
                       OR       AL,4
                       MOV      AH,AL
                       MOV      AL,6
                       OUT      DX,AX

                       MOV      DL,0C4H          ;SWITCH TO BPS MODE
                       MOV      AL,0BH
                       OUT      DX,AL
                       INC      DL
                       IN       AL,DX
                       DEC      DL

                       MOV      BX,CS:[BANK]
                       MOV      AH,BL
                       XOR      AH,2
                       MOV      DX,3C4H
                       MOV      AL,0EH
                       OUT      DX,AX

                       STI
                       POP      DX
                       POP      BX
                       POP      AX

                       RET
VGA_BANK               ENDP

;THIS ROUTINE SETS THE VGA PALETTE
;THE FIRST ARGUMENT ON THE STACK IS A FAR POINTER TO
;THE PALETTE DATA. THE SECOND ARGUMENT IS THE NUMBER OF COLOURS.
VGA_PALETTE            PROC     NEAR
                       PUSH     BP
                       MOV      BP,SP
                       PUSH     DS
                       PUSH     ES
                       MOV      AX,CS
                       MOV      ES,AX

                       MOV      SI,[BP + _AOFF + 0]    ;OFFSET OF SOURCE
                       MOV      DS,[BP + _AOFF + 2]    ;SEGMENT OF SOURCE

                       MOV      CX,[BP + _AOFF + 4]    ;NUMBER OF COLOURS

                       CMP      CX,0                   ;CHECK FOR NASTIES
                       JG       GVP0
                       JMP      GVPX

GVP0:                  MOV      DX,03C6H
                       MOV      AL,0FFH
                       OUT      DX,AL
```

10-10 Continued.

```
                MOV     BX,0

GVP1:           PUSH    CX
                MOV     DX,03C8H
                MOV     AL,BL
                INC     BX
                OUT     DX,AL

                INC     DX

                LODSB
                SHR     AL,1
                SHR     AL,1
                OUT     DX,AL

                LODSB
                SHR     AL,1
                SHR     AL,1
                OUT     DX,AL

                LODSB
                SHR     AL,1
                SHR     AL,1
                OUT     DX,AL

                POP     CX
                LOOP    GVP1

GVPX:           POP     ES
                POP     DS
                POP     BP
                RETF
VGA_PALETTE     ENDP

;THIS ROUTINE SETS THE VGA OVERSCAN.
VGA_OVERSCAN    PROC    NEAR
                PUSH    BP
                MOV     BP,SP
                MOV     AX,1001H
                MOV     BX,[BP + _AOFF + 0]
                XCHG    BH,BL
                INT     10H
                POP     BP
                RETF
VGA_OVERSCAN    ENDP

;THIS ROUTINE SELECTS THE EGA 16 COLOUR MODE
EGA_ON          PROC    NEAR
                PUSH    BP
                MOV     BP,SP
                PUSH    DS

EGA480:         MOV     CS:[V_EGAWIDE],640
```

10-10 Continued.

```
                      MOV      CS:[V_EGADEEP],480
                      MOV      CS:[V_EGABYTES],80

                      MOV      CX,640                    ;DEPTH OF SCREEN
                      SUB      DX,DX
                      MOV      SI,OFFSET SCREENTABLE

        EGA_ON2:      PUSH     DX
                      MOV      AX,80                     ;WIDTH OF SCREEEN
                      MUL      DX
                      MOV      CS:[SI],AX
                      ADD      SI,2
                      POP      DX
                      INC      DX
                      LOOP     EGA_ON2

                      MOV      AX,0012H
                      INT      10H

                      POP      DS
                      POP      BP
                      RETF
        EGA_ON        ENDP

        ;THIS ROUTINE DISPLAYS AN EGA LINE
        EGA_LINE      PROC     NEAR
                      PUSH     BP
                      MOV      BP,SP
                      PUSH     DS
                      PUSH     ES

                      MOV      SI,[BP + _AOFF + 0]       ;OFFSET OF SOURCE
                      MOV      DS,[BP + _AOFF + 2]       ;SEGMENT OF SOURCE
                      MOV      BX,[BP + _AOFF + 6]       ;GET LINE NUMBER
                      CMP      BX,CS:[V_EGADEEP]
                      JGE      SHOWEGAX

                      SHL      BX,1
                      MOV      DI,CS:[SCREENTABLE+BX]

                      MOV      AX,0A000H
                      MOV      ES,AX
                      MOV      BX,[BP + _AOFF + 4]       ;LENGTH OF MOVE IN BYTES

                      MOV      CX,BX
                      EGAPLANE            1
                      CLD
                      PUSH     DI
        REPNE         MOVSB
                      POP      DI

                      MOV      CX,BX
```

10-10 Continued.

```
                    EGAPLANE         2
                    PUSH     DI
          REPNE     MOVSB
                    POP      DI

                    MOV      CX,BX
                    EGAPLANE         4
                    PUSH     DI
          REPNE     MOVSB
                    POP      DI

                    MOV      CX,BX
                    EGAPLANE         8

                    PUSH     DI
          REPNE     MOVSB
                    POP      DI
                    EGAPLANE         0FH


SHOWEGAX:           POP      ES
                    POP      DS
                    POP      BP
                    RETF
EGA_LINE            ENDP

;THIS ROUTINE SETS THE EGA PALETTE
EGA_PALETTE         PROC     NEAR
                    PUSH     BP
                    MOV      BP,SP
                    PUSH     DS
                    PUSH     ES

                    MOV      SI,[BP + _AOFF + 6]      ;OFFSET OF SOURCE
                    MOV      DS,[BP + _AOFF + 8]      ;SEGMENT OF SOURCE

                    MOV      CX,[BP + _AOFF + 4]      ;NUMBER OF COLOURS
                    CMP      CX,16
                    JLE      EGA_PALETTE1
                    MOV      CX,16

EGA_PALETTE1:       PUSH     CX
                    MOV      BX,0000H

EGA_PALETTE2:       PUSH     CX
                    LODSB
                    SHR      AL,1
                    SHR      AL,1
                    MOV      DH,AL
                    LODSB
                    SHR      AL,1
                    SHR      AL,1
                    MOV      CH,AL
                    LODSB
```

10-10 Continued.

```
                        SHR     AL,1
                        SHR     AL,1
                        MOV     CL,AL
                        MOV     AX,1010H
                        INT     10H
                        INC     BX
                        POP     CX
                        LOOP    EGA_PALETTE2

                        POP     CX
                        MOV     BX,0000H

EGA_PALETTE3:           PUSH    CX
                        MOV     AX,1000H
                        INT     10H
                        ADD     BX,0101H
                        POP     CX
                        LOOP    EGA_PALETTE3

                        POP     ES
                        POP     DS
                        POP     BP
                        RETF
EGA_PALETTE             ENDP

;THIS ROUTINE DESELECTS THE EGA 16 COLOUR MODE
EGA_OFF                 PROC    NEAR
                        MOV     AX,0003H
                        INT     10H
                        RETF
EGA_OFF                 ENDP

;THIS ROUTINE SELECTS THE 2 COLOUR MODE
MONO_ON                 PROC    NEAR
                        PUSH    BP
                        MOV     BP,SP
                        PUSH    DS
                        PUSH    ES

                        MOV     CS:[V_MONOWIDE],640
                        MOV     CS:[V_MONODEEP],480
                        MOV     CS:[V_MONOBYTES],80

                        MOV     AX,0012H
                        INT     10H

                        MOV     CX,480
                        SUB     DX,DX
                        MOV     SI,OFFSET SCREENTABLE

MONO_ON1:               PUSH    DX
                        MOV     AX,80
```

10-10 Continued.

```
                MUL     DX
                MOV     CS:[SI],AX
                ADD     SI,2
                POP     DX
                INC     DX
                LOOP    MONO_ON1

                POP     ES
                POP     DS
                POP     BP
                SUB     AX,AX
                RETF
MONO_ON         ENDP

;THIS FUNCTION PERFORMS VARIOUS GRAPHIC OPERATIONS
;       ARGUMENTS       -       FUNCTION CODE
;                       -       VARIABLE
;
;       FUNCTIONS       -       0       RETURN SCREEN SEG
;                       -       1       RETURN OFFSET TO SCREEN TABLE
;                       -       2       RETURN MONOCHROME SCREEN WIDTH
;                       -       3       RETURN MONOCHROME SCREEN DEPTH
;                       -       4       INVERT FRAME RECT - ARGS ON STACK
;
MONO_FUNCTIONS  PROC    NEAR
                PUSH    BP
                MOV     BP,SP
                PUSH    DS
                PUSH    ES

                CMP     WORD PTR [BP + _AOFF + 0],0000H
                JNE     MF1

                MOV     AX,MONO_SCREENSEG
                JMP     MF_EXIT

MF1:            CMP     WORD PTR [BP + _AOFF + 0],0001H
                JNE     MF2

                MOV     AX,OFFSET SCREENTABLE-8
                JMP     MF_EXIT

MF2:            CMP     WORD PTR [BP + _AOFF + 0],0002H
                JNE     MF3

                MOV     AX,MONO_WIDE
                JMP     MF_EXIT

MF3:            CMP     WORD PTR [BP + _AOFF + 0],0003H
                JNE     MF4

                MOV     AX,MONO_DEEP
```

10-10 Continued.

```
                    JMP       MF_EXIT

MF4:                CMP       WORD PTR [BP + _AOFF + 0],0004H
                    JE        MF5
                    JMP       MF_EXIT

MF5:                MOV       AX,MONO_SCREENSEG
                    MOV       ES,AX

                    MOV       BX,[BP + _AOFF + 4]       ;GET TOP
                    SHL       BX,1
                    MOV       DI,CS:[SCREENTABLE+BX]

                    MOV       BX,[BP + _AOFF + 2]       ;GET LEFT
                    MOV       CX,[BP + _AOFF + 6]       ;GET RIGHT
                    SUB       CX,BX

MF5A:               PUSH      BX
                    AND       BX,0007H
                    MOV       AL,CS:[MASKTABLE+BX]
                    POP       BX

                    PUSH      BX
                    SHR       BX,1
                    SHR       BX,1
                    SHR       BX,1
                    XOR       ES:[DI+BX],AL
                    POP       BX
                    INC       BX
                    LOOP      MF5A

                    MOV       BX,[BP + _AOFF + 4]       ;GET TOP
                    INC       BX
                    MOV       CX,[BP + _AOFF + 8]       ;GET BOTTOM
                    DEC       CX
                    SUB       CX,BX

MF5B:               PUSH      BX
                    SHL       BX,1
                    MOV       DI,CS:[SCREENTABLE+BX]
                    MOV       BX,[BP + _AOFF + 2]       ;GET LEFT
                    PUSH      BX
                    AND       BX,0007H
                    MOV       AL,CS:[MASKTABLE+BX]
                    POP       BX
                    PUSH      BX
                    SHR       BX,1
                    SHR       BX,1
                    SHR       BX,1
                    XOR       ES:[DI+BX],AL
                    POP       BX
                    MOV       BX,[BP + _AOFF + 6]       ;GET RIGHT
```

10-10 Continued.

```
                DEC     BX
                PUSH    BX
                AND     BX,0007H
                MOV     AL,CS:[MASKTABLE+BX]
                POP     BX
                PUSH    BX
                SHR     BX,1
                SHR     BX,1
                SHR     BX,1
                XOR     ES:[DI+BX],AL
                POP     BX
                POP     BX
                INC     BX
                LOOP    MF5B

                MOV     BX,[BP + _AOFF + 8]     ;GET BOTTOM
                DEC     BX
                SHL     BX,1
                MOV     DI,CS:[SCREENTABLE+BX]

                MOV     BX,[BP + _AOFF + 2]     ;GET LEFT
                MOV     CX,[BP + _AOFF + 6]     ;GET RIGHT
                SUB     CX,BX

MF5D:           PUSH    BX
                AND     BX,0007H
                MOV     AL,CS:[MASKTABLE+BX]
                POP     BX

                PUSH    BX
                SHR     BX,1
                SHR     BX,1
                SHR     BX,1
                XOR     ES:[DI+BX],AL
                POP     BX
                INC     BX
                LOOP    MF5D

MF_EXIT:        POP     ES
                POP     DS
                POP     BP

                RETF
MONO_FUNCTIONS  ENDP

MASKTABLE       DB      80H,40H,20H,10H,08H,04H,02H,01H

MONO_LINE       PROC    NEAR
                PUSH    BP
                MOV     BP,SP

                PUSH    DS
```

10-10 Continued.

```
                PUSH    ES

                MOV     AX,0A000H              ;POINT TO THE SCREEN
                MOV     ES,AX

                MOV     CX,[BP + _AOFF + 6]    ;GET THE WIDTH OF MOVE
                CMP     CX,CS:[V_MONOBYTES]
                JL      MONO_LINE1
                MOV     CX,CS:[V_MONOBYTES]

MONO_LINE1:     MOV     SI,[BP + _AOFF + 0]    ;OFFSET OF BITMAP
                MOV     DS,[BP + _AOFF + 2]    ;SEGMENT OF BITMAP
                MOV     BX,[BP + _AOFF + 4]    ;NUMBER OF LINE
                SHL     BX,1

                CLD                            ;CLEAR DIRECTION FLAG
                MOV     DI,CS:[SCREENTABLE + BX]
        REPNE   MOVSB                          ;DO THE MOVE

                POP     ES
                POP     DS

                POP     BP
                RETF
MONO_LINE       ENDP

;THIS ROUTINE DESELECTS THE 2 COLOUR MODE
MONO_OFF        PROC    NEAR
                MOV     AX,0003H
                INT     10H
                SUB     AX,AX
                RETF
MONO_OFF        ENDP

;THIS IS A LINE START LOOKUP TABLE

SCREENTABLE     DW      1600 DUP(?)       ;LINE START TABLE
BANK            DW      ?

CODE            ENDS
                END
```

10-10 Continued.

Expanding the Trident driver

You can add modes to TRIDENT.ASM in the same way you can to
TSENG.ASM. Adjust the code that sets up the screen table to reflect the
screen dimensions of the mode you're interested in and change the code
that switches screen modes up in VGA_ON. It currently looks like this:

```
        MOV     AX,005CH
        INT     10H
```

The value loaded into AX determines the graphics mode to be used. Here's a list of modes supported by the Trident 8900 series chips:

```
005CH   640×400, 256 colors
005DH   640×480, 256 colors
005EH   800×600, 256 colors
0062H   1024×768, 256 colors
005BH   800×600, 16 colors
005FH   1024×768, 16 colors
```

As with the Tseng driver, note that you'll have to handle page switching part way through each image plane if you decide to work with the 1024×768 pixel, 16 color mode.

An ATI VGA Wonder driver

The most notable thing about the ATI VGA cards is that they seem to be the recipients of more advertising than all other VGA cards combined. While no better or worse than the previous two cards in their 256-color modes, the most recent ATI card, the ATI XL, is one of the few low-priced display devices to offer a true color mode. This mode is discussed in the next section.

The ATI.ASM screen driver, illustrated in FIG. 10-11, is very much like the previous two drivers. It uses switched pages and essentially the same logic to manage them.

The ATI.ASM driver implements the card's 640×400 pixel, 256-color mode.

```
;
;               Graphic Workshop ATI screen driver
;               Copyright (C) 1989, 1991 Alchemy Mindworks Inc.
;


VERSION         EQU     2               ;VERSION NUMBER
SUBVERSION      EQU     1               ;SUBVERSION NUMBER

_AOFF           EQU     6               ;STACK OFFSET

RGB_WIDE        EQU     640
RGB_DEEP        EQU     480
RGB_SCREENSEG   EQU     0A000H
VGA_WIDE        EQU     1024            ;WIDTH OF VGA SCREEN IN PIXELS
VGA_DEEP        EQU     768             ;DEPTH OF VGA SCREEN IN PIXELS
VGA_SCREENSEG   EQU     0A000H          ;SEGMENT OF VGA SCREEN
EGA_WIDE        EQU     640             ;WIDTH OF EGA SCREEN IN PIXELS
EGA_DEEP        EQU     480             ;DEPTH OF EGA SCREEN IN PIXELS
EGA_BYTES       EQU     80              ;WIDTH OF EGA SCREEN IN BYTES
EGA_SCREENSEG   EQU     0A000H          ;SEGMENT OF EGA SCREEN
```

10-11 The source code for ATI.ASM.

```
MONO_WIDE        EQU      640              ;WIDTH OF MONO SCREEN IN PIXELS
MONO_DEEP        EQU      480              ;DEPTH OF MONO SCREEN IN PIXELS
MONO_BYTES       EQU      80               ;WIDTH OF MONO SCREEN IN BYTES
MONO_SCREENSEG   EQU      0A000H           ;SEGMENT OF MONO SCREEN

;THIS MACRO SELECTS AN EGA PLANE
EGAPLANE         MACRO    ARG1
                 MOV      AL,2
                 MOV      DX,03C4H
                 OUT      DX,AL
                 INC      DX
                 MOV      AL,ARG1
                 OUT      DX,AL
                 ENDM

CODE             SEGMENT PARA PUBLIC 'CODE'
                 ASSUME  CS:CODE

                 ORG      0000H            ;ORIGIN FOR LOADABLE DRIVER

                 DB       'ALCHDRV2'       ;SIGNATURE - DON'T CHANGE THIS

;THE FOLLOWING ARE THE POINTERS TO THE CALLABLE ROUTINES AND THE COMMON
;DATA. THE SEGMENTS ARE FILLED IN BY GRAPHIC WORKSHOP. DON'T CHANGE ANYTHING.
DISPATCH         PROC     FAR
                 DW       VGA_ON           ;FAR POINTER TO VGA MODE SELECT
                 DW       ?
                 DW       VGA_LINE         ;FAR POINTER TO VGA LINE DISPLAY
                 DW       ?
                 DW       VGA_OFF          ;FAR POINTER TO VGA MODE DESELECT
                 DW       ?
                 DW       VGA_PALETTE      ;FAR POINTER TO VGA PALETTE SET
                 DW       ?
                 DW       VGA_OVERSCAN     ;FAR POINTER TO VGA OVERSCAN SET
                 DW       ?
                 DW       EGA_ON           ;FAR POINTER TO EGA MODE SELECT
                 DW       ?
                 DW       EGA_LINE         ;FAR POINTER TO EGA LINE DISPLAY
                 DW       ?
                 DW       EGA_OFF          ;FAR POINTER TO EGA MODE DESELECT
                 DW       ?
                 DW       EGA_PALETTE      ;FAR POINTER TO EGA PALETTE SET
                 DW       ?
                 DW       MONO_ON          ;FAR POINTER TO MONO MODE SELECT
                 DW       ?
                 DW       MONO_FUNCTIONS   ;FAR POINTER TO MONO PAGE DISPLAY
                 DW       ?
                 DW       MONO_LINE
                 DW       ?
                 DW       MONO_OFF         ;FAR POINTER TO MONO MODE DESELECT
                 DW       ?
                 DW       0,0
```

10-11 Continued.

An ATI VGA Wonder driver   **439**

```
                DW          0,0
                DW          0,0
                DW          0
                DW          0
V_VGAWIDE       DW          VGA_WIDE        ;VGA SCREEN WIDTH
V_VGADEEP       DW          VGA_DEEP        ;VGA SCREEN DEPTH
V_VGASCRNSEG    DW          VGA_SCREENSEG   ;VGA SCREEN SEGMENT
V_EGAWIDE       DW          EGA_WIDE        ;EGA SCREEN WIDTH
V_EGADEEP       DW          EGA_DEEP        ;EGA SCREEN DEPTH
V_EGABYTES      DW          EGA_BYTES       ;EGA SCREEN 3YTES
V_EGASCRNSEG    DW          EGA_SCREENSEG   ;EGA SCREEN SEGMENT
V_MONOWIDE      DW          MONO_WIDE       ;MONO SCREEN WIDTH
V_MONODEEP      DW          MONO_DEEP       ;MONO SCREEN DEPTH
V_MONOBYTES     DW          MONO_BYTES      ;BYTE WIDTH ON MONOCHROME SCREEN
V_MONOSCRNSEG   DW          MONO_SCREENSEG  ;MONOCHROME SCREEN SEGMENT
                DW          VERSION
                DW          SUBVERSION
                DB          'ATI 640x400  v2.1      ',0
DISPATCH        ENDP

VGAMODETABLE    DW          320,200
                DW          640,400
                DW          -1,-1

EGAMODETABLE    DW          -1,-1

MONOMODETABLE   DW          -1,-1

;THIS ROUTINE SELECTS THE VGA 256 COLOUR MODE
VGA_ON          PROC        NEAR
                PUSH        BP
                MOV         BP,SP
                PUSH        DS

                CMP         WORD PTR [BP + _AOFF + 0],320
                JG          EXT_ON
                CMP         WORD PTR [BP + _AOFF + 2],200
                JG          EXT_ON

                MOV         CS:[V_VGAWIDE],320
                MOV         CS:[V_VGADEEP],200
                MOV         CX,200                      ;DEPTH OF SCREEN
                SUB         DX,DX
                MOV         SI,OFFSET SCREENTABLE

VGA_ON1:        PUSH        DX
                MOV         AX,320                      ;WIDTH OF SCREEEN
                MUL         DX
                MOV         CS:[SI],AX
                ADD         SI,2
                POP         DX
                INC         DX
```

10-11 Continued.

```
                LOOP     VGA_ON1

                MOV      AX,0013H
                INT      10H

                JMP      EXT_EXIT

EXT_ON:         MOV      CS:[V_VGAWIDE],640
                MOV      CS:[V_VGADEEP],400

                MOV      CX,400                          ;DEPTH OF SCREEN
                SUB      BX,BX                           ;ZERO LINE COUNTER
                MOV      SI,OFFSET SCREENTABLE           ;POINT TO TABLE

EXT_1:          PUSH     CX
                MOV      AX,640                          ;WIDTH OF SCREEEN
                MUL      BX                              ;TIMES LINE NUMBER

                AND      DX,00FFH

                CMP      AX,(0FFFEH-640)                  ;SEE IF WE WILL
                JB       EXT_2

                MOV      DH,0FFH

EXT_2:          MOV      CS:[SI],AX                      ;SAVE THE VALUES
                MOV      CS:[SI+2],DX                    ;IN OUR LOOKUP TABLE
                ADD      SI,4                            ;AND POINT TO THE
                INC      BX                              ;NEXT LINE AND
                POP      CX                              ;ENTRY
                LOOP     EXT_1

                MOV      AX,0061H
                INT      10H

                MOV      AX,0C000H
                MOV      ES,AX
                MOV      AX,ES:[0010H]
                MOV      CS:[ATIREG],AX

                MOV      CS:[BANK],0000H

EXT_EXIT:       POP      DS
                POP      BP
                RETF
VGA_ON          ENDP

;THIS ROUTINE DISPLAYS A VGA LINE
VGA_LINE        PROC     NEAR
                PUSH     BP
                MOV      BP,SP
```

10-11 Continued.

```
              PUSH     DS
              PUSH     ES

              CMP      CS:[V_VGAWIDE],320
              JNE      EXTSHOW

              MOV      SI,[BP + _AOFF + 0]      ;OFFSET OF SOURCE
              MOV      DS,[BP + _AOFF + 2]      ;SEGMENT OF SOURCE

              MOV      BX,[BP + _AOFF + 6]      ;GET LINE NUMBER
              CMP      BX,200
              JG       VGASHOW2

              SHL      BX,1
              MOV      DI,CS:[SCREENTABLE+BX]

              CLD
              MOV      CX,[BP + _AOFF + 4]      ;LENGTH OF MOVE IN BYTES
              CMP      CX,0
              JE       VGASHOW2

              CMP      CX,320
              JL       VGASHOW1
              MOV      CX,320
VGASHOW1:     MOV      AX,0A000H
              MOV      ES,AX
       REPNE  MOVSB

VGASHOW2:     JMP      EXTSHOWX

EXTSHOW:      CMP      WORD PTR [BP + _AOFF + 6],400
              JL       EXTSHOW1
              JMP      EXTSHOWX

EXTSHOW1:     MOV      SI,[BP + _AOFF + 0]      ;OFFSET OF SOURCE
              MOV      DS,[BP + _AOFF + 2]      ;SEGMENT OF SOURCE
              MOV      CX,[BP + _AOFF + 4]      ;LENGTH OF MOVE IN BYTES

              CMP      CX,640                   ;IS IT TOO LONG?
              JL       EXTSHOW2

              MOV      CX,640

EXTSHOW2:     MOV      BX,[BP + _AOFF + 6]      ;GET INDEX INTO LINE TABLE
              SHL      BX,1
              SHL      BX,1

              MOV      DI,CS:[SCREENTABLE + BX]
              MOV      AX,CS:[SCREENTABLE + 2 + BX]

              CALL     VGA_BANK
```

10-11 Continued.

```
                    CMP       AH,00H
                    JNE       EXTSHOW3

                    MOV       AX,0A000H              ;POINT TO VIDEO BUFFER
                    MOV       ES,AX                  ;WITH ES

                    CLD

           REPNE    MOVSB                            ;MOVE IN THE LINE DATA
                    JMP       EXTSHOWX

EXTSHOW3:           MOV       AX,0A000H              ;POINT TO VIDEO BUFFER
                    MOV       ES,AX                  ;WITH ES

                    PUSH      CX
                    MOV       AX,DI
                    MOV       CX,0000H
                    SUB       CX,AX
                    MOV       BX,CX

                    CMP       CX,[BP + _AOFF + 4]    ;ARE THERE ENOUGH BYTES LEFT?
                    JL        EXTSHOW4               ;IF SO, GO JUMP THE FRAME

                    MOV       CX,[BP + _AOFF + 4]
                    CLD
           REPNE    MOVSB                            ;MOVE IN THE LINE DATA

                    POP       CX
                    JMP       EXTSHOWX

EXTSHOW4:           CLD
           REPNE    MOVSB                            ;MOVE IN THE LINE DATA

                    POP       CX
                    SUB       CX,BX
                    CMP       CX,0
                    JLE       EXTSHOWX

                    MOV       BX,[BP + _AOFF + 6]    ;GET INDEX INTO LINE TABLE
                    SHL       BX,1
                    SHL       BX,1
                    MOV       AX,CS:[SCREENTABLE + 2 + BX]
                    INC       AX

                    CALL      VGA_BANK

                    MOV       AX,0A000H
                    MOV       ES,AX

                    MOV       DI,0

                    CLD
```

10-11 Continued.

```
        REPNE   MOVSB                        ;MOVE IN THE LINE DATA

EXTSHOWX:       POP     ES
                POP     DS
                POP     BP
                RETF
VGA_LINE        ENDP

;THIS ROUTINE DESELECTS THE VGA 256 COLOUR MODE
VGA_OFF         PROC    NEAR
                MOV     AX,1200H
                MOV     BX,0031H
                INT     10H

                MOV     AX,0003H

                INT     10H
                RETF
VGA_OFF         ENDP

VGA_BANK        PROC    NEAR
                CMP     AX,CS:[BANK]
                JNE     VGABANK1
                RET

VGABANK1:       MOV     CS:[BANK],AX

                PUSH    AX
                PUSH    CX
                PUSH    DX

                MOV     DX,CS:[ATIREG]

                MOV     CX,AX
                CLI
                MOV     AL,0B2H
                OUT     DX,AL
                INC     DL
                IN      AL,DX
                MOV     AH,AL
                AND     AH,0E1H
                SHL     CL,1
                OR      AH,CL
                MOV     AL,0B2H
                DEC     DL
                OUT     DX,AX
                STI

                POP     DX
                POP     CX
                POP     AX
```

10-11 Continued.

```
                        RET
VGA_BANK                ENDP

;THIS ROUTINE SETS THE VGA PALETTE
VGA_PALETTE             PROC    NEAR
                        PUSH    BP
                        MOV     BP,SP
                        PUSH    DS
                        PUSH    ES
                        MOV     AX,CS
                        MOV     ES,AX

                        MOV     SI,[BP + _AOFF + 0]    ;OFFSET OF SOURCE
                        MOV     DS,[BP + _AOFF + 2]    ;SEGMENT OF SOURCE

                        MOV     CX,[BP + _AOFF + 4]    ;NUMBER OF COLOURS

                        CMP     CX,0                   ;CHECK FOR NASTIES
                        JG      GVP0
                        JMP     GVPX

GVP0:                   MOV     DX,03C6H
                        MOV     AL,0FFH
                        OUT     DX,AL

                        MOV     BX,0

GVP1:                   PUSH    CX
                        MOV     DX,03C8H
                        MOV     AL,BL
                        INC     BX
                        OUT     DX,AL

                        INC     DX

                        LODSB
                        SHR     AL,1
                        SHR     AL,1
                        OUT     DX,AL

                        LODSB
                        SHR     AL,1
                        SHR     AL,1
                        OUT     DX,AL

                        LODSB
                        SHR     AL,1
                        SHR     AL,1
                        OUT     DX,AL

                        POP     CX
```

10-11 Continued.

```
                    LOOP      GVP1

GVPX:               POP       ES
                    POP       DS
                    POP       BP
                    RETF
VGA_PALETTE         ENDP


;THIS ROUTINE SETS THE VGA OVERSCAN.
VGA_OVERSCAN        PROC      NEAR
                    PUSH      BP
                    MOV       BP,SP
                    MOV       AX,1001H
                    MOV       BX,[BP + _AOFF + 0]
                    XCHG      BH,BL
                    INT       10H
                    POP       BP
                    RETF
VGA_OVERSCAN        ENDP


;THIS ROUTINE SELECTS THE EGA 16 COLOUR MODE
EGA_ON              PROC      NEAR
                    PUSH      BP
                    MOV       BP,SP
                    PUSH      DS

EGA480:             MOV       CS:[V_EGAWIDE],640
                    MOV       CS:[V_EGADEEP],480
                    MOV       CS:[V_EGABYTES],80

                    MOV       CX,480          ;DEPTH OF SCREEN
                    SUB       DX,DX
                    MOV       SI,OFFSET SCREENTABLE

EGA_ON2:            PUSH      DX
                    MOV       AX,80           ;WIDTH OF SCREEEN
                    MUL       DX
                    MOV       CS:[SI],AX
                    ADD       SI,2
                    POP       DX
                    INC       DX
                    LOOP      EGA_ON2

                    MOV       AX,0012H
                    INT       10H

                    POP       DS
                    POP       BP
                    RETF
EGA_ON              ENDP


;THIS ROUTINE DISPLAYS AN EGA LINE
```

10-11 Continued.

```
;THE FIRST ARGUMENT ON THE STACK (2 WORDS) IS A FAR POINTER TO
;THE LINE. THE SECOND ARGUMENT IS THE LENGTH OF THE LINE IN BYTES
EGA_LINE          PROC    NEAR
                  PUSH    BP
                  MOV     BP,SP
                  PUSH    DS
                  PUSH    ES

                  MOV     SI,[BP + _AOFF + 0]      ;OFFSET OF SOURCE
                  MOV     DS,[BP + _AOFF + 2]      ;SEGMENT OF SOURCE
                  MOV     BX,[BP + _AOFF + 6]      ;GET LINE NUMBER
                  CMP     BX,CS:[V_EGADEEP]
                  JGE     SHOWEGAX

                  SHL     BX,1
                  MOV     DI,CS:[SCREENTABLE+BX]

                  MOV     AX,0A000H
                  MOV     ES,AX
                  MOV     BX,[BP + _AOFF + 4]      ;LENGTH OF MOVE IN BYTES

                  MOV     CX,BX
                  EGAPLANE          1
                  CLD
                  PUSH    DI
          REPNE   MOVSB
                  POP     DI

                  MOV     CX,BX
                  EGAPLANE          2
                  PUSH    DI
          REPNE   MOVSB
                  POP     DI

                  MOV     CX,BX
                  EGAPLANE          4
                  PUSH    DI
          REPNE   MOVSB
                  POP     DI

                  MOV     CX,BX
                  EGAPLANE          8
                  PUSH    DI
          REPNE   MOVSB
                  POP     DI
                  EGAPLANE          0FH

SHOWEGAX:         POP     ES
                  POP     DS
                  POP     BP
                  RETF
EGA_LINE          ENDP
```

10-11 Continued.

```
;THIS ROUTINE SETS THE EGA PALETTE
;THE FIRST ARGUMENT ON THE STACK IS A FAR POINTER TO
;THE PALETTE DATA. THE SECOND ARGUMENT IS THE NUMBER OF COLOURS.
EGA_PALETTE     PROC    NEAR
                PUSH    BP
                MOV     BP,SP
                PUSH    DS
                PUSH    ES

                MOV     SI,[BP + _AOFF + 6]     ;OFFSET OF SOURCE
                MOV     DS,[BP + _AOFF + 8]     ;SEGMENT OF SOURCE

                MOV     CX,[BP + _AOFF + 4]     ;NUMBER OF COLOURS
                CMP     CX,16
                JLE     EGA_PALETTE1
                MOV     CX,16

EGA_PALETTE1:   PUSH    CX
                MOV     BX,0000H

EGA_PALETTE2:   PUSH    CX
                LODSB
                SHR     AL,1
                SHR     AL,1
                MOV     DH,AL
                LODSB
                SHR     AL,1
                SHR     AL,1
                MOV     CH,AL
                LODSB
                SHR     AL,1
                SHR     AL,1
                MOV     CL,AL
                MOV     AX,1010H
                INT     10H
                INC     BX
                POP     CX
                LOOP    EGA_PALETTE2

                POP     CX
                MOV     BX,0000H

EGA_PALETTE3:   PUSH    CX
                MOV     AX,1000H
                INT     10H
                ADD     BX,0101H
                POP     CX
                LOOP    EGA_PALETTE3

                POP     ES
                POP     DS
                POP     BP
```

10-11 Continued.

```
                    RETF
EGA_PALETTE         ENDP


;THIS ROUTINE DESELECTS THE EGA 16 COLOUR MODE
EGA_OFF             PROC    NEAR
                    MOV     AX,0003H
                    INT     10H
                    RETF
EGA_OFF             ENDP


;THIS ROUTINE SELECTS THE 2 COLOUR MODE
MONO_ON             PROC    NEAR
                    PUSH    BP
                    MOV     BP,SP
                    PUSH    DS
                    PUSH    ES

                    MOV     CS:[V_MONOWIDE],640
                    MOV     CS:[V_MONODEEP],480
                    MOV     CS:[V_MONOBYTES],80

                    MOV     AX,0012H
                    INT     10H

                    MOV     CX,480
                    SUB     DX,DX
                    MOV     SI,OFFSET SCREENTABLE

MONO_ON1:           PUSH    DX
                    MOV     AX,80
                    MUL     DX
                    MOV     CS:[SI],AX
                    ADD     SI,2
                    POP     DX
                    INC     DX
                    LOOP    MONO_ON1

                    POP     ES
                    POP     DS
                    POP     BP
                    SUB     AX,AX
                    RETF
MONO_ON             ENDP


;THIS FUNCTION PERFORMS VARIOUS GRAPHIC OPERATIONS
;       ARGUMENTS       -       FUNCTION CODE
;                       -       VARIABLE
;
;       FUNCTIONS       -       0       RETURN SCREEN SEG
;                       -       1       RETURN OFFSET TO SCREEN TABLE
;                       -       2       RETURN MONOCHROME SCREEN WIDTH
;                       -       3       RETURN MONOCHROME SCREEN DEPTH
```

10-11 Continued.

```
;                       -    4       INVERT FRAME RECT - ARGS ON STACK
;                       -    5       RETURN OFFSET OF VGAMODETABLE
;                       -    6       RETURN OFFSET OF EGAMODETABLE
;                       -    7       RETURN OFFSET OF MONOMODETABLE
;                       -    8       RETURN OFFSET OF RGBMODETABLE
;
MONO_FUNCTIONS  PROC    NEAR
                PUSH    BP
                MOV     BP,SP
                PUSH    DS
                PUSH    ES

                CMP     WORD PTR [BP + _AOFF + 0],0000H
                JNE     MF1

                MOV     AX,MONO_SCREENSEG
                JMP     MF_EXIT

MF1:            CMP     WORD PTR [BP + _AOFF + 0],0001H
                JNE     MF2

                MOV     AX,OFFSET SCREENTABLE-8
                JMP     MF_EXIT

MF2:            CMP     WORD PTR [BP + _AOFF + 0],0002H
                JNE     MF3

                MOV     AX,MONO_WIDE
                JMP     MF_EXIT

MF3:            CMP     WORD PTR [BP + _AOFF + 0],0003H
                JNE     MF4

                MOV     AX,MONO_DEEP
                JMP     MF_EXIT

MF4:            CMP     WORD PTR [BP + _AOFF + 0],0004H
                JE      MF5.
                JMP     MF6

MF5:            MOV     AX,MONO_SCREENSEG
                MOV     ES,AX

                MOV     BX,[BP + _AOFF + 4]     ;GET TOP
                SHL     BX,1
                MOV     DI,CS:[SCREENTABLE+BX]

                MOV     BX,[BP + _AOFF + 2]     ;GET LEFT
                MOV     CX,[BP + _AOFF + 6]     ;GET RIGHT
                SUB     CX,BX

MF5A:           PUSH    BX
```

10-11 Continued.

```
                    AND       BX,0007H
                    MOV       AL,CS:[MASKTABLE+BX]
                    POP       BX

                    PUSH      BX
                    SHR       BX,1
                    SHR       BX,1
                    SHR       BX,1
                    XOR       ES:[DI+BX],AL
                    POP       BX
                    INC       BX
                    LOOP      MF5A

                    MOV       BX,[BP + _AOFF + 4]      ;GET TOP
                    INC       BX
                    MOV       CX,[BP + _AOFF + 8]      ;GET BOTTOM
                    DEC       CX
                    SUB       CX,BX

MF5B:               PUSH      BX
                    SHL       BX,1
                    MOV       DI,CS:[SCREENTABLE+BX]
                    MOV       BX,[BP + _AOFF + 2]      ;GET LEFT
                    PUSH      BX
                    AND       BX,0007H
                    MOV       AL,CS:[MASKTABLE+BX]
                    POP       BX
                    PUSH      BX
                    SHR       BX,1
                    SHR       BX,1
                    SHR       BX,1
                    XOR       ES:[DI+BX],AL
                    POP       BX
                    MOV       BX,[BP + _AOFF + 6]      ;GET RIGHT
                    DEC       BX
                    PUSH      BX
                    AND       BX,0007H
                    MOV       AL,CS:[MASKTABLE+BX]
                    POP       BX
                    PUSH      BX
                    SHR       BX,1
                    SHR       BX,1
                    SHR       BX,1
                    XOR       ES:[DI+BX],AL
                    POP       BX
                    POP       BX
                    INC       BX
                    LOOP      MF5B

                    MOV       BX,[BP + _AOFF + 8]      ;GET BOTTOM
                    DEC       BX
                    SHL       BX,1
```

10-11 Continued.

```
                MOV     DI,CS:[SCREENTABLE+BX]

                MOV     BX,[BP + _AOFF + 2]     ;GET LEFT
                MOV     CX,[BP + _AOFF + 6]     ;GET RIGHT
                SUB     CX,BX

MF5D:           PUSH    BX
                AND     BX,0007H
                MOV     AL,CS:[MASKTABLE+BX]
                POP     BX

                PUSH    BX
                SHR     BX,1
                SHR     BX,1
                SHR     BX,1
                XOR     ES:[DI+BX],AL
                POP     BX
                INC     BX
                LOOP    MF5D

MF6:            CMP     WORD PTR [BP + _AOFF + 0],0005H
                JNE     MF7

                MOV     AX,OFFSET VGAMODETABLE
                JMP     MF_EXIT

MF7:            CMP     WORD PTR [BP + _AOFF + 0],0006H
                JNE     MF8

                MOV     AX,OFFSET EGAMODETABLE
                JMP     MF_EXIT

MF8:            CMP     WORD PTR [BP + _AOFF + 0],0007H
                JNE     MF_EXIT

                MOV     AX,OFFSET MONOMODETABLE
                JMP     MF_EXIT

MF_EXIT:        POP     ES
                POP     DS
                POP     BP
                RETF
MONO_FUNCTIONS  ENDP

MASKTABLE       DB      80H,40H,20H,10H,08H,04H,02H,01H

MONO_LINE       PROC    NEAR
                PUSH    BP
                MOV     BP,SP

                PUSH    DS
                PUSH    ES
```

10-11 Continued.

```
                MOV     AX,0A000H           ;POINT TO THE SCREEN
                MOV     ES,AX

                MOV     CX,[BP + _AOFF + 6] ;GET THE WIDTH OF MOVE
                CMP     CX,CS:[V_MONOBYTES]
                JL      MONO_LINE1
                MOV     CX,CS:[V_MONOBYTES]

MONO_LINE1:     MOV     SI,[BP + _AOFF + 0] ;OFFSET OF BITMAP
                MOV     DS,[BP + _AOFF + 2] ;SEGMENT OF BITMAP
                MOV     BX,[BP + _AOFF + 4] ;NUMBER OF LINE
                SHL     BX,1

                CLD                         ;CLEAR DIRECTION FLAG
                MOV     DI,CS:[SCREENTABLE + BX]
        REPNE   MOVSB                       ;DO THE MOVE

                POP     ES
                POP     DS
                POP     BP
                RETF
MONO_LINE       ENDP

;THIS ROUTINE DESELECTS THE 2 COLOUR MODE
MONO_OFF        PROC    NEAR
                MOV     AX,0003H
                INT     10H
                SUB     AX,AX
                RETF
MONO_OFF        ENDP

;THIS IS A LINE START LOOKUP TABLE

SCREENTABLE     DW      800 DUP(?)          ;LINE START TABLE
BANK            DW      ?
ATIREG          DW      ?

CODE            ENDS
                END
```

10-11 Continued.

Expanding the ATI driver

ATI chips support a variety of additional, higher-resolution screen modes.
You can drive them by modifying the logic that generates the screen table
and changing the mode number in the screen mode switching code. At
present it looks like this:

```
        MOV   AX,0061H
        INT   10H

        MOV   AX,0C000H
        MOV   ES,AX
```

```
MOV    AX,ES:[0010H]
MOV    CS:[ATIREG],AX
```

The mode argument is in the AX register before the INT 10H call. The latter four lines of code locate the register base for the card, which is stored in the BIOS area.

The following is a list of mode numbers to get into the various ATI graphics modes.

0061H	640×400, 256 colors
0062H	640×480, 256 colors
0063H	800×600, 256 colors
0064H	1024×768, 256 colors
0054H	800×600, 16 colors
0055H	1024×768, 16 colors

Several additional graphic modes are available on recent ATI cards. One of them is the RGB color mode, mode 72, which is discussed momentarily. Another, mode 65, is a 1024×768, 16-color mode in which the display memory is structured like the lines of a 16-color BMP file, rather than in planes. This appears to have been implemented because it makes it possible to write a blindingly fast Windows driver, this being format in which Windows likes to deal with bitmaps internally. This mode is not discussed in this book.

You can get more information about writing programs to drive ATI's cards by contacting ATI Technologies, Inc., 3761 Victoria Park Ave., Scarborough, Ontario M1W 3S2, Canada.

An ATI XL True Color screen driver

An ATI XL card with 1Mb of memory on board offers one of the few true color modes available without the heavy financing for a Targa board or something else equally stratospheric. While this mode (mode 72) does not have the color resolution of a high-end Targa board, it does offer a significant improvement over using palette driven VGA modes to look at RGB images.

The hardware of a VGA card is confronted with a number of limitations and restrictions in dealing with true RGB pictures. A VGA card is based on 6-bit digital-to-analog converters, these being the chips that convert numerical color data to analog electrical levels to drive your monitor. Such a card also has a finite amount of memory and a relatively small page frame through which to access it. If you consider the amount of memory required by even a modest size RGB file, you can appreciate how much real estate the screen buffer of an RGB display card would occupy.

Thus far, all the examples of RGB color in this book have required 3 bytes per pixel. In fact, if you're willing to live with somewhat reduced color resolution, 15 bits of color rather than 24, you can squeeze a full RGB pixel into 2 bytes. Figure 10-12 illustrates the relationship between a traditional 3-byte RGB pixel and a 2-byte, 15-bit pixel.

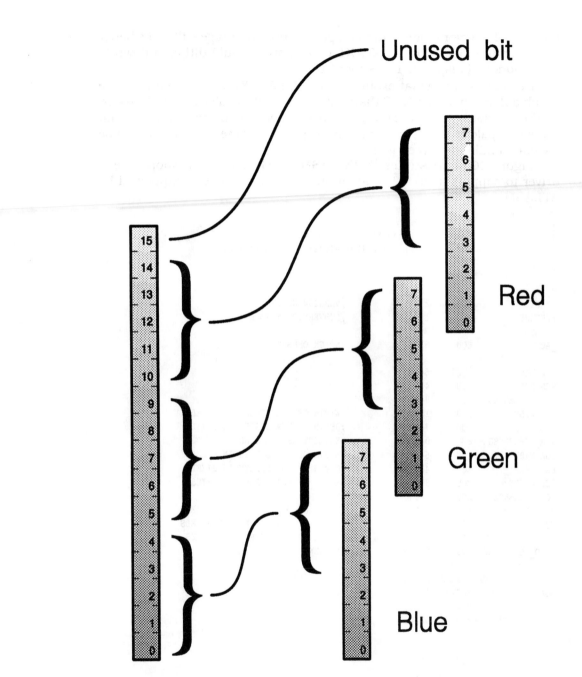

10-12 How a mode 72 pixel is structured.

A 15-bit pixel uses only the five most significant bits of each of the original 8-bit color-intensity values of a 24-bit pixel. This doesn't actually make that much of a difference to the appearance of images so displayed. While this amounts to 3 bits less resolution per pixel than a VGA card in one of its 256-color modes can manage, a true color image still looks better displayed in mode 72 of an ATI XL card than it would dithered down to 256 colors and displayed in a super VGA mode.

Despite its somewhat exotic nature, the ATI XL card doesn't behave much differently in mode 72 than it does in the 256-color mode discussed in the previous section. The pixels are all words instead of bytes and there's no palette to set, but for the most part the same type of code can be used to handle the screen lines.

Figure 10-13 illustrates ATIXL.ASM, a Graphic Workshop screen driver to support mode 72 in addition to the other modes supported by ATI.ASM.

```
;
;                    Graphic Workshop ATI XL screen driver
;                    Copyright (C) 1989, 1991 Alchemy Mindworks Inc.
;


VERSION             EQU     2                       ;VERSION NUMBER
SUBVERSION          EQU     1                       ;SUBVERSION NUMBER

_AOFF               EQU     6                       ;STACK OFFSET

RGB_WIDE            EQU     640
RGB_DEEP            EQU     480
RGB_SCREENSEG       EQU     0A000H
VGA_WIDE            EQU     1024                    ;WIDTH OF VGA SCREEN IN PIXELS
VGA_DEEP            EQU     768                     ;DEPTH OF VGA SCREEN IN PIXELS
VGA_SCREENSEG       EQU     0A000H                  ;SEGMENT OF VGA SCREEN
EGA_WIDE            EQU     640                     ;WIDTH OF EGA SCREEN IN PIXELS
EGA_DEEP            EQU     480                     ;DEPTH OF EGA SCREEN IN PIXELS
EGA_BYTES           EQU     80                      ;WIDTH OF EGA SCREEN IN BYTES
EGA_SCREENSEG       EQU     0A000H                  ;SEGMENT OF EGA SCREEN
MONO_WIDE           EQU     640                     ;WIDTH OF MONO SCREEN IN PIXELS
MONO_DEEP           EQU     480                     ;DEPTH OF MONO SCREEN IN PIXELS
MONO_BYTES          EQU     80                      ;WIDTH OF MONO SCREEN IN BYTES
MONO_SCREENSEG      EQU     0A000H                  ;SEGMENT OF MONO SCREEN

;THIS MACRO SELECTS AN EGA PLANE
EGAPLANE            MACRO   ARG1
                    MOV     AL,2
                    MOV     DX,03C4H
                    OUT     DX,AL
                    INC     DX
                    MOV     AL,ARG1
                    OUT     DX,AL
                    ENDM

;THIS MACRO COMPRESSES AN RGB TRIPLET AT DS:SI INTO A 15-BIT WORD IN AX
RGB2AX             MACRO
                    MOV     DX,0000H
```

10-13 The source code for ATIXL.ASM.

```
                LODSB

                MOV     CL,3
                SHR     AL,CL
                AND     AX,001FH
                MOV     CL,10
                SHL     AX,CL

                OR      DX,AX

                LODSB

                MOV     CL,3
                SHR     AL,CL
                AND     AX,001FH
                MOV     CL,5
                SHL     AX,CL

                OR      DX,AX

                LODSB

                MOV     CL,3
                SHR     AL,CL
                AND     AX,001FH
                OR      DX,AX
                MOV     AX,DX
                ENDM

CODE            SEGMENT PARA PUBLIC 'CODE'
                ASSUME  CS:CODE

                ORG     0000H           ;ORIGIN FOR LOADABLE DRIVER

                DB      'ALCHDRV2'       ;SIGNATURE - DON'T CHANGE THIS

;THE FOLLOWING ARE THE POINTERS TO THE CALLABLE ROUTINES AND THE COMMON
;DATA. THE SEGMENTS ARE FILLED IN BY GRAPHIC WORKSHOP. DON'T CHANGE ANYTHING.
DISPATCH        PROC    FAR
                DW      VGA_ON          ;FAR POINTER TO VGA MODE SELECT
                DW      ?
                DW      VGA_LINE        ;FAR POINTER TO VGA LINE DISPLAY
                DW      ?
                DW      VGA_OFF         ;FAR POINTER TO VGA MODE DESELECT
                DW      ?
                DW      VGA_PALETTE     ;FAR POINTER TO VGA PALETTE SET
                DW      ?
                DW      VGA_OVERSCAN    ;FAR POINTER TO VGA OVERSCAN SET
                DW      ?
                DW      EGA_ON          ;FAR POINTER TO EGA MODE SELECT
                DW      ?
                DW      EGA_LINE        ;FAR POINTER TO EGA LINE DISPLAY
```

10-13 Continued.

```
                DW      ?
                DW      EGA_OFF         ;FAR POINTER TO EGA MODE DESELECT
                DW      ?
                DW      EGA_PALETTE     ;FAR POINTER TO EGA PALETTE SET
                DW      ?
                DW      MONO_ON         ;FAR POINTER TO MONO MODE SELECT
                DW      ?
                DW      MONO_FUNCTIONS  ;FAR POINTER TO MONO FUNCTIONS
                DW      ?
                DW      MONO_LINE       ;FAR POINTER TO MONO LINE DISPLAY
                DW      ?
                DW      MONO_OFF        ;FAR POINTER TO MONO MODE DESELECT
                DW      ?
                DW      RGB_ON          ;FAR POINTER TO RGB MODE SELECT
                DW      ?
                DW      RGB_LINE        ;FAR POINTER TO RGB LINE DISPLAY
                DW      ?
                DW      RGB_OFF         ;FAR POINTER TO RGB MODE DESELECT
                DW      ?
V_RGBWIDE       DW      RGB_WIDE
V_RGBDEEP       DW      RGB_DEEP
V_VGAWIDE       DW      VGA_WIDE        ;VGA SCREEN WIDTH
V_VGADEEP       DW      VGA_DEEP        ;VGA SCREEN DEPTH
V_VGASCRNSEG    DW      VGA_SCREENSEG   ;VGA SCREEN SEGMENT
V_EGAWIDE       DW      EGA_WIDE        ;EGA SCREEN WIDTH
V_EGADEEP       DW      EGA_DEEP        ;EGA SCREEN DEPTH
V_EGABYTES      DW      EGA_BYTES       ;EGA SCREEN BYTES
V_EGASCRNSEG    DW      EGA_SCREENSEG   ;EGA SCREEN SEGMENT
V_MONOWIDE      DW      MONO_WIDE       ;MONO SCREEN WIDTH
V_MONODEEP      DW      MONO_DEEP       ;MONO SCREEN DEPTH
V_MONOBYTES     DW      MONO_BYTES      ;BYTE WIDTH ON MONOCHROME SCREEN
V_MONOSCRNSEG   DW      MONO_SCREENSEG  ;MONOCHROME SCREEN SEGMENT
                DW      VERSION
                DW      SUBVERSION
                DB      'ATI XL 640x480  v2.1 ',0
DISPATCH        ENDP

VGAMODETABLE    DW      320,200
                DW      640,400
                DW      -1,-1

EGAMODETABLE    DW      -1,-1

MONOMODETABLE   DW      -1,-1


;THIS FUNCTION SELECTS THE RGB DISPLAY MODE
RGB_ON          PROC    NEAR
                PUSH    BP
                PUSH    DS
                PUSH    ES

                MOV     CX,480                          ;DEPTH OF SCREEN
```

10-13 Continued.

```
            SUB       BX,BX                           ;ZERO LINE COUNTER
            MOV       SI,OFFSET SCREENTABLE           ;POINT TO TABLE

RGBON_1:    PUSH      CX
            MOV       AX,1280                         ;WIDTH OF SCREEEN
            MUL       BX                              ;TIMES LINE NUMBER

            AND       DX,00FFH

            CMP       AX,(0FFFEH-1280)     ;SEE IF WE WILL
            JB        RGBON_2

            MOV       DH,0FFH

RGBON_2:    MOV       CS:[SI],AX                      ;SAVE THE VALUES
            MOV       CS:[SI+2],DX                    ;IN OUR LOOKUP TABLE
            ADD       SI,4                            ;AND POINT TO THE
            INC       BX                              ;NEXT LINE AND
            POP       CX                              ;ENTRY
            LOOP      RGBON_1

            MOV       AX,0072H
            INT       10H

            MOV       AX,0C000H
            MOV       ES,AX
            MOV       AX,ES:[0010H]
            MOV       CS:[ATIREG],AX

            MOV       CS:[BANK],0000H

            POP       ES
            POP       DS
            POP       BP
            RETF
RGB_ON      ENDP

;THIS FUNCTION TURNS OFF THE RGB MODE
RGB_OFF       PROC      NEAR
              PUSH      BP
              PUSH      DS
              PUSH      ES

              MOV       AX,1200H
              MOV       BX,0031H
              INT       10H

              MOV       AX,0003H
              INT       10H

              POP       ES
              POP       DS
```

10-13 Continued.

```
                POP     BP
                RETF
RGB_OFF         ENDP


;THIS FUNCTION DISPLAYS ONE RGB LINE
RGB_LINE        PROC    NEAR
                PUSH    BP
                MOV     BP,SP
                PUSH    DS
                PUSH    ES

                MOV     SI,[BP + _AOFF + 0]
                MOV     DS,[BP + _AOFF + 2]

                MOV     CX,[BP + _AOFF + 4]
                CMP     CX,640
                JL      RGBLINE_1

                MOV     CX,640

RGBLINE_1:      MOV     AX,RGB_SCREENSEG
                MOV     ES,AX

                MOV     BX,[BP + _AOFF + 6]
                SHL     BX,1
                SHL     BX,1
                MOV     DI,CS:[SCREENTABLE + BX]
                MOV     AX,CS:[SCREENTABLE + 2 + BX]

                CLD

                CALL    VGA_BANK
                CMP     AH,00H
                JNE     RGBLINE_3

RGBLINE_2:      PUSH    CX
                RGB2AX
                STOSW
                POP     CX
                LOOP    RGBLINE_2

                JMP     RGBLINE_X

RGBLINE_3:      PUSH    CX
                RGB2AX
                STOSW
                CMP     DI,0000H
                JNE     RGBLINE_4

                MOV     AX,CS:[BANK]
                INC     AX
                CALL    VGA_BANK
```

10-13 Continued.

```
RGBLINE_4:      POP     CX
                LOOP    RGBLINE_3

RGBLINE_X:      POP     ES
                POP     DS
                POP     BP
                RETF
RGB_LINE        ENDP

;THIS ROUTINE SELECTS THE VGA 256 COLOUR MODE
VGA_ON          PROC    NEAR
                PUSH    BP
                MOV     BP,SP
                PUSH    DS

                CMP     WORD PTR [BP + _AOFF + 0],320
                JG      EXT_ON
                CMP     WORD PTR [BP + _AOFF + 2],200
                JG      EXT_ON

                MOV     CS:[V_VGAWIDE],320
                MOV     CS:[V_VGADEEP],200
                MOV     CX,200                  ;DEPTH OF SCREEN
                SUB     DX,DX
                MOV     SI,OFFSET SCREENTABLE

VGA_ON1:        PUSH    DX
                MOV     AX,320                  ;WIDTH OF SCREEEN
                MUL     DX
                MOV     CS:[SI],AX
                ADD     SI,2
                POP     DX
                INC     DX
                LOOP    VGA_ON1

                MOV     AX,0013H
                INT     10H

                JMP     EXT_EXIT

EXT_ON:         MOV     CS:[V_VGAWIDE],640
                MOV     CS:[V_VGADEEP],400

                MOV     CX,400                  ;DEPTH OF SCREEN
                SUB     BX,BX                   ;ZERO LINE COUNTER
                MOV     SI,OFFSET SCREENTABLE   ;POINT TO TABLE

EXT_1:          PUSH    CX
                MOV     AX,640                  ;WIDTH OF SCREEEN
                MUL     BX                      ;TIMES LINE NUMBER

                AND     DX,00FFH
```

10-13 Continued.

```
            CMP     AX,(0FFFEH-640)                  ;SEE IF WE WILL
            JB      EXT_2

            MOV     DH,0FFH

EXT_2:      MOV     CS:[SI],AX                       ;SAVE THE VALUES
            MOV     CS:[SI+2],DX                     ;IN OUR LOOKUP TABLE
            ADD     SI,4                             ;AND POINT TO THE
            INC     BX                               ;NEXT LINE AND
            POP     CX                               ;ENTRY
            LOOP    EXT_1

            MOV     AX,0061H
            INT     10H

            MOV     AX,0C000H
            MOV     ES,AX
            MOV     AX,ES:[0010H]
            MOV     CS:[ATIREG],AX

            MOV     CS:[BANK],0000H

EXT_EXIT:   POP     DS
            POP     BP
            RETF
VGA_ON      ENDP

;THIS ROUTINE DISPLAYS A VGA LINE
VGA_LINE    PROC    NEAR
            PUSH    BP
            MOV     BP,SP

            PUSH    DS
            PUSH    ES

            CMP     CS:[V_VGAWIDE],320
            JNE     EXTSHOW

            MOV     SI,[BP + _AOFF + 0]     ;OFFSET OF SOURCE
            MOV     DS,[BP + _AOFF + 2]     ;SEGMENT OF SOURCE

            MOV     BX,[BP + _AOFF + 6]     ;GET LINE NUMBER
            CMP     BX,200
            JG      VGASHOW2

            SHL     BX,1
            MOV     DI,CS:[SCREENTABLE+BX]

            CLD
            MOV     CX,[BP + _AOFF + 4]     ;LENGTH OF MOVE IN BYTES
            CMP     CX,0
            JE      VGASHOW2
```

10-13 Continued.

```
                     CMP     CX,320
                     JL      VGASHOW1

                     MOV     CX,320

VGASHOW1:            MOV     AX,0A000H
                     MOV     ES,AX
           REPNE     MOVSB

VGASHOW2:            JMP     EXTSHOWX

EXTSHOW:             CMP     WORD PTR [BP + _AOFF + 6],400
                     JL      EXTSHOW1
                     JMP     EXTSHOWX

EXTSHOW1:            MOV     SI,[BP + _AOFF + 0]      ;OFFSET OF SOURCE
                     MOV     DS,[BP + _AOFF + 2]      ;SEGMENT OF SOURCE
                     MOV     CX,[BP + _AOFF + 4]      ;LENGTH OF MOVE IN BYTES

                     CMP     CX,640                   ;IS IT TOO LONG?
                     JL      EXTSHOW2

                     MOV     CX,640

EXTSHOW2:            MOV     BX,[BP + _AOFF + 6]      ;GET INDEX INTO LINE TABLE
                     SHL     BX,1
                     SHL     BX,1

                     MOV     DI,CS:[SCREENTABLE + BX]
                     MOV     AX,CS:[SCREENTABLE + 2 + BX]

                     CALL    VGA_BANK

                     CMP     AH,00H
                     JNE     EXTSHOW3

                     MOV     AX,0A000H                ;POINT TO VIDEO BUFFER
                     MOV     ES,AX                    ;WITH ES

                     CLD
           REPNE     MOVSB                            ;MOVE IN THE LINE DATA
                     JMP     EXTSHOWX

EXTSHOW3:            MOV     AX,0A000H                ;POINT TO VIDEO BUFFER
                     MOV     ES,AX                    ;WITH ES

                     PUSH    CX
                     MOV     AX,DI
                     MOV     CX,0000H
                     SUB     CX,AX
                     MOV     BX,CX
```

10-13 Continued.

```
                CMP     CX,[BP + _AOFF + 4]      ;ARE THERE ENOUGH BYTES LEFT?
                JL      EXTSHOW4                 ;IF SO, GO JUMP THE FRAME

                MOV     CX,[BP + _AOFF + 4]
                CLD
        REPNE   MOVSB                            ;MOVE IN THE LINE DATA

                POP     CX
                JMP     EXTSHOWX


EXTSHOW4:       CLD
        REPNE   MOVSB                                    ;MOVE IN THE LINE DATA

                POP     CX
                SUB     CX,BX
                CMP     CX,0
                JLE     EXTSHOWX

                MOV     BX,[BP + _AOFF + 6]      ;GET INDEX INTO LINE TABLE
                SHL     BX,1
                SHL     BX,1
                MOV     AX,CS:[SCREENTABLE + 2 + BX]
                INC     AX

                CALL    VGA_BANK

                MOV     AX,0A000H
                MOV     ES,AX

                MOV     DI,0

                CLD
        REPNE   MOVSB                                    ;MOVE IN THE LINE DATA

EXTSHOWX:       POP     ES
                POP     DS
                POP     BP
                RETF
VGA_LINE        ENDP

;THIS ROUTINE DESELECTS THE VGA 256 COLOUR MODE
VGA_OFF         PROC    NEAR
                MOV     AX,1200H
                MOV     BX,0031H
                INT     10H

                MOV     AX,0003H
                INT     10H
                RETF
VGA_OFF         ENDP


VGA_BANK        PROC    NEAR
```

10-13 Continued.

```
                        CMP     AX,CS:[BANK]
                        JNE     VGABANK1
                        RET

VGABANK1:               MOV     CS:[BANK],AX

                        PUSH    AX
                        PUSH    CX
                        PUSH    DX

                        MOV     DX,CS:[ATIREG]

                        MOV     CX,AX
                        CLI
                        MOV     AL,0B2H
                        OUT     DX,AL
                        INC     DL

                        IN      AL,DX
                        MOV     AH,AL
                        AND     AH,0E1H
                        SHL     CL,1
                        OR      AH,CL
                        MOV     AL,0B2H
                        DEC     DL
                        OUT     DX,AX
                        STI

                        POP     DX
                        POP     CX
                        POP     AX

                        RET
VGA_BANK                ENDP

;THIS ROUTINE SETS THE VGA PALETTE
VGA_PALETTE             PROC    NEAR
                        PUSH    BP
                        MOV     BP,SP
                        PUSH    DS
                        PUSH    ES
                        MOV     AX,CS
                        MOV     ES,AX

                        MOV     SI,[BP + _AOFF + 0]     ;OFFSET OF SOURCE
                        MOV     DS,[BP + _AOFF + 2]     ;SEGMENT OF SOURCE

                        MOV     CX,[BP + _AOFF + 4]     ;NUMBER OF COLOURS

                        CMP     CX,0                    ;CHECK FOR NASTIES
                        JG      GVP0
                        JMP     GVPX
```

10-13 Continued.

```
GVP0:        MOV      DX,03C6H
             MOV      AL,0FFH
             OUT      DX,AL

             MOV      BX,0

GVP1:        PUSH     CX
             MOV      DX,03C8H
             MOV      AL,BL
             INC      BX
             OUT      DX,AL

             INC      DX

             LODSB
             SHR      AL,1
             SHR      AL,1
             OUT      DX,AL

             LODSB
             SHR      AL,1
             SHR      AL,1
             OUT      DX,AL

             LODSB
             SHR      AL,1
             SHR      AL,1
             OUT      DX,AL

             POP      CX
             LOOP     GVP1

GVPX:        POP      ES
             POP      DS
             POP      BP
             RETF
VGA_PALETTE  ENDP

;THIS ROUTINE SETS THE VGA OVERSCAN.
VGA_OVERSCAN PROC     NEAR
             PUSH     BP
             MOV      BP,SP
             MOV      AX,1001H
             MOV      BX,[BP + _AOFF + 0]
             XCHG     BH,BL
             INT      10H
             POP      BP
             RETF
VGA_OVERSCAN ENDP

;THIS ROUTINE SELECTS THE EGA 16 COLOUR MODE
EGA_ON       PROC     NEAR
```

10-13 Continued.

```
                    PUSH        BP
                    MOV         BP,SP
                    PUSH        DS

EGA480:             MOV         CS:[V_EGAWIDE],640
                    MOV         CS:[V_EGADEEP],480
                    MOV         CS:[V_EGABYTES],80

                    MOV         CX,480          ;DEPTH OF SCREEN
                    SUB         DX,DX
                    MOV         SI,OFFSET SCREENTABLE

EGA_ON2:            PUSH        DX
                    MOV         AX,80           ;WIDTH OF SCREEEN
                    MUL         DX
                    MOV         CS:[SI],AX
                    ADD         SI,2
                    POP         DX
                    INC         DX
                    LOOP        EGA_ON2

                    MOV         AX,0012H
                    INT         10H

                    POP         DS
                    POP         BP
                    RETF
EGA_ON              ENDP

;THIS ROUTINE DISPLAYS AN EGA LINE
;THE FIRST ARGUMENT ON THE STACK (2 WORDS) IS A FAR POINTER TO
;THE LINE. THE SECOND ARGUMENT IS THE LENGTH OF THE LINE IN BYTES
EGA_LINE            PROC        NEAR
                    PUSH        BP
                    MOV         BP,SP
                    PUSH        DS
                    PUSH        ES

                    MOV         SI,[BP + _AOFF + 0]     ;OFFSET OF SOURCE
                    MOV         DS,[BP + _AOFF + 2]     ;SEGMENT OF SOURCE
                    MOV         BX,[BP + _AOFF + 6]     ;GET LINE NUMBER
                    CMP         BX,CS:[V_EGADEEP]
                    JGE         SHOWEGAX

                    SHL         BX,1
                    MOV         DI,CS:[SCREENTABLE+BX]

                    MOV         AX,0A000H
                    MOV         ES,AX
                    MOV         BX,[BP + _AOFF + 4]     ;LENGTH OF MOVE IN BYTES

                    MOV         CX,BX
```

10-13 Continued.

```
                EGAPLANE         1
                CLD
                PUSH     DI
        REPNE   MOVSB
                POP      DI

                MOV      CX,BX
                EGAPLANE         2
                PUSH     DI
        REPNE   MOVSB
                POP      DI

                MOV      CX,BX
                EGAPLANE         4
                PUSH     DI
        REPNE   MOVSB
                POP      DI

                MOV      CX,BX
                EGAPLANE         8
                PUSH     DI
        REPNE   MOVSB
                POP      DI
                EGAPLANE         0FH


SHOWEGAX:       POP      ES
                POP      DS
                POP      BP
                RETF
EGA_LINE        ENDP

;THIS ROUTINE SETS THE EGA PALETTE
;THE FIRST ARGUMENT ON THE STACK IS A FAR POINTER TO
;THE PALETTE DATA. THE SECOND ARGUMENT IS THE NUMBER OF COLOURS.
EGA_PALETTE     PROC     NEAR
                PUSH     BP
                MOV      BP,SP
                PUSH     DS
                PUSH     ES

                MOV      SI,[BP + _AOFF + 6]     ;OFFSET OF SOURCE
                MOV      DS,[BP + _AOFF + 8]     ;SEGMENT OF SOURCE

                MOV      CX,[BP + _AOFF + 4]     ;NUMBER OF COLOURS
                CMP      CX,16
                JLE      EGA_PALETTE1
                MOV      CX,16

EGA_PALETTE1:   PUSH     CX
                MOV      BX,0000H

EGA_PALETTE2:   PUSH     CX
```

10-13 Continued.

```
                              LODSB
                              SHR       AL,1
                              SHR       AL,1
                              MOV       DH,AL
                              LODSB
                              SHR       AL,1
                              SHR       AL,1
                              MOV       CH,AL
                              LODSB
                              SHR       AL,1
                              SHR       AL,1
                              MOV       CL,AL
                              MOV       AX,1010H
                              INT       10H
                              INC       BX
                              POP       CX
                              LOOP      EGA_PALETTE2

                              POP       CX
                              MOV       BX,0000H

        EGA_PALETTE3:         PUSH      CX
                              MOV       AX,1000H
                              INT       10H
                              ADD       BX,0101H
                              POP       CX
                              LOOP      EGA_PALETTE3

                              POP       ES
                              POP       DS
                              POP       BP
                              RETF
        EGA_PALETTE           ENDP

        ;THIS ROUTINE DESELECTS THE EGA 16 COLOUR MODE
        EGA_OFF               PROC      NEAR
                              MOV       AX,0003H
                              INT       10H
                              RETF
        EGA_OFF               ENDP

        ;THIS ROUTINE SELECTS THE 2 COLOUR MODE
        MONO_ON               PROC      NEAR
                              PUSH      BP
                              MOV       BP,SP
                              PUSH      DS
                              PUSH      ES

                              MOV       CS:[V_MONOWIDE],640
                              MOV       CS:[V_MONODEEP],480
                              MOV       CS:[V_MONOBYTES],80
```

10-13 Continued.

```
                    MOV     AX,0012H
                    INT     10H

                    MOV     CX,480
                    SUB     DX,DX
                    MOV     SI,OFFSET SCREENTABLE

MONO_ON1:           PUSH    DX
                    MOV     AX,80
                    MUL     DX
                    MOV     CS:[SI],AX
                    ADD     SI,2
                    POP     DX
                    INC     DX
                    LOOP    MONO_ON1

                    POP     ES
                    POP     DS
                    POP     BP
                    SUB     AX,AX
                    RETF
MONO_ON             ENDP

;THIS FUNCTION PERFORMS VARIOUS GRAPHIC OPERATIONS
;        ARGUMENTS           -       FUNCTION CODE
;                            -       VARIABLE
;
;        FUNCTIONS           -       0       RETURN SCREEN SEG
;                            -       1       RETURN OFFSET TO SCREEN TABLE
;                            -       2       RETURN MONOCHROME SCREEN WIDTH
;                            -       3       RETURN MONOCHROME SCREEN DEPTH
;                            -       4       INVERT FRAME RECT - ARGS ON STACK
;                            -       5       RETURN OFFSET OF VGAMODETABLE
;                            -       6       RETURN OFFSET OF EGAMODETABLE
;                            -       7       RETURN OFFSET OF MONOMODETABLE
;                            -       8       RETURN OFFSET OF RGBMODETABLE
;
MONO_FUNCTIONS PROC NEAR
                    PUSH    BP
                    MOV     BP,SP
                    PUSH    DS
                    PUSH    ES

                    CMP     WORD PTR [BP + _AOFF + 0],0000H
                    JNE     MF1

                    MOV     AX,MONO_SCREENSEG
                    JMP     MF_EXIT

MF1:                CMP     WORD PTR [BP + _AOFF + 0],0001H
                    JNE     MF2
```

10-13 Continued.

```
                        MOV       AX,OFFSET SCREENTABLE-8
                        JMP       MF_EXIT

MF2:                    CMP       WORD PTR [BP + _AOFF + 0],0002H
                        JNE       MF3

                        MOV       AX,MONO_WIDE
                        JMP       MF_EXIT

MF3:                    CMP       WORD PTR [BP + _AOFF + 0],0003H
                        JNE       MF4

                        MOV       AX,MONO_DEEP
                        JMP       MF_EXIT

MF4:                    CMP       WORD PTR [BP + _AOFF + 0],0004H
                        JE        MF5
                        JMP       MF6

MF5:                    MOV       AX,MONO_SCREENSEG
                        MOV       ES,AX

                        MOV       BX,[BP + _AOFF + 4]      ;GET TOP
                        SHL       BX,1
                        MOV       DI,CS:[SCREENTABLE+BX]

                        MOV       BX,[BP + _AOFF + 2]      ;GET LEFT
                        MOV       CX,[BP + _AOFF + 6]      ;GET RIGHT
                        SUB       CX,BX

MF5A:                   PUSH      BX
                        AND       BX,0007H
                        MOV       AL,CS:[MASKTABLE+BX]
                        POP       BX

                        PUSH      BX
                        SHR       BX,1
                        SHR       BX,1
                        SHR       BX,1
                        XOR       ES:[DI+BX],AL
                        POP       BX
                        INC       BX
                        LOOP      MF5A

                        MOV       BX,[BP + _AOFF + 4]      ;GET TOP
                        INC       BX
                        MOV       CX,[BP + _AOFF + 8]      ;GET BOTTOM
                        DEC       CX
                        SUB       CX,BX

MF5B:                   PUSH      BX
```

10-13 Continued.

```
        SHL     BX,1
        MOV     DI,CS:[SCREENTABLE+BX]
        MOV     BX,[BP + _AOFF + 2]      ;GET LEFT
        PUSH    BX
        AND     BX,0007H
        MOV     AL,CS:[MASKTABLE+BX]
        POP     BX
        PUSH    BX

        SHR     BX,1
        SHR     BX,1
        SHR     BX,1
        XOR     ES:[DI+BX],AL
        POP     BX
        MOV     BX,[BP + _AOFF + 6]      ;GET RIGHT
        DEC     BX
        PUSH    BX
        AND     BX,0007H
        MOV     AL,CS:[MASKTABLE+BX]
        POP     BX
        PUSH    BX
        SHR     BX,1
        SHR     BX,1
        SHR     BX,1
        XOR     ES:[DI+BX],AL
        POP     BX
        POP     BX
        INC     BX
        LOOP    MF5B

        MOV     BX,[BP + _AOFF + 8]      ;GET BOTTOM
        DEC     BX
        SHL     BX,1
        MOV     DI,CS:[SCREENTABLE+BX]

        MOV     BX,[BP + _AOFF + 2]      ;GET LEFT
        MOV     CX,[BP + _AOFF + 6]      ;GET RIGHT
        SUB     CX,BX

MF5D:   PUSH    BX
        AND     BX,0007H
        MOV     AL,CS:[MASKTABLE+BX]
        POP     BX

        PUSH    BX
        SHR     BX,1
        SHR     BX,1
        SHR     BX,1
        XOR     ES:[DI+BX],AL
        POP     BX
        INC     BX
        LOOP    MF5D
```

10-13 Continued.

```
MF6:            CMP     WORD PTR [BP + _AOFF + 0],0005H
                JNE     MF7

                MOV     AX,OFFSET VGAMODETABLE
                JMP     MF_EXIT

MF7:            CMP     WORD PTR [BP + _AOFF + 0],0006H
                JNE     MF8

                MOV     AX,OFFSET EGAMODETABLE
                JMP     MF_EXIT

MF8:            CMP     WORD PTR [BP + _AOFF + 0],0007H
                JNE     MF_EXIT

                MOV     AX,OFFSET MONOMODETABLE
                JMP     MF_EXIT

MF_EXIT:        POP     ES
                POP     DS
                POP     BP
                RETF
MONO_FUNCTIONS  ENDP

MASKTABLE       DB      80H,40H,20H,10H,08H,04H,02H,01H

MONO_LINE       PROC    NEAR
                PUSH    BP
                MOV     BP,SP

                PUSH    DS
                PUSH    ES

                MOV     AX,0A000H               ;POINT TO THE SCREEN
                MOV     ES,AX

                MOV     CX,[BP + _AOFF + 6]     ;GET THE WIDTH OF MOVE
                CMP     CX,CS:[V_MONOBYTES]
                JL      MONO_LINE1
                MOV     CX,CS:[V_MONOBYTES]

MONO_LINE1:     MOV     SI,[BP + _AOFF + 0]     ;OFFSET OF BITMAP
                MOV     DS,[BP + _AOFF + 2]     ;SEGMENT OF BITMAP
                MOV     BX,[BP + _AOFF + 4]     ;NUMBER OF LINE
                SHL     BX,1

                CLD                             ;CLEAR DIRECTION FLAG
                MOV     DI,CS:[SCREENTABLE + BX]
        REPNE   MOVSB                           ;DO THE MOVE

                POP     ES
                POP     DS
```

10-13 Continued.

```
                  POP      BP
                  RETF
MONO_LINE         ENDP

;THIS ROUTINE DESELECTS THE 2 COLOUR MODE
MONO_OFF          PROC     NEAR
                  MOV      AX,0003H
                  INT      10H
                  SUB      AX,AX
                  RETF
MONO_OFF          ENDP

;THIS IS A LINE START LOOKUP TABLE

SCREENTABLE       DW       960 DUP(?)          ;LINE START TABLE
BANK              DW       ?
ATIREG            DW       ?

CODE              ENDS
                  END
```

10-13 Continued.

The ATIXL.ASM driver adds pointers in the dispatch table to handle
the RGB functions and, of course, the code that they point to. The
RGB_ON function creates a screen table and sets up the screen mode, just
as with the other drivers in this chapter. The RGB_LINE function does
most of the work. It uses the RGB2AX macro to pack the 3-byte RGB pixels that are passed to it into 2-byte pixels in a format that the ATI XL hardware will like the look of. While this conversion does slow down the display
a bit, it's much quicker than it would seem, as all that's involved is some
bit shifting, something a PC's processor can do pretty quickly.

You'll note that the approach to dealing with lines that cross page
boundaries is different in RGB_LINE than it was in the VGA_LINE function discussed in the previous two drivers. Rather than work out the split
point, this function merely copies the words to the screen buffer until the
DI register hits 0, indicating the end of a page. It then changes pages and
copies in the rest of the line.

There's little point in using the ATI XL driver with READGIF2, in that
GIF files don't support RGB color at the moment. Figure 10-14 is the
source code for READPCX2, which allows you to display 24-bit PCX files
using the ATI XL driver from FIG. 10-13.

There's not much happening in READPCX2 that hasn't already
turned up in earlier programs. The PCX files are handled as they were in
chapter 8. Rather than converting them from planar lines to gray-scale
palette lines, they're converted into 24-bit color lines with 3 bytes per
pixel, which is the form that the driver expects.

As with READGIF2, the READPCX2 program uses direct calls to DOS
to allocate memory in order to provide itself with a portable way to load
screen drivers.

```
/*
        24 bit PCX reader - copyright (c) 1991
        Version using device independant screen drivers
        Alchemy Mindworks Inc.
*/

#include "stdio.h"
#include "dos.h"
#include "alloc.h"

/*                              uncomment this line if you
#include "memmangr.h"           will be linking in the memory manager
*/

#define GOOD_READ       0       /* return codes */
#define BAD_FILE        1
#define BAD_READ        2
#define MEMORY_ERROR    3
#define WRONG_BITS      4
#define NO_DRIVER       5

#define SCREENWIDE      320     /* mode 13 screen dimensions */
#define SCREENDEEP      200
#define STEP            32      /* size of a step when panning */

#define HOME            0x4700  /* cursor control codes */
#define CURSOR_UP       0x4800
#define CURSOR_LEFT     0x4b00
#define CURSOR_RIGHT    0x4d00
#define END             0x4f00
#define CURSOR_DOWN     0x5000

#define RGB_RED         0
#define RGB_GREEN       1
#define RGB_BLUE        2
#define RGB_SIZE        3

#define greyvalue(r,g,b)        (((r*30)/100) + ((g*59)/100) + ((b*11)/100))

typedef struct {
        int width,depth,bytes,bits;
        int (*setup)();
        int (*closedown)();
        } FILEINFO;

typedef struct {
        char manufacturer;
        char version;
        char encoding;
        char bits_per_pixel;
        int xmin,ymin;
        int xmax,ymax;
```

10-14 The source code for READPCX2.ASM.

```
                int hres;
                int vres;
                char palette[48];
                char reserved;
                char colour_planes;
                int bytes_per_line;
                int palette_type;
                char filler[58];
                } PCXHEAD;

typedef struct {
                int (*vga_on)();
                int (*vga_line)();
                int (*vga_off)();
                int (*vga_palette)();
                int (*vga_overscan)();
                int (*ega_on)();
                int (*ega_line)();
                int (*ega_off)();
                int (*ega_palette)();
                int (*mono_on)();
                int (*mono_functions)();
                int (*mono_line)();
                int (*mono_off)();
                int (*rgb_on)();
                int (*rgb_line)();
                int (*rgb_off)();
                int rgb_wide;
                int rgb_deep;
                int vga_wide;
                int vga_deep;
                int vga_screenseg;
                int ega_wide;
                int ega_deep;
                int ega_bytes;
                int ega_screenseg;
                int mono_wide;
                int mono_deep;
                int mono_bytes;
                int mono_screenseg;
                int driver_version;
                int driver_subversion;
                char name[25];
                } GRAFDRIVER;

GRAFDRIVER *loadDriver(char *s);
char *farPtr(char *p,long l);
char *getline(unsigned int n);
int dosetup(FILEINFO *fi);
int doclosedown(FILEINFO *fi);
int putline(char *p,unsigned int n);
char *dosalloc(unsigned int n);
```

10-14 Continued.

```
        GRAFDRIVER *gd;
        FILEINFO fi;
        char *buffer=NULL;

        main(argc,argv)
                int argc;
                char *argv[];
        {
                FILE *fp;
                static char results[6][16] = {  "Ok",
                                                "Bad file",
                                                "Bad read",
                                                "Memory error",
                                                "Too few colours",
                                                "No driver mode"
                                                };

                char path[80];
                int r;

                if(argc > 2) {
                        strmfe(path,argv[2],"DRV");
                        if((gd=loadDriver(path))== NULL) {
                                printf("Error loading driver %s\n",path);
                                exit(1);
                        }
                        strmfe(path,argv[1],"PCX");
                        strupr(path);
                        if((fp = fopen(path,"rb")) != NULL) {
                                fi.setup=dosetup;
                                fi.closedown=doclosedown;
                                r=unpackpcx(fp,&fi);
                                printf("\%s",results[r]);
                                fclose(fp);
                        } else printf("Error opening %s",path);
                } else puts("Argument:       path to a PCX file");

        }

        /* unpack an PCX file */
        unpackpcx(fp,fi)
                FILE *fp;
                FILEINFO *fi;
        {
                PCXHEAD pcx;
                char *p,*pr;
                int i,j,bytes;

                if(fread((char *)&pcx,1,sizeof(PCXHEAD),fp) == sizeof(PCXHEAD) &&
                    pcx.manufacturer==10) {
                        if(pcx.bits_per_pixel==8 && pcx.colour_planes==3) {
                                bytes=pcx.bytes_per_line;
                                fi->width=pcx.xmax-pcx.xmin+1;
                                fi->depth=pcx.ymax-pcx.ymin+1;
```

10-14   Continued.

```
                    fi->bytes=bytes*RGB_SIZE;

                    if((p=dosalloc(fi->bytes)) == NULL) return(MEMORY_ERROR);

                    if((pr=dosalloc(fi->bytes)) == NULL) {
                            dosfree(p);
                            return(MEMORY_ERROR);
                    }

                    if((fi->setup)(fi) != GOOD_READ) {
                            dosfree(pr);
                            dosfree(p);
                            return(MEMORY_ERROR);
                    }

                    for(i=0;i<fi->depth;++i) {
                            for(j=0;j<RGB_SIZE;++j) {
                                    if(readpcxline(p+(j*bytes),fp,bytes) != bytes) {
                                            freebuffer();
                                            dosfree(pr);
                                            dosfree(p);
                                            return(BAD_READ);
                                    }
                            }

                            for(j=0;j<fi->width;++j) {
                                    pr[j*RGB_SIZE+RGB_RED]=p[j];
                                    pr[j*RGB_SIZE+RGB_GREEN]=p[RGB_GREEN*bytes+j];
                                    pr[j*RGB_SIZE+RGB_BLUE]=p[RGB_BLUE*bytes+j];
                            }
                            putline(pr,i);
                    }
                    (fi->closedown)(fi);
                    freebuffer();
                    dosfree(pr);
                    dosfree(p);
            } else return(WRONG_BITS);
    } else return(BAD_READ);
    return(GOOD_READ);
}

/* read and decode a PCX line into p */
readpcxline(p,fp,bytes)
        char *p;
        FILE *fp;
        int bytes;
{
        int n=0,c,i;

        do {
                c=fgetc(fp) & 0xff;
                if((c & 0xc0) == 0xc0) {
```

10-14 Continued.

```
                                        i=c & 0x3f;
                                        c=fgetc(fp);
                                        while(i--) p[n++]=c;
                        }
                        else p[n++]=c;
                } while(n < bytes);
                return(n);
        }


/* This function is called before an image is decompressed. It must
   allocate memory, put the display in graphic mode and so on. */
dosetup(fi)
        FILEINFO *fi;
{
        if(!getbuffer((long)fi->bytes*(long)fi->depth,fi->bytes,fi->depth))
            return(MEMORY_ERROR);

        if(gd->rgb_on==NULL) {
                freebuffer();
                return(NO_DRIVER);
        }
        (gd->rgb_on)(fi->width,fi->depth);

        return(GOOD_READ);
}


/* This function is called after an image has been unpacked. It must
   display the image and allocate memory. */
doclosedown(fi)
        FILEINFO *fi;
{
        int screenwide,screendeep;
        int c,i,n,x=0,y=0;

        screenwide=gd->rgb_wide;
        screendeep=gd->rgb_deep;
        if(fi->width > screenwide) n=screenwide;
        else n=fi->width;

        do {
                for(i=0;i<screendeep;++i) {
                        c=y+i;
                        if(c>=fi->depth) break;
                            (gd->rgb_line)(getline(y+i)+(x*RGB_SIZE),n,i);
                }
                c=GetKey();
                switch(c) {
                        case CURSOR_LEFT:
                                if((x-STEP) > 0) x-=STEP;
                                else x=0;
                                break;
                        case CURSOR_RIGHT:
```

10-14 Continued.

```
                        if((x+STEP+screenwide) < fi->width) x+=STEP;
                        else if(fi->width > screenwide)
                            x=fi->width-screenwide;
                        else x=0;
                        break;
                case CURSOR_UP:
                        if((y-STEP) > 0) y-=STEP;
                        else y=0;
                        break;
                case CURSOR_DOWN:
                        if((y+STEP+screendeep) < fi->depth) y+=STEP;
                        else if(fi->depth > screendeep)
                            y=fi->depth-screendeep;
                        else y=0;
                        break;
                case HOME:
                        x=y=0;
                        break;
                case END:
                        if(fi->width > screenwide)
                            x=fi->width-screenwide;
                        else x=0;
                        if(fi->depth > screendeep)
                            y=fi->depth-screendeep;
                        else y=0;
                        break;
        }
} while(c != 27);

freebuffer();

(gd->rgb_off)();

return(GOOD_READ);

}

/* get one extended key code */
GetKey()
{
        int c;

        c = getch();
        if(!(c & 0x00ff)) c = getch() << 8;
        return(c);
}

/* make file name with specific extension */
strmfe(new,old,ext)
        char *new,*old,*ext;
{
        while(*old != 0 && *old != '.') *new++=*old++;
```

10-14 Continued.

```
            *new++='.';
            while(*ext) *new++=*ext++;
            *new=0;
    }

GRAFDRIVER *loadDriver(s)              /* load an external graphics driver */
        char *s;
{
        GRAFDRIVER *gd;
        char *grafDriver=NULL;
        FILE *fp;
        long l;
        char b[8];
        unsigned int seg;

        if((fp=fopen(s,"rb")) != NULL) {
                fseek(fp,0L,SEEK_END);
                l=ftell(fp);
                rewind(fp);

                fread(b,1,8,fp);
                if(!memcmp(b,"ALCHDRV2",8)) {
                        l-=8L;
                        if(l < 0xffffL &&
                           (grafDriver=dosalloc((unsigned int)l)) != NULL) {
                                if(fread(grafDriver,1,(unsigned int)l,fp)==
                                   (unsigned int)l) {
                                        gd=(GRAFDRIVER *)grafDriver;
                                        seg=FP_SEG(grafDriver);

                                        if(gd->vga_on != NULL) {
                                                grafDriver[2]=seg;
                                                grafDriver[3]=(seg >> 8);
                                                grafDriver[6]=seg;
                                                grafDriver[7]=(seg >> 8);
                                                grafDriver[10]=seg;
                                                grafDriver[11]=(seg >> 8);
                                                grafDriver[14]=seg;
                                                grafDriver[15]=(seg >> 8);
                                                grafDriver[18]=seg;
                                                grafDriver[19]=(seg >> 8);
                                        }
                                        if(gd->ega_on != NULL) {
                                                grafDriver[22]=seg;
                                                grafDriver[23]=(seg >> 8);
                                                grafDriver[26]=seg;
                                                grafDriver[27]=(seg >> 8);
                                                grafDriver[30]=seg;
                                                grafDriver[31]=(seg >> 8);
                                                grafDriver[34]=seg;
                                                grafDriver[35]=(seg >> 8);
                                        }
```

10-14 Continued.

```
                                    if(gd->mono_on != NULL) {
                                            grafDriver[38]=seg;
                                            grafDriver[39]=(seg >> 8);
                                            grafDriver[42]=seg;
                                            grafDriver[43]=(seg >> 8);
                                            grafDriver[46]=seg;
                                            grafDriver[47]=(seg >> 8);
                                            grafDriver[50]=seg;
                                            grafDriver[51]=(seg >> 8);
                                    }

                                    if(gd->rgb_on != NULL) {
                                            grafDriver[54]=seg;
                                            grafDriver[55]=(seg >> 8);
                                            grafDriver[58]=seg;
                                            grafDriver[59]=(seg >> 8);
                                            grafDriver[62]=seg;
                                            grafDriver[63]=(seg >> 8);
                                    }
                            }
                            else {
                                    dosfree(grafDriver);
                                    grafDriver=NULL;
                            }
                    }
                }
                fclose(fp);
        }
        return((GRAFDRIVER *)grafDriver);
}


/* if you don't use in the memory manager, these functions
   will stand in for it */

#if !MEMMANGR

char *dosalloc(n)
        unsigned int n;
{
        union REGS r;

        n+=8;
        r.x.ax=0x4800;
        r.x.bx=1+(n>>4);
        int86(0x21,&r,&r);
        if(r.x.cflag) return(NULL);
        else return(MK_FP(r.x.ax,0x0008));
}

dosfree(p)
        char *p;
```

10-14 Continued.

```
{
        union REGS r;
        struct SREGS sr;

        r.x.ax=0x4900;
        sr.es=FP_SEG(p);
        int86x(0x21,&r,&r,&sr);
}

/* return a far pointer plus a long integer */
char *farPtr(p,l)
        char *p;
        long l;
{
        unsigned int seg,off;

        seg = FP_SEG(p);
        off = FP_OFF(p);
        seg += (off / 16);
        off &= 0x000f;
        off += (unsigned int)(l & 0x000fL);
        seg += (l / 16L);
        p = MK_FP(seg,off);
        return(p);
}

/* save one line to memory */
putline(p,n)
        char *p;
        unsigned int n;
{
        if(n >= 0 && n < fi.depth)
            memcpy(farPtr(buffer,(long)n*(long)fi.bytes),p,fi.bytes);
}

/* get one line from memory */
char *getline(n)
        unsigned int n;
{
        return(farPtr(buffer,(long)n*(long)fi.bytes));
}

#pragma warn -par
getbuffer(n,bytes,lines)
        unsigned long n;
        int bytes,lines;
{
        union REGS r;

        r.x.ax=0x4800;
        r.x.bx=1+(int)(n>>4);
        int86(0x21,&r,&r);
```

10-14 Continued.

```
            if(r.x.cflag) return(0);
            else {
                    buffer=MK_FP(r.x.ax,0x0000);
                    return(1);
            }
    }

freebuffer()
{
        union REGS r;
        struct SREGS sr;

        if(buffer != NULL) {
                r.x.ax=0x4900;
                sr.es=FP_SEG(buffer);
                int86x(0x21,&r,&r,&sr);
        }
        buffer=NULL;
}
#endif /* !MEMMANGR */
```

10-14 Continued.

In order to view HUMBIRD.PCX, one of the example files that comes on the disk set for this book, type the following command line.

        READPCX2 HUMBIRD.PCX ATIXL.DRV

The display should look something like the one in FIG. 10-15, although it will be somewhat more colorful.

The hummingbird picture has the dimensions 479×318 pixels, for a total unpacked size of 457K. This should fit in normal DOS memory along with READPCX2 if you have nothing else taking up any space. It's a tight squeeze under DOS 3, but DOS 5 makes it a bit easier to manage. You certainly will not be able to view it using conventional memory if you're running from within the Turbo C integrated development environment or shelled out of another application.

A Paradise True Color screen driver

The latest generation of high-end Paradise cards, based on the D series of Western Digital chips, has support for a RAMDAC, a true color digital-to-analog converter with 15-bit color support. If you have a Paradise card with 1Mb of memory and a RAMDAC on board, you can look at true color images in 640×480 or 800×600 pixel resolution. Like the conventional palette-driven Paradise super VGA modes, the true color modes can switch pages at the ends of lines, making the code to drive one both easier to write and faster to run.

The structure of the screen data for the Paradise true color modes is identical to that of the ATI-XL driver discussed in the previous section.

10-15 The hummingbird revisited, as it looks in READPCX2 using the ATIXL.DRV driver.

Figure 10-16 shows the code for PARA-15.ASM—PARADISE.ASM driver from earlier in this chapter with the addition of code to handle the 640×480 pixel true color mode.

You can use the PARA-15 driver with READPCX2, discussed earlier. To look at the hummingbird 24-bit PCX file, you would run it like this:

READPCX2 HUMBIRD.PCX PARA-15.DRV

You can add the 800×600 pixel true color mode to PARA-15.ASM pretty effortlessly. The mode number for the 640×480 pixel true color mode is 62H. Change this to 63H for the 800×600 pixel mode and change the screen dimensions in the code accordingly.

```
;
;               Graphic Workshop Paradise screen driver
;               Copyright (C) 1989, 1991 Alchemy Mindworks Inc.
;               Includes 15-bit true colour support
;


VERSION         EQU     2               ;VERSION NUMBER
SUBVERSION      EQU     1               ;SUBVERSION NUMBER

_AOFF           EQU     6               ;STACK OFFSET

RGB_WIDE        EQU     640
```

10-16 The source code for PARA-15.ASM.

```
RGB_DEEP          EQU     480
RGB_SCREENSEG     EQU     0A000H
VGA_WIDE          EQU     640             ;WIDTH OF VGA SCREEN IN PIXELS
VGA_DEEP          EQU     400             ;DEPTH OF VGA SCREEN IN PIXELS
VGA_SCREENSEG     EQU     0A000H          ;SEGMENT OF VGA SCREEN
EGA_WIDE          EQU     640             ;WIDTH OF EGA SCREEN IN PIXELS
EGA_DEEP          EQU     480             ;DEPTH OF EGA SCREEN IN PIXELS
EGA_BYTES         EQU     80              ;WIDTH OF EGA SCREEN IN BYTES
EGA_SCREENSEG     EQU     0A000H          ;SEGMENT OF EGA SCREEN
MONO_WIDE         EQU     800             ;WIDTH OF MONO SCREEN IN PIXELS
MONO_DEEP         EQU     600             ;DEPTH OF MONO SCREEN IN PIXELS
MONO_BYTES        EQU     80              ;WIDTH OF MONO SCREEN IN BYTES
MONO_SCREENSEG    EQU     0A000H          ;SEGMENT OF MONO SCREEN

PROA_REG          EQU     9               ;PROA REGISTER

;THIS MACRO COMPRESSES AN RGB TRIPLET AT DS:SI INTO A 15-BIT WORD IN AX
RGB2AX            MACRO
                  MOV     DX,0000H
                  LODSB

                  MOV     CL,3
                  SHR     AL,CL
                  AND     AX,001FH
                  MOV     CL,10
                  SHL     AX,CL

                  OR      DX,AX

                  LODSB

                  MOV     CL,3
                  SHR     AL,CL
                  AND     AX,001FH
                  MOV     CL,5
                  SHL     AX,CL

                  OR      DX,AX
                  LODSB

                  MOV     CL,3
                  SHR     AL,CL
                  AND     AX,001FH
                  OR      DX,AX
                  MOV     AX,DX
                  ENDM

;THIS MACRO SELECTS AN EGA PLANE
EGAPLANE          MACRO   ARG1
                  MOV     AL,2
                  MOV     DX,03C4H
                  OUT     DX,AL
```

10-16 Continued.

```
                        INC     DX
                        MOV     AL,ARG1
                        OUT     DX,AL
                        ENDM

;SET THE PROA REGISTER TO THE VALUE IN AL
SET_PROA        MACRO
                        PUSH    AX
                        MOV     DX,03CEH
                        MOV     AX,050FH
                        OUT     DX,AX
                        POP     AX
                        MOV     AH,AL
                        MOV     AL,PROA_REG
                        OUT     DX,AX
                        MOV     AX,000FH
                        OUT     DX,AX
                        ENDM

CODE            SEGMENT PARA PUBLIC 'CODE'
                ASSUME  CS:CODE

                ORG     0000H           ;ORIGIN FOR LOADABLE DRIVER

                DB      'ALCHDRV2'

;THE FOLLOWING ARE THE POINTERS TO THE CALLABLE ROUTINES AND THE COMMON
;DATA. THE SEGMENTS ARE FILLED IN BY GRAPHIC WORKSHOP. DON'T CHANGE ANYTHING.
DISPATCH        PROC    FAR
                DW      VGA_ON          ;FAR POINTER TO VGA MODE SELECT
                DW      ?
                DW      VGA_LINE        ;FAR POINTER TO VGA LINE DISPLAY
                DW      ?
                DW      VGA_OFF         ;FAR POINTER TO VGA MODE DESELECT
                DW      ?
                DW      VGA_PALETTE     ;FAR POINTER TO VGA PALETTE SET
                DW      ?
                DW      VGA_OVERSCAN    ;FAR POINTER TO VGA OVERSCAN SET
                DW      ?
                DW      EGA_ON          ;FAR POINTER TO EGA MODE SELECT
                DW      ?
                DW      EGA_LINE        ;FAR POINTER TO EGA LINE DISPLAY
                DW      ?
                DW      EGA_OFF         ;FAR POINTER TO EGA MODE DESELECT
                DW      ?
                DW      EGA_PALETTE     ;FAR POINTER TO EGA PALETTE SET
                DW      ?
                DW      MONO_ON         ;FAR POINTER TO MONO MODE SELECT
                DW      ?
                DW      MONO_FUNCTIONS  ;FAR POINTER TO MONO PAGE DISPLAY
                DW      ?
                DW      MONO_LINE
```

10-16 Continued.

```
              DW       ?
              DW       MONO_OFF          ;FAR POINTER TO MONO MODE DESELECT
              DW       ?
              DW       RGB_ON
              DW       ?
              DW       RGB_LINE
              DW       ?
              DW       RGB_OFF
              DW       ?
V_RGBWIDE     DW       RGB_WIDE          ;RGB SCREEN WIDTH
V_RGBDEEP     DW       RGB_DEEP          ;RGB SCREEN DEPTH
V_VGAWIDE     DW       VGA_WIDE          ;VGA SCREEN WIDTH
V_VGADEEP     DW       VGA_DEEP          ;VGA SCREEN DEPTH
V_VGASCRNSEG  DW       VGA_SCREENSEG     ;VGA SCREEN SEGMENT
V_EGAWIDE     DW       EGA_WIDE          ;EGA SCREEN WIDTH
V_EGADEEP     DW       EGA_DEEP          ;EGA SCREEN DEPTH
V_EGABYTES    DW       EGA_BYTES         ;EGA SCREEN BYTES
V_EGASCRNSEG  DW       EGA_SCREENSEG     ;EGA SCREEN SEGMENT
V_MONOWIDE    DW       MONO_WIDE         ;MONO SCREEN WIDTH
V_MONODEEP    DW       MONO_DEEP         ;MONO SCREEN DEPTH
V_MONOBYTES   DW       MONO_BYTES        ;BYTE WIDTH ON MONOCHROME SCREEN
V_MONOSCRNSEG DW       MONO_SCREENSEG    ;MONOCHROME SCREEN SEGMENT
              DW       VERSION
              DW       SUBVERSION
              DB       'Paradise D Version 2.1 ',0
DISPATCH      ENDP


RGBMODETABLE  DW       640,480
              DW       -1,-1


VGAMODETABLE  DW       320,200
              DW       640,400
              DW       -1,-1


EGAMODETABLE  DW       640,480
              DW       800,600
              DW       -1,-1


MONOMODETABLE DW       640,480
              DW       800,600
              DW       -1,-1


RGB_ON        PROC     NEAR
              PUSH     BP
              MOV      BP,SP
              PUSH     DS
              PUSH     ES

              MOV      CS:[V_RGBWIDE],640
              MOV      CS:[V_RGBDEEP],480
              MOV      CS:[CODEPAGE],0FFFFH
              MOV      CX,CS:[V_RGBDEEP]                ;DEPTH OF SCREEN
```

10-16 Continued.

```
                SUB     BX,BX                           ;ZERO LINE COUNTER
                MOV     SI,OFFSET SCREENTABLE           ;POINT TO TABLE

RGB480_1:       PUSH    CX
                MOV     AX,CS:[V_RGBWIDE]               ;WIDTH OF SCREEEN
                SHL     AX,1
                MUL     BX                              ;TIMES LINE NUMBER

                MOV     CL,4                            ;SHIFT HIGH ORDER
                SHL     DX,CL                           ;WORD OVER BY A BYTE
                AND     DX,00F0H

                CMP     AX,(0FFFEH-1280)        ;SEE IF WE WILL
                JB      RGB480_2                        ;HIT A 64K BOUNDARY
                SUB     AX,1000H                        ;AND ADJUST THE
                INC     DX                              ;HIGH ORDER WORD

RGB480_2:       MOV     CS:[SI],AX                      ;SAVE THE VALUES
                MOV     CS:[SI+2],DX                    ;IN OUR LOOKUP TABLE
                ADD     SI,4                            ;AND POINT TO THE
                INC     BX                              ;NEXT LINE AND
                POP     CX                              ;ENTRY
                LOOP    RGB480_1

                MOV     AX,0062H
                INT     10H
                MOV     CS:[CODEPAGE],0FFFFH

                POP     ES
                POP     DS
                POP     BP
                RETF
RGB_ON          ENDP

RGB_OFF         PROC    NEAR
                PUSH    BP
                PUSH    DS
                PUSH    ES

                MOV     AX,1200H
                MOV     BX,0031H
                INT     10H

                MOV     AX,0003H
                INT     10H

                POP     ES
                POP     DS
                POP     BP
                RETF
RGB_OFF         ENDP
```

10-16 Continued.

```
RGB_LINE        PROC    NEAR
                PUSH    BP
                MOV     BP,SP
                PUSH    DS
                PUSH    ES

                MOV     SI,[BP + _AOFF + 0]
                MOV     DS,[BP + _AOFF + 2]

                MOV     CX,[BP + _AOFF + 4]
                CMP     CX,CS:[V_RGBWIDE]
                JL      RGBLINE_1

                MOV     CX,CS:[V_RGBWIDE]

RGBLINE_1:      MOV     AX,0A000H
                MOV     ES,AX

                MOV     BX,[BP + _AOFF + 6]
                CMP     BX,CS:[V_RGBDEEP]
                JGE     RGBLINE_EXIT

                SHL     BX,1
                SHL     BX,1
                MOV     DI,CS:[SCREENTABLE + BX]
                MOV     AX,CS:[SCREENTABLE + 2 + BX]

                CMP     CS:[CODEPAGE],AX
                JE      RGBLINE_2

                MOV     CS:[CODEPAGE],AX
                SET_PROA                        ;SET HIGH ORDER WORD

RGBLINE_2:      MOV     AX,0A000H               ;POINT TO VIDEO BUFFER
                MOV     ES,AX                   ;WITH ES

RGBLINE_3:      PUSH    CX
                RGB2AX
                STOSW
                POP     CX
                LOOP    RGBLINE_3

RGBLINE_EXIT:   POP     ES
                POP     DS
                POP     BP
                RETF
RGB_LINE        ENDP


;THIS ROUTINE SELECTS THE VGA 256 COLOUR MODE
VGA_ON          PROC    NEAR
                PUSH    BP
```

10-16 Continued.

```
                    MOV       BP,SP
                    PUSH      DS

                    CMP       WORD PTR [BP + _AOFF + 0],320
                    JG        PARA_ON
                    CMP       WORD PTR [BP + _AOFF + 2],200
                    JG        PARA_ON

                    MOV       CS:[V_VGAWIDE],320
                    MOV       CS:[V_VGADEEP],200
                    MOV       CX,200                  ;DEPTH OF SCREEN
                    SUB       DX,DX
                    MOV       SI,OFFSET SCREENTABLE

VGA_ON1:            PUSH      DX
                    MOV       AX,320                  ;WIDTH OF SCREEEN
                    MUL       DX
                    MOV       CS:[SI],AX
                    ADD       SI,2
                    POP       DX
                    INC       DX

                    LOOP      VGA_ON1

                    MOV       AX,0013H
                    INT       10H

                    JMP       PARA_EXIT

PARA_ON:            MOV       CS:[V_VGAWIDE],VGA_WIDE
                    MOV       CS:[V_VGADEEP],VGA_DEEP
                    MOV       CS:[CODEPAGE],0FFFFH

                    MOV       CX,400                  ;DEPTH OF SCREEN
                    SUB       BX,BX                   ;ZERO LINE COUNTER
                    MOV       SI,OFFSET SCREENTABLE   ;POINT TO TABLE

PVGAG1:             PUSH      CX
                    MOV       AX,640                  ;WIDTH OF SCREEN
                    MUL       BX                      ;TIMES LINE NUMBER

                    MOV       CL,4                    ;SHIFT HIGH ORDER
                    SHL       DX,CL                   ;WORD OVER BY A BYTE
                    AND       DX,0070H

                    CMP       AX,(0FFFEH-640)          ;SEE IF WE WILL
                    JB        PVGAG2                  ;HIT A 64K BOUNDARY
                    SUB       AX,1000H                ;AND ADJUST THE
                    INC       DX                      ;HIGH ORDER WORD

PVGAG2:             MOV       CS:[SI],AX              ;SAVE THE VALUES
                    MOV       CS:[SI+2],DX            ;IN OUR LOOKUP TABLE
```

10-16 Continued.

```
                ADD     SI,4                        ;AND POINT TO THE
                INC     BX                          ;NEXT LINE AND
                POP     CX                          ;ENTRY
                LOOP    PVGAG1

                MOV     AX,005EH
                INT     10H

PARA_EXIT:      POP     DS
                POP     BP
                RETF
VGA_ON          ENDP

;THIS ROUTINE DISPLAYS A VGA LINE
VGA_LINE        PROC    NEAR
                PUSH    BP
                MOV     BP,SP

                PUSH    DS
                PUSH    ES

                CMP     V_VGAWIDE,320
                JNE     PARASHOW

                MOV     SI,[BP + _AOFF + 0]     ;OFFSET OF SOURCE
                MOV     DS,[BP + _AOFF + 2]     ;SEGMENT OF SOURCE

                MOV     BX,[BP + _AOFF + 6]     ;GET LINE NUMBER
                CMP     BX,200

                JGE     PSHOWVGAX

                SHL     BX,1
                MOV     DI,CS:[SCREENTABLE+BX]

                CLD
                MOV     CX,[BP + _AOFF + 4]     ;LENGTH OF MOVE IN BYTES
                CMP     CX,0
                JE      PSHOWVGAX               ;CHECK FOR NASTIES
                CMP     CX,320
                JL      SHOWVGA1
                MOV     CX,320
SHOWVGA1:       MOV     AX,VGA_SCREENSEG
                MOV     ES,AX
        REPNE   MOVSB

                JMP     PSHOWVGAX

PARASHOW:       CMP     WORD PTR [BP + _AOFF + 6],400
                JGE     PSHOWVGAX               ;IS THIS A LEGAL LINE?
                MOV     SI,[BP + _AOFF + 0]     ;OFFSET OF SOURCE
                MOV     DS,[BP + _AOFF + 2]     ;SEGMENT OF SOURCE
```

10-16 Continued.

```
                    MOV      CX,[BP + _AOFF + 4]      ;LENGTH OF MOVE IN BYTES

                    CMP      CX,640                   ;IS IT TOO LONG?
                    JL       PSHOWVGA0

                    MOV      CX,640

PSHOWVGA0:          MOV      BX,[BP + _AOFF + 6]      ;GET INDEX INTO LINE TABLE
                    SHL      BX,1
                    SHL      BX,1

                    MOV      DI,CS:[SCREENTABLE + BX]
                    MOV      AX,CS:[SCREENTABLE + 2 + BX]
                    CMP      CS:[CODEPAGE],AX
                    JE       PSHOWVGA1
                    MOV      CS:[CODEPAGE],AX
                    SET_PROA                          ;SET HIGH ORDER WORD

PSHOWVGA1:          MOV      AX,0A000H                ;POINT TO VIDEO BUFFER
                    MOV      ES,AX                    ;WITH ES

                    CLD
           REPNE    MOVSB                             ;MOVE IN THE LINE DATA

PSHOWVGAX:          POP      ES
                    POP      DS
                    POP      BP
                    RETF
VGA_LINE            ENDP

;THIS ROUTINE DESELECTS THE VGA 256 COLOUR MODE
VGA_OFF             PROC     NEAR
                    MOV      AX,1200H
                    MOV      BX,0031H
                    INT      10H

                    MOV      AX,0003H
                    INT      10H
                    RETF
VGA_OFF             ENDP

;THIS ROUTINE SETS THE VGA PALETTE
VGA_PALETTE         PROC     NEAR
                    PUSH     BP
                    MOV      BP,SP
                    PUSH     DS
                    PUSH     ES

                    MOV      SI,[BP + _AOFF + 0]      ;OFFSET OF SOURCE
                    MOV      DS,[BP + _AOFF + 2]      ;SEGMENT OF SOURCE

                    MOV      CX,[BP + _AOFF + 4]      ;NUMBER OF COLOURS
```

10-16 Continued.

```
              CMP     CX,0                    ;CHECK FOR NASTIES
              JG      GVP0
              JMP     GVPX

GVP0:         MOV     DX,03C6H
              MOV     AL,0FFH
              OUT     DX,AL

              MOV     BX,0

GVP1:         PUSH    CX
              MOV     DX,03C8H
              MOV     AL,BL
              INC     BX
              OUT     DX,AL

              INC     DX

              LODSB
              SHR     AL,1
              SHR     AL,1
              OUT     DX,AL

              LODSB
              SHR     AL,1
              SHR     AL,1
              OUT     DX,AL

              LODSB
              SHR     AL,1
              SHR     AL,1
              OUT     DX,AL

              POP     CX
              LOOP    GVP1

GVPX:         POP     ES
              POP     DS
              POP     BP
              RETF
VGA_PALETTE   ENDP

;THIS ROUTINE SETS THE VGA OVERSCAN.

VGA_OVERSCAN  PROC    NEAR
              PUSH    BP
              MOV     BP,SP

              MOV     AX,1001H
              MOV     BX,[BP + _AOFF + 0]
              XCHG    BH,BL
              INT     10H
```

10-16 Continued.

```
                          POP       BP
                          RETF
         VGA_OVERSCAN     ENDP

         ;THIS ROUTINE SELECTS THE EGA 16 COLOUR MODE
         EGA_ON           PROC      NEAR
                          PUSH      BP
                          MOV       BP,SP
                          PUSH      DS

         EGA480:          CMP       WORD PTR [BP + _AOFF + 2],640
                          JG        EGA600
                          CMP       WORD PTR [BP + _AOFF + 2],480
                          JG        EGA600

                          MOV       CS:[V_EGAWIDE],640
                          MOV       CS:[V_EGADEEP],480
                          MOV       CS:[V_EGABYTES],80

                          MOV       CX,480          ;DEPTH OF SCREEN
                          SUB       DX,DX
                          MOV       SI,OFFSET SCREENTABLE

         EGA_ON2:         PUSH      DX
                          MOV       AX,80           ;WIDTH OF SCREEEN
                          MUL       DX
                          MOV       CS:[SI],AX
                          ADD       SI,2
                          POP       DX
                          INC       DX
                          LOOP      EGA_ON2

                          MOV       AX,0012H
                          INT       10H

                          JMP       EGA_EXIT

         EGA600:          MOV       CS:[V_EGAWIDE],800
                          MOV       CS:[V_EGADEEP],600
                          MOV       CS:[V_EGABYTES],100

                          MOV       CX,600          ;DEPTH OF SCREEN
                          SUB       DX,DX
                          MOV       SI,OFFSET SCREENTABLE

         EGA_ON3:         PUSH      DX
                          MOV       AX,100          ;WIDTH OF SCREEEN
                          MUL       DX
                          MOV       CS:[SI],AX
                          ADD       SI,2
                          POP       DX
                          INC       DX
```

10-16 Continued.

```
                    LOOP        EGA_ON3

                    MOV         AX,0058H
                    INT         10H

EGA_EXIT:           POP         DS
                    POP         BP
                    RETF
EGA_ON              ENDP

;THIS ROUTINE DISPLAYS AN EGA LINE
EGA_LINE            PROC        NEAR
                    PUSH        BP
                    MOV         BP,SP
                    PUSH        DS
                    PUSH        ES

                    MOV         SI,[BP + _AOFF + 0]     ;OFFSET OF SOURCE
                    MOV         DS,[BP + _AOFF + 2]     ;SEGMENT OF SOURCE
                    MOV         BX,[BP + _AOFF + 6]     ;GET LINE NUMBER
                    CMP         BX,CS:[V_EGADEEP]
                    JGE         SHOWEGAX

                    SHL         BX,1
                    MOV         DI,CS:[SCREENTABLE+BX]

                    MOV         AX,0A000H
                    MOV         ES,AX
                    MOV         BX,[BP + _AOFF + 4]     ;LENGTH OF MOVE IN BYTES

                    MOV         CX,BX
                    EGAPLANE            1
                    CLD
                    PUSH        DI
        REPNE       MOVSB
                    POP         DI

                    MOV         CX,BX
                    EGAPLANE            2
                    PUSH        DI
        REPNE       MOVSB
                    POP         DI

                    MOV         CX,BX
                    EGAPLANE            4
                    PUSH        DI
        REPNE       MOVSB
                    POP         DI

                    MOV         CX,BX
                    EGAPLANE            8
                    PUSH        DI
        REPNE       MOVSB
```

10-16 Continued.

```
                    POP     DI
                    EGAPLANE        0FH

SHOWEGAX:           POP     ES
                    POP     DS
                    POP     BP
                    RETF
EGA_LINE            ENDP

;THIS ROUTINE SETS THE EGA PALETTE
EGA_PALETTE         PROC    NEAR
                    PUSH    BP
                    MOV     BP,SP
                    PUSH    DS
                    PUSH    ES

                    MOV     SI,[BP + _AOFF + 6]     ;OFFSET OF SOURCE
                    MOV     DS,[BP + _AOFF + 8]     ;SEGMENT OF SOURCE

                    MOV     CX,[BP + _AOFF + 4]     ;NUMBER OF COLOURS
                    CMP     CX,16
                    JLE     EGA_PALETTE1
                    MOV     CX,16

EGA_PALETTE1:       PUSH    CX
                    MOV     BX,0000H

EGA_PALETTE2:       PUSH    CX
                    LODSB
                    SHR     AL,1
                    SHR     AL,1
                    MOV     DH,AL
                    LODSB
                    SHR     AL,1
                    SHR     AL,1
                    MOV     CH,AL
                    LODSB
                    SHR     AL,1
                    SHR     AL,1
                    MOV     CL,AL
                    MOV     AX,1010H
                    INT     10H
                    INC     BX
                    POP     CX
                    LOOP    EGA_PALETTE2

                    POP     CX
                    MOV     BX,0000H

EGA_PALETTE3:       PUSH    CX
                    MOV     AX,1000H
                    INT     10H
```

10-16 Continued.

```
                ADD       BX,0101H
                POP       CX
                LOOP      EGA_PALETTE3

                POP       ES
                POP       DS
                POP       BP
                RETF
EGA_PALETTE     ENDP

;THIS ROUTINE DESELECTS THE EGA 16 COLOUR MODE

EGA_OFF         PROC      NEAR
                MOV       AX,0003H
                INT       10H
                RETF
EGA_OFF         ENDP

;THIS ROUTINE SELECTS THE 2 COLOUR MODE
MONO_ON         PROC      NEAR
                PUSH      BP
                MOV       BP,SP
                PUSH      DS
                PUSH      ES

                CMP       WORD PTR [BP + _AOFF + 2],640
                JG        MONO600
                CMP       WORD PTR [BP + _AOFF + 2],480
                JG        MONO600

                MOV       CS:[V_MONOWIDE],640
                MOV       CS:[V_MONODEEP],480
                MOV       CS:[V_MONOBYTES],80

                MOV       AX,0012H
                INT       10H

                MOV       CX,480
                SUB       DX,DX
                MOV       SI,OFFSET SCREENTABLE
MONO_ON1:       PUSH      DX
                MOV       AX,80
                MUL       DX
                MOV       CS:[SI],AX
                ADD       SI,2
                POP       DX
                INC       DX
                LOOP      MONO_ON1

                JMP       MONOEXIT

MONO600:        MOV       CS:[V_MONOWIDE],800
```

10-16 Continued.

```
                    MOV     CS:[V_MONODEEP],600
                    MOV     CS:[V_MONOBYTES],100

                    MOV     AX,0059H
                    INT     10H

                    MOV     CX,600
                    SUB     DX,DX
                    MOV     SI,OFFSET SCREENTABLE

MONO_ON3:           PUSH    DX
                    MOV     AX,100
                    MUL     DX
                    MOV     CS:[SI],AX
                    ADD     SI,2
                    POP     DX
                    INC     DX
                    LOOP    MONO_ON3

MONOEXIT:           POP     ES
                    POP     DS
                    POP     BP
                    SUB     AX,AX
                    RETF
MONO_ON             ENDP

;THIS FUNCTION PERFORMS VARIOUS GRAPHIC OPERATIONS
;       ARGUMENTS         -       FUNCTION CODE
;                         -       VARIABLE
;
;       FUNCTIONS         -       0       RETURN SCREEN SEG
;                         -       1       RETURN OFFSET TO SCREEN TABLE
;                         -       2       RETURN MONOCHROME SCREEN WIDTH
;                         -       3       RETURN MONOCHROME SCREEN DEPTH
;                         -       4       INVERT FRAME RECT - ARGS ON STACK
;                         -       5       RETURN OFFSET OF VGAMODETABLE
;                         -       6       RETURN OFFSET OF EGAMODETABLE
;                         -       7       RETURN OFFSET OF MONOMODETABLE
;                         -       8       RETURN OFFSET OF RGBMODETABLE
;
MONO_FUNCTIONS  PROC    NEAR
                PUSH    BP
                MOV     BP,SP
                PUSH    DS
                PUSH    ES

                CMP     WORD PTR [BP + _AOFF + 0],0000H
                JNE     MF1

                MOV     AX,MONO_SCREENSEG
                JMP     MF_EXIT
```

10-16 Continued.

```
MF1:            CMP     WORD PTR [BP + _AOFF + 0],0001H
                JNE     MF2

                MOV     AX,OFFSET SCREENTABLE-8
                JMP     MF_EXIT

MF2:            CMP     WORD PTR [BP + _AOFF + 0],0002H
                JNE     MF3

                MOV     AX,MONO_WIDE
                JMP     MF_EXIT

MF3:            CMP     WORD PTR [BP + _AOFF + 0],0003H
                JNE     MF4

                MOV     AX,MONO_DEEP
                JMP     MF_EXIT

MF4:            CMP     WORD PTR [BP + _AOFF + 0],0004H
                JE      MF5
                JMP     MF6

MF5:            MOV     AX,MONO_SCREENSEG
                MOV     ES,AX

                MOV     BX,[BP + _AOFF + 4]     ;GET TOP
                SHL     BX,1
                MOV     DI,CS:[SCREENTABLE+BX]

                MOV     BX,[BP + _AOFF + 2]     ;GET LEFT
                MOV     CX,[BP + _AOFF + 6]     ;GET RIGHT
                SUB     CX,BX

MF5A:           PUSH    BX
                AND     BX,0007H
                MOV     AL,CS:[MASKTABLE+BX]
                POP     BX

                PUSH    BX
                SHR     BX,1
                SHR     BX,1
                SHR     BX,1
                XOR     ES:[DI+BX],AL
                POP     BX
                INC     BX
                LOOP    MF5A

                MOV     BX,[BP + _AOFF + 4]     ;GET TOP
                INC     BX
                MOV     CX,[BP + _AOFF + 8]     ;GET BOTTOM
                DEC     CX
                SUB     CX,BX
```

10-16 Continued.

```
MF5B:           PUSH    BX
                SHL     BX,1
                MOV     DI,CS:[SCREENTABLE+BX]
                MOV     BX,[BP + _AOFF + 2]      ;GET LEFT
                PUSH    BX
                AND     BX,0007H
                MOV     AL,CS:[MASKTABLE+BX]
                POP     BX
                PUSH    BX
                SHR     BX,1
                SHR     BX,1
                SHR     BX,1
                XOR     ES:[DI+BX],AL
                POP     BX
                MOV     BX,[BP + _AOFF + 6]      ;GET RIGHT
                DEC     BX
                PUSH    BX
                AND     BX,0007H
                MOV     AL,CS:[MASKTABLE+BX]
                POP     BX
                PUSH    BX
                SHR     BX,1
                SHR     BX,1
                SHR     BX,1
                XOR     ES:[DI+BX],AL
                POP     BX
                POP     BX
                INC     BX
                LOOP    MF5B

                MOV     BX,[BP + _AOFF + 8]      ;GET BOTTOM
                DEC     BX
                SHL     BX,1
                MOV     DI,CS:[SCREENTABLE+BX]

                MOV     BX,[BP + _AOFF + 2]      ;GET LEFT
                MOV     CX,[BP + _AOFF + 6]      ;GET RIGHT
                SUB     CX,BX

MF5D:           PUSH    BX
                AND     BX,0007H
                MOV     AL,CS:[MASKTABLE+BX]
                POP     BX

                PUSH    BX
                SHR     BX,1
                SHR     BX,1
                SHR     BX,1
                XOR     ES:[DI+BX],AL
                POP     BX
                INC     BX
                LOOP    MF5D
```

10-16 Continued.

```
MF6:            CMP     WORD PTR [BP + _AOFF + 0],0005H
                JNE     MF7

                MOV     AX,OFFSET VGAMODETABLE
                JMP     MF_EXIT

MF7:            CMP     WORD PTR [BP + _AOFF + 0],0006H
                JNE     MF8

                MOV     AX,OFFSET EGAMODETABLE
                JMP     MF_EXIT

MF8:            CMP     WORD PTR [BP + _AOFF + 0],0007H
                JNE     MF9

                MOV     AX,OFFSET MONOMODETABLE
                JMP     MF_EXIT

MF9:            CMP     WORD PTR [BP + _AOFF + 0],0008H
                JNE     MF_EXIT

                MOV     AX,OFFSET RGBMODETABLE
                JMP     MF_EXIT

MF_EXIT:        POP     ES
                POP     DS
                POP     BP
                RETF
MONO_FUNCTIONS  ENDP

MASKTABLE       DB      80H,40H,20H,10H,08H,04H,02H,01H

MONO_LINE       PROC    NEAR
                PUSH    BP
                MOV     BP,SP

                PUSH    DS
                PUSH    ES

                MOV     AX,0A000H               ;POINT TO THE SCREEN
                MOV     ES,AX

                MOV     CX,[BP + _AOFF + 6]     ;GET THE WIDTH OF MOVE
                CMP     CX,CS:[V_MONOBYTES]
                JL      MONO_LINE1
                MOV     CX,CS:[V_MONOBYTES]

MONO_LINE1:     MOV     SI,[BP + _AOFF + 0]     ;OFFSET OF BITMAP
                MOV     DS,[BP + _AOFF + 2]     ;SEGMENT OF BITMAP
                MOV     BX,[BP + _AOFF + 4]     ;NUMBER OF LINE
                SHL     BX,1
```

10-16 Continued.

```
                CLD                                    ;CLEAR DIRECTION FLAG
                MOV     DI,CS:[SCREENTABLE + BX]
        REPNE   MOVSB                                  ;DO THE MOVE

                POP     ES
                POP     DS

                POP     BP
                RETF
MONO_LINE       ENDP

;THIS ROUTINE DESELECTS THE 2 COLOUR MODE
MONO_OFF        PROC    NEAR
                MOV     AX,0003H
                INT     10H
                SUB     AX,AX
                RETF
MONO_OFF        ENDP

;THIS IS A LINE START LOOKUP TABLE

SCREENTABLE     DW      960 DUP(?)       ;LINE START TABLE
CODEPAGE        DW      0

CODE            ENDS
                END
```
10-16 Continued.

Using screen drivers

In addition to the drivers discussed in this chapter, there is a whole library of drivers included with Graphic Workshop. If you don't buy the companion disks for this book, you can still find Graphic Workshop fairly easily, as it's shareware that turns up on most bulletin boards.

The Graphic Workshop screen drivers are stored as resources in a file called GWSDRV.RES. You can find a complete description of these resources and how they're used in my book *Graphical User Interface Programming*, TAB Book 3875. However, you don't need to get inside them to be able to swipe a few drivers.

Graphic Workshop's resource files are managed using a program called RMOVER, which is included with the Graphic Workshop package. You can see all the resources in GWSDRV.RES by doing this:

RMOVER GWSDRV.RES /L

The /L option instructs RMOVER to list the resources in the resource file it's given as its first argument.

Figure 10-17 illustrates the RMOVER resource list for the default GWSDRV.RES file that comes with Graphic Workshop.

You can extract any resource from this list using RMOVER. For example, the ATI XL driver in GWSDRV.RES is arguably preferable to the one

```
Resource mover version 1.3 - copyright (c) 1990 Alchemy Mindworks Inc.
-----------------------------------------------------------------------
Description: Resource file created by RMOVER
19 resource(s)
```

Rsrc 0000 - type:GRAF - nmbr:000000015 - 01052 bytes Amstrad 16 col 640x200
Rsrc 0001 - type:GRAF - nmbr:000000005 - 05319 bytes ATI Wonder 256K v2.0
Rsrc 0002 - type:GRAF - nmbr:000000007 - 05491 bytes ATI Wonder 512K 2.0
Rsrc 0003 - type:GRAF - nmbr:000000019 - 06089 bytes ATI XL 1024k v2.1
Rsrc 0004 - type:GRAF - nmbr:000000006 - 03595 bytes Dell super-VGA 256K 2.0
Rsrc 0005 - type:GRAF - nmbr:000000017 - 03680 bytes Dell super-VGA 512K 2.0
Rsrc 0006 - type:GRAF - nmbr:000000014 - 03756 bytes Paradise Pro Card V2.1
Rsrc 0007 - type:GRAF - nmbr:000000003 - 03731 bytes Paradise Plus Card 2.1
Rsrc 0008 - type:GRAF - nmbr:000000009 - 06053 bytes Hercules TIGA 31.5k 2.0
Rsrc 0009 - type:GRAF - nmbr:000000008 - 04423 bytes Trident 256K VGA 2.0
Rsrc 0010 - type:GRAF - nmbr:000000010 - 06039 bytes Trident 512K VGA 2.0
Rsrc 0011 - type:GRAF - nmbr:000000011 - 05332 bytes Tseng 4000 640x480 2.1
Rsrc 0012 - type:GRAF - nmbr:000000012 - 05540 bytes Tseng 4000 800x600 2.1
Rsrc 0013 - type:GRAF - nmbr:000000013 - 04758 bytes Tseng 4000 1024x768 2.1
Rsrc 0014 - type:GRAF - nmbr:000000001 - 01187 bytes VGA 360 x 480 2.0
Rsrc 0015 - type:GRAF - nmbr:000000002 - 01015 bytes VGA 320x400 2.0
Rsrc 0016 - type:GRAF - nmbr:000000016 - 02488 bytes VGA in pseudo 640x480
Rsrc 0017 - type:GRAF - nmbr:000000018 - 05361 bytes Video Seven 256K V2.1
Rsrc 0018 - type:GRAF - nmbr:000000004 - 05455 bytes Video Seven 1024i 2.1

10-17 Graphic Workshop's RMOVER resource list for GWSDRV.RES.

discussed in this chapter, as it supports more of the ATI cards super VGA screen modes. To extract it you would type:

RMOVER GWSDRV.RES /E /FATI-XL.RES /N19 /TGRAF

The /E option instructs RMOVER to extract a resource to a new file. The /F option specifies the name of the new file. The /N option specifies the number of the resource to be extracted. Note that this is the number from the center column of the RMOVER listing, not the one at the far left. Finally, the /T option specifies the type of resource to be extracted. This is always GRAF for screen drivers. The four-character type definition is case sensitive.

Every resource file begins with a file header. Every resource also has a header of its own. When you extract a single resource into a file, as done here, the two headers together occupy 85 bytes at the beginning of the file. The rest of the file is the screen driver itself.

You can dispense with the header pretty quickly using debug. Here's how this would be done for ATI-XL.RES.

1. Load the file into DEBUG by typing DEBUG ATI-XL.RES.
2. Find out how big the file is. The size will be in the CX register immediately after it has been loaded. You can see what's in the registers by issuing the R command at the dash prompt. In this example it's 181EH.

3. Subtract the size of the header from this value. It's 0055H bytes. You can use DEBUG's internal hexadecimal calculator to do this. Issue the command H181E,0055 at the dash prompt.
4. The resulting value, 17C9H, is the true size of the driver. You must load this number into the CX register. Issue the command RCX at the dash prompt and type in the new value for the CX register.
5. You must give DEBUG a new name for the driver. Issue the command NATI-XL.DRV at the dash prompt.
6. Write the driver out to the new file by issuing the command W155 at the dash prompt. This tells DEBUG to write 17C9H bytes to the file starting at 0155H. Note that DEBUG always loads binary files starting at location 0100H, rather than 0000H.
7. Issue the command Q at the dash prompt to get back to DOS.

This procedure creates ATI-XL.DRV, which can be used just like any of the assembled drivers discussed in this chapter.

As an aside, you might also use the code discussed in this chapter to write drivers for use with Graphic Workshop. More information about creating driver resources may be found in the Graphic Workshop documentation, or by looking at the section of *Graphical User Interface Programming* that deals with resource management.

11
Printing graphics

A penny saved is a penny.
—Murphy's Laws of Computers

Hard copy has a long tradition in human civilization. Trees have been dying to preserve peoples' words and images long before laser printers arrived to do a decent job of reproducing them. One might speculate how different history might have been if the span of time between the invention of movable type and that of good, cheap personal photocopiers and other hard copy devices hadn't been so great. One might imagine Martin Luther faxing his proclamation instead of nailing it up. All the great, partially suppressed underground Victorian literature could have been uploaded to bulletin boards rather than being hawked in darkened alleys or smuggled across the channel from France.

This lacks the romance of history, to be sure, but when you're shivering in a darkened alley in London peddling scurrilous books at two in the morning, history doesn't seem all that interesting to begin with.

The technology that produces really worthwhile hard copy from a computer is relatively new. Allowing that you ignore dot matrix printers (which this chapter does), affordable laser printers have been around for only a few years. Printers that generate color output that is both affordable and not too ugly to gaze at without eye protection are even newer.

This latter point is relative, to be sure. The color PostScript printers discussed in this chapter have prices that hover around $10,000. Even at this high price, they're a lot less expensive than commercial printing for proofs and very short print runs.

Specifically, this chapter discusses code to print graphics to the following general classes of devices:

- Hewlett-Packard LaserJet Plus compatible printers
- Monochrome PostScript printers
- Color PostScript printers
- Hewlett-Packard PaintJet compatible color inkjet printers

LaserJet Plus compatible printers encompass a pretty broad spectrum of low-cost personal lasers. The LaserJet's set of escape sequences has been duplicated by countless manufacturers because it's so easy to work with. The more recent Hewlett-Packard LaserJet II and LaserJet III laser printers also behave as LaserJet Plus printers for the sake of this discussion.

Just about all the laser printers that aren't LaserJets are PostScript printers, and a growing number of them are both—being able to emulate both a LaserJet Plus and a PostScript device. PostScript is a very sophisticated and intensely complex printer control language developed by Adobe. While a complete discussion of PostScript is beyond the scope of this book, this chapter gets into those areas of PostScript that are specific to printing graphics.

Color PostScript printers are by no means common, nor are they particularly cheap. The most frequently encountered one is the QMS ColorScript 100, which prints using sheets of film coated with colored wax. This chapter looks at printing color bitmapped graphics to a color PostScript printer. If you have access to one, the results are dazzling.

Finally, for those of us without ten grand to drop on a color printer, there are Hewlett-Packard PaintJet printers and a few HP compatibles, most notably the ones made by Kodak. While lacking the resolution and color management of a ColorScript, color inkjet printers offer you pretty respectable results if you know how to make them behave. They cost about a tenth of what a color PostScript printer does.

As noted earlier, this chapter does not deal with dot matrix graphics printing, which is an entirely separate can of worms. If you wish to uncan it, you'll find a complete discussion of the can openers required in *Bitmapped Graphics*.

LaserJet Plus printing

Aside from being pretty inexpensive, LaserJets are among the easiest printers to program for. While they use mysterious escape sequences instead of readable text, as is the case when dealing with PostScript, the format in which a LaserJet wants to see bitmaps is pretty much the same as the one in which they're naturally stored. Printing a bitmap really involves little more than positioning the printing cursor at the right spot on the virtual page of a LaserJet, sending down the bitmapped lines with an escape sequence preceding each one and finally sending a form-feed character to eject the page.

The commands that handle these functions are part of the printer control language of a LaserJet, called PCL. A bit unimaginative, PCL actually does stand for *printer control language*.

There are a number of refinements to this model when you attempt to apply it to some real-world code, of course.

To begin with, a LaserJet-compatible printer requires a minimum of 1Mb of memory to handle full-page graphics. The original Hewlett-Packard LaserJet came with 512K and some really low-cost LaserJet-compatible printers still do. The LaserJet Plus was, in fact, the version that came with a full megabyte of memory.

The second thing to keep in mind is that a LaserJet has no meaningful halftoning facilities built into its control language. Unless you specifically provide a way for it to do halftoning by downloading pre-halftoned pictures, a LaserJet is able to print only monochrome graphics. The program in this section looks at one way around this problem.

A LaserJet supports four resolution modes for printing graphics. While the print engine supports 300 dots per inch, it can print graphics at 75, 100, 150, and 300 dots per inch, essentially allowing you to have the printer increase the size of your pictures for you.

Figure 11-1 illustrates the four resolution modes of a LaserJet.

There's nothing particularly clever in the way a LaserJet increases the size of graphics. In one sense, you can look on it as integral scaling. At 300 dots per inch, each pixel of the graphic being printed is reproduced by 1 dot of the laser. At 150 dots per inch, each pixel is handled by a 2×2 dot block. At 100 dots per inch, each pixel is handled by a 3×3 dot block, and so on. Obviously, as the resolution of a graphic decreases it occupies more space. It also gets chunkier looking as the individual pixels become more noticeable. At 75 dots per inch, a LaserJet has much the same resolution as an 8-pin dot matrix printer, although its dots are a lot cleaner.

Also, note that laser printers always produce perfectly square dots; that is, dots having a one-to-one aspect ratio. This usually is not the case for dot matrix printers.

It's arguably easiest to begin looking at LaserJet graphic printing by discussing how to print a monochrome graphic. Since this is really the only graphics a LaserJet knows how to print, the code to handle color graphics as gray-scale images really involves a lot of data transformation to get everything into a black-and-white image, followed by the same code used to handle monochrome printing.

In order to print a monochrome bitmapped graphic to a LaserJet, you must do the following things:

1. Position the printer's cursor
2. Tell the printer to expect some graphics
3. Send the start of line escape sequence
4. Send a line of graphic information
5. Repeat steps 3 and 4 a lot

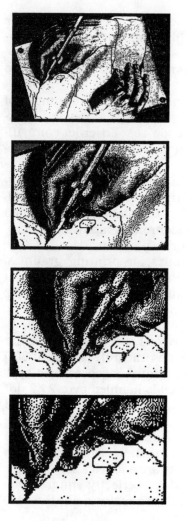

11-1 The four resolution modes of a LaserJet Plus.

6. Tell the printer not to expect any more graphics
7. Tell the printer to eject its page

The code to handle these operations isn't much more complex than this list. Assuming that you've loaded a suitable monochrome image into a buffer using the memory manager calls discussed earlier in this book and that fi is a pointer to a FILEINFO struct that defines it, this will immortalize it in carbon:

```
char *p;
int i,n;

p_string("\033E");
p_string("\033*t300R");
p_string("\033*p20X");
```

```
p_string("\033*p20Y");
p_string("\033*r1A");

n=pixels2bytes(fi->width);

for(i=0;i<fi->depth;++i) {
    p=getline(i);
    sprintf(b,"\033*b%dW",n);
    p_string(b);
    p_buff(p,n);
}

p_string("\033*rB");
p_string("\014");
```

A number of things are happening here that probably need a bit of explaining. The first is the function p_string.

Sending a lot of binary data to a laser printer isn't something to be done lightly. Many of the approaches to printing that are fairly safe when you're dealing with a few lines of text tend to fall apart when they're confronted with full-page graphics. For example, the accepted way to print from within a C program is to use the streamed file functions and write to the handle stdprn. This doesn't work in printing graphics, as DOS turns out not to check for the status of the printer until after it has printed to it. It checks for errors, not for printer readiness.

Laser printers object to this.

Printing directly through the BIOS is an altogether more agreeable way to get data to the printer, as the BIOS allows you to see if the printer port is busy before you send anything to it.

The p_char function illustrates how to communicate with the printer functions of the BIOS from within a C-language program. The first INT 17H call waits for the printer's busy flag to be clear. The second one sends the character to be printed to the printer port. The value of PRINTERPORT defines the port to be used. This should be 0 for LPT1, 1 for LPT2 and so on.

```
p_char(c)
    int c;
{
    union REGS r;

    do {
        r.h.ah = 2;
        r.x.dx = PRINTERPORT;
        int86(0x17,&r,&r);
    } while(!(r.h.ah & 0x80));

    r.h.ah = 0;
    r.h.al = c;
```

```
    r.x.dx = PRINTERPORT;
    int86(0x17,&r,&r);
}
```

Two useful functions call p_char. The first, p_string, sends a null-terminated C text string to the printer.

```
p_string(s)
    char *s;
{
    while(*s) p_char(*s++);
}
```

The second, p_buff, sends a specified number of bytes to the printer.

```
p_buff(s,l)
    char *s;
    int l;
{
    while(l-) p_char(*s++);
}
```

The second issue of importance in the LaserJet printing code is that rather ominous looking list of escape sequences. The PCL language that drives LaserJet printers is controlled by the escape character (character 27, or 033 octal) followed by some rather indecipherable arguments. The printer interprets properly formed escape sequences, rather than printing them.

In fact, the LaserJet supports a rich language of escape sequences, of which the ones required to print graphics represent only a small subset. This discussion leaves out most of its repertoire because they're designed for other applications. In the previous example, the following escape sequences are used.

The string "\033E" resets the printer, disposing of any previously downloaded fonts, pictures or text. It also undoes the work of previous escape sequences. You should send one of these things before you begin printing a new page. It's important not to send one if you're printing a picture as part of a larger page.

The string "\033*t300R" sets the resolution for the graphic image about to be printed. In this case, it is 300 dots per inch. The 300 could be replaced with 150, 100 or 75.

The strings "\033*p20X" and "\033*p20Y" set the horizontal and vertical location respectively of the upper left corner of the graphic to be printed. While there are other escape sequences provided by the Laser-Jet's PCL language to specify these coordinates in more commonly used units, these two strings are probably the most convenient, as they work in printer dots. Each dot is $1/300$ inch across. This graphic will be printed 20 dots right and down from the upper left corner of the printable area of the page.

It's important to note that laser printers can't print right out to the edges of the paper.

The string "\033*r1A" tells the printer that graphics are imminent. It instructs the printer to begin the graphic at the location defined by the previous two cursor position strings.

The string "\033*b%dW" is sent before each printed line. The %d format should be a decimal number that represents the number of bytes of data for the line to be printed. The printer interprets the subsequent bytes as a line of graphic information. When enough bytes have been sent to fill one line, it stops looking for graphics and moves its cursor down by 1 dot in the current resolution and back to the left edge of the current graphic area, ready to accept the next line.

The string "\033*rB" tells the printer that no more graphics are forthcoming for the moment. Finally, "\014" is a form feed; it causes the LaserJet to print everything in its memory to paper and send the page rumbling into its output tray.

As an aside, you can write a much more involved LaserJet printing function than the one previously discussed if you want to reduce the printing time of certain types of graphics. In a sense, you can compress them by splitting lines with a lot of white space into multiple smaller lines. In its simplest sense, such a function could, for example, look for lines with one or more all-white bytes at their ends and shorten them appropriately, so that only those areas that actually print something are sent.

You could further refine this to use the cursor-positioning escape sequences discussed earlier to send multiple short lines, should your code detect a line having white bytes interspersed with details.

This approach to printing can save you some time if you frequently print graphics having a lot of white space in them. It might take more time if you often print complex graphics. With the numerous escape sequences required to handle this type of coding, you might wind up sending more bytes per line than would be required to print graphics normally.

If you become fairly proficient with LaserJet graphics, you might want to see if you can come up with an algorithm to implement this.

Printing color graphics to a LaserJet

You can't print color graphics to a LaserJet in color—LaserJets don't support color. You can print them in gray scales or halftones if you can find a way to manage the halftoning process. Your LaserJet will not help you in this regard, as LaserJets are very dogmatic and don't believe in the existence of gray.

There are numerous approaches to handling halftones on a computer.

Among the most common ones are dithering and synthetic mechanical halftoning. Dithering was mentioned in earlier chapters. There's a complete discussion of monochrome dithering in *Bitmapped Graphics*.

Figure 11-2 illustrates the same picture handled as a PostScript gray-scale halftone, a really ugly Bayer dither, a rather more acceptable error-diffused dither, and, finally, as a simple mechanical halftone. You'll need the dithering code from *Bitmapped Graphics* to implement the two middle options. The final one can be performed by the program about to be discussed.

In commercial printing, gray-scale images are reproduced through a rather arcane process called photographic halftoning or *screening*. You can see the result of it in any newspaper photograph. Gray areas in a halftone are actually created by using small spots of varying size, which is how a PostScript printer does halftones, something to be discussed later in this chapter.

In creating photographic halftones, a continuous-tone photograph is printed through a plastic screen with a fine crosshatch of black lines on it. You can achieve much the same results by simply drawing a matrix of very small spots to represent the pixels of a gray-scale image, with the size of each spot being determined by the brightness of its corresponding pixel.

In practice, there are a few catches to this. The first is that the apparent gray level of a halftone isn't linear. A gray-scale picture, as created earlier in this book to display on a monitor, would look very washed out and flat if it were to be printed directly. The second is that drawing all those little spots on a PC would take forever if you were to attempt it using traditional drawing functions.

You can sneak around both of these problems by using lookup tables. In the first case, it's fairly easy to create a table of values that can remap linear gray levels to something more in keeping with the true gray-scale capabilities of a laser printer. If you were to plot such a table, the resulting curve would look like the one in FIG. 11-3.

The lookup table to do halftoning is even sneakier. It's a table of variable size spots. The most readily understood such table is one that represents 64 gray levels. It consists of 8 bytes per entry, with each 8 bytes representing an 8×8 pixel bitmap. Each bitmap defines one spot, with the spot size decreasing as you work your way up the table.

Having a table of variable size spots, it's possible to construct monochrome image lines such that eight monochrome planes can represent one gray-scale line. The monochrome lines in this case will also be eight times longer than the original source line in pixels.

In essence, this provides a reasonably quick way to draw halftone spots on a LaserJet. In fact, halftoning done this way doesn't look as good as PostScript halftones. The PostScript halftoning algorithm is a lot smarter. It also puts a very severe upper limit on the size of the images you

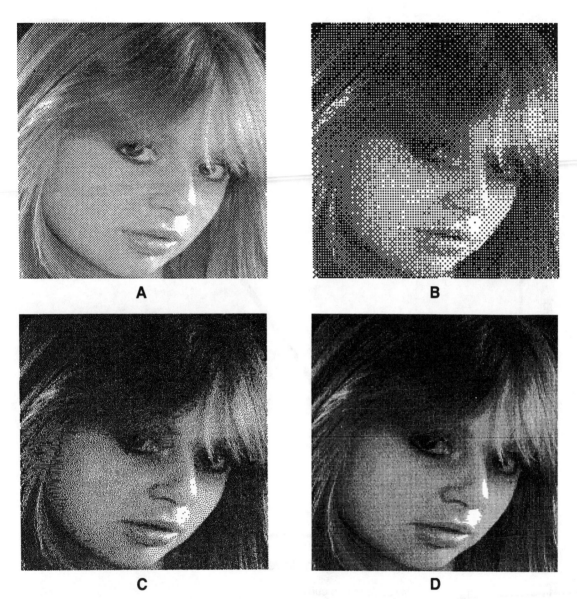

11-2 (A) A 256-color image printed as a PostScript halftone, (B) a Bayer dither, (C) an error diffused dither, and (D) as a mechanical halftone.

can print. Using a 64-entry spot table, the dimensions of your source image will be multiplied by 8. Using a 16-entry table, they will be multiplied by 4.

This is still a lot better than not being able to print gray-scale images at all.

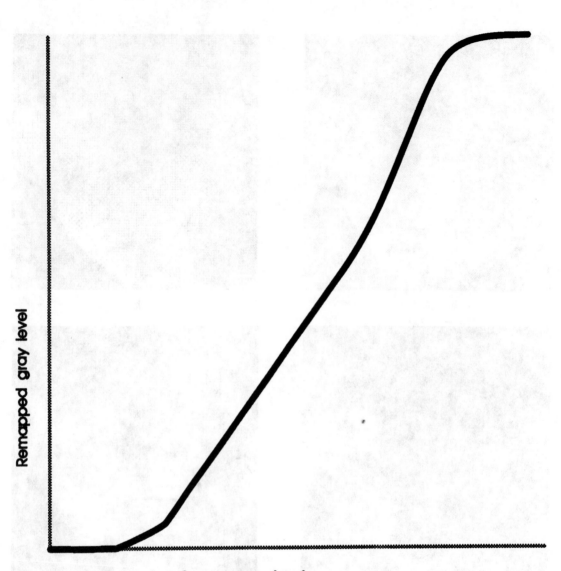

11-3 A precompensation gray-scale remap curve.

Figure 11-4 illustrates the same picture printed with both a 16- and 64-entry halftone spot table.

The program to handle LaserJet printing is called PRNTGIF1. As you might expect, it prints GIF files. You can use the printing functions from PRNTGIF1 to print from another file format if you like. The printing code is pretty well self-contained, and easily portable. It's all illustrated in FIG. 11-5.

If you've been through chapter 2 and understand how GIF files work,

11-4 (A) A 256-color image printed as a 16-level mechanical halftone, and

(B) as a 64-level mechanical halftone.

```
/*

        GIF printer - copyright (c) 1991
        LaserJet Plus version
        Alchemy Mindworks Inc.
*/

#include "stdio.h"
#include "dos.h"
#include "alloc.h"

/*                                      uncomment this line if you
#include "memmangr.h"                   will be linking in the memory manager
*/

#define GOOD_READ        0      /* return codes */
#define BAD_FILE         1
#define BAD_READ         2
#define UNEXPECTED_EOF   3
#define BAD_CODE         4
#define BAD_FIRSTCODE    5
#define BAD_ALLOC        6
#define BAD_SYMBOLSIZE   7

#define RGB_RED          0
#define RGB_GREEN        1
#define RGB_BLUE         2
#define RGB_SIZE         3

#define NO_CODE         -1

#define PRINTERPORT      0      /* 0=LPT1, 1=LPT2, 2=LPT3 */

#define pixels2bytes(n)    ((n+7)/8)

typedef struct {
        char sig[6];
        unsigned int screenwidth,screendepth;
        unsigned char flags,background,aspect;
        } GIFHEADER;

typedef struct {
        unsigned int left,top,width,depth;
        unsigned char flags;
        } IMAGEBLOCK;

typedef struct {
        int width,depth,bytes,bits;
        int flags;
        int background;
        char palette[768];
        int (*setup)();
        int (*closedown)();
```

11-5   The source code for PRNTGIF1.

```
            int (*saveline)();
            int (*savext)();
            } FILEINFO;

typedef struct {
            char blocksize;
            char flags;
            unsigned int delay;
            char transparent_colour;
            char terminator;
            } CONTROLBLOCK;

typedef struct {
            char blocksize;
            unsigned int left,top;
            unsigned int gridwidth,gridheight;
            char cellwidth,cellheight;
            char forecolour,backcolour;
            } PLAINTEXT;

typedef struct {
            char blocksize;
            char applstring[8];
            char authentication[3];
            } APPLICATION;

char *farPtr(char *p,long l);
char *getline(unsigned int n);

int putextension(FILE *fp);
int saveline(char *p,unsigned int n);
int dosetup(FILEINFO *fi);
int doclosedown(FILEINFO *fi);

char masktable[8]={0x80,0x40,0x20,0x10,0x08,0x04,0x02,0x01};

char halftone_16[]= {
        0x00,0x00,0x00,0x00,0x00,0x02,0x00,0x00,
        0x00,0x06,0x00,0x00,0x00,0x06,0x02,0x00,
        0x00,0x06,0x06,0x00,0x00,0x07,0x06,0x00,
        0x00,0x07,0x06,0x02,0x00,0x07,0x0e,0x02,
        0x04,0x07,0x0e,0x02,0x04,0x07,0x0f,0x02,
        0x04,0x07,0x0f,0x06,0x04,0x0f,0x0f,0x06,
        0x06,0x0f,0x0f,0x06,0x06,0x0f,0x0f,0x07,
        0x06,0x0f,0x0f,0x0f,0x0f,0x0f,0x0f,0x0f
        };

char halftone_64[]= {
        0x00,0x00,0x00,0x00,0x00,0x00,0x00,0x00,
        0x00,0x00,0x00,0x08,0x00,0x00,0x00,0x00,
        0x00,0x00,0x00,0x18,0x00,0x00,0x00,0x00,
        0x00,0x00,0x00,0x18,0x08,0x00,0x00,0x00,
```

11-5 Continued.

```
0x00,0x00,0x00,0x18,0x18,0x00,0x00,0x00,
0x00,0x00,0x00,0x1c,0x18,0x00,0x00,0x00,
0x00,0x00,0x00,0x1c,0x18,0x08,0x00,0x00,
0x00,0x00,0x00,0x1c,0x38,0x08,0x00,0x00,
0x00,0x00,0x08,0x1c,0x38,0x08,0x00,0x00,
0x00,0x00,0x08,0x1c,0x3c,0x08,0x00,0x00,
0x00,0x00,0x08,0x1c,0x3c,0x18,0x00,0x00,
0x00,0x00,0x08,0x3c,0x3c,0x18,0x00,0x00,
0x00,0x00,0x0c,0x3c,0x3c,0x18,0x00,0x00,
0x00,0x00,0x0c,0x3e,0x3c,0x18,0x00,0x00,
0x00,0x00,0x0c,0x3e,0x3e,0x18,0x00,0x00,
0x00,0x00,0x0c,0x3e,0x3e,0x1c,0x00,0x00,
0x00,0x00,0x0c,0x3e,0x3e,0x3c,0x00,0x00,
0x00,0x00,0x1c,0x3e,0x3e,0x3c,0x00,0x00,
0x00,0x00,0x1e,0x3e,0x3e,0x3c,0x00,0x00,
0x00,0x00,0x1e,0x3e,0x3e,0x3e,0x00,0x00,
0x00,0x00,0x3e,0x3e,0x3e,0x3e,0x00,0x00,
0x00,0x02,0x3e,0x3e,0x3e,0x3e,0x00,0x00,
0x00,0x02,0x3f,0x3e,0x3e,0x3e,0x00,0x00,
0x00,0x02,0x3f,0x3e,0x3e,0x3e,0x20,0x00,
0x00,0x02,0x3f,0x3e,0x3e,0x7e,0x20,0x00,
0x00,0x02,0x7f,0x3e,0x3e,0x7e,0x20,0x00,
0x00,0x06,0x7f,0x3e,0x3e,0x7e,0x20,0x00,
0x00,0x06,0x7f,0x3f,0x3e,0x7e,0x20,0x00,
0x00,0x06,0x7f,0x3f,0x3e,0x7e,0x30,0x00,
0x00,0x06,0x7f,0x7f,0x3e,0x7e,0x30,0x00,
0x00,0x0e,0x7f,0x7f,0x3e,0x7e,0x30,0x00,
0x00,0x0e,0x7f,0x7f,0x3f,0x7e,0x30,0x00,
0x00,0x0e,0x7f,0x7f,0x3f,0x7e,0x38,0x00,
0x00,0x0e,0x7f,0x7f,0x7f,0x7e,0x38,0x00,
0x00,0x1e,0x7f,0x7f,0x7f,0x7e,0x38,0x00,
0x00,0x1e,0x7f,0x7f,0x7f,0x7e,0x3c,0x00,
0x00,0x3e,0x7f,0x7f,0x7f,0x7e,0x3c,0x00,
0x00,0x3e,0x7f,0x7f,0x7f,0x7e,0x3e,0x00,
0x00,0x3e,0x7f,0x7f,0x7f,0x7f,0x3e,0x00,
0x00,0x3f,0x7f,0x7f,0x7f,0x7f,0x3e,0x00,
0x00,0x7f,0x7f,0x7f,0x7f,0x7f,0x3e,0x00,
0x00,0x7f,0x7f,0x7f,0x7f,0x7f,0x3f,0x00,
0x00,0x7f,0x7f,0x7f,0x7f,0x7f,0x7f,0x00,
0x08,0x7f,0x7f,0x7f,0x7f,0x7f,0x7f,0x00,
0x08,0x7f,0x7f,0xff,0x7f,0x7f,0x7f,0x00,
0x08,0x7f,0x7f,0xff,0x7f,0x7f,0x7f,0x08,
0x18,0x7f,0x7f,0xff,0x7f,0x7f,0x7f,0x08,
0x18,0x7f,0x7f,0xff,0xff,0x7f,0x7f,0x08,
0x18,0x7f,0x7f,0xff,0xff,0x7f,0x7f,0x18,
0x1c,0x7f,0x7f,0xff,0xff,0x7f,0x7f,0x18,
0x1c,0x7f,0x7f,0xff,0xff,0x7f,0x7f,0x1c,
0x1c,0x7f,0x7f,0xff,0xff,0xff,0x7f,0x1c,
0x3c,0x7f,0x7f,0xff,0xff,0xff,0x7f,0x1c,
0x3c,0x7f,0x7f,0xff,0xff,0xff,0x7f,0x1e,
0x3c,0x7f,0xff,0xff,0xff,0xff,0x7f,0x1e,
0x3c,0x7f,0xff,0xff,0xff,0xff,0x7f,0x3e,
```

11-5 Continued.

```
        0x3e,0x7f,0xff,0xff,0xff,0xff,0x7f,0x3e,
        0x3e,0x7f,0xff,0xff,0xff,0xff,0x7f,0x7e,
        0x7e,0x7f,0xff,0xff,0xff,0xff,0x7f,0x7e,
        0x7e,0xff,0xff,0xff,0xff,0xff,0x7f,0x7e,
        0x7e,0xff,0xff,0xff,0xff,0xff,0xff,0x7e,
        0xfe,0xff,0xff,0xff,0xff,0xff,0xff,0x7e,
        0xff,0xff,0xff,0xff,0xff,0xff,0xff,0x7e,
        0xff,0xff,0xff,0xff,0xff,0xff,0xff,0xff
        };

char remap[]={
        0x00,0x00,0x00,0x01,0x01,0x01,0x02,0x02,
        0x02,0x03,0x03,0x03,0x04,0x04,0x04,0x05,
        0x05,0x05,0x06,0x06,0x06,0x07,0x07,0x07,
        0x08,0x08,0x08,0x09,0x09,0x09,0x0a,0x0a,
        0x0a,0x0b,0x0b,0x0b,0x0c,0x0c,0x0c,0x0d,
        0x0d,0x0e,0x0e,0x0f,0x0f,0x10,0x10,0x11,
        0x11,0x12,0x12,0x13,0x13,0x14,0x14,0x15,
        0x15,0x15,0x16,0x16,0x17,0x18,0x19,0x1a,
        0x1b,0x1c,0x1d,0x1e,0x1f,0x20,0x20,0x21,
        0x22,0x23,0x23,0x24,0x25,0x27,0x27,0x28,
        0x29,0x2a,0x2b,0x2c,0x2d,0x2e,0x2f,0x2f,
        0x30,0x31,0x32,0x33,0x34,0x35,0x36,0x37,
        0x38,0x39,0x3a,0x3a,0x3b,0x3c,0x3d,0x3e,
        0x3f,0x40,0x41,0x42,0x43,0x44,0x45,0x46,
        0x47,0x48,0x49,0x4a,0x4b,0x4c,0x4d,0x4e,
        0x50,0x51,0x52,0x53,0x55,0x56,0x57,0x58,
        0x59,0x5a,0x5b,0x5d,0x5e,0x5f,0x60,0x61,
        0x63,0x64,0x65,0x66,0x67,0x69,0x6a,0x6b,
        0x6c,0x6e,0x70,0x72,0x73,0x74,0x76,0x78,
        0x7a,0x7c,0x7e,0x80,0x82,0x84,0x86,0x88,
        0x8a,0x8c,0x8f,0x91,0x93,0x95,0x98,0x9a,
        0x9c,0x9f,0xa1,0xa4,0xa6,0xa9,0xab,0xae,
        0xb0,0xb2,0xb3,0xb5,0xb7,0xb9,0xba,0xbc,
        0xbd,0xbe,0xc0,0xc2,0xc4,0xc6,0xc8,0xca,
        0xcc,0xce,0xd0,0xd2,0xd4,0xd6,0xd9,0xdb,
        0xdd,0xe0,0xe3,0xe6,0xe8,0xeb,0xed,0xed,
        0xee,0xee,0xef,0xef,0xf0,0xf0,0xf1,0xf1,
        0xf2,0xf2,0xf3,0xf3,0xf4,0xf4,0xf4,0xf5,
        0xf5,0xf5,0xf6,0xf6,0xf6,0xf7,0xf7,0xf7,
        0xf8,0xf8,0xf8,0xf9,0xf9,0xf9,0xfa,0xfa,
        0xfa,0xfb,0xfb,0xfb,0xfc,0xfc,0xfc,0xfd,
        0xfd,0xfd,0xfe,0xfe,0xfe,0xff,0xff,0xff,
        };

FILEINFO fi;
char *buffer=NULL;

char greypalette[256];
int resolution=300;
int halftonesize=64;
```

11-5 Continued.

```
main(argc,argv)
        int argc;
        char *argv[];
{

        FILE *fp;
        static char results[8][16] = {   "Ok",
                                         "Bad file",
                                         "Bad read",
                                         "Unexpected end",
                                         "Bad LZW code",
                                         "Bad first code",
                                         "Memory error",
                                         "Bad symbol size"
                                         };
        char path[81];
        int i,r;

        if(argc > 1) {
                for(i=0;i<argc;++i) {
                        if(!stricmp(argv[i],"/R300")) resolution=300;
                        else if(!stricmp(argv[i],"/R150")) resolution=150;
                        else if(!stricmp(argv[i],"/R100")) resolution=100;
                        else if(!stricmp(argv[i],"/R75")) resolution=75;
                        else if(!stricmp(argv[i],"/H16")) halftonesize=16;
                        else if(!stricmp(argv[i],"/H64")) halftonesize=64;
                }
                strmfe(path,argv[1],"GIF");
                if((fp = fopen(path,"rb")) != NULL) {
                        fi.setup=dosetup;
                        fi.closedown=doclosedown;
                        fi.saveline=saveline;
                        fi.savext=putextension;
                        r=unpackgif(fp,&fi);
                        printf("\%s",results[r]);
                        fclose(fp);
                } else printf("Error opening %s",path);
        } else puts("Argument:       path to a GIF file");
}

/* this function is called when the GIF decoder encounters an extension */
putextension(fp)
        FILE *fp;
{

        PLAINTEXT pt;
        CONTROLBLOCK cb;
        APPLICATION ap;
        int n,i;

        clrscr();
        switch(fgetc(fp)) {
                case 0x0001:                    /* plain text descriptor */
                        if(fread((char *)&pt,1,sizeof(PLAINTEXT),fp)
```

11-5 Continued.

```
                              == sizeof(PLAINTEXT)) {

                    do {
                             if((n=fgetc(fp)) != EOF) {
                                     for(i=0;i<n;++i) fgetc(fp);
                             }
                    } while(n > 0 && n != EOF);
            } else puts("Error reading plain text block");
            break;
case 0x00f9:                /* graphic control block */
            if(fread((char *)&cb,1,sizeof(CONTROLBLOCK),fp)
                != sizeof(CONTROLBLOCK))
                        puts("Error reading control block");
            break;
case 0x00fe:                /* comment extension */
            do {
                    if((n=fgetc(fp)) != EOF) {
                            for(i=0;i<n;++i) fgetc(fp);
                    }
            } while(n > 0 && n != EOF);
            break;
case 0x00ff:                /* application extension */
            if(fread((char *)&ap,1,sizeof(APPLICATION),fp)
                == sizeof(APPLICATION)) {
                    do {
                            if((n=fgetc(fp)) != EOF) {
                                    for(i=0;i<n;++i) fgetc(fp);
                            }
                    } while(n > 0 && n != EOF);
            } else puts("Error reading application block");
            break;
default:                    /* something else */
            n=fgetc(fp);
            for(i=0;i<n;++i) fgetc(fp);
            break;
            }
            getch();
}


/* unpack a GIF file */
unpackgif(fp,fi)
        FILE *fp;
        FILEINFO *fi;
{
        GIFHEADER gh;
        IMAGEBLOCK iblk;
        long t;
        int b,c;

        /* make sure it's a GIF file */
        if(fread((char *)&gh,1,sizeof(GIFHEADER),fp) != sizeof(GIFHEADER) ||
            memcmp(gh.sig, "GIF", 3)) return(BAD_FILE);
```

11-5 Continued.

```
/* get screen dimensions */
fi->width=gh.screenwidth;
fi->depth=gh.screendepth;
fi->bits=(gh.flags & 0x0007) + 1;
fi->background=gh.background;
/* get colour map if there is one */
if (gh.flags & 0x80) {
        c = 3 * (1 << ((gh.flags & 7) + 1));
        if(fread(fi->palette,1,c,fp) != c) return(BAD_READ);
}

/* step through the blocks */
while((c=fgetc(fp))==',' || c=='!' || c==0) {

        /* if it's an image block... */
        if (c == ',') {
                /* get the start of the image block */
                if(fread(&iblk,1,sizeof(IMAGEBLOCK),fp) !=
                    sizeof(IMAGEBLOCK)) return(BAD_READ);

                /* get the image dimensions */
                fi->width=iblk.width;
                fi->depth=iblk.depth;

                if(fi->bits==1) fi->bytes=pixels2bytes(fi->width);
                else fi->bytes=fi->width;

                /* get the local colour map if there is one */
                if(iblk.flags & 0x80) {
                        b = 3*(1<<((iblk.flags & 0x0007) + 1));
                        if(fread(fi->palette,1,b,fp) != c) return(BAD_READ);
                        fi->bits=(iblk.flags & 0x0007) + 1;
                }

                /* get the initial code size */
                if((c=fgetc(fp))==EOF) return(BAD_FILE);

                fi->flags=iblk.flags;

                /* do the setup procedure */
                if(fi->setup != NULL) {
                if((t=(fi->setup)(fi)) != GOOD_READ)
                    return(t);
        }

        /* unpack the image */
        t=unpackimage(fp,c,fi);

        /* do the close down procedure */
        if(fi->closedown != NULL) (fi->closedown)(fi);

        /* quit if there was an error */
```

11-5 Continued.

```
                        if(t != GOOD_READ) return(t);
            }
                /* otherwise, it's an extension */
                else if(c == '!') (fi->savext)(fp);
        }
        return(GOOD_READ);
}

/* unpack an LZW compressed image */
unpackimage(fp,bits,fi)
        FILE *fp;
        int bits;
        FILEINFO *fi;
{
        int bits2;          /* Bits plus 1 */
        int codesize;       /* Current code size in bits */
        int codesize2;      /* Next codesize */
        int nextcode;       /* Next available table entry */
        int thiscode;       /* Code being expanded */
        int oldtoken;       /* Last symbol decoded */
        int currentcode;    /* Code just read */
        int oldcode;        /* Code read before this one */
        int bitsleft;       /* Number of bits left in *p */
        int blocksize;      /* Bytes in next block */
        int line=0;         /* next line to write */
        int byte=0;         /* next byte to write */
        int pass=0;         /* pass number for interlaced pictures */

        char *p;            /* Pointer to current byte in read buffer */
        char *q;            /* Pointer past last byte in read buffer */
        char b[255];        /* Read buffer */
        char *u;            /* Stack pointer into firstcodestack */
        char *linebuffer;   /* place to store the current line */

        static char firstcodestack[4096]; /* Stack for first codes */
        static char lastcodestack[4096];  /* Stack for previous code */
        static int codestack[4096];       /* Stack for links */

        static int wordmasktable[] = {  0x0000,0x0001,0x0003,0x0007,
                                        0x000f,0x001f,0x003f,0x007f,
                                        0x00ff,0x01ff,0x03ff,0x07ff,
                                        0x0fff,0x1fff,0x3fff,0x7fff
                                        };

        static int inctable[] = { 8,8,4,2,0 }; /* interlace increments */
        static int startable[] = { 0,4,2,1,0 };  /* interlace starts */

        p=q=b;
        bitsleft = 8;

        if (bits < 2 || bits > 8) return(BAD_SYMBOLSIZE);
        bits2 = 1 << bits;
```

11-5 Continued.

```
nextcode = bits2 + 2;
codesize2 = 1 << (codesize = bits + 1);
oldcode=oldtoken=NO_CODE;

if((linebuffer=malloc(fi->width)) == NULL) return(BAD_ALLOC);

/* loop until something breaks */
for(;;) {
        if(bitsleft==8) {
                if(++p >= q &&
                (((blocksize = fgetc(fp)) < 1) ||
                (q=(p=b)+fread(b,1,blocksize,fp))< (b+blocksize)))) {
                        free(linebuffer);
                        return(UNEXPECTED_EOF);
                }
                bitsleft = 0;
        }
        thiscode = *p;
        if ((currentcode=(codesize+bitsleft)) <= 8) {
                *p >>= codesize;
                bitsleft = currentcode;
        }
        else {
                if(++p >= q &&
                  (((blocksize = fgetc(fp)) < 1) ||
                  (q=(p=b)+fread(b,1,blocksize,fp)) < (b+blocksize)))) {
                        free(linebuffer);
                        return(UNEXPECTED_EOF);
                }
                thiscode |= *p << (8 - bitsleft);
                if(currentcode <= 16) *p >>= (bitsleft=currentcode-8);
                else {
                        if(++p >= q &&
                          (((blocksize = fgetc(fp)) < 1) ||
                          (q=(p=b) + fread(b,1,blocksize,fp)) < (b+blocksize)))) {
                                free(linebuffer);
                                return(UNEXPECTED_EOF);
                        }
                        thiscode |= *p << (16 - bitsleft);
                        *p >>= (bitsleft = currentcode - 16);
                }
        }
        thiscode &= wordmasktable[codesize];
        currentcode = thiscode;

        if(thiscode == (bits2+1)) break;    /* found EOI */
        if(thiscode > nextcode) {
                free(linebuffer);
                return(BAD_CODE);
        }

        if(thiscode == bits2) {
```

11-5 Continued.

```
                    nextcode = bits2 + 2;
                    codesize2 = 1 << (codesize = (bits + 1));
                    oldtoken = oldcode = NO_CODE;
                    continue;
            }

        u = firstcodestack;

        if(thiscode==nextcode) {
                if(oldcode==NO_CODE) {
                        free(linebuffer);
                        return(BAD_FIRSTCODE);
                }
                *u++ = oldtoken;
                thiscode = oldcode;
        }

        while (thiscode >= bits2) {
                *u++ = lastcodestack[thiscode];
                thiscode = codestack[thiscode];
        }

        oldtoken = thiscode;
        do {
                linebuffer[byte++]=thiscode;
                if(byte >= fi->width) {
                        (fi->saveline)(linebuffer,line);
                        byte=0;

                        /* check for interlaced image */
                        if(fi->flags & 0x40) {
                                line+=inctable[pass];
                                if(line >= fi->depth)
                                        line=startable[++pass];
                        } else ++line;
                }

                if (u <= firstcodestack) break;
                thiscode = *--u;
        } while(1);

        if(nextcode < 4096 && oldcode != NO_CODE) {
                codestack[nextcode] = oldcode;
                lastcodestack[nextcode] = oldtoken;
                if (++nextcode >= codesize2 && codesize < 12)
                        codesize2 = 1 << ++codesize;
        }
        oldcode = currentcode;
    }
    free(linebuffer);
    return(GOOD_READ);
}
```

11-5 Continued.

```
/* This function is called before an image is decompressed. It must
   allocate memory, put the display in graphic mode and so on. */
dosetup(fi)
        FILEINFO *fi;
{
        if(!getbuffer((long)fi->bytes*(long)fi->depth,fi->bytes,fi->depth))
            return(BAD_ALLOC);

        makegreypalette();
        return(GOOD_READ);
}


/* This function is called after an image has been unpacked. It must
   display the image and deallocate memory. */
doclosedown(fi)
        FILEINFO *fi;
{
        char b[32],*p;
        int a,c,i,j,k,n;

        sprintf(b,"\x1b*t%uR",resolution);
        p_string("\033E");
        p_string(b);
        p_string("\x1b*p20X");
        p_string("\x1b*p20Y");
        p_string("\x1b*r1A");

        if(fi->bits==1) n=pixels2bytes(fi->width);
        else {
                if(halftonesize==16) n=pixels2bytes(fi->width)<<2;
                else n=pixels2bytes(fi->width)<<3;
        }

        for(i=0;i<fi->depth;++i) {
                printf("\rPrinting line %u     ",i);
                p=getline(i);
                if(fi->bits==1) {
                        sprintf(b,"\x1b*b%dW",n);
                        p_string(b);
                        p_buff(p,n);
                }
                else {
                        if(halftonesize==16) {
                                for(j=0;j<4;++j) {
                                        sprintf(b,"\x1b*b%dW",n);
                                        p_string(b);
                                        for(k=0;k<n;++k) {
                                                c=(*p++ >> 4);
                                                a = ((halftone_16[c*4+j] << 4) & 0xf0);
                                                c=(*p++ >> 4);
                                                a |= (halftone_16[c*4+j] & 0x0f);
                                                p_char(~a);
```

11-5 Continued.

```
                                    }
                                }
                            }
                            else {
                                for(j=0;j<8;++j) {
                                    sprintf(b,"\x1b*b%dW",n);
                                    p_string(b);
                                    for(k=0;k<n;++k) {
                                        c=p[k] >> 2;
                                        p_char(~halftone_64[c*8+j]);
                                    }
                                }
                            }
                        }
                    }
                }
        p_string("\x1b*rB");
        p_string("\014");

        freebuffer();
        return(GOOD_READ);
}

/* send a C language string to the printer */
p_string(s)
        char *s;
{
        while(*s) p_char(*s++);
}

/* send a buffer to the printer */
p_buff(s,l)
        char *s;
        int l;
{
        while(l--) p_char(*s++);
}

/* send a character to the printer */
p_char(c)
        int c;
{
        union REGS r;

        do {
                r.h.ah = 2;
                r.x.dx = PRINTERPORT;
                int86(0x17,&r,&r);
        } while(!(r.h.ah & 0x80));

        r.h.ah = 0;
        r.h.al = c;
        r.x.dx = PRINTERPORT;
```

11-5 Continued.

```
          int86(0x17,&r,&r);
}

/* make file name with specific extension */
strmfe(new,old,ext)
          char *new,*old,*ext;
{
          while(*old != 0 && *old != '.') *new++=*old++;
          *new++='.';
          while(*ext) *new++=*ext++;
          *new=0;
}

makegreypalette()
{
          double f;
          char *palette;
          int i,n;

          n=1<<fi.bits;
          palette=fi.palette;
          for(i=0;i<n;++i) {
                    f= (0.30 * (double)*palette++) +
                       (0.59 * (double)*palette++) +
                       (0.11 * (double)*palette++);
                    greypalette[i]=remap[(char)f];
          }
}

/* convert GIF line to buffered line and save it */
saveline(p,n)
          char *p;
          unsigned int n;
{
          char *pr;
          int i;

          printf("\rReading line %u       ",n);
          if(fi.bits==1) {
                    if((pr=malloc(fi.bytes)) != NULL) {
                              memset(pr,0xff,fi.bytes);
                              for(i=0;i<fi.width;++i) {
                                        if(p[i]) pr[i>>3] &= ~masktable[i & 0x0007];
                                        else pr[i>>3] |= masktable[i & 0x0007];
                              }
                              putline(pr,n);
                              free(pr);
                    }
          }
          else {
                    for(i=0;i<fi.width;++i) p[i]=greypalette[p[i]];
                    putline(p,n);
```

11-5 Continued.

```
        }
}

/* if you don't use in the memory manager, these functions
   will stand in for it */

#if !MEMMANGR

/* return a far pointer plus a long integer */
char *farPtr(p,l)
        char *p;
        long l;
{
        unsigned int seg,off;

        seg = FP_SEG(p);
        off = FP_OFF(p);
        seg += (off / 16);
        off &= 0x000f;
        off += (unsigned int)(l & 0x000fL);
        seg += (l / 16L);
        p = MK_FP(seg,off);
        return(p);
}

/* save one line to memory */
putline(p,n)
        char *p;
        unsigned int n;
{

        if(n >= 0 && n < fi.depth)
                memcpy(farPtr(buffer,(long)n*(long)fi.bytes),p,fi.bytes);
}

/* get one line from memory */
char *getline(n)
        unsigned int n;
{
        return(farPtr(buffer,(long)n*(long)fi.bytes));
}

#pragma warn -par
getbuffer(n,bytes,lines)
        unsigned long n;
        int bytes,lines;
{
        if((buffer=farmalloc(n)) == NULL) return(0);
        else return(1);
}

freebuffer()
```

11-5 Continued.

```
{
        if(buffer != NULL) farfree(buffer);
        buffer=NULL;
}
#endif /* !MEMMANGR */
```

11-5 Continued.

you'll have little trouble understanding what PRNTGIF1 is up to. It
unpacks the file passed to it as a command line argument and then calls
the printing code in `doclosedown` to drive a LaserJet. Monochrome
images are converted to planar image lines and printed directly. Color GIF
files are converted to gray scale and used to assemble halftone lines. The
halftone tables are stored up in `halftone_16` and `halftone_64`
respectively. The `remap` table does contrast expansion, as discussed earlier. Since there are only 256 possible gray-scale values for an 8-bit GIF
file, it's convenient to use a lookup table to handle the gray-scale conversion too. It lives in `graypalette`, as filled in by the `makegraypalette`
function.

There are several command line switches for PRNTGIF1 to select its
various options, as follows:

/R75	Print at 75 dots per inch
/R100	Print at 100 dots per inch
/R150	Print at 150 dots per inch
/R300	Print at 300 dots per inch
/H16	Use the 16-entry halftone spot table
/H64	Use the 64-entry halftone spot table

It defaults to using the 64-entry halftone table and 300 dot per inch
printing.

While the halftoning procedure discussed here is one way to print halftones on a LaserJet, it might not prove to be the best for your applications.
Its size limit is a bit of a restriction, for one thing. You might want to look at
implementing the dithering code from *Bitmapped Graphics* to print
directly to a LaserJet.

PostScript printing

The printer control language for PostScript printers is really a programming language, unlike PCL. It's a bit like the FORTH language, except it
has been fine-tuned to drive a laser printer. PostScript offers most of the
things you'd expect in a conventional programming language, such as C.
This includes a stack (actually, several of them), subroutines, dynamic
variable allocation, type checking, and so on.

PostScript is an interpreted language. A PostScript printer is really a
language interpreter with a print engine attached instead of a monitor. As
each line of PostScript code is downloaded to your printer, the printer's
firmware tries to make sense of it.

In sending text or graphics to a PostScript printer, the software that drives the printer essentially writes a program in the PostScript language that defines whatever's to be on the page. You might think of this as being similar to creating a PC screen by writing a program that puts characters and symbols on your monitor at certain locations.

In fact, most software that drives PostScript printers does not use much of the capability of the PostScript language. In many cases, all you'll really want to do is to place some text and pictures on a page, eject the page, and move on to the next one. It doesn't take much understanding of PostScript to do this.

Even a little bit of PostScript, however, is likely to make your brain hurt to some extent. There are several good reasons for this, not the least of which is that PostScript is a postfix language. It also embodies a number of somewhat troublesome concepts peculiar to effectively handling large graphic objects. This latter issue really doesn't concern the code in this chapter, as the PostScript programs involved in sending the odd picture to a PostScript printer are pretty trivial. The former one probably does. Postfix notation is something only a computer could love.

Here's a very simple PostScript operation:

```
100 100 moveto
(pig's breakfast) show
```

This bit of PostScript code would cause the string "pig's breakfast" to be printed at location (100,100) on the current page in the current font. The default unit of measurement under PostScript is a point, which is about $1/72$ inch. Points are used to measure type size, and PostScript is very much into typography.

Point (0,0) is the lower left corner of the page being printed.

While the PostScript operators moveto and show are pretty easy to understand, you'll notice that their arguments precede them, which is how postfix languages work. As it scans each line of input, a PostScript interpreter pushes everything it finds that is not an operator onto the stack and executes all the operators. Each operator knows how many things it should find on the stack. For example, the operator moveto knows that there should be two things awaiting it on the stack and that both of these things should be numbers. It pops these numbers from the stack and uses them as arguments.

PostScript operators don't know what has been pushed onto the stack before they're called. They know only what they expect to see.

PostScript code is not all that easy to write and very nearly impossible to read if you didn't write it to begin with. However, it is extremely flexible and very convenient to work with when you want to hide some in a program and send it out to a printer now and then.

One of the many PostScript operators is image, which serves to print bitmapped graphics. The image operator reads binary information from somewhere and arranges it in a rectangular matrix on the current page. While complex high-end PostScript devices can have image set up to receive its image data from one of a number of places, in this example it will receive it from the printer port.

A graphic to be printed on a PostScript printer consists of a very small PostScript program, an enormous amount of hexadecimal data, and the instruction showpage, which causes the current page to be imaged and printed. The first part has the code to make the image operator work. It also has a few bits of glue to handle halftoning and positioning of the image on the page being created. This is an example of a program used to print a monochrome image to a PostScript printer. In this case, the graphic has the dimensions 576×720 pixels.

```
/bytes 72 def
/width 576 def
/height 720 def
/pixwidth 553.8 def
/pixheight 692.3 def
/picstr bytes string def
/dopic {
gsave width height 1
[width 0 0 height neg 0 height]
{currentfile picstr readhexstring pop}
image grestore } def
/showname {
/Courier findfont 12 scalefont setfont
20 20 moveto (WATERFAL.GIF) show
} def
showname
25 50 translate pixwidth pixheight scale
dopic
5B41416F1088F2...

%% lots of hex numbers

...7A7B5507091A1A
showpage
```

While it's not necessary to understand everything that's going on in this bit of code in order to use it (and, in fairness, it's beyond the scope of this book to explain it fully) you can work through its operation superficially without an excessive amount of head scratching. The first three lines of the program define the image dimensions. The next two define the area it occupies on the page. The /pixstr definition creates a buffer for the PostScript interpreter to store one line of the image while it's working.

The /dopic declaration is actually a subroutine. It's called to print the picture. It creates a "transformation matrix" for the image being printed that defines how its coordinates should map to those of the paper. There's a whole chapter in the Adobe PostScript book on transformation matrices. Suffice it to say that this is how they should look if you'll be printing bitmaps the right way around.

The line of dopic enclosed in curly brackets is a function that image calls to get the data for the picture it's printing. It reads hexadecimal numbers from the current file and puts their binary values into the buffer `pic str`. The current file, in the case of a PostScript laser, is the data coming from the printer port.

The `/showname` declaration is another subroutine. It's used to print the name of the file in 12-point Courier type at the bottom of the page.

The second-to-last line of the PostScript code sets the location and size of the image to be printed.

Just as with the LaserJet graphics-printing program discussed earlier in this chapter, once you have the printer-dependent parts of a PostScript driver working properly, you need never look at them again. Inasmuch as the code in this chapter provides you with all the PostScript commands you need to print graphics, you should not have to worry about what the previous code means.

Printing gray-scale images to a PostScript printer is not a lot more difficult than printing monochrome ones, in that PostScript handles the half-toning. You can allow it to do so with its own default halftone spot procedure or you can provide one for it. If you leave it to its own devices, it should choose a spot procedure most in keeping with the capabilities of the particular laser printer engine you'll be printing to.

There are a few holes in the reality of this that may prompt you to specifically select the halftone spot characteristics of your output. To begin with, many PostScript printers have questionable choices for their default screen sizes. All other things being equal, a screen with more spots per inch will reproduce small details better but will also handle fewer distinct levels of gray. A well-chosen spot size and shape on a 300 dot per inch laser printer should be able to represent about 32 distinct levels of gray.

Some PostScript lasers seem to have had their halftone characteristics defined for printers with brand new, perfectly aligned print engines. As a laser printer's engine ages, things like xerographic dot gain and the alignment of its laser can deteriorate the quality of the halftone spots it produces, ultimately degrading its halftones. This will be a lot more noticeable if the spot characteristics were chosen with the assumption that only people with maintenance agreements stretching well into the next century deserve to own laser printers.

Finally, if you'll be printing halftone graphics for subsequent photocopying, note that most photocopiers cannot do a very good job of reproducing the approximately 50 spot-per-inch screens that PostScript lasers typically default to. Coarser screens usually leave you with better looking copies.

While you should experiment with different spot sizes to get a feel for what looks acceptable on your laser, 45 spots per inch, called a "45-line screen" in commercial printing, is a good place to start.

Figure 11-6 illustrates the result of printing with varying screen sizes.

Printing color pictures to a color PostScript printer, such as the QMS ColorScript 100, turns out to be no more complicated than printing gray-scale images to a conventional PostScript laser. Color PostScript can convert RGB color into first-class CYMK color, so there's no need to perform any complex color-model conversion or black removal.

Figure 11-7 is the source code for PRNTGIF2. This program prints GIF files to either a monochrome or a color PostScript device. It can handle images with between 1 and 8 bits of color.

For the most part, PRNTGIF2 works just like PRNTGIF1. The only differences lie in the actual printing code, which must speak PostScript

11-6 (A) PostScript output using a 50-line screen,

(B) a 45-line screen, and

(C) a 30-line screen.

rather than PCL. There are three small PostScript programs stashed at the top of the listing, one each for monochrome images, gray-scale images, and color images to be sent to a color printer. In each case, they use C-language `printf` formats to handle the dimensions and other dependent parameters for the images being printed.

```
/*
            GIF printer - copyright (c) 1991
            PostScript version
            Alchemy Mindworks Inc.
*/

#include "stdio.h"
#include "dos.h"
#include "alloc.h"

/*                              uncomment this line if you
#include "memmangr.h"           will be linking in the memory manager
*/

#define GOOD_READ          0    /* return codes */
#define BAD_FILE           1
#define BAD_READ           2
#define UNEXPECTED_EOF     3
#define BAD_CODE           4
#define BAD_FIRSTCODE      5
#define BAD_ALLOC          6
#define BAD_SYMBOLSIZE     7

#define RGB_RED            0
```

11-7 The source code for PRNTGIF2.

```
                    #define RGB_GREEN        1
                    #define RGB_BLUE         2
                    #define RGB_SIZE         3

                    #define NO_CODE          -1

                    #define PRINTERPORT      0         /* 0=LPT1, 1=LPT2, 2=LPT3 */

                    #define pixels2bytes(n)    ((n+7)/8)

                    typedef struct {
                            char sig[6];
                            unsigned int screenwidth,screendepth;
                            unsigned char flags,background,aspect;
                            } GIFHEADER;

                    typedef struct {
                            unsigned int left,top,width,depth;
                            unsigned char flags;
                            } IMAGEBLOCK;

                    typedef struct {
                            int width,depth,bytes,bits;
                            int flags;
                            int background;
                            char palette[768];
                            char name[81];
                            int (*setup)();
                            int (*closedown)();
                            int (*saveline)();
                            int (*savext)();
                            } FILEINFO;

                    typedef struct {
                            char blocksize;
                            char flags;
                            unsigned int delay;
                            char transparent_colour;
                            char terminator;
                            } CONTROLBLOCK;

                    typedef struct {
                            char blocksize;
                            unsigned int left,top;
                            unsigned int gridwidth,gridheight;
                            char cellwidth,cellheight;
                            char forecolour,backcolour;
                            } PLAINTEXT;

                    typedef struct {
                            char blocksize;
                            char applstring[8];
```

11-7 Continued.

```
            char authentication[3];
            } APPLICATION;

char *farPtr(char *p,long l);
char *getline(unsigned int n);

int putextension(FILE *fp);
int saveline(char *p,unsigned int n);
int dosetup(FILEINFO *fi);
int doclosedown(FILEINFO *fi);

char masktable[8]={0x80,0x40,0x20,0x10,0x08,0x04,0x02,0x01};

char c256pshd_colour[]=
            "/screensize %d def\r\n"
            "/width %d def\r\n"
            "/height %d def\r\n"
            "/pixwidth %f def\r\n"
            "/pixheight %f def\r\n"
            "/picstr 3 width mul string def\r\n"
            "screensize 0 ne {\r\n"
            "screensize 45 { abs exch abs 2 copy add 1 gt\r\n"
            "{ 1 sub dup mul exch 1 sub dup mul add 1 sub }\r\n"
            "{ dup mul exch dup mul add 1 exch sub }\r\n"
            "ifelse } setscreen\r\n"
            "} if\r\n"
            "/dopic {\r\n"
            "gsave width height 8\r\n"
            "[width 0 0 height neg 0 height]\r\n"
            "{currentfile picstr readhexstring pop}\r\n"
            "false 3 colorimage grestore } def\r\n"
            "/showname {\r\n"
            "/Courier findfont 12 scalefont setfont\r\n"
            "20 20 moveto (%s) show\r\n"
            "} def\r\n"
            "showname\r\n"
            "40 100 translate pixwidth pixheight scale\r\n"
            "dopic\r\n";

char c256pshd[]=
            "/screensize %d def\r\n"
            "/width %d def\r\n"
            "/height %d def\r\n"
            "/pixwidth %f def\r\n"
            "/pixheight %f def\r\n"
            "/picstr width string def\r\n"
            "screensize 0 ne {\r\n"
            "screensize 45 { abs exch abs 2 copy add 1 gt\r\n"
            "{ 1 sub dup mul exch 1 sub dup mul add 1 sub }\r\n"
            "{ dup mul exch dup mul add 1 exch sub }\r\n"
            "ifelse } setscreen\r\n"
            "} if\r\n"
```

11-7 Continued.

```
                    "/dopic {\r\n"
                    "gsave width height 8\r\n"
                    "[width 0 0 height neg 0 height]\r\n"
                    "{currentfile picstr readhexstring pop}\r\n"
                    "image grestore } def\r\n"
                    "/showname {\r\n"
                    "/Courier findfont 12 scalefont setfont\r\n"
                    "20 20 moveto (%s) show\r\n"
                    "} def\r\n"
                    "showname\r\n"
                    "40 50 translate pixwidth pixheight scale\r\n"
                    "dopic\r\n";

        char monopshd[]=
                    "/bytes %d def\r\n"
                    "/width %d def\r\n"
                    "/height %d def\r\n"
                    "/pixwidth %f def\r\n"
                    "/pixheight %f def\r\n"
                    "/picstr bytes string def\r\n"
                    "/dopic {\r\n"
                    "gsave width height 1\r\n"
                    "[width 0 0 height neg 0 height]\r\n"
                    "{currentfile picstr readhexstring pop}\r\n"
                    "image grestore } def\r\n"
                    "/showname {\r\n"
                    "/Courier findfont 12 scalefont setfont\r\n"
                    "20 20 moveto (%s) show\r\n"
                    "} def\r\n"
                    "showname\r\n"
                    "25 50 translate pixwidth pixheight scale\r\n"
                    "dopic\r\n";

        char remap[]={
                0x00,0x00,0x00,0x01,0x01,0x01,0x02,0x02,
                0x02,0x03,0x03,0x03,0x04,0x04,0x04,0x05,
                0x05,0x05,0x06,0x06,0x06,0x07,0x07,0x07,
                0x08,0x08,0x08,0x09,0x09,0x09,0x0a,0x0a,
                0x0a,0x0b,0x0b,0x0b,0x0c,0x0c,0x0c,0x0d,
                0x0d,0x0e,0x0e,0x0f,0x0f,0x10,0x10,0x11,
                0x11,0x12,0x12,0x13,0x13,0x14,0x14,0x15,
                0x15,0x15,0x16,0x16,0x17,0x18,0x19,0x1a,
                0x1b,0x1c,0x1d,0x1e,0x1f,0x20,0x20,0x21,
                0x22,0x23,0x23,0x24,0x25,0x27,0x27,0x28,
                0x29,0x2a,0x2b,0x2c,0x2d,0x2e,0x2f,0x2f,
                0x30,0x31,0x32,0x33,0x34,0x35,0x36,0x37,
                0x38,0x39,0x3a,0x3a,0x3b,0x3c,0x3d,0x3e,
                0x3f,0x40,0x41,0x42,0x43,0x44,0x45,0x46,
                0x47,0x48,0x49,0x4a,0x4b,0x4c,0x4d,0x4e,
                0x50,0x51,0x52,0x53,0x55,0x56,0x57,0x58,
                0x59,0x5a,0x5b,0x5d,0x5e,0x5f,0x60,0x61,
                0x63,0x64,0x65,0x66,0x67,0x69,0x6a,0x6b,
```

11-7 Continued.

```
        0x6c,0x6e,0x70,0x72,0x73,0x74,0x76,0x78,
        0x7a,0x7c,0x7e,0x80,0x82,0x84,0x86,0x88,
        0x8a,0x8c,0x8f,0x91,0x93,0x95,0x98,0x9a,
        0x9c,0x9f,0xa1,0xa4,0xa6,0xa9,0xab,0xae,
        0xb0,0xb2,0xb3,0xb5,0xb7,0xb9,0xba,0xbc,
        0xbd,0xbe,0xc0,0xc2,0xc4,0xc6,0xc8,0xca,
        0xcc,0xce,0xd0,0xd2,0xd4,0xd6,0xd9,0xdb,
        0xdd,0xe0,0xe3,0xe6,0xe8,0xeb,0xed,0xed,
        0xee,0xee,0xef,0xef,0xf0,0xf0,0xf1,0xf1,
        0xf2,0xf2,0xf3,0xf3,0xf4,0xf4,0xf4,0xf5,
        0xf5,0xf5,0xf6,0xf6,0xf6,0xf7,0xf7,0xf7,
        0xf8,0xf8,0xf8,0xf9,0xf9,0xf9,0xfa,0xfa,
        0xfa,0xfb,0xfb,0xfb,0xfc,0xfc,0xfc,0xfd,
        0xfd,0xfd,0xfe,0xfe,0xfe,0xff,0xff,0xff,
        };

FILEINFO fi;
char *buffer=NULL;

char greypalette[256];
int resolution=300;
int printcolour=0;
int screensize=0;

main(argc,argv)
        int argc;
        char *argv[];
{
        FILE *fp;
        static char results[8][16] = {  "Ok",
                                        "Bad file",
                                        "Bad read",
                                        "Unexpected end",
                                        "Bad LZW code",
                                        "Bad first code",
                                        "Memory error",
                                        "Bad symbol size"
                                        };
        char path[81];
        int i,r;

        if(argc > 1) {
                for(i=0;i<argc;++i) {
                        if(!stricmp(argv[i],"/R300")) resolution=300;
                        else if(!stricmp(argv[i],"/R150")) resolution=150;
                        else if(!stricmp(argv[i],"/R100")) resolution=100;
                        else if(!stricmp(argv[i],"/R75")) resolution=75;
                        else if(!stricmp(argv[i],"/COL")) printcolour=1;
                        else if(!memicmp(argv[i],"/S",2)) screensize=atoi(argv[i]+2);
                }

                strmfe(path,argv[1],"GIF");
```

11-7 Continued.

```
                    strupr(path);
                    strcpy(fi.name,path);
                    if((fp = fopen(path,"rb")) != NULL) {
                            fi.setup=dosetup;
                            fi.closedown=doclosedown;
                            fi.saveline=saveline;
                            fi.savext=putextension;
                            r=unpackgif(fp,&fi);
                            printf("\%s",results[r]);
                            fclose(fp);
                    } else printf("Error opening %s",path);
            } else puts("Argument:      path to a GIF file");
}

/* This function is called when the GIF decoder encounters an extension */
putextension(fp)
        FILE *fp;
{
        PLAINTEXT pt;
        CONTROLBLOCK cb;
        APPLICATION ap;
        int n,i;

        clrscr();
        switch(fgetc(fp)) {
                case 0x0001:                /* plain text descriptor */
                        if(fread((char *)&pt,1,sizeof(PLAINTEXT),fp)
                           == sizeof(PLAINTEXT)) {

                                do {
                                        if((n=fgetc(fp)) != EOF) {
                                                for(i=0;i<n;++i) fgetc(fp);
                                        }
                                } while(n > 0 && n != EOF);
                        } else puts("Error reading plain text block");
                        break;
                case 0x00f9:                /* graphic control block */
                        if(fread((char *)&cb,1,sizeof(CONTROLBLOCK),fp)
                           != sizeof(CONTROLBLOCK))
                                puts("Error reading control block");
                        break;
                case 0x00fe:                /* comment extension */
                        do {
                                if((n=fgetc(fp)) != EOF) {
                                        for(i=0;i<n;++i) fgetc(fp);
                                }
                        } while(n > 0 && n != EOF);
                        break;
                case 0x00ff:                /* application extension */
                        if(fread((char *)&ap,1,sizeof(APPLICATION),fp)
                           == sizeof(APPLICATION)) {
                                do {
```

11-7 Continued.

```
                                        if((n=fgetc(fp)) != EOF) {
                                                for(i=0;i<n;++i) fgetc(fp);
                                        }
                                } while(n > 0 && n != EOF);
                        } else puts("Error reading application block");
                        break;
                default:                        /* something else */
                        n=fgetc(fp);
                        for(i=0;i<n;++i) fgetc(fp);
                        break;
        }

        getch();
}

/* unpack a GIF file */
unpackgif(fp,fi)
        FILE *fp;
        FILEINFO *fi;
{

        GIFHEADER gh;
        IMAGEBLOCK iblk;
        long t;
        int b,c;

        /* make sure it's a GIF file */
        if(fread((char *)&gh,1,sizeof(GIFHEADER),fp) != sizeof(GIFHEADER) ||
            memcmp(gh.sig, "GIF", 3)) return(BAD_FILE);

        /* get screen dimensions */
        fi->width=gh.screenwidth;
        fi->depth=gh.screendepth;
        fi->bits=(gh.flags & 0x0007) + 1;
        fi->background=gh.background;
        /* get colour map if there is one */
        if (gh.flags & 0x80) {
                c = 3 * (1 << ((gh.flags & 7) + 1));
                if(fread(fi->palette,1,c,fp) != c) return(BAD_READ);
        }
        /* step through the blocks */
        while((c=fgetc(fp))==',' || c=='!' || c==0) {

                /* if it's an image block... */
                if (c == ',') {
                        /* get the start of the image block */
                        if(fread(&iblk,1,sizeof(IMAGEBLOCK),fp) !=
                            sizeof(IMAGEBLOCK)) return(BAD_READ);

                        /* get the image dimensions */
                        fi->width=iblk.width;
                        fi->depth=iblk.depth;

                        if(fi->bits==1) fi->bytes=pixels2bytes(fi->width);
```

11-7 Continued.

```
                              else {
                                      if(printcolour) fi->bytes=fi->width*RGB_SIZE;
                                      else fi->bytes=fi->width;
                              }

                              /* get the local colour map if there is one */
                              if(iblk.flags & 0x80) {
                                      b = 3*(1<<((iblk.flags & 0x0007) + 1));
                                      if(fread(fi->palette,1,b,fp) != c) return(BAD_READ);
                                      fi->bits=(iblk.flags & 0x0007) + 1;
                              }

                              /* get the initial code size */
                              if((c=fgetc(fp))==EOF) return(BAD_FILE);

                              fi->flags=iblk.flags;
                              /* do the setup procedure */
                              if(fi->setup != NULL) {
                                      if((t=(fi->setup)(fi)) != GOOD_READ)
                                              return(t);
                              }

                              /* unpack the image */
                              t=unpackimage(fp,c,fi);

                              /* do the close down procedure */
                              if(fi->closedown != NULL) (fi->closedown)(fi);

                              /* quit if there was an error */
                              if(t != GOOD_READ) return(t);
                      }
                      /* otherwise, it's an extension */
                      else if(c == '!') (fi->savext)(fp);
              }
              return(GOOD_READ);
      }

      /* unpack an LZW compressed image */
      unpackimage(fp,bits,fi)
              FILE *fp;
              int bits;
              FILEINFO *fi;
      {
              int bits2;              /* Bits plus 1 */
              int codesize;          /* Current code size in bits */
              int codesize2;         /* Next codesize */
              int nextcode;          /* Next available table entry */
              int thiscode;          /* Code being expanded */
              int oldtoken;          /* Last symbol decoded */
              int currentcode;       /* Code just read */
              int oldcode;           /* Code read before this one */
              int bitsleft;          /* Number of bits left in *p */
```

11-7 Continued.

```
int blocksize;        /* Bytes in next block */
int line=0;           /* next line to write */
int byte=0;           /* next byte to write */
int pass=0;           /* pass number for interlaced pictures */

char *p;              /* Pointer to current byte in read buffer */
char *q;              /* Pointer past last byte in read buffer */
char b[255];          /* Read buffer */
char *u;              /* Stack pointer into firstcodestack */
char *linebuffer;     /* place to store the current line */

static char firstcodestack[4096];  /* Stack for first codes */
static char lastcodestack[4096];   /* Stack for previous code */
static int codestack[4096];        /* Stack for links */

static int wordmasktable[] = {  0x0000,0x0001,0x0003,0x0007,
                                0x000f,0x001f,0x003f,0x007f,
                                0x00ff,0x01ff,0x03ff,0x07ff,
                                0x0fff,0x1fff,0x3fff,0x7fff
                                };

static int inctable[] = { 8,8,4,2,0 }; /* interlace increments */
static int startable[] = { 0,4,2,1,0 };  /* interlace starts */

p=q=b;
bitsleft = 8;

if (bits < 2 || bits > 8) return(BAD_SYMBOLSIZE);
bits2 = 1 << bits;
nextcode = bits2 + 2;
codesize2 = 1 << (codesize = bits + 1);
oldcode=oldtoken=NO_CODE;

if((linebuffer=malloc(fi->width)) == NULL) return(BAD_ALLOC);

/* loop until something breaks */
for(;;) {
        if(bitsleft==8) {
                if(++p >= q &&
                (((blocksize = fgetc(fp)) < 1) ||
                (q=(p=b)+fread(b,1,blocksize,fp))< (b+blocksize))) {
                        free(linebuffer);
                        return(UNEXPECTED_EOF);
                }
                bitsleft = 0;
        }
        thiscode = *p;
        if ((currentcode=(codesize+bitsleft)) <= 8) {
                *p >>= codesize;
                bitsleft = currentcode;
        }
        else {
```

11-7 Continued.

```
                    if(++p >= q &&
                      (((blocksize = fgetc(fp)) < 1) ||
                       (q=(p=b)+fread(b,1,blocksize,fp)) < (b+blocksize))) {
                            free(linebuffer);
                            return(UNEXPECTED_EOF);
                    }
                    thiscode |= *p << (8 - bitsleft);
                    if(currentcode <= 16) *p >>= (bitsleft=currentcode-8);
                    else {
                            if(++p >= q &&
                              (((blocksize = fgetc(fp)) < 1) ||
                               (q=(p=b) + fread(b,1,blocksize,fp)) < (b+blocksize))) {
                                    free(linebuffer);
                                    return(UNEXPECTED_EOF);
                            }
                            thiscode |= *p << (16 - bitsleft);
                            *p >>= (bitsleft = currentcode - 16);
                    }
            }
    thiscode &= wordmasktable[codesize];
    currentcode = thiscode;

    if(thiscode == (bits2+1)) break;      /* found EOI */
    if(thiscode > nextcode) {
            free(linebuffer);
            return(BAD_CODE);
    }

    if(thiscode == bits2) {
            nextcode = bits2 + 2;
            codesize2 = 1 << (codesize = (bits + 1));
            oldtoken = oldcode = NO_CODE;
            continue;
    }

    u = firstcodestack;

    if(thiscode==nextcode) {
            if(oldcode==NO_CODE) {
                    free(linebuffer);
                    return(BAD_FIRSTCODE);
            }
            *u++ = oldtoken;
            thiscode = oldcode;
    }

    while (thiscode >= bits2) {
            *u++ = lastcodestack[thiscode];
            thiscode = codestack[thiscode];
    }

    oldtoken = thiscode;
```
11-7 Continued.

```
        do {
                linebuffer[byte++]=thiscode;
                if(byte >= fi->width) {
                        (fi->saveline)(linebuffer,line);
                        byte=0;

                        /* check for interlaced image */
                        if(fi->flags & 0x40) {
                                line+=inctable[pass];
                                if(line >= fi->depth)
                                        line=startable[++pass];
                        } else ++line;
                }

                if (u <= firstcodestack) break;
                thiscode = *--u;
        } while(1);

        if(nextcode < 4096 && oldcode != NO_CODE) {
                codestack[nextcode] = oldcode;
                lastcodestack[nextcode] = oldtoken;
                if (++nextcode >= codesize2 && codesize < 12)
                    codesize2 = 1 << ++codesize;
        }
        oldcode = currentcode;
    }
    free(linebuffer);
    return(GOOD_READ);
}

/* This function is called before an image is decompressed. It must
   allocate memory, put the display in graphic mode and so on. */
dosetup(fi)
        FILEINFO *fi;
{

        if(!getbuffer((long)fi->bytes*(long)fi->depth,fi->bytes,fi->depth))
            return(BAD_ALLOC);

        makegreypalette();

        return(GOOD_READ);
}

/* This function is called after an image has been unpacked. It must
   display the image and deallocate memory. */
doclosedown(fi)
        FILEINFO *fi;
{
        static char s[768];
        char *p;
        int i,j,k=0,n;

        if(fi->bits==1) p=monopshd;
```

11-7 Continued.

```
else {
        if(printcolour) p=c256pshd_colour;
        else p=c256pshd;
}

switch(resolution) {
        case 75:
                if(fi->bits==1)
                        sprintf(s,p,fi->bytes,fi->bytes<<3,fi->depth,
                                (double)fi->width/1.04,(double)fi->depth/1.04,fi->name);
                else
                        sprintf(s,p,screensize,
                                fi->width,fi->depth,(double)fi->width/1.04,
                                (double)fi->depth/1.04,fi->name);
                p_string(s);
                break;
        case 100:
                if(fi->bits==1)
                        sprintf(s,p,fi->bytes,fi->bytes<<3,fi->depth,
                                (double)fi->width/1.39,(double)fi->depth/1.39,fi->name);
                else
                        sprintf(s,p,screensize,
                                fi->width,fi->depth,(double)fi->width/1.39,
                                (double)fi->depth/1.39,fi->name);
                p_string(s);
                break;
        case 150:
                if(fi->bits==1)
                        sprintf(s,p,fi->bytes,fi->bytes<<3,fi->depth,
                                (double)fi->width/2.08,(double)fi->depth/2.08,fi->name);
                else
                        sprintf(s,p,screensize,
                                fi->width,fi->depth,(double)fi->width/2.08,
                                (double)fi->depth/2.08,fi->name);
                p_string(s);
                break;
        case 300:
                if(fi->bits==1)
                        sprintf(s,p,fi->bytes,fi->bytes<<3,fi->depth,
                                (double)fi->width/4.16,(double)fi->depth/4.16,fi->name);
                else
                        sprintf(s,p,screensize,
                                fi->width,fi->depth,(double)fi->width/4.16,
                                (double)fi->depth/4.16,fi->name);
                p_string(s);
                break;
}

for(i=0;i<fi->depth;++i) {
        printf("\rPrinting line %u      ",i);
        p=getline(i);
        if(fi->bits==1) {
```

11-7 Continued.

```
                        for(j=0;j<fi->bytes;++j) {
                                sprintf(s,"%02.2X",p[j] & 0xff);
                                p_string(s);
                                if(k++==16) {
                                        p_string("\r\n");
                                        k=0;
                                }
                        }
                }
                else {
                        if(printcolour) {
                                for(j=0;j<fi->width;++j) {
                                        n=p[j]*RGB_SIZE;
                                        sprintf(s,"%02.2X%02.2X%02.2X",
                                                fi->palette[n+RGB_RED],
                                                fi->palette[n+RGB_GREEN],
                                                fi->palette[n+RGB_BLUE]);
                                        p_string(s);
                                        if(k++==16) {
                                                p_string("\r\n");
                                                k=0;
                                        }
                                }
                        }
                        else {
                                for(j=0;j<fi->bytes;++j) {
                                        sprintf(s,"%02.2X",p[j] & 0xff);
                                        p_string(s);
                                        if(k++==16) {
                                                p_string("\r\n");
                                                k=0;
                                        }
                                }
                        }
                }
        }
        p_string("\r\nshowpage\r\n");

        freebuffer();
        return(GOOD_READ);
}

/* send a C language string to the printer */
p_string(s)
        char *s;
{
        while(*s) p_char(*s++);
}

/* send a buffer to the printer */
p_buff(s,l)
        char *s;
```

11-7 Continued.

```
        int l;
{
        while(l--) p_char(*s++);
}


/* send a character to the printer */
p_char(c)
        int c;
{
        union REGS r;

        do {
                r.h.ah = 2;
                r.x.dx = PRINTERPORT;
                int86(0x17,&r,&r);
        } while(!(r.h.ah & 0x80));

        r.h.ah = 0;
        r.h.al = c;
        r.x.dx = PRINTERPORT;
        int86(0x17,&r,&r);
}

/* make file name with specific extension */
strmfe(new,old,ext)
        char *new,*old,*ext;
{
        while(*old != 0 && *old != '.') *new++=*old++;
        *new++='.';
        while(*ext) *new++=*ext++;
        *new=0;
}


makegreypalette()
{
        double f;
        char *palette;
        int i,n;

        n=1<<fi.bits;
        palette=fi.palette;
        for(i=0;i<n;++i) {
                f= (0.30 * (double)*palette++) +
                    (0.59 * (double)*palette++) +
                    (0.11 * (double)*palette++);
                greypalette[i]=remap[(char)f];
        }
}

/* convert GIF line to buffered line and save it */
saveline(p,n)
        char *p;
```

11-7 Continued.

```
        unsigned int n;
{
        char *pr;
        int i;
        printf("\rReading line %u      ",n);
        if(fi.bits==1) {
                if((pr=malloc(fi.bytes)) != NULL) {
                        memset(pr,0xff,fi.bytes);
                        for(i=0;i<fi.width;++i) {
                                if(p[i]) pr[i>>3] |= masktable[i & 0x0007];
                                else pr[i>>3] &= ~masktable[i & 0x0007];
                        }
                        putline(pr,n);
                        free(pr);
                }
        }
        else {
                if(printcolour) putline(p,n);
                else {
                        for(i=0;i<fi.width;++i) p[i]=greypalette[p[i]];
                        putline(p,n);
                }
        }
}

/* if you don't use in the memory manager, these functions
   will stand in for it */

#if !MEMMANGR

/* return a far pointer plus a long integer */
char *farPtr(p,l)
        char *p;
        long l;
{
        unsigned int seg,off;

        seg = FP_SEG(p);
        off = FP_OFF(p);
        seg += (off / 16);
        off &= 0x000f;
        off += (unsigned int)(l & 0x000fL);
        seg += (l / 16L);
        p = MK_FP(seg,off);
        return(p);
}

/* save one line to memory */
putline(p,n)
        char *p;
        unsigned int n;
{
```

11-7 Continued.

```
                if(n >= 0 && n < fi.depth)
                        memcpy(farPtr(buffer,(long)n*(long)fi.bytes),p,fi.bytes);
        }


        /* get one line from memory */
        char *getline(n)
                unsigned int n;
        {
                return(farPtr(buffer,(long)n*(long)fi.bytes));
        }
        #pragma warn -par
        getbuffer(n,bytes,lines)
                unsigned long n;
                int bytes,lines;
        {
                if((buffer=farmalloc(n)) == NULL) return(0);
                else return(1);
        }


        freebuffer()
        {
                if(buffer != NULL) farfree(buffer);
                buffer=NULL;
        }
        #endif /* !MEMMANGR */
```

11-7 Continued.

While this program, like PRNTGIF1, offers four resolutions to print with, PostScript is happy to scale pictures to any size you like. These four modes result in the minimum possible scaling aberrations, however, just as with a LaserJet. Using the 75 dot per inch mode, for example, makes all the pixels big and chunky, but it won't introduce any interference into the printed picture, something that would probably happen if you used a scale factor that was not an even submultiple of the dot pitch of the print engine.

The resolution mode and other options for PRNTGIF2 are set by command line switches. Here's a list of them:

/R75	Print at 75 dots per inch
/R100	Print at 100 dots per inch
/R150	Print at 150 dots per inch
/R300	Print at 300 dots per inch
/COL	Print to a color PostScript printer
/Sn	Set the screen size

The value of n for the /S command line switch should be the number of screen spots per inch you'd like your graphic to print at, or 0 for the default internal screen of the printer. As it's set up in FIG. 11-7, the PRNTGIF2 program defaults to printing to a monochrome PostScript laser at 300 dots per inch using the default internal screen of the printer for gray-scale images.

The data for a PostScript bitmapped image is sent as lines of unbroken two-digit hexadecimal numbers. In theory you could just send all the data in a single line. In practice, most PostScript printers have finite line buffers, and it's worth making sure that there's a carriage return every so often.

The `readhexstring` PostScript operator is called once for each hexadecimal line in the image. A line is defined as the number of hex entries required to complete a line of the graphic in question. Carriage returns in the PostScript code are thus ignored. It reads as many values as will fit in `picstr` and then passes the string to `image`. This all works if the number of hexadecimal digits reflects the number of bytes `image` has been led to expect. If it does not, `readhexstring` will read past the end of the hexadecimal image data and eats the `showpage` operator that follows. Specifically, it will ignore everything that it does not regard as being a legitimate hexadecimal character. It will interpret `showpage` as being the number AEH, these being the only two characters in the word "showpage" that are actually hexadecimal digits.

This won't happen to PRNTGIF2 unless you modify it and cause it to miscalculate the number of bytes of image information it should print. If you do, you'll cause your printer to lock up, as it will have reached the end of its program without encountering enough hexadecimal data to satisfy the `image` instruction.

There are two useful things to have around if you take to experimenting with PostScript. The first is a text file called SHOWPAGE.TXT that contains the word "showpage" followed by a carriage return. If you suspect that your PostScript printer has not received a `showpage` operator, or destroyed the one you sent it, and is idling with its memory full of graphics, do this from the DOS prompt:

    COPY SHOWPAGE.TXT LPT1

This sends the printer a `showpage` operator. If it's on line and working, the current page will be ejected.

If you manage to actually lock up your printer, such as by sending it an inadequate amount of data for the `image` operator, you can derail the PostScript interpreter's current task by sending it a control-C character. You might want to create this little program. I call it PBREAK.

```
#include "stdio.h"
#include "dos.h"

main()
{       p_char(3);
}

p_char(c)
    int c;
{
    union REGS r;
```

```
    int i=0x8000;
    do {
        r.h.ah = 2;
        r.x.dx = 0;
        int86(0x17,&r,&r);
    } while(!(r.h.ah & 0x80) && i-);
    r.h.ah = 0;
    r.h.al = c;
    r.x.dx = 0;
    int86(0x17,&r,&r);
}
```

If you lock up your printer, run this thing from the DOS prompt a few times. Most contemporary PostScript printers have status displays to tell you whether the PostScript interpreter is processing or idle. After a few shots from PBREAK, the display should indicate that the printer is idle. If your printer doesn't have a way to communicate its present condition to you, you can see if it's working properly by sending it a showpage operator, as previously discussed. The resulting page will be blank and can be reused.

There's a lot more to printing graphics to a PostScript printer than is discussed here. If you'd like to learn more about PostScript programming, consult the *PostScript Language Reference Manual*, second edition, by Adobe Systems. It's published by Addison-Wesley, ISBN 0-201-18127-4.

PaintJet printing

The Hewlett-Packard PaintJet color inkjet printers offer a way to have color output without necessarily becoming hopelessly broke in the process. They can't touch the quality of a ColorScript 100 color PostScript printer, but starting at under $1000 on the street, they're a pretty good compromise between superb, expensive color and no color at all.

In addition to real PaintJets, there are several printers that emulate the PaintJet's escape sequences, most notably is the Kodak Diconix 4. If you have such a printer, the code discussed in this section is applicable to your hardware.

Unlike a ColorScript, which can print in any of 16 million colors, a PaintJet can print only in 8 colors—actually, it can really only print in 4 colors: cyan, magenta, yellow, and black. It can synthesize red, green, and blue from these. Its eighth color is white, which it comes by without much effort.

Despite its somewhat reduced palette, a PaintJet can print remarkably convincing color images if you're prepared to cheat a bit and hold them at arm's length when you look at them. The cheating involved is the application of color dithering.

While color dithering is discussed in greater detail in chapter 12, it's probably worth getting into a bit of the theory to better explain what the program in this section is doing. You might want to look at chapter 12 as well if you really want to get a handle on the concepts involved. Some of them are a bit slippery.

The problem confronting a 256-color image that finds itself looking down the barrel of PaintJet is that not only need it reduce its palette down to 8 colors; it doesn't even get to choose the colors involved. However, the 8 colors are each as unlike all the other colors in the palette as they can be. In terms that will make more sense after you've read chapter 12, each one has the maximum possible distance in color space from all the others.

The 8 colors can be represented as RGB values like this:

Color	Red	Green	Blue
Black	0	0	0
Red	255	0	0
Green	0	255	0
Yellow	255	255	0
Blue	0	0	255
Magenta	255	0	255
Cyan	0	255	255
White	255	255	255

To understand how the complex palette of a 256-color GIF file might be reduced to this simple palette, it's necessary to dispense with the 256-color palette entirely. The GIF file must be transformed into a 24-bit RGB image with each pixel having its own color value. This is very easy to do. If fi is a pointer to a FILEINFO struct for the image in question, this is how you'd do the conversion. This example assumes there's lots of memory available, as it doesn't check the results of calling malloc.

```
char *source,*dest;
int i,j;

dest=malloc(fi->width*RGB_SIZE);
for(i=0;i<fi->depth;++i) {
    source=getline(i);
    for(j=0;j<fi->width;++j)
        memcpy(dest+(j*RGB_SIZE),
            fi->palette+(p[j]*RGB_SIZE),
            RGB_SIZE);
    /* do something with the RGB line in dest */
}
```

This process is a memory hog. It increases the size of the unpacked image by a factor of 3.

Having created a suitable RGB source image, you can begin to look at how it's to be dithered. Let's say that the first pixel in the image has the

RGB values (12,240,240), which would make it a slightly orange color. Looking at the above chart of color values, it would seem to be closest to yellow. If it's compared to yellow, it produces a difference in the 3 colors of (12, –16, –16). This is called the color "error."

Having found the closest color for this pixel, the dithering code replaces the real pixel with the RGB values for yellow. It then "diffuses" the error to surrounding pixels.

Error diffusion in dithering is handled by the application of a dithering "filter." There are lots of these about. The code in this chapter uses the Floyd-Steinberg filter, which is fairly fast. It's drawn as a diagram like this:

```
      X   7
  3   5   1
```

Each of the characters in the filter diagram represents a pixel. The X pixel is the current one. The numbered pixels are the pixels with which the current pixel communicates. The numbers represent the proportion of the error to be added to the surrounding pixels. Because these values add up to 16, these numbers are the numerators of fractions having 16 as their denominators.

Having derived an RGB error of (12, –16, –16) then, the pixel immediately to the right of the current one would receive $7/16$ of the error. The one immediately below it would receive $5/16$ of the error, and so on. This being the first pixel in the row, the pixel below the current one and to the left, represented in the map by 3, doesn't exist and would be ignored.

Having diffused the error for 1 pixel, the filter would be shifted over to the right by 1 and the process repeated.

The result of error diffusion dithering is to cause the average color values of consecutive pixels in the dithered image to approximate the average color of the same area of pixels in the source image, even if the individual pixels may be grossly different. While this doesn't result in perfect color reproduction by any means, it's usually surprisingly good. To be sure, it's the best you can manage with a PaintJet.

The PRNTGIF3 program in FIG. 11-8 illustrates the GIF file printing program modified one last time, this time to drive a PaintJet.

```
/*
        GIF printer - copyright (c) 1991
        PaintJet version
        Alchemy Mindworks Inc.
*/

#include "stdio.h"
#include "dos.h"
#include "alloc.h"

/*                              uncomment this line if you
#include "memmangr.h"           will be linking in the memory manager
```

11-8 The source code for PRNTGIF3.

```
*/

#define GOOD_READ          0         /* return codes */
#define BAD_FILE           1
#define BAD_READ           2
#define UNEXPECTED_EOF     3
#define BAD_CODE           4
#define BAD_FIRSTCODE      5
#define BAD_ALLOC          6
#define BAD_SYMBOLSIZE     7


#define RGB_RED            0
#define RGB_GREEN          1
#define RGB_BLUE           2
#define RGB_SIZE           3


#define NO_CODE           -1


#define PRINTERPORT        0         /* 0=LPT1, 1=LPT2, 2=LPT3 */
#define LINECOUNT          3         /* number of lines in a floyd dither */


#define pixels2bytes(n)    ((n+7)/8)


typedef struct {
        char sig[6];
        unsigned int screenwidth,screendepth;
        unsigned char flags,background,aspect;
        } GIFHEADER;

typedef struct {
        unsigned int left,top,width,depth;
        unsigned char flags;
        } IMAGEBLOCK;

typedef struct {
        int width,depth,bytes,bits;
        int flags;
        int background;
        char palette[768];
        int (*setup)();
        int (*closedown)();
        int (*saveline)();
        int (*savext)();
        } FILEINFO;


typedef struct {
        char blocksize;
        char flags;
        unsigned int delay;
        char transparent_colour;
        char terminator;
        } CONTROLBLOCK;
```

11-8 Continued.

```
typedef struct {
        char blocksize;
        unsigned int left,top;
        unsigned int gridwidth,gridheight;
        char cellwidth,cellheight;
        char forecolour,backcolour;
        } PLAINTEXT;

typedef struct {
        char blocksize;
        char applstring[8];
        char authentication[3];
        } APPLICATION;

char *farPtr(char *p,long l);
char *getline(unsigned int n);

char fixedpalette[]={
         0,  0,  0,
       255,  0,  0,
         0,255,  0,
       255,255,  0,
         0,  0,255,
       255,  0,255,
         0,255,255,
       255,255,255
        };

int putextension(FILE *fp);
int saveline(char *p,unsigned int n);
int dosetup(FILEINFO *fi);
int doclosedown(FILEINFO *fi);

char masktable[8]={0x80,0x40,0x20,0x10,0x08,0x04,0x02,0x01};

FILEINFO fi;
char *buffer=NULL;

main(argc,argv)
        int argc;
        char *argv[];
{
        FILE *fp;
        static char results[8][16] = {  "Ok",
                                        "Bad file",
                                        "Bad read",
                                        "Unexpected end",
                                        "Bad LZW code",
                                        "Bad first code",
                                        "Memory error",
                                        "Bad symbol size"
                                        };
```

11-8 Continued.

```
        char path[81];
        int r;

        if(argc > 1) {
                strmfe(path,argv[1],"GIF");
                if((fp = fopen(path,"rb")) != NULL) {
                        fi.setup=dosetup;
                        fi.closedown=doclosedown;
                        fi.saveline=saveline;
                        fi.savext=putextension;
                        r=unpackgif(fp,&fi);
                        printf("\%s",results[r]);
                        fclose(fp);
                } else printf("Error opening %s",path);
        } else puts("Argument:        path to a GIF file");

}


/* This function is called when the GIF decoder encounters an extension */
putextension(fp)
        FILE *fp;
{

        PLAINTEXT pt;
        CONTROLBLOCK cb;
        APPLICATION ap;
        int n,i;

        clrscr();
        switch(fgetc(fp)) {
                case 0x0001:                /* plain text descriptor */
                        if(fread((char *)&pt,1,sizeof(PLAINTEXT),fp)
                            == sizeof(PLAINTEXT)) {

                                do {
                                        if((n=fgetc(fp)) != EOF) {
                                                for(i=0;i<n;++i) fgetc(fp);
                                        }
                                } while(n > 0 && n != EOF);
                        } else puts("Error reading plain text block");
                        break;
                case 0x00f9:                /* graphic control block */
                        if(fread((char *)&cb,1,sizeof(CONTROLBLOCK),fp)
                            != sizeof(CONTROLBLOCK))
                                puts("Error reading control block");
                        break;
                case 0x00fe:                /* comment extension */
                        do {
                                if((n=fgetc(fp)) != EOF) {
                                        for(i=0;i<n;++i) fgetc(fp);
                                }
                        } while(n > 0 && n != EOF);
                        break;
                case 0x00ff:                /* application extension */
```

11-8 Continued.

```
                                 if(fread((char *)&ap,1,sizeof(APPLICATION),fp)
                                     == sizeof(APPLICATION)) {
                                     do {
                                            if((n=fgetc(fp)) != EOF) {
                                                  for(i=0;i<n;++i) fgetc(fp);
                                            }
                                     } while(n > 0 && n != EOF);
                                 } else puts("Error reading application block");
                                 break;
                      default:                   /* something else */
                                 n=fgetc(fp);
                                 for(i=0;i<n;++i) fgetc(fp);
                                 break;
             }
         getch();
    }

    /* unpack a GIF file */
    unpackgif(fp,fi)
         FILE *fp;
         FILEINFO *fi;
    {
         GIFHEADER gh;
         IMAGEBLOCK iblk;
         long t;
         int b,c;

         /* make sure it's a GIF file */
         if(fread((char *)&gh,1,sizeof(GIFHEADER),fp) != sizeof(GIFHEADER) ||
             memcmp(gh.sig, "GIF", 3)) return(BAD_FILE);

         /* get screen dimensions */
         fi->width=gh.screenwidth;
         fi->depth=gh.screendepth;
         fi->bits=(gh.flags & 0x0007) + 1;
         fi->background=gh.background;
         /* get colour map if there is one */
         if (gh.flags & 0x80) {
                 c = 3 * (1 << ((gh.flags & 7) + 1));
                 if(fread(fi->palette,1,c,fp) != c) return(BAD_READ);
         }

         /* step through the blocks */
         while((c=fgetc(fp))==',' || c=='!' || c==0) {

                 /* if it's an image block... */
                 if (c == ',') {
                         /* get the start of the image block */
                         if(fread(&iblk,1,sizeof(IMAGEBLOCK),fp) !=
                             sizeof(IMAGEBLOCK)) return(BAD_READ);

                         /* get the image dimensions */
```

11-8 Continued.

```
                    fi->width=iblk.width;
                    fi->depth=iblk.depth;

                    if(fi->bits==1) fi->bytes=pixels2bytes(fi->width);
                    else fi->bytes=fi->width*RGB_SIZE;

                    /* get the local colour map if there is one */
                    if(iblk.flags & 0x80) {
                            b = 3*(1<<((iblk.flags & 0x0007) + 1));
                            if(fread(fi->palette,1,b,fp) != c) return(BAD_READ);
                            fi->bits=(iblk.flags & 0x0007) + 1;
                    }

                    /* get the initial code size */
                    if((c=fgetc(fp))==EOF) return(BAD_FILE);
                    fi->flags=iblk.flags;

                    /* do the setup procedure */
                    if(fi->setup != NULL) {
                            if((t=(fi->setup)(fi)) != GOOD_READ)
                                return(t);
                    }

                    /* unpack the image */
                    if((t=unpackimage(fp,c,fi)) != GOOD_READ)
                        return(t);

                    /* do the close down procedure */
                    if(fi->closedown != NULL) {
                            if((t=(fi->closedown)(fi)) != GOOD_READ)
                                return(t);
                    }
            }
            /* otherwise, it's an extension */
            else if(c == '!') (fi->savext)(fp);
        }
        return(GOOD_READ);
}


/* unpack an LZW compressed image */
unpackimage(fp,bits,fi)
        FILE *fp;
        int bits;
        FILEINFO *fi;
{
        int bits2;          /* Bits plus 1 */
        int codesize;       /* Current code size in bits */
        int codesize2;      /* Next codesize */
        int nextcode;       /* Next available table entry */
        int thiscode;       /* Code being expanded */
        int oldtoken;       /* Last symbol decoded */
        int currentcode;    /* Code just read */
```

11-8 Continued.

```
int oldcode;          /* Code read before this one */
int bitsleft;         /* Number of bits left in *p */
int blocksize;        /* Bytes in next block */
int line=0;           /* next line to write */
int byte=0;           /* next byte to write */
int pass=0;           /* pass number for interlaced pictures */

char *p;              /* Pointer to current byte in read buffer */
char *q;              /* Pointer past last byte in read buffer */
char b[255];          /* Read buffer */
char *u;              /* Stack pointer into firstcodestack */
char *linebuffer;     /* place to store the current line */

static char firstcodestack[4096];  /* Stack for first codes */
static char lastcodestack[4096];   /* Stack for previous code */
static int codestack[4096];        /* Stack for links */

static int wordmasktable[] = {  0x0000,0x0001,0x0003,0x0007,
                                0x000f,0x001f,0x003f,0x007f,
                                0x00ff,0x01ff,0x03ff,0x07ff,
                                0x0fff,0x1fff,0x3fff,0x7fff

                              };

static int inctable[] = { 8,8,4,2,0 }; /* interlace increments */
static int startable[] = { 0,4,2,1,0 };  /* interlace starts */

p=q=b;
bitsleft = 8;

if (bits < 2 || bits > 8) return(BAD_SYMBOLSIZE);
bits2 = 1 << bits;
nextcode = bits2 + 2;
codesize2 = 1 << (codesize = bits + 1);
oldcode=oldtoken=NO_CODE;

if((linebuffer=malloc(fi->width)) == NULL) return(BAD_ALLOC);

/* loop until something breaks */
for(;;) {
        if(bitsleft==8) {
                if(++p >= q &&
                (((blocksize = fgetc(fp)) < 1) ||
                (q=(p=b)+fread(b,1,blocksize,fp))< (b+blocksize))) {
                        free(linebuffer);
                        return(UNEXPECTED_EOF);
                }
                bitsleft = 0;
        }
        thiscode = *p;
        if ((currentcode=(codesize+bitsleft)) <= 8) {
                *p >>= codesize;
```

11-8 Continued.

```
                bitsleft = currentcode;
        }
        else {
                if(++p >= q &&
                  (((blocksize = fgetc(fp)) < 1) ||
                  (q=(p=b)+fread(b,1,blocksize,fp)) < (b+blocksize))) {
                        free(linebuffer);
                        return(UNEXPECTED_EOF);
                }
                thiscode |= *p << (8 - bitsleft);
                if(currentcode <= 16) *p >>= (bitsleft=currentcode-8);
                else {
                        if(++p >= q &&
                          (((blocksize = fgetc(fp)) < 1) ||
                          (q=(p=b) + fread(b,1,blocksize,fp)) < (b+blocksize))) {
                                free(linebuffer);
                                return(UNEXPECTED_EOF);
                        }
                        thiscode |= *p << (16 - bitsleft);
                        *p >>= (bitsleft = currentcode - 16);
                }
        }
        thiscode &= wordmasktable[codesize];
        currentcode = thiscode;

        if(thiscode == (bits2+1)) break;     /* found EOI */
        if(thiscode > nextcode) {
                free(linebuffer);
                return(BAD_CODE);
        }

        if(thiscode == bits2) {
                nextcode = bits2 + 2;
                codesize2 = 1 << (codesize = (bits + 1));
                oldtoken = oldcode = NO_CODE;
                continue;
        }

        u = firstcodestack;

        if(thiscode==nextcode) {
                if(oldcode==NO_CODE) {
                        free(linebuffer);
                        return(BAD_FIRSTCODE);
                }
                *u++ = oldtoken;
                thiscode = oldcode;
        }

        while (thiscode >= bits2) {
                *u++ = lastcodestack[thiscode];
                thiscode = codestack[thiscode];
```

11-8 Continued.

```
                  }

                  oldtoken = thiscode;
                  do {
                          linebuffer[byte++]=thiscode;
                          if(byte >= fi->width) {
                                  (fi->saveline)(linebuffer,line);
                                  byte=0;

                                  /* check for interlaced image */
                                  if(fi->flags & 0x40) {
                                          line+=inctable[pass];
                                          if(line >= fi->depth)
                                                  line=startable[++pass];
                                  } else ++line;
                          }

                          if (u <= firstcodestack) break;
                          thiscode = *--u;
                  } while(1);

                  if(nextcode < 4096 && oldcode != NO_CODE) {
                          codestack[nextcode] = oldcode;
                          lastcodestack[nextcode] = oldtoken;
                          if (++nextcode >= codesize2 && codesize < 12)
                              codesize2 = 1 << ++codesize;
                  }
                  oldcode = currentcode;
          }
          free(linebuffer);
          return(GOOD_READ);
}


/* This function is called before an image is decompressed. It must
   allocate memory, put the display in graphic mode and so on. */
dosetup(fi)
          FILEINFO *fi;
{
          if(!getbuffer((long)fi->bytes*(long)fi->depth,fi->bytes,fi->depth))
              return(BAD_ALLOC);

          return(GOOD_READ);
}


/* This function is called after an image has been unpacked. It must
   display the image and deallocate memory. */
doclosedown(fi)
          FILEINFO *fi;
{
          char b[32],*p,*linebuf[3];
          int i,j,k,l,n;
```

11-8 Continued.

```
if(fi->bits==1) {
        p_string("\033E");
        p_string("\x1b*t75R");
        p_string("\x1b*p20X");
        p_string("\x1b*p20Y");
        p_string("\x1b*r1A");

        n=pixels2bytes(fi->width);

        for(i=0;i<fi->depth;++i) {
                printf("\rPrinting line %u       ",i);
                p=getline(i);
                sprintf(b,"\x1b*b%dW",n);
                p_string(b);
                p_buff(p,n);
        }
}
else {
        if((i=ditherimage(fi)) != GOOD_READ) return(i);

        l=pixels2bytes(fi->width);

        for(i=0;i<3;++i) {
                if((linebuf[i]=malloc(l)) == NULL) {
                        freebuffer();
                        return(BAD_ALLOC);
                }
        }

        p_string("\033E");
        p_string("\x1b*t75R");
        p_string("\x1b*p20X");
        p_string("\x1b*p20Y");
        p_string("\x1b*r1A");

        sprintf(b,"\x1b*r%dS",fi->width);
        p_string(b);

        p_string("\x1b*r3U");
        p_string("\x1b*b0M");
        p_string("\x1b*b50Y");

        for(i=0;i<fi->depth;++i) {
        printf("\rPrinting line %u       ",i);
        p=getline(i);

        for(j=0;j<3;++j)
            memset(linebuf[j],0,l);

        for(j=0;j<fi->width;++j) {
                n=getPaintjetColour(p);
                for(k=0;k<3;++k) {
```

11-8 Continued.

```
                              if(n & (1<<k)) linebuf[k][j>>3] |= masktable[j & 0x0007];
                    }
                         p+=RGB_SIZE;
            }

                    sprintf(b,"\033*b%uV",1);
                    p_string(b);
                    p_buff(linebuf[0],1);

                    sprintf(b,"\033*b%uV",1);
                    p_string(b);
                    p_buff(linebuf[1],1);

                    sprintf(b,"\033*b%uW",1);
                    p_string(b);
                    p_buff(linebuf[2],1);
            }
        }

        p_string("\x1b*rB");
        p_string("\014");

        freebuffer();
        return(GOOD_READ);
}

getPaintjetColour(p)
        char *p;
{
        int i;

        for(i=0;i<8;++i) {
                if(!memcmp(p,fixedpalette+(i*RGB_SIZE),RGB_SIZE))
                    return(i);
        }
        return(7);
}

ditherimage(fi)
        FILEINFO *fi;
{
        char *p,*linebuf[LINECOUNT];
        int i,j,n,max[RGB_SIZE],min[RGB_SIZE],mid[RGB_SIZE];
        int r,g,b,mr,mg,mb,w;

        w=fi->width*RGB_SIZE;

        for(i=0;i<LINECOUNT;++i) {
                if((linebuf[i]=malloc(w)) == NULL) return(BAD_ALLOC);
        }
        for(i=0;i<RGB_SIZE;++i) {
                min[i]=255;
```

11-8 Continued.

```
            max[i]=0;
}

for(i=0;i<fi->depth;++i) {
        printf("\rRemapping line %u    ",i);
        p=getline(i);
        for(j=0;j<fi->width;++j) {
                n=j*RGB_SIZE;
                r=p[n+RGB_RED];
                g=p[n+RGB_GREEN];
                b=p[n+RGB_BLUE];
                if(r < min[RGB_RED]) min[RGB_RED]=r;
                if(g < min[RGB_GREEN]) min[RGB_GREEN]=g;
                if(b < min[RGB_BLUE]) min[RGB_BLUE]=b;
                if(r > max[RGB_RED]) max[RGB_RED]=r;
                if(g > max[RGB_GREEN]) max[RGB_GREEN]=g;
                if(b > max[RGB_BLUE]) max[RGB_BLUE]=b;
        }
}

for(i=0;i<RGB_SIZE;++i) mid[i]=(max[i]+min[i])>>1;

for(i=0;i<fi->depth;++i) {
        printf("\rDithering line %u    ",i);
        memcpy(linebuf[0],getline(i),w);
        if((i+1) < fi->depth) memcpy(linebuf[1],getline(i+1),w);

        p=linebuf[0];
        for(j=0;j<fi->width;++j) {
                r=p[RGB_RED];
                if(r > mid[RGB_RED]) mr=255;
                else mr=0;

                g=p[RGB_GREEN];
                if(g > mid[RGB_GREEN]) mg=255;
                else mg=0;

                b=p[RGB_BLUE];
                if(b > mid[RGB_BLUE]) mb=255;
                else mb=0;

                p[RGB_RED]=mr;
                p[RGB_GREEN]=mg;
                p[RGB_BLUE]=mb;

                diffuseFloyd(linebuf[0],linebuf[1],j,i,r,g,b,mr,mg,mb,fi->width,fi->depth);

                p+=RGB_SIZE;
        }

        putline(linebuf[0],i);
        if((i+1) < fi->depth) putline(linebuf[1],i+1);
```

11-8 Continued.

```
}

for(i=0;i<LINECOUNT;++i) free(linebuf[i]);
return(GOOD_READ);

}

diffuseFloyd(line1,line2,x,y,r,g,b,mr,mg,mb,width,depth)
        char *line1,*line2;
        int x,y,r,g,b;
        int mr,mg,mb;
        int width,depth;
{

        int dr,dg,db;

        dr=r-mr;
        dg=g-mg;
        db=b-mb;

        if((x+1) < width) {
                line1[((x+1)*RGB_SIZE)+RGB_RED]  =addb(line1[((x+1)*RGB_SIZE)+RGB_RED],((dr*7)/16));
                line1[((x+1)*RGB_SIZE)+RGB_GREEN]=addb(line1[((x+1)*RGB_SIZE)+RGB_GREEN],((dg*7)/16));
                line1[((x+1)*RGB_SIZE)+RGB_BLUE] =addb(line1[((x+1)*RGB_SIZE)+RGB_BLUE],((db*7)/16));
        }

        if((x-1) > 0 && (y+1) < depth) {
                line2[((x-1)*RGB_SIZE)+RGB_RED]  =addb(line2[((x-1)*RGB_SIZE)+RGB_RED],((dr*3)/16));
                line2[((x-1)*RGB_SIZE)+RGB_GREEN]=addb(line2[((x-1)*RGB_SIZE)+RGB_GREEN],((dg*3)/16));
                line2[((x-1)*RGB_SIZE)+RGB_BLUE] =addb(line2[((x-1)*RGB_SIZE)+RGB_BLUE],((db*3)/16));
        }

        if((x+1) < width && (y+1) < depth) {
                line2[((x+1)*RGB_SIZE)+RGB_RED]  =addb(line2[((x+1)*RGB_SIZE)+RGB_RED],((dr*1)/16));
                line2[((x+1)*RGB_SIZE)+RGB_GREEN]=addb(line2[((x+1)*RGB_SIZE)+RGB_GREEN],((dg*1)/16));
                line2[((x+1)*RGB_SIZE)+RGB_BLUE] =addb(line2[((x+1)*RGB_SIZE)+RGB_BLUE],((db*1)/16));
        }

        if((y+1) < depth) {
                line2[(x*RGB_SIZE)+RGB_RED]  =addb(line2[(x*RGB_SIZE)+RGB_RED],((dr*5)/16));
                line2[(x*RGB_SIZE)+RGB_GREEN]=addb(line2[(x*RGB_SIZE)+RGB_GREEN],((dg*5)/16));
                line2[(x*RGB_SIZE)+RGB_BLUE] =addb(line2[(x*RGB_SIZE)+RGB_BLUE],((db*5)/16));
        }
}

/* add two bytes, clamp to byte range */
addb(n1,n2)
        int n1,n2;
{

        int n;

        n=n1+n2;
        if(n<0) n=0;
```

11-8 Continued.

```
                else if(n > 255) n=255;
                return(n);
        }


/* send a C language string to the printer */
p_string(s)
                char *s;
        {
                while(*s) p_char(*s++);
        }


/* send a buffer to the printer */
p_buff(s,l)
                char *s;
                int l;
        {
                while(l--) p_char(*s++);
        }


/* send a character to the printer */
p_char(c)
                int c;
        {
                union REGS r;

                do {
                        r.h.ah = 2;
                        r.x.dx = PRINTERPORT;
                        int86(0x17,&r,&r);
                } while(!(r.h.ah & 0x80));

                r.h.ah = 0;
                r.h.al = c;
                r.x.dx = PRINTERPORT;
                int86(0x17,&r,&r);
        }


/* make file name with specific extension */
strmfe(new,old,ext)
                char *new,*old,*ext;
        {
                while(*old != 0 && *old != '.') *new++=*old++;
                *new++='.';
                while(*ext) *new++=*ext++;
                *new=0;
        }


/* convert GIF line to buffered line and save it */
saveline(p,n)
                char *p;
                unsigned int n;
        {
```

11-8 Continued.

```
            char *pr;
            int i;

            printf("\rReading line %u       ",n);
            if(fi.bits==1) {
                    if((pr=malloc(fi.bytes)) != NULL) {
                            memset(pr,0xff,fi.bytes);
                            for(i=0;i<fi.width;++i) {
                                    if(p[i]) pr[i>>3] &= ~masktable[i & 0x0007];
                                    else pr[i>>3] |= masktable[i & 0x0007];
                            }
                            putline(pr,n);
                            free(pr);
                    }
            }
            else {
                    if((pr=malloc(fi.bytes)) != NULL) {
                            memset(pr,0x00,fi.bytes);
                            for(i=0;i<fi.width;++i) {
                                    memcpy(pr+(i*RGB_SIZE),
                                            fi.palette+(p[i]*RGB_SIZE),
                                            RGB_SIZE);
                            }
                            putline(pr,n);
                            free(pr);
                    }
            }
    }

/* if you don't use in the memory manager, these functions
   will stand in for it */

#if !MEMMANGR

/* return a far pointer plus a long integer */
char *farPtr(p,l)
        char *p;
        long l;
{
        unsigned int seg,off;

        seg = FP_SEG(p);
        off = FP_OFF(p);
        seg += (off / 16);
        off &= 0x000f;
        off += (unsigned int)(l & 0x000fL);
        seg += (l / 16L);
        p = MK_FP(seg,off);
        return(p);
}
/* save one line to memory */
putline(p,n)
```

11-8 Continued.

```
        char *p;
        unsigned int n;
{

        if(n >= 0 && n < fi.depth)
                memcpy(farPtr(buffer,(long)n*(long)fi.bytes),p,fi.bytes);
}

/* get one line from memory */
char *getline(n)
        unsigned int n;
{
        return(farPtr(buffer,(long)n*(long)fi.bytes));
}

#pragma warn -par
getbuffer(n,bytes,lines)
        unsigned long n;
        int bytes,lines;
{
        if((buffer=farmalloc(n)) == NULL) return(0);
        else return(1);
}

freebuffer()
{
        if(buffer != NULL) farfree(buffer);
        buffer=NULL;
}
#endif /* !MEMMANGR */
```

11-8 Continued.

The native language of PaintJet printers is actually an extension of
the basic PCL language with which LaserJets communicate. Printing a
monochrome graphic to a PaintJet involves precisely the same escape
sequences as were used to print black-and-white pictures to LaserJet
printers in PRNTGIF1, at the beginning of this chapter.

The initial escape sequences for printing in color are also the same as
those used for printing monochrome images to a LaserJet. The line handling is done differently, however.

The 8 primary colors that a PaintJet likes to deal with are numbered 0
though 7. The numbers 0 through 7, when represented in binary, look like
this:

	Bit 0	**Bit 1**	**Bit 2**
0	0	0	0
1	1	0	0
2	0	1	0
3	1	1	0
4	0	0	1

5	1	0	1
6	0	1	1
7	1	1	1

If you compare this chart to the one that specified the RGB values for the 8 basic PaintJet colors, you'll notice that the set bits in this table correspond to the RGB components set to 255 in the earlier one.

The PaintJet expects to have each line of color information sent to it as three monochrome planes, in which the bit values of each pixel in each plane will form color numbers from 0 through 7. While a weird and complex way of handling color numbers, it does allow a whole line of color values to be downloaded to the printer without any wasted data.

You can see this at work in the `doclosedown` function of PRNTGIF3.

Because it wants to deal with RGB images, PRNTGIF3 requires a lot of memory. If you'll be working with source images having dimensions much beyond 320×200 pixels, plan to link the memory manager discussed in the appendix to your code.

There are a number of things to keep in mind when you're printing color graphics to a PaintJet. The most important is that the process uses voluminous quantities of ink. The quality of the graphics a PaintJet can generate will vary enormously with the state of its ink supply. If one of the colors of ink is approaching exhaustion, which is a common state of affairs, as they don't all get used at the same rate, you'll notice streaks and color shifts in your output.

Some subjects print better than others as well. Pictures with a lot of fine details in them often lose their details in the dithering process. Surprisingly, dithering to 8 colors isn't particularly unkind to large areas of graduated color. Flesh tones and such fair reasonably well.

Finally, because PaintJets squirt liquid ink at their pages, printing large areas of ink, such as bitmapped graphics, tends to get the paper soggy, far more so than printing text would. When the pages dry out, they might have wrinkled a bit. You can minimize this effect by using something better than conventional bond photocopier paper in your PaintJet.

If you'd like more information about driving a PaintJet, you might want to contact Hewlett-Packard for a document called *Flare, PaintJet XL, PCL Software Developer's Guide*.

Driving printers

The discussion of graphic printing in this chapter has been, of necessity, fairly basic. There are entire books available that discuss the nuances of both PCL and PostScript.

Having said this, the code discussed here gives you the tools to implement graphic printing for any application in which you merely have to generate hard copy of some pictures. The other things that the printers discussed here do, such as their text and graphic-manipulation facilities, fall into other areas.

Once you have the code in this chapter working, you might want to create versions of some of the printer programs to deal with other file formats. If you'll be working with 24-bit images and have access to a color PostScript printer, you should certainly create a version of PRNTGIF2 to handle Targa, TIFF or one of the other 24-bit formats. The results are exceedingly impressive.

As with display cards, there are a lot of dissimilar hard copy devices about. Beyond PostScript and PCL devices, which all behave in compatible, predictable ways, the proprietary dot matrix standards are numerous. You might want to consider supporting printers in the same way that the code in chapter 10 supported VGA cards, that is, with loadable drivers.

There's a discussion of loadable printer drivers in my book *Graphical User Interface Programming*, Windcrest book 3875. These are the driver resources used by Graphic Workshop. Among other things, Graphic Workshop includes a loadable driver to handle PaintJets.

12
Color dithering and quantization

Sacred cows make better burgers.

—GRAFFITI

One of the least obvious graphic operations in this book is the translation between true color RGB images and palette-driven pictures, such as GIF files. As mentioned in previous chapters, this isn't a perfect translation at the best of times in that it involves disposing of a surfeit of color information.

With a degree of stealth and cunning, the excess can be disposed of in a way that is as unobjectionable as possible.

There are, in fact, several distinct problems in reducing the number of colors in a 24-bit image to something that can fit in a 256-color palette-driven image. Such a translation involves the following steps:

- Find a good 256-color palette
- Remap the 24-bit pixels to it
- Diffuse the color errors so the results don't look like a medieval tapestry after the moths have gotten to it

The first problem is the nastiest. You'll probably appreciate its true nastiness more fully once you have a handle on what the whole process is.

If you read the section of chapter 11 about color dithering to drive a PaintJet printer, you might be familiar with some of the ideas in this chapter.

Color remapping

In a 24-bit color image it's fair to assume that every pixel represents a unique color. In attempting to create a 256-color image from a 24-bit image, the code that generates the palette driven picture must replace each of the original 24-bit pixels with a palette index value, so that the palette colors represented are as close as possible to the source pixels.

This can be further refined through color dithering, something discussed briefly in chapter 11, and is dealt with in greater detail in this chapter.

The choice of a really good palette is tricky, and can wait for the moment. Let's begin the discussion of this process by assuming that the palette already exists and that it represents 256 colors that are evenly distributed across the visible spectrum. As it happens, this is not a particularly good way to handle color remapping, but it's a start.

The three color indices of an RGB color value can be represented in 3-dimensional space, a concept often referred to as *color space*. Figure 12-1 illustrates a model of color space.

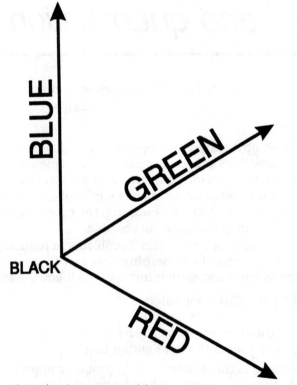

12-1 A color space model.

You can plot any RGB color on the color space model, representing the values of the three numbers involved as distances along the three axes. Having done so, there will be a point in the intervening space that represents the location of the color in question. Figure 12-2 illustrates this.

Because every distinct color is defined as a unique point in color space, two different colors have a distance in color space between them.

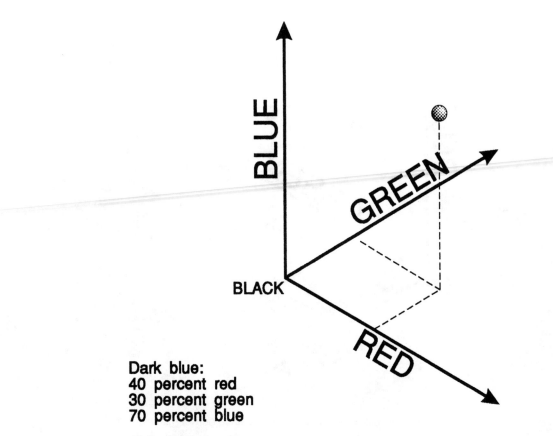

Dark blue:
40 percent red
30 percent green
70 percent blue

12-2   A point in color space.

Figure 12-3 illustrates how this looks.

Color space distance is measurable using a fairly simple formula. Allowing that there are two RGB colors represented by `r1`, `g1`, and `b1` for the first color and `r2`, `g2`, and `b2` for the second, how you would figure out the color distance between them follows:

```
unsigned long distance;

distance =   3L*(long)(r1-r2)*(long)(r1-r2) +
             4L*(long)(g1-g2)*(long)(g1-g2) +
             2L*(long)(b1-b2)*(long)(b1-b2);
```

If you know how to work out the difference between two colors, you can find the color in a palette that most closely matches the color of an RGB pixel by finding the palette color that represents the shortest color distance from the RGB pixel in question.

This is, in fact, a very time-consuming process. Reducing a 24-bit image down to 256 colors involves performing the preceding calculation up to 256 times for each pixel in the source image. The code in this chap-

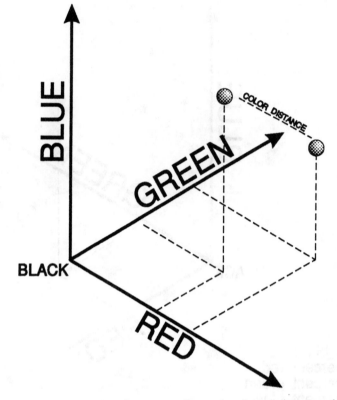

12-3   Two points in color space with a color distance between them.

ter takes a while to run. Allowing that the destination palette for the image to be created already exists (this example uses an evenly distributed 256-color palette) it's possible to replace all the 24-bit pixels in an RGB image with palette indices with this procedure, called *remapping* an image. The results are almost always breathtakingly awful. They'll be more so at the moment, as the palette being used probably won't suit the picture particularly well.

The problem with remapping a picture this way is that in most cases there is some color distance between each pixel in the source picture and the best available palette color that replaces it. This is called the *color error*. It can be represented as an RGB value, that is, as the difference between the two red values, the difference between the two green values, and the difference between the two blue values. Note that unlike a real RGB color value, these numbers could be negative.

In simply remapping a picture, the color errors are thrown away, which is why remapping rarely looks very good, especially in images scanned from photographs. There are simply too many colors in such a source image to make replacing them with a fixed palette workable.

There is a way to make a 256-color image look like it has more colors than it really does. You can dither it. Specifically, you diffuse the color errors over its pixels, resulting in the illusion of more colors than there really are.

Dithering is something mentioned in hushed whispers among people who work with graphics. It sounds mysterious. In fact, it's pretty easy to understand if you look at it in its simplest sense. Dithering is a way to mix colors in a medium that doesn't really let you mix colors.

On a computer monitor driven by a display card with a finite palette, only those colors in the display card's palette are available. However, you can synthesize other colors by painting areas of the screen with a mixture of different color dots. For example, you could make part of your screen look green by setting all the odd-numbered dots to yellow and all the even-numbered dots to blue. This is dithering. If you've used Microsoft Windows, you'll have seen a lot of dithering going on. Microsoft Windows dithers up any colors its fixed palette isn't able to provide.

In Microsoft Windows, all the dithering uses regular patterns of alternating colored pixels. You can apply the idea of dithering to the irregular pixels of a scanned image as well.

The process of dithering images being remapped is called *error diffusion*. Error diffusion is handled using a diffusion "filter" of which there are quite a few around. The most commonly encountered one is the Floyd-Steinberg filter. It's drawn like this:

```
        X    7
   3    5    1
```

In this diagram, the X represents the pixel to be remapped. The other numbers represent adjacent pixels. The 5, for example, is the pixel one line down and immediately below the pixel being remapped. In looking at error diffusion filter diagrams, any pixels that extend beyond the edges of the picture are ignored.

In this filter all the numbers add up to 16. The numbers represent the numerators of fractions whose denominators are 16. These fractions represent the proportion of the total error to be diffused to each of the pixels in the diagram.

To apply this filter to remapping an image, then, you would begin with the first pixel in the source 24-bit picture. Having found the nearest match for it in the destination palette, you would derive a color error for the two RGB values by subtracting the destination red value from the source red value, the destination green value from the source green value, and the destination blue value from the source blue value. We'll call these three numbers rd, gd, and bd respectively.

Having derived the color error for the pixel being remapped, it can be replaced by the palette entry in question.

Looking at the filter diagram, the pixel to the immediate right of the one being remapped should receive $7/16$ of the color error. As such, you would find the red value for this pixel and add (rd * 7) / 16 to it. The same thing can be done for the green and blue values. Having done this, you would repeat the process for any other pixels affected by this filter. The pixel indicated by 3 would be ignored in this case, as it extends beyond the left edge of the picture if you're working with the first pixel in a line.

Having remapped and diffused one pixel, the filter moves right by 1 pixel and the whole circus can start again.

In remapping a 24-bit image down to 256 colors, most of the individual pixels will exhibit decided color errors when they're compared to the colors of the source image. However, if you compare an area of pixels in an error-diffused 256-color image to the same area in its source 24-bit image, the aggregate color error should be negligible. Inasmuch as our eyes don't see the individual pixels, but tend to average their individual color values over larger areas, error diffusion succeeds in creating the illusion of intermediate colors that don't really exist in the palette of an error-diffused picture.

This effect works better if you dither larger source images, as the individual pixels are not as noticeable. In fact, as discussed in *Bitmapped Graphics*, error-diffused dithering can produce distinctly better results if you scale a source image up and then dither it.

The results of error-diffused dithering are also affected by the filter you use. A filter that communicates with a larger number of pixels usually produces more attractive results, as it is less likely to make the picture look as if it has a pattern built into it. The Stucki filter, for example, usually does much better work than the Floyd-Steinberg filter. It looks like this:

```
            X   8   4
  2   4     8   4   2
  1   2     4   2   1
```

The Stucki filter works with fractions of the color error in which the denominator is 42, the sum of all of the numbers in the filter diagram. It's pretty slow as compared to the Floyd-Steinberg filter.

The Burkes filter is somewhere between the two preceding filters. It looks like this:

```
            X   8   4
  2   4     8   4   2
```

If you get seriously into image manipulation using error diffused dithering, you'll probably get a feel for the types of images that benefit from a more complex filter. You'll also find that there are some images that don't take to being filtered at all and look best if they're just remapped. For the most part, these are pictures that have been generated digitally, rather than by scanning a photograph. Some ray traced pictures don't look very good after they've been dithered, for example, and fare much better if you just remap them.

A 24-bit PCX preview

As discussed earlier, looking at 24-bit pictures without a display card that handles true color is a bit troublesome. There are several approaches to the problem, all of which make trade-offs between image fidelity and the amount of time it takes to get something more than a wait message on your screen. A gray-scale display is the fastest approach, but it dispenses with all the color information.

An arguably better approach to previewing true color images is to do a quick color dither. The time involved in performing color dithering increases with the number of bits of color in the destination palette. However, by the careful use of some enlightened cheating, you can reduce the dithering time inordinately. The cheat consists of choosing a fixed 8-color palette in which all the colors consist of RGB colors having either 0 or 255 for each color value.

These eight colors can be represented as follows:

Color	Red	Green	Blue
Black	0	0	0
Red	255	0	0
Green	0	255	0
Yellow	255	255	0
Blue	0	0	255
Magenta	255	0	255
Cyan	0	255	255
White	255	255	255

Error diffusion theory suggests that even though this palette is pretty small, using it will result in a fair approximation of the colors in a 24-bit source image. In fact, you'd have to have a source image of pretty substantial dimensions, with a matching monitor, before the dithered colors would really start to look reasonably close to the source colors. However, as a quick preview of the colors in a 24-bit file, this approach works pretty well.

Figure 12-4 illustrates the source code for PVIEWPCX. This program reads a 24-bit PCX file and displays an 8-color dither in VGA mode 13H.

```
/*
        24 bit PCX preview with dithering - copyright (c) 1991
        Alchemy Mindworks Inc.
*/

#include "stdio.h"
#include "dos.h"
#include "alloc.h"

/*                              uncomment this line if you
#include "memmangr.h"           will be linking in the memory manager
```

12-4 The source code for PVIEWPCX.

```
*/

        #define GOOD_READ       0       /* return codes */
        #define BAD_FILE        1
        #define BAD_READ        2
        #define MEMORY_ERROR    3
        #define WRONG_BITS      4

        #define SCREENWIDE      320     /* mode 13 screen dimensions */
        #define SCREENDEEP      200
        #define STEP            32      /* size of a step when panning */

        #define HOME            0x4700  /* cursor control codes */
        #define CURSOR_UP       0x4800
        #define CURSOR_LEFT     0x4b00
        #define CURSOR_RIGHT    0x4d00
        #define END             0x4f00
        #define CURSOR_DOWN     0x5000

        #define RGB_RED         0
        #define RGB_GREEN       1
        #define RGB_BLUE        2
        #define RGB_SIZE        3

        #define FLOYD           1
        #define BURKES          2
        #define STUCKI          3

        #define LINECOUNT       4

        typedef struct {
                int width,depth,bytes,bits;
                char palette[768];
                int (*setup)();
                int (*closedown)();
                } FILEINFO;

        typedef struct {
                char manufacturer;
                char version;
                char encoding;
                char bits_per_pixel;
                int xmin,ymin;
                int xmax,ymax;
                int hres;
                int vres;
                char palette[48];
                char reserved;
                char colour_planes;
                int bytes_per_line;
                int palette_type;
                char filler[58];
```

12-4 Continued.

```
                    } PCXHEAD;

        char *farPtr(char *p,long l);
        char *getline(unsigned int n);
        int dosetup(FILEINFO *fi);
        int doclosedown(FILEINFO *fi);
        int putline(char *p,unsigned int n);

        char fixedpalette[]={
                  0,   0,   0,
                255,   0,   0,
                  0, 255,   0,
                255, 255,   0,
                  0,   0, 255,
                255,   0, 255,
                  0, 255, 255,
                255, 255, 255
                };

        FILEINFO fi;
        char *buffer=NULL;

        main(argc,argv)
                int argc;
                char *argv[];
        {
                FILE *fp;
                static char results[5][16] = {  "Ok",
                                                "Bad file",
                                                "Bad read",
                                                "Memory error",
                                                "Too few colours"
                                                };
                char path[80];
                int r;

                if(argc > 1) {
                        strmfe(path,argv[1],"PCX");
                        strupr(path);
                        if((fp = fopen(path,"rb")) != NULL) {
                                fi.setup=dosetup;
                                fi.closedown=doclosedown;
                                r=unpackpcx(fp,&fi);
                                printf("\%s",results[r]);
                                fclose(fp);
                        } else printf("Error opening %s",path);
                } else puts("Argument:       path to a PCX file");
        }

        /* unpack an PCX file */
        unpackpcx(fp,fi)
                FILE *fp;
```

12-4 Continued.

```
        FILEINFO *fi;
{
        PCXHEAD pcx;

char *p,*pr;
int i,j,bytes;

if(fread((char *)&pcx,1,sizeof(PCXHEAD),fp) == sizeof(PCXHEAD) &&
   pcx.manufacturer==10) {
        if(pcx.bits_per_pixel==8 && pcx.colour_planes==3) {
                bytes=pcx.bytes_per_line;
                fi->width=pcx.xmax-pcx.xmin+1;
                fi->depth=pcx.ymax-pcx.ymin+1;
                fi->bytes=bytes*RGB_SIZE;

                if((p=malloc(fi->bytes)) == NULL) return(MEMORY_ERROR);

                if((pr=malloc(fi->bytes)) == NULL) {
                        free(p);
                        return(MEMORY_ERROR);
                }

                if((fi->setup)(fi) != GOOD_READ) {
                        free(pr);
                        free(p);
                        return(MEMORY_ERROR);
                }

                for(i=0;i<fi->depth;++i) {
                        for(j=0;j<RGB_SIZE;++j) {
                                if(readpcxline(p+(j*bytes),fp,bytes) != bytes) {
                                        freebuffer();
                                        free(pr);
                                        free(p);
                                        return(BAD_READ);
                                }
                        }

                        for(j=0;j<fi->width;++j) {
                                pr[j*RGB_SIZE+RGB_RED]=p[j];
                                pr[j*RGB_SIZE+RGB_GREEN]=p[RGB_GREEN*bytes+j];
                                pr[j*RGB_SIZE+RGB_BLUE]=p[RGB_BLUE*bytes+j];
                        }

                        putline(pr,i);
                }
                (fi->closedown)(fi);
                freebuffer();
                free(pr);
                free(p);
        } else return(WRONG_BITS);
} else return(BAD_READ);
return(GOOD_READ);
```

12-4 Continued.

```
                    }

                    /* read and decode a PCX line into p */
                    readpcxline(p,fp,bytes)
                            char *p;
                            FILE *fp;
                            int bytes;
                    {
                            int n=0,c,i;
            do {
                    c=fgetc(fp) & 0xff;
                    if((c & 0xc0) == 0xc0) {
                            i=c & 0x3f;
                            c=fgetc(fp);
                            while(i--) p[n++]=c;
                    }
                    else p[n++]=c;
            } while(n < bytes);
            return(n);
    }


/* This function is called after the BMHD and CMAP chunks have
   been read but before the BODY is unpacked */
dosetup(fi)
        FILEINFO *fi;
{
        if(!getbuffer((long)fi->bytes*(long)fi->depth,fi->bytes,fi->depth))
            return(MEMORY_ERROR);

        return(GOOD_READ);
}


/* This function is called after an image has been unpacked. It must
   display the image and deallocate memory. */
doclosedown(fi)
        FILEINFO *fi;
{
        union REGS r;
        int c,i,n,x=0,y=0;

        ditherimage(fi);

        r.x.ax=0x0013;
        int86(0x10,&r,&r);

        setvgapalette(fi->palette,1<<fi->bits,0);

        if(fi->width > SCREENWIDE) n=SCREENWIDE;
        else n=fi->width;

        do {
                for(i=0;i<SCREENDEEP;++i) {
```

12-4 Continued.

```
                        c=y+i;
                        if(c>=fi->depth) break;
                        memcpy(MK_FP(0xa000,SCREENWIDE*i),getline(c)+x,n);
                }
                c=GetKey();
                switch(c) {
                        case CURSOR_LEFT:
                                if((x-STEP) > 0) x-=STEP;
                                else x=0;
                                break;
                        case CURSOR_RIGHT:
                                if((x+STEP+SCREENWIDE) < fi->width) x+=STEP;
                                else if(fi->width > SCREENWIDE)
                                        x=fi->width-SCREENWIDE;
                                else x=0;
                                break;
                        case CURSOR_UP:
                                if((y-STEP) > 0) y-=STEP;
                                else y=0;
                                break;
                        case CURSOR_DOWN:
                                if((y+STEP+SCREENDEEP) < fi->depth) y+=STEP;
                                else if(fi->depth > SCREENDEEP)
                                        y=fi->depth-SCREENDEEP;
                                else y=0;
                                break;
                        case HOME:
                                x=y=0;
                                break;
                        case END:
                                if(fi->width > SCREENWIDE)
                                        x=fi->width-SCREENWIDE;
                                else x=0;
                                if(fi->depth > SCREENDEEP)
                                        y=fi->depth-SCREENDEEP;
                                else y=0;
                                break;
                }
        } while(c != 27);

        freebuffer();

        r.x.ax=0x0003;
        int86(0x10,&r,&r);
        return(GOOD_READ);
}

/* get one extended key code */
GetKey()
{
        int c;
        c = getch();
```

12-4 Continued.

```
                if(!(c & 0x00ff)) c = getch() << 8;
                return(c);
        }


        /* set the VGA palette and background */
        setvgapalette(p,n,b)
                char *p;
                int n,b;
        {

                union REGS r;
                int i;

                outp(0x3c6,0xff);
                for(i=0;i<n;++i) {
                        outp(0x3c8,i);
                        outp(0x3c9,(*p++) >> 2);
                        outp(0x3c9,(*p++) >> 2);
                        outp(0x3c9,(*p++) >> 2);
                }
                r.x.ax=0x1001;
                r.h.bh=b;
                int86(0x10,&r,&r);
        }


        /* make file name with specific extension */
        strmfe(new,old,ext)
                char *new,*old,*ext;
        {

                while(*old != 0 && *old != '.') *new++=*old++;
                *new++='.';
                while(*ext) *new++=*ext++;
                *new=0;
        }


        ditherimage(fi)
                FILEINFO *fi;
        {

                char *p,*linebuf[LINECOUNT];
                int i,j,n,max[RGB_SIZE],min[RGB_SIZE],mid[RGB_SIZE];
                int r,g,b,mr,mg,mb,w;

                w=fi->width*RGB_SIZE;

                for(i=0;i<LINECOUNT;++i) {
                        if((linebuf[i]=malloc(w)) == NULL) return(MEMORY_ERROR);
                }

                for(i=0;i<RGB_SIZE;++i) {
                        min[i]=255;
                        max[i]=0;
                }
```

12-4 Continued.

```
for(i=0;i<fi->depth;++i) {
        printf("\rRemapping line %u      ",i);
        p=getline(i);
        for(j=0;j<fi->width;++j) {
                n=j*RGB_SIZE;
                r=p[n+RGB_RED];
                g=p[n+RGB_GREEN];
                b=p[n+RGB_BLUE];
                if(r < min[RGB_RED]) min[RGB_RED]=r;
                if(g < min[RGB_GREEN]) min[RGB_GREEN]=g;
                if(b < min[RGB_BLUE]) min[RGB_BLUE]=b;
                if(r > max[RGB_RED]) max[RGB_RED]=r;
                if(g > max[RGB_GREEN]) max[RGB_GREEN]=g;
                if(b > max[RGB_BLUE]) max[RGB_BLUE]=b;
        }
}

for(i=0;i<RGB_SIZE;++i) mid[i]=(max[i]+min[i])>>1;

for(i=0;i<fi->depth;++i) {
        printf("\rDithering line %u      ",i);
        memcpy(linebuf[0],getline(i),w);
        if((i+1) < fi->depth) memcpy(linebuf[1],getline(i+1),w);

        p=linebuf[0];
        for(j=0;j<fi->width;++j) {
                r=p[RGB_RED];
                if(r > mid[RGB_RED]) mr=255;
                else mr=0;

                g=p[RGB_GREEN];
                if(g > mid[RGB_GREEN]) mg=255;
                else mg=0;

                b=p[RGB_BLUE];
                if(b > mid[RGB_BLUE]) mb=255;
                else mb=0;

                n=0;
                if(mr) n |= 0x0001;
                if(mg) n |= 0x0002;
                if(mb) n |= 0x0004;

                linebuf[LINECOUNT-1][j]=n;

                diffuseFloyd(linebuf[0],linebuf[1],j,i,r,g,b,mr,mg,mb,fi->width,fi->depth);

                p+=RGB_SIZE;
        }

        putline(linebuf[LINECOUNT-1],i);
        if((i+1) < fi->depth) putline(linebuf[1],i+1);
```

12-4 Continued.

```
        }

        for(i=0;i<LINECOUNT;++i) free(linebuf[i]);
        memcpy(fi->palette,fixedpalette,24);
        fi->bits=3;

        return(GOOD_READ);
}

diffuseFloyd(line1,line2,x,y,r,g,b,mr,mg,mb,width,depth)
        char *line1,*line2;
        int x,y,r,g,b;
        int mr,mg,mb;
        int width,depth;
{
        int dr,dg,db;

        dr=r-mr;
        dg=g-mg;
        db=b-mb;

        if((x+1) < width) {
                line1[((x+1)*RGB_SIZE)+RGB_RED]  =addb(line1[((x+1)*RGB_SIZE)+RGB_RED],((dr*7)/16));
                line1[((x+1)*RGB_SIZE)+RGB_GREEN]=addb(line1[((x+1)*RGB_SIZE)+RGB_GREEN],((dg*7)/16));
                line1[((x+1)*RGB_SIZE)+RGB_BLUE] =addb(line1[((x+1)*RGB_SIZE)+RGB_BLUE],((db*7)/16));
        }

        if((x-1) > 0 && (y+1) < depth) {
                line2[((x-1)*RGB_SIZE)+RGB_RED]  =addb(line2[((x-1)*RGB_SIZE)+RGB_RED],((dr*3)/16));
                line2[((x-1)*RGB_SIZE)+RGB_GREEN]=addb(line2[((x-1)*RGB_SIZE)+RGB_GREEN],((dg*3)/16));
                line2[((x-1)*RGB_SIZE)+RGB_BLUE] =addb(line2[((x-1)*RGB_SIZE)+RGB_BLUE],((db*3)/16));
        }

        if((x+1) < width && (y+1) < depth) {
                line2[((x+1)*RGB_SIZE)+RGB_RED]  =addb(line2[((x+1)*RGB_SIZE)+RGB_RED],((dr*1)/16));
                line2[((x+1)*RGB_SIZE)+RGB_GREEN]=addb(line2[((x+1)*RGB_SIZE)+RGB_GREEN],((dg*1)/16));
                line2[((x+1)*RGB_SIZE)+RGB_BLUE] =addb(line2[((x+1)*RGB_SIZE)+RGB_BLUE],((db*1)/16));
        }

        if((y+1) < depth) {
                line2[(x*RGB_SIZE)+RGB_RED]  =addb(line2[(x*RGB_SIZE)+RGB_RED],((dr*5)/16));
                line2[(x*RGB_SIZE)+RGB_GREEN]=addb(line2[(x*RGB_SIZE)+RGB_GREEN],((dg*5)/16));
                line2[(x*RGB_SIZE)+RGB_BLUE] =addb(line2[(x*RGB_SIZE)+RGB_BLUE],((db*5)/16));
        }
}

addb(n1,n2)         /* add two bytes, clamp to byte range */
        int n1,n2;
{
        int n;

        n=n1+n2;
```

12-4 Continued.

```
            if(n<0) n=0;
            else if(n > 255) n=255;
            return(n);
}


/* if you don't use in the memory manager, these functions
    will stand in for it */

#if !MEMMANGR

/* return a far pointer plus a long integer */
char *farPtr(p,l)
            char *p;
            long l;
{
            unsigned int seg,off;

            seg = FP_SEG(p);
            off = FP_OFF(p);
            seg += (off / 16);
            off &= 0x000f;
            off += (unsigned int)(l & 0x000fL);
            seg += (l / 16L);
            p = MK_FP(seg,off);
            return(p);
}

/* save one line to memory */
putline(p,n)
            char *p;
            unsigned int n;
{
            if(n >= 0 && n < fi.depth)
                memcpy(farPtr(buffer,(long)n*(long)fi.bytes),p,fi.bytes);
}

/* get one line from memory */
char *getline(n)
            unsigned int n;
{
            return(farPtr(buffer,(long)n*(long)fi.bytes));
}
#pragma warn -par
getbuffer(n,bytes,lines)
            unsigned long n;
            int bytes,lines;
{
            if((buffer=farmalloc(n)) == NULL) return(0);
            else return(1);
}

freebuffer()
```

12-4 Continued.

```
{
        if(buffer != NULL) farfree(buffer);
        buffer=NULL;
}
#endif /* !MEMMANGR */
```
12-4 Continued.

The PVIEWPCX program loads a 24-bit PCX file, as discussed in chapter 8. It then dithers and remaps the file to the eight colors defined in `fixedpalette`. Note that in this case it's not necessary to actually compute the color distance between the source and remapped colors because each of the remapped color values are 0 or 255. Having dithered the image, PVIEWPCX uses the display code that appeared in the early file-reader programs in this book to display the image on your screen.

The results of all this are passable in mode 13H. They look a lot better in a 16-color display mode, such as mode 12H because the resulting pixels will be a lot smaller. You might want to modify PVIEWPCX to use the screen drivers discussed in chapter 10.

Color quantization

The discussion of color dithering deftly ignored the issue of finding a suitable palette with which to remap a 24-bit image. All the examples of color dithering discussed thus far have used fixed palettes, that is, palettes chosen without regard to the colors in the images to be remapped. For reasons discussed earlier, this approach doesn't work very well. In most cases, it will result in dithered images in which the error diffusion process has to handle artificially large color errors.

It's possible to strategically choose a destination palette based on the actual dispersal of colors in a source 24-bit image. For example, if you wanted to dither a picture of a green frog sitting on a green leaf in a jungle, most of the colors in the palette should ideally be green. More to the point, they should be drawn from the source image.

The choice of colors in an ideally selected palette would be those that appear most frequently in the source image, and those that are the most unique. If a function could be found to judge colors on this basis, you could sort all the colors in the source image in order of these criteria and lop off the first 256.

This process of choosing a palette is called *quantization*. The algorithm that does it is called a *median cut*, and was first devised by Paul Heckbert in 1982. It's somewhat complex, involving another journey into the trackless, desolate void of color space.

The following discussion of median-cut color quantization deals with the theory of it in pretty general terms in the interest of being understandable by people who don't usually count on their fingers in exponential notation or complex numbers. If you'd like a deeper insight into the process, consult the reference at the end of this chapter.

If you'll be abstracting the quantization code later in this chapter, you'll probably find that you don't have to understand how the algorithm works at all.

The first problem in coming up with a well chosen 256-color palette is to determine the colors that actually exist in the source image and how frequently each one is used. The most practical way of doing this is to create a table, or `histogram`, of all the colors.

There are 16 million possible colors in a 24-bit image, which would make for a rather large histogram. If the color resolution is reduced somewhat, so that only the most significant bits of color are used, the size of the histogram can be pruned to more manageable dimensions. Because it is exceedingly convenient for the resulting array to fit in a single memory segment, we use 4 bits of color resolution. There are three color values per entry (one each for the red, green, and blue components) for a total of 12 bits. This will result in a histogram with 4096 possible entries, 4096 being 2^{12}.

Initially, the histogram can be seen as an array of 4096 long integers, all set to 0. In fact, each entry is a complex structure, as it also must ultimately contain the RGB values for the color it represents. It can be filled in by scanning through all the pixels in the source and reducing each pixel to a 12-bit value, that is, to three 4-bit color indices. Each of the resulting 12-bit numbers can be regarded as being an index into the histogram table. Each time an index is derived from a pixel, the corresponding entry in the histogram should be incremented.

Allowing for the accuracy of the table (12 bits rather than 24) the final histogram will reflect the frequency of each color in the source image. In fact, each entry in the histogram really specifies the frequency of a clump of 4096 similar colors; but this is close enough for the purposes of this algorithm. Keep in mind that there will be only 256 colors in the destination image.

Color space, as discussed at the beginning of this chapter, is finite. It runs from black to white, or rather, from point (0,0,0) through to point (255,255,255). This can be seen in FIG. 12-5.

Actually, since the color resolution was reduced to 4 bits for each of the three color components, white is really represented by the color (15,15,15) because in this 12-bit color, 15 represents a color component that is fully on. Color space looks like FIG. 12-6 now.

In order to come up with a palette having 256 colors, color space must be divided into 256 smaller spaces. If you regard color space as being a cube, you can regard each of the 256 eventual palette entries as being a smaller cube within the larger cube. The ideal palette would be one in which the volume of each of the 256 eventual cubes reflects the widest dispersal of colors represented by the color frequency histogram.

The algorithm that performs this carving up of color space is Paul Heckbert's median-cut algorithm, and it recursively subdivides the principal cube of color space until a suitable number of smaller cubes has been

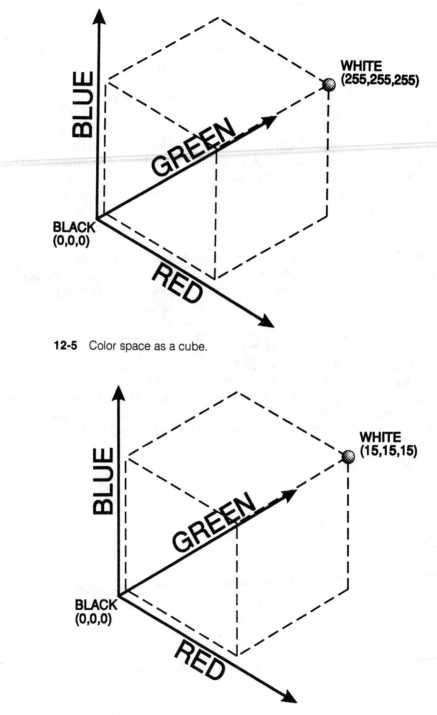

12-5 Color space as a cube.

12-6 Color space for 12-bit color.

obtained. You can see what is happening if you look at the creation of one smaller cube carved from the whole cube of color space.

In this example we'll assume that there are actually 4096 used entries in the histogram to keep the numbers simple. In practice, there will probably be far fewer. The calculations involved actually work with the number of colors used rather than the size of the histogram table.

The initial cube—all of the color space—has a minimum color value of (0,0,0)—black—and a maximum color value of (15,15,15)—white. In scanning through the list of colors in the histogram, one of the three color components will be found to have the greatest difference between its minimum and maximum values. If this color turns out to be blue, the entries in the histogram would be initially sorted in order of their blue values.

The code should now scan through the histogram and add up the blue components until the sum reaches half the total blue value of the entire histogram. This sum is the median for the blue size of the cube. Splitting the color space at this point would produce two smaller solids. Having done this, the process can be repeated for each of the two smaller divisions of color space until 256 solids exist in the color space. The color coordinates of these solids represent the 256 best colors for remapping the source image.

Quantizing and dithering 24-bit PCX images

The DITHRPCX program in FIG. 12-7 illustrates code that quantizes and dithers a 24-bit PCX file down to your choice of 16 through 256 colors and displays the results in mode 13H on a VGA card. It uses the Heckbert median-cut quantization algorithm and color dithering discussed in this chapter. In fact, it implements all three filters mentioned have.

```
/*
        24 bit PCX reader with dithering - copyright (c) 1991
        Alchemy Mindworks Inc.
*/

#include "stdio.h"
#include "dos.h"
#include "alloc.h"

/*                              uncomment this line if you
#include "memmangr.h"           will be linking in the memory manager
*/

#define GOOD_READ       0       /* return codes */
#define BAD_FILE        1
#define BAD_READ        2
#define MEMORY_ERROR    3
#define WRONG_BITS      4

#define SCREENWIDE      320     /* mode 13 screen dimensions */
```

12-7 The source code for DITHRPCX.

```
#define SCREENDEEP        200
#define STEP              32      /* size of a step when panning */

#define HOME              0x4700  /* cursor control codes */
#define CURSOR_UP         0x4800
#define CURSOR_LEFT       0x4b00
#define CURSOR_RIGHT      0x4d00
#define END               0x4f00
#define CURSOR_DOWN       0x5000

#define RGB_RED           0
#define RGB_GREEN         1
#define RGB_BLUE          2
#define RGB_SIZE          3

#define FLOYD             1
#define BURKES            2
#define STUCKI            3

#define LINECOUNT         4

#define COLOR_ARRAY_SIZE       4096
#define BITS_PER_PRIM_COLOR    4
#define MAX_PRIM_COLOR         0x0f

#define BIG_DISTANCE 1000000L

#define DIST(r1,g1,b1,r2,g2,b2) \
          (long) (3L*(long)((r1)-(r2))*(long)((r1)-(r2)) + \
                  4L*(long)((g1)-(g2))*(long)((g1)-(g2)) + \
                  2L*(long)((b1)-(b2))*(long)((b1)-(b2)))

typedef struct {
        int width,depth,bytes,bits;
        char palette[768];
        int (*setup)();
        int (*closedown)();
        } FILEINFO;

typedef struct {
        char manufacturer;
        char version;
        char encoding;
        char bits_per_pixel;
        int xmin,ymin;
        int xmax,ymax;
        int hres;
        int vres;
        char palette[48];
        char reserved;
        char colour_planes;
        int bytes_per_line;
        int palette_type;
```

12-7 Continued.

```
                char filler[58];
        } PCXHEAD;

typedef struct QCOLOUR {
        char RGB[3];
        char NewColorIndex;
        long Count;
        struct QCOLOUR *Pnext;
        } QCOLOUR;

typedef struct {
        char RGBMin[3],RGBWidth[3];
        unsigned int NumEntries;        /* Number of QCOLOUR in linked list below. */
        long Count;                     /* Total number of pixels in all the entries. */
        QCOLOUR *QuantizedColors;
        } NEWCOLOUR;

char *farPtr(char *p,long l);
char *getline(unsigned int n);
int dosetup(FILEINFO *fi);
int doclosedown(FILEINFO *fi);
int putline(char *p,unsigned int n);
int SortCmpRtn(QCOLOUR **Entry1, QCOLOUR **Entry2);
int quantize(int width,int depth,int *ColorMapSize,char *OutputColorMap,char *(*proc)());

FILEINFO fi;
char *buffer=NULL;
int dithertype=FLOYD;
int ditherbits=8;
int SortRGBAxis;                        /* used by quantize */

main(argc,argv)
        int argc;
        char *argv[];
{
        FILE *fp;
        static char results[5][16] = {  "Ok",
                                        "Bad file",
                                        "Bad read",
                                        "Memory error",
                                        "Too few colours"
                                        };
        char path[80];
        int i,r;
        if(argc > 1) {
                for(i=0;i<argc;++i) {
                        if(!memicmp(argv[i],"/C",2)) ditherbits=atoi(argv[i]+2);
                        else if(!stricmp(argv[i],"/F")) dithertype=FLOYD;
                        else if(!stricmp(argv[i],"/B")) dithertype=BURKES;
                        else if(!stricmp(argv[i],"/C")) dithertype=STUCKI;
                }
                if(ditherbits < 4) ditherbits=4;
```

12-7 Continued.

```
                    if(ditherbits > 8) ditherbits=8;
                    strmfe(path,argv[1],"PCX");
                    strupr(path);
                    if((fp = fopen(path,"rb")) != NULL) {
                            fi.setup=dosetup;
                            fi.closedown=doclosedown;
                            r=unpackpcx(fp,&fi);
                            printf("\%s",results[r]);
                            fclose(fp);
                    } else printf("Error opening %s",path);
            } else puts("Argument:        path to a PCX file");
    }


    /* unpack an PCX file */
    unpackpcx(fp,fi)
            FILE *fp;
            FILEINFO *fi;
    {
            PCXHEAD pcx;
            char *p,*pr;
            int i,j,bytes;

            if(fread((char *)&pcx,1,sizeof(PCXHEAD),fp) == sizeof(PCXHEAD) &&
               pcx.manufacturer==10) {
                    if(pcx.bits_per_pixel==8 && pcx.colour_planes==3) {
                            bytes=pcx.bytes_per_line;
                            fi->width=pcx.xmax-pcx.xmin+1;
                            fi->depth=pcx.ymax-pcx.ymin+1;
                            fi->bytes=bytes*RGB_SIZE;

                            if((p=malloc(fi->bytes)) == NULL) return(MEMORY_ERROR);

                            if((pr=malloc(fi->bytes)) == NULL) {
                                    free(p);
                                    return(MEMORY_ERROR);
                            }

                            if((fi->setup)(fi) != GOOD_READ) {
                                    free(pr);
                                    free(p);
                                    return(MEMORY_ERROR);
                            }

                            for(i=0;i<fi->depth;++i) {
                                    for(j=0;j<RGB_SIZE;++j) {
                                            if(readpcxline(p+(j*bytes),fp,bytes) != bytes) {
                                                    freebuffer();
                                                    free(pr);
                                                    free(p);
                                                    return(BAD_READ);
                                            }
```

12-7 Continued.

```
                                        }
                                for(j=0;j<fi->width;++j) {
                                        pr[j*RGB_SIZE+RGB_RED]=p[j];
                                        pr[j*RGB_SIZE+RGB_GREEN]=p[RGB_GREEN*bytes+j];
                                        pr[j*RGB_SIZE+RGB_BLUE]=p[RGB_BLUE*bytes+j];
                                }

                                putline(pr,i);
                        }
                        (fi->closedown)(fi);
                        freebuffer();
                        free(pr);
                        free(p);
                } else return(WRONG_BITS);
        } else return(BAD_READ);
        return(GOOD_READ);
}


/* read and decode a PCX line into p */
readpcxline(p,fp,bytes)
        char *p;
        FILE *fp;
        int bytes;
{

        int n=0,c,i;

        do {
                c=fgetc(fp) & 0xff;
                if((c & 0xc0) == 0xc0) {
                        i=c & 0x3f;
                        c=fgetc(fp);
                        while(i--) p[n++]=c;
                }
                else p[n++]=c;
        } while(n < bytes);
        return(n);

}
/* this function is called after the BMHD and CMAP chunks have
   been read but before the BODY is unpacked */
dosetup(fi)
        FILEINFO *fi;
{
        if(!getbuffer((long)fi->bytes*(long)fi->depth,fi->bytes,fi->depth))
            return(MEMORY_ERROR);

        return(GOOD_READ);
}


/* This function is called after an image has been unpacked. It must
   display the image and deallocate memory. */
doclosedown(fi)
```

12-7 Continued.

```
        FILEINFO *fi;
{

        union REGS r;
        int c,i,n,x=0,y=0;

        ditherfile(fi);
        r.x.ax=0x0013;
        int86(0x10,&r,&r);

        setvgapalette(fi->palette,1<<fi->bits,0);

        if(fi->width > SCREENWIDE) n=SCREENWIDE;
        else n=fi->width;

        do {
                for(i=0;i<SCREENDEEP;++i) {
                        c=y+i;
                        if(c>=fi->depth) break;
                        memcpy(MK_FP(0xa000,SCREENWIDE*i),getline(c)+x,n);
                }
                c=GetKey();
                switch(c) {
                        case CURSOR_LEFT:
                                if((x-STEP) > 0) x-=STEP;
                                else x=0;
                                break;
                        case CURSOR_RIGHT:
                                if((x+STEP+SCREENWIDE) < fi->width) x+=STEP;
                                else if(fi->width > SCREENWIDE)
                                    x=fi->width-SCREENWIDE;
                                else x=0;
                                break;
                        case CURSOR_UP:
                                if((y-STEP) > 0) y-=STEP;
                                else y=0;
                                break;
                        case CURSOR_DOWN:
                                if((y+STEP+SCREENDEEP) < fi->depth) y+=STEP;
                                else if(fi->depth > SCREENDEEP)
                                    y=fi->depth-SCREENDEEP;
                                else y=0;
                                break;
                        case HOME:
                                x=y=0;
                                break;
                        case END:
                                if(fi->width > SCREENWIDE)
                                    x=fi->width-SCREENWIDE;
                                else x=0;
                                if(fi->depth > SCREENDEEP)
                                    y=fi->depth-SCREENDEEP;
                                else y=0;
```

12-7 Continued.

```
                        break;
                }
        } while(c != 27);

        freebuffer();

        r.x.ax=0x0003;
        int86(0x10,&r,&r);
        return(GOOD_READ);
}

/* get one extended key code */

GetKey()
{
        int c;

        c = getch();
        if(!(c & 0x00ff)) c = getch() << 8;
        return(c);
}

/* set the VGA palette and background */
setvgapalette(p,n,b)
        char *p;
        int n,b;
{
        union REGS r;
        int i;

        outp(0x3c6,0xff);
        for(i=0;i<n;++i) {
                outp(0x3c8,i);
                outp(0x3c9, (*p++) >> 2);
                outp(0x3c9, (*p++) >> 2);
                outp(0x3c9, (*p++) >> 2);
        }
        r.x.ax=0x1001;
        r.h.bh=b;
        int86(0x10,&r,&r);
}

/* make file name with specific extension */
strmfe(new,old,ext)
        char *new,*old,*ext;
{
        while(*old != 0 && *old != '.') *new++=*old++;
        *new++='.';
        while(*ext) *new++=*ext++;
        *new=0;
}


ditherfile(fi)
```

12-7 Continued.

```
        FILEINFO *fi;
{

        char *linebuf[LINECOUNT];
        int i,j,n;
        unsigned int r,g,b;
        unsigned int mr,mg,mb;

        fi->bits=ditherbits;
        n=1<<fi->bits;

        for(i=0;i<LINECOUNT;++i) {
                if((linebuf[i]=malloc(fi->bytes))==NULL)
                    return(MEMORY_ERROR);
        }

        if(!quantize(fi->width,fi->depth,&n,fi->palette,getline)) {
                for(j=0;j<LINECOUNT;++j)
                    if(linebuf[j] != NULL) free(linebuf[j]);
                return(MEMORY_ERROR);
        }
}

printf("%u colours used\n",n);

for(i=0;i<fi->depth;++i) {
        printf("\rDithering line %u",i);

        memcpy(linebuf[0],getline(i),fi->width*RGB_SIZE);
        if((i+1) < fi->depth ) memcpy(linebuf[1],getline(i+1),fi->width*RGB_SIZE);
        if((i+2) < fi->depth ) memcpy(linebuf[2],getline(i+2),fi->width*RGB_SIZE);
        for(j=0;j<fi->width;++j) {
                r=linebuf[0][(j*RGB_SIZE)+RGB_RED];
                g=linebuf[0][(j*RGB_SIZE)+RGB_GREEN];
                b=linebuf[0][(j*RGB_SIZE)+RGB_BLUE];

                linebuf[3][j]=findNearestMatch(r,g,b,&mr,&mg,&mb,fi->palette,n);

                switch(dithertype) {
                        case FLOYD:
                                diffuseFloyd(linebuf[0],linebuf[1],j,i,r,g,b,mr,mg,mb,fi->width,fi->depth
                                break;
                        case BURKES:
                                diffuseBurkes(linebuf[0],linebuf[1],j,i,r,g,b,mr,mg,mb,fi->width,fi->depth
                                break;
                        case STUCKI:
                                diffuseStucki(linebuf[0],linebuf[1],linebuf[2],j,i,r,g,b,mr,mg,mb,fi->w:
                                break;
                }

                putline(linebuf[3],i);
                if((i+1) < fi->depth) putline(linebuf[1],i+1);
                if((i+2) < fi->depth) putline(linebuf[2],i+2);
        }
```

12-7 Continued.

```
        }
        for(i=0;i<LINECOUNT;++i) free(linebuf[i]);
}


quantize(width,depth,colourcount,OutputColorMap,proc)
        int width,depth;                /* image dimensions */
        int *colourcount;               /* new palette size */
        char *OutputColorMap;           /* new palette */
        char *(*proc)();                /* procedure to get a line */
{
        char *p;
        unsigned int i,j;
        int Index;
        int NewColorMapSize;
        int NumOfEntries;
        long cRed,cGreen,cBlue;
        NEWCOLOUR *NewColorSubdiv;

        QCOLOUR *ColorArrayEntries, *QuantizedColor;

        if((ColorArrayEntries = (QCOLOUR *)malloc(sizeof(QCOLOUR) * COLOR_ARRAY_SIZE)) == NULL) return(0);
        if((NewColorSubdiv = (NEWCOLOUR *)malloc(sizeof(NEWCOLOUR) * 256)) == NULL) {
                free((char *)ColorArrayEntries);
                return(0);
        }

        for(i=0;i<COLOR_ARRAY_SIZE;i++) {
                ColorArrayEntries[i].RGB[RGB_RED] = i >> (2 * BITS_PER_PRIM_COLOR);
                ColorArrayEntries[i].RGB[RGB_GREEN] = (i >> BITS_PER_PRIM_COLOR) & MAX_PRIM_COLOR;
                ColorArrayEntries[i].RGB[RGB_BLUE] = i & MAX_PRIM_COLOR;
                ColorArrayEntries[i].Count = 0L;
        }

        for(i=0;i<depth;++i) {
                p=(proc)(i);
                for(j=0;j<width;++j) {
                        Index = (((int)p[RGB_RED] >> (8 - BITS_PER_PRIM_COLOR)) << (2 * BITS_PER_PRIM_COLOR)) +
                                (((int)p[RGB_GREEN] >> (8 - BITS_PER_PRIM_COLOR)) << BITS_PER_PRIM_COLOR) +
                                ((int)p[RGB_BLUE] >> (8 - BITS_PER_PRIM_COLOR)));
                        ColorArrayEntries[Index].Count++;
                        p+=RGB_SIZE;
                }
        }

        for(i=0;i<256;i++) {
                NewColorSubdiv[i].QuantizedColors = NULL;
                NewColorSubdiv[i].Count = 0L;
                NewColorSubdiv[i].NumEntries = 0;
                for(j=0;j<RGB_SIZE;++j) {
                        NewColorSubdiv[i].RGBMin[j] = 0;
                        NewColorSubdiv[i].RGBWidth[j] = 255;
                }
```

12-7 Continued.

```
                }

        for (i=0;i<COLOR_ARRAY_SIZE;i++)
                if(ColorArrayEntries[i].Count > 0) break;
        QuantizedColor = NewColorSubdiv[0].QuantizedColors = &ColorArrayEntries[i];
        NumOfEntries = 1;
        while(++i < COLOR_ARRAY_SIZE)
                if(ColorArrayEntries[i].Count > 0) {
                        QuantizedColor->Pnext=&ColorArrayEntries[i];
                        QuantizedColor = &ColorArrayEntries[i];
                        NumOfEntries++;
                }
        QuantizedColor->Pnext = NULL;

        NewColorSubdiv[0].NumEntries = NumOfEntries;/* Different sampled colors. */
        NewColorSubdiv[0].Count = (long)width * (long)depth;              /* Pixels. */
        NewColorMapSize = 1;
        if(dividemap(NewColorSubdiv, *colourcount,&NewColorMapSize) == 0) {
                free((char *)ColorArrayEntries);
                free((char *)NewColorSubdiv);
                return(0);
        }
        if(NewColorMapSize < *colourcount) {
                for(i=NewColorMapSize;i<*colourcount;i++)
                        OutputColorMap[(i*3)+RGB_RED]=
                        OutputColorMap[(i*3)+RGB_GREEN]=
                        OutputColorMap[(i*3)+RGB_BLUE]=0;

        }

        for(i=0;i<NewColorMapSize;i++) {
                if((j=NewColorSubdiv[i].NumEntries) > 0) {
                        QuantizedColor = NewColorSubdiv[i].QuantizedColors;

                cRed=cGreen=cBlue=0;
                while(QuantizedColor) {
                        QuantizedColor->NewColorIndex=i;
                        cRed+=QuantizedColor->RGB[RGB_RED];
                        cGreen+=QuantizedColor->RGB[RGB_GREEN];
                        cBlue+=QuantizedColor->RGB[RGB_BLUE];
                        QuantizedColor=QuantizedColor->Pnext;
                }
                OutputColorMap[(i*RGB_SIZE)+RGB_RED]=(int)(cRed<<(8-BITS_PER_PRIM_COLOR))/j;
                OutputColorMap[(i*RGB_SIZE)+RGB_GREEN]=(int)(cGreen<<(8-BITS_PER_PRIM_COLOR))/j;
                OutputColorMap[(i*RGB_SIZE)+RGB_BLUE]=(int)(cBlue<<(8-BITS_PER_PRIM_COLOR))/j;
        }
    }

free((char *)ColorArrayEntries);
free((char *)NewColorSubdiv);
*colourcount = NewColorMapSize;
return(1);
}
```

12-7 Continued.

```
/* do median cut - return false if not enough memory */
dividemap(NewColorSubdiv,ColorMapSize,NewColorMapSize)
        NEWCOLOUR *NewColorSubdiv;
        int ColorMapSize,*NewColorMapSize;
{
        unsigned int i,j;
        int MaxSize,Index=0;
        unsigned int NumEntries,MinColor,MaxColor;
        long Sum,Count;
        QCOLOUR *QuantizedColor, **SortArray;

        while(ColorMapSize>*NewColorMapSize) {
                MaxSize=-1;
                for(i=0;i<*NewColorMapSize;i++) {
                        for(j=0;j<3;j++) {
                                if(((int)NewColorSubdiv[i].RGBWidth[j]) > MaxSize && NewColorSubdiv[i].NumEntrie
                                        MaxSize = NewColorSubdiv[i].RGBWidth[j];
                                        Index = i;
                                        SortRGBAxis = j;
                                }
                        }
                }

                if(MaxSize == -1) return(1);

                if((SortArray=(QCOLOUR **)malloc(sizeof(QCOLOUR *) * NewColorSubdiv[Index].NumEntries)) == NULL)

                for(j=0,QuantizedColor=NewColorSubdiv[Index].QuantizedColors;
                    j < NewColorSubdiv[Index].NumEntries && QuantizedColor != NULL;
                    j++,QuantizedColor=QuantizedColor->Pnext)
                        SortArray[j]=QuantizedColor;

                qsort(SortArray,NewColorSubdiv[Index].NumEntries,sizeof(QCOLOUR *),SortCmpRtn);

                for(j=0;j<NewColorSubdiv[Index].NumEntries-1;j++)
                        SortArray[j]->Pnext = SortArray[j+1];
                SortArray[NewColorSubdiv[Index].NumEntries-1]->Pnext=NULL;
                NewColorSubdiv[Index].QuantizedColors=QuantizedColor=SortArray[0];
                free((char *)SortArray);

                Sum = NewColorSubdiv[Index].Count / 2 - QuantizedColor -> Count;
                NumEntries = 1;
                Count=QuantizedColor->Count;
                while((Sum-=QuantizedColor->Pnext->Count) >= 0 &&
                      QuantizedColor->Pnext != NULL &&
                      QuantizedColor->Pnext->Pnext != NULL) {
                        QuantizedColor = QuantizedColor->Pnext;
                        NumEntries++;
                        Count+=QuantizedColor->Count;
                }
```

12-7 Continued.

```
                    MaxColor = QuantizedColor->RGB[SortRGBAxis];                    /* Max. of first half. */
                    MinColor = QuantizedColor->Pnext->RGB[SortRGBAxis];                /* of second. */
                    MaxColor <<=(8-BITS_PER_PRIM_COLOR);
                    MinColor <<=(8-BITS_PER_PRIM_COLOR);

                    NewColorSubdiv[*NewColorMapSize].QuantizedColors = QuantizedColor->Pnext;
                    QuantizedColor->Pnext = NULL;
                    NewColorSubdiv[*NewColorMapSize].Count = Count;
                    NewColorSubdiv[Index].Count -= Count;
                    NewColorSubdiv[*NewColorMapSize].NumEntries = NewColorSubdiv[Index].NumEntries - NumEntries;
                    NewColorSubdiv[Index].NumEntries = NumEntries;
                    for(j=0;j<3;j++) {
                            NewColorSubdiv[*NewColorMapSize].RGBMin[j] = NewColorSubdiv[Index].RGBMin[j];
                            NewColorSubdiv[*NewColorMapSize].RGBWidth[j] = NewColorSubdiv[Index].RGBWidth[j];
                    }
                    NewColorSubdiv[*NewColorMapSize].RGBWidth[SortRGBAxis] =
                        NewColorSubdiv[*NewColorMapSize].RGBMin[SortRGBAxis] +
                        NewColorSubdiv[*NewColorMapSize].RGBWidth[SortRGBAxis] -
                        MinColor;
                    NewColorSubdiv[*NewColorMapSize].RGBMin[SortRGBAxis] = MinColor;

                    NewColorSubdiv[Index].RGBWidth[SortRGBAxis] =
                        MaxColor - NewColorSubdiv[Index].RGBMin[SortRGBAxis];

                    (*NewColorMapSize)++;
            }

            return(1);
}

/* compare function to sort colour entries */
int SortCmpRtn(Entry1,Entry2)
        QCOLOUR **Entry1,**Entry2;
{
        return(*Entry1)->RGB[SortRGBAxis]-(*Entry2)->RGB[SortRGBAxis];
}

diffuseStucki(line1,line2,line3,x,y,r,g,b,mr,mg,mb,width,depth)
        char *line1,*line2,*line3;
        int x,y,r,g,b;
        int mr,mg,mb;
        int width,depth;
{
        int dr,dg,db;

        dr=r-mr;
        dg=g-mg;
        db=b-mb;

        if((x+1) < width) {
```

12-7 Continued.

```
                line1[((x+1)*RGB_SIZE)+RGB_RED]  =addb(line1[((x+1)*RGB_SIZE)+RGB_RED],((dr*8)/42));
                line1[((x+1)*RGB_SIZE)+RGB_GREEN]=addb(line1[((x+1)*RGB_SIZE)+RGB_GREEN],((dg*8)/42));
                line1[((x+1)*RGB_SIZE)+RGB_BLUE] =addb(line1[((x+1)*RGB_SIZE)+RGB_BLUE],((db*8)/42));
        }

        if((x+2) < width) {
                line1[((x+1)*RGB_SIZE)+RGB_RED]  =addb(line1[((x+1)*RGB_SIZE)+RGB_RED],((dr*4)/42));
                line1[((x+1)*RGB_SIZE)+RGB_GREEN]=addb(line1[((x+1)*RGB_SIZE)+RGB_GREEN],((dg*4)/42));
                line1[((x+1)*RGB_SIZE)+RGB_BLUE] =addb(line1[((x+1)*RGB_SIZE)+RGB_BLUE],((db*4)/42));
        }

        if((x-2) > 0 && (y+1) < depth) {
                line2[((x-2)*RGB_SIZE)+RGB_RED]  =addb(line2[((x-2)*RGB_SIZE)+RGB_RED],((dr*2)/42));
                line2[((x-2)*RGB_SIZE)+RGB_GREEN]=addb(line2[((x-2)*RGB_SIZE)+RGB_GREEN],((dg*2)/42));
                line2[((x-2)*RGB_SIZE)+RGB_BLUE] =addb(line2[((x-2)*RGB_SIZE)+RGB_BLUE],((db*2)/42));
        }

        if((x-1) > 0 && (y+1) < depth) {
                line2[((x-1)*RGB_SIZE)+RGB_RED]  =addb(line2[((x-1)*RGB_SIZE)+RGB_RED],((dr*4)/42));
                line2[((x-1)*RGB_SIZE)+RGB_GREEN]=addb(line2[((x-1)*RGB_SIZE)+RGB_GREEN],((dg*4)/42));
                line2[((x-1)*RGB_SIZE)+RGB_BLUE] =addb(line2[((x-1)*RGB_SIZE)+RGB_BLUE],((db*4)/42));
        }

        if((y+1) < depth) {
                line2[(x*RGB_SIZE)+RGB_RED]  =addb(line2[(x*RGB_SIZE)+RGB_RED],((dr*8)/42));
                line2[(x*RGB_SIZE)+RGB_GREEN]=addb(line2[(x*RGB_SIZE)+RGB_GREEN],((dg*8)/42));
                line2[(x*RGB_SIZE)+RGB_BLUE] =addb(line2[(x*RGB_SIZE)+RGB_BLUE],((db*8)/42));
        }

        if((x+1) < width && (y+1) < depth) {
                line2[((x+1)*RGB_SIZE)+RGB_RED]  =addb(line2[((x+1)*RGB_SIZE)+RGB_RED],((dr*4)/42));
                line2[((x+1)*RGB_SIZE)+RGB_GREEN]=addb(line2[((x+1)*RGB_SIZE)+RGB_GREEN],((dg*4)/42));
                line2[((x+1)*RGB_SIZE)+RGB_BLUE] =addb(line2[((x+1)*RGB_SIZE)+RGB_BLUE],((db*4)/42));
        }

        if((x+2) < width && (y+1) < depth) {
                line2[((x+2)*RGB_SIZE)+RGB_RED]  =addb(line2[((x+2)*RGB_SIZE)+RGB_RED],((dr*2)/42));
                line2[((x+2)*RGB_SIZE)+RGB_GREEN]=addb(line2[((x+2)*RGB_SIZE)+RGB_GREEN],((dg*2)/42));
                line2[((x+2)*RGB_SIZE)+RGB_BLUE] =addb(line2[((x+2)*RGB_SIZE)+RGB_BLUE],((db*2)/42));
        }

        if((x-2) > 0 && (y+2) < depth) {
                line3[((x-2)*RGD_SIZE)+RGB_RED]  =addb(line3[((x-2)*RGB_SIZE)+RGB_RED],((dr*1)/42));
                line3[((x-2)*RGB_SIZE)+RGB_GREEN]=addb(line3[((x-2)*RGB_STZE)+RGB_GREEN],((dg*1)/42));
                line3[((x-2)*RGB_SIZE)+RGB_BLUE] =addb(line3[((x-2)*RGB_SIZE)+RGB_BLUE],((db*1)/42));
        }

        if((x-1) > 0 && (y+2) < depth) {
                line3[((x-1)*RGB_SIZE)+RGB_RED]  =addb(line3[((x-1)*RGB_SIZE)+RGB_RED],((dr*2)/42));
                line3[((x-1)*RGB_SIZE)+RGB_GREEN]=addb(line3[((x-1)*RGB_SIZE)+RGB_GREEN],((dg*2)/42));
                line3[((x-1)*RGB_SIZE)+RGB_BLUE] =addb(line3[((x-1)*RGB_SIZE)+RGB_BLUE],((db*2)/42));
        }
```

12-7 Continued.

```
        if((y+2) < depth) {
                line3[(x*RGB_SIZE)+RGB_RED]   =addb(line3[(x*RGB_SIZE)+RGB_RED],((dr*4)/42));
                line3[(x*RGB_SIZE)+RGB_GREEN]=addb(line3[(x*RGB_SIZE)+RGB_GREEN],((dg*4)/42));
                line3[(x*RGB_SIZE)+RGB_BLUE]  =addb(line3[(x*RGB_SIZE)+RGB_BLUE],((db*4)/42));
        }

        if((x+1) < width && (y+2) < depth) {
                line3[((x+1)*RGB_SIZE)+RGB_RED]   =addb(line3[((x+1)*RGB_SIZE)+RGB_RED],((dr*2)/42));
                line3[((x+1)*RGB_SIZE)+RGB_GREEN]=addb(line3[((x+1)*RGB_SIZE)+RGB_GREEN],((dg*2)/42));
                line3[((x+1)*RGB_SIZE)+RGB_BLUE]  =addb(line3[((x+1)*RGB_SIZE)+RGB_BLUE],((db*2)/42));
        }

        if((x+2) < width && (y+2) < depth) {
                line3[((x+2)*RGB_SIZE)+RGB_RED]   =addb(line3[((x+2)*RGB_SIZE)+RGB_RED],((dr*1)/42));
                line3[((x+2)*RGB_SIZE)+RGB_GREEN]=addb(line3[((x+2)*RGB_SIZE)+RGB_GREEN],((dg*1)/42));
                line3[((x+2)*RGB_SIZE)+RGB_BLUE]  =addb(line3[((x+2)*RGB_SIZE)+RGB_BLUE],((db*1)/42));
        }
}

diffuseBurkes(line1,line2,x,y,r,g,b,mr,mg,mb,width,depth)
        char *line1,*line2;
        int x,y,r,g,b;
        int mr,mg,mb;
        int width,depth;
{

        int dr,dg,db;

        dr=r-mr;
        dg=g-mg;
        db=b-mb;

        if((x+1) < width) {
                line1[((x+1)*RGB_SIZE)+RGB_RED]   =addb(line1[((x+1)*RGB_SIZE)+RGB_RED],((dr*8)/32));
                line1[((x+1)*RGB_SIZE)+RGB_GREEN]=addb(line1[((x+1)*RGB_SIZE)+RGB_GREEN],((dg*8)/32));
                line1[((x+1)*RGB_SIZE)+RGB_BLUE]  =addb(line1[((x+1)*RGB_SIZE)+RGB_BLUE],((db*8)/32));
        }

        if((x+2) < width) {
                line1[((x+2)*RGB_SIZE)+RGB_RED]   =addb(line1[((x+2)*RGB_SIZE)+RGB_RED],((dr*4)/32));
                line1[((x+2)*RGB_SIZE)+RGB_GREEN]=addb(line1[((x+2)*RGB_SIZE)+RGB_GREEN],((dg*4)/32));
                line1[((x+2)*RGB_SIZE)+RGB_BLUE]  =addb(line1[((x+2)*RGB_SIZE)+RGB_BLUE],((db*4)/32));
        }

        if((x-2) > 0 && (y+1) < depth) {
                line2[((x-2)*RGB_SIZE)+RGB_RED]   =addb(line2[((x-2)*RGB_SIZE)+RGB_RED],((dr*2)/32));
                line2[((x-2)*RGB_SIZE)+RGB_GREEN]=addb(line2[((x-2)*RGB_SIZE)+RGB_GREEN],((dg*2)/32));
                line2[((x-2)*RGB_SIZE)+RGB_BLUE]  =addb(line2[((x-2)*RGB_SIZE)+RGB_BLUE],((db*2)/32));
        }

        if((x-1) > 0 && (y+1) < depth) {
                line2[((x-1)*RGB_SIZE)+RGB_RED]   =addb(line2[((x-1)*RGB_SIZE)+RGB_RED],((dr*4)/32));
                line2[((x-1)*RGB_SIZE)+RGB_GREEN]=addb(line2[((x-1)*RGB_SIZE)+RGB_GREEN],((dg*4)/32));
```

12-7 Continued.

```
                    line2[((x-1)*RGB_SIZE)+RGB_BLUE] =addb(line2[((x-1)*RGB_SIZE)+RGB_BLUE],((db*4)/32));
        }

        if((y+1) < depth) {
                line2[(x*RGB_SIZE)+RGB_RED]   =addb(line2[(x*RGB_SIZE)+RGB_RED],((dr*8)/32));
                line2[(x*RGB_SIZE)+RGB_GREEN]=addb(line2[(x*RGB_SIZE)+RGB_GREEN],((dg*8)/32));
                line2[(x*RGB_SIZE)+RGB_BLUE] =addb(line2[(x*RGB_SIZE)+RGB_BLUE],((db*8)/32));
        }

        if((x+1) < width && (y+1) < depth) {
                line2[((x+1)*RGB_SIZE)+RGB_RED]   =addb(line2[((x+1)*RGB_SIZE)+RGB_RED],((dr*4)/32));
                line2[((x+1)*RGB_SIZE)+RGB_GREEN]=addb(line2[((x+1)*RGB_SIZE)+RGB_GREEN],((dg*4)/32));
                line2[((x+1)*RGB_SIZE)+RGB_BLUE] =addb(line2[((x+1)*RGB_SIZE)+RGB_BLUE],((db*4)/32));
        }

        if((x+2) < width && (y+1) < depth) {
                line2[((x+2)*RGB_SIZE)+RGB_RED]   =addb(line2[((x+2)*RGB_SIZE)+RGB_RED],((dr*2)/32));
                line2[((x+2)*RGB_SIZE)+RGB_GREEN]=addb(line2[((x+2)*RGB_SIZE)+RGB_GREEN],((dg*2)/32));
                line2[((x+2)*RGB_SIZE)+RGB_BLUE] =addb(line2[((x+2)*RGB_SIZE)+RGB_BLUE],((db*2)/32));
        }
}

diffuseFloyd(line1,line2,x,y,r,g,b,mr,mg,mb,width,depth)
        char *line1,*line2;
        int x,y,r,g,b;
        int mr,mg,mb;
        int width,depth;
{

        int dr,dg,db;

        dr=r-mr;
        dg=g-mg;
        db=b-mb;

        if((x+1) < width) {
                line1[((x+1)*RGB_SIZE)+RGB_RED]   =addb(line1[((x+1)*RGB_SIZE)+RGB_RED],((dr*7)/16));
                line1[((x+1)*RGB_SIZE)+RGB_GREEN]=addb(line1[((x+1)*RGB_SIZE)+RGB_GREEN],((dg*7)/16));
                line1[((x+1)*RGB_SIZE)+RGB_BLUE] =addb(line1[((x+1)*RGB_SIZE)+RGB_BLUE],((db*7)/16));
        }

        if((x-1) > 0 && (y+1) < depth) {
                line2[((x-1)*RGB_SIZE)+RGB_RED]   =addb(line2[((x-1)*RGB_SIZE)+RGB_RED],((dr*3)/16));
                line2[((x-1)*RGB_SIZE)+RGB_CREEN]=addb(line2[((x-1)*RGB_SIZE)+RGB_GREEN],((dg*3)/16));
                line2[((x-1)*RGB_SIZE)+RGB_BLUE] =addb(line2[((x-1)*RGB_SIZE)+RGB_BLUE],((db*3)/16));
        }

        if((x+1) < width && (y+1) < depth) {
                line2[((x+1)*RGB_SIZE)+RGB_RED]   =addb(line2[((x+1)*RGB_SIZE)+RGB_RED],((dr*1)/16));
                line2[((x+1)*RGB_SIZE)+RGB_GREEN]=addb(line2[((x+1)*RGB_SIZE)+RGB_GREEN],((dg*1)/16));
                line2[((x+1)*RGB_SIZE)+RGB_BLUE] =addb(line2[((x+1)*RGB_SIZE)+RGB_BLUE],((db*1)/16));
        }
```

12-7 Continued.

```
        if((y+1) < depth) {
                line2[(x*RGB_SIZE)+RGB_RED]  =addb(line2[(x*RGB_SIZE)+RGB_RED],((dr*5)/16));
                line2[(x*RGB_SIZE)+RGB_GREEN]=addb(line2[(x*RGB_SIZE)+RGB_GREEN],((dg*5)/16));
                line2[(x*RGB_SIZE)+RGB_BLUE] =addb(line2[(x*RGB_SIZE)+RGB_BLUE],((db*5)/16));
        }
}

addb(n1,n2)         /* add two bytes, clamp to byte range */
        int n1,n2;
{
        int n;

        n=n1+n2;
        if(n<0) n=0;
        else if(n > 255) n=255;
        return(n);

}

findNearestMatch(r,g,b,mr,mg,mb,p,n)
        int r,g,b,*mr,*mg,*mb;
        char *p;
        int n;
{
        char *pp;
        long mdist,tdist;
        int i,pn=0;

        mdist=BIG_DISTANCE;

        pp=p;
        for(i=0;i<n;++i) {
                tdist=DIST(r,g,b,pp[RGB_RED],pp[RGB_GREEN],pp[RGB_BLUE]);
                if(tdist < mdist) {
                        mdist=tdist;
                        pn=i;
                }
                pp+=RGB_SIZE;
        }
        p+=(pn*RGB_SIZE);
        *mr=p[RGB_RED];
        *mg=p[RGB_GREEN];
        *mb=p[RGB_BLUE];
        return(pn);
}

/* if you don't use in the memory manager, these functions
   will stand in for it */

#if !MEMMANGR

/* return a far pointer plus a long integer */
```

12-7 Continued.

```
char *farPtr(p,l)
        char *p;
        long l;
{
        unsigned int seg,off;

        seg = FP_SEG(p);
        off = FP_OFF(p);
        seg += (off / 16);
        off &= 0x000f;
        off += (unsigned int)(l & 0x000fL);
        seg += (l / 16L);
        p = MK_FP(seg,off);
        return(p);
}

/* save one line to memory */
putline(p,n)
        char *p;
        unsigned int n;
{
        if(n >= 0 && n < fi.depth)
            memcpy(farPtr(buffer,(long)n*(long)fi.bytes),p,fi.bytes);
}

/* get one line from memory */
char *getline(n)
        unsigned int n;
{
        return(farPtr(buffer,(long)n*(long)fi.bytes));
}

#pragma warn -par
getbuffer(n,bytes,lines)
        unsigned long n;
        int bytes,lines;
{
        if((buffer=farmalloc(n)) == NULL) return(0);
        else return(1);
}

freebuffer()
{
        if(buffer != NULL) farfree(buffer);
        buffer=NULL;
}
#endif /* !MEMMANGR */
```

12-7 Continued.

The DITHRPCX program actually stores its images as real RGB lines, using 3 bytes per pixel. Its quantization function also requires a fairly substantial buffer in which to store its histogram table. For this reason, you'll probably find that you'll need to compile DITHRPCX with the memory manager (see the appendix) book linked to it.

There are a number of command line switches available in DITHRPCX, as follows:

/Cn   Display the source image dithered down to n bits, where n is somewhere between 4 and 8.

/F   Use the Floyd-Steinberg dithering filter.

/B   Use the Burkes dithering filter.

/S   Use the Stucki dithering filter.

Because DITHRPCX actually does color-distance calculations for each of the pixels it remaps, it's pretty slow. Its speed decreases as the number of colors it's asked to scan through increases. A picture with the dimensions of a mode 13H VGA screen can take 15 minutes or so to dither to 256 colors on a 25-MHz, 386 system.

While DITHRPCX illustrates how to use the quantization and dithering code, chances are you'll want to abstract these functions for use in something a bit less transitory. Waiting 15 minutes just to view a picture may seem a bit futile. You'll probably want to quantize your source files down and save the resulting pictures in other files.

References:

Heckbert, Paul. 1982. *Color Image Quantization for frame buffer display*. pp. 297 – 307. SIGGRAPH.

The quantization function in this chapter is derived from some first-rate code by Gershon Elber, which turned up on a bulletin board. It also borrows a bit from David Rowley's QRT2GIF utility, which uses Michael Mauldin's median-cut code.

Appendix
The memory manager

The example programs in this book all default to conventional DOS memory for storing images. This works well for images of modest size; unfortunately, images rarely stay modest, and the least modest ones are usually the most interesting.

A 640×480 pixel, 256-color GIF file requires 300K of memory in order to unpack. If you write a small viewer or other program to work with GIF files, there will probably be sufficient conventional memory in an otherwise unencumbered system with 640K of conventional memory.

An 800×600 pixel picture with 256 colors requires almost half a megabyte. You can be reasonably sure that this will not be available after the program that works with the image has loaded.

Images with 24 bits of color can swell to require enormous tracts of memory without half trying.

All the programs in this book can be made to use an external memory management package that deals with the allocation and access of memory buffers larger than what is available in conventional DOS memory. In each of them you'll find a commented out #include statement at the top of the file, like this:

```
/*
#include "memmangr.h"
*/
```

If you uncomment this line and create a project file for the program that links it to the code discussed in this appendix, the limitations of conventional memory are banished into the nether reaches from which they first appeared in the early eighties.

At the very least, they'll be reduced to sullen, mewling little specters that lurk in the shadows of your applications. The memory manager allows you to get around the logistics of using alternate types of storage. Admittedly, it cannot generate storage where none exists.

After DOS and your program are loaded, the unused memory up to 640K is called the *heap*. It's available for your program to use for storage. Every time you call `malloc` or one of its descendants, some of the heap is parceled out to your program.

The heap is very useful when you need small, transitory buffers. However, it has several limitations when discussing buffers large enough in which to store an entire image. To begin with, if you allocate a big buffer in conventional memory you might find that there's no memory left to allocate to small line buffers, buffers for drivers, and other scratch space. Just because these buffers are small doesn't mean that they are unimportant.

Secondly, you might find, as alluded to, that even a fairly large heap isn't large enough.

Finally, large buffers (those that occupy more than one memory segment) require some connivance to address, as discussed in chapter 1.

For these reasons, applications that work with graphics should embody an approach to memory allocation that lets them use alternatives to conventional memory for large pictures.

There are three alternatives to conventional memory—extended, expanded, and virtual memory, as discussed in chapter 1.

The code in this chapter essentially provides four functions to replace the `getbuffer`, `freebuffer`, `getline`, and `putline` functions that appear throughout this book. These new versions of the memory management functions will be smarter than the ones that have appeared earlier in that they are flexible and transparent. In essence, with the memory manager code linked to a program, the program can say "get me a buffer" without really caring where the buffer is stored. It doesn't need to know that there is not enough conventional memory to provide the buffer the program asked for. The memory manager, upon sensing that this is the case, uses whatever extra memory it has been told exists.

The memory manager code used in this chapter is a simplified version of the memory manager from Graphic Workshop.

The memory manager source

To use the memory manager, you must have MEMMANGR.H included in any programs that call it. You must also link MEMMANGR.OBJ and XMEM.OBJ, discussed here, to your program using a project file. Create a library with these two object modules, MEMMANGR.LIB, using TLIB. Here's the command line to do so:

TLIB MEMMANGR +MEMMANGR.OBJ +XMEM.OBJ

Using a library leaves you with one less object module to keep track of.
Figure A-1 lists the complete MEMMANGR.H file.

```
/* memory manager header */

#define CONVENTIONAL    0
#define VIRTUAL         1
#define EXTENDED        2
#define EXPANDED        3

#define TEMPFILE        "TEMP$$$$.$$$"

#define malloc(n) dosalloc(n)
#define free(p)         dosfree(p)

#define MEMMANGR        1

typedef struct {
        int functions;
        int (*test)();
        int (*init)();
        int (*alloc)();
        int (*free)();
        char *(*get)();
        int (*put)();
        int (*null_one)();
        int (*null_two)();
        int (*null_three)();
        int (*null_four)();
        int flags;
        int version;
        int subversion;
        char name[25];
        } XMEM;

typedef struct {
        unsigned long length;
        unsigned int sourceH;
        unsigned long sourceOff;
        unsigned int destH;
        unsigned long destOff;
        } XMOVE;

int getbuffer(unsigned long n,unsigned int bytes,unsigned int depth);
void freebuffer(void);
int putline(char *p,unsigned int n);
```

A-1   The source for MEMMANGR.H.

```
char *getline(unsigned int n);
char *farPtr(char *,long l);

char *dosalloc(unsigned int n);
void dosfree(char *p);

unsigned long ptr2long(char *p);

int emsTest(void);
int emsInit(void);
int emsAlloc(unsigned int size,unsigned int bytes,unsigned int lines);
int emsFree(void);
char *emsGet(int n);
int emsPut(char *p,int n);

int virTest(void);
int virInit(void);
int virAlloc(unsigned int size,unsigned int bytes,unsigned int lines);
int virFree(void);
char *virGet(int n);
int virPut(char *p,int n);

int xmsTest(void);
int xmsInit(void);
int xmsAlloc(unsigned int size,unsigned int bytes,unsigned int lines);
int xmsFree(void);
char *xmsGet(int n);
int xmsPut(char *p,int n);

int cnvTest(void);
int cnvInit(void);
int cnvAlloc(unsigned int size,unsigned int bytes,unsigned int lines);
int cnvFree(void);
char *cnvGet(int n);
int cnvPut(char *p,int n);

#if MEMDATA
XMEM xmem;
unsigned int memorytype=VIRTUAL;
unsigned int memorylines;
unsigned int memorybytes;
char *IMbuffer;
int emsPageframe;
int IMhandle;
unsigned int *emsLinestart;
char *IMlinebuffer;
#else
extern XMEM xmem;
extern unsigned int memorytype;
extern unsigned int memorylines;
extern unsigned int memorybytes;
extern char *IMbuffer;
```

A-1 Continued.

```
extern int emsPageframe;
extern int IMhandle;
extern unsigned int *emsLinestart;
extern char *IMlinebuffer;
#endif
```

A-1 Continued.

The memory manager is written entirely in C, with the exception of some glue required to interface to an extended memory driver. For reasons that become clearer in a moment, this is much easier to handle in assembly language. The C-language part of the memory manager, MEM-MANGR.C, is shown in FIG. A-2.

```
#define MEMDATA          1
#include "stdio.h"
#include "dos.h"
#include "fcntl.h"
#include "stdlib.h"
#include "memmangr.h"

getbuffer(n,bytes,depth)
        unsigned long n;
        unsigned int bytes,depth;
{
        IMbuffer=NULL;

        memorylines=depth;
        memorybytes=bytes;

        setextra(&xmem,CONVENTIONAL);
        if((xmem.test)()) {
                if((xmem.init)()) {
                        if((xmem.alloc)((int)(n/1024L)+1,bytes,depth)) return(1);
                }
        }

        setextra(&xmem,memorytype);
        if((xmem.test)()) {
                if((xmem.init)()) {
                        if((xmem.alloc)((int)(n/1024L)+1,bytes,depth)) return(1);
                        else return(0);
                } else return(0);
        } else return(0);
}

void freebuffer()
{
        (xmem.free)();
}

putline(p,n)
```

A-2 The source for MEMMANGR.C.

```
        char *p;
        unsigned int n;
{
        (xmem.put) (p,n);
}

char *getline(n)
        unsigned int n;
{
        return((xmem.get)(n));
}

/* retrun a far pointer plus a long integer */
char *farPtr(p,l)
        char *p;
        long l;
{
        unsigned int seg,off;

        seg = FP_SEG(p);
        off = FP_OFF(p);
        seg += (off / 16);
        off &= 0x000f;
        off += (unsigned int)(l & 0x000fL);
        seg += (l / 16L);
        p = MK_FP(seg,off);
        return(p);
}

emsTest()
{
        int fh;
        union REGS rg;

        if((fh=open("EMMXXXX0",O_RDONLY,&fh)) ==-1) return(0);

        rg.h.ah = 0x44;
        rg.h.al = 0x00;
        rg.x.bx = fh;
        int86(0x21,&rg,&rg);
        close(fh);
        if(rg.x.cflag) return(0);
        if(rg.x.dx & 0x80) return(1);
        else return(0);
}

emsInit()
{
        union REGS rg;

        rg.h.ah = 0x40;
        int86(0x67,&rg,&rg);
```

A-2 Continued.

```c
        if(rg.h.ah != 0) return(0);

        rg.h.ah = 0x41;
        int86(0x67,&rg,&rg);
        if(rg.h.ah != 0) return(0);

        emsPageframe=rg.x.bx;
        return(1);
}

#pragma warn -par
emsAlloc(size,bytes,lines)
        unsigned int size,bytes,lines;
{
        union REGS rg;
        int i,offset=0,page=0;

        IMhandle=-1;

        if((emsLinestart=(unsigned int *)dosalloc(4*lines)) == NULL) return(0);
        for(i=0;i<lines;++i) {
                emsLinestart[i<<1]=offset;
                emsLinestart[(i<<1)+1]=page;
                offset+=bytes;
                if((offset+bytes) > 0x4000) {
                        ++page;
                        offset=0;
                }

        }

        rg.h.ah=0x42;
        int86(0x67,&rg,&rg);
        if(rg.x.cflag || rg.x.dx < (page + 1)) {
                dosfree((char *)emsLinestart);
                return(0);
        }

        rg.h.ah = 0x43;
        rg.x.bx = page+1;
        int86(0x67,&rg,&rg);
        if(rg.h.ah) {
                dosfree((char *)emsLinestart);
                return(0);
        }
        IMhandle=rg.x.dx;
        return(1);
}

char *emsGet(n)
        int n;
{
```

A-2 Continued.

```
        union REGS rg;

        rg.h.ah = 0x44;
        rg.h.al = 0;
        rg.x.bx = emsLinestart[(n<<1)+1];
        rg.x.dx = IMhandle;
        int86(0x67,&rg,&rg);
        if(rg.h.ah != 0) return(NULL);
        else return(MK_FP(emsPageframe,emsLinestart[n<<1]));
}


emsPut(p,n)
        char *p;
        int n;
{
        union REGS rg;

        rg.h.ah = 0x44;
        rg.h.al = 0;
        rg.x.bx = emsLinestart[(n<<1)+1];
        rg.x.dx = IMhandle;
        int86(0x67,&rg,&rg);
        if(rg.h.ah == 0) memcpy(MK_FP(emsPageframe,emsLinestart[n<<1]),p,memorybytes);
        return(1);
}


emsFree()
{
        union REGS rg;

        rg.h.ah = 0x45;
        rg.x.dx = IMhandle;
        int86(0x67,&rg,&rg);

        dosfree((char *)emsLinestart);
}
virTest()
{
        return(1);
}

virInit()
{
        return(1);
}

#pragma warn -par
virAlloc(size,bytes,lines)
        unsigned int size,bytes,lines;
{
        union REGS r;
        struct SREGS sg;
```

A-2 Continued.

```
            char *p,s[81];
            int i;

            IMhandle=-1;

            if((IMlinebuffer=dosalloc(bytes))==NULL) return(0);

            p=getenv("TEMP");
            s[0]=0;
            if(p != NULL) strcpy(s,getenv("TEMP"));
            strcat(s,TEMPFILE);

            r.x.ax=0x3c00;
            r.x.cx=0;
            r.x.dx=FP_OFF(s);
            sg.ds=FP_SEG(s);
            int86x(0x21,&r,&r,&sg);
            if(r.x.cflag) {
                    dosfree(IMlinebuffer);
                    return(0);
            } else IMhandle=r.x.ax;

            memset(IMlinebuffer,0,bytes);

            for(i=0;i<lines;++i) {
                    r.x.ax=0x4000;
                    r.x.bx=IMhandle;
                    r.x.cx=bytes;
                    r.x.dx=FP_OFF(IMlinebuffer);
                    sg.ds=FP_SEG(IMlinebuffer);
                    int86x(0x21,&r,&r,&sg);
                    if(r.x.cflag != 0 || r.x.ax != r.x.cx) {
                            dosfree(IMlinebuffer);
                            r.x.ax=0x3e00;
                            r.x.bx=IMhandle;
                            int86(0x21,&r,&r);
                            remove(s);
                            return(0);
                    }
            }
            return(1);
}

char *virGet(n)
        int n;
{
        union REGS r;
        struct SREGS sg;
        unsigned long l;

        l=(long)memorybytes*(long)n;

        r.h.ah=0x42;
```

A-2 Continued.

```
                r.h.al=SEEK_SET;
                r.x.bx=IMhandle;
                r.x.cx=(unsigned int)(l >> 16);
                r.x.dx=(unsigned int)l;
                int86x(0x21,&r,&r,&sg);
                if(r.x.cflag) return(NULL);

                r.x.ax=0x3f00;
                r.x.bx=IMhandle;
                r.x.cx=memorybytes;
                r.x.dx=FP_OFF(IMlinebuffer);
                sg.ds=FP_SEG(IMlinebuffer);
                int86x(0x21,&r,&r,&sg);
                if(r.x.cflag || r.x.ax != r.x.cx) return(NULL);
                else return(IMlinebuffer);
}

virPut(p,n)
                char *p;
                int n;
{

                union REGS r;
                struct SREGS sg;
                unsigned long l;

                l=(long)memorybytes*(long)n;

                r.h.ah=0x42;
                r.h.al=SEEK_SET;
                r.x.bx=IMhandle;
                r.x.cx=(unsigned int)(l >> 16);
                r.x.dx=(unsigned int)l;
                int86x(0x21,&r,&r,&sg);
                if(r.x.cflag) return(0);

                r.x.ax=0x4000;
                r.x.bx=IMhandle;
                r.x.cx=memorybytes;
                r.x.dx=FP_OFF(p);
                sg.ds=FP_SEG(p);
                int86x(0x21,&r,&r,&sg);
                if(r.x.cflag || r.x.ax != r.x.cx) return(0);
                else return(r.x.ax);
}

virFree()
{
                union REGS r;
                char *p,s[81];

                dosfree(IMlinebuffer);
                r.x.ax=0x3e00;
```

A-2 Continued.

```
                r.x.bx=IMhandle;
                int86(0x21,&r,&r);

                p=getenv("TEMP");
                s[0]=0;
                if(p != NULL) strcpy(s,getenv("TEMP"));
                strcat(s,TEMPFILE);

                remove(s);
                return(0);
}


xmsTest()
{
                int i;

                i=get_xmem();
                if(i >= 0x0200 && i != -1) return(1);
                else return(0);
}


xmsInit()
{
                return(1);
}


#pragma warn -par
xmsAlloc(size,bytes,lines)
        unsigned int size,bytes,lines;
{
                IMhandle=-1;

                if((IMlinebuffer=dosalloc(bytes))==NULL) return(0);

                IMhandle=alloc_xmem(size+1);
                if(IMhandle == -1) {
                        dosfree(IMlinebuffer);
                        return(0);
                } else return(1);
}


char *xmsGet(n)
        int n;
{
                XMOVE xmove;

                xmove.length = (long)memorybytes;
                xmove.sourceH=IMhandle;
                xmove.sourceOff=(long)n*(long)memorybytes;
                xmove.destH=0;
                xmove.destOff=ptr2long(IMlinebuffer);
                if(!move_xmem(&xmove)) return(NULL);
```

A-2 Continued.

```
                else return(IMlinebuffer);
        }
xmsPut(p,n)
                char *p;
                int n;
        {
                XMOVE xmove;

                xmove.length = (long)memorybytes;
                xmove.sourceH=0;
                xmove.sourceOff=ptr2long(p);
                xmove.destH=IMhandle;
                xmove.destOff=(long)n*(long)memorybytes;
                if(!move_xmem(&xmove)) return(0);
                else return(1);
        }


xmsFree()
        {
                if(IMhandle != -1) dealloc_xmem(IMhandle);
        }


cnvTest()
        {
                return(1);
        }


cnvInit()
        {
                return(1);
        }


#pragma warn -par
cnvAlloc(size,bytes,lines)
                unsigned int size,bytes,lines;
        {
                union REGS r;

                r.x.ax=0x4800;
                r.x.bx=1+((long)size*64);
                int86(0x21,&r,&r);

                if(r.x.cflag) return(0);
                else {
                        IMbuffer=MK_FP(r.x.ax,0x0000);
                        return(1);
                }
        }


char *cnvGet(n)
                int n;
        {
```

A-2 Continued.

```
                    if(n >= 0 && n < memorylines)
                        return(farPtr(IMbuffer,(long)n*(long)memorybytes));
                    else return(NULL);
        }


cnvPut(p,n)
            char *p;
            int n;
        {

            if(n >= 0 && n < memorylines)
                memcpy(farPtr(IMbuffer,(long)n*(long)memorybytes),p,memorybytes);
        }


cnvFree()
        {
            union REGS r;
            struct SREGS sr;

            if(IMbuffer != NULL) {
                    r.x.ax=0x4900;
                    sr.es=FP_SEG(IMbuffer);
                    int86x(0x21,&r,&r,&sr);
            }
        }


setextra(xmem,n)
            XMEM *xmem;
            int n;
        {

            switch(n) {
                    case EXPANDED:
                            xmem->test=emsTest;
                            xmem->init=emsInit;
                            xmem->alloc=emsAlloc;
                            xmem->free=emsFree;
                            xmem->get=emsGet;
                            xmem->put=emsPut;
                            strcpy(xmem->name,"Expanded");
                            break;
                    case EXTENDED:
                            xmem->test=xmsTest;
                            xmem->init=xmsInit;
                            xmem->alloc=xmsAlloc;
                            xmem->free=xmsFree;
                            xmem->get=xmsGet;
                            xmem->put=xmsPut;
                            strcpy(xmem->name,"Extended");
                            break;
                    case VIRTUAL:
                            xmem->test=virTest;
                            xmem->init=virInit;
```

A-2 Continued.

```
                    xmem->alloc=virAlloc;
                    xmem->free=virFree;
                    xmem->get=virGet;
                    xmem->put=virPut;
                    strcpy(xmem->name,"Virtual");
                    break;
            case CONVENTIONAL:
                    xmem->test=cnvTest;
                    xmem->init=cnvInit;
                    xmem->alloc=cnvAlloc;
                    xmem->free=cnvFree;
                    xmem->get=cnvGet;
                    xmem->put=cnvPut;
                    strcpy(xmem->name,"Conventional");
                    break;
        }
}
char *dosalloc(n)
        unsigned int n;
{
        union REGS r;

        n+=8;
        r.x.ax=0x4800;
        r.x.bx=1+(n>>4);
        int86(0x21,&r,&r);
        if(r.x.cflag) return(NULL);
        else return(MK_FP(r.x.ax,0x0008));
}

void dosfree(p)
        char *p;
{
        union REGS r;
        struct SREGS sr;

        r.x.ax=0x4900;
        sr.es=FP_SEG(p);
        int86x(0x21,&r,&r,&sr);
}
```

A-2 Continued.

Figure A-3 illustrates the assembly language interface for extended memory, called XMEM.ASM. You must assemble this with MASM or TASM to create XMEM.OBJ.

There's not much to modify in the memory manager, and unless you're particularly curious about what it's up to, you can compile and assemble its components, link them to the programs you're interested in, and not think of them any further.

```
;
;                     Extended memory control functions
;                     Copyright (c) 1989 Alchemy Mindworks Inc.
;


VERSION         EQU     1                               ;VERSION
SUBVERSION      EQU     0                               ;SUBVERSION


_AOFF           EQU     6                               ;FAR STACK OFFSET

;THIS MACRO FETCHES THE DATA SEGEMENT
DATASEG         MACRO
                PUSH    AX
                MOV     AX,_DATA
                MOV     DS,AX
                POP     AX
                ENDM


XMEM_TEXT       SEGMENT BYTE PUBLIC 'CODE'
                ASSUME  CS:XMEM_TEXT,DS:_DATA


;THIS FUNCTION INITIALIZES THE DRIVER
;               CALLED AS
;               get_xmem();
;
;               Returns the version number or -1 if no driver
;
                PUBLIC  _get_xmem
_get_xmem       PROC    FAR
                PUSH    BP
                MOV     BP,SP

                MOV     AX,4300H
                INT     2FH
                CMP     AL,80H
                JE      GETX1

                MOV     AX,0FFFFH
                JMP     GETX2

GETX1:          MOV     AX,4310H

                INT     2FH
                MOV     WORD PTR CS:[_CONTOFF],BX
                MOV     WORD PTR CS:[_CONTSEG],ES

                XOR     AX,AX
                CALL    CS:[CONTROL]

GETX2:          DATASEG
```

A-3 The source for XMEM.ASM.

```
                POP     BP
                RET
_get_xmem       ENDP


;THIS FUNCTION MOVES EXTENDED MEMORY
;               CALLED AS
;               move_xmem(p);
;               p = pointer to move structure
;                       /* returns true if successful */
;
                PUBLIC  _move_xmem
_move_xmem      PROC    FAR
                PUSH    BP
                MOV     BP,SP

                MOV     SI,[BP + _AOFF + 0]     ;OFFSET OF STRUCTURE
                MOV     DS,[BP + _AOFF + 2]     ;SEGMENT OF STRUCTURE

                MOV     AH,11
                CALL    CS:[CONTROL]

                DATASEG
                POP     BP
                RET
_move_xmem      ENDP

;THIS FUNCTION DEALLOCATES EXTENDED MEMORY
;               CALLED AS
;               dealloc_xmem(h);
;               int h;  /* handle to deallocate */
;                       /* returns true if successful */
;
                PUBLIC  _dealloc_xmem
_dealloc_xmem   PROC    FAR
                PUSH    BP
                MOV     BP,SP

                MOV     DX,[BP + _AOFF + 0]     ;OFFSET OF DESTINATION
                MOV     AH,10
                CALL    CS:[CONTROL]

                DATASEG
                POP     BP
                RET
_dealloc_xmem   ENDP

;THIS FUNCTION ALLOCATES EXTENDED MEMORY
;               CALLED AS
;               alloc_xmem(n);
;               int n;  /* number of kilobytes to allocate */
;                       /* returns handle or -1 if error */
;
```

A-3 Continued.

```
                PUBLIC   _alloc_xmem
_alloc_xmem     PROC     FAR
                PUSH     BP
                MOV      BP,SP

                MOV      DX,[BP + _AOFF + 0]     ;OFFSET OF DESTINATION
                MOV      AH,9
                CALL     CS:[CONTROL]

                OR       AX,AX
                JZ       ALLOC1

                MOV      AX,DX
                JMP      ALLOC2

ALLOC1:         MOV      AX,0FFFFH

ALLOC2:         DATASEG
                POP      BP
                RET
_alloc_xmem     ENDP

;THIS FUNCTION CONVERTS A POINTER TO AN INTEL LONG
;               CALLED AS
;               long ptr2long(p);
;               char *p
;
                PUBLIC   _ptr2long
_ptr2long       PROC     FAR
                PUSH     BP
                MOV      BP,SP

                MOV      AX,[BP + _AOFF + 0]     ;OFFSET OF POINTER
                MOV      DX,[BP + _AOFF + 2]     ;SEGMENT OF POINTER

                DATASEG
                POP      BP
                RET
_ptr2long       ENDP

;THIS FUNCTION IS A DUMMY RETURN FOR UNSET PROCEDURES
_DUMMY          PROC     FAR
                MOV      AX,0FFFFH
                RET
_DUMMY          ENDP

CONTROL         LABEL    DWORD
_CONTOFF        DW       _DUMMY
_CONTSEG        DW       XMEM_TEXT

XMEM_TEXT       ENDS

DGROUP          GROUP    _DATA,_BSS
```

A-3 Continued.

```
_DATA           SEGMENT WORD PUBLIC 'DATA'

_DATA           ENDS

_BSS            SEGMENT WORD PUBLIC 'BSS'
_BSS            ENDS
                END
```
A-3 Continued.

Inside the memory manager

The memory manager attempts to allocate memory in two stages. It begins by checking to see if there's enough conventional memory available to allocate to the buffer. If there isn't, it will attempt to allocate some type of extra memory. The type of extra memory it attempts to allocate is defined by the contents of the integer `memorytype`. The program that calls the memory manager should set this value to one of three constants before it calls `getbuffer`: EXTENDED, EXPANDED, or VIRTUAL.

It's not really practical to attempt to detect what type of extra memory is available when `getbuffer` is called. It's quite possible, and pretty common, for there to be both extended and expanded memory available. It makes a lot more sense to allow the users of your software to define the type of extra memory they want to use.

It's not advisable under some versions of the Turbo C and Borland C++ languages to mix calls to the library for conventional memory allocation functions (`malloc` and such) with calls directly to the DOS INT 21H memory allocation function. However, since allocated buffers with predictable offsets are required if you wish to use loadable machine-language drivers (something that isn't portable among the various versions of Turbo C and Borland C++ if you call `malloc`) it's preferable to use direct DOS memory allocation. For this reason, MEMMANGR.H includes macros to redefine any calls to `malloc` and `free` as calls to `dosalloc` and `dosfree`, which are part of MEMMANGR.H.

There are two things to remember. Make sure that your code doesn't sneak around these macros, and make calls to the C-language allocation functions. For example, avoid using `farmalloc` or `calloc`. Secondly, note that some versions of the Borland languages won't let you allocate memory directly if the program you're running is in the integrated development environment. You'll have to step out to DOS to run programs that use the memory manager if you encounter this difficulty.

There's another quirk of the Borland languages as they apply to memory allocation that you should probably be aware of. Some of the versions of the integrated development environment get positively outraged if you allocate expanded memory from a program running under one. While such a program functions normally if you run it from the DOS prompt, it might crash the integrated development environment. If you find this happening, develop your code with the memory manager configured to use virtual memory. Obviously, it needn't run this way once you're out of the integrated development environment.

The current extra memory type can be set by your programs by including a statement like this one in your code before making any calls to getbuffer:

```
memorytype=EXTENDED;
```

This example has told the memory manager to use extended memory if it can't allocate enough DOS memory. A text description of the currently used memory type can be found in the string xmem.name.

There is a limitation to the memory manager as it stands that you should keep in mind, and which you may wish to mention in the documentation for your applications if they use it. Specifically, the memory manager can only allocate a buffer from one type of memory at a time. As such, if your program attempts to allocate 3Mb of memory and your computer has 500K of unused conventional memory and 2.5Mb of unused extended memory, the allocation request will fail.

This crops up a lot in systems that claim to have 1Mb of memory. What this really means is that they have 1Mb memory chips, of which 640K is assigned as DOS memory and the remaining 384K is available as extended or expanded memory. The largest available buffer for the memory manager to use on such a system would be either the conventional memory heap or the 384K of extra memory, but not a combination of both.

Finally, note that as it stands the getbuffer function of the memory manager can only allocate one buffer at a time.

Virtual memory

The memory manager defaults to using virtual memory, which is a big disk file. However, it will put the disk file anywhere you like—you can send it to a RAM disk if you have one. If getbuffer is called and subsequently decides that a virtual memory buffer is called for, it will look at the DOS environment for a variable called TEMP. If it finds one, it will create the path to its virtual memory scratch file using the argument to TEMP as the path. As such, if you have a RAM drive set up as drive H, you can force the memory manager to write its temporary files to drive H by putting the following command in the AUTOEXEC.BAT file of your system:

```
SET TEMP = H:\
```

When getbuffer is called to allocate a virtual memory buffer, it works out the total number of bytes in the buffer by multiplying the number of bytes in a line by the number of lines and writes this much empty data to a temporary file. It creates a complete file first in case the lines being written to it don't appear in ascending order, as would be the case if they were emerging from an interlaced GIF file or a BMP file.

When the memory manager writes a line to a virtual memory buffer, it determines the file position by multiplying the number of bytes in a line by the line to be accessed, seeks to that point in the file and writes one line. It finds a line to fetch in the same way.

When a virtual memory buffer is deallocated, its temporary file is deleted. The memory manager also frees up an internal line buffer that it uses to store individual lines being transferred.

While virtual memory is the slowest of the three extra memory types, it's the least likely one to encounter driver problems, hardware conflicts, and other potential user problems. All that's required to make it work is lots of drive space.

Extended memory

Extended memory uses memory that lives above 1Mb on a PC's address bus. It's only accessible on machines having 16- or 32-bit address buses, that is, machines based on 80286 or better processors. Systems that are based on the 8088 processor can't use extended memory, and should be taken into a nearby field and blown up as soon as possible.

This is a very bourgeois attitude, to be sure.

Extended memory is managed by an extended memory driver, which serves to provide a consistent interface to applications that call for it. It also allows multiple applications to deal with the same pool of extended memory, inasmuch as the driver sticks around even though the applications that call it may come and go.

There's a catch to this, of course. If you allocate extended memory and then terminate the application that asked for the buffer in question without deallocating the memory, the allocated memory effectively becomes orphaned, or inaccessible until you reboot your computer. Unlike memory allocated from the conventional DOS heap, extended memory is not automatically deallocated when an application returns control to DOS.

There's a second catch to using extended memory. Earlier versions of DOS came with a handy RAM disk driver called VDISK.SYS. A bit of a memory imperialist, VDISK.SYS assumed that it would be the only user of any extended memory it came across. If you have VDISK.SYS in your system, applications running on your computer will not be able to use extended memory. More recent versions of DOS have replaced VDISK.SYS with RAMDRIVE.SYS, which is a bit more respectful of its limitations. It can coexist with other applications that use extended memory.

Dealing with the extended memory driver is a bit complex—you can see what's happening if you look at XMEM.ASM. The get_xmem function uses INT 2FH, the extended memory driver's private interrupt, to inquire as to its health. If AX contains the value 4300H when this call is made, a properly loaded extended memory driver will return with the high-order bit set in AL. Subsequently calling the driver with AX set to 4310H prompts it to return a pointer to itself in ES:BX. All subsequent communication with the driver can be carried out by calling the code addressed by this pointer.

Buffers of extended memory are allocated in chunks of 1K. You can request one by calling `alloc_xmem` and passing it the number of kilobytes you have in mind. It returns a handle to your memory, or – 1 if you're asking for more memory than you deserve. You can subsequently deallocate extended memory by passing this handle to `dealloc_xmem`.

Extended memory handles are integers, and really just serve as notes to the extended memory driver to tell it which allocated buffer you're interested in. Because extended memory lives beyond the range of normal PC memory addressing, you must ask the driver to move data in and out of an extended memory buffer.

Extended memory access requests are handled by passing the address of an XMOVE struct to `move_xmem`. An XMOVE struct looks like this:

```
typedef struct {
        unsigned long length;
        unsigned int sourceH;
        unsigned long sourceOff;
        unsigned int destH;
        unsigned long destOff;
        } XMOVE;
```

The extended memory driver moves data between memory pointed to by handles. Handle 0 is considered to be conventional memory. As such, if `handle` is an extended-memory handle returned by `alloc_xmem`, p is a pointer to a line of image data, and xmove is an XMOVE struct, this is how you'd move 1 byte of data into extended memory:

```
xmove.length=(long)1;
xmove.sourceH=0;
xmove.sourceOff=ptr2long(p);
xmove.destH=handle;
xmove.destOff=0L;
move_xmem(&xmove);
```

This example assumes that the data is to be moved into the extended memory buffer starting with the first byte of the buffer. You could put it somewhere else by specifying the offset into the buffer as the value in `xmove.destOff`.

You can move data from extended memory to conventional memory by reversing the handle and offset arguments.

```
xmove.length=(long)1;
xmove.sourceH=handle;
```

```
xmove.sourceOff=0L
xmove.destH=0;
xmove.destOff=ptr2long(p);
move__xmem(&xmove);
```

The `ptr2long` function accepts a C-language pointer and returns a long integer, something of a convenience, as the offset in an XMOVE structure is actually the 32 bits of a conventional pointer when a conventional memory buffer is involved.

Extended memory is fast, flexible and easy to work with. It's a bit tricky to debug, though, as you can't find out if something has been transferred to extended memory by just booting up DEBUG and having a look at it.

Expanded memory

As discussed in chapter 1, expanded memory uses a small page frame in the conventional memory address space to provide access to a large pool of page-switched extra memory. It's a decided hack that was perpetrated back before 80286 processors were commonly available to sneak around the original PC memory crunch.

Because the page size of the expanded memory page frame is fixed, the problem of storing image lines in expanded memory is similar to that of displaying 256-color image lines on a super VGA card with inflexible memory paging. The end of a page usually does not happen to fall between the lines being stored in it.

In writing image lines to expanded memory, the page breaks can be dealt with in one of two ways. Those lines that would overlap the ends of pages can be allowed to do so. This makes the most efficient use of expanded memory, but it makes the code to read and write lines to it more cumbersome and slower than it needs to be. Alternately, lines that would overlap the end of a page can be promoted to the next allocated page, wasting the partial line on the previous page.

Expanded memory is allocated in 16K pages. Therefore, wasting a few bytes of it at the end of allocated pages rarely affects the amount of memory that gets allocated. It's worth throwing away a few bytes in order to have the additional speed provided by the latter approach. Unless the cosmic overlords and statistical probability are really out to get you, there's no actual memory penalty involved in doing so.

If it turns out that the cosmic overlords really are out to get you, and these extra few bytes entail the use of an extra page of memory in a particularly pathological case, it will temporarily waste 16K of memory, a nominal penalty at worst.

The best way to manage expanded memory that is to be used to store image lines is to create a table of page and offset values in conventional memory that indicate where each line is to go, again as was done in driving the graphic modes of super VGA cards. Each entry in the table consists of two integers that hold the offset into the page frame and the page in which each line resides. In fact, you could get by with 3 bytes per entry, but multiplying by four is a great deal faster.

The expanded-memory page frame is 16K long for traditional small-page expanded memory. It can live anywhere in the conventional memory address space. A common location for it is at segment C800H.

Expanded memory is addressed through a driver. Locating the driver is a little weird. Here's the official voodoo for getting its attention:

```
union REGS rg;
int fh;

if((fh=open("EMMXXXX0",O_RDONLY,&fh))==-1)
return(0);

rg.h.ah = 0x44;
rg.h.al = 0x00;
rg.x.bx = fh;
int86(0x21,&rg,&rg);
close(fh);
```

If an expanded memory driver is available, attempting to open a file called "EMMXXXX0" for reading will prove successful, even though no such file actually exists. Subsequently, testing the resulting file handle's characteristics will indicate that it's a device, rather than a file. That's what the int86 call is up to; this can lead you to speculate on the type of thinking that would come up with something like this.

Having determined the existence of a driver, expanded memory can be dealt with using INT 67H, the officially sanctioned expanded memory interrupt.

This is how you can make sure that the aforementioned expanded memory driver is actually connected to some memory:

```
MOV     AH,40H
INT     67H
```

If the AH register contains 0, all is well.

This call returns the total number of available expanded memory pages:

```
MOV     AH,42H
INT     67H
```

If the carry flag is clear, the DX register will contain the total number of available pages.

This call tells you where the expanded memory page frame resides:

```
MOV     AH,41H
INT     67H
```

If the AL register contains 0, the BX register contains the segment of the page frame. The offset of the page frame is always 0.

This call allocates n pages of expanded memory:

```
MOV     AH,43H
MOV     BX,n
INT     67H
```

This call returns a handle to the allocated memory in the DX register if the AH register returns with 0.

Here's how to free up some allocated expanded memory:

```
MOV     AH,45H
MOV     DX,handle
INT     67H
```

Inasmuch as the expanded memory page frame is located in the conventional memory address space, it can be read from and written to using conventional large-model pointers. If p is a pointer and pageframe is an integer containing the page frame segment, you can address the expanded memory page frame this way:

```
p=MK_FP(pageframe,0);
```

You might want to have a look at the expanded memory code in the memory manager for a more detailed look at what it takes to work with expanded memory. Specifically, have a look at how the page changes are handled. You can cause page n of an allocated expanded memory buffer to appear in the page frame like this:

```
MOV     AX,4400H
MOV     BX,n
MOV     DX,handle
INT     67H
```

The logic for selecting pages, in this case based on the contents of the line table discussed earlier, is illustrated by the memory manager code that deals with expanded memory.

Glossary

ATI   Super VGA display cards manufactured by ATI Technologies.

BMP   The bitmapped file format used by Microsoft Windows 3.

buffer   An allocated area of memory used for storage.

chunk   One logical data element in an IFF/LBM image file.

color map   A lookup table of RGB color values.

color number   A crude way of representing color values, as used by EGA cards.

dithering   The process of creating the illusion of colors that don't exist by mixing patterns of colors which do.

driver   A block of loadable code that interfaces common functional code to specific hardware.

EGA card   The IBM enhanced graphics adapter and compatibles thereof. The EGA card supports a 640 × 350 pixel, 16-color graphics mode.

EMS   See *expanded memory*.

escape sequence   A sequence of characters preceded by ASCII character 27 (escape), which some printers will interpret as a command rather than as literal data. Escape sequences are used to control LaserJets and other PCL printers.

expanded memory   Extra memory arranged as pages and accessed through a high-memory page frame.

extended memory   Extra memory located on the extended memory bus of 80286 and better processors and accessed through direct 16-bit addressing.

extension block A logical data element of a GIF file that contains something other than image information.

far pointer A 32-bit pointer that includes both an offset and a segment component, and is thus able to address any location in conventional memory.

GIF The file format created by CompuServe for use in storing scanned images.

halftone A representation of continuous tone (gray-scale) images in black and white by using variable size spots to represent gray levels.

header A block of data that precedes an image file and defines its characteristics.

Huffman encoding A type of image-file compression originally implemented to be manageable using hardware encoding and decoding circuitry.

IFF The image file format originally devised by Commodore for use on its Amiga computers.

LaserJet A laser printer created by Hewlett Packard, controlled by the PCL printer control language.

LBM A variation on the IFF file format used by the Electronic Arts' *Deluxe Paint* package.

lookup table An array of objects used to provide the return values of a function that would either be too slow to calculate in real time or for which there is no obvious mathematical or algorithmic relationship between the argument and the returned values.

LZW compression A data compression algorithm first postulated by Lempil-Ziv and Welch which uses a table of variable strings and tokens.

Marble Madness The only practical use the author has thus far encountered for an Amiga.

mask Data used to selectively adjust the contents of an existing bit field.

memory page A section of a larger pool of memory that can be made visible or invisible to the conventional memory address bus, such that multiple pages of memory can be accessed through a small area of the bus.

mode 13H The 320×200 pixel, 256-color display mode of a VGA card.

MSP The old monochrome image file format of the Microsoft Windows 2 *Paint* applications.

PackBits The image file run-length compression procedure originated on the Macintosh and currently used by TIFF and IFF/LBM files.

page frame The area of the conventional memory address bus through which paged memory is accessed.

palette see *color map*.

Paradise The trade name of VGA cards and VGA support chips manufactured by Western Digital Imaging.

PCX The image file format originated by Z-Soft for their *PC Paintbrush* software.

PIC The image file format used by the *PC Paint/Pictor* paint software.

pixel One dot in a bitmapped image.

planar An image that consists of one or more interleaved image planes.

pointer An object that defines the location of another object in memory.

Postfix A programming structure in which the arguments to functions appear before the functions that use them.

PostScript The printer control language created by Adobe Systems.

preview A small secondary image that contains a scaled-down version of the principal image in an image file. A preview image allows the contents of an image file to be examined without the entire file being unpacked.

prototype A C-language convention that allows the number and type of the arguments to a function to be defined before compiling a source file.

quantizing The process of algorithmically reducing the number of distinct colors in a bitmapped image.

ray tracing A technique for creating bitmapped images from vector drawings or theoretical data. In this technique, one or more light sources are postulated. Software then calculates how the rays from the light sources will be absorbed or reflected by the objects in the model.

record A logical data element of a WordPerfect Graphic file.

RGB The way in which additive color is specified, that is, as sequences of red, green, and blue color components.

Run-length compression A form of image file compression in which redundant data is replaced by tokens.

scan line One horizontal row of pixels in a bitmapped image, corresponding to one horizontal line on a monitor's cathode ray tube.

string-table compression See *LZW compression*.

super VGA card A display adapter that supports a superset of the display modes provided by a standard IBM VGA card.

tag A logical data element of a TIFF file.

Targa The display adapters and supporting file formats created by Truevision.

TIFF The tagged image file format.

Trident A manufacturer of super VGA cards and chips.

true color A bitmapped image file in which each pixel in the image is expressed as a distinct color, rather than as a palette index.

Tseng Labs A manufacturer of super VGA chips.

VGA Video Graphics Array, the designation for a type of display adapters by IBM.

virtual memory The process of using a disk file to simulate memory.

WPG The WordPerfect graphic file format.

XMS See *extended memory*.

Index

Other Bestsellers of Related Interest

BIT-MAPPED GRAPHICS—Steve Rimmer

This is one of the first books to cover the specific graphic file formats used by popular paint and desktop publishing packages. It shows you how to pack and unpack bit-map image files so you can import and export them to other applications. And, it helps you sort through available file formats, standards, patches, and revision levels, using commercial-quality C code to explore bit-mapped graphics and effectively deal with image files. 504 pages, 131 illustrations. Book No. 3558, $26.95 paperback, $38.95 hardcover

MACINTOSH SYSTEM 7: The Complete Sourcebook—Gordon M. Campbell

Campbell shows off some of the exciting new features of System 7 and offers tips for upgrading your hardware and software. This is your best guide to the first major development in the Macintosh since its introduction in 1984. With this book by your keyboard, you can count on clear skies and smooth sailing, for either upgrade or installation. 320 pages, illustrated. Book No. 4074, $32.95 paperback only

MS-DOS® BATCH FILE PROGRAMMING
—3rd Edition—Ronny Richardson

Now updated to cover DOS 5.0, this book explores the power of .BAT—the PC user's key to total system control. Richardson shows how to boost productivity dramatically with simple step-saving programs. He discusses two of the most often customized system batch files, AUTOEXEC.BAT and CONFIG.SYS. You can then progress to creating your own batch files in order to make your computer run more smoothly and do exactly what you want it to do. 440 pages, 186 illustrations. Book No. 3916, $26.95 paperback, $36.95 hardcover

BUILD YOUR OWN 386/386SX COMPATIBLE AND SAVE A BUNDLE—2nd Edition
—Aubrey Pilgrim

Assemble an 80386 microcomputer at home using mail-order parts that cost a lot less today than they did several years ago. Absolutely no special technical know-how is required—only a pair of pliers, a couple of screwdrivers, and this detailed, easy-to-follow guide. 248 pages, 79 illustrations. Book No. 4089, $18.95 paperback, $29.95 hardcover

MS-DOS® BATCH FILE UTILITIES
—Ronny Richardson

Featuring more than 200 of the best batch file programs available for the PC, this is the most complete source of documentation available for batch file utilities currently offered as shareware or in the public domain. Arranged alphabetically and meticulously cross-referenced by category, this valuable reference features detailed descriptions and instructions for ALL commercial batch files on the DOS market today. 368 pages, 275 illustrations. Book No. 3915, $29.95 paperback, $36.95 hardcover

FOXPRO® : The Master Reference
—2nd Edition
—Robin Stark and Shelley Satonin

Design and run powerful, customized databases in no time using all the exciting new features of FoxPro. This alphabetical guide to every FoxPro command and function covers all versions through 2.0—more than 350 entries in all. Its innovative three-part indexing system leads you quickly to all commands, functions, and examples found in the book. 512 pages, 135 illustrations. Book No. 4056, $24.95 paperback only

**101+ FOXPRO® AND dBASE® IV
USER-DEFINED FUNCTIONS**—Philip Steele

Whether you've already written many lines of database code and just want to improve your code or you want to develop more complex applications for distribution in the corporate marketplace, this book's for you. It contains professional guidelines for writing and developing UDFs that will eliminate repetitive database programming tasks. A companion disk, offered on an order form at the end of the book, contains all the UDFs used in the book. 368 pages, 159 illustrations. Book No. 3951, $22.95 paperback only

**COMPUTER SECURITY HANDBOOK
—2nd Edition**—Richard H. Baker

This edition emphasizes practical, affordable measures that protect networks and database servers, featuring all-new coverage of virus control methods, the 1986 Computer Fraud and Abuse Act, and recent case studies of security problems. You'll find complete information on prevention and cure of viruses, electronic eavesdropping, personnel controls, identifying your most vulnerable points, password perils, security planning, and how a computer can protect itself. 432 pages, 70 illustrations. Book No. 3592, $24.95 paperback, $34.95 hardcover

Enclosed is your diskette containing the bit-mapped graphics source code for IBM and compatible PCs

Your disk should contain eight files:

HUMBIRD.ZIP	OBJECT.ZIP
GRAFWK61.ZIP	ZIPPER.COM
DTPC14.ZIP	ZOE.GIF
SOURCE.ZIP	README.TXT

Create a new subdirectory on your hard drive to copy the files into. To create a subdirectory, type:

`MKDIR directory-name`

and press Enter at your C:\ prompt. directory-name is the desired name of the directory.

To copy all of the files, simply place your disk in drive A and type:

`COPY A:*.* C:\directory-name`

and press Enter. *directory-name* is the name of the directory that you just created.

The five .ZIP archive files on the disk need to be uncompressed before you can use them. (*Note:* You need to have about 3.5Mb of free space on your hard drive to store the uncompressed files.) ZIPPER.COM is the program used to uncompress the files. (You also can use PKUNZIP.) To use ZIPPER, make sure that the directory containing ZIPPER.COM and the .ZIP files is the current directory. Type:

`CD C:\directory-name`

You must use ZIPPER on each of the .ZIP files—wildcards will not work properly. (PKUNZIP users can use wildcards.) The syntax for ZIPPER is:

`ZIPPER filename`

where *filename* is the name of the file that you want to uncompress. Do not use the .ZIP extension in the filename, it is assumed.